NURSE PRACTITIONER'S
BUSINESS PRACTICE and LEGAL GUIDE

Fifth Edition

CAROLYN BUPPERT, CRNP, JD
Attorney
Boulder, Colorado

JONES & BARTLETT
LEARNING

World Headquarters
Jones & Bartlett Learning
5 Wall Street
Burlington, MA 01803
978-443-5000
info@jblearning.com
www.jblearning.com

Jones & Bartlett Learning books and products are available through most bookstores and online booksellers. To contact Jones & Bartlett Learning directly, call 800-832-0034, fax 978-443-8000, or visit our website, www.jblearning.com.

Substantial discounts on bulk quantities of Jones & Bartlett Learning publications are available to corporations, professional associations, and other qualified organizations. For details and specific discount information, contact the special sales department at Jones & Bartlett Learning via the above contact information or send an email to specialsales@jblearning.com.

Production Credits
Executive Publisher: William Brottmiller
Senior Editor: Amanda Martin
Associate Managing Editor: Sara Bempkins
Production Editor: Amanda Clerkin
Marketing Communications Manager: Katie Hennessy
VP, Manufacturing and Inventory Control: Therese Connell
Composition: Laserwords Private Limited, Chennai, India
Cover Design: Kristin E. Parker
Rights Clearance Editor: Maria Leon Maimone
Cover Image: © lenetstan/ShutterStock, Inc.
Printing and Binding: Edwards Brothers Malloy
Cover Printing: Edwards Brothers Malloy

To order this product, use ISBN: 978-1-284-05091-2

Library of Congress Cataloging-in-Publication Data
Library of Congress Cataloging-in-Publication Data unavailable at time of printing.

6048

Printed in the United States of America
18 17 16 15   10 9 8 7 6 5 4

Contents

Preface

This text contains the answers to many questions asked of me in my 23 years of practice as an attorney. I specialize in legal issues affecting nurse practitioners. The questions came from nurse practitioners, employers of nurse practitioners, hospital and nursing facility executives, student nurse practitioners and their professors, other attorneys, bureaucrats, and legislators conducting hearings about bills that addressed nurse practitioners.

Nurse practitioners frequently ask questions such as these:

- A physician (or hospital or group) wants to hire me to do [fill in a particular healthcare service]. Can I legally do that?
- An insurance company refuses to pay the bill for a patient's visit with me. What can I do?
- A hospital bought my group's practice. The hospital is not sure what to do with me. How can I help them understand what nurse practitioners can offer?
- What should be covered in my employment contract?
- Can I incorporate in a business with physicians?
- I have been working in a trauma center for 4 years. Now I hear that my notes need to be cosigned by a physician. Is that true?
- An Internet-based pharmacist refuses to fill a prescription I wrote because I am not a physician. I have the legal authority to prescribe in my state. What can I do?
- I have been working without a contract. Now the company wants me to be on call three nights a week. Do I have to do it?
- I am writing a paper for my "nurse practitioner role" class on legislative issues affecting nurse practitioners. What are these issues?
- How can I get on a health plan's provider panel?
- A group wants to pay me a base salary plus a percentage of billings over $250,000. Is this reasonable?
- What does "incident to a physician's professional services" mean?
- How do I start my own practice?
- I know nothing about how billing is done. Can you tell me how to get reimbursed for my services?

Legislators and bureaucrats frequently ask such questions as these:

- How is a nurse practitioner different from a registered nurse?
- Which states allow nurse practitioners to practice independently?
- How does a nurse practitioner know when to consult a physician?

- Does a physician have to supervise everything a nurse practitioner does?
- In how many states can nurse practitioners write prescriptions?

Employers of nurse practitioners frequently ask such questions as these:

- I want the nurse practitioner to see my hospitalized patients. Can we get reimbursed for that?
- How can we get paid by Medicare for patient visits to the nurse practitioner?
- We want to put nurse practitioners in nursing homes. What can the nurse practitioner do? Admit patients? Perform the yearly visit? Perform illness-related visits? Recertify?
- Who is liable if the nurse practitioner makes a mistake: the nurse practitioner or the physician?

Other attorneys ask such questions as these:

- A nursing home I represent has hired a nurse practitioner to do administrative work and to see patients. How can we bill for his or her services?
- My clients want to start a network of nurse practitioner practices. What can you tell me about that? Do you know anything about Florida [fill in any state] law on nurse practitioners?

Some of the questioners have become clients, and I have done the necessary legal research to answer their questions and have completed the necessary legal documents to carry out their plans. Others will now benefit from the work done for those clients.

Nurse practitioners who read this book will have a solid knowledge base to use, whether it be in developing an employment relationship, undertaking a business venture, giving testimony before the state legislature, composing a letter to an insurance company about an unpaid bill, teaching at a school of nursing, or serving as president of a state or national organization. My hope is that once nurse practitioners have this base of knowledge about the business of health care and the legal foundation upon which nurse practitioners function, they can hasten the advancement of their careers.

CHAPTER 1

What Is a Nurse Practitioner?

Individuals who have never experienced the care of a nurse practitioner (NP)—whether they are physicians, reporters, lawmakers, bureaucrats, lobbyists, or new patients—often request clarification about just who NPs are and what they do.

It is their combination of the skills of both a physician and a nurse that seems to confuse people. Yet it is that combination of skills that makes an NP unique.

Definition of Nurse Practitioner

The term *nurse practitioner* has been given a variety of definitions.

- According to a state NP organization, "Nurse practitioners are registered professional nurses who are prepared, through advanced graduate education and clinical training, to provide a range of health services, including the diagnosis and management of common as well as complex medical conditions to individuals of all ages."[1]
- According to a national NP organization, "NPs are quickly becoming the health partner of choice for millions of Americans. As clinicians that blend clinical expertise in diagnosing and treating health conditions with an added emphasis on disease prevention and health management, NPs bring a comprehensive perspective to health care."[2]
- A board of nursing defines an NP as follows: "A nurse practitioner (NP) is an RN [registered nurse] who has earned a separate license as an NP through additional education and experience in a distinct specialty area of practice. Nurse practitioners may diagnose, treat, and prescribe for a patient's condition that falls within their specialty areas of practice. This is done in collaboration with a licensed physician qualified in the specialty involved and in accordance with an approved written practice agreement and protocols. Nurse practitioners are autonomous and do not practice under the supervision of the collaborating physician."[3]
- According to federal law, "Nurse practitioner means a nurse practitioner who performs such services as such individual is legally authorized to perform (in the state in which the individual performs such services) in accordance with state laws and who meets such training, education, and experience required as the Secretary has prescribed in regulations" [42 U.S.C.A. § 1395x(aa)(5)(A)].
- In California state law, "nurse practitioner means a registered nurse who possesses additional preparation and skills in physical diagnosis, psych-social assessment, and

management of health-illness needs in primary health care and who has been prepared in a program conforming to board standards as specified in Section 1484" [CAL. CODE REGS. tit. 16, § 1480(a)].

For state-by-state definitions of the term *nurse practitioner*, see **Appendix 1-A**.

An NP, by Any Other Name . . .

Other designations sometimes given to NPs include physician extender, mid-level practitioner, nonphysician practitioner, and advanced practice nurse. For a state-by-state listing of official terms for NPs, see **Appendix 1-B**.

Physician Extender

The term *physician extender* is used by physicians' associations and publications aimed at the physician market and usually refers collectively to NPs, clinical nurse specialists, nurse anesthetists, nurse midwives, and physician assistants.

Mid-Level Practitioner

The term *mid-level practitioner* is used by some physician groups, some states, and the federal government in the Code of Federal Regulation sections dealing with Drug Enforcement Administration (DEA) registration. The DEA defines a mid-level practitioner as follows:

> The term mid-level practitioner means an individual practitioner other than a physician, dentist, veterinarian, or podiatrist, who is licensed, registered, or otherwise permitted by the United States or the jurisdiction in which he/she practices to dispense controlled dangerous substances in the course of professional practice. Examples of mid-level practitioners include, but are not limited to, healthcare providers such as nurse practitioners, nurse midwives, nurse anesthetists, clinical nurse specialists, and physician assistants who are authorized to dispense controlled substances by the state in which they practice.
>
> Citation: 21 C.F.R. § 1300.01(b).

Some state laws provide a definition of mid-level practitioner. For example, in Minnesota, "'Mid-level practitioner' means a nurse practitioner, nurse midwife, nurse anesthetist, advanced clinical nurse specialist, or physician assistant" [MINN. STAT. § 144.1501(f)].

Nonphysician Practitioner

The term *nonphysician practitioner* is used by the Centers for Medicare & Medicaid Services and Medicare administrative contractors. Here is the definition from one administrator's website[4]:

> For Medicare purposes, the term nonphysician practitioner (NPP) includes:
>
> ■ Nurse practitioner or clinical nurse specialist, as those terms are defined in section 1861(aa)(5) of the Social Security Act, who is working in collaboration with the physician in accordance with State law
>
> ■ Certified nurse-midwife, as defined in section 1861(gg) of the Social Security Act, as authorized by State law

- A physician assistant, as defined in section 1861(aa)(5) of the Social Security Act, under the supervision of the physician

Advanced Practice Nurse

Advanced practice nurse is an umbrella term used by some states and some nursing associations to cover, collectively, NPs, clinical nurse specialists, nurse midwives, and nurse anesthetists. NPs differ from other advanced practice nurses in that they offer a wider range of services to a wider portion of the population. Other advanced practice nurses compare with NPs in the following ways:

- *Nurse anesthetist*: Narrow range of services (preoperative assessment, administration of anesthesia, management of postanesthesia recovery) to a narrow base of patients (people having anesthesia).
- *Clinical nurse specialist*: Medium range of services (consultation, research, education, administration, coordination of care, case management, direct care within the definition of a registered nurse) to a narrow patient base (people under the care of a medical specialist).
- *Certified nurse midwife*: Narrow range of services (well-women gynecologic care, management of pregnancy and childbirth, antepartum and postpartum care) to a medium-sized base of patients (childbearing women).
- *Nurse practitioner*: Wide range of services (evaluation, diagnosis, treatment, education, risk assessment, health promotion, case management, coordination of care, counseling) to a wide base of patients, depending upon area of certification; a family nurse practitioner can have a patient base of any age, gender, or problem.

Services Provided by NPs

NPs may perform any service authorized by a state nurse practice act. Some nurse practice acts are so broad as to allow any service agreed upon by an NP and collaborating physician. Generally, NP services include:

- Obtaining medical histories and performing physical examinations
- Diagnosing and treating health problems
- Ordering and interpreting laboratory tests and X-rays
- Prescribing medications and other treatments
- Providing prenatal care and family planning services
- Providing well-child care and immunizations
- Providing gynecologic examinations and Pap smears
- Providing education about health risks, illness prevention, and health maintenance
- Providing counseling regarding the need for compliance with a diagnostic and/or treatment plan, course of illness, side effects of treatment, and/or prognosis
- Coordinating care and case management

Typically, an NP has the following duties and responsibilities:

- Conducts comprehensive medical and social history of individuals, including those who are healthy and those with acute illnesses and chronic diseases

- Conducts physical examination of individuals, either comprehensive or problem focused
- Orders, performs, and interprets laboratory tests for screening and for diagnosing
- Prescribes medications
- Performs therapeutic or corrective measures, including urgent care
- Refers individuals to appropriate specialist nurses, physicians, or other healthcare providers
- Makes independent decisions regarding management and treatment of medical problems identified
- Performs various invasive/clinical procedures such as suturing, biopsy of skin lesions, and endometrial biopsy, depending upon education, training, patient needs, and written agreement with physician collaborator
- Prescribes and orders appropriate diet and other forms of treatment, such as physical therapy
- Provides information, instruction, and counseling on health maintenance, health promotion, social problems, illness prevention, illness management, and medication use
- Evaluates the effectiveness of instruction and counseling and provides additional instruction and counseling as necessary
- Initiates and participates in research studies and projects
- Teaches groups of clients about health-related topics
- Provides outreach health education services in the community
- Serves as preceptor for medical, nursing, NP, or physician assistant students
- Accepts after-hours calls and handles after-hours problems on a rotating schedule
- Participates in development of pertinent health education materials
- Participates in development of clinical practice guidelines
- Initiates and maintains follow-up of noncompliant patients
- Makes client home visits and provides care in the home as necessary
- Makes hospital visits and follows hospital care of established patients
- Consults with other healthcare providers about established clients who have been admitted to hospital, home care, rehabilitation, or nursing homes
- Corresponds with insurers, employers, government agencies, and other healthcare providers about established clients as necessary
- Manages care of clients; develops plan of treatment and/or follow-up and monitors progress, determines when referral to another provider is necessary, makes necessary arrangements for further care, determines when hospital admission or emergency room visit is necessary, and determines when illness is resolved
- Assesses social/economic factors for each client and tailors care to those factors
- Manages care of clients in a way that balances quality and cost
- Tracks outcome of interventions and alters interventions to achieve optimum results
- Obtains informed consent from clients as appropriate and necessary
- Maintains familiarity with community resources and connects clients with appropriate resources
- Contracts with clients regarding provider responsibilities and client responsibilities
- Supervises and teaches registered nurses and nonlicensed healthcare workers

- Participates in community programs and health fairs, school programs, and workplace programs
- Represents the practice or the profession as an NP before local and state governing bodies, agencies, and private businesses as needed

Preparation and License Requirements

All NPs are registered nurses (RNs) with education beyond the basic requirements for RN licensure. Most NPs have master's degrees, and some have doctorates. Master's degrees for NPs are required by law in 34 states. NPs without master's degrees have completed a program that meets requirements of state law.

State-required qualifications vary widely. For example, in Alaska, NPs must have completed a 1-year academic course, have an RN license, be certified by a national certifying agency, and have 30 hours of continuing education every 2 years. In Pennsylvania, NPs must have an RN license, a master's degree, certification by a national organization, must provide evidence of continuing competence in medical diagnosis and therapeutics, and must have 30 hours of continuing education per year and 45 hours of advanced pharmacology. Federal law defers to state law regarding NP qualifications (42 C.F.R. § 440.166).

In 45 states, NPs are required by state law to take and pass a national certification exam. A state requirement that an NP be nationally certified leads to a requirement of master's education because the certifying agencies of adult and pediatric NPs require a master's degree to sit for the certification examination.

Initials

Among the initials used to designate NPs are CRNP (certified registered nurse practitioner); ANP-C (adult nurse practitioner–certified); CPNP (certified pediatric nurse practitioner); CGNP (certified geriatric nurse practitioner); RN, CS (registered nurse, certified specialist); ARNP (advanced registered nurse practitioner); and APRN (advanced practice registered nurse).

Areas of Practice

NPs may be certified in the following areas:

- Adult primary care
- Family primary care
- Geriatric primary care
- Neonatal care
- Obstetrics and gynecology
- Pediatric primary care
- Pediatric acute care
- Acute care
- Primary care of school-aged children

- Family planning
- Emergency health care
- Maternal child health
- Mental health/psychiatric care
- Critical care
- Oncology
- Palliative care
- Rehabilitation
- Community health
- Occupational health

Not all categories are recognized in all states.

According to the APRN Consensus Model (2008):

> APRNs are educated in one of the four roles and in at least one of six population foci: family/individual across the lifespan, adult-gerontology, neonatal, pediatrics, women's health/gender-related or psych/mental health.[5]

Legal History of NPs

Before the emergence of advanced practice nurses, the legal scope of nurses' practice excluded the diagnosis and treatment of medical problems. Nurses carried out physicians' orders. In the mid-1970s, some state nurse practice acts were amended to include "nursing diagnoses" in the scope of nursing practice. A nursing diagnosis "limits the diagnostic process to those diagnoses that represent human responses to actual or potential health problems that are within the legal scope of nursing practice."[6]

When a physician shortage arose in the 1960s, it became evident that the shortage and the limitations on nurses' making medical diagnoses were restricting access to health care for people in medically underserved areas. Certain nurses and physicians joined forces to solve the problem. One answer was the NP.

The first NP educational program was a joint effort between Henry K. Silver, a pediatrician, and Loretta C. Ford, then a nursing professor, at the University of Colorado in 1965. Their project was one of many efforts to deal with a physician shortage. The first NPs began practicing in the late 1960s.

As the concept was envisioned, NPs would make not only nursing diagnoses but also medical diagnoses. Further, they would treat patients with medical therapeutics, ordering pharmacotherapeutics and other treatments. It became necessary to broaden the legal scope of nursing practice.

As soon as NPs began to emerge from the training programs, a body of law emerged governing NP licensure and scope of practice. Idaho was the first state to revise its regulations to allow diagnosis and treatment by nurses.

By the mid-1970s, state legislators began to consider proposed laws regarding prescriptive authority for NPs. In some states, the prescriptive authority was granted through the regulatory process; in others, it was granted through the legislative process. By 2006, NPs had achieved some degree of prescriptive privileges in all states and the District of Columbia.

The main legal goal of NPs for 30 years was achieved. The next legal hurdle became evident with the enrollment of a large percentage of the population into managed-care plans. While NPs had the authority to bill for services to patients covered by Medicare and Medicaid, they were not necessarily credentialed as providers by the managed-care plans. So, NPs met with executives at managed-care organizations and attempted to persuade them to allow NPs to be "primary care providers" for the plans. As of 2013, that had been achieved, for the most part, in most states. The next legal hurdle is achieving the legal authority to medically manage patients within an NP's scope of practice, without mandated physician collaboration. While NPs in some states may practice without a collaborative practice agreement with a physician, the majority of states still require some form of physician involvement in NP practice.

Demographics

There are over 157,000 NPs in the United States, according to the American Academy of Nurse Practitioners.[2]

NPs in Primary Care

The concept of the NP emerged from a need for more primary care providers in underserved areas of the nation. While many NPs work in specialty and acute care settings, many provide primary care.

Because health plans designate certain generalist physicians—pediatricians, internists, and family practitioners—as primary care providers (PCPs) for groups of patients, it is important for NPs to be included in the definition of PCP. It is also important for NPs to be included as providers who can be a "medical home" for a patient.

Definition of Primary Care

The following are definitions of primary care.

According to a national health policy think tank, the National Academy of Sciences' Institute of Medicine,

- "Primary care is the provision of integrated, accessible healthcare services by clinicians who are accountable for addressing a large majority of personal healthcare needs, developing a sustained partnership with patients, and practicing in the context of family and community."[7]

A nurse practice act written by a state agency defines primary health care as:

- "that which occurs when a consumer makes contact with a healthcare provider who assumes responsibility and accountability for the continuity of health care regardless of the presence or absence of disease" [CAL. CODE REGS. tit. 16 § 1480(b)].

A state legislature's definition is:

- "the health care which clients receive at the first point of contact with the healthcare system and [that] is continuous and comprehensive. Primary health care includes health promotion, prevention of disease and disability, health maintenance, rehabilitation, identification of health problems, management of health problems, and referral" [Code Me. R. § 02 380 008(G)].

Finally, here is a definition provided by the American Academy of Family Physicians:

- "Primary care is that care provided by physicians specifically trained for and skilled in comprehensive first contact and continuing care for persons with any undiagnosed sign, symptom, or health concern (the 'undifferentiated' patient) not limited by problem origin (biological, behavioral, or social), organ system, gender, or diagnosis. Primary care includes health promotion, disease prevention, health maintenance, counseling, patient education, diagnosis, and treatment of acute and chronic illnesses in a variety of healthcare settings (e.g., office, inpatient, critical care, long-term care, home care, day care, etc.). Primary care is performed and managed by a personal physician, utilizing other health professionals, consultation and/or referral as appropriate."[8] The American Academy of Family Physicians has five definitions of primary care. One of them acknowledges that providers other than physicians provide primary care.

Primary care itself is not controversial. Who performs primary care is somewhat controversial. Who receives reimbursement for primary care is very controversial.

Legal Authority of NPs to Be Primary Care Providers

Some state laws specifically authorize NPs to be PCPs; that is, to be designated as the individual responsible for the primary care of a patient enrolled in a managed-care plan.

An example of one such law is Maryland's, which provides that "... each member [of a health maintenance organization] shall have an opportunity to select a primary physician or a certified nurse practitioner from among those available to the health maintenance organization...." (Md Health-General Code Ann. § 19-705.1).

In Maryland, a clause in the state law governing health maintenance organizations had been construed as prohibiting anyone other than a physician from being a PCP. Maryland NPs went to the legislature asking for a change in that law. In 2003, the change was made, and the language cited here was enacted.

In some states, no law prohibits an NP from being designated as a PCP.

NPs as Team Members in Secondary and Tertiary Care

Whereas the role of NP was originally contemplated to be in primary care, more and more NPs are working for specialists and in hospitals. For those NPs, state law on scope of practice and reimbursement and federal law on reimbursement are most relevant.

NP Versus Physician Assistant: What Is the Difference?

While NPs and physician assistants (PAs) may function very similarly and may, in some states, be interchangeable in terms of job description, there are differences between them in legal definition, scope of practice, licensure, and independence of practice. PAs practice medicine under the supervision of a physician, never independently, as far as the law is concerned. PAs are true physician extenders. NPs practice under their own licenses and in some states may practice independent of physician involvement. NPs may be physician extenders or practice independently, depending upon state law.

Definition and Scope of Practice of PAs, Compared with NPs

By definition, a PA is a healthcare provider who practices medicine with physician supervision. NPs define themselves as nurses with a broadened scope of practice and do not define themselves as physician-supervised professionals.

PAs include in descriptions of their duties taking medical histories, performing physical examinations, ordering and interpreting laboratory tests, diagnosing and treating illnesses, assisting at surgery, prescribing and/or dispensing medication, and counseling patients.[9] NPs would include all of these activities in their scope of practice, with the exception of assisting in surgery. While some NPs assist in surgery under practice agreements with physicians, it is not so common an activity that it is universally included in the scope of practice of NPs. NPs usually include special attention to healthcare maintenance and illness prevention in their statements of scope of practice. The nurse practice act of at least one state, Oregon, includes hospital admission in the scope of NP practice.

The scope of a PA's practice corresponds with a supervising physician's practice, with the understanding that the supervising physician will handle the more complicated medical cases. PAs are authorized to prescribe medications in all 50 states, the District of Columbia, and Guam.[9]

Physician Involvement with PA Practice

PAs acknowledge their status as physician extenders. According to the American Academy of Physician Assistants, "By design, physicians and PAs work together as a team, and all PAs practice medicine with physician supervision."[9]

The *Guidelines for Physician/Physician Assistant Practice*,[10] adopted by the American Medical Association House of Delegates in 1995, state the following:

1. The physician is responsible for managing the health care of patients in all practice settings.
2. Healthcare services delivered by physicians and PAs must be within the scope of each practitioner's authorized practice as defined by state law.
3. The physician is ultimately responsible for coordinating and managing the care of patients and, with the appropriate input of the PA, ensuring the quality of health care provided to patients.
4. The physician is responsible for the supervision of the PA in all settings.
5. The role of the PA in the delivery of health care should be defined through mutually agreed-upon guidelines that are developed by the physician and the PA and based on the physician's delegatory style.

6. The physician must be available for consultation with the PA at all times, either in person or through telecommunication system or other means.
7. The extent of the involvement by the PA in the assessment and implementation of treatment will depend on the complexity and acuity of the patient's condition and the training and experience and preparation of the PA as adjudged by the physician.
8. Patients should be made clearly aware at all times whether they are being cared for by a physician or a PA.
9. The physician and PA together should review all delegated patient services on a regular basis, as well as the mutually agreed-upon guidelines for practice.
10. The physician is responsible for clarifying and familiarizing the PA with his or her supervising methods and style of delegating patient care.

Demographics

As of June 2013, there were approximately 86,500 individuals in clinical practice as PAs.[9]

Education

PAs are educated in programs that use the medical model and are designed to complement physician training. The American Academy of Physician Assistants describes PA education in the following way: PA education includes instruction in core sciences including anatomy, physiology, biochemistry, pharmacology, physical diagnosis, pathophysiology, microbiology, clinical laboratory science, behavioral science, and medical ethics. PAs also complete more than 2000 hours of clinical rotations, with an emphasis on primary care in ambulatory clinics, physician offices, and acute or long-term care facilities. Rotations include family medicine, internal medicine, obstetrics and gynecology, pediatrics, general surgery, emergency medicine, and psychiatry.[9]

Licensure Requirements

According to the American Academy of Physician Assistants, "Before PAs can practice, they must apply for and obtain authorization from the state. In most states and DC, this authorization process is called 'licensure,' but in one state (OH) it is called 'registration.'"[9] For licensure, PAs must graduate from an accredited PA program and pass a national certifying examination.

Certification Requirements

To maintain national certification, PAs must log 100 hours of continuing medical education (CME) every 2 years. CME requirements to maintain state authorization to practice vary from state to state. PAs sit for recertification every 6 years. See **Table 1-1** for a comparison of PAs, NPs, and physicians according to basic and continuing education.

History of PAs

As with NPs, the birth of the concept of PAs came after a physician shortage was recognized in the mid-1960s. Dr. Eugene Stead of Duke University Medical Center established the first PA program, using already trained Navy corpsmen. He based his program on a fast-track training program for physicians during World War II.

Table 1-1	Nurse Practitioners' Education, License, and Certification Contrasted with That of Other Primary Care Providers					
Health Professional	*Years of College*	*Undergraduate Degree or Other Education*	*Graduate Degree*	*License*	*Continuing Education (Minimum)*	*Certification (Renewal)*
Nurse practitioner	2–4	AA, BS, or RN diploma	Master's degree or doctorate required in 32 states	Yes (RN plus specific area of NP certica-tion)	75 hours/ 5 years	Yes, every 5 years
Physician assistant	2–4	BS or certificate	Not required, but the major-ity of PA programs are master's-level programs	Yes	100 hours/ 2 years	Yes, every 6 years
Primary care physician	4	BA/BS	Doctor of medicine or osteopathy required in all states	Yes (MD or DO)	50 hours/ year	Optional

Abbreviations: AA, associate of arts degree; BA, bachelor of arts degree; BS, bachelor of science degree; DO, doctor of osteopathic medicine; MD, doctor of medicine; RN, registered nurse.

Source: Data from the American Nurses Credentialing Center, American Academy of Physician Assistants and American Academy of Family Physicians.

NP Versus Physician: What Is the Difference?

NPs differ from physicians in definition, scope of practice, and education.

Definition and Scope of Practice of Physicians

A physician is a provider of medical care according to the laws of the individual states. An example of state law defining the practice of medicine is New Jersey's statute:

> The phrase "the practice of medicine or surgery" and the phrase "the practice of medicine and surgery" shall include the practice of any branch of medicine and/ or surgery and any method of treatment of human ailment, disease, pain, injury, deformity, mental or physical condition, and the term "physician and surgeon" or "physician or surgeon" shall be deemed to include practitioners in any branch of medicine and/or surgery or method of treatment of human ailment, disease,

pain, injury, deformity, mental or physical condition. Within the meaning of this act, except as herein otherwise specifically provided, and except for the purposes of the exemptions hereinafter contained in Sections 45:9-14.1 to 45:9-14.10, inclusive, the practice of medicine and/or surgery shall be deemed to include the inter alia, the practice of osteopathy...

Citation: N.J. Stat. Ann. § 45:9-5.1.

Educational Requirements of Physicians

Physicians have 4 years of medical education. See Table 1-1 for a comparison of NPs, physicians, and PAs on requirements for basic education, continuing education, licensure, and certification.

NP Versus Registered Nurse: What Is the Difference?

NPs and RNs differ in definition, scope of practice, education, and physician supervision.

Definition of RN

The legal definition of an RN is provided by the laws of the states. Michigan, for example, defines nursing and registered nurse as follows:

The "practice of nursing" means the systematic application of substantial specialized knowledge and skill derived from the biological, physical, and behavioral sciences, to the care, treatment, counsel, and health teaching of individuals who are experiencing changes in the normal health processes or who require assistance in the maintenance of health and the prevention or management of illness, injury, or disability. . . ."Registered professional nurse" or "RN" means an individual licensed under this article to engage in the practice of nursing which scope of practice includes the teaching, direction, and supervision of less skilled personnel in the performance of delegated nursing activities.

Citation: Mich. Comp. Laws § 333.17201.

Scope of Practice of RNs

Nursing typically includes a variety of acts, described under state law. The nursing acts described here are taken from the law of North Dakota:

The performance of acts utilizing specialized knowledge, skills, and abilities for people in a variety of settings. The term includes the following acts, which may not be deemed to include acts of medical diagnosis or treatment or the practice of medicine as defined in Chapter 43–17.

   a. The maintenance of health and prevention of illness
   b. Diagnosing human responses to actual or potential health problems
   c. Providing supportive and restorative care and nursing treatment, medication administration, health counseling and teaching, case finding and

referral of persons who are ill, injured, or experiencing changes in the normal health processes

d. Administration, teaching, supervision, delegation, and evaluation of health and nursing practices

e. Collaboration with other healthcare professionals in the implementation of the total healthcare regimen and execution of the healthcare regimen prescribed by a healthcare practitioner licensed to order healthcare regimens

Citation: N.D. Cent. Code § 43-12.1-02(5).

Education of RNs

An RN has 2–4 years of college education and may have a master's degree, a doctorate degree, or other advanced training over and above the basic education.

Supervision of RNs

Supervision is generally not mandated by law for those activities within the scope of nursing practice. To provide medical care, such as administering prescription medication, an RN needs an order from a healthcare provider authorized by law to give orders or prescribe medication.

NP Versus Clincial Nurse Specialist: What Is the Difference?

While NPs and clinical nurse specialists (CNSs) both are advanced practice nurses, they focus on different forms of patient care. While NPs manage patients in offices, nursing facilities, homes, and hospitals, CNSs traditionally have worked in hospitals, as resources for other clinicians. Psychiatric/mental health CNSs traditionally have performed direct patient care, as therapists. In the past 10 years, programs for psych/mental health NPs have emerged, so now, both NPs and CNSs manage patients with psychiatric diagnoses. The distinction between CNSs and NPs is important to advanced practice nurses, but probably not so important to those who are not in the field.

Definition and Scope of Practice of CNSs

The definition and scope of practice of a clinical nurse specialist (CNS) are specified by state law. For example, Maine law defines the scope of practice of a CNS as follows:

> The certified clinical nurse specialist applies research-based knowledge, skills, and experience to intervene in human responses to complex health and illness problems. The certified clinical nurse specialist (1) provides case management skills to coordinate comprehensive health services and ensure continuity of care, (2) evaluates client progress in attaining expected outcomes, (3) consults with other healthcare providers to influence care of clients, effect change in symptoms, and enhance the ability of others to provide health care, (4) performs additional functions specific to the specialty areas. In addition to the above, the

certified psychiatric clinical nurse specialist may independently assess, diagnose, and therapeutically intervene in complex mental health problems using psychotherapy and other interventions.

Citation: CODE ME. R. § 02 380 Chapter 8.

Education of CNSs

CNSs have, at minimum, a master's degree in nursing and may have a doctorate degree.

Physician Supervision of CNSs

CNSs have no requirement for physician supervision unless they have prescriptive authority, in which case there often are collaboration or supervision requirements specified by state law. See **Table 1-2** for a comparison of NPs, CNSs, and other types of advanced practice nurses in terms of education and licensure.

Where Do Nurse Practitioners Practice?

NPs practice in health maintenance organizations, independent or collaborative private practices, hospitals and affiliated clinics, emergency departments, family planning clinics, college health services, school clinics, convenient care clinics, employee health clinics, nursing and long-term care facilities, homeless shelters, hospices, and home-based care services.

Notes

1. Nurse Practitioner Association of Maryland. (2009). Media packet. Retrieved from http://www.npamonline.org/associations/9774/files/NPAM%20Media%20packet.10.2009.pdf
2. American Association of Nurse Practitioners. (n.d.). What's an np? Retrieved from http://www.aanp.org/all-about-nps/what-is-an-np
3. New York State Education Department Office of the Professions. (2013, September 24). Nursing. Retrieved from http://www.op.nysed.gov/prof/nurse
4. Palmetto GBA Medicare. (2013, October 8). Who qualifies as a non-physician practitioner (NPP)? Retrieved from http://www.palmettogba.com/palmetto/providers.nsf/DocsCat/Providers~Jurisdiction%2011%20Home%20Health%20and%20Hospice~Resources~FAQs~Home%20Health~8GKMQC6571?open&navmenu=Resources%7C%7C
5. National Council of State Boards of Nursing. (2008, July 7). The consensus model for APRN regulation, licensure, accreditation, certification, and education. Retrieved from https://www.ncsbn.org/4213.htm
6. Smith, C. M., & Maurer, F. A. (1995). *Community health nursing: Theory and practice*. Philadelphia, PA: W. B. Saunders.
7. Institute of Medicine. (1996). Primary care: American's health in a new era. Washington, DC: IOM Division of Healthcare Services.
8. American Academy of Family Physicians. (n.d.). Primary care. Retrieved from http://www.aafp.org/about/policies/all/primary-care.html
9. American Academy of Physician Assistants. (n.d.). What is a PA? Retrieved from http://www.aapa.org/the_pa_profession/what_is_a_pa.aspx
10. American Medical Association. (1995, June). Guidelines for physician/physician assistant practice. Retrieved from http://www.aapa.org/uploadedFiles/content/The_PA_Profession/Federal_and_State_Affairs/Resource_Items/AMA-Guidelines.pdf

Table 1-2 Nurse Practitioners' Educational and Professional Credentials Contrasted with Those of Other Advanced Practice Nurses

Type of APN	Years of College	Years of Training	Undergraduate Degree	Graduate Degree	License	Continuing Education	Renewal of Certification
Nurse anesthetist	4	2	BA/BS	Master's degree	Yes, RN plus nurse anesthetist	40 hours/2 years	Yes, as CRNA by NPCRNA
Nurse midwife	4	2	BA/BS	Master's degree or doctorate	Yes, RN plus nurse midwife	20 hours/5 years with other recertification options available	Yes, as nurse midwife by AMCB
Nurse psychotherapist	4	2, plus 100 hours of supervised practice	BA/BS	Master's degree	Yes, RN plus nurse psychotherapist	75 hours/5 years	Yes, as CNS by ANCC
Nurse practitioner	4	2	BA/BS	Master's degree or doctorate required in 32 states	Yes, RN plus nurse practitioner	Varies with certifying body; 75 hours/5 years (ANCC)	Yes, as NP by ANCC, PNCB, or NCC

Abbreviations: APN, advanced practice nurse; AMCB, American Midwifery Certification Board; ANCC, American Nurses Credentialing Center; BA, bachelor of arts degree; BS, bachelor of science degree; CRNA, certified registered nurse anesthetist; NBCRNA, National Board of Certification and Recertification of Nurse Anesthetists; NCC, National Certification Corporation; PNCB, Pediatric Nursing Certification Board; RN, registered nurse.

Source: Data from the American Nurses Credentialing Center, American Association of Nurse Anesthetists, and American College of Nurse Midwives websites.

State-by-State Definitions of Nurse Practitioner

State-by-state definitions of nurse practitioner, including citation of code section:

Alabama

Advanced practice nurse. A registered nurse that has gained additional knowledge and skills through successful completion of an organized program of nursing education that prepares nurses for advanced practice roles and has been certified by the Board of Nursing to engage in the practice of advanced practice nursing.

Citation: ALA. CODE § 34-21-81(3).

Practice as a certified registered nurse practitioner (CRNP) means the performance of nursing skills by a registered nurse who has demonstrated by certification that he or she has advanced knowledge and skills in the delivery of nursing services within a health care system that provides for consultation, collaborative management, or referral as indicated by the health status of the client.

Citation: ALA. CODE § 34-21-81(4a).

Alaska

"Advanced nurse practitioner" means a registered nurse authorized to practice in the state who, because of specialized education and experience, is certified to perform acts of medical diagnosis and the prescription and dispensing of medical, therapeutic, or corrective measures under regulations adopted by the Board of Nursing.

Citation: ALASKA STAT. § 08.68.850.

Arizona

"Registered nurse practitioner" means a registered nurse who:

a. Is certified by the board.
b. Has completed a nurse practitioner education program approved or recognized by the board and educational requirements prescribed by the board by rule.
c. If applying for certification after July 1, 2004, holds national certification as a nurse practitioner from a national certifying body recognized by the board.
d. Has an expanded scope of practice within a specialty area that includes:
    i. Assessing clients, synthesizing and analyzing data, and understanding and applying principles of health care at an advanced level.
    ii. Managing the physical and psychosocial health status of clients.
    iii. Analyzing multiple sources of data, identifying alternative possibilities as to the nature of a healthcare problem and selecting, implementing and evaluating appropriate treatment.
    iv. Making independent decisions in solving complex client care problems.
    v. Diagnosing, performing diagnostic and therapeutic procedures, and prescribing, administering and dispensing therapeutic measures, including legend drugs, medical devices, and controlled substances within the scope of registered nurse practitioner practice on meeting the requirements established by the board.
    vi. Recognizing the limits of the nurse's knowledge and experience and planning for situations beyond the nurse's knowledge, educational preparation and expertise by consulting with or referring clients to other healthcare providers when appropriate.
    vii. Delegating to a medical assistant pursuant to § 32-1456.
    viii. Performing additional acts that require education and training as prescribed by the board and that are recognized by the nursing profession as proper to be performed by a nurse practitioner.

Citation: Ariz. Rev. Stat. Ann. § 32-1601(19).

Arkansas

(1)(a) Any person holding a license to practice as a registered nurse and possessing the educational qualifications required under subsection (b) of this section to be licensed as a registered nurse practitioner may, upon application and payment of necessary fees to the Arkansas State Board of Nursing, be licensed as a registered nurse practitioner and have the right to use the title of "registered nurse practitioner" and the abbreviation "RNP."

2. No other person shall assume such a title or use such an abbreviation or any other words, letters, signs, or devices to indicate that the person using them is a registered nurse practitioner.

b. In order to be licensed as a registered nurse practitioner, a registered nurse must hold a certificate or academic degree evidencing successful completion of the educational program of an accredited school of nursing or other nationally recognized accredited program recognized by the board as meeting the requirements of a nurse practitioner program…

Citation: ARK. CODE ANN. § 17-87-303.

California

The Legislature finds that various and conflicting definitions of the nurse practitioner are being created by state agencies and private organizations within California. The Legislature also finds that the public is harmed by conflicting usage of the title of nurse practitioner and lack of correspondence between use of the title and qualifications of the registered nurse using the title. Therefore, the Legislature finds the public interest served by the determination of the legitimate use of the title "nurse practitioner" by registered nurses.

Citation: CAL. BUS. & PROF. CODE § 2834.

"Nurse practitioner" means a registered nurse who possesses additional preparation and skills in physical diagnosis, psycho-social assessment, and management of health-illness needs in primary health care, and who has been prepared in a program conforming to board standards as specified in Section 1484.

Citation: CAL. CODE REGS. tit. 16, § 1480(a).

Colorado

"Practice of advanced practice nurse" means an expanded scope of professional nursing in a scope, role, and population focus approved by the board, with or without compensation or personal profit, and includes the practice of professional nursing.

Citation: COLO. REV. STAT. ANN. § 12-38-103-8.5a.

The board shall establish the advanced practice registry and shall require that a nurse applying for registration identify his or her role and population focus. The board shall establish reasonable criteria for designation of specific role and population foci based on currently accepted professional standards. A nurse who is included in the advanced practice registry has the right to use the title "advanced practice nurse" or, if authorized by the board, to use the title "certified nurse midwife", "clinical nurse specialist", "certified registered nurse anesthetist", or "nurse practitioner". These titles may be abbreviated as "A.P.N.", "C.N.M.", "C.N.S.", "C.R.N.A.", or "N.P.", respectively. It is unlawful for any person to use any of the titles or abbreviations listed in this subsection (3) unless included in the registry and authorized by the board to do so.

Citation: COLO. REV. STAT. ANN. § 12-38-111.5(3).

Connecticut

Advanced nursing practice is defined as the performance of advanced level nursing practice activities which, by virtue of post-basic specialized education and experience, are appropriate to and may be performed by an advanced practice registered nurse.

Citation: CONN. GEN. STAT. ANN. § 20-87a (West).

Delaware

"Advanced practice nurse" means an individual whose education and certification meet criteria established by the Board of Nursing who is currently licensed as a registered nurse and has a master's degree or a postbasic program certificate in a clinical nursing specialty with national certification. When no national certification at the advanced level exists, a master's degree in a clinical nursing specialty will qualify an individual for advanced practice nurse licensure. "Advanced practice nurse" shall include, but not be limited to, nurse practitioners, certified registered nurse anesthetists, certified nurse midwives, or clinical nurse specialists. Advanced practice nursing is the application of nursing principles, including those described in subsection (o) of this section, at an advanced level and includes:

a. For those advanced practice nurses who do not perform independent acts of diagnosis or prescription, the authority as granted within the scope of practice rules and regulations promulgated by the Board of Nursing; and

b. For those advanced practice nurses performing independent acts of diagnosis and/or prescription with the collaboration of a licensed physician, dentist, podiatrist, or licensed Delaware health care delivery system without written guidelines or protocols and within the scope of practice as defined in the rules and regulations promulgated by the Joint Practice Committee and approved by the Board of Medical Licensure and Discipline.

Citation: DEL. CODE ANN. tit. 24, § 1902 (b)(1).

District of Columbia

"Practice of advanced practice registered nursing" means the performance of advanced-level nursing actions, with or without compensation, by a licensed registered nurse with advanced education, knowledge, skills, and scope of practice who has been certified to perform such actions by a national certifying body acceptable to the Board of Nursing. The practice of advanced practice registered nursing includes:

A. Advanced assessment;
B. Medical diagnosis;
C. Prescribing;
D. Selecting, administering, and dispensing therapeutic measures;
E. Treating alterations of the health status; and
F. Carrying out other functions identified in Subchapter VI of this chapter and in accordance with procedures required by this chapter.

Citation: D.C. Stat. § 3-1201.02 (02).

Florida

"Advanced registered nurse practitioner" means any person licensed in this state to practice professional nursing and certified in advanced or specialized nursing practice, including certified registered nurse anesthetists, certified nurse midwives, and nurse practitioners.

Citation: Fla. Stat. Ann. § 464.003(3).

Georgia

"Advanced nursing practice" means practice by a registered professional nurse who meets those educational, practice, certification requirements, or any combination of such requirements, as specified by the board and includes certified nurse midwives, nurse practitioners, certified registered nurse anesthetists, clinical nurse specialists in psychiatric/mental health, and others recognized by the board.

Citation: Ga. Code Ann. § 43-26-3(1).

a. A nurse practitioner is a registered professional nurse who is recognized by the Board to engage in advanced practice registered nursing.
b. The nurse practitioner practices in a manner consistent with Chapter 410-13 of the Georgia Board of Nursing Rules and Regulations.

Citation: Ga. Comp. R. & Regs. § r. 410-12-.03(1).

Hawaii

"Advanced practice registered nurse" means a registered nurse who has met the qualifications for advanced practice registered nurse set forth in this chapter and through rules of the board, which shall include educational requirements.

Citation: Haw. Rev. Stat. § 457-2.

"Advanced practice registered nurse (APRN)" means a registered nurse licensed to practice in this State who has met the qualifications set forth in Chapter 457, HRS, and this subchapter, who, because of advanced education and specialized training, is authorized to assess, screen, diagnose, order, utilize, or perform medical, therapeutic, preventive or corrective measures.

Citation: Haw. Admin. § 16-89-2.

Idaho

"Advanced practice registered nurse" means a registered nurse licensed in this state who has gained additional specialized knowledge, skills and experience through a program of study recognized or defined by the board. An advanced practice registered nurse is authorized to perform advanced nursing practice, which may include the prescribing, administering and dispensing of therapeutic pharmacologic agents, as defined by board rules. An advanced practice registered nurse shall perform only those acts as provided by the board and for which the individual is educationally prepared.

Citation: Idaho Code § 54-1402(1).

Illinois

a. Advanced practice nursing by certified nurse practitioners, certified nurse anesthetists, certified nurse midwives, or clinical nurse specialists is based on knowledge and skills acquired throughout an advanced practice nurse's nursing education, training, and experience.
b. Practice as an advanced practice nurse means a scope of nursing practice, with or without compensation, and includes the registered nurse scope of practice.
c. The scope of practice of an advanced practice nurse includes, but is not limited to, each of the following:
    1. Advanced nursing patient assessment and diagnosis.
    2. Ordering diagnostic and therapeutic tests and procedures, performing those tests and procedures when using health care equipment, and interpreting and using the results of diagnostic and therapeutic tests

and procedures ordered by the advanced practice nurse or another health care professional.

3. Ordering treatments, ordering or applying appropriate medical devices, and using nursing medical, therapeutic, and corrective measures to treat illness and improve health status.
4. Providing palliative and end-of-life care.
5. Providing advanced counseling, patient education, health education, and patient advocacy.
6. Prescriptive authority as defined in Section 65-40 of this Act.
7. Delegating selected nursing activities or tasks to a licensed practical nurse, a registered nurse, or other personnel.

Citation: ILL. COMP. STAT. § 65/65-30.

Indiana

"Advanced practice nurse" means (1) a nurse practitioner; (2) a nurse midwife; or (3) a clinical nurse specialist; who is a registered nurse qualified to practice nursing in a specialty role based upon the additional knowledge and skill gained through a formal organized program of study and clinical expertise, or the equivalent as determined by the board, which does not limit but extends or expands the function of the nurse, which may be initiated by the client or provider in settings that shall include hospital outpatient clinics and health maintenance organizations.

Citation: IND. CODE ANN. § 25-23-1-1(b).

Iowa

"Advanced registered nurse practitioner (ARNP)" means a nurse with current licensure as a registered nurse in Iowa or who is licensed in another state and recognized for licensure in this state pursuant to the nurse licensure compact contained in 2000 Iowa Acts, House File 2105, section 8, and is also registered in Iowa to practice in an advanced role. The ARNP is prepared for an advanced role by virtue of additional knowledge and skills gained through a formal advanced practice education program of nursing in a specialty area approved by the board. In the advanced role, the nurse practices nursing assessment, intervention, and management within the boundaries of the nurse-client relationship. Advanced nursing practice occurs in a variety of settings, within an interdisciplinary health care team, which provide for consultation, collaborative management, or referral. The ARNP may perform selected medically delegated functions when a collaborative practice agreement exists.

Citation: IOWA ADMIN. CODE § r. 655-6.1(152).

"Certified nurse practitioner" is an ARNP educated in the discipline of nursing who has advanced knowledge of nursing, physical and psychosocial assessment, appropriate interventions and management of health care, and who possesses evidence of current certification by a national professional nursing certifying body approved by the board.

Citation: Iowa Admin. Code § r. 655-6.1(152).

Kansas

"Advanced practice registered nurse" or "APRN" means a professional nurse who holds a license from the board to function as a professional nurse in an advanced role, and this advanced role shall be defined by rules and regulations adopted by the board in accordance with the KSA 65-1130 and amendments thereto.

Citation: Kan. Stat. Ann. § 65-1113(g).

Kentucky

"Advanced practice registered nurse" means a certified nurse practitioner, certified nurse anesthetist, certified nurse midwife, or clinical nurse specialist, who is licensed to engage in advance practice registered nursing pursuant to KRS 314.042 and certified in at least one (1) population focus.

Citation: Ky. Rev. Stat. Ann. § 314.011(7).

Louisiana

"Advanced practice registered nurse" or "APRN" means a licensed registered nurse who is certified by a nationally recognized certifying body, such as the American Nurses Credentialing Center, as having an advanced nursing specialty as described in this Part and who meets the criteria for an advanced practice registered nurse as established by the board. In the absence of the availability of a national certification examination in a selected clinical area, the board may establish commensurate requirements. An advanced practice registered nurse shall include, but not be limited to, the following:

a. Certified nurse midwife or "CNM"
b. Certified registered nurse anesthetist or "CRNA"
c. Clinical nurse specialist or "CNS"
d. Nurse practitioner or "NP"

Citation: La. Rev. Stat. Ann. § 37:913 (1).

Maine

"Advanced practice registered nursing" (A.P.R.N.) means the practice of a registered professional nurse who, on the basis of specialized education and experience, is authorized under these rules to deliver expanded professional health care.

"Certified nurse practitioner" (C.N.P.) means a registered professional nurse who has received post-graduate education designed to prepare the nurse for advanced practice registered nursing in a specialty area in nursing that has a defined scope of practice and has been certified in the clinical specialty by a national certifying organization acceptable to the Board.

Citation: Code Me. R. § 02 380 008(1).

Maryland

"Nurse practitioner" means a registered nurse who by reason of certification under these regulations may engage in the activities authorized by these regulations.

Citation: Md. Regs. Code. § 10.27.07.01.B(4).

Massachusetts

Nurse authorized to practice in the expanded role means a nurse with:

a. current licensure as a registered nurse in the Commonwealth;
b. advanced nursing knowledge and clinical skills acquired through an appropriate nursing education program, as described in 244 CMR 4.13 or, until April 15, 1993, as acquired through appropriate education and clinical experience, or their equivalent, as described in 244 CMR 4.14 and
c. current certification in a specific practice area as described in 244 CMR 4.13.

Citation: 244 Mass. Admin. Code § 4.05.

Michigan

The board of nursing may issue a specialty certification to a registered professional nurse who has advanced training beyond that required for initial licensure and who has demonstrated competency through examination or other evaluative processes and who practices in one of the following health profession specialty fields: nurse midwifery, nurse anesthetist, or nurse practitioner.

Citation: Mich. Comp. Laws § 333.17210.

"Certified nurse practitioner" means an individual licensed as a registered professional nurse under part 172 who has been issued a specialty certification as a nurse practitioner by the board of nursing under Section 17210.

Citation: Mich. Comp. Laws § 333.2701(c).

Minnesota

"Advanced practice registered nurse," abbreviated APRN, means an individual licensed as a registered nurse by the board and certified by a national nurse certification organization acceptable to the board to practice as a clinical nurse specialist, nurse anesthetist, nurse-midwife, or nurse practitioner.

Citation: MINN. STAT. § 148.171(3).

Mississippi

An "advanced practice registered nurse" is a person who is licensed or holds the privilege to practice under this article and who is certified in advanced practice registered nurse or specialized nursing practice and includes certified nurse midwives, certified registered nurse anesthetists and certified nurse practitioners.

Citation: MISS. NURSING PRACTICE LAW §73-15-5(11).

Missouri

"Advanced practice registered nurse," a nurse who has education beyond the basic nursing education and is certified by a nationally recognized professional organization as a certified nurse practitioner, certified nurse midwife, certified registered nurse anesthetist, or a certified clinical nurse specialist. The board shall promulgate rules specifying which nationally recognized professional organization certifications are to be reorganized for the purposes of this section. Advanced practice nurses and only such individuals may use the title "Advanced Practice Registered Nurse" and the abbreviation "APRN."

Citation: MO. REV STAT. § 335.016(2).

Montana

1. Nurse practitioner (NP) practice means the independent and/or collaborative management of primary and/or acute health care of individuals, families, and communities including:
   a. assessing the health status of individuals and families using methods appropriate to the client population and area of practice such as health history taking, physical examination, and assessing developmental health problems.
   b. instituting and facilitating continuity of health care to clients, including:
      i. ordering durable medical equipment, treatments and modalities, and diagnostic tests;
      ii. receiving and interpreting results of diagnostic procedures;
      iii. making medical and nursing diagnoses; and
      iv. working with clients to promote their understanding of and compliance with therapeutic regimens.
   c. promoting wellness and disease prevention programs;
   d. referring clients to a physician or other healthcare provider, when appropriate;

e. providing instruction and counseling to individuals, families, and groups in the areas of health promotion and maintenance, including involving such persons in planning for their health care; and

f. working in collaboration with other health care providers and agencies to provide and, where appropriate, coordinate services to individuals and families.

2. Every licensed NP shall abide by the practice standards and guidelines established by an NP national professional organization as identified by the NP.

Citation: Mont. Code Ann. 24.159.1470.

Nebraska

Nurse practitioner means a registered nurse certified as described in Section 38-2317 and licensed under the Advanced Practice Registered Nurse Practice Act to practice as a nurse practitioner.

Citation: Neb. Rev. Stat. § 38-2312.

Nevada

"Advanced practice registered nurse" means a registered professional nurse who has specialized skill, knowledge and experience obtained from an organized formal program of training and who is authorized in special conditions as defined by NAC 632.255 to 632.295, inclusive, to provide designated services in addition to those which a registered nurse is authorized to perform.

Citation: Nev. Admin. Code § 632.020.

New Hampshire

"Advanced practice registered nurse" or "APRN" means a registered nurse currently licensed by the board under RSA 326-B:18.

Citation: N.H. Rev. Stat. Ann. § 326-B:2.I.

New Jersey

"Advanced practice nurse" means a person who holds a certification in accordance with section 8 or 9 of P.L. 1991, c.377 (C.45:11-47 or 45.11-48).

Citation: N.J. Stat. Ann. § 45:11-23.d.

Whenever the titles or designations "nurse practitioner," "clinical nurse specialist," or "nurse practitioner/clinical nurse specialist" occur or any reference is made thereto in any law, contract or document, the same shall be deemed to mean or refer to the title or designation "advanced practice nurse."

Citation: N.J. Stat. Ann. § 45:11-46.c.

New Mexico

"Certified nurse practitioner" means a registered nurse who is licensed by the board for advanced practice as a certified registered nurse practitioner and whose name and pertinent information are entered on the list of certified registered nurse practitioners maintained by the board.

Citation: N.M. Stat. Ann. § 61-3-3.E.

New York

The practice of registered professional nursing by a nurse practitioner, certified under section six thousand nine hundred ten of this article, may include the diagnosis of illness and physical conditions and the performance of therapeutic and corrective measures within a specialty area of practice, in collaboration with a licensed physician qualified to collaborate in the specialty involved, provided such services are performed in accordance with a written practice agreement and written practice protocols.

Citation: N.Y. Educ. Law, Art. 139 § 6902.3(a).

North Carolina

"Advanced Practice Registered Nurse (APRN)" means a nurse practitioner, nurse anesthetist, nurse-midwife or clinical nurse specialist.

Citation: N.C. Admin. Code tit. 21, r. § 36.0120(5).

"Nurse Practitioner" or "NP" means a currently licensed registered nurse approved to perform medical acts consistent with the nurse's area of nurse practitioner academic educational preparation and national certification under an agreement with a licensed physician for ongoing supervision, consultation, collaboration and evaluation of the medical acts performed. Such medical acts are in addition to those nursing acts performed by virtue of registered nurse (RN) licensure. The NP is held accountable under the RN license for those nursing acts that he or she may perform.

Citation: N.C. Admin. Code tit. 21, r. § 36.0801.

North Dakota

"Advanced practice registered nurse" means an individual who holds a current license to practice in this state as an advanced practice registered nurse within one of the roles of certified nurse practitioner, certified registered nurse anesthetist, certified nurse midwife, or certified clinical nurse specialist, and who functions in one of the population foci as approved by the board.

Citation: N.D. Cent. Code § 43-12.1-02(1).

Ohio

(J) "Certified nurse practitioner" means a registered nurse who holds a valid certificate of authority issued under this chapter that authorizes the practice of nursing as a certified nurse practitioner in accordance with Section 4723.43 of the Revised Code and rules adopted by the board of nursing.

(O) "Advanced practice registered nurse" means a certified registered nurse anesthetist, clinical nurse specialist, certified nurse-midwife, or certified nurse practitioner.

Citation: OHIO REV. CODE ANN. § 4723.01.

Oklahoma

"Advanced practice nurse" means a licensed registered nurse:

a. who has completed an advanced practice registered nursing education program for one of four recognized advanced practice registered roles,
b. who has passed a national certification examination recognized by the Board that measures the advanced practice registered nurse role and specialty competencies and who maintains recertification in the role and specialty through a national certification program,
c. who has acquired advanced clinical knowledge and skills in preparation for providing both direct and indirect care to patients; however, the defining factor for all Advanced Practice Registered Nurses is that a significant component of the education and practice focuses on direct care of individuals,
d. whose practice builds on the competencies of Registered Nurses by demonstrating a greater depth and breadth of knowledge, a greater synthesis of data, and increased complexity of skills and interventions,
e. who has obtained a license as an Advanced Practice Registered Nurse in one of the following roles: Certified Registered Nurse Anesthetist, Certified Nurse-Midwife, Clinical Nurse Specialist, or Certified Nurse Practitioner.

Citation: OKLA. STAT. ANN., § 59-567.3.5.

Oregon

"Nurse practitioner" (NP) means an advanced practice registered nurse who is certified by the Board to independently assume responsibility and accountability for the care of clients. The title nurse practitioner and population foci of practice shall not be used unless the individual is certified by the Board.

Citation: OR. ADMIN. § R. 851-050-0000(21).

Pennsylvania

Certified Registered Nurse Practitioner —A professional nurse licensed in this Commonwealth who is certified by the Board in a specialty and who, while functioning in the expanded role as a professional nurse, performs acts of medical diagnosis or prescription of medical therapeutic or corrective measures in collaboration with a physician licensed to practice in this Commonwealth and in accordance with the act and this subchapter. Nothing in this subchapter is to be deemed to limit or prohibit a professional nurse from engaging in those activities which constitute the practice of professional nursing as defined in section 2 of the act (63 P. S. § 212).

Citation: 49 Pa. Code § 21.251.

Rhode Island

"Certified registered nurse practitioner" is an advanced practice nurse utilizing independent knowledge of physical assessment and management of health care and illnesses. The practice includes prescriptive privileges. The practice includes collaboration with other licensed healthcare professionals including, but not limited to, physicians, pharmacists, podiatrists, dentists, and nurses.

Citation: R.I. Gen. Laws § 5-34-3(3).

South Carolina

"Nurse Practitioner" or "NP" means a registered nurse who has completed an advanced formal education program at the master's level acceptable to the board, and who demonstrates advanced knowledge and skill in assessment and management of physical and psychosocial health, illness status of persons, families, and groups. Nurse practitioners who perform delegated medical acts must have a supervising physician or dentist who is readily available for consultation and shall operate within the approved written protocols.

Citation: 2 S.C. Code Ann. § 40-33-20(41).

South Dakota

"Nurse practitioner," a provider duly authorized under this chapter to practice the specialty of nurse practitioner as defined in 36-9A-12.

Citation: S.D. Codified Laws § 36-9A-1(5).

Tennessee

"Advanced practice nurse" means a registered nurse with a master's degree or higher in a nursing specialty and national specialty certification as a nurse practitioner, nurse anesthetist, nurse midwife, or clinical nurse specialist.

Citation: Tenn. Code Ann. § 63-7-126(a).

Texas

Advanced practice nurse—A registered nurse approved by the board to practice as an advanced practice nurse based on completing an advanced educational program acceptable to the board. The term includes a nurse practitioner, nurse-midwife, nurse anesthetist, and a clinical nurse specialist. The advanced practice nurse is prepared to practice in an expanded role to provide health care to individuals, families, and/or groups in a variety of settings including but not limited to homes, hospitals, institutions, offices, industry, schools, community agencies, public and private clinics, and private practice. The advanced practice nurse acts independently and/or in collaboration with other health care professionals in the delivery of health care services.

Citation: 22 Tex. Admin. Code § 222.1(3).

Utah

"Practice of advanced practice registered nursing" means the practice of nursing within the generally recognized scope and standards of advanced practice registered nursing as defined by rule and consistent with professionally recognized preparation and education standards of an advanced practice registered nurse by a person licensed under this chapter as an advanced practice registered nurse. Advanced practice nursing includes:

a. maintenance and promotion of health and prevention of disease;
b. diagnosis, treatment, correction, consultation, or referral for common health problems; and
c. prescription or administration of prescription drugs or devices, including:
    i. local anesthesia;
    ii. Schedule IV-V controlled substances; and
    iii. Schedule II-III controlled substances in accordance with a consultation and referral plan.

Citation: Utah Code Ann. § 58-31b-102(13).

Vermont

"Advanced practice registered nurse" or "APRN" means a licensed registered nurse authorized to practice in this state who, because of specialized education and experience, is endorsed to perform acts of medical diagnosis and to prescribe medical, therapeutic, or corrective measures under administrative rules adopted by the board.

Citation: Vt. Stat. Ann. tit. 26, § 1572(4).

Virginia

"Nurse practitioner" means a registered nurse who has met the requirements for licensure as a nurse practitioner as stated in 18 VAC 90-30.

Citation: 18 Va. Code Ann. § 90-40-10.

Washington

1. A licensed advanced registered nurse practitioner (ARNP) is a registered nurse prepared in a formal educational program to assume primary responsibility for continuous and comprehensive management of a broad range of patient care, concerns, and problems.
2. The ARNP is prepared and qualified to assume primary responsibility and accountability for the care of patients.
3. ARNP practice is grounded in nursing and incorporates the use of independent judgment as well as collaborative interaction with other health care professionals when indicated in the assessment and management of wellness and health conditions as appropriate to the ARNP's area of practice and certification.
4. The ARNP functions within his or her scope of practice according to the commission approved certification program and standards of care developed by professional organizations.

Citation: Wash. Admin. Code § 246-840-300(1-4).

West Virginia

"Nurse practitioner" means a registered nurse qualified by virtue of his or her education and credentials and approved by the West Virginia Board of Examiners for registered professional nurses to practice as an advanced practice nurse independently or in a collaborative relationship with a physician.

Citation: W. Va. Code § 9-4B-1(c).

"Advanced nurse practitioner" means a registered nurse with substantial theoretical knowledge in a specialized area of nursing practice and proficient clinical utilization of the knowledge in implementing the nursing process, and who has met the further requirements of title 19, legislative rules for West Virginia board of examiners for registered professional nurses, series 7, who has mutually agreed upon association in writing with a physician and has been selected by or assigned to the person and has primary responsibility for treatment and care of the person.

Citation: W. Va. Code § 16-30-3(c).

Wisconsin

"Nurse practitioner" means a registered nurse licensed under Ch. 441 or in a party state, as defined in § 441.50(2)(j), whose practice of professional nursing under § 441.001(4) includes performance of delegated medical services under the supervision of a physician, dentist, or podiatrist.

Citation: Wis. Stat. § 255.06(d).

Wyoming

"Advanced practice registered nurse (APRN)" means a nurse who:

A. May prescribe, administer, dispense, or provide nonprescriptive and prescriptive medications including prepackaged medications, except schedule I drugs as defined in W.S. 35-7-1013 and 34-7-1014;

B. Has responsibility for the direct care and management of patients and clients in relation to their human needs, disease states and therapeutic and technological interventions;

C. Has a master's degree in nursing, or an advanced practice registered nurse specialty or has completed an accredited advanced practice registered nurse educational program prior to January 1, 1999; and

D. Has completed an advanced program of study in a specialty area in an accredited nursing program, has taken and passed a national certification examination in the same area and has been granted recognition by the board to practice as an APRN.

Citation: Wyo. Stat. Ann. § 33-21-120(a)(i).

State-by-State Titles for Nurse Practitioners

ALABAMA: Certified Registered Nurse Practitioner (CRNP)

ALASKA: Advanced Nurse Practitioner (ANP)

ARIZONA: Registered Nurse Practitioner (RNP)

ARKANSAS: Advanced or Registered Nurse Practitioner (RNP)

CALIFORNIA: Nurse Practitioner (NP)

COLORADO: Nurse Practitioner (NP) or Advanced Practice Nurse (APN)

CONNECTICUT: Advanced Practice Registered Nurse (APRN) or Certified Nurse Practitioner (CNP)

DELAWARE: Advanced Practice Nurse (APN), Nurse Practitioner (NP), or Advanced Registered Nurse Practitioner (ARNP)

DISTRICT OF COLUMBIA: Advanced Practice Registered Nurse (APRN)

FLORIDA: Advanced Registered Nurse Practitioner (ARNP)

GEORGIA: Advanced Practice Registered Nurse (APRN) or Nurse Practitioner (NP)

HAWAII: Advanced Practice Registered Nurse (APRN)

IDAHO: Advanced Practice Registered Nurse (APRN)

ILLINOIS: Advanced Practice Nurse (APN)

INDIANA: Advanced Practice Nurse (APN) or Nurse Practitioner (NP)

IOWA: Advanced Registered Nurse Practitioner (ARNP) or Certified Nurse Practitioner (CNP)

KANSAS: Advanced Practice Registered Nurse (APRN)

KENTUCKY: Advanced Practice Registered Nurse (APRN)

LOUISIANA: Advanced Practice Registered Nurse (APRN)

MAINE: Advanced Practice Registered Nurse (APRN) or Certified Nurse Practitioner (CNP)

MARYLAND: Certified Registered Nurse Practitioner (CRNP)

MASSACHUSETTS: Nurse Practitioner (NP)

MICHIGAN: Certified Nurse Practitioner (CNP)

MINNESOTA: Advanced Practice Registered Nurse Practitioner (APRN) or Nurse Practitioner (NP)

MISSISSIPPI: Advanced Practice Registered Nurse (APRN)

MISSOURI: Advanced Practice Registered Nurse (APRN)

MONTANA: Advanced Practice Registered Nurse (APRN) or Nurse Practitioner (NP)

NEBRASKA: Nurse Practitioner (NP)

NEVADA: Advanced Practice Registered Nurse (APRN)

NEW HAMPSHIRE: Advanced Practice Registered Nurse (APRN)

NEW JERSEY: Advanced Practice Nurse (APN)

NEW MEXICO: Certified Nurse Practitioner (CNP)

NEW YORK: Nurse Practitioner (NP)

NORTH CAROLINA: Advanced Practice Registered Nurse (APRN) or Nurse Practitioner (NP)

NORTH DAKOTA: Advanced Practice Registered Nurse (APRN) or Nurse Practitioner (NP)

OHIO: Certified Nurse Practitioner (CNP) or Advanced Practice Registered Nurse (APRN)

OKLAHOMA: Advanced Practice Nurse (APN) or Advanced Registered Nurse Practitioner (ARNP)

OREGON: Nurse Practitioner (NP)

PENNSYLVANIA: Certified Registered Nurse Practitioner (CRNP)

RHODE ISLAND: Certified Registered Nurse Practitioner (RNP)

SOUTH CAROLINA: Nurse Practitioner (NP)

SOUTH DAKOTA: Nurse Practitioner (NP)

TENNESSEE: Advanced Practice Nurse (APN) or Certified Nurse Practitioner (CNP)

TEXAS: Advanced Practice Nurse (APN)

UTAH: Advanced Practice Registered Nurse (APRN)

VERMONT: Advanced Practice Registered Nurse (APRN)

VIRGINIA: Nurse Practitioner (NP)

WASHINGTON: Advanced Registered Nurse Practitioner (ARNP)

WEST VIRGINIA: Advanced Nurse Practitioner (ANP) or Nurse Practitioner (NP)

WISCONSIN: Nurse Practitioner (NP)

WYOMING: Advanced Practice Registered Nurse (APRN)

CHAPTER 2

Legal Scope of Nurse Practitioner Practice

Having an adequate legal description of nurse practitioners' (NPs') scope of practice according to state law is important for the following reasons:

1. To allow NPs to perform at their level of education and training
2. To avoid any charges of practicing medicine without a license
3. To avoid imputation of liability for medical malpractice to someone other than the NP, usually a physician
4. To place accountability for both benefits and harm to patients squarely on the NP
5. To provide a basis for inclusion of NPs in the legal definition of primary care providers, which is necessary for admission to provider panels
6. To establish that the NP is a professional entity, not just a "nonphysician," a "physician extender," or whatever an agency, employer, or delegating physician decides an NP is
7. To get reimbursement for physician services, when provided by an NP

State law is the most powerful source of authority for professional practice. However, federal agencies and private businesses may have policies on NP scope of practice, and professional societies may have accepted certain tasks, functions, and decisions as part of NP scope of practice.

Professional Association Definition of Scope of Practice

Some associations define the scope of practice for NPs in general or for individual NPs. For example, the American Academy of Nurse Practitioners' statement on scope of practice says:

> Nurse practitioners are licensed independent practitioners who practice in ambulatory, acute, and long-term care settings as primary and/or specialty care providers. According to their practice specialty, they provide nursing and medical services to individuals, families, and groups. In addition to diagnosing and managing acute episodic and chronic illnesses, NPs emphasize health promotion and disease prevention. Services include but are not limited to ordering, conducting, and interpreting diagnostic and laboratory tests, prescription of pharmacologic agents and treatments and nonpharmacologic therapies. Teaching and counseling individuals, families, and groups are a major part of nurse practitioners'

practice. As licensed independent practitioners, nurse practitioners practice autonomously and in collaboration with healthcare professionals and other individuals to diagnose, treat, and manage the patient's health problems. They serve as healthcare resources, interdisciplinary consultants, and patient advocates.[1]

Statutory Versus Regulatory Scope of NP Practice

Some states define scope of practice in statutes enacted by the state legislature. In other states, the legislature gives the board of nursing the authority to define the scope of NP practice. Either way is enforceable, and regulations carry the same force of law as statutes.

Some states describe scope of practice specifically, and some define it generally. State statutes describing NP scope of practice fall into six categories:

1. Scope of practice is clearly defined by statute.
2. Scope of practice is clearly defined by regulation.
3. Scope of practice is vaguely defined by statute.
4. Scope of practice is not defined.
5. Scope of practice is defined by exception from a state law prohibiting the practice of medicine without a license.
6. Scope of practice is defined by the individual physician, who may delegate to an NP by law.

The first category is the most secure for the NP.

At a time when NPs are viewed by some physicians as competitors, the first response to competitive pressures is often for physicians to point to state law and ask for strict interpretation. For example, physicians' associations may counter NPs' efforts to be designated as primary care providers (PCPs) for managed-care organizations or a patient's "medical home" by claiming that state law does not explicitly authorize NPs to perform the necessary functions. Then, only NPs in states where the NP scope of practice is clearly defined as including medical diagnosis and treatment, prescription of medication, and oversight of comprehensive healthcare services for patients will have legal grounds for arguing that NPs should be admitted to provider panels as PCPs or designated a "medical home."

A vaguely worded nurse practice act that states, for example, that the scope of NP practice includes "acts of advanced nursing practice" will not provide sound legal basis for arguments that NPs should be admitted to managed-care provider panels or receive fees for providing physician services. It is difficult to argue to managed-care executives, state administrators, and legislators that "acts of nursing practice" are the acts necessary to perform physician services.

Physician Challenges to NPs' Scope of Practice

An example of a physician challenge to NPs' scope of practice is a 1984 Missouri court case, *Sermchief v. Gonzales* [660 S.W.2d 683 (Mo. 1984)]. That case, which the NPs won only after it went to the state's supreme court, could be repeated in other states today where state law is not specific enough about the authority of NPs to diagnose and treat.

In *Sermchief*, two obstetric-gynecologic NPs were working in a family planning clinic under written protocols with the clinic's physicians. The NPs were taking histories, performing physical examinations, treating minor illnesses, and prescribing contraceptives. There was no specific charge of malpractice, but rather the Missouri Board of Medicine charged that the NPs were practicing medicine without a license.

The lower court agreed and found that the NPs were practicing medicine without a license. However, the Missouri Supreme Court, after analyzing the nurse practice act, noted that the legislature had deleted a requirement that a physician directly supervise nursing functions and decided that by that deletion the legislature had intended to broaden the scope of nursing.

The NPs eventually prevailed in the case, but that will not necessarily help NPs in other states if there is no express statutory authority for NPs' medical functions. NPs need a clear statutory definition of the scope of practice that includes medical diagnoses and treatment and prescriptive authority.

Need for Clarity of Scope of Practice

Some state laws describe scope of practice succinctly and others go into great detail. Longer is not necessarily better, and vague language should be avoided. Consider Oklahoma's statute on nurse practitioner scope of practice.

> "Certified Nurse Practitioner" is an Advanced Practice Registered Nurse who performs in an expanded role in the delivery of health care:
>
> a. consistent with advanced educational preparation as a Certified Nurse Practitioner in an area of specialty,
> b. functions within the Certified Nurse Practitioner scope of practice for the selected area of specialization, and
> c. is in accord with the standards for Certified Nurse Practitioners as identified by the certifying body and approved by the Board.
>
> A Certified Nurse Practitioner shall be eligible, in accordance with the scope of practice of the Certified Nurse Practitioner, to obtain recognition as authorized by the Board to prescribe, as defined by the rules promulgated by the Board pursuant to this section and subject to the medical direction of a supervising physician. This authorization shall not include dispensing drugs, but shall not preclude, subject to federal regulations, the receipt of, the signing for, or the dispensing of professional samples to patients.
>
> *Citation:* OKLA. STAT. ANN. tit. 59, § 567.3a(6).

Under Oklahoma's statutory definition of NP scope of practice, an NP can prescribe, but it is unclear what else an NP can do. To prove that the NP can make medical diagnoses, the NP would need to produce transcripts and course descriptions, as well as information from the certifying body on the scope of practice. Oklahoma's Administrative Code provides a detailed description of NP scope of practice, however. The Oklahoma Administrative Code states the following:

The Certified Nurse Practitioner's scope of practice includes the full scope of nursing practice and practice in an expanded role as follows:

1. The Certified Nurse Practitioner (CNP) provides comprehensive health care to clients across the life span.
2. The CNP is responsible and accountable for the continuous and comprehensive management of a broad range of health services, which include, but are not limited to:
   A. promotion and maintenance of health;
   B. prevention of illness and disability;
   C. diagnosis and prescription of medications, treatments, and devices for acute and chronic conditions and diseases;
   D. management of health care during acute and chronic phases of illness;
   E. guidance and counseling services;
   F. consultation and/or collaboration with other health care providers and community resources;
   G. referral to other health care providers and community resources.

Citation: Okla. Admin. Code § 485:10–15.6(b)

An example of a comprehensive description of scope of practice is Pennsylvania's law:

When acting in collaboration with a physician as set forth in a collaborative agreement and within the CRNP's specialty, a CRNP may:

1. Perform comprehensive assessments of patients and establish medical diagnoses.
2. Order, perform and supervise diagnostic tests for patients and, to the extent the interpretation of diagnostic tests is within the scope of the CRNP's specialty and consistent with the collaborative agreement, may interpret diagnostic tests.
3. Initiate referrals to and consultations with other licensed professional health care providers, and consult with other licensed professional health care providers at their request.
4. Develop and implement treatment plans, including issuing orders to implement treatment plans. However, only a CRNP with current prescriptive authority approval may develop and implement treatment plans for pharmaceutical treatments.
5. Complete admission and discharge summaries.
6. Order blood and blood components for patients.
7. Order dietary plans for patients.
8. Order home health and hospice care.
9. Order durable medical equipment.
10. Issue oral orders to the extent permitted by the health care facilities' by-laws, rules, regulations or administrative policies and guidelines.

11. Make physical therapy and dietitian referrals.
12. Make respiratory and occupational therapy referrals.
13. Perform disability assessments for the program providing temporary assistance to needy families (TANF).
14. Issue homebound schooling certifications.
15. Perform and sign the initial assessment of methadone treatment evaluations, provided that any order for methadone treatment shall be made only by a physician.

Citation: 49 PA CODE § 21.251.

See **Exhibit 2-1** for a breakdown of elements of NP practice found in various state laws. See **Appendix 2-A** for the law of each of the states regarding NP scope of practice.

Exhibit 2-1   Specific Functions Included in States' Definitions of NP Scope of Practice

Diagnose	OR	MT	IL	VT
AL	PA	ND	IN	WA
AZ	SC	ND	KS	WI
CO	SD	NE	KY	WY
CT	UT	NV	LA	
DC	VT	NH	MD	**Admit to Hospital**
FL	WA	NJ	MA	AL
GA		NY	ME	AZ
HI	**Treat**	NC	MN	HI
IA	AL	OK	MO	OR
ID	AZ	OR	MS	WA
IL	CO	PA	NC	
IN	CT	SC	NC	**Refer**
LA	DE	SD	ND	AL
ME	DC	UT	NE	AZ
MD	FL	VT	NH	CO
MA	GA	WA	NJ	DC
MN	ID		NM	DE
MS	IL	**Prescribe**	NV	HI
MT	IN	AL	NY	IN
NC	KS	AZ	OH	KY
ND	KY	CO	OK	LA
NE	LA	CT	OR	ME
NH	ME	DE	PA	MD
NH	MD	DC	RI	MN
NJ	MA	FL	SC	MT
NV	MS	GA	SD	NC
NY	MN	IA	TX	NE
OK	MO	ID	UT	NH

Refer	Order Tests	Assist in Surgery
NJ	AL	HI
NV	AZ	
OK	CO	**Perform Palliative Care**
OR	DC	IL
PA	DE	
SD	FL	**Order Durable Medical Equipment**
UT	GA	
WA	HI	MT
	IA	PA
Teach	IL	
AL	KY	**Order Restraints**
DE	MA	SD
HI	MD	
IA	ME	
IL	MT	
IN	NE	
KS	NJ	
LA	NC	
ME	PA	
MT	WA	
NV	WI	
NC		
ND	**Perform Procedures**	
NH	WA	
OK		
OR	**Remove Epidural Catheter**	
SD	DE	

NP Scope of Practice Compared with Registered Nurse Scope of Practice

NP scope of practice usually includes medical diagnosis and treatment, while registered nurse (RN) scope of practice usually includes "nursing diagnosis" and "nursing interventions" or "nursing treatments."

Compare Oregon's scope of practice for an RN to Oregon's scope of practice for an NP. Oregon's law on scope of practice for an RN states:

> The Board recognizes that the scope of practice for the registered nurse encompasses a variety of roles, including, but not limited to:
>
> a. Provision of client care;
> b. Supervision of others in the provision of care;

   c. Development and implementation of health care policy;

   d. Consultation in the practice of nursing;

   e. Nursing administration;

   f. Nursing education;

   g. Case management;

   h. Nursing research;

   i. Teaching health care providers and prospective healthcare providers;

   j. Specialization in advanced practice;

   k. Nursing informatics.

Citation: Or. Admin. § R. 851-045-0060.

Oregon's board of nursing has elegantly defined the scope of NP practice as follows:

   . . .

3. The nurse practitioner provides holistic health care to individuals, families, and groups across the life span in a variety of settings, including hospitals, long-term care facilities, and community-based settings.

4. Within his or her specialty, the nurse practitioner is responsible for managing health problems encountered by the client and is accountable for health outcomes. This process includes:

   a. Assessment;

   b. Diagnosis;

   c. Development of a plan;

   d. Intervention;

   e. Evaluation.

5. The nurse practitioner is independently responsible and accountable for the continuous and comprehensive management of a broad range of health care, which may include:

   a. Promotion and maintenance of health;

   b. Prevention of illness and disability;

   c. Assessment of clients, synthesis and analysis of data, and application of nursing principles and therapeutic modalities;

   d. Management of health care during acute and chronic phases of illness;

   e. Admission of his/her clients to hospitals and long-term care facilities and management of client care in these facilities;

   f. Counseling;

   g. Consultation and/or collaboration with other care providers and community resources;

   h. Referral to other healthcare providers and community resources;

   i. Management and coordination of care;

   j. Use of research skills;

   k. Diagnosis of health/illness status;

    l. Prescribing, dispensing, and administration of therapeutic devices and measures, including legend drugs and controlled substances as provided in Division 56 of the Oregon Nurse Practice Act, consistent with the definition of the practitioner's specialty category and scope of practice.

    6. The nurse practitioner's scope of practice includes teaching the theory and practice of advanced practice nursing.

    7. The nurse practitioner is responsible for recognizing limits of knowledge and experience, and for resolving situations beyond his/her nurse practitioner expertise by consulting with or referring clients to other healthcare providers.

    8. The nurse practitioner will only provide healthcare services within the nurse practitioner's scope of practice for which he/she is educationally prepared and for which competency has been established and maintained. Educational preparation includes academic course work, workshops or seminars, provided both theory and clinical experience are included.

Citation: Or. Admin. § R. 851-050-0005.

In California, the scope of practice of an NP is defined as that of an RN:

> The nurse practitioner shall function within the scope of practice as specified in the Nursing Practice Act and as it applies to all registered nurses.

Citation: Cal. Code Reg. tit. 16 §1485.

An NP or RN gets the authority to perform medical acts through standardized procedures developed with physicians. Here is a statement from the California Board of Professional Nursing website about the scope of practice of a nurse practitioner:

> The NP does not have an additional scope of practice beyond the usual RN scope and must rely on standardized procedures for authorization to perform overlapping medical functions (CCR Section 1485). Section 2725 of the Nursing Practice Act (NPA) provides authority for nursing functions that are also essential to providing primary health care which do not require standardized procedures. Examples include physical and mental assessment, disease prevention and restorative measures, performance of skin tests and immunization techniques, and withdrawal of blood, as well as authority to initiate emergency procedures.

> Nurse practitioners frequently ask if they really need standardized procedures. The answer is that they do when performing overlapping medical functions. Standardized procedures are the legal authority to exceed the usual scope of RN practice. Without standardized procedures the NP is legally very vulnerable, regardless of having been certified as a RN, who has acquired additional skills as a certified nurse practitioner.[2]

In general, NPs may make medical diagnoses and initiate and perform medical treatments, while RNs may not. RNs may make nursing diagnoses, carry out physician or NP orders, and perform nursing treatments, as well as many other functions. Ideally, NPs have clear authority under state law to perform comprehensive evaluations, make medical diagnoses, order tests, initiate and perform medical therapies, including the prescribing of medication, and admit patients to hospitals.

NP and Physician Scope of Practice Compared

When NP scope of practice is defined to include medical diagnosis, medical treatment, prescriptive authority, and admission of patients to hospitals, as in Oregon law, there is little legal difference between NP and physician scope of practice. However, in most states, medical scope of practice is defined more broadly than the scope of practice for any other healthcare professional. Consider Mississippi's definition of the practice of medicine:

> The practice of medicine shall mean to suggest, recommend, prescribe, or direct for the use of any person, any drug, medicine, appliance, or other agency, whether material or not material, for the cure, relief, or palliation of any ailment or disease of the mind or body, or for the cure or relief of any wound or fracture or other bodily injury or deformity, or the practice of obstetrics or midwifery, after having received, or with the intent of receiving therefore, either directly or indirectly, any bonus, gift, profit, or compensation; provided, that nothing in this section shall apply to females engaged solely in the practice of midwifery.
>
> *Citation:* Miss. Code Ann. § 73-25-33.

The liberal use of the word "any" differentiates the physician scope of practice from the NP scope of practice. There are no laws that authorize as wide a scope of practice for NPs as the Mississippi law authorizes for physician practice.

An Individual NP's Portfolio

Individual NPs may want to develop portfolios—compilations of documentation of the NP's education, training, and experience. The portfolio often is a binder containing pages, which may be removed and copied as needed.

There are at least three good reasons to keep a portfolio. First, in many states, NPs must submit to the Board of Nursing a written agreement stating the services the NP is authorized to perform. NPs may want to perform procedures, such as colposcopy or suturing. Boards require NPs to document that they are qualified to perform such procedures. Qualifications might include formal course work, informal course work, or formal or informal one-to-one preceptorship experience. NPs can find it difficult to document such training, especially if the NP learned how to perform a procedure years ago from a physician while on the job. If NPs document the teaching at the time it is done, through a letter or form signed and dated by the instructor, the NP can produce the document as needed many years later, assuming the NP keeps such documents in a safe place—in the portfolio.

Second, some states' laws defer to scope of practice statements adopted by professional organizations. For example, Texas law states the following:

> The advanced practice nurse provides a broad range of health services, the scope of which shall be based upon educational preparation, continued advanced practice experience, and the accepted scope of professional practice of the particular specialty area. Advanced practice nurses practice in a variety of settings and, according to their practice specialties and roles, they provide a broad range of healthcare services to a variety of patient populations.
>
> 1. The scope of practice of particular specialty areas shall be defined by national professional specialty organizations or advanced practice nursing organizations recognized by the Board. The advanced practice nurse may perform only those functions which are within that scope of practice and which are consistent with the Nursing Practice Act, Board rules, and other laws and regulations of the State of Texas.
>
> *Citation:* TX ADMIN. CODE § 221.12.

NPs living in states with laws similar to Texas should have the scope and standards of practice established by the national organization representing the NP's specialty in their portfolios.

For example, if an NP in Texas is certified by the American Academy of Nurse Practitioners (AANP), the NP should keep in his/her portfolio a 1-page document from the AANP website titled *Scope of Practice for Nurse Practitioners.* The document states, in part:

> Nurse Practitioners are licensed independent practitioners who practice in ambulatory, acute and long-term care as primary and/or specialty care providers. According to their practice specialty they provide nursing and medical services to individuals, families, and groups. In addition to diagnosing and managing acute episodic and chronic illnesses, nurse practitioners emphasize health promotion and disease prevention. Services include, but are not limited to ordering, conducting, supervising, and interpreting diagnostic and laboratory tests, and prescription of pharmacologic agents and nonpharmacologic therapies. Teaching and counseling individuals, families, and groups are a major part of nurse practitioner practice.[1]

Third, some nurses are using their portfolios in place of resumes when interviewing for jobs. A portfolio could include the following:

- Statement of career goals
- Description of special interests or abilities

- Description of special projects conducted by the individual
- Articles or reports written by the individual
- Articles written about the individual
- Brochures from previous practices
- Testimonials or letters of appreciation from patients
- Letters of reference from former employers or coworkers
- Awards, honors, or distinction earned by the individual
- Transcripts
- Diplomas
- Certificates of certification as advanced practice nurse
- Nursing and advanced practice nursing (APN) license
- Photo of the individual
- Certificates of continuing education or training
- Letters of recommendation
- Letters, forms, or photographs documenting one-on-one training
- Listing of former jobs or projects
- National Provider Identifier and any other provider numbers needed for reimbursement
- Drug Enforcement Agency (DEA) number and state controlled substances prescriber number
- Certificate of professional liability insurance
- Copy of state law addressing NP scope of practice, prescribing, qualifications, and physician collaboration requirements, if any
- Previous written agreements, if state law requires physician collaboration
- Outcomes data, if the NP or an employer has tracked the NP's outcomes
- Data on performance measures, if the NP has participated in Medicare's Quality Reporting System or other quality measurement programs
- Productivity data, if the NP or an employer has tracked visits, revenues, and collections
- Patient satisfaction data, if the NP or an employer has tracked patient satisfaction

Finally, it saves time if one keeps the documents related to one's professional practice in one place.

Mandated Physician Involvement with NP Practice

In some states, there is no legal requirement for physician involvement in NP practice. However, in the majority of states, there is some legal requirement for physician involvement. That involvement may be "supervision," "collaboration," or some other form. It may be limited to situations where the NP is prescribing medications, or it may be required for all advanced practice.

See **Exhibit 2-2** for a chart listing requirements of physician involvement by state. For text of state laws regarding physician involvement, see **Appendix 2-B**.

Exhibit 2-2   Physician Involvement Required for NP Practice

Collaborate	Supervise	Protocols	None
AL	FL	AL	AK
AR	MI	AR	AZ
CT	ME*	CA	CO
DE	SC	FL	DC
GA	OK	GA	HI
IA+	TN	KS	ID
IL		MA	KY
IN	**Delegate**	NJ	ME**
KS	GA	NY	MT
LA	MI	SC	ND
MA	MN	TX	NH
MD	SC		NM
MN	WV	**Referral**	NV
MO		**Process**	OR
MS	**Direct**	AK	RI
NC	OK		UT***
ND	AR		VT**
NE			WA
NJ			WY
NY			
OH			
OH			
PA			
SD			
VA			
VT*			
WV			
WI			

+Iowa Administrative Code requires collaboration for medical functions; however, the Board of Nursing's position is that advanced registered nurse practitioners function independently.
*First 24 months of practice only.
**After 24 months.
***Consultation/referral plan required to prescribe Schedules II–III controlled substances.

Some states require that NPs practice using written protocols. Some states require a written agreement between the NP and the physician that states how the physician will participate in NP practice, what medications the NP may prescribe, what procedures an NP may perform, how often a physician will review NP documentation, and under what circumstances an NP must contact a physician. A protocol is a written instrument that guides the NP in collecting data from the patient and recommends specific action based upon the collected data. It consists of mutually agreed upon medical guidelines between the physician and the NP that define their individual and shared responsibilities. The protocol is considered a standard because it provides a guideline for a minimum level of safe practice in specific situations.[3]

Exhibit 2-3 is an example of a protocol.

Exhibit 2-3   Urinary Tract Infection Protocol: Initial Visit

I. RATIONALE
    This protocol will assist in the differentiation between pyelonephritis and urinary tract symptoms sufficiently to eradicate the symptoms per se rather than an attempt to eradicate any bacteriuria that may or may not be present. The design of the protocol for urinary tract infection (UTI) encompasses these principles.

II. SYMPTOMS
    A. CYSTITIS
        1. FEMALE PATIENTS
            Order a STAT clean catch urinalysis (UA) for female patients with any of the following symptoms;
            a. Dysuria
            b. Frequency
            c. Urgency
            d. Inability to empty bladder completely
        2. Male patients
            Male patients with any of the above symptoms should be seen by a physician, not by an NP, unless they have a uretheral discharge (possible venereal disease (VD)—follow VD protocol).

    B. PYELONEPHRITIS
        1. In addition to the above symptoms, patients with pyelonephritis may have:
            a. Fever greater than 100.0° F, or
            b. Flank pains, or
            c. Chills, or
            d. Nausea, vomiting, or abdominal pain.
        2. Continue with protocol through the physical exam with these patients, but then consult supervising physician before deciding on treatment.

III. HISTORY
    A. Consult supervising physician if patient has:
        1. A history of kidney problems, or
        2. Is currently pregnant. To ascertain this, always ask for last menstrual period (LMP) date and record for all female patients.
        3. Diabetes or insulin.
        4. Three or more UTIs in past 12 months.

    B. Continue with UTI protocol, but also refer patient to gynecology practitioner if history of:

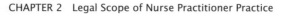

      1. Vaginal discharge, or

      2. Perineal inflammation.

IV. PHYSICAL EXAM

   A. Perform the following examinations:

      1. Abdominal

      2. Costovertebral angle (CVA) tenderness

      3. Temperature

   B. Consult supervising physician if findings of:

      1. Fever greater than 100.0° F, or

      2. CVA tenderness.

V. LAB TESTS

INITIAL URINALYSIS

   A. Consult supervising physician if:

      1. Casts

      2. Red blood cells (RBCs) or protein are positive (with associated white blood cell (WBC) abnormality).

   B. If UA shows 10 or more WBCs/hpf and patient is symptomatic, give patient antibiotic prescription as described in the treatment section.

   C. If UA revealed 0–10 WBCs, review symptoms. If the symptoms are definite and very severe, treat with antibiotics; if symptoms are vague and poorly defined, then give patient symptomatic treatment as described in the treatment section and consider referral to gynecology for pelvic.

   D. Should the initial UA be "positive": (defined in guidelines below), then give patient a repeat UA slip for the abnormality found with instructions to have the UA one week following completion of treatment.

   Positive UA findings are defined as:

   Casts: any except occasional hyaline or rare granular
   RBCs > 3 (if not menstruating) and WBC < 5
   Protein > trace and WBC < 5

VI. TREATMENT

ANTIBACTERIAL TREATMENT
To be given if initial UA reveals 10 or more WBC/hpf, or in any case where symptoms are severe, even if UA revealed, WBC/hpf.

   A. Prescribe appropriate antibiotic drug (see below).

   B. Instruct patient to call in if symptoms do not subside within 72 hours. If patient does call back, information for treatment failure instructions.

SYMPTOMATIC TREATMENT
To be given only if initial UA reveals, 10 WBC/hpf, and patient has minimal or uncertain symptoms. Consider gynecology referral for pelvic.

   A. Prescribe either Propantheline 15 mg #20 sig: 1-2 QID prn or Belladonna with Pb tabs #15, sig: 1 tab QID prn.

B.   Instruct patient to call in if symptoms persist beyond 72 hours or if symptoms worsen at any time.

VII. REPEAT URINALYSIS
A.   Consult supervising physician if UA shows casts.
B.   If repeat UA conforms abnormality (protein and/or RBC as listed below) refer to Proteinuria and/or Hematuria protocols.

Positive UA findings are defined as:

Casts: any, except occasional hyaline or rare granular
RBCs > 3 (if not menstruating) and WBC < 5
Protein > trace and WBC < 5

UTI PROTOCOL: ANTIBIOTIC TREATMENT

A.   If organism found in patient's urine is not listed in the table below, consult supervising physician for treatment.
B.   If this is the first antibiotic course (initial visit), assume E. coli and use the first listed drug to which patient is not allergic, as listed for E. coli in the drug table on the following page.
C.   If this is a second antibiotic course (treatment failure), go to the first drug for the organism listed that is not the same as that previously used and to which the patient is not allergic. If the patient is allergic to all drugs listed, consult supervising physician for treatment.
D.   Prescribe according to the prescription table which follows:
1.   If symptoms have been present within the past 48 hours, use 1 dose treatment.
2.   If symptoms have been present longer than 48 hours, use 5-day treatment.
3.   If symptoms persist after treatment with first drug, repeat UA and culture and consult supervising physician.

UTI PROTOCOL: TREATMENT FAILURE

If the patient calls in with persisted or recurrent symptoms after the first course of antibiotic treatment, obtain a clean catch urine specimen for UA and culture and sensitivity.

If the UA is negative, wait for the culture results before treating. If the UA is positive, treat with the next drug listed on the Antibiotic Prescription Table and review treatment choice when the culture and sensitivity results are available.

If culture is positive and patients symptoms are improving, stay with the same antibiotic. If not responding after 3 days, switch to a new antibiotic based on culture sensitivity.

Adapted from protocol developed by: _____, NP

_____, MD

(List names of nurse practitioners and physicians who developed the standardized procedure, including the protocol section.)

ANTIBIOTIC PRESCRIPTION TABLE

Organism	Drug	
E. Coli	Septra DS, AmoxicillinProteus mirabilis	Macrodantin, Keflex
Aerobacter	Septra DS, MacrodantinKlebsiella	Keflex, Ciprofloxacin
Enterococcus	Ampicillin	*Consult MD if allergic
Pseudomonas	Ciprofloxacin	(Usually not seen in out-patient setting)

Dosages	
SEPTRA DS	#3 PO at once or 1 bid × 5 days
AMOXICILLIN	500 mg 3 gms PO at once or 250 mg 1 tid × 5 days
MACRODANTIN	100 mg qid × 5 day
KEFLEX	250 mg qid × 5 day
CIPROFLOXACIN	250 mg qid × 5 day

Source: California Board of Registered Nursing. Available at http://www.rn.ca.gov. Retrieved May 30, 2013.

Notes

1. American Academy of Nurse Practitioners. (2013). Scope of practice for nurse practitioners. Retrieved from http://www.aanp.org/images/documents/publications/scopeofpractice.pdf
2. California Board of Registred Nursing. (2011.). General information: Nurse practitioner practice. Retrieved from http://www.rn.ca.gov/pdfs/regulations/npr-b-23.pdf
3. Phillips, R. S. (1985). Nurse practitioners: Their scope of practice and theories of liability. *Journal of Legal Medicine, 6,* 391–414.

Scope of Practice

In some states scope of practice is specified by statute; in other states it is specified by regulation. Both statutes and regulations carry the same legal weight. Statutes are laws made by the legislature; they are also changed by a vote of the legislature. Regulations are executive agency–made law; they can be changed by the agency or overridden by statute.

The following are excerpts from state law. For the complete language, see each state's Nurse Practice Act, usually available online through the state's Board of Nursing website.

Alabama

Practice as a certified registered nurse practitioner (CRNP) means the performance of nursing skills by a registered nurse who has demonstrated by certification that he or she has advanced knowledge and skills in the delivery of nursing services within a healthcare system that provides for consultation, collaborative management, or referral as indicated by the health status of the client.

Citation: ALA. CODE § 34-21-81(4a).

1. Functions and activities of certified registered nurse practitioners. The certified registered nurse practitioner is responsible for the continuous and comprehensive management of a broad range of health services for which the certified registered nurse practitioner is educationally prepared and for which competency is maintained, with physician collaboration as decribed in these rules. These services include but are not restricted to the following:
   a. Evaluate current health status and risk factors of individuals based on comprehensive health history and physical examination and assessment.
   b. Formulate a working diagnosis, develop and implement a treatment plan, and evaluate and modify therapeutic regimens to promote positive patient outcomes.
   c. Prescribe, administer and provide therapeutic measures, tests, procedures, and drugs.

    d. Counsel, teach and assist individuals and families to assume responsibility for self-care in prevention of illness, health maintenance, and health restoration.

    e. Consult with and refer to other healthcare providers as appropriate.

2. A standard protocol approved by the Board of Nursing and State Board of Medical Examiners shall address permissible functions and activities specific to the advanced practice of the certified registered nurse practitioner.

3. A certified registered nurse practitioner may, after the successful completion of an organized program of study and supervised clinical practice, carry out functions beyond the nurse practitioner educational preparation provided the functions are approved by the Board of Nursing as being within the legal scope of practice for a certified registered nurse practitioner. Such functions shall be submitted to the Joint Committee for consideration for inclusion on the standard protocol.

4. Request for additional functions to be added to the protocol may be submitted to the Joint Committee for consideration.

5. A certified registered nurse practitioner may write admission orders for inpatients as directed by the physician and subsequent orders in accordance with established protocols and institutional policies.

Citation: Ala. Admin. Code r. 610-X-5-.10.

Alaska

The board recognizes advanced and specialized acts of nursing practice as those described in the scope of practice statements for nurse practitioners certified by national certification bodies recognized by the board.

Citation: Alaska Admin. Code, § 44.430.

Authority AS 08.68.100(a)

Arizona

Nurse practitioners

- Examine patients and establish medical diagnoses by client history, physical exam, and other criteria
- For a patient who requires the services of a health care facility: admit the patient to healthcare facilities, manage the care the patient receives in the facility, and discharge the patient from the facility
- Order and interpret laboratory, radiographic, and other diagnostic tests, and perform those tests that the RNP is qualified to perform
- Identify, develop, implement, and evaluate a plan of care for a patient to promote, maintain, and restore health

- Perform therapeutic procedures that the RNP is qualified to perform
- Prescribe treatments
- If authorized under R4-19-511, prescribe and dispense drugs and devices
- Perform additional acts that the RNP is qualified to perform

Citation: Ariz. Admin. Code § R4-19-508.

Arkansas

"Practice of advanced nurse practitioner nursing" means the performance for compensation of nursing skills by a registered nurse who, as demonstrated by national certification, has advanced knowledge and practice skills in the delivery of nursing services.

Citation: Ark. Code Ann. § 17-87-102.(4)(B)(i).

"Practice of registered nurse practitioner nursing" means the delivery of health care services for compensation in collaboration with and under the direction of a licensed physician or under the direction of protocols developed with a licensed physician.

Citation: Ark. Code Ann. § 17-87-102.(8)(A).

California

Nothing in this article shall be construed to limit the scope of practice of a registered nurse authorized pursuant to this chapter.

Citation: Cal. Bus. & Prof. Code § 2837.

Nothing in this article shall be construed to limit the scope of practice of the registered nurse authorized pursuant to the Business and Professions Code, Divison 2, Chapter 6. The nurse practitioner shall function within the scope of practice as specified in the Nurse Practice Act and as it applies to all registered nurses.

Citation: Cal. Code Reg. tit.16, § 1485.

Colorado

In order to enhance the cost efficiency and continuity of care, an advanced practice nurse may, within his or her scope of practice and within the advanced practice nurse-patient relationship, sign an affidavit, certification, or similar document that:

- I. Documents a patient's current health status;
- II. Authorizes continuing treatment, tests, services, or equipment; or
- III. Gives advance directives for end-of-life care.

b. Such affidavit, certification, or similar document may not:

    I. Be the prescription of medication unless the advanced practice nurse has been granted prescriptive authority pursuant to section 12-38-111.6; or

    II. Be in conflict with other requirements of law.

Citation: COLO. REV. STAT.§12-38-111.5(7)(A).

"Practice of professional nursing" means the performance of both independent nursing functions and delegated medical functions in accordance with accepted practice standards. Such functions include the initiation and performance of nursing care through health promotion, supportive or restorative care, disease prevention, diagnosis and treatment of human disease, ailment, pain, injury, deformity, and physical or mental condition using specialized knowledge, judgment, and skill involving the application of biological, physical, social, and behavioral science principles required for licensure as a professional nurse pursuant to section 12-38-111.

The "practice of professional nursing" shall include the performance of such services as:

    I.   Evaluating health status through the collection and assessment of health data;

    II. Health teaching and health counseling;

    III. Providing therapy and treatment that is supportive and restorative to life and well-being either directly to the patient or indirectly through consultation with, delegation to, supervision of, or teaching of others;

    IV. Executing delegated medical functions;

    V. Referring to medical or community agencies those patients who need further evaluation or treatment;

    VI. Reviewing and monitoring therapy and treatment plans.

Citation: Colo. Rev. Stat. Ann. § 12-38-103 (10)(a) and (b).

A nurse who meets the definition of advanced practice nurse . . . may be granted prescriptive authority as a function in addition to those defined in Section 12-38-103(10).

Citation: Colo. Rev. Stat. Ann. § 12-38-111.5.

The scope of practice for an advanced practice nurse may be determined by the board in accordance with this article.

Citation: Colo. Rev. Stat. Ann. § 12-38-111.6(8)(a).

Connecticut

Advanced nursing practice is defined as the performance of advanced level nursing practice activities, which by virtue of post-basic specialized education and experience are appropriate to and may be performed by an Advanced

Practice Registered Nurse. The advanced practice registered nurse performs acts of diagnosis and treatment of alteration in health status as described in subsection (a) of this section, and shall collaborate with a physician licensed to practice medicine in this state. In all settings, the advanced practice registered nurse may, in collaboration with a physician licensed to practice medicine in this state, prescribe, dispense, and administer medical therapeutics and corrective measures and may request, sign for, receive, and dispense drugs in the form of professional samples. . . .

Citation: CONN. GEN. STAT. ANN § 20-87a.

Delaware

"Independent practice by an advanced practice nurse" shall include those advance practice nurses who practice and prescribe without written guidelines or protocols but with a collaborative agreement with a licensed physician, dentist, podiatrist, or licensed Delaware health care delivery system and with the approval of the Joint Practice Committee.

Citation: DEL. CODE ANN. TIT. 24, § 1902(g).

Generic functions of the Advanced Practice Nurse with the Specialized Scope of Practice include, but are not limited to:

- Eliciting detailed health history(s)
- Defining nursing problem(s)
- Performing physical examination(s)
- Collecting and performing laboratory tests
- Interpreting laboratory data
- Initiating requests for essential laboratory procedures
- Initiating requests for essential x-rays
- Screening patients to identify abnormal problems
- Initiating referrals to appropriate resources and services as necessary
- Initiating or modifying treatment and medications within established guidelines
- Assessing and reporting changes in the health of individuals, families, and communities
- Providing health education through teaching and counseling
- Planning and/or instituting health care programs in the community with other health care professionals and the public
- Delegating tasks appropriately
- Prescribing medications and treatments independently pursuant to Rules and Regulations . . .
- Removing epidural catheters

Citation: DEL. NURSING REGS. tit. 24, ch 1900, § 8.7.

District of Columbia

The advanced practice registered nurse may perform actions of medical diagnosis, treatment, prescription, and other functions authorized by this subchapter.

Citation: D.C. Stat. § 3-1206.01(a).

An advanced practice registered nurse may:

1. Initiate, monitor, and alter drug therapies;
2. Initiate appropriate therapies or treatments;
3. Make referrals for appropriate therapies or treatments; and
4. Perform additional functions within his or her specialty determined in accordance with rules and regulations promulgated by the board.

Citation: D.C. Stat. § 3-1206.04.

"Practice of advanced practice registered nursing" means the performance of advanced-level nursing actions, with or without compensation, by a licensed registered nurse with advanced education, knowledge, skills, and scope of practice who has been certified to perform such actions by a national certifying body acceptable to the Board of Nursing. The practice of advanced practice registered nursing includes:

A. Advanced assessment;
B. Medical diagnosis;
C. Prescribing;
D. Selecting, administering, and dispensing therapeutic measures;
E. Treating alterations of the health status; and
F. Carrying out other functions identified in subchapter VI of this chapter and in accordance with procedures required by this chapter.

Citation: D.C. Stat. § 3-1201.02(2).

Florida

An advanced registered nurse practitioner shall perform those functions authorized in this section within the framework of an established protocol that is filed with the board upon biennial license renewal and within 30 days after entering into a supervisory relationship with a physician or changes to the protocol. The board shall review the protocol to ensure compliance with applicable regulatory standards for protocols. The board shall refer to the department licensees submitting protocols that are not compliant with the regulatory standards for protocols. A practitioner currently licensed under chapter 458, chapter 459, or chapter 466 shall maintain supervision for directing the specific course of medical treatment. Within the established framework, an advanced registered nurse practitioner may:

a. Monitor and alter drug therapies.
b. Initiate appropriate therapies for certain conditions.
c. Perform additional functions as may be determined by rule . . .
d. Order diagnostic tests and physical and occupational therapy.

Citation: FLA. STAT. Ch. 464.012(3).

All categories of Advanced Registered Nurse Practitioner may perform functions listed in Section 464.012(3), F.S. The scope of practice for all categories of ARNP's shall include those functions which the ARNP has been educated to perform including the monitoring and altering of drug therapies, and initiation of appropriate therapies, according to the established protocol and consistent with the practice setting.

Citation: FLA. ADMIN REGISTER & FLA. ADMIN CODE. Ch. 064B9-4.009.

Within the context of advanced or specialized nursing practice, the advanced registered nurse practitioner may perform acts of nursing diagnosis and nursing treatment of alterations of the health status. The advanced registered nurse practitioner may also perform acts of medical diagnosis and treatment, prescription, and operation which are identified and approved by a joint committee composed of three members appointed by the Board of Nursing, two of whom must be advanced registered nurse practitioners; three members appointed by the Board of Medicine, two of whom must have had work experience with advanced registered nurse practitioners; and the State Surgeon General or the State Surgeon General's designee.

Citation: FLA. STAT. Ch. 464.003(2).

Georgia

The nurse practitioner provides advanced practice nursing care and medical services specific to the nurse practitioner respective specialty to individuals, families, and groups, emphasizing health promotion and disease prevention as well as the diagnosis and management of acute and chronic diseases. The nurse practitioner collaborates as necessary with a variety of individuals to diagnose and manage clients' healthcare problems.

Citation: GA. COMP. R. & REGS. r. 410-12-.03(2)(a).

The advanced practice registered nurse is authorized to perform advanced nursing functions and certain medical acts which include, but are not limited to, ordering drugs, treatments, and diagnostic studies as provided in O.C.G.A. 43-24-26.1 and Chapter 410.13.

Citation: GA. COMP. R. & REGS. r. 410-12-.01(4b).

Hawaii

In addition to those functions specified for the registered nurse, and in accordance with appropriate nationally recognized standards of practice, the advanced practice registered nurse may perform the following generic acts which include, but are not limited to:

1. Provide direct nursing care by utilizing advanced practice scientific knowledge, skills, nursing and related theories to assess, plan, and implement appropriate health and nursing care to patients;
2. Provide indirect care. Plan, guide, evaluate, and direct the nursing care given by other personnel associated with the health care team;
3. Teach, counsel, or plan care for individuals or group, utilizing a synthesis of advanced skills, theories, and knowledge of biologic, pharmacologic, physical, sociocultural and psychological aspects of care to accomplish desired objectives;
4. Serve as a consultant and resource of advanced clinical knowledge and skills to those involved directly or indirectly in patient care;
5. Participate in joint and periodic evaluation of services rendered including, but not limited to, chart reviews, case reviews, patient evaluations, and outcome of case statistics;
6. Establish collaborative, consultative, and referral networks as appropriate with other health care professionals. Patients who require care beyond the scope of practice of an APRN shall be referred to an appropriate health care provider;
7. Manage the plan of care prescribed for the patient;
8. Initiate and maintain accurate records and authorize appropriate regulatory and other legal documents;
9. Recognize, develop, and implement professional and community educational programs related to health care;
10. Conduct research and analyze the health needs of individuals and populations and design programs which target at-risk groups and cultural and environmental factors which foster health and prevent illness;
11. Participate in policy analysis and development of new policy initiative in the area of practice specialty; and
12. Contribute to the development, maintenance, and change of health care delivery systems to improve quality of health care services and consumer access to services.

Citation: Haw. Admin. R. §16-89-81(b).

Nurse practitioner scope of practice, depending on area of specialty, may include, but is not limited to:

A. Evaluate the physical and psychosocial health status of patients through a comprehensive health history and physical examination, or mental status examination, using skills of observation, inspection, palpation, percussion, and auscultation, and using diagnostic instruments or procedures that are basic to the clinical evaluation of physical, developmental, and psychological signs and symptoms;

B. Order, interpret, or perform diagnostic, screening, and therapeutic examinations, tests and procedures.
C. Formulate a diagnosis;
D. Plan, implement, and evaluate care;
E. Order or utilize medical, therapeutic, or corrective measures, including, but not limited to, rehabilitation therapies, medical nutritional therapy, social services and psychological and other medical services;
F. Monitor the effectiveness of therapeutic interventions;
G. Assist in surgery; and
H. Admit and discharge clients for inpatient care at facilities licensed as hospitals, long term care facilities or hospice.

Citation: HAW. ADMIN. R. § 16-89-81(c)(1).

Practice as an advanced practice registered nurse means the scope of nursing in a category approved by the board, regardless of compensation or personal profit, and includes the registered nurse scope of practice. The scope of an advanced practice registered nurse includes but is not limited to advanced assessment and the diagnosis, prescription, selection, and administration of therapeutic measures including over the counter drugs, legend drugs, and controlled substances within the advanced practice registered nurse's role and specialty-appropriate education and certification.

Citation: HAW. REV. STAT. § 457-a.

Idaho

An advanced practice registered nurse is authorized to perform advanced nursing practice, which may include the prescribing, administering and dispensing of therapeutic pharmacologic agents, as defined by board rules. An advanced practice registered nurse shall perform only those acts as provided by the board and for which the individual is educationally prepared.

Citation: IDAHO CODE § 54-1402(1).

Advanced Practice Registered Nurse. Means a registered nurse licensed in this state who has gained additional specialized knowledge, skills and experience through a graduate or post-graduate program of study as defined herein and is authorized to perform advanced nursing practice, which may include acts of diagnosis and treatment, and the prescribing, administering and dispensing of therapeutic pharmacologic and non-pharmacologic agents, as defined herein.

Citation: IDAHO ADMIN. CODE §23.01.01: 271.02.

Illinois

a. Advanced practice nursing by certified nurse practitioners, certified nurse anesthetists, certified nurse midwives, or clinical nurse specialists is based on knowledge and skills acquired throughout an advanced practice nurse's nursing education, training, and experience.

b. Practice as an advanced practice nurse means a scope of nursing practice, with or without compensation, and includes the registered nurse scope of practice.

c. The scope of practice of an advanced practice nurse includes, but is not limited to, each of the following:

   1. Advanced nursing patient assessment and diagnosis.
   2. Ordering diagnostic and therapeutic tests and procedures, performing those tests and procedures when using health care equipment, and interpreting and using the results of diagnostic and therapeutic tests and procedures ordered by the advanced practice nurse or another health care professional.
   3. Ordering treatments, ordering or applying appropriate medical devices, and using nursing medical, therapeutic, and corrective measures to treat illness and improve health status.
   4. Providing palliative and end-of-life care.
   5. Providing advanced counseling, patient education, health education, and patient advocacy.
   6. Prescriptive authority as defined in Section 65-40 of this Act.
   7. Delegating selected nursing activities or tasks to a licensed practical nurse, a registered nurse, or other personnel.

Citation: 225 Ill. Comp. Stat. § 65/65-30.

Indiana

"Nurse practitioner" means an advanced practice nurse who provides advanced levels of nursing client care in a specialty role, who meets the requirements of the advanced practice nurse as outlined in Section 3 of this rule.

Citation: Ind. Admin. Code tit. 848, r. 4-1-4.

[Indiana law does not use the words "scope of practice," but describes "standards for each nurse practitioner" as follows:]

1. Assess clients by using advanced knowledge and skills to:
    A. identify abnormal conditions;
    B. diagnose health problems;
    C. develop and implement nursing treatment plans;

D. evaluate patient outcomes; and

E. collaborate with or refer to a practitioner, as defined in IC 25-23-1-19.4, in managing the plan of care.

2. Use advanced knowledge and skills in teaching and guiding clients and other health team members.

3. Use appropriate critical thinking skills to make independent decisions, commensurate with the autonomy, authority, and responsibility of a nurse practitioner.

4. Function within the legal boundaries of their advanced practice area and shall have and utilize knowledge of the statutes and rules governing their advanced practice area; including the following:

A. State and federal drug laws and regulations.

B. State and federal confidentiality laws and regulations.

C. State and federal medical records access laws.

5. Consult and collaborate with other members of the health team as appropriate to provide reasonable client care, both acute and ongoing.

6. Recognize the limits of individual knowledge and experience, and consult with or refer clients to other health care providers as appropriate.

7. Retain professional accountability for any delegated intervention, and delegate interventions only as authorized by IC 25-23-1 and this title.

8. Maintain current knowledge and skills in the nurse practitioner area.

9. Conduct an assessment of clients and families, which may include health history, family history, physical examination, and evaluation of health risk factors.

10. Assess normal and abnormal findings obtained from the history, physical examination, and laboratory results.

11. Evaluate clients and families regarding development, coping ability, and emotional and social well-being.

12. Plan, implement, and evaluate care.

13. Develop individualized teaching plans with each client based on health records.

14. Counsel individuals, families, and groups about health and illness and promote attention to wellness.

15. Participate in periodic or joint evaluations of services rendered, including, but not limited to, the following:

A. Chart reviews.

B. Client evaluations.

C. Outcome statistics.

16. Conduct and apply research findings appropriate to the area of practice.

17. Participate, when appropriate, in the joint review of the plan of care.

Citation: IND. ADMIN. CODE tit. 848, r. 4-2-1.

The board shall establish a program under which advanced practice nurses who meet the requirements established by the board are authorized to prescribe legend drugs, including controlled substances (as defined in IC 35-48-1).

b. The authority granted by the board under this section:
   1. expires on October 31 of the odd-numbered year following the year the authority was granted or renewed; and
   2. is subject to renewal indefinitely for successive periods of two (2) years.

c. The rules adopted under section 7 of this chapter concerning the authority of advanced practice nurses to prescribe legend drugs must do the following:
   1. Require an advanced practice nurse or a prospective advanced practice nurse who seeks the authority to submit an application to the board.
   2. Require, as a prerequisite to the initial granting of the authority, the successful completion by the applicant of a graduate level course in pharmacology providing at least two (2) semester hours of academic credit.
   3. Require, as a condition of the renewal of the authority, the completion by the advanced practice nurse of the continuing education requirements set out in section 19.7 of this chapter.

Citation: IND. CODE §25-23-1-19.5(a).

Iowa

In the advanced role, the nurse practices nursing assessment, intervention, and management within the boundaries of the nurse-client relationship. Advanced nursing practice occurs in a variety of settings within an interdisciplinary healthcare team, which provides for consultation, collaborative management, and referral. The ARNP may perform selected medically designated functions when a collaborative practice agreement exists.

Citation: IOWA ADMIN. CODE r. 655-6.1(152).

Kansas

Each "advanced practice registered nurse" (APRN), as defined by K.S.A. 65-1113 and amendments thereto, shall function in an expanded role to provide primary, secondary, and tertiary health care in the APRN's category of advanced practice. Each APRN shall be authorized to make independent decisions about advanced practice nursing needs of families, patients, and clients and medical decisions based on the authorization for collaborative practice with one or more physicians. This regulation shall not be deemed to require the immediate and physical presence of the physician when care is given by an APRN. Each APRN shall be directly accountable and responsible to the consumer.

Citation: KAN. ADMIN. REGS. § 60-11-101(a).

Each advanced registered nurse practitioner in the category of nurse practitioner shall function in an expanded role at a specialized level, through the application of advanced knowledge and skills and shall be authorized to perform the following:

a. Provide health promotion and maintenance, disease prevention, and independent nursing diagnosis, as defined in K.S.A. 65-1113(b) and amendments thereto, and treatment, as defined in K.S.A. 65-1113(c) and amendments thereto, of acute and chronic diseases;

b. develop and manage the medical plan of care for patients or clients, based on the authorization for collaborative practice;

c. provide health care services for which the nurse practitioner is educationally prepared and for which competency has been established and maintained. Educational preparation may include academic coursework, workshops, institutes, and seminars if theory or clinical experience, or both, are included;

d. provide health care for individuals by managing health problems encountered by patients and clients; and

e. provide innovation in evidence-based nursing practice based upon advanced clinical expertise, decision making, and leadership skills and serve as a consultant, researcher, and patient advocate for individuals, families, groups, and communities to achieve quality, cost-effective patient outcomes and solutions.

Citation: Kan. Admin. Regs. § 60-11-104.

An advanced practice registered nurse may prescribe drugs pursuant to a written protocol as authorized by a responsible physician.

Citation: Kan. Stat. Ann. § 65-1130(d).

Kentucky

"Advanced practice registered nursing" means the performance of additional acts by registered nurses who have gained added knowledge and skills through an approved organized postbasic program of study and clinical experience; and who are certified by the American Nurses' Association or other nationally established organizations or agencies recognized by the board to certify registered nurses for advanced practice registered nursing as a certified nurse practitioner, certified nurse anesthetist, certified nurse midwife, or clinical nurse specialist; and who are certified in at least one (1) population focus. The additional acts shall, subject to approval of the board, include but not be limited to, prescribing treatment, drugs, devices, and ordering diagnostic tests. Advanced practice registered nurses who engage in these additional acts shall be authorized to issue prescriptions for and dispense nonscheduled legend drugs as defined in KRS 217.905 and to issue prescriptions for but not to dispense Schedules II through V controlled substances as classified in KRS 218A.060, 218A.070, 218A.080,

218A.090, 218A.100, 218A.110, 218A.120, and 218A.130, under the conditions set forth in KRS 314.042 and regulations promulgated by the Kentucky Board of Nursing on or before August 15, 2006.

a. Prescriptions issued by advanced practice registered nurses for Schedule II controlled substances classified under KRS 218A.060 shall be limited to a seventy-two (72)-hour supply without any refill. Prescriptions issued under this subsection for psychostimulants may be written for a thirty (30)-day supply only by an advanced practice registered nurse certified in psychiatric-mental health nursing who is providing services in a health facility as defined in KRS Chapter 216B or in a regional mental health-mental retardation services program as defined in KRS Chapter 210.

b. Prescriptions issued by advanced practice registered nurses for Schedule III controlled substances classified under KRS 218A.080 shall be limited to a thirty (30)-day supply without any refill. Prescriptions issued by advanced practice registered nurses for Schedules IV and V controlled substances classified under KRS 218A.100 and 218A.120 shall be limited to the original prescription and refills not to exceed a six (6)-month supply. . . .

Citation: Ky. Rev. Stat. Ann. § 314.011(8).

The practice of the advanced practice registered nurse shall be in accordance with the standards and functions defined in the following scope and standards of practice statements for each specialty area.

- In the performance of advanced practice registered nursing, the advanced practice registered nurse shall seek consultation or referral in those situations outside the advanced practice registered nurse's scope of practice.
- Advanced practice registered nursing shall include prescribing medications and ordering treatments, devices, and diagnostic tests which are consistent with the scope and standard of practice of the advanced practice registered nurse.

Advanced practice registered nursing shall not preclude the practice by the advanced practice registered nurse of registered nursing practice as defined in KRS 314.011(5).

Citation: 201 Ky. Admin. Regs. § 20:057 Sections 2–5.

Louisiana

An advanced practice registered nurse shall practice as set forth in R.S. 37:913(3)(a) and the standards set forth in these administrative rules. The patient services provided by an APRN shall be in accord with the educational preparation of that APRN. . . .

Standards of practice are essential for safe practice by the APRN and shall be in accordance with the published professional standards for each recognized specialty and/or functional role. The core standards for all categories of advanced practice registered nurses include, but are not limited to:

1. an APRN shall meet the standards of practice for registered nurses as defined in LAC 46:XLVII.3901-3915;
2. an APRN shall assess patients at an advanced level, identify abnormal conditions, analyze and synthesize data to establish a diagnosis, develop and implement treatment plans, and evaluate patient outcomes;
3. the APRN shall use advanced knowledge and skills in providing patients and health team members with guidance and teaching;
4. an APRN shall use critical thinking and independent decision-making at an advanced level commensurate with the autonomy, authority, and responsibility of the specialty and functional role while working with patients and their families in meeting health care needs;
5. an APRN shall demonstrate knowledge of the statutes and rules governing advanced registered nursing practice and function within the legal boundaries of the appropriate advanced registered nursing practice role;
6. an APRN shall demonstrate knowledge of and apply current nursing research findings relevant to the advanced nursing specialty and functional role;
7. an APRN shall make decisions to solve patient care problems and select medical treatment regimens in collaboration with a licensed physician or dentist; and
8. an APRN shall retain professional accountability for his/her actions and/or interventions.

Citation: LA. ADMIN. CODE tit. 46, § XLVII-4513.

a. "Advanced practice registered nursing" means nursing by a certified registered nurse anesthetist, certified nurse midwife, clinical nurse specialist, or nurse practitioner which is based on knowledge and skills acquired in a basic nursing education program, licensure as a registered nurse, and a minimum of a master's degree with a concentration in the respective advanced practice nursing specialty which includes both didactic and clinical components, advanced knowledge in nursing theory, physical and psychosocial assessment, nursing interventions, and management of health care. Advanced practice registered nursing includes:

   i. Assessing patients, analyzing and synthesizing data, and knowledge of and applying nursing principles at an advanced level.
   ii. Providing guidance and teaching.
   iii. Working with patients and families in meeting health care needs.
   iv. Collaborating with other health care providers.
   v. Managing patients' physical and psychosocial health-illness status with regard to nursing care.
   vi. Utilizing research skills.

vii. Analyzing multiple sources of data and performing certain acts of medical diagnosis in accordance with the collaborative practice agreement.

viii. Making decisions in solving patient care problems and selecting treatment regimens in collaboration with a licensed physician, dentist, or other health care provider as indicated.

ix. Consulting with or referring patients to licensed physicians, dentists, and other health care providers in accordance with a collaborative practice agreement.

b. Advanced practice registered nursing may include certain acts of medical diagnosis, in accordance with R.S. 37:913(8) and (9), or medical prescriptions of therapeutic or corrective nature, prescribing assessment studies, legend and certain controlled drugs, therapeutic regimens, medical devices and appliances, receiving and distributing a therapeutic regimen of prepackaged drugs prepared and labeled by a licensed pharmacist, and free samples supplied by a drug manufacturer, and distributing drugs for administration to and use by other individuals within the scope of practice as defined by the board and in accordance with this Paragraph.

Citation: La. Rev. Stat. § 37:913(3).

Maine

The certified nurse practitioner shall provide only those health care services for which the certified nurse practitioner is educationally and clinically prepared, and for which competency has been maintained. The Board reserves the right to make exceptions. Such health care services, for which the certified nurse practitioner is independently responsible and accountable, include:

1. obtaining a complete health data base that includes a health history, physical examination, and screening and diagnostic evaluation
2. interpreting health data by identifying wellness and risk factors and variations from norms
3. diagnosing and treating common diseases and human responses to actual and potential health problems
4. counseling individuals and families
5. consulting and/or collaborating with other healthcare providers and community resources
6. referring client to other health care providers and community resources.

Citation: Code Me. R. § 02 380 3.

"Advanced practice registered nursing" means the delivery of expanded professional health care by an advanced practice registered nurse that is:

B. Within the advanced practice registered nurse's scope of practice as specified by the board of rulemaking, taking into consideration any national standards that exists; and

C. In accordance with the standards of practice for advanced practice registered nurses as specified by the board by rulemaking, taking into consideration any national standards that may exist. Advanced practice registered nursing includes consultation with or referral to medical and other health care providers when required by client health care needs.

A certified nurse practitioner or a certified nurse midwife who qualified as an advanced practice registered nurse may prescribe and dispense drugs or devices, or both, in accordance with rules adopted by the board.

A certified nurse practitioner who qualified as an advanced practice registered nurse must practice, for at least 24 months, under the supervision of a licensed physician or a supervising nurse practitioner or must be employed by a clinic or hospital that has a medical director who is a licensed physician. The certified nurse practitioner shall submit written evidence to the board upon completion of the required clinical experience.

Citation: ME. REV. STAT. ANN. tit. 32, § 2102-2A.

Maryland

A. A nurse practitioner may perform independently the following functions:
1. A comprehensive physical assessment of patients;
2. In accordance with Family Law Article, §2-301, Annotated Code of Maryland, certify to the clerk of the court that a:
   a. 16 or 17 year old individual, who wants to get married without parental consent, has been examined and found to be pregnant or has given birth to a child; or
   b. 15 year old individual, who has parental consent to be married, has been examined and found to be pregnant or has given birth to a child;
3. In accordance with Transportation Article, §13-704, Annotated Code of Maryland, certify to the Department of Transportation that an individual needs special consideration for certain health reasons;
4. In accordance with Health General Article, §4-208, Annotated Code of Maryland, complete the date of birth and medical information required on a birth certificate;
5. In accordance with Health General Article, §4-212, Annotated Code of Maryland, complete a death certificate if:
   a. The medical examiner does not take charge of the body; and
   b. The deceased was under the care of the nurse practitioner;

6. In accordance with Health General Article, §13-704, Annotated Code of Maryland, conduct education and training to certify individuals for the Insect Sting Emergency Treatment Program;

7. Establish medical diagnosis for common short-term and chronic stable health problems;

8. In accordance with Health General Article, §4-212, Annotated Code of Maryland, file a replacement death certificate;

9. In accordance with Health General Article, §5-601, Annotated Code of Maryland, issue a "do not resuscitate order" on a Maryland Emergency Medical Services form.

10. Order, perform, and interpret laboratory and diagnostic tests;

11. Order and perform diagnostic, therapeutic, and corrective measures;

12. Prescribe drugs;

13. Provide emergency care;

14. Refer patients to appropriate licensed physicians or other health care providers as needed; and

15. In accordance with Health General Article, §5-602, Annotated Code of Maryland, witness an advance directive.

B. A nurse practitioner may practice only in the area of specialization in which certified.

C. Nothing in this chapter limits or prohibits a registered nurse from performing those functions which constitute the practice of registered nursing as defined by law.

Citation: MD. REGS. CODE. 10 § 27.07.02.

Massachusetts

The practice of registered nurses shall include, but not be limited to:

1. the application of nursing theory to the development, implementation, evaluation, and modification of plans of nursing care for individuals, families and communities;

2. coordination and management of resources of care delivery;

3. management, direction and supervision of the practice of nursing, including the delegation of selected activities to unlicensed assistive personnel.

Advanced practice nurse regulations which govern the ordering of tests, therapeutics, and prescribing of medications shall be promulgated by the board of nursing and in conjunction with the board of medicine.

Citation: MASS. GEN LAWS CH 112 § 80B.

The area of practice of a nurse practitioner includes:

a. Assessing the health status of individuals and families by obtaining health and medical histories, performing physical examinations, diagnosing health and developmental problems, and caring for patients suffering from acute and chronic diseases by managing therapeutic regimens according to guidelines approved and developed in compliance with 244 CMR § 4.22.

Citation: CODE MASS REGS Tit. 244 § 4.26(a).

Michigan

[There is no statutory or regulatory scope of practice for NPs. Physicians may delegate at their discretion.]:

Subject to subsections (2) to (6), a licensee who holds a license other than a health profession subfield license may delegate to a licensed or unlicensed individual who is otherwise qualified by education, training or experience the performance of selected acts, tasks or functions where the acts, tasks, or functions fall within the scope of practice of the licensee's profession and will be performed under the licensee's supervision. A licensee shall not delegate an act, task, or function under this section if the act, task, or function, under standards of acceptable and prevailing practice, requires the level of education, skill, and judgment required of the licensee under this article.

Citation: MICH. COMP. LAWS § 333.16215(1).

Minnesota

"Nurse practitioner practice" means, within the context of collaborative management:

1. diagnosing, directly managing, and preventing acute and chronic illness and disease; and
2. promoting wellness, including providing non-pharmacologic treatment. The certified nurse practitioner is certified for advanced registered nurse practice in a specific field of nurse practitioner practice.

Citation: MINN. STAT. ANN. § 148.171(11).

The "practice of advanced practice registered nursing" means the performance of clinical nurse specialist practice, nurse-midwife practice, nurse practitioner, or registered nurse anesthetist practice as defined in subdivisions 5, 10, 11, and 21. The practice includes functioning as a direct care provider, case manager, consultant, educator, and researcher. The practice of advanced practice registered nursing also includes accepting referrals from, consulting with, cooperating with, or referring to all other types of health care providers, including but not limited to physicians, chiropractors, podiatrists, and dentists, provided that the advanced practice registered nurse and the other provider are practicing within their scopes of practice as defined in state law. The advanced practice registered nurse must practice within a health care system that provides for consultation, collaborative management, and referral as indicated by the health status of the patient.

Citation: MINN. STAT. ANN. § 148.171(13).

Mississippi

"Advanced nursing practice" means, in addition to the practice of professional nursing, the performance of advanced-level nursing approved by the board which, by virtue of graduate education and experience are appropriately performed by an advanced practice registered nurse. The advanced practice registered nurse may diagnose, treat, and manage medical conditions. This may include prescriptive authority as identified by the board.

Citation: MISS. NURSING PRACTICE LAW §73-15-5(4).

Missouri

RNs recognized by the MSBN as being eligible to practice as an APRN shall function clinically within the professional scope and standards of their advanced practice nursing clinical specialty area and consistent with their formal advanced nursing education and national certification, if applicable, or within their education, training, knowledge, judgment, skill, and competence as an RN.

Citation: MO. CODE REGS. ANN. tit. 20, § 2200-4.100(4)(A)(2).

The methods of treatment and the authority to administer, dispense, or prescribe drugs delegated in a collaborative practice arrangement between a collaborating physician and collaborating APRN shall be within the scope of practice of each professional and shall be consistent with each professional's skill, training, education, competence, licensure, and/or certification and shall not be further delegated to any person except that the individuals identified in sections 338.095 and 338.198, RSMo, may communicate prescription drug orders to a pharmacist.

Citation: MO. CODE REGS. ANN. tit. 20, § 2200-4.200.

(3)(A) When a collaborative practice arrangement is utilized to provide health care services for conditions other than acute self-limited or well-defined problems, the collaborating physician, or other physician designated in the collaborative practice arrangement, shall examine and evaluate the patient and approve or formulate the plan of treatment for new or significantly changed conditions as soon as is practical, but in no case more than two (2) weeks after the patient has been seen by the collaborating APRN or RN.

Citation: MO. CODE REGS. ANN. tit. 20, § 2200-4.200 (3)(H).

Montana

Nurse practitioner practice means the independent and/or collaborative management of primary and/or acute health care of individuals, families, and communities including:

a. assessing the health status of individuals and families using methods appropriate to the client population and area of practice such as health history taking, physical examination, and assessing developmental health problems;
b. instituting and facilitating continuity of health care to clients, including:
    i. ordering durable medical equipment, treatments and modalities, and diagnostic tests;
    ii. receiving and interpreting results of diagnostic procedures;
    iii. making medical and nursing diagnoses; and
    iv. working with clients to promote their understanding of and compliance with therapeutic regimens.
c. promoting wellness and disease prevention programs;
d. referring clients to a physician or other health care provider, when appropriate;
e. providing instruction and counseling to individuals, families, and groups in the areas of health promotion and maintenance, including involving such persons in planning for their health care; and
f. working in collaboration with other health care providers and agencies to provide and, where appropriate, coordinate services to individuals and families.

Citation: MONT. ADMIN. R. § 24.159.1470(1).

Nebraska

An advanced practice registered nurse practitioner may provide healthcare services within specialty areas.

1. A nurse practitioner may provide health care services within specialty areas. A nurse practitioner shall function by establishing collaborative, consultative, and referral networks as appropriate with other health care professionals. Patients who require care beyond the scope of practice of a nurse practitioner shall be referred to an appropriate health care provider.
2. Nurse practitioner practice means health promotion, health supervision, illness prevention and diagnosis, treatment, and management of common health problems and acute and chronic conditions, including:
    a. Assessing patients, ordering diagnostic tests and therapeutic treatments, synthesizing and analyzing data, and applying advanced nursing principles;
    b. Dispensing, incident to practice only, sample medication which are provided by the manufacturer and are provided at no charge to the patient; and

   c. Prescribing therapeutic measures and medications, relating to health conditions within the scope of practice. Any limitation on the prescribing authority of the advanced practice registered nurse for controlled substances listed in Schedule II of Section 28-405 shall be recorded in the integrated practice agreement. . . .

Citation: NEB. REV. STAT. § 38-2315.

Nevada

[Effective through June 30, 2014.]

1. The Board may issue a license to practice as an advanced practice registered nurse to a registered nurse who has completed an educational program designed to prepare a registered nurse to:
   a. Perform designated acts of medical diagnosis;
   b. Prescribe therapeutic or corrective measures; and
   c. Prescribe controlled substances, poisons, dangerous drugs and devices, and who meets the other requirements established by the Board for such licensure.
2. An advanced practice registered nurse may:
   a. Engage in selected medical diagnosis and treatment; and
   b. If authorized pursuant to NRS 639.2351, prescribe controlled substances, poisons, dangerous drugs and devices.
3. The Board shall adopt regulations:
   a. Specifying the training, education and experience necessary for licensure as an advanced practice registered nurse.
   b. Delineating the authorized scope of practice of an advanced practice registered nurse
   c. Establishing the procedure for application for licensure as an advanced practice registered nurse.

Citation: NEV. REV. STAT. § 632.237, as amended May 2013 by AB 170.

An advanced practice registered nurse may perform the following acts in addition to the functions of a registered nurse if the advanced practice registered nurse is properly prepared and the acts are currently within the standard of practice for his or her role and population of focus:

1. Systematically assess the health status of person and families by:
   a. Taking, recording and interpreting medical histories and performing physical examinations; and
   b. Performing or initiating selected diagnostic procedures.

2. Based on information obtained in the assessment of a person's health, manage the care of selected persons and families with common, acute, recurrent or long-term health problems. Management may include:
   a. Initiation of a program of treatment;
   b. Evaluation of responses to health problems and programs of treatment;
   c. Informing a person or family of the status of the patient's health and alternatives for care;
   d. Evaluation of compliance with a program of treatment agreed upon by the person or family and the advanced practice registered nurse.;
   e. Modification of programs of treatment based on the response of the person or family to treatment;
   f. Referral to appropriate providers of health care; and
   g. Commencement of care required to stabilize a patient in an emergency.
3. Any other act if:
   a. The advanced practice registered nurse is certified to perform that act by an organization recognized by the Board;
   b. The performance of the act was taught in the program of education attended by the advanced practice registered nurse;
   c. The performance of the act was taught in a comprehensive program of instruction successfully completed by the advanced practice registered nurse, which included clinical experience;
   d. The act is within the scope of practice of an advanced practice registered nurse as determined by the Board; or
   e. The advanced practice registered nurse is trained to perform that act by a physician or another advanced practice registered nurse and the act:
      1. Has been described as being performed by an advanced practice registered nurse in two or more national nursing publications, national nursing practice guidelines or national standards for nursing practice, or any combination thereof, which are listed in the *Cumulative Index to Nursing and Allied Health Literature*, as adopted by referenced in NAC 632.1110; or
      2. Has been individually approved by the Board.

Citation: Nev. Admin. Code § 632.255.

New Hampshire

I. Advanced practice registered nursing by nurse practitioners shall consist of a combination of knowledge and skills acquired in basic nursing education. The APRN scope of practice, with or without compensation or personal profit, shall be limited to:

    a. Performing acts of advanced assessment, diagnosing, prescribing, selecting, administering, and providing therapeutic measures and treatment regimes;

    b. Obtaining consultation, planning, and implementing collaborative management, referral, or transferring the care of the client as appropriate; and

    c. Providing such functions common to a nurse practitioner for which the APRN is educationally and experientially prepared and which are consistent with standards established by a national credentialing or certification body recognized by the National Council of State Boards of Nursing and approved by the board in the appropriate APRN role and specialty.

II. An APRN shall practice within standards consistent with standards established by a national credentialing or certification body recognized by the National Council of State Boards of Nursing and approved by the board in the appropriate APRN role and specialty. The board shall not approve a new advanced practice specialty category that has not been developed by a national credentialing or certifying body recognized by the National Council of State Board of Nursing without approval of the legislature under RSA 332-G:6. Each APRN shall be accountable to clients and the board:

    a. For complying with this chapter and the quality of advanced nursing care rendered;

    b. For recognizing limits of knowledge and experience and planning for the management of situations beyond the APRN's expertise; and

    c. For consulting with or referring clients to other healthcare providers as appropriate.

III. An APRN shall have plenary authority to possess, compound, prescribe, administer, and dispense and distribute to clients controlled and non-controlled drugs within the scope of the APRN's practice as defined by this chapter. Such authority may be denied, suspended, or revoked by the board after notice and the opportunity for hearing, upon proof that the authority has been abused.

IV. Any expansion of the scope of practice shall be adopted by legislation in accordance with RSA 332-G:6.

Citation: N.H. Rev. Stat. Ann. § 326-B:11.

New Jersey

    a. In addition to all other tasks which a registered professional nurse may, by law, perform, an advanced practice nurse may manage preventive care services, and diagnose and manage deviations from wellness and long-term illnesses, consistent with the needs of the patient and within the scope of practice of the advanced practice nurse, by:

    1. initiating laboratory and other diagnostic tests;

2. prescribing or ordering medications and devices, as authorized by subsections b. and c. of this section;
3. prescribing and ordering treatments, including referrals to other licensed health care professionals, and performing specific procedures in accordance with the provisions of this subsection.

Citation: N.J. Stat. Ann. § 45:11-49.a.

New Mexico

Certified nurse practitioners who have fulfilled requirements for prescriptive authority may prescribe in accordance with the rules, regulations, guidelines, and formularies for individual certified nurse practitioners promulgated by the board.

Citation: N.M. Stat. Ann. § 61-3-23.2.C.

Certified nurse practitioners may:

1. Perform an expanded practice that is beyond the scope of practice of professional registered nursing;
2. Practice independently and make decisions regarding health care needs of the individual, family, or community and carry out health regimens, including the prescription and dispensing of dangerous drugs and controlled substances included in Schedule II through V of the Controlled Dangerous Substances Act; and
3. Serve as a primary acute, chronic long-term and end-of-life health care provider and as necessary collaborate with licensed medical doctors, osteopathic physicians, or podiatrists.

Citation: N.M. Stat. Ann. § 61-3-23.2.B.

New York

The practice of registered professional nursing by a nurse practitioner, certified under section six thousand nine hundred ten of this article, may include the diagnosis of illness and physical conditions and the performance of therapeutic and corrective measures within a specialty area of practice, in collaboration with a licensed physician qualified to collaborate in the specialty involved, provided such services are performed in accordance with a written practice agreement and written practice protocols.

Citation: N.Y. Educ. Law, Art. 139 § 6902.3(a).

Prescriptions for drugs, devices, and immunizing agents may be issued . . . in accordance with the practice agreement and practice protocols.

Citation: N.Y. Educ. Law Art. 139 § 6902.3(b).

North Carolina

A nurse practitioner shall be held accountable by both Boards for the continuous and comprehensive management of a broad range of personal health services for which the nurse practitioner is educationally prepared and for which competency has been maintained, with physician supervision as described in Rule .0810 of this Section. These services include but are not restricted to:

1. Promotion and maintenance of health;
2. Prevention of illness and disability;
3. Diagnosis, treating, and managing acute and chronic illnesses;
4. Guidance and counseling of both individuals and families;
5. Prescribing, administering, and dispensing therapeutic measures, tests, procedures and drugs;
6. Planning for situations beyond the nurse practitioner's expertise, and consulting with and referring to other health care providers as appropriate; and
7. Evaluating health outcomes.

Citation: N.C. Admin Code tit. 21, r. 36.0802.

North Dakota

1. Practice as an advanced practice registered nurse may include:
   a. Perform a comprehensive assessment of clients and synthesize and analyze data within a nursing framework;
   b. Identify, develop, plan, and maintain evidence-based, client-centered nursing care;
   c. Prescribe a therapeutic regimen of health care, including diagnosing, prescribing, administering, and dispensing legend drugs and controlled substances;
   d. Evaluate prescribed health care regimen;
   e. Participate in nursing care management according to chapter 54-05-04 relating to standards for assignment and delegation and section 54-05-02-02.2 assigning of nursing interventions;
   f. Promote a safe and therapeutic environment;
   g. Provide health teaching and counseling to promote, attain, and maintain the optimum health level of clients;
   h. Communicate and collaborate with the interdisciplinary team in the management of health care and the implementation of the total health care regimen;
   i. Manage and evaluate the clients' physical and psychosocial health-illness status;
   j. Manage, supervise, and evaluate the practice of nursing;
   k. Utilize evolving client information management systems;

  l. Integrate quality improvement principles in the delivery and evaluation of client care;

  m. Teach the theory and practice of nursing;

  n. Analyze, synthesize, and apply research outcomes in practice; and

  o. Integrate the principles of research in practice.

2. Notwithstanding the above, all services rendered by the licensee shall be commensurate with the academic preparation, knowledge, skills, and abilities of the advanced practice licensed nurse's experience, continuing education, and demonstrated competencies. The nurse must recognize individual limits of knowledge, skills, and abilities and plan for situations beyond the licensee's expertise.

Citation: N.D. ADMIN. CODE § 54-05-03.1-03.2.

Ohio

A certified nurse-midwife, certified nurse practitioner, certified registered nurse anesthetist, or clinical nurse specialist shall do all of the following:

1. Function within the scope of practice of nursing for a registered nurse as set forth in division (b) of section 4723.01 of the Revised Code and the rules of the board.
2. Function within the nurse's applicable scope of practice as set forth in section 4723.43 of the Revised Code and the rules of the board.
3. Practice in accordance with section 4723.481 of the Revised Code and Chapter 4723-9 of the Administrative Code if the individual holds a certificate to prescribe.

Citation: OHIO REV. CODE ANN. § 4723-4-053(A).

Oklahoma

A Certified Nurse Practitioner shall be eligible, in accordance with the scope of practice of the Certified Nurse Practitioner, to obtain recognition as authorized by the Board to prescribe, as defined by the rules promulgated by the Board pursuant to this section and subject to the medical direction of a supervising physician. This authorization shall not include dispensing drugs, but shall not preclude, subject to federal regulations, the receipt of, the signing for, or the dispensing of professional samples to patients.

The Certified Nurse Practitioner accepts responsibility, accountability, and obligation to practice in accordance with usual and customary advanced practice nursing standards and functions as defined by the scope of practice/role definition statements for the advanced registered nurse practitioner.

Citation: OKLA. STAT. ANN. tit. 59, § 567.3a (6).

The Certified Nurse Practitioner's (CNP) scope of practice includes the full scope of nursing practice and practice in an expanded role as follows:

1. The Certified Nurse Practitioner (CNP) provides comprehensive health care to clients across the life span.
2. The CNP is responsible and accountable for the continuous and comprehensive management of a broad range of health services, which include, but are not limited to:
   A. promotion and maintenance of health;
   B. prevention of illness and disability;
   C. diagnosis and prescription of medications, treatments, and devices for acute and chronic conditions and diseases;
   D. management of health care during acute and chronic phases of illness;
   E. guidance and counseling services;
   F. consultation and/or collaboration with other healthcare providers and community resources;
   G. referral to other healthcare providers and community resources.
3. The CNP will provide services based upon education, experience, and national certification. It is the responsibility of the licensee to document competency of any act, based upon education, experience and certification.
4. The scope of practice as previously defined is incorporated into the following specialty categories and further delineates the population served:
   A. Adult CNP (acute and/or primary) provides health care to adolescents and adults.
   B. Family CNP provides health care to persons across the lifespan.
   C. Geriatric CNP provides health care to older adults.
   D. Neonatal CNP provides health care to neonates and infants.
   E. Pediatric CNP (acute and/or primary) provides health care to persons from newborn to young adulthood.
   F. Women's Health Care CNP provides health care to adolescent and adult females. Care may also be provided to males with reproductive health needs or problems.
   G. Acute Care CNP provides health care to adults who are acutely or critically ill.
   H. The Adult Psychiatric and Mental Health CNP provides acute and chronic psychiatric and mental health care to persons age 13 or older.
   I. The Family Psychiatric and Mental Health CNP provides acute and chronic psychiatric and mental health care to persons across the lifespan.
   J. The Acute Care Pediatric CNP provides health care to persons from newborn to young adulthood with complex acute, critical, and chronic health conditions.
5. Effective January 1, 2016, the applicant for initial APRN licensure or APRN licensure by endorsement as a CNP shall hold certification in at least one of the following population foci: family/individual across the lifespan,

adult-gerontology (acute and/or primary), neonatal, pediatrics (acute and/or primary), women's health/gender related, or psychiatric/mental health.

Citation: OKLA. ADMIN. CODE § 485:10-15-6(c).

Oregon

. . .

3. The nurse practitioner provides holistic health care to individuals, families, and groups across the life span in a variety of settings, including hospitals, long-term care facilities, and community-based settings.
4. Within his or her specialty, the nurse practitioner is responsible for managing health problems encountered by the client and is accountable for health outcomes. This process includes:
   a. Assessment;
   b. Diagnosis;
   c. Development of a plan;
   d. Intervention;
   e. Evaluation.
5. The nurse practitioner is independently responsible and accountable for the continuous and comprehensive management of a broad range of health care, which may include:
   a. Promotion and maintenance of health;
   b. Prevention of illness and disability;
   c. Assessment of clients, synthesis and analysis of data and application of nursing principles and therapeutic modalities;
   d. Management of health care during acute and chronic phases of illness;
   e. Admission of his/her clients to hospitals and/or health services including but not limited to home health, hospice, long term care, and drug and alcohol treatment;
   f. Counseling;
   g. Consultation and/or collaboration with other care providers and community resources;
   h. Referral to other health care providers and community resources;
   i. Management and coordination of care;
   j. Use of research skills;
   k. Diagnosis of health/illness status;
   l. Prescribing, dispensing, and administration of therapeutic devices and measures including legend drugs and controlled substances as provided in Division 56 of the Oregon Nurse Practice Act, consistent with the definition of the practitioner's specialty category and scope of practice.
6. The nurse practitioner scope of practice includes teaching the theory and practice of advanced practice nursing.

7. The nurse practitioner is responsible for recognizing limits of knowledge and experience, and for resolving situations beyond his/her nurse practitioner expertise by consulting with or referring clients to other health care providers.

8. The nurse practitioner will only provide health care services within the nurse practitioner's scope of practice for which he/she is educationally prepared and for which competency has been established and maintained. Educational preparation includes academic course work, workshops or seminars, provided both theory and clinical experience are included.

Citation: Or. Admin. R. § 851-050-0005.

Pennsylvania

A CRNP . . . while functioning in the expanded role as a professional nurse, performs acts of medical diagnosis or prescription of medical therapeutics or corrective measures in collaboration with a physician licensed to practice.

Citation: 49 Pa. Code § 21.251.

a. A CRNP may collaborate only with physicians who hold a current license to practice in this Commonwealth.

b. When acting in collaboration with a physician as set forth in a collaborative agreement and within the CRNP's specialty, a CRNP may:
   1. Perform comprehensive assessments of patients and establish medical diagnoses.
   2. Order, perform and supervise diagnostic tests for patients and, to the extent the interpretation of diagnostic tests is within the scope of the CRNP's specialty and consistent with the collaborative agreement, may interpret diagnostic tests.
   3. Initiate referrals to and consultations with other licensed professional health care providers, and consult with other licensed professional health care providers at their request.
   4. Develop and implement treatment plans, including issuing orders to implement treatment plans. However, only a CRNP with current prescriptive authority approval may develop and implement treatment plans for pharmaceutical treatments.
   5. Complete admission and discharge summaries.
   6. Order blood and blood components for patients.
   7. Order dietary plans for patients.
   8. Order home health and hospice care.
   9. Order durable medical equipment.

10. Issue oral orders to the extent permitted by the health care facilities' by-laws, rules, regulations or administrative policies and guidelines.
11. Make physical therapy and dietitian referrals.
12. Make respiratory and occupational therapy referrals.
13. Perform disability assessments for the program providing temporary assistance to needy families (TANF).
14. Issue homebound schooling certifications.
15. Perform and sign the initial assessment of methadone treatment evaluations, provided that any order for methadone treatment shall be made only by a physician.

Citation: 49 PA CODE §21.282a(a) and (b).

Rhode Island

"Certified registered nurse practitioner" (RNP) means an advanced practice nurse utilizing independent knowledge of physical assessment and management of health care and illnesses. The practice includes prescriptive privileges, and collaboration with other licensed healthcare professionals, including, but not limited to, physicians, pharmacists, podiatrists, dentists, and nurses. Such collaboration is not required to be pursuant to a written collaboration agreement, with a specific designation physician, or at the same physical location as a collaborating practitioner.

Citation: R.I. R. R5-34-NUR/ED 1.10.

South Carolina

In addition to those activities considered the practice of nursing, an APRN may perform delegated medical acts.

Citation: S.C. CODE ANN. § 40-33-20(5).

"Delegated medical acts" means additional acts delegated by a physician or dentist to the NP, CNM, or CNS and may include formulating a medical diagnosis and initiating, continuing, and modifying therapies, including prescribing drug therapy, under approved written protocols ... Delegated medical acts must be agreed to jointly by both the Board of Nursing and the Board of Medical Examiners. Delegated medical acts must be performed under the general supervision of a physician or dentist who must be readily available for consultation.

Citation: S.C. CODE ANN. § 40-33-20(23).

South Dakota

A nurse practitioner may perform the following overlapping scope of advanced practice nursing and medical functions pursuant to § 36-9A-15, including:

1. The initial medical diagnosis and the institution of a plan of therapy or referral;
2. The prescription of medications and provision of drug samples or a limited supply of labeled medications, including controlled drugs or substances listed in Schedule II in Chapter 34-20B for one period of not more than thirty days for treatment of causative factors and symptoms. Medications or sample drugs provided to patients shall be accompanied with written administration instructions and appropriate documentation shall be entered in the patient's medical record;
3. The writing of a chemical or physical restraint order when the patient may do personal harm or harm others;
4. The completion and signing of official documents such as death certificates, birth certificates, and similar documents required by law;
5. The performance of a physical examination for participation in athletics and the certification that the patient is healthy and able to participate in athletics.

Citation: S.D. CODIFIED LAWS § 36-9A-12.

The nurse practitioner or nurse midwife advanced practice nursing functions include:

1. Providing advanced nursing assessment, nursing intervention, and nursing case management;
2. Providing advanced health promotion and maintenance education and counseling to clients, families, and other members of the health care team;
3. Utilizing research findings to evaluate and implement changes in nursing practice, programs, and policies; and
4. Recognizing limits of knowledge and experience, planning for situations beyond expertise, and consulting with or referring clients to other health care providers as appropriate.

These advanced practice nursing functions are under the jurisdiction of the Board of Nursing.

Citation: S.D. CODIFIED LAWS § 36-9A-13.1.

Tennessee

There is no description of the scope of practice for a nurse practitioner in Tennessee law, other than the authority to write and sign prescriptions and/or issue drugs.

Citation: [for prescriptive authority] TENN. CODE ANN. § 63-7-123(a) and (b)(2).

Texas

The advanced practice nurse provides a broad range of health services, the scope of which shall be based upon educational preparation, continued advanced practice experience and the accepted scope of professional practice of the particular specialty area. Advanced practice nurses practice in a variety of settings and, according to their practice specialty and role, they provide a broad range of health care services to a variety of patient populations.

1. The scope of practice of particular specialty areas shall be defined by national professional specialty organizations or advanced practice nursing organizations recognized by the Board. The advanced practice nurse may perform only those functions which are within that scope of practice and which are consistent with the Nursing Practice Act, Board rules, and other laws and regulations of the State of Texas.

2. The advanced practice nurse's scope of practice shall be in addition to the scope of practice permitted a registered nurse and does not prohibit the advanced practice nurse from practicing in those areas deemed to be within the scope of practice of a registered nurse.

Citation: 22 Texas Admin. Code § 221.12.

Utah

"Practice of advanced practice registered nursing" means the practice of nursing within the generally recognized scope and standards of advanced practice registered nursing as defined by rule and consistent with professionally recognized preparation and education standards of an advanced practice registered nurse by a person licensed under this chapter as an advanced practice registered nurse. Advanced practice registered nursing includes:

a. maintenance and promotion of health and prevention of disease;
b. diagnosis, treatment, correction, consultation, or referral for common health problems; and
c. prescription or administration of prescription drugs or devices, including:
    i. local anesthesia
    ii. schedule IV-V controlled substances; and
    iii. schedule II-III controlled substances in accordance with a consultation and referral plan.

Citation: Utah Code Ann. § 58-31b-102(13).

Vermont

"Advanced practice registered nurse" or "APRN" means a licensed registered nurse, authorized to practice in this state who, because of specialized education and experience is endorsed to perform acts of medical diagnosis and to prescribe medical, therapeutic, or corrective measures under administrative rules adopted by the board.

Citation: Vt. Stat. Ann. tit. 26, § 1572(4).

An APRN practices an expanded scope of nursing, which includes the registered nurse scope of practice. The scope of an APRN includes assessing at an advanced level, diagnosing, prescribing, giving medical and nursing orders, and evaluating care.

Citation: Vt. Board of Nursing Admin Rules 15.2(3).

Virginia

A nurse practitioner licensed in a category other than certified registered nurse anesthetist shall be authorized to render care in collaboration with a licensed patient care team physician as part of a patient care team.

Citation: 18 Va. Admin. Code § 90-30-120A.

Washington

An advanced registered nurse practitioner, under his license, may perform for compensation nursing care, as that term is usually understood, of the ill, injured, or infirm and in the course thereof, she or he may do the following things that shall not be done by a person not so licensed, except as provided in RCW 18.79.260 and 18.79.270:

1. Perform specialized and advanced levels of nursing as recognized jointly by the medical and nursing professions, as defined by the commission;
2. Prescribe legend drugs and Schedule V controlled substances, as defined in the Uniform Controlled Substances Act, chapter 69.50 RCW, and Schedule II through IV subject to RCW 18.79.240(1)(r) or (s) within the scope of practice defined by the commission;
3. Perform all acts provided in RCW 18.79.260;
4. Hold himself out to the public or designate himself as an advanced registered nurse practitioner or as a nurse practitioner.

Citation: Wash. Rev. Code § 18.79.250.

1. A licensed advanced registered nurse practitioner (ARNP) is a registered nurse prepared in a formal educational program to assume primary responsibility for continuous and comprehensive management of a broad range of patient care, concerns, and problems.
2. The ARNP is prepared and qualified to assume primary responsibility and accountability for the care of patients.

3. ARNP practice is grounded in nursing and incorporates the use of independent judgment as well as collaborative interaction with other health care professionals when indicated in the assessment and management of wellness and health conditions as appropriate to the ARNP's area of practice and certification.
4. The ARNP functions within his or her scope of practice according to the commission approved certification program and standards of care developed by professional organizations.
5. The ARNP shall obtain instruction, supervision, and consultation as necessary before implementing new or unfamiliar techniques or practices.
6. Performing within the scope of the ARNP's knowledge, experience, and practice, the licensed ARNP may perform the following:
    a. Examine patients and establish diagnoses by patient history, physical examination, and other methods of assessment;
    b. Admit, manage, and discharge patients to and from healthcare facilities;
    c. Order, collect, perform, and interpret diagnostic tests;
    d. Manage health care by identifying, developing, implementing, and evaluating a plan of care and treatment for patients;
    e. Prescribe therapies and medical equipment;
    f. Prescribe medications when granted authority under this chapter;
    g. Refer patients to other healthcare practitioners, services or facilities; and
    h. Perform procedures or provide care services that are within the scope of practice according to the commission approved certification program.

Citation: WASH. ADMIN. CODE § 246-840-300.

West Virginia

"Advanced Practice Registered Nurse" (APRN) means a registered nurse who has acquired clinical knowledge and skills preparing him or her to independently provide direct and indirect care to patients, who has completed a board approved graduate-level education program and who has passed a board approved national certification examination.

Citation: W.VA. CODE ST. R. tit. 19, § 19-7-2.1.Wisconsin.

The intent of the board of nursing in adopting rules in this chapter is to specify education, training, or experience that a registered nurse must satisfy to call himself or herself an advanced practice nurse; to establish appropriate education, training, and examination requirements that an advanced practice nurse must satisfy to qualify for a certificate to issue prescription orders; to define the scope of practice within which an advanced practice nurse prescriber may issue prescription orders; to specify the classes of drugs, individual drugs, or devices that may not be prescribed by an advanced practice nurse prescriber; to specify the conditions to be met for a registered nurse to administer a drug prescribed or directed by an advanced practice nurse prescriber; to establish procedures for maintaining a certificate to issue prescription orders, including requirements for continuing education; and to establish the minimum amount of malpractice insurance required of an advanced practice nurse prescriber.

Citation: WIS. ADMIN. CODE § N8.01(2).

To promote case management, the advanced practice nurse prescriber may order laboratory testing, radiographs or electrocardiograms appropriate . . . to his or her education, training, or experience.

Citation: WISC. ADMIN. CODE § N8.10(6).

Wyoming

"Advanced practice registered nurse (APRN)" means a nurse who:

A. May prescribe, administer, dispense or provide nonprescriptive and prescriptive medications including prepackaged medications, except Schedule I drugs as defined in W.S. 35-7-1013 and 35-7-1014;
B. Has responsibility for the direct care and management of patients and clients in relation to their human needs, disease states and therapeutic and technological interventions;
C. Has a master's degree in nursing, or an advanced practice registered nurse specialty or has completed an accredited advanced practice registered nurse educational program prior to January 1, 1999; and
D. Has completed an advanced program of study in a specialty area in an accredited nursing program, has taken and passed a national certification examination in the same area, and has been granted recognition by the board to practice as an APRN.

Citation: WYO. STAT. ANN. §33-21-120(a)(i).

a. The advanced practice registered nurse is subject at all times to the established Standards of Nursing Practice as stated in Chapter 3 of these rules and regulations, the standards and scope of practice established by national professional organizations, and/or accrediting agencies representing the various core, role and population focus areas of advanced practice registered nursing, and the Wyoming Nurse Practice Act.
b. The board recognizes advanced practice registered nurse core, role and population focus areas described in the scope of practice statements for advanced practice registered nurses issued by national professional organizations and/or accrediting agencies.

Citation: WYO. BOARD OF NURSING RULES CHAPTER 4 § Section 7.

Physician Collaboration

Alabama

COLLABORATION. A formal relationship between one or more certified registered nurse practitioners and certified nurse midwives and a physician or physicians under which these nurses may engage in advanced practice nursing as evidenced by written protocols approved in accordance with the requirements of this article or exempted in accordance with requirements of this article. The term collaboration does not require direct, on-site supervision of the activities of a certified registered nurse practitioner or a certified nurse midwife by the collaborating physician. The term does require such professional oversight and direction as may be required by the rules and regulations of the State Board of Medical Examiners and the Board of Nursing.

Citation: ALA. CODE § 34-21-81(5).

Requirements for collaborative practice by physicians and certified registered nurse practitioners:

1. The collaborating physician shall:
   a. Provide professional medical oversight and direction to the certified registered nurse practitioner.
   b. Be readily available for direct communication or by radio, telephone or telecommunications.
   c. Be readily available for consultation or referrals of patients from the certified registered nurse practitioner.
2. In the event the collaborating physician is not readily available, provisions shall be made for medical coverage by a physician who is pre-approved by the State Board of Medical Examiners and is familiar with these rules.
3. If the certified registered nurse practitioner is to perform duties at a site away from the collaborating physician, the written protocol shall clearly specify the circumstances and provide written verification of physician availability for consultation, referral, or direct medical intervention in emergencies and after hours, if indicated.

4. The collaborating physician shall be present with the certified registered nurse practitioner in an approved collaborative practice site for not less than ten percent (10%) of the certified registered nurse practitioner's scheduled hours in the collaborative practice as specified in the protocol application. In addition, the collaborating physician shall visit each approved collaborative practice site not less than quarterly. The collaborating physicians with the Alabama Department of Public Health and county health departments are exempt from this requirement.

5. The certified registered nurse practitioner's scheduled hours in licensed acute care hospitals, licensed skilled nursing facilities, licensed special-care assisted living facilities, and licensed assisted living facilities are not subject to the required minimum hours for physician presence.

6. If the certified registered nurse practitioner's scheduled weekly collaborative practice hours are:

   a. Thirty or more hours per week, the certified registered nurse practitioner shall be present in an approved practice site with the collaborating or covering physician for time equal to ten percent (10%) of the certified registered nurse practitioner's scheduled weekly hours. Cumulative hours may accrue on a monthly basis.

   b. Less than 30 hours per week, the certified registered nurse practitioner shall be present in an approved practice site with the collaborating or covering physician for time equal to ten percent (10%) of the certified registered nurse practitioner's scheduled weekly hours. Cumulative hours may accrue on a quarterly basis.

7. The collaborating physician shall provide notice in writing to the State Board of Medical Examiners of the commencement or termination of a collaborative practice agreement as required by Rule 540-X-8-.04(4).

8. The Joint Committee may, at its discretion, waive the requirements of written verification of physician availability upon documentation of exceptional circumstances. Employees of the Alabama Department of Public Health and county health departments are exempt from the requirements of written verification of physician availability.

9. A written standard protocol specific to the specialty practice area of the certified registered nurse practitioner and the specialty practice area of the collaborating physician, approved and signed by both the collaborating physician and the certified registered nurse practitioner, shall:

   a. Identify all sites where the certified registered nurse practitioner will practice within the collaboration protocol.

   b. Identify the physician's principal practice site.

   c. Be maintained at each practice site.

   d. Include a formulary of drugs, devices, medical treatments, tests and procedures that may be prescribed, ordered, and implemented by the certified registered nurse practitioner consistent with these rules and which are appropriate for the collaborative practice setting.

e. Include a pre-determined plan for emergency services.

f. Specify the process by which the certified registered nurse practitioner shall refer a patient to a physician other than the collaborating physician.

g. Specify a plan for quality assurance management with established patient outcome indicators for evaluation of the clinical practice of the certified registered nurse practitioner and include review of no less than ten percent (10%) of medical records plus all adverse outcomes. Documentation of quality assurance review shall be readily retrievable, identify records that were selected for review, include a summary of findings, conclusions, and, if indicated, recommendations for change. Quality assurance monitoring may be performed by designated personnel, with final results presented to the physician and certified registered nurse practitioner for review.

Citation: ALA. ADMIN. CODE r. 610-X-5-.08.

Alaska

If intending to deliver health care services to the public, must submit with the application for initial authorization a consultation and referral plan; the plan must

A. describe the applicant's clinical practice;

B. identify the expected client population focus area, which is within the scope of practice of the applicant;

C. list the applicant's method of routine consultations and referrals, the method of documenting routine consultations and referrals in the patient record, and the names and titles of health care providers that the applicant will use for routine consultations and referrals;

D. list the applicant's method for emergency referrals; and

E. *repealed 10/3/2011;*

F. describe the process for quality assurance the applicants will use to evaluate the applicant's practice, including

   i. the use of standards that apply to the area of practice;

   ii. present or past review of the practice;

   iii. use of preestablished criteria; and

   iv. a written evaluation of the quality assurance review with a plan for corrective action, if indicated, and follow-up;

Citation: ALASKA ADMIN. CODE tit. 12, § 44.400(5)(c).

Arizona

"Collaborate" means to establish a relationship for consultation or referral with one or more licensed physicians on an as-needed basis. Supervision of the activities of a registered nurse practitioner by the collaborating physician is not required.

Citation: ARIZ. ADMIN. CODE § R4-19-101.

Arkansas

A collaborative practice agreement shall include, but not be limited to, provisions addressing: (1) The availability of the collaborating physician for consultation or referral or both; (2) Methods of management of the collaborative practice, which shall include protocols for prescriptive authority; (3) Coverage of the health care needs of a patient in the emergency absence of the advanced practice nurse or physician; and (4) Quality assurance.

Citation: Ark. Code Ann. § 17-87-310(C).

California

Neither this chapter nor any other provision of law shall be construed to prohibit a nurse practitioner from furnishing or ordering drugs or devices when all of the following apply:

a. The drugs or devices are furnished or ordered by a nurse practitioner in accordance with standardized procedures or protocols developed by the nurse practitioner and the supervising physician and surgeon when the drugs or devices furnished or ordered are consistent with the practitioner's educational preparation or for which clinical competency has been established and maintained.

b. The nurse practitioner is functioning pursuant to standardized procedure, as defined by Section 2725, or protocol. The standardized procedure or protocol shall be developed and approved by the supervising physician and surgeon, the nurse practitioner, and the facility administrator or the designee.

c. 1. The standardized procedure or protocol covering the furnishing of drugs or devices shall specify which nurse practitioners may furnish or order drugs or devices, which drugs or devices may be furnished or ordered, under what circumstances, the extent of physician and surgeon supervision, the method of periodic review of the nurse practitioner's competence, including peer review, and review of the provision of the standardized procedure.

   2. In addition to the requirements in paragraph (1), for Schedule II controlled substance protocols, the provision for furnishing Schedule II controlled substances shall address the diagnosis of the illness, injury, or condition for which the Schedule II controlled substance is to be furnished.

d. The furnishing or ordering of drugs or devices by a nurse practitioner occurs under physician and surgeon supervision. Physician and surgeon supervision shall not be construed to require the physical presence of the physician, but does include (1) collaboration on the development of the standardized procedure, (2) approval of the standardized procedure, and (3) availability by telephonic contact at the time of patient examination by the nurse practitioner.

e. For purposes of this section, no physician and surgeon shall supervise more than four nurse practitioners at one time.

f. 1. Drugs or devices furnished or ordered by a nurse practitioner may include Schedule II through Schedule V controlled substances under the California Uniform Controlled Substances Act . . . and shall be further limited to those drugs agreed upon by the nurse practitioner and physician and surgeon and specified in the standardized procedure.

   2. When Schedule II or III controlled substances . . . are furnished or ordered by a nurse practitioner, the controlled substances shall be furnished or ordered in accordance with a patient-specific protocol approved by the treating or supervising physician. A copy of the section of the nurse practitioner's standardized procedure relating to controlled substances shall be provided, upon request, to any licensed pharmacist who dispenses drugs or devices, when there is uncertainty about the nurse practitioner furnishing the order.

g. 1. The board has certified in accordance with Section 2836.3 that the nurse practitioner has satisfactorily completed (1) at least six month's physician and surgeon-supervised experience in the furnishing or ordering of drugs or devices, and (2) a course in pharmacology covering the drugs or devices to be furnished or ordered under this section.

   2. Nurse practitioners who are certified by the board and hold an active furnishing number, who are authorized through standardized procedures or protocols to furnish Schedule II controlled substances, and who are registered with the United States Drug Enforcement Administration, shall complete, as part of their continuing education requirements, a course including Schedule II controlled substances based on the standards developed by the board. The board shall establish the requirements for satisfactory completion of this subdivision.

h. Use of the term "furnishing" in this section, in health facilities defined in Section 1250 of the Health and Safety Code, shall include (1) the ordering of a drug or device in accordance with the standardized procedure and (2) transmitting an order of a supervising physician and surgeon.

i. "Drug order" or "order" for purposes of this section means an order for medication which is dispensed to or for an ultimate user, issued by a nurse practitioner as an individual practitioner, within the meaning of Section 1306.02 of Title 21 of the Code of Federal Regulations. Notwithstanding any other provision of law, (1) a drug order issued pursuant to this section shall be treated in the same manner as a prescription of the supervising physician; (2) all references to "prescription" in this code and the Health and Safety Code shall include drug orders issued by nurse practitioners; and (3) the signature of a nurse practitioner on a drug order issued in accordance with this section shall be deemed to be the signature of a prescriber for purposes of this code and the Health and Safety Code.

Citation: Ann. Cal. Bus. & Prof. Code § 2836.1.

Furnishing or ordering of drugs or devices by nurse practitioners is defined to mean the act of making a pharmaceutical agent or agents available to the patient in strict accordance with a standardized procedure. All nurse practitioners who are authorized pursuant to Section 2836.1 to furnish or issue drug orders for controlled substances shall register with the United States Drug Enforcement Administration.

Citation: ANN. CAL. BUS. & PROF. CODE § 2836.2.

Colorado

An advanced practice nurse shall practice in accordance with the standards of the appropriate national professional nursing organization and have a safe mechanism for consultation or collaboration with a physician or, when appropriate, referral to a physician. Advanced practice nursing also includes, when appropriate, referral to other health care providers.

Citation: COLO. REV. STAT. ANN. § 12-38-111.5(6).

Connecticut

. . . "[C]ollaboration" means a mutually agreed upon relationship between an advanced practice registered nurse and a physician who is educated, trained, or has relevant experience that is related to the work of such advanced practice registered nurse. The collaboration shall address a reasonable and appropriate level of consultation and referral, coverage for the patient in the absence of the advanced practice registered nurse, a method to review patient outcomes, and a method of disclosure of the relationship to the patient. Relative to the exercise of prescriptive authority, the collaboration between an advanced practice registered nurse and a physician shall be in writing and shall address the level of Schedule II and III controlled substances that the advanced practice registered nurse may prescribe and provide a method to review patient outcomes, including, but not limited to, the review of medical therapeutics, corrective measures, laboratory tests, and other diagnostic procedures that the advanced practice registered nurse may prescribe, dispense, and administer.

Citation: CONN. GEN. STAT. ANN. § 20-87(b).

Delaware

Advanced practice nurses shall operate in collaboration with a licensed physician, dentist, podiatrist, or licensed Delaware health care delivery system to cooperate, coordinate, and consult with each other as appropriate pursuant to a collaborative agreement defined in the rules and regulations promulgated by the Board of Nursing, in the provision of health care to their patients. Advanced practice nurses desiring to practice independently or to prescribe independently must do so pursuant to Title 24, § 1906(a)(20) of Title 24.

Citation: Del. Code Ann. tit. 24, § 1902(b)(1b).

The "Joint Practice Committee" with the approval of the Board of Medical Licensure and Discipline shall have the authority to grant, restrict, suspend or revoke practice or independent practice authority and the Joint Practice Committee with the approval of the Board of Medical Licensure and Discipline shall be responsible for promulgating rules and regulations to implement the provisions of this chapter regarding "advanced practice nurses" who have been granted authority for independent practice and/or independent prescriptive authority.

Citation: Del. Code Ann. tit. 24, § 1906(20).

Those individuals who wish to engage in independent practice without written guidelines or protocols and/or wish to have independent prescriptive authority shall apply for such privilege or privileges to the Joint Practice Committee and do so only in collaboration with a licensed physician, dentist, podiatrist, or licensed Delaware health care delivery system. This does not include those individuals who have protocols and/or waivers approved by the Board of Medical Licensure and Discipline.

Citation: Del. Code Ann. tit. 24, § 1902(b)(2).

District of Columbia

   a. Generally, advanced practice registered nurses shall carry out acts of advanced registered nursing in collaboration with a licensed health care provider.
   d. Notwithstanding the provisions of this section, hospitals, facilities, and agencies, in requiring specific levels of collaboration and licensed health care providers in agreeing to the levels of collaboration, shall apply reasonable, nondiscriminatory standards, free of anticompetitive intent or purpose, in accordance with Chapter 14 of Title 2, Chapter 45 of Title 28, and § 44-507.

Citation: D.C. Stat. § 3-1206.03.

Florida

An Advanced Registered Nurse Practitioner shall only perform medical acts of diagnosis, treatment, and operation pursuant to a protocol between the ARNP and a Florida-licensed medical doctor, osteopathic physician, or dentist. The degree and method of supervision, determined by the ARNP and the physician or dentist, shall be specifically identified in the written protocol and shall be appropriate for prudent health care providers under similar circumstances. General supervision by the physician or dentist is required, unless these rules set a different level of supervision for a particular act. The number of persons to be supervised shall be limited to insure that an acceptable standard of medical care is rendered in consideration of the following factors:

a. Risk to patient;
b. Educational preparation, specialty, and experience of the parties to the protocol;
c. Complexity and risk of the procedures;
d. Practice setting; and
e. Availability of the physician or dentist.

Citation: FLA. ADMIN. CODE Ch. 64B9-4.010(1).

Georgia

A nurse protocol agreement between a physician and an advanced practice registered nurse pursuant to this Code section shall:

1. Be between an advanced practice registered nurse who is in a comparable specialty area or field as that of the delegating physician;
2. Contain a provision for immediate consultation between the advanced practice registered nurse and the delegating physician; if the delegating physician is not available, the delegating physician for purposes of consultation may designate another physician who concurs with the terms of the nurse protocol agreement;
3. Identify the parameters under which delegated acts may be performed by the advanced practice registered nurse, including without limitation the number of refills which may be ordered, the kinds of diagnostic studies which may be ordered, the extent to which radiographic image tests may be ordered, and the circumstances under which a prescription drug order may be executed. In the event the delegating physician authorizes the advanced practice registered nurse to order an X-ray, ultrasound, or radiographic imaging test, the nurse protocol agreement shall contain provisions whereby such X-ray, ultrasound, or radiographic imaging test shall be read and interpreted by a physician who is trained in the reading and interpretation of such tests; a report of such X-ray, ultrasound, or radiographic imaging test may be reviewed by the advanced practice registered nurse; and a copy of such report shall be forwarded to the delegating physician, except that such provision for an ultrasound shall not be required for an advanced practice registered nurse acting within his or her scope of practice as authorized by Code Sections 43-26-3 and 43-26-5.
4. Require documentation either in writing or by electronic means or other medium by the advanced practice registered nurse or those acts performed by the advanced practice registered nurse which are specific to the medical act authorized by the delegating physician;

5. Include a schedule for periodic review by the delegating physician of patient records. Such patient records review may be achieved with a sampling of such records as determined by the delegating physician;

6. Provide for patient evaluation or follow-up examination by the delegating physician or other physician designated by the delegating physician pursuant to paragraph (2) of this subsection, with the frequency of such evaluation or follow-up examination based on the nature, extent, and scope of the delegated act or acts as determined by the delegating physician in accordance with paragraph (3) of this subsection and accepted standards of medical practice as determined by the board;

7. Be reviewed, revised, or updated annually by the delegating physician and the advanced practice registered nurse;

8. Be available for review upon written request to the advanced practice registered nurse by the Georgia Board of Nursing or to the physician by the board; and

9. Provide that a patient who received a prescription drug order for any controlled substance pursuant to a nurse protocol agreement shall be evaluated or examined by the delegating physician or other physician designated by the delegating physician pursuant to paragraph (2) of this subsection on at least a quarterly basis or at a more frequent interval as determined by the board.

   d. A written prescription drug order issued pursuant to this Code section shall be signed by the advanced practice registered nurse and shall be on a form which shall include, without limitation, the names of the advanced practice registered nurse and delegating physician who are parties to the nurse protocol agreement, the patient's name and address, the drug or device ordered, directions with regard to the taking and dosage of the drug or use of the device, and the number of refills. A prescription drug order which is transmitted either electronically or via facsimile shall conform to the requirements set out in paragraphs (1) and (2) of Subsection (c) of Code Section 26-4-80, respectively.

Citation: GA CODE ANN. § 43-34-25(b).

Hawaii

"Collaborate" means a process in which an APRN works with other members of the health care team to deliver health care services.

Citation: HAW. ADMIN. R § 16-89-2.

Idaho

An advanced practice registered nurse collaborates with other health professionals in providing health care.

Citation: IDAHO CODE § 54-1402(1).

Illinois

a. A written collaborative agreement is required for all advanced practice nurses engaged in clinical practice, except for advanced practice nurses who are authorized to practice in a hospital or ambulatory surgical treatment center.

a-5. If an advanced practice nurse engages in clinical practice outside of a hospital or ambulatory surgical treatment center in which he or she is authorized to practice, the advanced practice nurse must have a written collaborative agreement.

b. A written collaborative agreement shall describe the working relationship of the advanced practice nurse with the collaborating physician or podiatrist and shall authorize the categories of care, treatment, or procedures to be performed by the advanced practice nurse. A collaborative agreement with a dentist must be in accordance with subsection (c-10) of this Section. Collaboration does not require an employment relationship between the collaborating physician and advanced practice nurse.

Collaboration means the relationship under which an advanced practice nurse works with a collaborating physician or podiatrist in an active clinical practice to deliver health care services in accordance with (i) the advanced practice nurse's training, education, and experience and (ii) collaboration and consultation as documented in a jointly developed written collaborative agreement.

The agreement shall promote the exercise of professional judgment by the advanced practice nurse commensurate with his or her education and experience. The services to be provided by the advanced practice nurse shall be services that the collaborating physician or podiatrist is authorized to and generally provides or may provide in his or her clinical medical or podiatric practice, except as set forth in subsections (b-5) or (c-5) of this Section. The agreement need not describe the exact steps that an advanced practice nurse must take with respect to each specific condition, disease, or symptom but must specify which authorized procedures require the presence of the collaborating physician or podiatrist as the procedures are being performed. The collaborative relationship under an agreement shall not be construed to require the personal presence of a physician or podiatrist at the place where the services are rendered.

Methods of communication shall be available for consultation with the collaborating physician or podiatrist in person or by telecommunications in accordance with established written guidelines as set forth in the written agreement.

b-5. Absent an employment relationship, a written collaborative agreement may not (1) restrict the categories of patients of an advanced practice nurse within the scope of the advanced practice nurses training and experience, (2) limit third party payors or government health programs, such as the medical assistance program or Medicare with which the advanced practice nurse contracts, or (3) limit the geographic area or practice location of the advanced practice nurse in this State.

c. Collaboration and consultation under all collaboration agreements shall be adequate if a collaborating physician or podiatrist does each of the following:

1. Participates in the joint formulation and joint approval of orders or guidelines with the advanced practice nurse and he or she periodically reviews such orders and the services provided patients under such orders in accordance with accepted standards of medical practice or podiatric practice and advanced practice nursing practice.

2. Provides collaboration and consultation with the advanced practice nurse at least once a month. In the case of anesthesia services provided by a certified registered nurse anesthetist, an anesthesiologist, physician, dentist, or podiatrist must participate through discussion of and agreement with the anesthesia plan and remain physically present and available on the premises during the delivery of anesthesia services for diagnosis, consultation, and treatment of emergency medical conditions.

3. Is available through telecommunications for consultation on medical problems, complications, or emergencies or patient referral. In the case of anesthesia services provided by a certified registered nurse anesthetist, an anesthesiologist, physician, dentist, or podiatrist must participate through discussion of and agreement with the anesthesia plan and remain physically present and available on the premises during the delivery of anesthesia services for diagnosis, consultation, and treatment of emergency medical conditions.

The agreement must contain provisions detailing notice for termination or change of status involving a written collaborative agreement, except when such notice is given for just cause. [Portions omitted.]

> *Citation:* 225 ILL. COMP. STAT. § 60/54.5 as amended by Public Act 098-0192, enacted August 6, 2013.

Indiana

An advanced practice nurse shall operate in collaboration with a licensed practitioner as evidenced by a practice agreement, or by privileges granted by the governing board of a hospital . . . with the advice of the medical staff of the hospital that sets forth the manner in which the advanced practice nurse and a licensed practitioner will cooperate, coordinate, and consult with each other in the provision of health care to their patients.

> *Citation:* IND. CODE ANN. § 25-23-1-19.4(b).

"Practitioner" means [for the purpose of the nurse practice act]:

- A licensed physician
- A veterinarian
- A dentist
- A podiatrist
- An optometrist
- An advanced practice nurse who meets the requirements of IC 25-23-1-19.5
- A physician assistant licensed under IC 25-27.5 who is delegated prescriptive authority under IC 25-27.5-5-6

Citation: IND. CODE ANN. § 16-42-19-5.

An advanced practice nurse may be authorized to prescribe legend drugs, including controlled substances, if the advanced practice nurse . . . (7) submits proof of collaboration with a licensed practitioner in the form of a written practice agreement that sets forth the manner in which the advanced practice nurse and licensed practitioner will cooperate, coordinate, and consult with each other in the provision of health care to patients. Practice agreements shall be in writing and shall also set forth provisions for the type of collaboration between the advanced practice nurse and the licensed practitioner and the reasonable and timely review by the licensed practitioner of the prescribing practices of the advanced practice nurse.

Citation: IND. ADMIN. CODE tit. 848, r. 5-1-1(7).

Iowa

The ARNP may perform selected medically designated functions when a collaborative practice agreement exists.

Citation: IOWA ADMIN. CODE r. 655-7.1(152).

Author's note: The Iowa Board of Nursing interprets Iowa law as not requiring physician involvement in nurse practitioner practice:

- "In Iowa, an ARNP may practice independently." *Source:* Iowa Board of Nursing website
- "An ARNP may have a collaborative agreement with a physician or physicians if their practice so warrants, but this agreement is not a requirement of the Iowa Board of Nursing."

Source: Iowa Board of Nursing Newsletter, Volume 28, Number 4

Author's note: The inconsistency between the regulatory language and the Board of Nursing statements seem to be related to whether an ARNP is performing medicine or nursing. Making medical diagnoses and treating with medical therapies (prescribing medications and ordering therapies) are medical functions, and therefore would require collaboration with a physician.

Kansas

An advanced practice registered nurse may prescribe drugs pursuant to a written protocol as authorized by a responsible physician. Each written protocol shall contain a precise and detailed medical plan of care for each classification of disease or injury for which the advanced practice registered nurse is authorized to prescribe and shall specify all drugs which may be prescribed by the advanced practice registered nurse. Any written prescription order shall include the name, address, and telephone number of the responsible physician. The advanced practice registered nurse may not dispense drugs, but may request, receive and sign for professional samples and may distribute professional samples to patients pursuant to written protocol as authorized by a responsible physician.

Citation: KAN. STAT. ANN. § 65-1130(d).

"Authorization for collaborative practice" shall mean that an ARNP is authorized to develop and manage the medical plan of care for patients or clients based upon an agreement developed jointly and signed by the ARNP and one or more physicians. Each ARNP and physician shall jointly review the authorization for collaborative practice annually. Each authorization for collaborative practice shall include a cover page containing the names and telephone numbers of the ARNP and the physician, their signatures, and the date of review by the ARNP and the physician. Each authorization for collaborative practice shall be maintained in either hard copy or electronic format at the ARNP's principal place of practice.

Citation: KAN. STAT. ANN. § 60-11-101(b).

Kentucky

Before an advanced practice registered nurse engages in the prescribing or dispensing of nonscheduled legend drugs as authorized under KRS 314.011(8), the advanced practice registered nurse shall enter into a written "Collaborative Agreement for Advanced Practice Registered Nurse's Prescriptive Authority for Nonscheduled Legend Drugs" (CAPA-NS) with a physician that defines the scope of the prescriptive authority for nonscheduled legend drugs.

Citation: [New legislation enacted February 2014 — no collaboration required for experienced NPs.] KY. REV. STAT. ANN. § 314.042(8).

Before an advanced registered nurse practitioner engages in the prescribing of Schedules II through V controlled substances as authorized by KRS 314.011(8), the advanced practice registered nurse practitioner shall enter into a written "Collaborative Agreement for the Advanced Practice Registered Nurse's Prescriptive Authority for Controlled Substances" (CAPA-CS) with a physician that defines the scope of the prescriptive authority for controlled substances [further requirements omitted].

Citation: KY. REV. STAT. ANN. § 314.042(9).

Louisiana

7. "Collaboration" means a cooperative working relationship with another licensed physician, dentist, or other health care providers to jointly contribute to providing patient care and may include, but not be limited to discussion of a patient's diagnosis and cooperation in the management and delivery of health care with each provider performing those activities that he is legally authorized to perform.

8. "Collaborative practice" means the joint management of the health care of a patient by an advanced practice registered nurse performing advanced practice registered nursing and one or more consulting physicians or dentists. Except as otherwise provided in R.S. 37:930, acts of medical diagnosis and prescription by an advanced practice registered nurse shall be in accordance with a collaborative practice agreement.

9. "Collaborative practice agreement" means a formal written statement addressing the parameters of the collaborative practice which are mutually agreed upon by the advanced practice registered nurse and one or more licensed physicians or dentists which shall include but not be limited to the following provisions:
   a. Availability of the collaborating physician or dentist for consultation or referral, or both.
   b. Methods of management of the collaborative practice which shall include clinical practice guidelines.
   c. Coverage of the health care needs of a patient during any absence of the advanced practice registered nurse, physician, or dentist.

Citation: La. Rev. Stat. Ann. § 37:913.

vi. The applicant shall . . . provide evidence of . . . [a] collaborative practice agreement . . . which shall include, but not be limited to:

a. A plan of accountability among the parties that: (i) defines the limited prescriptive authority of the APRN and the responsibilities of the collaborating physician or physicians; (ii) delineates a plan for possible hospital admissions and privileges which includes a statement that the collaborating physician must have said privileges at the same institution before an APRN can receive this determination at said institution; (iii) delineates mechanisms and arrangements for diagnostic and laboratory requests for testing; and (iv) delineates a plan for documentation of medical records;

b. clinical practice guidelines . . . shall contain documentation of the types of categories or schedules of drugs available and generic substitution for prescription and be in accordance with current standards of care and evidence-based practice for the APRN specialty and functional role and be: (i) mutually agreed upon by the APRN and collaborating physician; (ii) specific to the practice setting; (iii) maintained on site; and (iv) reviewed and signed at least annually by the APRN and physician to reflect current practice.

c. documentation of the availability of the collaborating physician when the physician is not physically present in the practice setting....

d. documentation shall be shown that patients are informed about how to access care when both the APRN and/or collaborating physicians are absent from the practice setting; and

e. an acknowledgment of the mutual obligation and responsibility of the APRN and collaborating physician to insure that all acts of limited prescriptive authority of the APRN are properly documented.

Citation: LA. ADMIN. CODE tit. 46, § XLVII.4513.

Maine

1. Requirements for initial approval to practice
   C. Submits evidence of a minimum of 1500 hours of practice in an expanded specialty nursing role within 5 years preceding application, or have completed a nurse practitioner program within 5 years preceding application. If more than 5 years have elapsed since completion of an advanced practice registered nurse program and the applicant does not meet the practice requirement of 1500 hours, the applicant shall complete 500 hours of clinical practice supervised by a physician or nurse practitioner in the same specialty area of practice.

2. For temporary approval [to practice] for graduates of nurse practitioner programs
   A. A nurse practitioner must practice for a minimum of 24 months under the supervision of a licensed physician, or a supervising nurse practitioner, or be employed by a clinic or hospital that has a medical director who is a licensed physician.
   B. The applicant shall identify a supervisory relationship with a licensed physician or nurse practitioner in the same practice category who will provide oversight for the nurse practitioner.

Citation: CODE ME. R. § 02 380 008 (Section 2).

Maryland

A. Before commencing practice, a nurse practitioner shall complete a Board-approved written attestation that:
   1. The nurse practitioner has an agreement for collaborating and consulting with a physician;
   2. States the name and license number of the physician;

3. The nurse practitioner shall refer to and consult with physicians and other health care providers as needed; and

4. The nurse practitioner shall practice in accordance with the standards of practice of:

   a. The American Academy of Nurse Practitioners; or

   b. Any other national nurse practitioner certifying body recognized by the Board.

B. The Board shall:

1. Maintain an approved written attestation; and

2. Make the approved written attestation available to the Board of Physicians on the request of the Board of Physicians.

C. If a nurse practitioner terminates or changes an agreement to collaborate, a new written attestation stating the name of the physician shall be submitted immediately, by mail or facsimile, to the Board.

Citation: MD. CODE tit. 10 § 27.07.04.

Massachusetts

1. All nurses practicing in an expanded role . . . shall practice in accordance with the written guidelines developed in collaboration with and mutually acceptable to the nurse and to:

   a. a physician expert by virtue of training or experience in the nurse's area of practice; or

   b. the appropriate medical staff and nursing administration staff of the institution employing the nurse.

2. In all cases the written guidelines shall designate a physician who shall provide medical direction as is customarily accepted in the specialty area. Guidelines may authorize the nurse's performance of any professional activities included within her area of practice. The guidelines shall:

   a. specifically describe the nature and scope of the nursing practice;

   b. describe the circumstances in which physician consultation or referral is required;

   c. describe the use of established procedures for the treatment of common medical conditions which the nurse may encounter; and

   d. include provisions for managing emergencies.

3. In addition to the requirements of 244 CMR 4.22(2), the guidelines pertaining to prescriptive practice shall:

   a. include a defined mechanism to monitor prescribing practices, including documentation of review with a supervising physician at least every three months;

   b. include protocols for initiation of intravenous therapies and Schedule II drugs;

c. specify the frequency of review of initial prescription of controlled substances; the initial prescription of Schedule II drugs must be reviewed by the physician within 96 hours; and

d. conform to M.G.L. c.94C, 105 CMR 700.000 et seq., and M.G.L. c.112, § 80E or § 80G, as applicable.

Citation: CODE MASS. REGS. tit. 244, § 4.22.

Michigan

Subject to subsections (2) to (6), a licensee who holds a license other than a health profession subfield license may delegate to a licensed or unlicensed individual who is otherwise qualified by education, training or experience the performance of selected acts, tasks, or functions where the acts, tasks, or functions fall within the scope of practice of the licensee's profession and will be performed under the licensee's supervision. A licensee shall not delegate an act, task, or function under this section if the act, task, or function, under standards of acceptable and prevailing practice, requires the level of education, skill, and judgment required of the licensee under this article.

Citation: MICH. COMP. LAWS § 333.16215(1).

Minnesota

"Collaborative management" is a mutually agreed-upon plan between an advanced practice registered nurse and one or more physicians or surgeons licensed under chapter 147 that designates the scope of collaboration necessary to manage the care of patients. The advanced practice registered nurse and the one or more physicians must have experience in providing care to patients with the same or similar medical problems.

Citation: MINN. STAT. ANN. § 148.171(6).

Mississippi

An advanced practice registered nurse shall perform those functions authorized in this section within a collaborative/consultative relationship with a dentist or physician with an unrestricted license to practice dentistry or medicine in this state and within an established protocol or practice guidelines, as appropriate, that is filed with the board upon license application, license renewal, after entering into a new collaborative/consultative relationship or making changes to the protocol or practice guidelines or practice site. The board shall review and approve the protocol to ensure compliance with applicable regulatory standards. The advanced practice registered nurse may not practice as an APRN if there is no collaborative/consultative relationship with a physician or dentist and a board approved protocol or practice guidelines.

Citation: Miss. Nursing Practice Law §73-15-20(3).

Missouri

Collaborative practice arrangements—Refers to written agreements, jointly agreed upon protocols, or standing orders, all of which shall be in writing, for the delivery of healthcare services.

Citation: Mo. Code Regs. Ann. tit. 20, § 2200-4.200 (1)(C).

A. The collaborating physician in a collaborative practice shall not be so geographically distanced from the collaborating RN or APRN as to create an impediment to effective collaboration in the delivery of healthcare services or the adequate review of those services.

B. The use of a collaborative practice arrangement by an APRN who provides health care services that include the diagnosis and initiation of treatment for acutely or chronically ill or injured persons shall be limited to practice locations where the collaborating physician, or other physician designated in the collaborative practice arrangement, is no further than fifty (50) miles by road, using the most direct route available, from the collaborating APRN if the APRN is practicing in federally-designated health professional shortage areas (HPSAs). Otherwise, in non-HPSAs, the collaborating physician and collaborating APRN shall practice within thirty (30) miles by road of one another.

C. An APRN who desires to enter into a collaborative practice arrangement at a location where the collaborating physician is not continuously present shall practice together at the same location with the collaborating physician continuously for a period of at least one (1) month before the collaborating APRN practices at a location where the collaborating physician is not present. It is the responsibility of the collaborating physician to determine and document the completion of the same location practice described in the previous sentence.

D. A collaborating physician shall not enter into a collaborative practice arrangement with more than three (3) full-time equivalent APRNs. This limitation shall not apply to collaborative arrangements of hospital employees providing inpatient care service in hospitals as defined in Chapter 197, RSMo, or population-based public health services as defined in this rule.

Citation: Mo. Code Regs. Ann. tit. 20, § 2200-4.200(2).

The methods of treatment and the authority to administer, dispense, or prescribe drugs delegated in a collaborative practice arrangement between a collaborating physician and collaborating APRN shall be within the scope of practice of each professional and shall be consistent with each professional's skill, training, education, competence, licensure, and/or certification and shall not be further delegated to any person except that the individuals identified in sections 338.095 and 338.198, RSMo, may communicate prescription drug orders to a pharmacist.

Citation: Mo. Code Regs. Ann. tit. 20, § 2200-4.200(3)(A).

C. The collaborating physician shall consider the level of skill, education, training, and competence of the collaborating RN or APRN and ensure that the delegated responsibilities contained in the collaborative practice arrangement are consistent with that level of skill, education, training, and competence.

D. Guidelines for consultation and referral to the collaborating physician or designated health care facility for services or emergency care that is beyond the education, training, competence, or scope of practice of the collaborating RN or APRN shall be established in the collaborative practice arrangement.

E. The methods of treatment, including any authority to administer or dispense drugs, delegated in a collaborative practice arrangement between a collaborating physician and a collaborating RN shall be delivered only pursuant to a written agreement, jointly agreed-upon protocols, or standing orders that shall describe a specific sequence of orders, steps, or procedures to be followed in providing patient care in specified clinical situations.

F. The methods of treatment, including any authority to administer, dispense, or prescribe drugs, delegated in a collaborative practice arrangement between a collaborating physician and a collaborating APRN shall be delivered only pursuant to a written agreement, jointly agree-upon protocols, or standing orders that are specific to the clinical conditions treated by the collaborating physician and collaborating APRN.

Citation: Mo. Code Regs. Ann. tit. 20, § 2200-4.200(3).

Methods of treatment delegated and authority to administer, dispense, or prescribe drugs shall be subject to the following:

1. The physician retains the responsibility for ensuring the appropriate administering, dispensing, prescribing, and control of drugs utilized pursuant to a collaborative practice arrangement in accordance with all state and federal statues, rules, or regulations....

Citation: Mo. Code Regs. Ann. tit. 20, § 2200-4.200(3)(G).

A. In order to assure true collaborative practice and to foster effective communication and review of services, the collaborating physician, or other physician designated in the collaborative practice arrangement, shall be immediately available for consultation to the collaborating RN or APRN at all times, either personally or via telecommunications.

B. The collaborative practice arrangement between a collaborating physician and a collaborating RN or APRN shall be signed and dated by the collaborating physician and collaborating RN or APRN before it is implemented, signifying that both are aware of its content and agree to follow the terms of the collaborative practice arrangement. The collaborative practice arrangement and any subsequent notice of termination shall be in writing and shall be maintained by the collaborating professionals for a minimum of eight (8) years after termination of the collaborative practice arrangement. The collaborative practice arrangement shall be reviewed at least annually and revised as needed by the collaborating physician and collaborating RN or APRN. Documentation of the annual review shall be maintained as part of the collaborative practice arrangement.

C. Within thirty (30) days of any change and with each physician's license renewal, the collaborating physician shall advise the Missouri State Board of Registration for the Healing Arts whether he/she is engaged in any collaborative practice agreement, including collaborative practice agreements delegating the authority to prescribe controlled substances and also report to the board the name of each licensed RN or APRN with whom he/she has entered into such agreement. A change shall include, but not be limited to, resignation or termination of the RN or APRN; change in practice locations; and addition or new collaborating professionals.

D. An RN or an APRN practicing pursuant to a collaborative practice arrangement shall maintain adequate and complete patient records in compliance with section 334.097, RSMo.

E. The collaborating physician shall complete a review of a minimum of ten percent (10%) of the total health care services delivered by the collaborating APRN. If the APRN's practice includes the prescribing of controlled substances, the physician shall review a minimum of twenty percent (20%) of the cases in which the APRN wrote a prescription for a controlled substance. If the controlled substance chart review meets the minimum total ten percent (10%) as described above, then the minimum review requirements have been met. The collaborating APRN's documentation shall be submitted for review to the collaborating physician at least every fourteen (14) days. This documentation submission may be accomplished in person or by other electronic means and reviewed by the collaborating physician. The collaborating physician must produce evidence of the chart review upon request of the Missouri State Board of Registration for the Healing Arts. This subsection shall not apply during the time the collaborating physician and collaborating APRN are practicing together as required in subsection (2)(C) above.

F. If a collaborative practice arrangement is used in clinical situations where a collaborating APRN provides health care services that include the diagnosis and initiation or treatment for acutely or chronically ill or injured persons, then the collaborating physician shall be present for sufficient periods of time, at least once every two (2) weeks, except in extraordinary circumstances that shall be documented, to participate in such review and to provide necessary medical direction, medical services, consultations, and supervision of the health care staff. In such settings, the use of a collaborative practice arrangement shall be limited to only an APRN.

G. The collaborating physician and collaborating RN or APRN shall determine an appropriate process of review and management of abnormal test results which shall be documented in the collaborative practice arrangement.

Citation: Mo. Code Regs. Ann. tit. 20, § 2200-4.200(4).

Montana

Nurse practitioner (NP) practice means the independent and/or collaborative management of primary and/or acute health care of individuals, families, and communities including . . . working in collaboration with other health care providers and agencies to provide and, where appropriate, coordinate services to individuals and families.

Citation: Mont. Admin. R. § 24.159.1470(f).

Nebraska

Collaboration means a process and relationship in which a nurse practitioner, together with other health professionals, delivers health care within the scope of authority of the various clinical specialty practices.

Citation: Neb. Rev. Stat. § 38-2308.

1. Integrated practice agreement means a written agreement between a nurse practitioner and a collaborating physician in which the nurse practitioner and the collaborating physician provide for the delivery of health care through an integrated practice. The integrated practice agreement shall provide that the nurse practitioner and the collaborating physician will practice collaboratively within the framework of their respective scopes of practice. Each provider shall be responsible for his or her individual decisions in managing the health care of patients. Integrated practice includes consultation, collaboration, and referral.

2. The nurse practitioner and the collaborating physician shall have joint responsibility for patient care, based upon the scope of practice of each practitioner. The collaborating physician shall be responsible for supervision of the nurse practitioner to ensure the quality of health care provided to patients.

3. For the purposes of this section:
   a. Collaborating physician means a physician or osteopathic physician licensed in Nebraska and practicing in the same geographic area and practice specialty, related specialty, or field of practice as the nurse practitioner; and
   b. Supervision means the ready availability of the collaborating physician for consultation and direction of the activities of the nurse practitioner within the nurse practitioner's defined scope of practice.

Citation: NEB. REV. STAT. § 38-2310.

Nevada

Note: Section 632.2555 has been repealed as of December 10, 2013.

New Hampshire

There is no requirement for physician collaboration for NP practice in New Hampshire.

New Jersey

An advanced practice nurse may order medications and devices in the inpatient setting, subject to the following condition:

1. the collaborating physician and advanced practice nurse shall address in the joint protocols whether prior consultation with the collaborating physician is required to initiate an order for a controlled dangerous substance;
2. the order is written in accordance with standing orders or joint protocols developed in agreement between a collaborating physician and the advanced practice nurse, or pursuant to the specific direction of a physician;
3. the advanced practice nurse authorizes the order by signing his or her own name, printing the name and certification number, and printing the collaborating physician's name;
4. the physician is present or readily available through electronic communications;
5. the charts and records of the patients treated by the advanced practice nurse are reviewed by the collaborating physician and the advanced practice nurse within the period of time specified by rule adopted by the Commissioner of Health and Senior Services pursuant to section 13 of P.L.1991, c.377 (C.45:11-52);
6. the joint protocols developed by the collaborating physician and the advanced practice nurse are reviewed, updated and signed at least annually by both parties; and
7. the advanced practice nurse has completed six contact hours of continuing professional education in pharmacology related to controlled substances, including pharmacologic therapy and addiction prevention and management,

in accordance with regulations adopted by the New Jersey Board of Nursing. The six contact hours shall be in addition to the New Jersey Board of Nursing pharmacology education requirements for advanced practice nurses related to initial certification and recertification of an advanced practice nurse as set forth in N.J.A.C.13:37-7.2 and 12:37-7.5.

c. An advanced practice nurse may prescribe medications and devices in all other medically appropriate settings, subject to the following conditions:

1. the collaborating physician and advanced practice nurse shall address in the joint protocols whether prior consultation with the collaborating physician is required to initiate a prescription for a controlled dangerous substance;

2. the prescription is written in accordance with standing orders or joint protocols developed in agreement between a collaborating physician and the advanced practice nurse, or pursuant to the specific direction of a physician;

3. the advanced practice nurse writes the prescription on a New Jersey Prescription Blank pursuant to P.L.2003, c.280 (C.45:14-40 et seq.), signs his name to the prescription and prints his name and certification number;

4. the prescription is dated and includes the name of the patient and the name, address, and telephone number of the collaborating physician;

5. the physician is present or readily available through electronic communications;

6. the charts and records of the patients treated by the advanced practice nurse are periodically reviewed by the collaborating physician and the advanced practice nurse;

7. the joint protocols developed by the collaborating physician and the advanced practice nurse are reviewed, updated, and signed at least annually by both parties; and

8. the advanced practice nurse has completed six contact hours of continuing professional education in pharmacology related to controlled substances, including pharmacologic therapy and addiction prevention and management, in accordance with regulations adopted by the New Jersey Board of Nursing. The six contact hours shall be in addition to New Jersey Board of Nursing pharmacology education requirements for advanced practice nurses related to initial certification and recertification of an advanced practice nurse as set forth in N.J.A.C.13:37-7.2 and 13:37-7.5.

d. The joint protocols employed pursuant to Subsections b. and c. of this section shall conform with standards adopted by the Director of the Division of Consumer Affairs pursuant to Section 12 of P.L.1991, c. 377 (C.45:11–51) or Section 10 of P.L.1999, c. 85 (C.45:11–49.2), as applicable.

Citation: N.J. Stat. Ann. § 45:11-49.

New Mexico

The Certified Nurse Practitioner makes independent decisions regarding the health care needs of the client and also makes independent decisions on carrying out health care regimens.

Citation: N.M. Admin. Code § 16.12.2.13.N(1).

New York

[A practice agreement between NP and a physician is required.]

Each practice agreement shall provide for patient records review by the collaborating physician in a timely fashion but in no event less often than every three months. The names of the nurse practitioner and the collaborating physician shall be clearly posted in the practice setting of the nurse practitioner.

Citation: N.Y. Educ. Law, Art. 139 § 6902.3(c).

No physician shall enter into practice agreements with more than four nurse practitioners who are not located on the same physical premises as the collaborating physician.

Citation: N.Y. Educ. Law, Art. 139 § 6902.3(e).

The practice protocol shall reflect current accepted medical and nursing practice. The protocols shall be filed with the department within ninety days of the commencement of the practice and may be updated periodically. The commissioner shall make regulations establishing the procedure for the review of protocols and the disposition of any issues arising from such review.

Citation: N.Y. Educ. Law, Art. 139 § 6902.3(d).

North Carolina

The following are the quality assurance standards for a collaborative practice agreement:

1. Availability: The primary or back-up supervising physician(s) and the nurse practitioner shall be continuously available to each other for consultation by direct communication or telecommunication.
2. Collaborative Practice Agreement:
   a. shall be agreed upon and signed by both the primary supervising physician and the nurse practitioner, and maintained in each practice site;
   b. shall be reviewed at least yearly. This review shall be acknowledged by a dated signature sheet, signed by both the primary supervising physician and the nurse practitioner, appended to the collaborative practice

agreement and available for inspection by members or agents of either Board;

c. shall include the drugs, devices, medical treatments, tests, and procedures that may be prescribed, ordered and performed by the nurse practitioner consistent with Rule .0809 of this Section; and

d. shall include a pre-determined plan for emergency services.

3. The nurse practitioner shall demonstrate the ability to perform medical acts as outlined in the collaborative practice agreement upon request by members or agents of either Board.

4. Quality Improvement Process.

a. The primary supervising physician and the nurse practitioner shall develop a process for the ongoing review of the care provided in each practice site including a written plan for evaluating the quality of care provided for one or more frequently encountered clinical problems.

b. This plan shall include a description of the clinical problem(s), an evaluation of the current treatment interventions, and if needed, a plan for improving outcomes within an identified timeframe.

c. The quality improvement process shall include scheduled meetings between the primary supervising physician and the nurse practitioner at least every six months. Documentation for each meeting shall:

   i. identify clinical problems discussed, including progress toward improving outcomes as stated in Sub-item (4)(b) of this Rule, and recommendations, if any, for changes in treatment plan(s);

   ii. be signed and dated by those who attended; and

   iii. be available for review by members or agents of either Board for the previous five calendar years and be retained by both the nurse practitioner and primary supervising physician.

5. Nurse Practitioner-Physician Consultation. The following requirements establish the minimum standards for consultation between the nurse practitioner and primary supervising physician(s):

a. During the first six months of a collaborative practice agreement between a nurse practitioner and the primary supervising physician, there shall be monthly meetings for the first six months to discuss practice relevant clinical issues and quality improvement measures.

b. Documentation of the meetings shall:

   i. identify clinical issues discussed and actions taken;

   ii. be signed and dated by those who attended; and

   iii. be available for review by members or agents of either Board for the previous five calendar years and be retained by both the nurse practitioner and primary supervising physician.

Citation: N.C. Admin. Code tit. 21, r. 36.0810.

North Dakota

There is no requirement for physician collaboration for APRN practice in North Dakota.

Ohio

A ... certified nurse practitioner, in collaboration with one or more physicians or podiatrists, may provide preventive and primary care services, provide services for acute illness, and evaluate and promote patient wellness within the nurse's nursing specialty, consistent with the nurse's education and certification, and in accordance with rules adopted by the board. A certified nurse practitioner who holds a certificate to prescribe issued under Section 4723.48 of the Revised Code may, in collaboration with one or more physicians or podiatrists, prescribe drugs and therapeutic devices in accordance with Section 4723.481 of the Revised Code. When a certified nurse practitioner is collaborating with a podiatrist, the nurse's scope of practice is limited to the procedures that the podiatrist has the authority under Section 4731.51 of the Revised Code to perform.

Citation: OHIO REV. CODE ANN. § 4723.43(C).

Oklahoma

A Certified Nurse Practitioner shall be eligible, in accordance with the scope of practice of the Certified Nurse Practitioner, to obtain recognition as authorized by the Board to prescribe ... subject to the medical direction of a supervising physician.

Citation: OKLA. STAT. ANN. tit. 59, § 567.3a(6).

Oregon

There is no requirement of physician collaboration.

Pennsylvania

Collaboration—A process in which a CRNP works with one or more physicians to deliver health care services within the scope of the CRNP's expertise. The process includes all of the following:
  i. Immediate availability of a licensed physician to a CRNP through direct communications or by radio, telephone or telecommunications.
  ii. A predetermined plan for emergency services.
  iii. A physician available to a CRNP on a regularly scheduled basis for referrals, review of the standards of medical practice incorporating consultation and chart review, drug and other medical protocols within the

practice setting, periodic updating in medical diagnosis and therapeutics and cosigning records when necessary to document accountability by both parties.

Citation: 49 Pa. Code § 21.251.

Rhode Island

"Certified registered nurse practitioner (RNP)" means an advanced practice nurse utilizing independent knowledge of physical assessment and management of health care and illnesses. The practice includes prescriptive privileges, and collaboration with other licensed healthcare professionals, including, but not limited to, physicians, pharmacists, podiatrists, dentists and nurses. Such collaboration is not required to be pursuant to a written collaboration agreement, with a specific designated physician, or at the same physical location as a collaborating physician.

Citation: R.I. R. § R5-34-NUR/ED 1.0(1.10).

South Carolina

. . . Nurse practitioners who perform delegated medical acts must have a supervising physician or dentist who is readily available for consultation and shall operate within the approved written protocols.

Citation: S.C. Code Ann. § 40-33-20(41).

"Approved written protocols" mean specific statements developed collaboratively by a physician or medical staff and a NP, CNM, or CNS that establishes physician delegation for medical aspects of care, including the prescription of medications.

Citation: S.C. Code Ann. § 40-33-20(10).

Delegated medical acts performed by a nurse practitioner, certified nurse-midwife, or clinical nurse specialist must be performed pursuant to an approved written protocol between the nurse and physician and must include . . . (a) this general information:

i. Name, address, and South Carolina license number of the nurse;
ii. Name, address, and South Carolina license number of the physician;
iii. Nature of practice and practice locations of the nurse and physician;
iv. Date the protocol was developed and dates the protocol was reviewed and amended;
v. Description of how consultation with the physician is provided and provision for backup consultation in the physician's absence.

b. This information for delegated medical acts:

i. The medical conditions for which therapies may be initiated, continued, or modified;

      ii. The treatments that may be initiated, continued, or modified;

    iii. The drug therapies that may be prescribed;

    iv. Situations that require direct evaluation by or referral to the physician.

2. The original protocol and any amendments to the protocol must be reviewed at least annually, dated and signed by the nurse and physician, and made available to the Board for review within 72 hours of request. Failure to produce protocols upon request of the board is considered misconduct and subjects the licensee to disciplinary action. A random audit of approved written protocols must be conducted by the board at least biennially.

3. Licensees who change practice settings or physicians, shall notify the board of the change within 15 business days and provide verification of approved written protocols. NPs, CNMs and CNSs who discontinue their practice shall notify the board within 15 days.

Citation: S.C. CODE ANN. § 43-33-34(D).

South Dakota

"Collaborative agreement" defined. The term, collaborative agreement, as used in this chapter, means a written agreement authored and signed by the nurse practitioner or nurse midwife and the physician with whom the nurse practitioner or nurse midwife is collaborating. A collaborative agreement defines or describes the agreed upon overlapping scope of advanced practice nursing and medical functions that may be performed, consistent with § 36-9A-12 or 36-9A-13, and contains such other information as required by the boards. A copy of each collaborative agreement shall be maintained on file with and be approved by the boards prior to performing any of the acts contained in the agreement.

Citation: S.D. CODIFIED LAWS § 36-9A-15.

Advanced practice nursing and medical functions—Collaborative agreement required. A nurse practitioner or nurse midwife may perform the overlapping scope of advanced practice nursing and medical functions only under the terms of a collaborative agreement with a physician licensed under Chapter 36-4. Any collaborative agreement shall be maintained on file with the boards. Collaboration may be by direct personal contact, or by a combination of direct personal contact and indirect contact via telecommunication, as may be required by the boards. If the collaborating physician named in a collaborative agreement becomes temporarily unavailable, the nurse practitioner or nurse midwife may perform the agreed upon overlapping scope of advanced practice nursing and medical functions in consultation with another licensed physician designated as a substitute.

Citation: S.D. CODIFIED LAWS § 36-9A-17.

Collaboration with a licensed physician or physicians. A nurse practitioner or nurse midwife may perform the overlapping scope of advanced practice nursing and medical functions defined in SDCL 36-9A-12 and 36-9A-13, in collaboration with a physician or physicians licensed under SDCL Chapter 36-4. Collaboration by direct personal contact with each collaborating physician must occur no less than twice each month unless it is established in the collaborative agreement that one of the twice monthly meetings may be held by telecommunication. Collaboration with each collaborating physician shall occur at least once per month by direct personal contact.

Citation: S.D. ADMIN. R. § 20:62:03:03.

Direct personal contact. For the purposes of this chapter, the term, direct personal contact, means that both the collaborating physician and the nurse practitioner or nurse midwife are physically present on site and available for the purposes of collaboration. When the collaborating physician is not in direct personal contact with the nurse practitioner or nurse midwife, the physician must be available by telecommunication. If the boards consider additional direct personal contact necessary for a nurse practitioner or nurse midwife, they shall set the terms of that additional collaboration and require inclusion of those terms in that nurse practitioner's or midwife's collaborative agreement as a condition for its approval.

Citation: S.D. ADMIN. R. § 20:62:03:04.

Collaboration—Separate practice location. In addition to the required two meetings per month, the collaborating physician must be physically present on-site every ninety days at each practice location. This requirement does not apply to locations where health care services are not routine to the setting, such as patient homes and school health screening events.

Citation: S.D. ADMIN. R. § 20:62:03:05.

Tennessee

b. 1. A nurse who has been issued a certificate of fitness as a nurse practitioner pursuant to § 63-7-207 and this section shall file a notice with the board, containing the name of the nurse practitioner, the name of the licensed physician having supervision, control, and responsibility for prescriptive services rendered by the nurse practitioner and a copy of the formulary describing the categories of legend drugs to be prescribed and/or issued by the nurse practitioner. The nurse practitioner shall be responsible for updating this information.

2. The nurse practitioner who holds a certificate of fitness shall be authorized to prescribe and/or issue controlled substances listed in Schedules II, III, IV, and V . . . upon joint adoption of physician supervisory rules concerning controlled substances. . . .

Citation: TENN. CODE ANN. § 63-7-123(b)(1)&(2).

Texas

The advanced practice nurse acts independently and/or in collaboration with the health team in the observation, assessment, diagnosis, intervention, evaluation, rehabilitation, care and counsel, and health teachings of persons who are ill, injured, or infirm or experiencing changes in normal health processes; and in the promotion and maintenance of health or prevention of illness.

Citation: 21 Tex. Admin. Code § 221.13(c).

When providing medical aspects of care, advanced practice nurses shall utilize mechanisms that provide authority for that care. These mechanisms may include, but are not limited to, protocols or other written authorization. This shall not be construed as requiring authority for nursing aspects of care.

1. Protocols or other written authorization shall promote the exercise of professional judgment by the advanced practice nurse commensurate with his/her education and experience. The degree of detail within protocols/policies/practice guidelines/clinical practice privileges may vary in relation to the complexity of the situations covered by such protocols, the advanced specialty area of practice, the advanced educational preparation of the individual, and the experience level of the individual advanced practice nurse.
2. Protocols or other written authorization:
   A. should be jointly developed by the advanced practice nurse and the appropriate physician(s);
   B. shall be signed by both the advanced practice nurse and the physician(s);
   C. shall be reviewed and re-signed at least annually;
   D. shall be maintained in the practice setting of the advanced practice nurse; and
   E. shall be made available as necessary to verify authority to provide medical aspects of care.
e. The advanced practice nurse shall retain professional accountability for advanced practice nursing care.

Citation: 21 Tex. Admin. Code § 221.13(d)&(e).

a. The APRN with full licensure and a valid prescription authorization number shall:
   1. order or prescribe only those drugs or devices that are:
      A. authorized by a prescriptive authority agreement or, if practicing in a facility-based practice, authorized by either a prescriptive authority agreement or protocols or other written authorization; and
      B. ordered or prescribed for patient populations within the accepted scope of professional practice for the APRN's license; and

2. comply with the requirements for chart reviews specified in the prescriptive authority agreement and periodic face to face meetings set forth in the prescriptive authority agreement; or

3. comply with the requirements set forth in protocols or other written authorization if ordering or prescribing drugs or devices under facility-based protocols or other written authorization.

b. Prescription Information. The format and essential elements of a prescription drug order shall comply with the requirements of the Texas State Board of Pharmacy. The following information must be provided on each prescription:

1. the patient's name and address;
2. the name, strength, and quantity of the drug to be dispensed;
3. directions to the patient regarding taking of the drug and the dosage;
4. the intended use of the drug, if appropriate;
5. the name, address, and telephone number of the physician with whom the APRN has a prescriptive authority agreement or facility-based protocols or other written authorization;
6. address and telephone number of the site at which the prescription drug order was issued;
7. the date of issuance;
8. the number of refills permitted;
9. the name, prescription authorization number, and original signature of the APRN who authorized the prescription drug order; and
10. the United States Drug Enforcement Administration numbers of the APRN and the delegating physician, if the prescription drug order is for a controlled substance.

c. Generic Substitution. The APRN shall authorize or prevent generic substitution on a prescription in compliance with the current rules of the Texas State Board of Pharmacy relating to generic substitution.

d. An APRN may order or prescribe medications for sexually transmitted diseases for partners of an established patient, if the APRN assesses the patient and determines that the patient may have been infected with a sexually transmitted disease. Nothing in this subsection shall be construed to require the APRN to issue prescriptions for partners of patients.

e. APRNs may order or prescribe only those medications that are FDA approved unless done through protocol registration in a United States Institutional Review Board or Expanded Access authorized clinical trial. "Off label" use, or prescription of FDA-approved medications for uses other than that indicated by the FDA, is permitted when such practices are:

1. within the current standard of care for treatment of the disease or condition; and
2. supported by evidence-based research.

f. The APRN with full licensure and a valid prescriptive authorization number shall cooperate with representatives of the Board and the Texas Medical Board during an inspection and audit relating to the operation and implementation of a prescriptive authority agreement.

Citation: 22 Tex. Admin. Code §224.4.

Utah

"Consultation and referral plan" means a written plan jointly developed by an advanced practice registered nurse and a consulting physician that permits the advanced practice registered nurse to prescribe schedule II-III controlled substances in consultation with the consulting physician.

Citation: Utah Code Ann. § 58-31b-102(5).

Vermont

Graduates with fewer than 24 months and 2,400 hours of license active advanced nursing practice shall have a formal agreement with a collaborating provider.

Citation: Vt. Board of Nursing Admin Rules 15.14.

a. A collaborating provider is:
    1. an APRN or
    2. a physician licensed to practice medicine under Title 26, Chapter 23, or
    3. an osteophathic physician licensed to practice under Title 26, Chapter 33.
b. The collaborating provider's license must be in good standing, and the collaborating provider shall practice in the same role and population focus or specialty as the new graduate APRN's area of certification.
c. An APRN collaborating provider shall have practiced in the same specialty for a minimum of four years. The Board, in its discretion, may waive the requirement that a collaborating provider be licensed in Vermont upon showing of necessity by the APRN. Any waiver granted under this section will only apply to providers currently licensed in the United States.

Citation: Vt. Board of Nursing Admin Rules 15.17.

Virginia

A nurse practitioner licensed in a category other than certified registered nurse anesthetist shall be authorized to render care in collaboration and consultation with a licensed patient care team physician as part of patient care team.

Citation: 18 Va. Admin. Code § 90-30-120.A.

A nurse practitioner with prescriptive authority may prescribe only within the scope of the written or electronic practice agreement with a patient care team physician.

Citation: 18 Va. Admin. Code § 90-40-90.

"Practice agreement" means a written or electronic agreement jointly developed by the patient care team physician and the nurse practitioner for the practice of the nurse practitioner that also describes the prescriptive authority of the nurse practitioner, if applicable.

Citation: 18 Va. Admin. Code § 90-40-10.

Washington

No physician collaboration is required by law for nurse practitioner practice in Washington.

West Virginia

The board may, in its discretion, authorize an advanced nurse practitioner to prescribe prescription drugs in a collaborative relationship with a physician licensed to practice in West Virginia and in accordance with applicable state and federal laws. An authorized advanced nurse practitioner may write or sign prescriptions or transmit prescriptions verbally or by other means of communication.

For purposes of this section an agreement to a collaborative relationship for prescriptive practice between a physician and an advanced practice registered nurse shall be set forth in writing. . . .

Collaborative agreements shall include, but not be limited to, the following:
1. Mutually agreed upon written guidelines or protocols for prescriptive authority as it applies to the advanced practice registered nurse's clinical practice;
2. Statements describing the individual and shared responsibilities of the advanced practice registered nurse and the physician pursuant to the collaborative agreement between them;
3. Periodic and joint evaluation of prescriptive practice; and
4. Periodic and joint review and updating of the written guidelines or protocols.

Citation: W.VA. Code Ann. § 30-7-15(a).

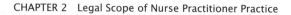

Wisconsin

Advanced practice nurse prescribers shall facilitate collaboration with other health care professionals, at least one of whom shall be a physician, through the use of modern communication techniques.

Citation: Wis. Admin. Code § N8.10(2).

Advanced practice nurse prescribers shall work in a collaborative relationship with a physician. The collaborative relationship is a process in which an advanced practice nurse prescriber is working with a physician, in each other's presence when necessary, to deliver health care services within the scope of the practitioner's professional expertise. The advanced practice nurse prescriber and the physician must document this relationship.

Citation: Wis. Admin. Code § N8.10(7).

Wyoming

There is no requirement for physician collaboration or supervision.

CHAPTER 3

State Regulation of Nurse Practitioner Practice

The law governing nurse practitioner (NP) definition, scope of practice, prescriptive authority, and requirement of physician collaboration, if any, may be enacted by a state legislature in great detail or in general terms. Alternatively, the state legislature may give authority to a licensing board to make the rules and regulations that govern NPs.

The state board that is likely to have the authority to make the rules regarding NPs is the board of nursing. In many states, the board of nursing makes the rules governing NP practice. In some states, however, the board of medicine has a role. See **Appendix 3-A** for a state-by-state list of the agencies that regulate NPs.

How Laws About NP Practice Evolve

State law takes two forms: statutes and regulations (sometimes referred to as rules). The legislature makes statutory law, and state agencies under the executive branch of government make regulations. Regulations cannot contradict statutes but often expand upon the statutes to include more detail of government administration.

When a member of the public wants to change a statute, the advocate must enlist the help of a state legislator, who can introduce a bill that will change the current statute. When a member of the public wants to change a regulation, the advocate must either convince the state agency that is responsible for the regulation to change the regulation or convince a legislator to introduce a bill that, if enacted, would override the regulation.

When an agency decides to change a regulation, the agency writes a new regulation, publishes the regulation in an official state publication, and invites comments from interested parties. The agency may or may not make changes to the proposed regulation based on comments received from interested parties. A proposed regulation becomes a final regulation—law—after it has been published in proposed form and comments have been reviewed. Final regulations are republished, in final form, in the state's "register," an official publication of the state.

What Is Regulated?

Much of the state law governing NPs appears in regulations; some law is statutory. The practice issues that come under state regulation are:

- Requirements for licensure
- Scope of practice

- Prescriptive authority
- Requirement of collaboration or supervision
- Basis for license suspension, revocation, or nonrenewal
- Reimbursement under Medicaid
- Reimbursement by indemnity insurers
- Requirements of educational programs
- Standards of practice

Licensure Requirements

State law governs the requirements for holding a professional license in the state. All states require NPs to hold state licenses as registered nurses (RNs). Thirty-three states require NPs to have master's degrees. Forty-five states require NPs to have obtained national certification.

Appendix 3-B lists state-by-state requirements for holding and maintaining an NP license.

Basis for Loss of License

State law, usually a regulation, specifies the criteria under which an NP's license may be revoked, suspended, or not renewed. Examples of some state laws follow. North Carolina and Pennsylvania make continuation of practice contingent upon following the rules of physician supervision. Rhode Island's law does not address physician collaboration or supervision but is concerned with practice-related safety issues.

More specific than most, North Carolina's law enforces the requirement of an NP to practice under physician supervision:

> . . . [A]ction may be taken . . . if one or more of the following is found:
>
> - That the nurse practitioner held himself or herself out or permitted another to represent the nurse practitioner as a licensed physician;
> - That the nurse practitioner has engaged or attempted to engage in the performance of medical acts other than according to the collaborative practice agreement.
>
> *Citation:* N.C. Admin. Code tit. 21 r. 36.0812.

In Pennsylvania, approval may be terminated by the board of nursing when, after notice and hearing, the board finds the registrant has "engaged in performance of medical functions and tasks other than at the direction of a physician licensed by the state board of medicine" (with exceptions), or "the registrant has performed a medical task or function which the registrant is not qualified by education to perform" (49 Pa. Code § 18.81).

In Rhode Island, grounds for revocation/suspension include:

a. Guilty of fraud or deceit in procuring or attempting to procure a license to practice nursing
b. Guilty of a crime of gross immorality
c. Unfit or incompetent by reason of negligence or habits

d. Habitually intemperate or . . . addicted to one of the habit-forming drugs
e. Mentally incompetent
f. Guilty of unprofessional conduct which includes:
    i. Abandonment of a patient
    ii. Willfully making and filing false reports or records in the practice of nursing
    iii. Willful omission to file reports or record nursing records or reports as required by law
    iv. Failure to furnish appropriate details of client's nursing needs to succeeding nurse legally qualified to provide continuing nursing services to a client
    v. Willful disregard of standards and failure to maintain standards of the nursing profession
    vi. Failure to comply with the provisions of Section 5-34-40(c) of the General Laws, as a nurse practitioner
g. Guilty of willfully or repeatedly violating any of the provisions of the act and/or the rules and regulations adopted thereunder.

Citation: R.I. Nursing Rules § 12.0.

State-by-State List of Agencies That Regulate Nurse Practitioners

ALABAMA: State Board of Medical Examiners and Board of Nursing

ALASKA: Board of Nursing

ARIZONA: Board of Nursing

ARKANSAS: Board of Nursing

CALIFORNIA: Board of Nursing

COLORADO: Board of Nursing

CONNECTICUT: Board of Nursing

DELAWARE: Board of Nursing and Board of Medical Licensure and Discipline

DISTRICT OF COLUMBIA: Board of Nursing

FLORIDA: Board of Nursing

GEORGIA: Board of Nursing

HAWAII: Board of Nursing

IDAHO: Board of Nursing

ILLINOIS: Board of Nursing

INDIANA: Board of Nursing

IOWA: Board of Nursing

KANSAS: Board of Nursing

KENTUCKY: Board of Nursing

LOUISIANA: Board of Nursing

MAINE: Board of Nursing

MARYLAND: Board of Nursing

MASSACHUSETTS: Board of Nursing

MICHIGAN: Board of Nursing

MINNESOTA: Board of Nursing

MISSISSIPPI: Board of Nursing

MISSOURI: Board of Nursing

MONTANA: Board of Nursing

NEBRASKA: Board of Nursing

NEVADA: Board of Nursing

NEW HAMPSHIRE: Board of Nursing

NEW JERSEY: Board of Nursing

NEW MEXICO: Board of Nursing

NEW YORK: Board of Nursing

NORTH CAROLINA: Board of Nursing

NORTH DAKOTA: Board of Nursing

OHIO: Board of Nursing

OKLAHOMA: Board of Nursing

OREGON: Board of Nursing

PENNSYLVANIA: Board of Nursing

RHODE ISLAND: Nurse Licensure Compact of the National Council of State Boards of Nursing; Nurse Registration and Nursing Education Board

SOUTH CAROLINA: Board of Nursing

SOUTH DAKOTA: Board of Nursing

TENNESSEE: Board of Nursing

TEXAS: Board of Nursing

UTAH: Board of Nursing

VERMONT: Board of Nursing

VIRGINIA: Board of Nursing

WASHINGTON: Nursing Care Quality Assurance Commission

WEST VIRGINIA: Board of Examiners for Registered Professional Nurses

WISCONSIN: Board of Nursing

WYOMING: Board of Nursing

State-by-State Nurse Practitioner Qualifications Required by Law

Alabama

- RN license
- Graduation from an organized program of study and clinical experience beyond basic educational preparation as a registered nurse that is recognized by the Board of Nursing and/or the appropriate specialty certifying agency
- Master's degree or higher in advanced practice nursing from an accredited program recognized by the Board
- Certification from a national certifying agency recognized by the Board of Nursing in the clinical specialty consistent with educational preparation and appropriate to the area of practice

Citation: ALA. ADMIN. CODE r. 610-X-5-.02.

Alaska

Requirements for initial authority to practice:

- A formal accredited graduate educational course of study in nursing that is a minimum of one academic year in length; prepares registered nurses to perform an expanded role in the delivery of health care; includes a combination of classroom instruction and a minimum of 500 separate, non-duplicated hours of supervised clinical practice; and if completed on or after January 1, 1998, has distinct course offerings of three graduate credits or more in advanced pathophysiology, advanced pharmacotherapeutics, and advanced physical assessment
- RN license
- Certification by a national certifying agency in the specialty area of nursing for which the applicant was educated

Requirement to maintain authority to practice:

- 30 contact hours of continuing education in the population focus of the nurse practitioner every two years

Citation: Alaska Admin. Code tit. 12, § 44.400.

Arizona

   A. An applicant for certification as a registered nurse practitioner (RNP) or clinical nurse specialist (CNS) in a specialty area, shall:

      1. Hold a current Arizona registered nurse (RN) license in good standing or an RN license in good standing from a compact party state with multi-state privileges

      2. Submit an application to Board that has

         a. Full name and any former names

         b. Current mailing address and telephone number

         c. Place and date of birth

         d. RN license number, application for RN license, or copy of a multistate compact RN license

         e. Social security number

         f. Current e-mail address

         g. Educational background

         h. Role and population focus…

         i. Current employer or practice setting…

         j. Evidence of national certification or recertification as an advanced practice nurse [additional requirements omitted]

Citation: Ariz. Admin. Code R4-19-505(1) and (2).

Arkansas

- Evidence of education approved by board
- National certification approved by board

Citation: Ark. Code Ann. § 17-87-302.

California

- RN license in California
- Successful completion of a program of study that conforms to the board standards or
- Certification by a national or state organization whose standards are equivalent to those set forth in Section 1484 or
- A nurse who has not completed a nurse practitioner program which meets board standards as specified in Section 1484, shall be able to provide:

○ Documentation of remediation of areas of deficiency in course content and/or clinical experience, and

 ○ Verification by a nurse practitioner and by a physician who meet the requirements for faculty members specified in Section 1484(c), of clinical competence in the delivery of primary health care

Citation: Cal. Code Regs. § 1482.

Colorado

- Completion of an appropriate graduate degree
- National certification from a nationally recognized agency

For prescriptive authority:

- Satisfactory completion of specific educational requirements in the use of controlled substances and prescription drugs, as established by the board, either as part of a degree program or in addition to a degree program
- Postgraduate experience as an APN in a relevant clinical setting . . . consisting of not less than 1800 hours to be completed within the immediately preceding five-year period. The preceptorship shall be conducted either with a physician or a physician and an advanced practice nurse who has prescriptive authority and experience in prescribing medications.
- Professional liability insurance
- A mechanism for consultation and referral
- A quality assurance plan
- Decision support tools
- Documentation of ongoing continuing education in pharmacology and safe prescribing

Citation: Colo. Rev. Code Ann. § 12-38-111.5 and 111.6.

Connecticut

- RN license
- Certification as NP from a national certifying body
- 30 hours education in pharmacology for advanced nursing practice
- If after December 31, 1994, master's degree

Citation: Conn. Gen. Stat. Ann. § 20-94a(a).

Delaware

The nurse practitioner designation is received after graduation from a master's program or from an accredited post-basic nurse practitioner certification program of at least one academic year in length in a nurse practitioner specialty.... The nurse practitioner must have national certification in an area of specialization at the advanced level by a certifying agency which meets the established criteria approved by the Delaware Board of Nursing.

Citation: DEL. ADMIN. CODE, TIT. 24 §8.4.

District of Columbia

- RN license
- Submit evidence of national certification or recertification, as applicable, by the ANCC or other national certifying body approved by the Board.
- Beginning with the 2006 renewal period, submit proof of completion of 15 contact hours of continuing education, which shall include a pharmacology component...
- Furnish proof...that the applicant has successfully completed a post-basic nursing education program applicable to the area of practice approved by the Boad or accredited by a nationally recognized body accepted by the Board and which is relevant to the nurse practitioner's area of practice.
- Receive a passing score on the national certification examination, offered by the ANCC or any other nationally recognized body accepted by the Board.

Citation: D.C. MUNICIPAL RULES §5903.5, 5904.1, and 5905.1.§ 3-1206.08.

Florida

- RN license
- Malpractice insurance
- One of the following:
  1. Completion of a formal postbasic educational program of at least one academic year, the purpose of which is to prepare nurses for advanced or specialized practice
  2. Certification by an appropriate specialty board
  3. Graduation from a program leading to a master's degree in a nursing clinical specialty area with preparation in specialized practitioner skills.

Citation: FLA. STAT. Ch. 464.012(1).

- Applicant shall submit proof of national advanced practice certification from an approved nursing specialty board. After July 1, 2006, applications for certification as an Advanced Registered Nurse Practitioner pursuant to Section 464.012(3), F.S., shall submit proof of current national advanced practice nurse certification from an approved nursing specialty board.
- Pursuant to Section 456.048, F.S., all ARNP's shall carry malpractice insurance or demonstrate proof of financial responsibility ... [and] proof as a condition of biennial renewal or reactivation.

Citation: FLA. ADMIN. CODE Ch. 64B9-4.002(5).

Georgia

- RN license
- Completed Board application with required fee
- Official transcript which verifies graduation with a master's or higher degree in nursing for the respective nurse practitioner specialty or a graduate level post-master's certificate in an advanced practice registered nurse practitioner specialty and evidence of advanced pharmacology within the curriculum or as a separate course, advanced physical assessment, and pathophysiology
- Verification of current national certification from the respective Board-recognized certifying organization
- The applicant must document one of the following within the four (4) years immediately preceding the date of current application:
  a. 500 hours of practice as an advanced practice registered nurse;
  b. graduation from a nursing education program or a graduate level post-master's certificate in an advanced practice registered nurse practitioner specialty;
  c. completion of a Georgia Board-approved advanced practice registered nurse reentry/refresher program.

Citation: GA. COMP. R. & REGS. § r.410-12-.03(3), and (4).

Hawaii

- A current, unencumbered RN license in the state of Hawaii
- Unencumbered RN license in all other states where licensed
- An unencumbered recognition as an advanced practice registered nurse or similar designation in all other states in which the nurse has a current and active recognition as an advanced practice registered nurse
- Completed an accredited graduate-level education program leading to a master's degree as a certified registered nurse anesthetist, a nurse midwife, a clinical nurse specialist, or a nurse practitioner
- A current, unencumbered certification of having passed a national certification examination that measures roles and population-focused competencies and is recognized by the board
- Maintained continued competencies through recertification in role and population-focused competencies through a national certification program recognized by the board
- Acquired advanced clinical knowledge and skills preparing the nurse to provide direct care to patients through a significant educational and practical concentration on the direct care of patients
- Demonstrated a greater breadth of knowledge, a greater synthesis of data, greater complexity of skills and interventions, and greater role autonomy than demonstrated by a registered nurse
- Been educationally prepared to assume responsibility and accountability for health promotion and maintenance and to assess, diagnose, and manage

patient problems through the use and prescription of pharmacologic and non-pharmacologic interventions
- Acquired clinical experience of sufficient depth and breadth to reflect the intended license
- Paid the appropriate fees

Citation: HAW. REV. STAT. ANN. § 457-8.5a.

- Completed application prescribed by the board
- Proof of unencumbered license as RN in other states
- Documentation relating to any disciplinary action ordered by or pending before any board of nursing
- Documentation regarding any criminal conviction within the past 20 years

Citation: HAW. ADMIN. R. § 16-89-83.

The requirements for prescriptive authority are as follows:
- Completed application for prescriptive authority for controlled or non-controlled substances provided by the board and submitted with all appropriate documents and required feeds
- Proof of a current, unencumbered license as a RN
- Proof of a current, unencumbered recognition or license as an advanced practice registered nurse
- Proof of successful completion of an accredited graduate-level nursing program with a significant educational and practical concentration on the direct care of patients, recognized by the board, leading to a master's degree
- Proof of successful completion of at least 30 contact hours, as part of a master's degree program from an accredited, board-recognized college or university, of advanced pharmacology education, including advanced pharmacotherapeutics that is integrated into the curriculum, within the three-year time period immediately preceding the date of application
- Payment of a fee

Citation: HAW. ADMIN. R. § 16-89-119.

Idaho

To practice:

- RN license
- Completion of an approved advanced practice registered nursing education program that meets the board requirements
- Passing results on the certification examination recognized by the board and have current certification from a national organization recognized by the board
- Be of sufficiently sound physical and mental health as will not impair or interfere with the ability to practice nursing
- Pay a licensing fee

Citation: IDAHO CODE § 54-1409.

To prescribe pharmacologic and non-pharmacologic agents:

- Currently licensed as an advanced practice registered nurse in Idaho
- Evidence of completion of thirty (30) contact hours of post-basic education in pharmacotherapeutics obtained as part of study within a formal educational program or continuing education program, which are related to the applicant's advanced practice category scope of practice
- Submit a completed, notarized application form provided by the Board
- Remit fees prescribed in Section 901

Citation: Idaho Admin. Code § 23.01.01.315.01(a).

Illinois

An applicant for licensure to practice as an advanced practice nurse must do each of the following:

- Submit a completed application and any fees as established by the Department
- Current licensure to practice as a registered professional nurse
- Successful completion of requirements need to practice as, and holds a current, national certification as, a nurse midwife, clinical nurse specialist, nurse practitioner, or certified registered nurse anesthetist from the appropriate national certifying body
- Proof of successful completion of a graduate degree appropriate for national certification in clinical advanced practice nursing specialty or a graduate degree or post-master's certificate from a graduate level program in a clinical advanced practice nursing specialty
- Have not violated the provisions of this Act concerning the grounds for disciplinary action
- Submit to a criminal history records check

Citation: 225 Ill. Comp. Stat. § 65/65-5.

Indiana

To practice:

- Graduation from a college or university accredited by the Commission on Recognition of Postsecondary Accreditation which prepares the registered nurse to practice as a nurse practitioner.
- A certificate program offered by a college or university accredited by the Commission on Recognition of Postsecondary Accreditation which prepares the registered nurse to practice as a nurse practitioner and meets the requirements of section 6 of this rule.

Citation: Ind. Admin. Code tit. 848, r. 4-1-4.

To prescribe:

- Submits an application with the required fee
- Active, unrestricted registered nurse license
- Proof of having met the requirements of all applicable laws for practice as an advanced practice nurse in the state of Indiana
- Baccalaureate or higher degree in nursing
- Completion of a graduate level pharmacology course consisting of at least two semester hours of academic credit from a college accredited by the Commission on Recognition of Postsecondary Accreditation, or
- Completion of 30 hours of continuing education in the past two years, including a minimum of at least eight actual contact hours of pharmacology
- Submits proof of collaboration with a licensed practitioner in the form of a written practice agreement that sets forth the manner in which the advanced practice nurse and licensed practitioner will cooperate, coordinate, and consult with each other in the provision of health care to patients.

Citation: IND. ADMIN. CODE tit. 848, r. 5-1-1.

Iowa

- Master's degree or completion of a formal advanced practice educational program of study in a nursing specialty area approved by the board and appropriate clinical experience as approved by the board
- An advanced registered nurse practitioner application which may be obtained from the office of the board
- A registration fee as established by the board
- Copy of the time-dated, advanced level certification by appropriate national certifying body evidencing that the applicant holds current certification in good standing
- Copy of official transcript directly from formal advanced practice educational program maintaining the records necessary to document that all requirements have been met in one of the specialty areas of nursing practice

Citation: IOWA ADMIN. CODE r. 655-7.2(4) and 655-7.2(5).

Kansas

Advanced practice registered nursing is based on knowledge and skills acquired in basic nursing education, licensure as a registered nurse and graduation from or completion of a master's or higher degree in one of the advanced practice registered nurse roles approved by the board of nursing.

Citation: KAN. STAT. §65-1130(c) (2).

- Completion of a formal, post-basic nursing education program located or offered in Kansas, approved by the board that prepares nurses to function in an expanded role for which application is made
- Completion of a formal, post-basic nursing education that is not located or offered in Kansas but is determined by the board to meet the standards for program approval
- Completion of a formal, post-basic nursing education program that could be no longer in existence but is determined by the board to meet standards for program approval by board at the time of graduation
- Hold a current license to practice as an advanced practice registered nurse in the role for which application is made and that meets the following criteria: was issued by a nursing licensing authority of another jurisdiction; and required completion of a program meeting standards equal to or greater than those established by K.A.R. 60-17-101 through 60-17-108
- Completion of a formal educational program of post-basic study and clinical experience that can be demonstrated by the applicant to have sufficiently prepared the applicant for practice in the role of advanced practice for which application is made
- Completion of 3 college hours in advanced pharmacology or the equivalent
- Completion of 3 college hours in advanced pathophysiology or the equivalent and 3 college hours in advanced health assessment or its equivalent

Applicant for a certificate of qualification as an advanced registered nurse practitioner who has not gained 1000 hours of advanced nursing practice during the five years preceding the date of application shall be required to successfully complete a refresher course as defined by the Board.

Citation: KAN. ADMIN. REGS. § 60-11-103.

Kentucky

- RN licensure or holding the privilege to practice as a registered nurse in this state and maintain current certification by the appropriate national organization or agency recognized by the board
- Completion of an organized post-basic program of study and clinical experience acceptable to the board
- Certification by a national established organization or agency recognized by the board
- Facility with English language

Citation: KY. REV. STAT. ANN. § 314.042.

Louisiana

To practice:

- RN license and there are no grounds for disciplinary proceedings
- Master's degree in appropriate program with concentration in a respective advanced practice nursing specialty and functional role or completion of a post master's concentration in the respective advanced nursing specialty and functional role from an accredited college or university that meets the curriculum guidelines established by the board
- Competed application form
- Submission of evidence of current certification in the respective advanced practice nursing specialty and functional role by a nationally recognized certifying body approved by the board.

Citation: La. Admin. Code tit. 46, § XLVII.4507.

To prescribe:

- Unencumbered, unrestricted, and valid RN licensure with no pending disciplinary proceedings
- APRN licensure
- Evidence of 500 hours of practice as a licensed ARNP or APRN applicant within 1 year in the clinical specialty for which applicant was educationally prepared immediately prior to applying for prescriptive and distributing authority
- Minimum of 45 contact hours of education (three credit hour academic course) in advanced pharmacotherapeutics
- Minimum of 45 contact hours (three credit hour academic course) in physiology/pathophysiology
- Collaborative practice agreement with one or more licensed collaborating physicians
- Each year, six contact hours of continuing education in pharmacotherapeutics

Citation: La. Admin. Code tit. 46, § XLVII.4513.

Maine

- RN license
- Successfully completed a formal education program that is acceptable to the board in an advanced nursing specialty area
- Evidence of current certification

Citation: Code Me. R. 32 M.R.S.A. § 2201-A.

A. A registered professional nurse who is approved by the Board to practice as an advanced practice registered nurse prior to January 1, 1996 is considered to have met the requirements of 32 M.R.S.A. Section 2201-A(2) and (3) regarding education and certification. ...

C. As of January 1, 2006, an applicant for initial approval as an advanced practice registered nurse in Maine must hold a master's degree with preparation in the specialty area for which application is made.

Citation: CODE ME. R. § 02 380 008 (Section 1)(2).

C. Submits evidence of a minimum of 1500 hours of practice in an expanded specialty nursing role within 5 years preceding application, or have completed a nurse practitioner program within 5 years preceding application. If more than 5 years have elapsed since completion of an advanced practice registered nurse program and the applicant does not meet the practice requirement of 1500 hours, the applicant shall complete 500 hours of clinical practice supervised by a physician or nurse practitioner in the same specialty area of practice.

Citation: CODE ME. R. § 02 380 008 (Section 2)(2).

1. For prescriptive and dispensing authority:
    A. If the applicant has not prescribed drugs within the past 2 years, the applicant shall provide evidence of satisfactory completion of 15 contact hours of pharmacology within the 2 years prior to applying for approval to practice.
    B. If the applicant has not prescribed drugs within the past 5 years, the applicant shall provide evidence of satisfactory completion of 45 contact hours (or 3 credits) of pharmacology within the 2 years prior to applying for approval to practice.

2A. For certified nurse practitioners with prescriptive authority in other US jurisdictions:
    1. Minimum of 200 hours of practice in an expanded specialty role within the preceding 2 years.
    2. 45 contact hours (or 3 credits) of pharmacology equivalent to the requirements set forth in Section 64(3)(A) and (B).
    B. If the applicant has not prescribed drugs within the past 2 years, the applicant shall provide evidence of satisfactory completion of 15 contact hours of pharmacology within the 2 years prior to applying for approval to practice.
    C. If the applicant has not prescribed drugs within the past 5 years, the applicant shall provide evidence of satisfactory completion of 45 contact hours (or 3 credits) of pharmacology within the 2 years prior to applying for approval to practice.

Citation: CODE ME. R. § 02 380 008 (Section 6).

Maryland

A. A nurse practitioner shall obtain certification from the Board before commencing practice.
B. An applicant for certification as a nurse practitioner shall:
   1. Hold a current license in good standing to practice registered nursing in Maryland or a compact state;
   2. Complete, in full, the application for certification as a nurse practitioner for each area in which certification is sought;
   3. As part of the application, submit to the Board:
      a. Documentation that the applicant has graduated from a Board-approved educational program for nurse practitioners; and
      b. Documentation of certification as a nurse practitioner by a nationally recognized certifying body recognized by the Board;
   4. Pay all fees established by the Board; and
   5. Pass a Board-approved examination.

Citation: Md. Regs. Code. 10 § 27.07.03.

Massachusetts

- RN license
- Advanced nursing knowledge and clinical skills acquired through an appropriate nursing education program
- Degree for preparation in advanced nursing practice from a graduate school approved by a national accrediting body acceptable to the board, or have received a certificate of completion of an educational program in advanced nursing practice approved by a national accrediting body acceptable to the board
- Current certification in practice area

Citation: Mass. Ann. Laws Ch. 112 § 80B and Code Mass. Regs. tit. 244, § 4.05 and 4.13(2).

Michigan

- RN license
- Submission of an application for certification in a specialty area of nursing
- Meets standards of advanced practice certification agencies

Citation: Mich. Admin. Code R338.10404.

Minnesota

- RN license
- Graduation from NP program

- Certification as NP by national certifying agency
- To prescribe, a written agreement with a physician

Citation: MINN. STAT. ANN. § 148.235 and 148.284.

Mississippi

- RN license
- Satisfactory completion of a formal post-basic educational program of at least one academic year.
- Graduation from a program leading to a master's or post-master's degree in a nursing clinical specialty area with a preparation in specialized practitioner skills.
- Certification by a board approved certifying body.

Citation: MISS. NURSING PRACTICE LAW §73-15-20(1).

Missouri

- RN license
- Evidence of successful completion of a graduate degree from an advanced nursing education program
- Certification in respective advanced practice nursing clinical specialty area by a nationally recognized certifying body
- Evidence of satisfactory, active, up-to-date certification/recertification/maintenance and/or continuing education/competency

For prescribing:

- Completion of three graduate credit hours of pharmacology offered by an accredited college or university within the last 5 years prior to the date of application to the board
- Evidence of a minimum of 800 hours of clinical practice in the advanced practice nursing clinical specialty area within two years prior to date of application to the board

For prescribing controlled substances:

- Completion of an advanced pharmacology course (45 units that shall include preceptorial experience in the prescription of drugs, medicines, and therapeutic devices with a qualified preceptor)
- Provide evidence of completion of at least 300 clock hours of preceptorial experience in the prescription of drugs, medicines, and therapeutic devices with a qualified preceptor
- Has had controlled substance prescriptive authority delegated in a collaborative practice agreement under section 334.104, RSMo, with a Missouri license

physician who has an unrestricted federal Drug Enforcement Administration (DEA) number

Citation: Mo. Code Regs. tit. 20, CSR 2200-4.100(2).

Montana

- RN license
- National certification in area of specialization
- Completion of post-basic professional nursing program in APN area
- Master's degree or post-graduate certificate from an accredited APRN program that provided a minimum of 250 hours of didactic instruction and a minimum of 500 hours of preceptorship

Citation: Mont. Admin. R. § 24.159.1414.

Nebraska

To practice:

- RN license
- Evidence of having successfully completed a graduate-level program in the clinical specialty area of nurse practitioner practice, which program is accredited by a national accrediting body
- Proof of having passed an examination pertaining to the specific nurse practitioner role or approved by the board with the approval of the department
- Evidence of having successfully completed 30 contact hours of education in pharmacotherapeutics
- Submission of proof of having passed an examination pertaining to the specific advanced practice registered nursing role in nursing adopted or approved by the boards

Citation: Neb. Rev. Stat. § 38-2317.

Nevada

- Completion of a program for an advanced practice registered nurse, at least one year in length, which must include, without limitation, didactic instruction and clinical experience with a qualified physician or advanced practice registered nurse, approved by the Board, and including advanced courses in the assessment of health of patients, pathophysiology, and the preparation for practice as an advanced practice registered nurse.
- Completed an advanced practice registered nurse program within two years of application of license.
- Completion of 1000 hours of practice, without the privilege of writing prescriptions, under the supervision of a qualified physician or advanced practice registered nurse.

- If previously licensed or certified as an advanced practice registered nurse in another state or jurisdiction, have maintained the licensure or certification in good standing.
- If completed a program after July 1, 1992, be certified as an advanced practice registered nurse by a nationally recognized certifying agency and hold a bachelor's degree in nursing from an accredited school.
- If completed an educational program after June 1, 2005, holds a master's or doctorate degree in nursing..

Citation: Nev. Admin. Code § 632.260.

New Hampshire

- Current and unencumbered RN license
- Current certification from a national certifying body
- Graduate degree in an accredited advanced registered nurse practitioner education program; or
- If graduated before July 1, 2004 from an APRN education program, be accredited by a national accrediting body
- Have used advanced practice nursing knowledge, judgment, and skills for at least 400 hours within the four years immediately preceding application
- If the applicant graduated from an advanced nurse practitioner program within two years of applying for application, they need:
- At least 30 educational contact hours to satisfy the requirements of RN continuing competence, and an additional 30 hours (five of which shall be in training in pharmacology appropriate to specialty), within two years immediately prior to date of applying

Citation: N.H. Code Admin. R. Ann. [NUR] § 302.04.

New Jersey

- Possess a current New Jersey registered professional nurse license in good standing and be certified by the Board as an advanced practice nurse
- Master's degree in nursing from a school accredited by a nursing accrediting association recognized by the U. S. Department of Education or master's in nursing and completed a post master's program that focuses on an advanced practice nursing specialty from a school accredited by a nursing accrediting association recognized by the U.S. Department of Education
- Completion of at least 39 hours in pharmacology
- Completion of six contact hours in pharmacology related to controlled dangerous substances, including pharmacologic therapy and addiction prevention and management

- Pass an advanced practice examination in his/her area of specialty offered by a national certifying agency that is accredited by the American Board of Nursing Specialties and/or the National Commission for Certifying Agencies.

> *Citation:* N.J. Admin. Code tit. 13, § 37:7.1-7.4.

New Mexico

- Current, unencumbered RN license
- Successful completion of a graduate level nursing program designed for the education and preparation of nurse practitioners as providers of primary, or acute, or chronic, or long-term, or end of life health care; it must be a master's degree if applying after January 1, 2001 for initial licensure
- National certification

> *Citation:* N.M. Admin. Code § 16.12.2.13.A.

To prescribe:

- 400 hours of work experience in which prescribing dangerous drugs has occurred within the two (2) years immediately preceding date of application
- Current state controlled substances registration and current DEA number
- Maintain a formulary of dangerous drugs and controlled substances that may be prescribed

> *Citation:* N.M. Admin. Code § 16.12.2.13.N(5)(a) and (b).

New York

- Nurse practitioner certificate that reflects specialty area
- Completion of an educational program registered by the Department of Education…which is designed and conducted to prepare graduates to practice as a nurse practitioner, or
- Certification as NP by a national certifying body, and
- At least 3 semester hours in pharmacology

> *Citation:* N.Y. Commissioner's Regulation. § 64.4.

North Carolina

To practice:

- Unrestricted license to practice as RN and unrestricted approval to practice as NP
- Successful completion of approved educational program
- Certified as a nurse practitioner by a national credentialing body
- Submission of any information deemed necessary to evaluate the application

- Beginning January 1, 2005 all registered nurses seeking first-time nurse practitioner registration in North Carolina shall hold a master's degree in Nursing or related field with primary focus on Nursing; have successfully completed a graduate-level nurse practitioner education program accredited by a national credentialing body; certification by nationally credentialing body.

Citation: N.C. Admin. Code tit. 21, § 36.0803.

To maintain license:

- 50 contact hours of continuing education each year beginning with the first renewal after initial approval to practice has been granted. At least 20 hours of the required 50 hours must be those for which the approval has been granted by the ANCC, or ACCME, other national credentialing bodies or practice relevant courses in an institution of higher learning.

Citation: N.C. Admin. Code tit. 21, § 36.0807.

North Dakota

- RN license
- Submit evidence of completion of an accredited graduate level APRN program in one of the four roles and with at least one population focus
- Current certification by a national organization in the APRN role and population foci appropriate to educational preparation
- Submit a scope of practice statement according to established board guidelines . . .

Citation: N.D. Admin. Code § 54-05-03.1-04.

To prescribe:

- Licensed as an advanced practice registered nurse in North Dakota
- Submit a notarized prescriptive authority application and pay the fee
- Submit a completed transcript with degree posted from an accredited graduate level advanced practice registered nurse program and which includes evidence of completion of advanced pharmacotherapy, physical assessment, and pathophysiology
- Evidence of completion of contact 30 hours of education or equivalent in pharmacotherapy related to specialty area, which has been obtained within a three-year period of time immediately prior to the date of application for prescriptive authority, or approved by the board

Citation: N.D. Admin. Code § 54-05-03.1-09.

Ohio

- RN license
- Graduate degree with a major in a nursing specialty . . .
- Evidence of passing the certification examination of a national certifying organization approved by the board

Citation: Ohio Rev. Code Ann. § 4723.41.

Oklahoma

- Successful completion of an advanced practice registered nursing education program in preparation for one of four recognized advanced practice registered nurse roles
- Nationally certified by body recognized by board of nursing
- Acquired advanced clinical knowledge and skills in preparation for providing both direct and indirect care to patients, with a significant component of the education focus on direct care of individuals.

Citation: Okla. Stat. Ann. tit. 59, § 567.3a(5).

Effective January 1, 2016 all applicatnts for initial licensure or licensure by endorsement as a certified nurse practitioner must hold a graduate level degree from an advanced practice education program accredited by or holding pending approval or candidacy status with the NLN Accreditation Commission or the Commission on Collegiate Nursing Education.

Citation: Okla. Admin. Code § 485:10-15-6.

Oregon

To practice:

- Unencumbered RN license.
- Master's or Doctorate degree in nursing from the Commission on Collegiate Nursing Education (CCNE) or National League for Nursing Accreditation Commision (NLNAC).
- Satisfactory completion of an NP program specific to the role and role population for which application is made.
- Meet the practice requirement of OAR 851-050-0004.
- As of January 1, 2011 provide verification of national certification that is congruent with Board recognition nurse practitioner role and population focus.

Citation: Or. Admin. § R. 851-050-0002.

- Completion of a nurse practitioner program within the past year; or within the past two years and a minimum of 192 hours of practice as a nurse practitioner; or 960 hours of nurse practitioner practice within the five years preceding certification application or renewal; or completion of a Board-supervised advanced practice re-entry program within two years immediately preceding issuance of certification under a limited or registered nurse license and a limited nurse practitioner certificate.
- Initial applicants must provide documentation of a minimum of 384 hours of registered nurse practice, which includes assessment and management of clients and is not completed as an academic clinical requirement or continuing education program. The applicant shall verify completion of the required hours before issuance of the nurse practitioner certificate. This requirement shall be waived for individuals practicing in the specialty area as a licensed certified nurse practitioner in another state for at least 384 hours in the advanced practice role. All practice hours claimed are subject to audit and disciplinary action for falsification.

Citation: OR. ADMIN. R. § 851-050-0004.

Pennsylvania

- Current unrestricted license as a professional nurse
- Completion of a master's or postmaster's nurse practitioner program
- National certification in the specialty in which the nurse is seeking certification
- A CRNP who holds an unrestricted certification to practice may apply for certification in an additional specialty if they meet the educational and National certification requirements for the specialty

Citation: 49 PA. CODE § 21.271.

a. A CRNP with prescriptive authority may, when acting in collaboration with a physician as set forth in a prescriptive authority collaborative agreement within the CRNP's specialty, prescribe and dispense drugs and give written or oral orders for drugs and other medical therapeutic or corrective measures. These orders may include:
   1. Orders for drugs, total parenteral nutrition and lipids, in accordance with § 21.284 and 21.285 (related to prescribing and dispensing parameters; and prescriptive authority collaborative agreements).
   2. Disposables and devices adjunctive to a treatment plan.
b. To obtain prescriptive authority approval, a CRNP shall:
   1. Successfully complete at least 45 hours of course work specific to advanced pharmacology in accordance with the following:
      i. The course work in advanced pharmacology may be either part of the CRNP education program or, if completed outside of the CRNP

education program, an additional course or courses taken from an educational program or programs approved by the Board.

    ii The course work in advanced level above a pharmacology course required by a professional nursing (RN) education program.

    iii. The course work shall have been completed within 5 years immediately preceding the date the applicant applies for initial prescriptive authority approval.

2. Submit an application for prescriptive authority approval to the Board.
3. Pay the fee set forth in § 21.253 (relating to fees).

c. A CRNP who has prescriptive authority shall complete at least 16 hours of Board-approved continuing education in pharmacology in the two years prior to the biennial renewal date of the certification. The CRNP shall verify completion of the continuing education when submitting a biennial renewal.

Citation: 49 PA CODE §21.283.

Rhode Island

- Be of good moral character
- RN license
- Completion of an approved accredited educational program resulting in a master's degree and/or an approved nurse practitioner course of study
- Passing of a national certifying examination recognized by the Board
- For applicants seeking licensure by endorsement, the licensing agency in each state in which the applicant holds or has held a registration or license must submit to the Board a statement confirming the applicant to be or have been in good standing.

Citation: R.I.R. § R5-34-NUR/ED 3.2.

To prescribe:

- Completion of 30 hours of education in pharmacology within 3 years prior to application

To maintain prescriptive privileges:

- Completion of 30 hours of continuing education in pharmacology every six years

Citation: R.I.R. § R5-34-NUR/ED 10.3, and 10.3(1).

South Carolina

- RN license
- Current specialty certification by a board-approved credentialing organization. New graduates shall provide evidence of certification within one year of program completion.

- Master's degree in nursing
- Declared specialty area of nursing practice and the specialty title to be used must be the title which is granted by the board-approved credentialing organization

To prescribe:

- 45 contact hours of education in pharmacotherapeutics within two years before application
- At least 15 hours of education in controlled substances

Citation: S.C. Code Ann. § 40-33-34(A) and (E).

South Dakota

- RN license
- Completion of an approved program for the preparation of NPs
- Passing examination that the boards in their discretion may require

Citation: S.D. Codified Laws § 36-9A-4.

Tennessee

- RN license
- Graduation from a program conferring a master's or higher in nursing in nursing specialty

Citation: Tenn. Comp. R. & Regs. tit. 11, Ch. 1000-4-.02(1).

- National certification in a nursing specialty of licensure to practice in Tennessee was obtained prior to July 1, 2005, or national certification in a nursing specialty and licensure as a registered nurse with the multistate licensure privilege to practice in Tennessee was obtained prior to July 1, 2005
- Current national specialty certification in the appropriate specialty area

Citation: Tenn. Comp. R. & Regs. tit. 11, Ch. 1000-4-.03(2).

Texas

- Current, valid, unencumbered license as registered nurse in Texas.
- Evidence of educational preparation.
- Minimum 400 hours of current practice within preceding 24 calendar months . . . unless graduated from appropriate program within the last 24 calendar months.
- 20 contact hours of continuing education within 24 calendar months.
- Continuing education in the advanced practice role and population-focus must meet the requirements of Chapter 216.

- Current certification in an advanced nursing role and specialty recognized by the board.

Citation: 22 Texas Admin. Code § 221.4.

For prescriptive authority:

- Full licensure from the Board to practice as an advanced practice registered nurse
- Have successfully completed courses in pharmacotherapeutics, advanced pathophysiology, advanced health assessment, and diagnosis and management of disease and conditions within the role and population focus area

Citation: 22 Texas Admin. Code § 222.2.

Utah

- Be in a condition of physical and mental health that will allow the applicant to practice safely as an advanced practice registered nurse
- Current registered nurse license in good standing
- Graduate degree in advanced practice registered nursing or a related area of specialized knowledge, or have completed a nurse anesthesia program in accordance with Subsection (4)(f)(ii)
- Successful completion of course work in patient assessment, diagnosis and treatment, and pharmacotherapeutics from an education program approved by the division in collaboration with the board, or a nurse anesthesia program which is approved by the Council on Accreditation of Nurse Anesthesia Educational Programs
- Passing of examinations as required by division rule made in collaboration with the board
- Certification by a program approved by the division in collaboration with the board

Citation: Utah Code Ann. § 58-31b-302(4).

Vermont

- RN license
- Completion of formal educational program approved by Board of Nursing. Programs shall include a supervised clinical component in the role and population focus of the applicant's certification. Completion of graduate level courses in: advanced pharmacotherapeutics; advanced patient assessment; and advanced pathophysiology
- Certification by national organization recognized by Board of Nursing

Citation: 26 V.S.A. § 1611.

Virginia

- Current, active RN license
- Graduate degree in nursing or in the appropriate nurse practitioner specialty from board-approved educational program
- Evidence of professional certification consistent with specialty area by an agency accepted by the board

Citation: 18 Va. Admin. Code § 90-30-80A.

For prescriptive authority:

- Current, unrestricted license as a nurse practitioner
- Evidence of conditioned professional certification as a nurse practitioner, or
- Completion of a graduate-level course in pharmacology or pharmacothera-peutics as part of NP program within five years prior to submission of the application, or
- Practice as NP for no less than 1000 hours and 15 continuing education units related to the area of practice for each of the two years prior to submission of the application, or
- Thirty hours of education in pharmacology or pharmacotherapuetics accept-able to the boards taken within five years prior to submission of the application. The 30 contact hours may be obtained in a formal academic setting as a discrete offering or as noncredit continuing education offerings and shall include the fol-lowing course content: Applicable federal and state laws; prescription writing; drug selection, dosage, and route; drug interactions; information resources; and clinical application of pharmacology related to specific scope of practice
- Practice agreement between NP and patient care team physician

Citation: 18 Va. Admin. Code § 90-40-40.

Washington

ARNP application requirements for new graduates of advanced registered nurse programs are as follows.

1. An applicant for licensure as an ARNP must meet the following requirements:
   a. Hold a registered nurse license in the state of Washington that is not subject to sanctions or restrictions by the commission;
   b. Have graduated from an advanced nursing education program within the past year;
      i. For new graduates of advanced nursing education programs in the United States, the program must be accredited by a nursing or nurs-ing-related accrediting organization recognized by the United States Department of Education (USDE) or the Council of Higher Educa-tion Accreditation (CHEA);

    ii. For new graduates of advanced nursing education programs outside the United States, the program must be equivalent to the advanced registered nurse education in Washington; and

  c. Hold certification from a commission-approved certification program as identified in WAC 246-840-302.

2. An applicant for ARNP licensure must:
   a. Apply for Washington state registered nurse licensure if not a current holder of the RN license;
   b. Submit a completed application to the commission;
   c. Submit the license fee as specified in WAC 246-840-990;
   d. Request the commission-approved certification program as identified in WAC 246-840-302;
   e. Request the advanced nursing educational program to send an official transcript directly to the commission showing all courses, grades, degree or certificate granted, official seal, and appropriate registrar or program director's signature;
   f. Submit documentation from the graduate program director or faculty identifying the area of practice, unless the area of practice is clearly indicated on the official transcript;
   g. Submit program objectives and course descriptions when requested by the commission; and
   h. Request a certificate or credential from a commission-approved credential evaluating service if the applicant is a new graduate educated outside the United States.

3. The ARNP applicant may petition the commission for an exemption to the requirement that application for licensure occur within one year of graduation if the applicant has had undue hardship.

Citation: Wash. Admin. Code § 246-840-340.

For prescriptive authority:

- Current license as an ARNP in Washington that is not subject to sanctions or restrictions issued by the commission
- Evidence of completion of 30 contact hours of education in pharmacotherapeutics within two-year time period immediately prior to application date for prescriptive authority. . . .

Citation: Wash. Admin. Code § 246-840-410.

West Virginia

- RN license
- Graduation from a graduate program. On and after January 2, 2015, verification must include evidence of completion of 3 separate graduate level courses

in advanced physiology and pathophysiology, advanced health assessment, and advanced pharmacology, which includes pharmacodynamics, pharmaco-kenetics and pharmacotherapeutics of all broad categories of agents, role and population focus of the education program
- Verification of successful completion of the appropriate APRN national certi-fication examination in the APRN role and population focus congruent with educational preparation

Citation: W. Va. Code St. R. § 19-7-3.

For prescriptive authority:

- Successfully completed an accredited course of instruction in pharmacology during undergraduate study
- Successfully completed an advanced pharmacotherapy graduate level course approved by the board of not less than 45 pharmacology contact hours
- Provide documentation of the use of pharmacotherapy in clinical practice in the education program
- Provide evidence of 15 pharmacology contact hours in advanced pharmaco-therapy completed within 2 years prior to application
- Written verification of an agreement to a collaborative relationship with a licensed physician holding a West Virginia license for prescriptive practice

Citation: W. Va. Code St. R. § 19-8-3(3.1).

Wisconsin

- RN license
- Certification by a national certifying body approved by the board as a nurse practitioner
- For applicants who receive certification after July 1, 1998, a master's degree in nursing or a related health field granted by a college or university accredited by a regional accrediting agency approved by the board of education in the state in which the college or university is located

Citation: Wisc. Admin. Code § N 8.02(1).

Wyoming

- RN license.
- Graduation of a state board approved nursing education program.
- Pass a board approved national nursing licensure examination.
- Not committed any acts that are grounds for disciplinary action or if so, the board may, at its discretion determine and after investigation determine that sufficient restitution has been made.

Citation: Wyo. Stat. Ann. § 33-21-127.

- RN license
- Completion of a pre-accredited or accredited graduate-level advanced practice registered nurse educational program; or an accredited advanced practice registered nurse educational program prior to January 1, 1999
- Provide documentation verifying national certification in the advanced practice registered nurse role and at least one population focus area of practice for which they are educationally prepared

> *Citation:* WYO. BOARD OF NURSING RULES CHAPTER 4 § Section 3.

For prescriptive authority:

- Recognition as an advanced practitioner of nursing in Wyoming
- Documentation of completion of a minimum of two semester credit hours, three quarter credit hours, or 30 contact hours of course work approved by the board in pharmacology and clinical management of drug therapy or pharmacotherapeutics within the five-year period immediately before the date of application
- Documentation of completion of 400 hours of advanced nursing practice in recognized areas of specialty within the two-year period immediately before the date of application
- Compliance with the standards of nursing practice, the rules and regulations, and the Act

> *Citation:* WYO. BOARD OF NURSING RULES CHAPTER 4 § Section 8.(C).

Federal Regulation of the Nurse Practitioner Profession

The federal government regulates nurse practitioner (NP) practice through statutes enacted by Congress and by regulations, policies, and guidelines written by federal agencies. Federal law may preempt state law, and when federal and state law conflict, federal law prevails. Where no federal law addresses an issue, or where Congress has expressly given the responsibility to the states to legislate an issue, state law controls.

Federal law addresses the following:

- Care of patients covered by Medicare
- Billing Medicare
- Care of patients covered by Medicaid
- Care of hospitalized patients insofar as participation by hospitals in the Medicare program is contingent on hospitals following certain regulations
- Care of residents in nursing homes
- In-office and hospital laboratories, under the Clinical Laboratory Improvement Amendments (CLIA)
- Self-referral by healthcare providers, under the Stark Acts
- Prescription of controlled substances, under the Drug Enforcement Administration (DEA)
- Reporting of successful malpractice lawsuits against NPs to the National Practitioner Data Bank (NPDB)
- Confidentiality of information about patients under the Health Insurance Portability and Accountability Act (HIPAA)
- Discrimination in hiring and firing
- Facility access for disabled people
- E-prescribing and electronic medical records

Federal law affects NPs both through what it states explicitly and what it does not.

Medicare

Because much of the funding for hospitals and much of the reimbursement for office practice comes from Medicare, federal statutes and regulations and policies from the Center for Medicare and Medicaid Services (CMS) have great impact on the interest of hospitals and medical practices that employ NP providers. For example, the Social Security Act, which governs Medicare and Medicaid, was written in 1965, before there were NPs. The Act frequently uses the term *physician* as if there is no other healthcare provider. Other healthcare providers have had to get Congress to pass acts to include them in the laws governing Medicare. The Act has been amended many times since the 1960s, but some relevant portions remain that give permission to physicians and only physicians to provide care.

NPs made progress in 1997 when an act of Congress authorized them to be reimbursed directly for the care of Medicare patients, regardless of setting. However, there still are sections of the federal law that have physician-only language. The Social Security Act still states that a physician must direct the care of hospitalized patients. In late 1997, the Health Care Financing Administration proposed new regulations for hospital participation in Medicare (62 Fed. Reg. 66726-66763). The regulations state that every Medicare patient must be under the care of a physician, dentist, podiatrist, optometrist, chiropractor, or psychologist. The regulation is based on a section of the Social Security Act that states the following:

> "Hospital" means an institution which has a requirement that every patient with
> respect to whom payment may be made under this title must be under the care
> of a physician, except that a patient receiving qualified psychologist services . . .
> may be under the care of a clinical psychologist with respect to such services to
> the extent permitted under state law.

Citation: 42 U.S.C.S. § 1395x(e)(4).

The regulation states that physicians, dentists, podiatrists, optometrists, chiropractors, or psychologists may delegate tasks to other qualified healthcare personnel to the extent recognized under state law or a state's regulatory mechanism (42 C.F.R. § 482.12). Because the proposed regulation does not use the term *nurse practitioner*, it is not clear that the regulation contemplates NPs practicing in hospitals. However, it can certainly be argued that NPs are "other qualified healthcare personnel." Hospitals wishing to serve patients covered by Medicare will want NPs to give care only as delegated by a physician. This may be a limitation for NPs in states where physician collaboration is not required.

NPs may want to lobby Congress for statutory language that specifically authorizes NP participation in the care of Medicare patients in hospitals, at home, in nursing homes, or in offices. Being relegated to the "other qualified personnel" bin is suboptimal for the NP profession. Other providers, most recently psychologists, have successfully lobbied for greater inclusion in the Social Security Act.

As of the date of publication of this text, the areas of federal law that still contain physician-only language are as follows:

- Nursing home law, which states that only a physician may be medical director and a physician must perform the initial comprehensive evaluation
- Home healthcare law, which states that a physician must order home care
- Hospice law, which states that only a physician may be the medical director

Medicare Reimbursement

In 1997, direct reimbursement to NPs, regardless of their geographic area of practice, was authorized by Congress. However, the specific procedures by which NPs are reimbursed are frequently revised and clarified as questions arise and answers are developed. For example, the Budget Reconciliation Act of 1997 removed the provision of the prior law that restricted reimbursement of NPs to those practicing in rural areas and also set the amount paid to 80% of either the lesser of the actual charge or 85% of the fee schedule amount provided under Section 1848. NPs who work for medical practices and who can fulfill the requirements of "incident to" or shared visit relationships with physicians can submit their work under a physician's provider number and will receive a full fee (not 85% of the physician fee). In general, however, an NP's work should be billed under the NP's provider number. Practitioners who are in doubt should seek an opinion from their Medicare payer or from an appropriate attorney.

What Is "Incident to"?

The full term is "incident to a physician's professional service." "Incident to" is a Medicare phrase, meaning services furnished as an "integral, although incidental, part of the physician's personal professional services in the course of diagnosis or treatment of an injury or illness."[1] To qualify under this definition, the services of nonphysicians must be rendered under a physician's "direct personal supervision." Nonphysicians must be employees of a physician or physician group, leased employees, or have an independent contractor relationship with a physician or physician group. Services must be furnished during a course of treatment where a physician performs an initial service and subsequent services of a frequency that reflects the physician's active participation in and management of a course of treatment. Direct personal supervision in the office setting does not mean that a physician must be in the same room.

However, to bill an incident to a physician's service, the physician must be in the same suite in the office as the NP at the time the NP performs the service to be billed under the physician's provider number.

Here is an example:

> A patient covered by Medicare visits a physician for the first time and the physician diagnoses high blood pressure. The physician asks the patient to return in a month for a follow-up visit with an NP employed by the physician. The physician is in another room in the office when the patient visits the NP. The NP evaluates and manages the patient's high blood pressure. Under the "incident to" rules, the NP's service (office visit, established patient) may be billed under the physician's provider number and the practice will receive 100% of the Physician Fee Schedule rate.

"Incident to" billing is applicable only in the office setting. However, if services are provided in a hospital, whether to inpatients, outpatients, or emergency room patients, there is a way to bill under a physician's provider number that is similar to "incident to billing," and the practice can receive 100% of the Physician Fee Schedule rate when NPs perform some of the service. "Shared visits" is a Medicare term for a situation in which both an NP and a physician in the same group provide evaluation and management services to a patient in a hospital. If the rules on "shared visits" are followed, the work of both the NP and the physician may be billed under the physician's provider number. The rules on shared visits are as follows:

- The NP and physician must belong to the same group; that is, be employed by the same entity.
- Both the NP and physician must document the evaluation and management service they provided to the same patient on the same day.
- Both the NP and physician must have a face-to-face visit with the patient that day.
- Shared visits apply only to evaluation and management services.

Federal Definition of Collaboration

Under federal law, the term "collaboration" means:

> A process in which a nurse practitioner works with a physician to deliver healthcare services within the scope of the practitioner's professional expertise, with medical direction and appropriate supervision as provided for in jointly developed guidelines or other mechanism as defined by the law of the State in which the services are performed.

Citation: 42 U.S.C.S. § 1395x(aa)(6).

The emergence of the NP as a primary provider rather than a supervised helper is not reflected in the Social Security Act. In the Act, an NP is someone to whom a physician may delegate certain tasks. State law either does not require collaboration or calls for "collaboration" but defines it without using the term "supervision." In contrast, federal law requires, through its definition of collaboration, "supervision." It would take an act of Congress to change this.

Medicare Fraud

CMS makes the rules regarding the care of Medicare patients and the billing of Medicare. The U.S. Justice Department enforces the rules. NPs who do not follow CMS's rules can expect to do poorly on audits and may be charged with Medicare fraud and/or abuse.

In the past few years, CMS has reevaluated Medicare's payment system, upgrading the reimbursement for some evaluation and management functions and downgrading the reimbursement for others. At the same time, CMS has clarified how providers, hospitals, and medical groups should bill, based on the services provided. Of particular interest to NPs are the guidelines jointly developed by CMS and the American Medical Association for coding office visits.

NPs can expect that their Medicare billing choices will be audited, and they will be expected to know the rules for choosing appropriate evaluation and management codes that correlate with the type of visit performed and the documentation recorded. NPs also can expect that the rules for Medicare will soon become the rules for billing in general. Recently, many NPs have been audited, and in some cases CMS has demanded the return of many thousands of dollars.

For the guidelines for coding office visits covered by Medicare, see **Appendix 4-A**. Medicare reimbursement and avoiding Medicare fraud and abuse are discussed in more detail elsewhere in the text. For information on specific questions regarding Medicare billing, consult the Medicare manuals, which can be downloaded from the CMS website (http://www.cms.hhs.gov).

Medicaid

The federal government has given most of the rule-making and administrative duties for Medicaid to the individual states, and, in most situations, state law controls Medicaid activities. However, the states must follow Federal Code 42 U.S.C.A. § 1396 in such matters as ensuring access to care and offering a choice of providers. Federal law provides that Medicaid will cover the services of pediatric NPs and family NPs, whether or not the NP is employed by or supervised by a physician [42 U.S.C.S. § 1396d(a)(xi)(21)].

The states also must follow CMS rules and regulations regarding administration of Medicaid. For example, states wishing to enroll all Medicaid recipients in managed care have had to apply to CMS for waivers that specify how the managed-care programs will be handled. It has been important for NPs in states that have applied for waivers to ensure that NPs are permitted to be primary care providers. If NPs are not included as providers in the language of state waivers approved by CMS, they can only care for Medicaid patients covered by traditional Medicaid, not patients in managed care. Thus, if all patients are in managed care, NPs who can care only for patients covered by traditional, fee-for-service Medicaid may find that there are no such patients.

NPs must apply to their state agency administering Medicaid for Medicaid provider numbers. More information on billing Medicaid is provided elsewhere in the text. For specific questions on Medicaid issues, contact the state Medicaid agency.

Nursing Homes

Under federal law that addresses patients covered by Medicare, residents of a skilled nursing facility must be provided with care under the supervision of a physician [42 U.S.C.S. § 1395i-3(b)(6)(A)]. The law states, "Skilled nursing facilities must require that the medical care of every resident be provided under the supervision of a physician" [42 U.S.C.S. § 1395i-3(b)(6)(A)] and "provide for having a physician available to furnish necessary medical care in case of emergency" [42 U.S.C.S. § 1395i-3(b)(6)(B)]. Physicians may delegate tasks to other qualified healthcare providers (42 C.F.R. 483).

Under federal law that addresses patients covered by Medicaid, nursing home residents may be provided care under the supervision of an NP. Medicaid law states the following:

> A nursing facility must require that the health care of every resident be provided under the supervision of a physician, or, at the option of a state, under the supervision of a nurse practitioner, clinical nurse specialist, or physician assistant who is not an employee of the facility but who is working in collaboration with a physician.

> *Citation:* 42 U.S.C.S. § 1396r(b)(6)(A).

Even if the care is supervised by an NP or a physician assistant, a nursing facility must have a physician "available to furnish necessary medical care in case of emergency" [42 U.S.C.S. § 1396r(b)(6)(B)]. And, as of the publication date of this text, only a physician may admit a patient to a skilled nursing facility.

In-Office and Hospital Laboratories Under the Clinical Laboratory Improvement Amendments

Office laboratories, no matter how small or limited in scope, are subject to federal oversight under the Clinical Laboratory Improvement Amendments (CLIA). State health departments often require office laboratories to meet certain requirements as well. Office laboratories are subject to state and federal inspection and approval. In offices where laboratory tests are limited to fecal occult blood (hemocult), urine pregnancy test, blood glucose, urinalysis (urine dip), and office microscopy, practices may obtain exemption from inspection. Nevertheless, offices must apply to CLIA for a letter of exemption.

Self-Referral by Healthcare Providers Under the Stark Acts

CMS has released rules regarding physician referral, entitled *Physicians' Referrals to Health Care Entities With Which They Have Financial Relationships*. These rules relate to the Ethics in Patient Referral Act of 1989 (42 U.S.C. § 1395nn), which was amended by the Omnibus Budget and Reconciliation Act of 1993 and incorporated into the Social Security Act [Social Security Act, 42 U.S.C.A. § 1877 and 1903(s)]. Collectively, these acts are commonly referred to as the "Stark Acts."

Under the Stark Acts, a physician cannot refer a patient covered by Medicare to a clinical laboratory with which the physician or an immediate family member of the physician has a financial relationship. Nor may a physician refer a patient to certain designated health services when the physician has a financial relationship with the facility offering the services. The designated health services include: (1) physical therapy services; (2) occupational therapy services; (3) radiation therapy services; (4) radiology services; (5) durable medical equipment and supplies; (6) parenteral and enteral nutrients; (7) prosthetics, orthotics, and prosthetic devices; (8) home health services; (9) outpatient prescription drugs; and (10) inpatient and outpatient hospital services. The Stark laws originally were aimed at physicians who own an interest in, for example, medical equipment companies or laboratories, and are in a position to profit when they refer patients for additional services. However, the Stark laws have been interpreted very broadly and now are being used to prohibit hospitals from rewarding physicians who refer patients to the hospitals.

For the purposes of the Stark Acts, referral is defined broadly. A physician may make a referral simply by including a service in the plan of care.

The Stark Acts have wide-ranging application. Just how Stark applies to many situations is still an evolving body of law.

CMS rules allow for certain exceptions from the self-referral prohibitions. For example, there is an exception for ownership and compensation for physicians' services "provided personally by or under the personal supervision of another physician in the same group practice . . . as the referring physician" [Social Security Act, 42 U.S.C.A. § 1877(b)(1)]. In other words, a physician may refer a patient to another physician in the same group practice without violating the self-referral law.

How Might Stark Affect NPs?

The Stark Acts are not aimed at NPs, but rather at physicians. However, if a physician requires an NP employee to refer to an entity with which the physician employer has a financial relationship, then the NP may become involved in an activity that violates the Stark Acts. If the referrals were found to be a violation of the Stark Act, the referrals would be imputed to the physician employing the NP, rather than the NP. On the other hand, if an NP employee is free to refer to the entity of his or her choice, and he or she independently chooses to refer to an entity in which his or her employer has a financial relationship, it is not clear that a Stark violation has taken place. The Office of the Inspector General has said that such cases would be evaluated based on the specific facts of the situation.

NPs and other healthcare providers wanting to start businesses that might lead to questions regarding the issues described in this section should consult with an attorney.

Anti-Kickback Statute

Under federal law, there are criminal penalties for individuals or entities that knowingly and willfully offer, pay, solicit, or receive remuneration (i.e., anything of value, in cash or in kind) in order to induce the referral of business reimbursable by a federal healthcare program. The statute prohibiting these activities -- kickbacks -- is at 42 U.S.C. 1320a-7b. Violations of the anti-kickback statute also may result in civil monetary penalties. The statute has been in existence since 1977. It applies to all kinds of healthcare providers and suppliers.

The law was enacted because Congress believed that payments tied to referrals increase the likelihood of overutilization of items and services, increase the cost of healthcare programs, lead to inappropriate referrals, and make competition unfair.

Examples of kickbacks include the following:

- Waiving deductibles and copayments for Medicare patients
- Paying an NP or physician a fee for referring a patient
- Accepting a fee for referring a patient

Implications for NPs

The federal prohibition on kickbacks applies to NPs. For example, what if an NP started a practice, asked a physician to be the collaborator, and promised to refer at least 50 patients per year to the physician as compensation for the services involved in being the collaborator? The promise to refer, combined with the actual referral of patients covered by Medicaid or Medicare, may be evidence of kickbacks in violation of federal law.

Prescription of Controlled Substances Under the DEA

The Drug Enforcement Administration (DEA) licenses healthcare providers who prescribe controlled dangerous substances. The DEA licenses NPs as "mid-level practitioners" (21 C.F.R. § 1301, 1304, and 1306.3). The DEA will assign an NP a DEA number if the NP has no felony on record, if the NP has a practice site, and if state law permits NPs to prescribe controlled substances. Controlled substances may be issued only by a practitioner who is authorized to prescribe controlled substances by the jurisdiction in which the practitioner is licensed to practice and has either registered or is exempt from registration.

Reporting to the National Practitioner Data Bank

Under federal law (42 C.F.R. § 60), malpractice insurers must report damage awards paid on behalf of physicians, dentists, NPs, and some other healthcare providers to the National Practitioner Data Bank (NPDB), a national repository of information on healthcare providers. The NPDB is discussed in more detail elsewhere in the text.

Patient Confidentiality

Federal law requires NPs and other healthcare providers to protect patient privacy and confidentiality. Specific federal laws protect the privacy of patients with substance abuse problems (42 U.S.C. § 290dd-2), patients with mental health problems (42 U.S.C. § 9501), and patients who are residents of nursing homes [42 U.S.C. § 1395e-3(C)(x)(A)(iv)].

Patient Privacy

Congress mandated the Department of Health and Human Services to promulgate rules governing privacy in health care under the Health Insurance Portability and Accountability Act (HIPAA) of 1996. The following are incidents that inspired Congress to pass the privacy protection requirements:

- A health system in Michigan accidentally posted the medical records of thousands of patients on the Internet (1999 report).
- A businessman purchased at auction the medical records of patients at a family practice in South Carolina and attempted to sell them back to the former patients (1991 report).
- Johnson & Johnson marketed a list of 5 million elderly women who had been treated for incontinence (1998 report).

Under the Final Rule ("Standards for Privacy of Individually Identifiable Health Information, Final Rule," *Federal Register*, December 28, 2000, pp. 82462-82829), any individual, organization, or facility that meets the definition of "covered entity" must do the following:

- Appoint a privacy officer
- Assess the office, hospital, or facility for potential for breaches of patient privacy
- Issue policies regarding handling and protection of patient information
- Conduct training for staff about the policies
- Monitor office or facility procedures for compliance with policies
- Get patients to authorize, in writing, any release of their individually identifiable information for marketing purposes
- Notify patients, in writing, of their rights under the rules, and make a good faith effort to get patients to sign an acknowledgment that they have received notice of their rights

- Provide patients with their own medical records, within 30 days of a patient's request

"Covered entities" include the following:

- Health plans
- Healthcare clearinghouses
- Healthcare providers who transmit any health information in electronic form in connection with a transaction

"Healthcare providers" include the following:

- Hospitals
- Skilled nursing facilities
- Comprehensive outpatient rehabilitation facilities
- Home health agencies
- Hospice programs
- NPs
- Certified nurse midwives
- Clinical nurse specialists
- Psychologists
- Clinical social workers
- Certified registered nurse anesthetists
- Physicians and physician assistants
- "...[A]nd any other person or organization who furnishes, bills, or is paid for health care in the normal course of business."

An individual healthcare provider—an NP, for example—need not personally transmit health information in electronic form for the rules to apply. If information is transmitted on the provider's behalf or by the provider's agency, the rules apply. The rules also apply to "business associates" of healthcare providers.

Basic requirements of the privacy rule are as follows:

- Providers and their staff are restricted to conveying the "minimum necessary information" about patients. "Minimum necessary" must be defined by organizational policy. Providers must establish policies that (1) identify the persons or classes of persons in the workforce who need access to protected patient information to do their jobs, (2) specify the information these workers may access, and (3) specify how information is protected from inspection by unauthorized individuals.
- If a provider wants to release patient information for marketing purposes, the provider must first explain to the patient how the information will be used, to whom it will be disclosed, and the time frame. The patient needs to authorize use of the information in writing. If the provider will be paid for releasing the patient's information, the provider must inform the patient of that fact.
- Providers may disclose health information to oversight agencies such as CMS without patient authorization. No authorization is required for victims of abuse, neglect, or domestic violence when state law mandates that the provider report abuse. No separate authorization is required when information is used for public health purposes or for organ and tissue donation. No authorization is required under certain circumstances involving law enforcement.

- There are special rules for psychotherapy notes. In general, patient authorization is required in order to disclose psychotherapy notes to carry out treatment, payment, or healthcare operations. Patients may authorize disclosure of their entire record. Such authorizations must include the name or class of the persons authorized to disclose and an expiration date or event.
- Providers must notify patients about how personal medical information may be used and disclosed, and how individuals may access their own information. Individuals have no right to three types of information about themselves: psychotherapy notes, information compiled in anticipation of civil or criminal litigation, and certain clinical laboratory information covered by the CLIA.
- Providers must accommodate reasonable requests from patients who want to restrict use of their information.

Discrimination in Hiring and Firing

Federal law prohibits discrimination based on race, color, sex, national origin, age, and disability. Title VII of the Civil Rights Act of 1964, which prohibits discrimination based on race, color, or national origin, applies to government employers and private employers with more than 15 employees. The Age Discrimination Act of 1967 prohibits discrimination based on age above 40 and applies to employers with more than 20 employees. The Equal Pay Act of 1963 prohibits wage discrimination between men and women and applies to most employers.

Requirements Under the Americans with Disabilities Act

Title I of the Americans with Disabilities Act of 1990 prohibits private employers from discriminating against qualified individuals in hiring, firing, advancement, compensation, job training, and conditions of employment. A disabled person is one who has a physical or mental impairment that substantially limits one or more major life activities. The Act applies to employers with more than 15 employees.

Note

1. Centers for Medicare and Medicaid Services. (May 5, 2013). Medicare benefit policy manual, Chapter 15, Sections 60.1–60.3. Retrieved from https://www.cms.gov/manuals/Downloads/bp102c15.pdf

Documentation Guidelines for Evaluation and Management Services

This is an update of the guidelines jointly produced by the American Medical Association (AMA) and the Health Care Financing Administration (HCFA) in May 1997. It appears on the Center for Medicare and Medicaid Services (CMS) website at http://www.cms.gov. It incorporates revisions to the gastrointestinal section of the general multisystem exam and the skin section of the single-organ system exam of the skin. These revisions were approved by the AMA and CMS in November 1997. This is not the final version of the guidelines. This version of the guidelines will be reviewed and may be amended before Medicare carriers begin to use it in compliance activities. NPs should check the CMS website periodically to determine whether revisions have been published.

Foreword

These guidelines were developed jointly by the American Medical Association (AMA) and the Health Care Financing Administration (HCFA), now known as the Center for Medicare and Medicaid Services (CMS). The stated goal was to provide physicians and claims reviewers with advice about preparing or reviewing documentation for Evaluation and Management services. In developing and testing the validity of these guidelines, special emphasis was placed on assuring that they:

- Are consistent with the clinical descriptors and definitions contained in Current Procedural Terminology (CPT);
- Would be widely accepted by clinicians and minimize any changes in record-keeping practices; and
- Would be interpreted and applied uniformly by users across the country.

This edition contains a substantial amount of new material and a number of significant revisions in material that appeared in the first edition. Because of the extensive changes, the section on examination should be read in its entirety. In this edition:

- The content of general multisystem examinations has been defined with greater clinical specificity.
- Documentation requirements for general multisystem examinations have been changed.
- For the first time, content and documentation requirements have been defined for examinations pertaining to ten organ systems. The content of these examinations was developed with the assistance of representatives from the specialties that frequently perform these examinations.
- Several editorial changes have been made in the definitions of the four types of examinations. This text also appears in CPT itself in the section headed "Evaluation and Management (E/M) Services Guidelines."
- The definition of an extended history of present illness has been expanded to include information about chronic or inactive conditions.

Documentation Guidelines for Evaluation and Management Services

I. Introduction

What Is Documentation and Why Is It Important?

Medical record documentation is required to record pertinent facts, findings, and observations about an individual's health history including past and present illnesses, examinations, tests, treatments, and outcomes. The medical record chronologically documents the care of the patient and is an important element contributing to high-quality care. The medical record facilitates:

- The ability of the physician and other healthcare professionals to evaluate and plan the patient's immediate treatment, and to monitor his/her health care over time;
- Communication and continuity of care among physicians and other healthcare professionals involved in the patient's care;
- Accurate and timely claims review and payment;
- Appropriate utilization review and quality of care evaluations; and
- Collection of data that may be useful for research and education.

An appropriately documented medical record can reduce many of the "hassles" associated with claims processing and may serve as a legal document to verify the care provided, if necessary.

What Do Payers Want and Why?

Because payers have a contractual obligation to enrollees, they may require reasonable documentation that services are consistent with the insurance coverage provided. They may request information to validate:

- The site of service;
- The medical necessity and appropriateness of the diagnostic and/or therapeutic services provided; and/or
- That services provided have been accurately reported.

II. General Principles of Medical Record Documentation

The principles of documentation listed below are applicable to all types of medical and surgical services in all settings. For Evaluation and Management (E/M) services, the nature and amount of physician work and documentation varies by type of service, place of service, and the patient's status. The general principles listed below may be modified to account for these variable circumstances in providing E/M services.

1. The medical record should be complete and legible.
2. The documentation of each patient encounter should include:

   - Reason for the encounter and relevant history, physical examination findings, and prior diagnostic test results;
   - Assessment, clinical impression, or diagnosis;
   - Plan for care; and
   - Date and legible identity of the observer.

3. If not documented, the rationale for ordering diagnostic and other ancillary services should be easily inferred.
4. Past and present diagnoses should be accessible to the treating and/or consulting physician.
5. Appropriate health risk factors should be identified.
6. The patient's progress, response to and changes in treatment, and revision of diagnosis should be documented.
7. The CPT and ICD-9-CM codes reported on the health insurance claim form or billing statement should be supported by the documentation in the medical record.

III. Documentation of E/M Services

This publication provides definitions and documentation guidelines for the three key components of E/M services and for visits that consist predominately of counseling or coordination of care. The three key components—history, examination, and medical decision making—appear in the descriptors for office and other outpatient services, hospital observation services, hospital inpatient services, consultations, emergency department services, nursing facility services, domiciliary care services, and home services. While some of the text of CPT has been repeated in this publication, the reader should refer to CPT for the complete descriptors for E/M services and instructions for selecting a level of service. Documentation guidelines are identified by the symbol "●DG."

The descriptors for the levels of E/M services recognize seven components that are used in defining the levels of E/M services. These components are:

- History,
- Examination,
- Medical decision making,
- Counseling,
- Coordination of care,
- Nature of presenting problem, and
- Time.

The first three of these components (i.e., history, examination, and medical decision making) are the key components in selecting the level of E/M services. In the case of visits that consist predominantly of counseling or coordination of care, time is the key or controlling factor to qualify for a particular level of E/M service.

Because the level of E/M service is dependent on two or three key components, performance and documentation of one component (e.g., examination) at the highest level does not necessarily mean that the encounter in its entirety qualifies for the highest level of E/M service.

These documentation guidelines for E/M services reflect the needs of the typical adult population. For certain groups of patients, the recorded information may vary slightly from that described here. Specifically, the medical records of infants, children, adolescents, and pregnant women may have additional or modified information recorded in each history and examination area.

As an example, newborn records may include under history of the present illness (HPI) the details of mother's pregnancy and the infant's status at birth; social history will focus on family structure; family history will focus on congenital anomalies and hereditary disorders in the family. In addition, the content of a pediatric examination will vary with the age and development of the child. Although not specifically defined in these documentation guidelines, these patient group variations on history and examination are appropriate.

Documentation of History

The levels of E/M services are based on four types of history (Problem Focused, Expanded Problem Focused, Detailed, and Comprehensive). Each type of history includes some or all of the following elements:

- Chief complaint (CC)
- History of present illness (HPI)
- Review of systems (ROS)
- Past, family, and/or social history (PFSH)

The extent of history of present illness, review of systems, and past, family, and/or social history that is obtained and documented is dependent upon clinical judgment and the nature of the presenting problem(s). The chart below shows the progression of the elements required for each type of history. To qualify for a given type of history all three elements in the table must be met. (A chief complaint is indicated at all levels.)

- •DG: *The CC, ROS, and PFSH may be listed as separate elements of history, or they may be included in the description of the history of the present illness.*
- •DG: *An ROS and/or a PFSH obtained during an earlier encounter does not need to be rerecorded if there is evidence that the physician reviewed and updated the previous information. This may occur when a physician updates his or her own record or in an institutional setting or group practice where many physicians use a common record. The review and update may be documented by:*
  - *Describing any new ROS and/or PFSH information or noting there has been no change in the information; and*
  - *Noting the date and location of the earlier ROS and/or PFSH.*

- •DG: *The ROS and/or PFSH may be recorded by ancillary staff or on a form completed by the patient. To document that the physician reviewed the information, there must be a notation supplementing or confirming the information recorded by others.*
- •DG: *If the physician is unable to obtain a history from the patient or other source, the record should describe the patient's condition or other circumstance that precludes obtaining a history.*

Definitions and specific documentation guidelines for each of the elements of history are listed below.

Chief Complaint (CC)

The CC is a concise statement describing the symptom, problem, condition, diagnosis, physician recommended return, or other factor that is the reason for the encounter, usually stated in the patient's words.

- •DG: *The medical record should clearly reflect the chief complaint.*

History of Present Illness (HPI)

The HPI is a chronological description of the development of the patient's present illness from the first sign and/or symptom or from the previous encounter to the present. It includes the following elements:

- Location
- Quality
- Severity
- Duration
- Timing
- Context
- Modifying factors
- Associated signs and symptoms

Brief and extended HPIs are distinguished by the amount of detail needed to accurately characterize the clinical problem(s).

A brief HPI consists of one to three elements of the HPI.

- •DG: *The medical record should describe one to three elements of the present illness (HPI).*

An extended HPI consists of at least four elements of the HPI or the status of at least three chronic or inactive conditions.

- •DG: *The medical record should describe at least four elements of the present illness (HPI), or the status of at least three chronic or inactive conditions.*

Review of Systems (ROS)

An ROS is an inventory of body systems obtained through a series of questions seeking to identify signs and/or symptoms that the patient may be experiencing or has experienced.

For purposes of ROS, the following systems are recognized:

- Constitutional symptoms (e.g., fever, weight loss)
- Eyes
- Ears, nose, mouth, throat
- Cardiovascular
- Respiratory
- Gastrointestinal
- Genitourinary
- Musculoskeletal
- Integumentary (skin and/or breast)
- Neurological
- Psychiatric
- Endocrine
- Hematologic/lymphatic
- Allergic/immunologic

A problem pertinent ROS inquires about the system directly related to the problem(s) identified in the HPI.

> •DG: *The patient's positive responses and pertinent negatives for the system related to the problem should be documented.*

An extended ROS inquires about the system directly related to the problem(s) identified in the HPI and a limited number of additional systems.

> •DG: *The patient's positive responses and pertinent negatives for two to nine systems should be documented.*

A complete ROS inquires about the system(s) directly related to the problem(s) identified in the HPI plus all additional body systems.

> •DG: *At least ten organ systems must be reviewed. Those systems with positive or pertinent negative responses must be individually documented. For the remaining systems, a notation indicating all other systems are negative is permissible. In the absence of such a notation, at least ten systems must be individually documented.*

Past, Family, and/or Social History (PFSH)

The PFSH consists of a review of three areas:

- Past history (the patient's past experiences with illnesses, operations, injuries, and treatments),
- Family history (a review of medical events in the patient's family, including diseases which may be hereditary or place the patient at risk), and
- Social history (an age-appropriate review of past and current activities).

For certain categories of E/M services that include only an interval history, it is not necessary to record information about the PFSH. Those categories are subsequent hospital care, follow-up inpatient consultations, and subsequent nursing facility care.

A pertinent PFSH is a review of the history area(s) directly related to the problem(s) identified in the HPI.

> •DG: *At least one specific item from any of the three history areas must be documented for a pertinent PFSH.*

A complete PFSH is a review of two or all three of the PFSH history areas, depending on the category of the E/M service. A review of all three history areas is required for services that by their nature include a comprehensive assessment or reassessment of the patient. A review of two of the three history areas is sufficient for other services.

> •DG: *At least one specific item from two of the three history areas must be documented for a complete PFSH for the following categories of E/M services: office or other outpatient services, established patient; emergency department; domiciliary care, established patient; and home care, established patient.*

> •DG: *At least one specific item from each of the three history areas must be documented for a complete PFSH for the following categories of E/M services: office or other outpatient services, new patient; hospital observation services; hospital inpatient services, initial care; consultations; comprehensive nursing facility assessments; domiciliary care, new patient; and home care, new patient.*

Documentation of Examination

The levels of E/M services are based on four types of examination:

- Problem Focused—a limited examination of the affected body area or organ system.
- Expanded Problem Focused—a limited examination of the affected body area or organ system and any other symptomatic or related body area(s) or organ system(s).
- Detailed—an extended examination of the affected body area(s) or organ system(s) and any other symptomatic or related body area(s) or organ system(s).
- Comprehensive—a general multisystem examination or complete examination of a single organ system and other symptomatic or related body area(s) or organ system(s).

These types of examinations have been defined for general multisystems and the following single organ systems:

- Cardiovascular
- Ears, nose, mouth, and throat
- Eyes
- Genitourinary (female)
- Genitourinary (male)

- Hematologic/lymphatic/immunologic
- Musculoskeletal
- Neurological
- Psychiatric
- Respiratory
- Skin

A general multisystem examination or a single organ system examination may be performed by any physician regardless of specialty. The type (general multisystem or single organ system) and content of examination are selected by the examining physician and are based upon clinical judgment, the patient's history, and the nature of the presenting problem(s).

The content and documentation requirements for each type and level of examination are summarized next and described in detail in tables found later in this chapter. In the tables, organ systems and body areas recognized by CPT for purposes of describing examinations are shown in the left column. The content, or individual elements, of the examination pertaining to that body area or organ system are identified by bullets (•) in the right column.

Parenthetical examples "(e.g., . . .)" have been used for clarification and to provide guidance regarding documentation. Documentation for each element must satisfy any numeric requirements (such as "Measurement of any three of the following seven . . .") included in the description of the element. Elements with multiple components but with no specific numeric requirement (such as "Examination of liver and spleen") require documentation of at least one component. It is possible for a given examination to be expanded beyond what is defined here. When that occurs, findings related to the additional systems and/or areas should be documented.

- •DG: *Specific abnormal and relevant negative findings of the examination of the affected or symptomatic body area(s) or organ system(s) should be documented. A notation of "abnormal" without elaboration is insufficient.*
- •DG: *Abnormal or unexpected findings of the examination of any asymptomatic body area(s) or organ system(s) should be described.*

- •DG: *A brief statement or notation indicating "negative" or "normal" is sufficient to document normal findings related to unaffected area(s) or asymptomatic organ system(s).*

General Multisystem Examinations

General multisystem examinations are described in detail beginning on page 176. To qualify for a given level of multisystem examination, the following content and documentation requirements should be met:

- Problem Focused Examination—should include performance and documentation of one to five elements identified by a bullet (•) in one or more organ system(s) or body area(s).

- Expanded Problem Focused Examination—should include performance and documentation of at least six elements identified by a bullet (•) in one or more organ system(s) or body area(s).
- Detailed Examination—should include at least six organ systems or body areas. For each system/area selected, performance and documentation of at least two elements identified by a bullet (•) are expected. Alternatively, a detailed examination may include performance and documentation of at least twelve elements identified by a bullet (•) in two or more organ systems or body areas.
- Comprehensive Examination—should include at least nine organ systems or body areas. For each system/area selected, all elements of the examination identified by a bullet (•) should be performed, unless specific directions limit the content of the examination. For each area/system, documentation of at least two elements identified by a bullet is expected.

Single Organ System Examinations

The single organ system examinations recognized by CPT are described in detail beginning on page 178. Variations among these examinations in the organ systems and body areas identified in the left columns and in the elements of the examinations described in the right columns reflect differing emphases among specialties. To qualify for a given level of single organ system examination, the following content and documentation requirements should be met:

- Problem Focused Examination—should include performance and documentation of one to five elements identified by a bullet (•), whether in a box with a shaded or unshaded border.
- Expanded Problem Focused Examination—should include performance and documentation of at least six elements identified by a bullet (•), whether in a box with a shaded or unshaded border.
- Detailed Examination—examinations other than the eye and psychiatric examinations should include performance and documentation of at least twelve elements identified by a bullet (•), whether in a box with a shaded or unshaded border. Eye and psychiatric examinations should include the performance and documentation of at least nine elements identified by a bullet (•), whether in a box with a shaded or unshaded border.
- Comprehensive Examination—should include performance of all elements identified by a bullet (•), whether in a shaded or unshaded box. Documentation of every element in each box with a shaded border and at least one element in each box with an unshaded border is expected.

Note

This is the most recent version of the guidelines, as of January 2011.

CONTENT AND DOCUMENTATION REQUIREMENTS

General Multisystem Examination

System/Body Area	Elements of Examination
Constitutional	• Measurement of any three of the following seven vital signs: (1) sitting or standing blood pressure, (2) supine blood pressure, (3) pulse rate and regularity, (4) respiration, (5) temperature, (6) height, (7) weight (may be measured and recorded by ancillary staff) • General appearance of patient (e.g., development, nutrition, body habitus, deformities, attention to grooming)
Eyes	• Inspection of conjunctivae and lids • Examination of pupils and irises (e.g., reaction to light and accommodation, size, and symmetry) • Ophthalmoscopic examination of optic discs (e.g., size, C/D ratio, appearance) and posterior segments (e.g., vessel changes, exudates, hemorrhages)
Ears, Nose, Mouth, and Throat	• External inspection of ears and nose (e.g., overall appearance and throat scars, lesions, masses) • Otoscopic examination of external auditory canals and tympanic membranes • Assessment of hearing (e.g., whispered voice, finger rub, tuning fork) • Inspection of nasal mucosa, septum, and turbinates • Inspection of lips, teeth, and gums • Examination of oropharynx: oral mucosa, salivary glands, hard and soft palates, tongue, tonsils, and posterior pharynx
Neck	• Examination of neck (e.g., masses, overall appearance, symmetry, tracheal position, crepitus) • Examination of thyroid (e.g., enlargement, tenderness, mass)
Respiratory	• Assessment of respiratory effort (e.g., intercostal retractions, use of accessory muscles, diaphragmatic movement) • Percussion of chest (e.g., dullness, flatness, hyperresonance) • Palpation of chest (e.g., tactile fremitus) • Auscultation of lungs (e.g., breath sounds, adventitious sounds, rubs)
Cardiovascular	• Palpation of heart (e.g., location, size, thrills) • Auscultation of heart with notation of abnormal sounds and murmurs Examination of: • Carotid arteries (e.g., pulse amplitude, bruits) • Abdominal aorta (e.g., size, bruits) • Femoral arteries (e.g., pulse amplitude, bruits) • Pedal pulses (e.g., pulse amplitude) • Extremities for edema and/or varicosities
Chest (Breasts)	• Inspection of breasts (e.g., symmetry, nipple discharge) • Palpation of breasts and axillae (e.g., masses or lumps, tenderness)
Gastrointestinal (Abdomen)	• Examination of abdomen with notation of presence of masses or tenderness • Examination of liver and spleen

System/Body Area	Elements of Examination
Gastrointestinal (Abdomen)	• Examination for presence or absence of hernia • Examination (when indicated) of anus, perineum, and rectum, including sphincter tone, presence of hemorrhoids, rectal masses • Obtain stool sample for occult blood test when indicated
Genitourinary	**MALE:** • Examination of the scrotal contents (e.g., hydrocele, spermatocele, tenderness of cord, testicular mass) • Examination of the penis • Digital rectal examination of prostate gland (e.g., size, symmetry, nodularity, tenderness) **FEMALE:** Pelvic examination (with or without specimen collection for smears and cultures), including: • Examination of external genitalia (e.g., general appearance, hair distribution, lesions) and vagina (e.g., general appearance, estrogen effect, discharge, lesions, pelvic support, cystocele, rectocele) • Examination of urethra (e.g., masses, tenderness, scarring) • Examination of bladder (e.g., fullness, masses, tenderness) • Cervix (e.g., general appearance, lesions, discharge) • Uterus (e.g., size, contour, position, mobility, tenderness, consistency, descent, or support) • Adnexa/parametria (e.g., masses, tenderness, organomegaly, nodularity)
Lymphatic	Palpation of lymph nodes in two or more areas: • Neck • Axillae • Groin • Other

Musculoskeletal	• Examination of gait and station
	• Inspection and/or palpation of digits and nails (e.g., clubbing, cyanosis, inflammatory conditions, petechiae, ischemia, infections, nodes)
	  • Examination of joints, bones, and muscles of one or more of the following six areas: (1) head and neck; (2) spine, ribs, and pelvis;(3) right upper extremity; (4) left upper extremity; (5) right lower extremity; and (6) left lower extremity. The examination of a given area includes:
	   – Inspection and/or palpation with notation of presence of any misalignment, asymmetry, crepitation, defects, tenderness, masses, effusions
	   – Assessment of range of motion with notation of any pain, crepitation, or contracture
	   – Assessment of stability with notation of any dislocation (luxation), subluxation, or laxity
	   – Assessment of muscle strength and tone (e.g., flaccid, cog wheel, spastic) with notation of any atrophy or abnormal movements

Skin	• Inspection of skin and subcutaneous tissue (e.g., rashes, lesions, ulcers) • Palpation of skin and subcutaneous tissue (e.g., induration, subcutaneous nodules, tightening)

System/Body Area	Elements of Examination
Neurological	• Test cranial nerves with notation of any deficits • Examination of deep tendon reflexes with notation of pathological reflexes (e.g., Babinski) • Examination of sensation (e.g., by touch, pin, vibration, proprioception)

Psychiatric	• Description of patient's judgment and insight
	• Brief assessment of mental status including:
	  – Orientation to time, place, and person
	  – Recent and remote memory
	  – Mood and affect (e.g., depression, anxiety, agitation)

Content and Documentation Requirements

Level of Exam	Perform and Document:
Problem Focused	One to five elements identified by a bullet.
Expanded Problem Focused	At least six elements identified by a bullet.
Detailed	At least two elements identified by a bullet from each of six areas/systems OR at least twelve elements identified by a bullet in two or more areas/systems.
Comprehensive	Perform all elements identified by a bullet in at least nine organ systems or body areas and document at least two elements identified by a bullet from each of nine areas/systems.

Cardiovascular Examination

System/Body Area	Elements of Examination
Constitutional	• Measurement of any three of the following seven vital signs: (1) sitting or standing blood pressure, (2) supine blood pressure, (3) pulse rate and regularity, (4) respiration, (5) temperature, (6) height, (7) weight (may be measured and recorded by ancillary staff) • General appearance of patient (e.g., development, nutrition, body habitus, deformities, attention to grooming)
Head and Face	
Eyes	• Inspection of conjunctivae and lids (e.g., xanthelasma)
Ears, Nose, Mouth, and Throat	• Inspection of teeth, gums, palate, and throat • Inspection of oral mucosa with notation of presence of pallor or cyanosis
Neck	• Examination of jugular veins (e.g., distension; a, v, or cannon a waves) • Examination of thyroid (e.g., enlargement, tenderness, mass)
Respiratory	• Assessment of respiratory effort (e.g., intercostal retractions, use of accessory muscles, diaphragmatic movement) • Auscultation of lungs (e.g., breath sounds, adventitious sounds, rubs)

Cardiovascular	• Palpation of heart (e.g., location, size, and forcefulness of the point of maximal impact; thrills; lifts; palpable S3 or S4)
	• Auscultation of heart including sounds, abnormal sounds, and murmurs
	• Measurement of blood pressure in two or more extremities when indicated (e.g., aortic dissection, coarctation)
	• Examination of:
	  – Carotid arteries (e.g., waveform, pulse amplitude, bruits, apicalcarotid delay)
	  – Abdominal aorta (e.g., size, bruits)
	  – Femoral arteries (e.g., pulse amplitude, bruits)
	  – Pedal pulses (e.g., pulse amplitude)
	  – Extremities for peripheral edema and/or varicosities

Chest (Breasts)	
Gastrointestinal (Abdomen)	• Examination of abdomen with notation of presence of masses (Abdomen) or tenderness • Examination of liver and spleen • Obtain stool sample for occult blood from patients who are being considered for thrombolytic or anticoagulant therapy.
Genitourinary	
Lymphatic	
Musculoskeletal	• Examination of the back with notation of kyphosis or scoliosis • Examination of gait with notation of ability to undergo exercise testing and/or participation in exercise programs • Assessment of muscle strength and tone (e.g., flaccid, cog wheel, spastic) with notation of any atrophy and abnormal movements
Extremities	• Inspection and palpation of digits and nails (e.g., clubbing, cyanosis, inflammation, petechiae, ischemia, infections, Osler's nodes)
Skin	• Inspection and/or palpation of skin and subcutaneous tissue (e.g., stasis dermatitis, ulcers, scars, xanthomas)

Neurological/ Psychiatric	• Brief assessment of mental status including: Psychiatric
	  – Orientation to time, place, and person
	  – Mood and affect (e.g., depression, anxiety, agitation)

Content and Documentation Requirements

Level of Exam	Perform and Document:
Problem Focused	One to five elements identified by a bullet.
Expanded Problem Focused	At least six elements identified by a bullet.
Detailed	At least twelve elements identified by a bullet.
Comprehensive	Perform all elements identified by a bullet; document every element in each box with a shaded border and at least one element in each box with an unshaded border.

Ear, Nose, Mouth, and Throat Examination

System/Body Area	Elements of Examination
Constitutional	• Measurement of any three of the following seven vital signs: (1) sitting or standing blood pressure, (2) supine blood pressure, (3) pulse rate and regularity, (4) respiration, (5) temperature, (6) height, (7) weight (may be measured and recorded by ancillary staff) • General appearance of patient (e.g., development, nutrition, body habitus, deformities, attention to grooming) • Assessment of ability to communicate (e.g., use of sign language or other communication aids) and quality of voice
Head and Face	• Inspection of head and face (e.g., overall appearance, scars, lesions, and masses) • Palpation and/or percussion of face with notation of presence or absence of sinus tenderness • Examination of salivary glands • Assessment of facial strength
Eyes	• Test ocular motility including primary gaze alignment
Ears, Nose, Mouth, and Throat	• Otoscopic examination of external auditory canals and tympanic membranes including pneumootoscopy with notation of mobility of membranes • Assessment of hearing with tuning forks and clinical speech reception thresholds (e.g., whispered voice, finger rub) • External inspection of ears and nose (e.g., overall appearance, scars, lesions, and masses) • Inspection of nasal mucosa, septum, and turbinates • Inspection of lips, teeth, and gums • Examination of oropharynx: oral mucosa, hard and soft palates, tongue, tonsils, and posterior pharynx (e.g., asymmetry, lesions, hydration of mucosal surfaces) • Inspection of pharyngeal walls and pyriform sinuses (e.g., pooling of saliva, asymmetry, lesions) • Examination by mirror of larynx including the condition of the epiglottis, false vocal cords, true vocal cords, and mobility of larynx (use of mirror not required in children) • Examination by mirror of nasopharynx including appearance of the mucosa, adenoids, posterior choanae, and eustachian tubes (use of mirror not required in children)
Neck	• Examination of neck (e.g., masses, overall appearance, symmetry, tracheal position, crepitus) • Examination of thyroid (e.g., enlargement, tenderness, mass)
Respiratory	• Inspection of chest including symmetry, expansion, and/or assessment of respiratory effort (e.g., intercostal retractions, use of accessory muscles, diaphragmatic movement) • Auscultation of lungs (e.g., breath sounds, adventitious sounds, rubs)
Cardiovascular	• Auscultation of heart with notation of abnormal sounds and murmurs • Examination of peripheral vascular system by observation (e.g., swelling, varicosities) and palpation (e.g., pulses, temperature, edema, tenderness)

Chest (Breasts)	
Gastrointestinal (Abdomen)	
Genitourinary	
Lymphatic	• Palpation of lymph nodes in neck, axillae, groin, and/or other location
Musculoskeletal	
Extremities	
Skin	

Neurological/ Psychiatric	• Test cranial nerves with notation of any deficits
	• Brief assessment of mental status including:
	  – Orientation to time, place, and person
	  – Mood and affect (e.g., depression, anxiety, agitation)

Content and Documentation Requirements

Level of Exam	*Perform and Document:*
Problem Focused	One to five elements identified by a bullet.
Expanded Problem Focused	At least six elements identified by a bullet.
Detailed	At least twelve elements identified by a bullet.
Comprehensive	Perform all elements identified by a bullet; document every element in each box with a shaded border and at least one element in each box with an unshaded border.

Eye Examination

System/Body Area	*Elements of Examination*
Constitutional	
Head and Face	
Eyes	• Test visual acuity (does not include determination of refractive error) • Gross visual field testing by confrontation • Test ocular motility including primary gaze alignment • Inspection of bulbar and palpebral conjunctivae • Examination of ocular adnexae including lids (e.g., ptosis or lagophthalmos), lacrimal glands, lacrimal drainage, orbits, and preauricular lymph nodes • Examination of pupils and irises including shape, direct and consensual reaction (afferent pupil), size (e.g., anisocoria), and morphology • Slit lamp examination of the corneas including epithelium, stroma, endothelium, and tear film • Slit lamp examination of the anterior chambers including depth, cells, and flare • Slit lamp examination of the lenses including clarity, anterior and posterior capsule, cortex, and nucleus

System/Body Area	Elements of Examination

Eyes	• Measurement of intraocular pressures (except in children and patients with trauma or infectious disease)
	• Ophthalmoscopic examination through dilated pupils (unless contraindicated) of:
	  – Optic discs including size, C/D ratio, appearance (e.g., atrophy, cupping, tumor elevation), and nerve fiber layer
	  – Posterior segments including retina and vessels (e.g., exudates and hemorrhages)

Ears, Nose, Mouth, and Throat	
Neck	
Respiratory	
Cardiovascular	
Chest (Breasts)	
Gastrointestinal (Abdomen)	
Genitourinary	
Lymphatic	
Musculoskeletal	
Extremities	
Skin	

Neurological/ Psychiatric	• Brief assessment of mental status including:
	  – Orientation to time, place, and person
	  – Mood and affect (e.g., depression, anxiety, agitation)

Content and Documentation Requirements

Level of Exam	Perform and Document:
Problem Focused	One to five elements identified by a bullet.
Expanded Problem Focused	At least six elements identified by a bullet.
Detailed	At least nine elements identified by a bullet.
Comprehensive	Perform all elements identified by a bullet; document every element in each box with a shaded border and at least one element in each box with an unshaded border.

Genitourinary Examination

System/Body Area	Elements of Examination
Constitutional	• Measurement of any three of the following seven vital signs:(1) sitting or standing blood pressure, (2) supine blood pressure, (3) pulse rate and regularity, (4) respiration, (5) temperature, (6) height, (7) weight (may be measured and recorded by ancillary staff) • General appearance of patient (e.g., development, nutrition, body habitus, deformities, attention to grooming)

Head and Face	
Eyes	
Ears, Nose, Mouth, and Throat	
Neck	• Examination of neck (e.g., masses, overall appearance, symmetry, tracheal position, crepitus) • Examination of thyroid (e.g., enlargement, tenderness, mass)
Respiratory	• Assessment of respiratory effort (e.g., intercostal retractions, use of accessory muscles, diaphragmatic movement) • Auscultation of lungs (e.g., breath sounds, adventitious sounds, rubs)
Cardiovascular	• Auscultation of heart with notation of abnormal sounds and murmurs • Examination of peripheral vascular system by observation (e.g., swelling, varicosities) and palpation (e.g., pulses, temperature, edema, tenderness)
Chest (Breasts)	[See genitourinary (female)]
Gastrointestinal (Abdomen)	• Examination of abdomen with notation of presence of masses or tenderness • Examination for presence or absence of hernia • Examination of liver and spleen • Obtain stool sample for occult blood test when indicated

Genitourinary	**MALE:**
	• Inspection of anus and perineum
	• Examination (with or without specimen collection for smears and cultures) of genitalia including:
	  – Scrotum (e.g., lesions, cysts, rashes)
	  – Epididymides (e.g., size, symmetry, masses)
	  – Testes (e.g., size, symmetry, masses)
	  – Urethral meatus (e.g., size, location, lesions, discharge)
	  – Penis (e.g., lesions, presence or absence of foreskin, foreskin retractability, plaque, masses, scarring, deformities)
	• Digital rectal examination including:
	  – Prostate gland (e.g., size, symmetry, nodularity, tenderness)
	  – Seminal vesicles (e.g., symmetry, tenderness, masses, enlargement)
	  – Sphincter tone, presence of hemorrhoids, rectal masses
	
	FEMALE:
	Includes at least seven of the following eleven elements identified:
	• Inspection and palpation of breasts (e.g., masses or lumps, tenderness, symmetry, nipple discharge)
	• Digital rectal examination including sphincter tone, presence of hemorrhoids, rectal masses
	• Pelvic examination (with or without specimen collection for smears and cultures) including:
	  – External genitalia (e.g., general appearance, hair distribution, lesions)
	  – Urethral meatus (e.g., size, location, lesions, prolapse)
	  – Urethra (e.g., masses, tenderness, scarring)
	  – Bladder (e.g., fullness, masses, tenderness)
	  – Vagina (e.g., general appearance, estrogen effect, discharge, lesions, pelvic support, cystocele, rectocele)

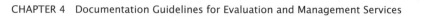

System/Body Area	Elements of Examination
	– Cervix (e.g., general appearance, lesions, discharge) – Uterus (e.g., size, contour, position, mobility, tenderness, consistency, descent, or support) – Adnexa/parametria (e.g., masses, tenderness, organomegaly, nodularity) – Anus and perineum
Lymphatic	• Palpation of lymph nodes in neck, axillae, groin, and/or other location
Musculoskeletal	
Extremities	
Skin	• Inspection and/or palpation of skin and subcutaneous tissue (e.g., rashes, lesions, ulcers)
Neurological/Psychiatric	• Brief assessment of mental status including: – Orientation (e.g., time, place, and person) – Mood and affect (e.g., depression, anxiety, agitation)

Content and Documentation Requirements

Level of Exam	Perform and Document:
Problem Focused	One to five elements identified by a bullet.
Expanded Problem Focused	At least six elements identified by a bullet.
Detailed	At least twelve elements identified by a bullet.
Comprehensive	Perform all elements identified by a bullet; document every element in each box with a shaded border and at least one element in each box with an unshaded border.

Hematologic/Lymphatic/Immunologic Examination

System/Body Area	Elements of Examination
Constitutional	• Measurement of any three of the following seven vital signs:(1) sitting or standing blood pressure, (2) supine blood pressure, (3) pulse rate and regularity, (4) respiration, (5) temperature, (6) height, (7) weight (may be measured and recorded by ancillary staff) • General appearance of patient (e.g., development, nutrition, body habitus, deformities, attention to grooming)
Head and Face	• Palpation and/or percussion of face with notation of presence or absence of sinus tenderness
Eyes	• Inspection of conjunctivae and lids
Ears, Nose, Mouth, and Throat	• Otoscopic examination of external auditory canals and tympanic membranes • Inspection of nasal mucosa, septum, and turbinates • Inspection of teeth and gums • Examination of oropharynx (e.g., oral mucosa, hard and soft palates, tongue, tonsils, posterior pharynx)
Neck	• Examination of neck (e.g., masses, overall appearance, symmetry, tracheal position, crepitus) • Examination of thyroid (e.g., enlargement, tenderness, mass)

Respiratory	• Assessment of respiratory effort (e.g., intercostal retractions, use of accessory muscles, diaphragmatic movement) • Auscultation of lungs (e.g., breath sounds, adventitious sounds, rubs)
Cardiovascular	• Auscultation of heart with notation of abnormal sounds and murmurs Examination of peripheral vascular system by observation (e.g., swelling, varicosities), and palpation (e.g., pulses, temperature, edema, tenderness)
Chest (Breasts)	
Gastrointestinal	• Examination of abdomen with notation of presence of masses or tenderness • Examination of liver and spleen
Genitourinary	
Lymphatic	• Palpation of lymph nodes in neck, axillae, groin, and/or other location
Musculoskeletal	
Extremities	• Inspection and palpation of digits and nails (e.g., clubbing, cyanosis, inflammation, petechiae, ischemia, infections, nodes)
Skin	• Inspecion and/or palpation of skin and subcutaneous tissue (e.g., rashes, lesions, ulcers, ecchymoses, bruises)
Neurological/Psychiatric	• Brief assessment of mental status including: – Orientation to time, place, and person – Mood and affect (e.g., depression, anxiety, agitation

Content and Documentation Requirements

Level of Exam	Perform and Document:
Problem Focused	One to five elements identified by a bullet.
Expanded Problem Focused	At least six elements identified by a bullet.
Detailed	At least twelve elements identified by a bullet.
Comprehensive	Perform all elements identified by a bullet; document every element in each box with a shaded border and at least one element in each box with an unshaded border.

Musculoskeletal Examination

System/Body Area	Elements of Examination
Constitutional	• Measurement of any three of the following seven vital signs: (1) sitting or standing blood pressure, (2) supine blood pressure, (3) pulse rate and regularity, (4) respiration, (5) temperature, (6) height, (7) weight (may be measured and recorded by ancillary staff) • General appearance of patient (e.g., development, nutrition, body habitus, deformities, attention to grooming)
Head and Face	
Eyes	

System/Body Area	Elements of Examination
Ears, Nose, Mouth, and Throat	
Neck	
Respiratory	
Cardiovascular	• Examination of peripheral vascular system by observation (e.g., swelling, varicosities) and palpation (e.g., pulses, temperature, edema, tenderness)
Chest (Breasts)	
Gastrointestinal (Abdomen)	
Genitourinary	
Lymphatic	• Palpation of lymph nodes in neck, axillae, groin, and/or other location

Musculoskeletal	• Examination of gait and station
	• Examination of joint(s), bone(s), and muscle(s)/tendon(s) of four of the following six areas: (1) head and neck; (2) spine, ribs, and pelvis; (3) right upper extremity; (4) left upper extremity; (5) right lower extremity; and (6) left lower extremity. The examination of a given area includes:
	  – Inspection, percussion, and/or palpation with notation of any misalignment, asymmetry, crepitation, defects, tenderness, masses, or effusions
	  – Assessment of range of motion with notation of any pain (e.g., straight leg raising), crepitation, or contracture
	  – Assessment of stability with notation of any dislocation (luxation), subluxation, or laxity
	  – Assessment of muscle strength and tone (e.g., flaccid, cog wheel, spastic) with notation of any atrophy or abnormal movements
	NOTE: For the comprehensive level of examination, all four of the elements identified by a bullet must be performed and documented for each of four anatomic areas. For the three lower levels of examination, each element is counted separately for each body area. For example, assessing range of motion in two extremities constitutes two elements.

Extremities	[See musculoskeletal and skin]
Skin	• Inspection and/or palpation of skin and subcutaneous tissue (e.g., scars, rashes, lesions, cafe-au-lait spots, ulcers) in four of the following six areas: (1) head and neck; (2) trunk; (3) right upper extremity; (4) left upper extremity; (5) right lower extremity; and (6) left lower extremity. NOTE: For the comprehensive level, the examination of four anatomic areas must be performed and documented. For the three lower levels of examination, each body area is counted separately. For example, inspection and/or palpation of the skin and subcutaneous tissue of two extremities constitutes two elements.

Neurological/Psychiatric	• Test coordination (e.g., finger/nose, heel/knee/shin, rapid alternating movements in the upper and lower extremities, evaluation of fine motor coordination in young children)
	• Examination of deep tendon reflexes and/or nerve stretch test with notation of pathological reflexes (e.g., Babinski)
	• Examination of sensation (e.g., by touch, pin, vibration, proprioception)
	• Brief assessment of mental status including:
	  – Orientation to time, place, and person
	  – Mood and affect (e.g., depression, anxiety, agitation)

Content and Documentation Requirements

Level of Exam	*Perform and Document:*
Problem Focused	One to five elements identified by a bullet.
Expanded Problem Focused	At least six elements identified by a bullet.
Detailed	At least twelve elements identified by a bullet.
Comprehensive	Perform all elements identified by a bullet; document every element in each box with a shaded border and at least one element in each box with an unshaded border.

Neurological Examination

System/Body Area	*Elements of Examination*
Constitutional	• Measurement of any three of the following seven vital signs: (1) sitting or standing blood pressure, (2) supine blood pressure, (3) pulse rate and regularity, (4) respiration, (5) temperature, (6) height, (7) weight (may be measured and recorded by ancillary staff) • General appearance of patient (e.g., development, nutrition, body habitus, deformities, attention to grooming)
Head and Face	
Ears, Nose, Mouth, and Throat	• Ophthalmoscopic examination of optic discs (e.g., size, C/D ratio, appearance) and posterior segments (e.g., vessel changes, exudates, hemorrhages)
Neck	
Respiratory	
Cardiovascular	• Examination of carotid arteries (e.g., pulse amplitude, bruits) • Auscultation of heart with notation of abnormal sounds and murmurs • Examination of peripheral vascular system by observation (e.g., swelling, varicosities) and palpation (e.g., pulses, temperature, edema, tenderness)
Chest (Breasts)	
Gastrointestinal (Abdomen)	

System/Body Area	Elements of Examination
Genitourinary	
Lymphatic	

Musculoskeletal	• Examination of gait and station
	• Assessment of motor function including:
	   − Muscle strength in upper and lower extremities
	   − Muscle tone in upper and lower extremities (e.g., flaccid, cog wheel, spastic) with notation of any atrophy or abnormal movements (e.g., fasciculation, tardive dyskinesia)

Extremities	[See musculoskeletal]
Skin	

Neurological/ Psychiatric	• Evaluation of higher integrative functions including:
	   − Orientation to time, place, and person
	   − Recent and remote memory
	   − Attention span and concentration
	   − Language (e.g., naming objects, repeating phrases, spontaneous speech)
	   − Fund of knowledge (e.g., awareness of current events, past history, vocabulary)
	• Test the following cranial nerves:
	   − 2nd cranial nerve (e.g., visual acuity, visual fields, fundi)
	   − 3rd, 4th, and 6th cranial nerves (e.g., pupils, eye movements)
	   − 5th cranial nerve (e.g., facial sensation, corneal reflexes)
	   − 7th cranial nerve (e.g., facial symmetry, strength)
	   − 8th cranial nerve (e.g., hearing with tuning fork, whispered voice, and/or finger rub)
	   − 9th cranial nerve (e.g., spontaneous or reflex palate movement)
	   − 11th cranial nerve (e.g., shoulder shrug strength)
	   − 12th cranial nerve (e.g., tongue protrusion)
	• Examination of sensation (e.g., by touch, pin, vibration, proprioception)
	• Examination of deep tendon reflexes in upper and lower extremities with notation of pathological reflexes (e.g., Babinski)
	• Test coordination (e.g., finger/nose, heel/knee/shin, rapid alternating movements in the upper and lower extremities, evaluation of fine motor coordination in young children)

Content and Documentation Requirements

Level of Exam	Perform and Document:
Problem Focused	One to five elements identified by a bullet.
Expanded Problem Focused	At least six elements identified by a bullet.
Detailed	At least twelve elements identified by a bullet.
Comprehensive	Perform all elements identified by a bullet; document every element in each box with a shaded border and at least one element in each box with an unshaded border.

Psychiatric Examination

System/Body Area	Elements of Examination
Constitutional	• Measurement of any three of the following seven vital signs:(1) sitting or standing blood pressure, (2) supine blood pressure, (3) pulse rate and regularity, (4) respiration, (5) temperature, (6) height, (7) weight (may be measured and recorded by ancillary staff) • General appearance of patient (e.g., development, nutrition, body habitus, deformities, attention to grooming)
Head and Face	
Ears, Nose, Mouth, and Throat	
Neck	
Respiratory	
Cardiovascular	
Chest (Breasts)	
Gastrointestinal (Abdomen)	
Genitourinary	
Lymphatic	
Musculoskeletal	• Assessment of muscle strength and tone (e.g., flaccid, cog wheel, spastic) with notation of any atrophy and abnormal movements • Examination of gait and station
Extremities	
Skin	
Neurological/ Psychiatric	• Description of speech including: rate, volume, articulation, coherence, and spontaneity with notation of abnormalities (e.g., perseveration, paucity of language) • Description of thought processes including: rate of thoughts, content of thoughts (e.g., logical vs. illogical, tangential), abstract reasoning, and computation • Description of associations (e.g., loose, tangential, circumstantial, intact) • Description of abnormal or psychotic thoughts including: hallucinations, delusions, preoccupation with violence, homicidal or suicidal ideation, and obsessions • Description of the patient's judgment (e.g., concerning everyday activities and social situations) and insight (e.g., concerning psychiatric condition)

Neurological/ Psychological	• Complete mental status examination including:
	  – Orientation to time, place, and person
	  – Recent and remote memory
	  – Attention span and concentration
	  – Language (e.g., naming objects, repeating phrases)
	  – Fund of knowledge (e.g., awareness of current events, past history, vocabulary)
	  – Mood and affect (e.g., depression, anxiety, agitation, hypo-mania, lability)

Content and Documentation Requirements

Level of Exam	Perform and Document:
Problem Focused	One to five elements identified by a bullet.
Expanded Problem Focused	At least six elements identified by a bullet.
Detailed	At least nine elements identified by a bullet.
Comprehensive	Perform all elements identified by a bullet; document every element in each box with a shaded border and at least one element in each box with an unshaded border.

Respiratory Examination

System/Body Area	Elements of Examination
Constitutional	• Measurement of any three of the following seven vital signs:(1) sitting or standing blood pressure, (2) supine blood pressure, (3) pulse rate and regularity, (4) respiration, (5) temperature, (6) height, (7) weight (may be measured and recorded by ancillary staff) • General appearance of patient (e.g., development, nutrition, body habitus, deformities, attention to grooming)
Head and Face	
Eyes	
Ears, Nose, Mouth, and Throat	• Inspection of nasal mucosa, septum, and turbinates • Inspection of teeth and gums • Examination of oropharynx (e.g., oral mucosa, hard and soft palates, tongue, tonsils, and posterior pharynx)
Neck	• Examination of neck (e.g., masses, overall appearance, symmetry, tracheal position, crepitus) • Examination of thyroid (e.g., enlargement, tenderness, mass) • Examination of jugular veins (e.g., distension; a, v, or cannon a waves)
Respiratory	• Inspection of chest with notation of symmetry and expansion • Assessment of respiratory effort (e.g., intercostal retractions, use of accessory muscles, diaphragmatic movement) • Percussion of chest (e.g., dullness, flatness, hyperresonance) • Palpation of chest (e.g., tactile fremitus) • Auscultation of lungs (e.g., breath sounds, adventitious sounds, rubs)
Cardiovascular	• Auscultation of heart including sounds, abnormal sounds, and murmurs • Examination of peripheral vascular system by observation (e.g., swelling, varicosities) and palpation (e.g., pulses, temperature, edema, tenderness)
Chest (Breasts)	
Gastrointestinal (Abdomen)	• Examination of abdomen with notation of presence of masses or tenderness • Examination of liver and spleen

Genitourinary	
Lymphatic	• Palpation of lymph nodes in neck, axillae, groin, and/or other location
Musculoskeletal	• Assessment of muscle strength and tone (e.g., flaccid, cog wheel, spastic) with notation of any atrophy and abnormal movements • Examination of gait and station
Extremities	• Inspection and palpation of digits and nails (e.g., clubbing, cyanosis, inflammation, petechiae, ischemia, infections, nodes)
Skin	• Inspection and/or palpation of skin and subcutaneous tissue (e.g., rashes, lesions, ulcers)

Neurological/ Psychiatric	• Brief assessment of mental status including:
	  – Orientation to time, place, and person
	  – Mood and affect (e.g., depression, anxiety, agitation)

Content and Documentation Requirements

Level of Exam	*Perform and Document:*
Problem Focused	One to five elements identified by a bullet.
Expanded Problem Focused	At least six elements identified by a bullet.
Detailed	At least twelve elements identified by a bullet.
Comprehensive	Perform all elements identified by a bullet; document every element in each box with a shaded border and at least one element in each box with an unshaded border.

Skin Examination

System/Body Area	*Elements of Examination*
Constitutional	• Measurement of any three of the following seven vital signs: (1) sitting or standing blood pressure, (2) supine blood pressure, (3) pulse rate and regularity, (4) respiration, (5) temperature, (6) height, (7) weight (may be measured and recorded by ancillary staff) • General appearance of patient (e.g., development, nutrition, body habitus, deformities, attention to grooming)
Head and Face	
Eyes	• Inspection of conjunctivae and lids
Ears, Nose, Mouth, and Throat	• Inspection of lips, teeth, and gums • Examination of oropharynx (e.g., oral mucosa, hard and soft palates, tongue, tonsils, posterior pharynx)
Neck	• Examination of thyroid (e.g., enlargement, tenderness, mass)
Respiratory	
Cardiovascular	• Examination of peripheral vascular system by observation (e.g., swelling, varicosities) and palpation (e.g., pulses, temperature, edema, tenderness)
Chest (Breasts)	

System/Body Area	Elements of Examination
Gastrointestinal (Abdomen)	• Examination of liver and spleen • Examination of anus for condyloma and other lesions
Genitourinary	
Lymphatic	• Palpation of lymph nodes in neck, axillae, groin, and/or other location
Musculoskeletal	
Extremities	• Inspection and palpation of digits and nails (e.g., clubbing, cyanosis, inflammation, petechiae, ischemia, infections, nodes)

Skin	• Palpation of scalp and inspection of hair of scalp, eyebrows, face, chest, pubic area (when indicated), and extremities
	• Inspection and/or palpation of skin and subcutaneous tissue (e.g., rashes, lesions, ulcers, susceptibility to and presence of photo damage) in eight of the following ten areas:
	  – Head, including the face
	  – Neck
	  – Chest, including breasts and axillae
	  – Abdomen
	  – Genitalia, groin, buttocks
	  – Back
	  – Right upper extremity
	  – Left upper extremity
	  – Right lower extremity
	  – Left lower extremity

Neurological/ Psychiatric	NOTE: For the comprehensive level, the examination of at least eight anatomic areas must be performed and documented. For the three lower levels of examination, each body area is counted separately. For example, inspection and/or palpation of the skin and subcutaneous tissue of the right upper extremity and the left upper extremity constitutes two elements.
	• Inspection of eccrine and apocrine glands of skin and subcutaneous tissue with identification and location of any hyperhidrosis, chromhidrosis, or bromhidrosis
	• Brief assessment of mental status including:
	  – Orientation to time, place, and person
	  – Mood and affect (e.g., depression, anxiety, agitation)

Content and Documentation Requirements

Level of Exam	Perform and Document:
Problem Focused	One to five elements identified by a bullet.
Expanded Problem Focused	At least six elements identified by a bullet.
Detailed	At least twelve elements identified by a bullet.
Comprehensive	Perform all elements identified by a bullet; document every element in each box with a shaded border and at least one element in each box with an unshaded border.

Documentation of the Complexity of Medical Decision Making

The levels of E/M services recognize four types of medical decision making (straightforward, low complexity, moderate complexity, and high complexity). Medical decision making refers to the complexity of establishing a diagnosis and/or selecting a management option as measured by:

- The number of possible diagnoses and/or the number of management options that must be considered;
- The amount and/or complexity of medical records, diagnostic tests, and/or other information that must be obtained, reviewed, and analyzed; and
- The risk of significant complications, morbidity and/or mortality, as well as comorbidities, associated with the patient's presenting problem(s), the diagnostic procedure(s), and/or the possible management options.

The chart on page 195 shows the progression of the elements required for each level of medical decision making. To qualify for a given type of decision making, two of the three elements in the table must be either met or exceeded.

Each of the elements of medical decision making is described below.

Number of Diagnoses or Management Options

The number of possible diagnoses and/or the number of management options that must be considered is based on the number and types of problems addressed during the encounter, the complexity of establishing a diagnosis, and the management decisions that are made by the physician.

Generally, decision making with respect to a diagnosed problem is easier than that for an identified but undiagnosed problem. The number and type of diagnostic tests employed may be an indicator of the number of possible diagnoses. Problems that are improving or resolving are less complex than those that are worsening or failing to change as expected. The need to seek advice from others is another indicator of complexity of diagnostic or management problems.

- •DG: *For each encounter, an assessment, clinical impression, or diagnosis should be documented. It may be explicitly stated or implied in documented decisions regarding management plans and/or further evaluation.*
    - *For a presenting problem with an established diagnosis the record should reflect whether the problem is: (a) improved, well controlled, resolving, or resolved; or, (b) inadequately controlled, worsening, or failing to change as expected.*
    - *For a presenting problem without an established diagnosis, the assessment or clinical impression may be stated in the form of differential diagnoses or as a "possible," "probable," or "rule out" (R/O) diagnosis.*

- •DG: *The initiation of, or changes in, treatment should be documented. Treatment includes a wide range of management options including patient instructions, nursing instructions, therapies, and medications.*

- •DG: *If referrals are made, consultations requested, or advice sought, the record should indi-cate to whom or where the referral or consultation is made or from whom the advice is requested.*

Amount and/or Complexity of Data To Be Reviewed

The amount and complexity of data to be reviewed is based on the types of diagnostic test-ing ordered or reviewed. A decision to obtain and review old medical records and/or obtain history from sources other than the patient increases the amount and complexity of data to be reviewed.

Discussion of contradictory or unexpected test results with the physician who performed or interpreted the test is an indication of the complexity of data being reviewed. On occa-sion the physician who ordered a test may personally review the image, tracing, or specimen to supplement information from the physician who prepared the test report or interpreta-tion; this is another indication of the complexity of data being reviewed.

- •DG: *If a diagnostic service (test or procedure) is ordered, planned, scheduled, or performed at the time of the E/M encounter, the type of service (e.g., lab or X-ray) should be documented.*
- •DG: *The review of lab, radiology, and/or other diagnostic tests should be documented. A simple notation such as "WBC elevated" or "chest X-ray unremarkable" is acceptable. Alternatively, the review may be documented by initialing and dating the report containing the test results.*
- •DG: *A decision to obtain old records or a decision to obtain additional history from the family, caretaker, or other source to supplement that obtained from the patient should be documented.*
- •DG: *Relevant findings from the review of old records, and/or the receipt of additional history from the family, caretaker, or other source to supplement that obtained from the patient should be documented. If there is no relevant information beyond that already obtained, that fact should be documented. A notation of "old records reviewed" or "additional history obtained from family" without elaboration is insufficient.*
- •DG: *The results of discussion of laboratory, radiology, or other diagnostic tests with the physician who performed or interpreted the study should be documented.*
- •DG: *The direct visualization and independent interpretation of an image, tracing, or specimen previously or subsequently interpreted by another physician should be documented.*

Risk of Significant Complications, Morbidity, and/or Mortality

The risk of significant complications, morbidity, and/or mortality is based on the risks associated with the presenting problem(s), the diagnostic procedure(s), and the possible management options.

- •DG: *Comorbidities/underlying diseases or other factors that increase the complexity of medical decision making by increasing the risk of complications, morbidity, and/or mortality should be documented.*
- •DG: *If a surgical or invasive diagnostic procedure is ordered, planned, or scheduled at the time of the E/M encounter, the type of procedure (e.g., laparoscopy) should be documented.*
- •DG: *If a surgical or invasive diagnostic procedure is performed at the time of the E/M encounter, the specific procedure should be documented.*
- •DG: *The referral for or decision to perform a surgical or invasive diagnostic procedure on an urgent basis should be documented or implied.*

The following table may be used to help determine whether the risk of significant complications, morbidity, and/or mortality is minimal, low, moderate, or high. Because the determination of risk is complex and not readily quantifiable, the table includes common clinical examples rather than absolute measures of risk. The assessment of risk of the presenting problem(s) is based on the risk related to the disease process anticipated between the present encounter and the next one. The assessment of risk of selecting diagnostic procedures and management options is based on the risk during and immediately following any procedures or treatment. The highest level of risk in any one category (presenting problem(s), diagnostic procedure(s), or management options) determines the overall risk.

Table of Risk

Number of Diagnoses or Management Options	Amount and/or Complexity of Data To Be Reviewed	Risk of Complications and/or Morbidity or Mortality	Type of Decision Making
Limited	Multiple	Extensive	Moderate
	Extensive	Minimal	High
	Minimal to None	Low	Straightforward
	Limited		Low Complexity
	Moderate		Moderate Complexity
			High Complexity

Table of Risk

Level of Risk	Presenting Problem(s)	Diagnostic Procedure(s) Ordered	Management Options Selected
Minimal	• One self-limited or minor problem, e.g., cold, insect bite, tinea corporis	• Laboratory tests requiring venipuncture • Chest X-rays • EKG/EEG • Urinalysis • Ultrasound, e.g., echocardiography • KOH prep	• Rest • Gargles • Elastic bandages • Superficial dressings
Low	• Two or more self-limited or minor problems • One stable chronic illness, e.g., well-controlled hypertension, noninsulin–dependent diabetes, cataract, BPH • Acute uncomplicated illness or injury, e.g., cystitis, allergic rhinitis, simple sprain	• Physiologic tests not under stress, e.g., pulmonary function tests • Noncardiovascular imaging studies with contrast, e.g., barium enema • Superficial needle biopsies • Clinical laboratory tests requiring arterial puncture • Skin biopsies	• Over-the-counter drugs • Minor surgery with no identified risk factors • Physical therapy • Occupational therapy • IV fluids without additives
Moderate	• One or more chronic illnesses with mild exacerbation, progression, or side effects of treatment • Two or more stable chronic illnesses • Undiagnosed new problem with uncertain prognosis, e.g., lump in breast • Acute illness with systemic symptoms, e.g., pyelonephritis, pneumonitis, colitis • Acute complicated injury, e.g., head injury with brief loss of consciousness	• Physiologic tests under stress, e.g., cardiac stress test, fetal contraction stress test • Diagnostic endoscopies with no identified risk factors • Deep needle or incisional biopsy • Cardiovascular imaging studies with contrast and no identified risk factors, e.g., arteriogram, cardiac catheterization • Obtain fluid from body cavity, e.g., lumbar puncture, thoracentesis, culdocentesis	• Minor surgery with identified risk factors • Elective major surgery (open, percutaneous, or endoscopic) with no identified risk factors • Prescription drug management • Therapeutic nuclear medicine • IV fluids with additives • Closed treatment of fracture or dislocation without manipulation

| High | • One or more chronic illnesses with severe exacerbation, progression, or side effects of treatment
• Acute or chronic illnesses or injuries that pose a threat to life or bodily function, e.g., multiple trauma, acute renal failure
• MI, pulmonary embolus, severe respiratory distress, progressive severe rheumatoid arthritis, psychiatric illness with potential threat to self or others, peritonitis, acute renal failure
• An abrupt change in neurologic status, e.g., seizure, TIA, weakness, sensory loss | • Cardiovascular imaging studies with contrast with identified risk factors
• Cardiac electrophysiological tests
• Diagnostic endoscopies with identified risk factors
• Discography | • Elective major surgery (open, percutaneous, or endoscopic) with identified risk factors
• Emergency major surgery (open, percutaneous, or endoscopic)
• Parenteral controlled substances
• Drug therapy requiring intensive monitoring for toxicity
• Decision not to resuscitate or to de-escalate care because of poor prognosis |

Documentation of an Encounter Dominated by Counseling or Coordination of Care

In the case where counseling and/or coordination of care dominates (more than 50%) the physician/patient and/or family encounter (face-to-face time in the office or other outpatient setting, floor/unit time in the hospital or nursing facility), time is considered the key or controlling factor to qualify for a particular level of E/M services.

> •DG: *If the physician elects to report the level of service based on counseling and/or coordination of care, the total length of time of the encounter (face-to-face or floor time, as appropriate) should be documented and the record should describe the counseling and/or activities to coordinate care.*

CHAPTER 5

Prescribing

Nurse practitioners (NPs) in 50 states and the District of Columbia have the legal authority to prescribe. The independence of NPs' prescriptive authority varies widely, and, in several states, words other than "prescribe" are used.

In 17 states and the District of Columbia, NPs have explicit legal authority to "prescribe," with no requirement for physician involvement. In one state (Utah), NPs need physician involvement only when prescribing Schedules II–III. In 33 states, NPs have explicit legal authority to prescribe but must have a collaborative relationship with a specific physician. In one state (Michigan), NPs do not have specific legal authority to prescribe, but the law permits physicians to delegate medical functions (see **Exhibit 5-1**). In 48 states and the District of Columbia, NPs may prescribe controlled substances. (See **Exhibit 5-2** for the states that fall into this category.) **Appendix 5-A** presents laws on prescriptive authority for each state.

Controlled Substances

Controlled dangerous substances are narcotics, depressants, stimulants, and hallucinogenic drugs covered under the Controlled Substances Act, a federal law. In 49 states and the District of Columbia, NPs may prescribe controlled substances.

Classification of Controlled Substances

There are five "schedules" of controlled substances:

- *Schedule I*: Schedule I substances have no accepted medical use in the United States and have high abuse potential. Examples are heroin, LSD, MDMA ("ecstasy"), marijuana, and peyote.
- *Schedule II*: Schedule II drugs have a high abuse potential with severe psychic or physical dependence liability and in general are substances that have therapeutic utility. Schedule II narcotics include morphine, codeine, fentanyl, hydromorphone (Dilaudid), meperidine (Demerol), methadone, pantopon, and opium. Stimulants such as amphetamines are included in Schedule II, as well as depressants such as pentobarbital.
- *Schedule III*: Schedule III drugs are stimulants and depressants with an abuse potential that is less than those drugs in Schedules I and II. Schedule III narcotics include mixtures of limited specified quantities of codeine with noncontrolled active ingredients (such as

Tylenol with codeine), and mixtures of amobarbital, pentobarbital, or secobarbital with other noncontrolled medicinal ingredients.

- *Schedule IV*: Schedule IV drugs have less abuse potential than Schedule III and include depressants such as alprazolam, phenobarbital, and chloral hydrate.
- *Schedule V*: Schedule V substances have less abuse potential than Schedule IV and include preparations containing limited quantities of certain narcotic and stimulant drugs generally given for antitussive, antidiarrheal, and analgesic purposes. Examples are buprenorphine and propylhexedrin.

A complete listing of the drugs controlled under the Controlled Substances Act may be found in Title 21, Code of Federal Regulations, Part 1300 to end, Sections 1308.11 through 1308.15. Prescribing references usually provide the class of each drug listed.

Exhibit 5-1   Forms of Prescriptive Authority

**Explicit Legal Authority to Prescribe/
No Physician Involvement Required**
Alaska
Arizona
Colorado
District of Columbia
Hawaii (Schedules III–V)
Idaho
Iowa
Kentucky
Maine
Montana
New Hampshire
New Mexico
North Dakota
Oregon
Rhode Island
South Dakota
Utah—except for Schedules II–III
Vermont
Washington
Wyoming

**Physician May Delegate Authority
to Prescribe**
Georgia
Michigan
Texas

**Explicit Legal Authority to Prescribe/
Physician Collaboration Required**
Alabama

Arkansas
California
Connecticut
Delaware
Florida
Georgia
Illinois
Indiana
Kansas
Louisiana
Maryland
Massachusetts
Minnesota
Mississippi
Missouri
Nebraska
Nevada
New Jersey
New York
North Carolina
Ohio
Oklahoma
Pennsylvania
South Carolina
Tennessee
Texas
Virginia
West Virginia
Wisconsin

Exhibit 5-2   State Regulations of NPs' Prescriptive Activity

---

NP May Prescribe Controlled Substances (except Schedule I, which are not used medically)

Alabama (Schedules III–V)
Alaska
Arizona
Arkansas (not Schedule I–II)
California
Colorado
Connecticut
Delaware
District of Columbia
Georgia (not Schedule I–II)
Hawaii
Idaho
Illinois
Indiana
Iowa
Kansas
Kentucky
Louisiana (not Schedule I–II, except for attention deficit disorder medications)
Maine
Maryland
Massachusetts
Michigan
Minnesota
Mississippi

Missouri (not Schedule I–II)
Montana
Nebraska
Nevada
New Hampshire
New Jersey
New Mexico
New York
North Carolina
North Dakota
Ohio
Oklahoma (not Schedule I–II)
Oregon
Pennsylvania
Rhode Island
South Carolina (not Schedule I–II)
South Dakota
Tennessee
Texas (not Schedule I–II)
Utah
Vermont
Virginia
Washington
West Virginia (not Schedule I–II)
Wisconsin
Wyoming

Drug Enforcement Administration Registration

The federal government—the Drug Enforcement Administration (DEA)—oversees NPs' prescribing of controlled substances. To prescribe controlled substances, an NP must register with the DEA and obtain a DEA number. The NP must use the DEA number on prescriptions for scheduled drugs.

DEA registration is one method of tracking healthcare providers' prescribing practices related to controlled substances. The DEA number is also a method of minimizing unauthorized prescribing; a person who is not authorized to prescribe but who wants to write a prescription for a controlled substance, has a prescription pad, and signs the name of an authorized prescriber will be unable to get the prescription filled if it does not include a DEA number.

Federal registration is based on the applicant's compliance with state and local laws. If a state requires a separate controlled substances license, an NP must obtain that license and submit a copy with the application for a DEA number. If state law does not authorize NPs to prescribe controlled substances, the DEA will not issue DEA numbers.

DEA registration costs $731 for a 3-year term. States may charge for registration as well. To apply for DEA registration, visit the DEA's website (http://www.deadiversion.usdoj.gov /drugreg). Once a DEA number is issued, a renewal application is automatically issued 45 days prior to expiration. Registrants must report, in writing, any change in business location to the DEA. DEA registration is issued in the NP's name at the business address.

Guidelines for Prescribing Legally

NPs should follow these general guidelines when prescribing:

1. Prescribe the right medicine at the right time for the right indication for the right patient.
2. If there is a practice protocol or guidelines in the facility, follow it.
3. If there is no facility-wide protocol, adhere to the standard of care in prescribing. The standard of care for prescribing may be assumed to be the *Physician's Desk Reference* or Epocrates (http://www.epocrates.com).
4. Before prescribing, ask a patient:
   - Are you pregnant?
   - Are you breastfeeding?
   - Are you allergic to any medications?
   - Have you taken [this medicine] before? Did it work? Did it give you any ill effects?
   - Do you have any liver or kidney problems?
   - What other medications are you on?
   - What other medical problems do you have?
5. Address any cross-sensitivities. For example, if a patient is allergic to penicillin, an NP probably should not prescribe Keflex, which has cross-sensitivities with penicillin.
6. Address any contraindications. For example, a patient with chronic hepatitis should not be prescribed a medication that has potential for liver damage unless it is a life or death situation and there is no other choice.
7. Address any drug interactions. For example, theophylline is antagonized by phenytoin and potentiated by macrolide antibiotics.
8. Inform the patient of potential side effects, and ask whether the patient wants to accept the risk of experiencing those side effects.
9. Instruct the patient to call or return if he or she notices any adverse change in his or her condition.

Other considerations when prescribing include the following:

- Can the patient afford the medication? If not, the NP should not count on the patient getting the prescription filled.
- Is the drug to be prescribed in the formulary for the agency or health maintenance organization?
- Is there potential for abuse of the medication? For example, a depressed patient may overdose on a prescribed medication, and a patient with a history of substance abuse may be seeking to continue the habit through a request for pain medication.

- Can the patient read? For example, the author had a personal experience where a patient was not responding to a variety of blood pressure medications. After much trial and error as well as discussion, it was revealed that the patient was not literate. The patient kept his wide assortment of medications on top of the refrigerator. He depended on his wife to dole out the proper medication to him, at the proper time and in the proper dose. When she was not available, which was often, he did not get his medication.

Resources

Buppert, C. (2010). *Prescribing: Avoiding legal pitfalls for NPs.* Law Office of Carolyn Buppert, P.C. Available for purchase at http://www.buppert.com/publications.html

State-by-State Law Prescriptive Authority

Alabama

[The] joint committee shall recommend model practice protocols to be used by certified registered nurse practitioners and certified nurse midwives and a formulary of legend drugs that may be prescribed by these advanced practice nurses, subject to approval by both the State Board of Medical Examiners and the Board of Nursing. The joint committee shall also recommend rules and regulations to establish the ratio of physicians to certified registered nurse practitioners and certified nurse midwives; provided, however, that the rules and regulations shall not limit the ratio to less than two nurse practitioners or midwives to one physician or one certified registered nurse practitioner and one certified nurse midwife to one physician and shall provide for exceptions. The joint committee shall also recommend rules and regulations that establish the manner in which a collaborating physician may designate a covering physician when temporarily unavailable as the collaborating physician.

Citation: Ala. § 34-21-87.

a. Certified registered nurse practitioners and certified nurse midwives, engaged in collaborative practice with physicians practicing under protocols approved in the manner prescribed by this article may prescribe legend drugs to their patients, subject to both of the following conditions:
   1. The drug type, dosage, quantity prescribed, and number of refills shall be authorized in an approved protocol signed by the collaborating physician; and
   2. The drug shall be on the formulary recommended by the joint committee and adopted by the State Board of Medical Examiners and the Board of Nursing.
b. A certified registered nurse practitioner or a certified nurse midwife may not initiate a call-in prescription in the name of a collaborating physician for any drug, whether legend or controlled substance, which the nurse practitioner

or certified nurse midwife is not authorized to prescribe under the protocol signed by the collaborating physician and certified registered nurse practitioner or certified nurse midwife and approved under this section unless the drug is specifically ordered for the patient by the physician, either in writing or by a verbal order which has been reduced to writing, and which has been signed by the physician within a time specified in the rules and regulations approved by the State Board of Medical Examiners and the Board of Nursing.

c. Registered nurses and licensed practical nurses are authorized to administer any legend drug that has been lawfully ordered or prescribed by an authorized practitioner including certified registered nurse practitioners, certified nurse midwives, and/or assistants to physicians.

Citation: Ala. Code § 34-21-86.

1. Certified registered nurse practitioners engaged in collaborative practice with physicians may be granted prescriptive authority upon submission of evidence of completion of an academic course in pharmacology or evidence of integration of pharmacology theory and clinical application in the certified registered nurse practitioner curriculum.

2. Certified registered nurse practitioners practicing under protocols approved in the manner prescribed by Code of Alabama, 1975, Section 34-21-80 et seq. may prescribe legend drugs to their patients, subject to the following conditions:

   a. The drug type, dosage, quantity prescribed, and number of refills shall be authorized in an approved protocol signed by the collaborating physician and the certified registered nurse practitioner. This requirement may be met if written prescriptions adhere to the standard recommended doses of legend drugs as identified in the *Physician's Desk Reference* or Product Information Insert, not to exceed the recommended treatment regimen periods.

   b. The drug shall be included in the formulary recommended by the Joint Committee and adopted by the Board of Nursing and the State Board of Medical Examiners.

3. A certified registered nurse practitioner shall not initiate a call-in prescription in the name of a collaborating physician for any drug, whether legend or controlled substance, which the certified registered nurse practitioner is not authorized to prescribe under the protocol signed by the collaborating physician and certified registered nurse practitioner and approved under this section unless the drug is specifically ordered for the patient by the physician, either in writing or by a verbal order which has been transcribed in writing, and which has been signed by the physician within seven working days or as otherwise specified by the Board of Nursing and the State Board of Medical Examiners.

4. A written prescription for any drug that the certified registered nurse practitioner is authorized to prescribe may be called in to a pharmacy, provided the prescription is entered into the patient's record and signed by the certified registered nurse practitioner.

5. The certified registered nurse practitioner in collaborative practice with prescriptive privileges shall not engage in prescribing for:
   a. Self.
   b. Immediate family members.
   c. Individuals who are not patients of the practice.

6. The certified registered nurse practitioner who is in collaborative practice and has prescriptive privileges may receive and sign for samples of legend drugs that are authorized in the approved formulary for the collaborative practice, provided the certified registered nurse practitioner complies with all applicable state and federal laws and regulations.

7. When prescribing legend drugs a certified registered nurse practitioner shall use a prescription format that includes all of the following:
   a. The name, medical practice site address and telephone number of the collaborating physician or covering physician.
   b. The certified registered nurse practitioner's name printed below or to the side of the physician's name.
   c. The medical practice site address and telephone number of the certified registered nurse practitioner if different from that of the collaborating physician.
   d. The certified registered nurse practitioner's registered nurse license number and identifying prescriptive authority number assigned by the Board of Nursing.
   e. The words "Product Selection Permitted" printed on one side of the prescription form directly beneath a signature line.
   f. The words "Dispense as written" printed on one side of the prescription form directly beneath a signature line.
   g. The date the prescription is issued to the patient.

Citation: Ala. Admin. Code r. 610-X-5-.11.

Upon receipt of a Qualified Alabama Controlled Substances Registration Certificate (QACSC) and a valid registration number issued by the United States Drug Enforcement Administration, a certified registered nurse practitioner (CRNP) or certified nurse midwife (CNM) may prescribe, administer, authorize for administration, or dispense only those controlled substances listed in Schedules III, IV, and V of Article 2, Chapter 2, of this title in accordance with rules adopted by the Board of Medical Examiners and any protocols, formularies, and medical regimens established by the board for regulation of a QACSC.

Citation: ALA. CODE §20-2-253(a).

Alaska

a. The Board will, in its discretion, authorize an advanced nurse practitioner or "ANP" to prescribe and dispense legend drugs in accordance with applicable state and federal laws.
b. *Repealed 3/28/2008.*
c. An advanced nurse practitioner who applies for authorization to prescribe and dispense drugs
   1. must be currently designated as an ANP in Alaska at the time of application;
   2. shall provide evidence of completion of 15 contact hours of education in advanced pharmacology and clinical management of drug therapy within the two-year period immediately before the date of application; and
   3. shall submit a completed application, as required in 12 AAC 44.400(a)(6) accompanied by the application fee established by 12 AAC 02.280.

> *Citation:* Alaska Admin. Code tit. 12, § 44.440.

There is no requirement for physician collaboration.

a. In addition to the legend drug prescriptive and dispensing authority under 12 AAC 44.440, the board will, in its discretion, authorize an advanced nurse practitioner or "ANP" to prescribe and dispense schedule 2-5 controlled substances in accordance with applicable state and federal laws if an applicant
   1. submits a completed application on a form provided by the department; the completed application must include the applicant's
      A. name, address, and phone number;
      B. authorization number as an ANP;
      C. date of birth;
      D. *repealed 12/27/2012;* and
      E. notarized signature certifying that the information in the application is correct to the best of the applicant's knowledge;
   2. *repealed 12/27/2012;* and
   3. pays the application fee established by 12 AAC 02.280.

> *Citation:* Alaska Admin. Code tit. 12, § 44.445.

Arizona

A. The Board shall authorize an RNP to prescribe and dispense (P&D) drugs and devices within the RNP's specialty area and category of practice only if the RNP does all of the following:
   1. Obtains authorization by the Board to practice as a registered nurse practitioner;
   2. Applies for prescribing and dispensing privileges on the application for registered nurse practitioner certification;

3. Submits a completed application on a form provided by the Board that contains all of the following information:
   a. Name, address, and home phone number;
   b. Arizona registered nurse license number, or copy of compact license;
   c. Nurse practitioner specialty;
   d. Nurse practitioner certification number issued by the Board;
   e. Business address and telephone number; and
   f. A sworn statement verifying the truthfulness of the information provided;
4. Submits evidence of completion of a minimum of 45 contact hours of education within the three years immediately preceding the application, covering one or both of the following topics:
   a. _____ Pharmacology
   b. _____ Clinical management of drug therapy, and
5. Submits the required fee.
B. An applicant who is denied P & D authority may request a hearing by filing a written request with the Board within 30 days of service of the Board's order denying the application for P & D authority. Board hearings shall comply with A.R.S. Title 41, Chapter 6, Article 10, and 4 A.A.C. 19, Article 6.

Citation: Ariz. Admin. Code R4-19-511.

A. An RNP granted P & D authority by the Board may:
   1. Prescribe drugs and devices;
   2. Provide for refill of prescription-only drugs and devices for one year from the date of the prescription.
B. An RNP with P & D authority who wishes to prescribe a controlled substance shall obtain a DEA registration number before prescribing a controlled substance. The RNP shall file the DEA registration number with the Board.
C. An RNP with a DEA registration number may prescribe:
   1. A Class II controlled substance as defined in the federal Uniform Controlled Substances Act, 21 U.S.C. § 801 et seq., or Arizona's Uniform Controlled Substances Act, A.R.S. Title 36, Chapter 27, but shall not prescribe refills of the prescription;
   2. A Class III or IV controlled substance, as defined in the federal Uniform Controlled Substances Act or Arizona's Uniform Controlled Substances Act, and may prescribe a maximum of five refills in six months; and
   3. A Class V controlled substance, as defined in the federal Uniform Controlled Substances Act or Arizona's Uniform Controlled Substances Act, and may prescribe refills for a maximum of one year.
D. An RNP whose DEA registration is revoked or expires shall not prescribe controlled substances. An RNP whose DEA registration is revoked or limited shall report the action to the Board.

E. In all outpatient settings or at the time of hospital discharge, an RNP with P & D authority shall personally provide a patient or the patient's representative with the name of the drug, directions for use, and any special instructions, precautions, or storage requirements necessary for safe and effective use of the drug if any of the following occurs:

1. A new drug is prescribed or there is a change in the dose, form, or direction for use in a previously prescribed drug;
2. In the RNP's professional judgment, these instructions are warranted; or
3. The patient or patient's representative requests instruction.

F. An RNP with P & D authority shall ensure that all prescription orders contain the following:

1. The RNP's name, address, telephone number, and specialty area;
2. The prescription date;
3. The name and address of the patient;
4. The full name of the drug, strength, dosage form, and directions for use;
5. The letters "DAW," or "dispense as written," "do not substitute," "medically necessary" or any similar statement on the face of the prescription form if intending to prevent substitution of the drug;
6. The RNP's DEA registration number, if applicable; and
7. The RNP's signature.

Citation: Ariz. Admin. Code R4-19-512.

Arkansas

An advanced practice nurse with a certificate of prescriptive authority may receive and prescribe drugs, medications, or therapeutic devices appropriate to an advanced practice nurse's area of practice in accordance with rules established by the Board.

Citation: Ark. Code Ann. § 17-87-310(b)(1).

An advanced practice nurse may prescribe Schedule III-V drugs.

Citation: Ark. Code Ann. § 17-87-310(b)(2).

The Arkansas State Board of Nursing may grant a certificate of prescriptive authority to an advanced practice nurse who:

- Submits proof of successful completion of a board-approved advanced pharmacology course that shall include preceptorial experience in the prescription of drugs, medicine, and therapeutic devices; and
- Has a collaborative practice with a physician, who is licensed under the Arkansas Medical Practices Act, §§ 17-95-201–7-95-207, 17-95-301–17-95-305, and 17-95-401–17-95-411, and who has a practice comparable in scope, specialty or expertise to that of the advanced practice nurse on file with the board.

Citation: Ark. Code Ann. § 17-87-310(a).

California

Neither this chapter nor any other provision of law shall be construed to prohibit a nurse practitioner from furnishing or ordering drugs or devices when all of the following apply:

a. The drugs or devices are furnished or ordered by a nurse practitioner in accordance with standardized procedures or protocols developed by the nurse practitioner and the supervising physician and surgeon when the drugs or devices furnished or ordered are consistent with the nurse practitioner's educational preparation or for which clinical competency has been established and maintained.

b. The nurse practitioner is functioning pursuant to standardized procedure, as defined by Section 2725, or protocol. The standardized procedure or protocol shall be developed and approved by the supervising physician and surgeon, the nurse practitioner, and the facility administrator or the designee.

c. 1. The standardized procedure or protocol covering the furnishing of drugs or devices shall specify which nurse practitioner may furnish or order drugs or devices, which drugs or devices may be furnished or ordered, under what circumstances, the extent of physician and surgeon supervision, the method of periodic review of the nurse practitioner's competence, including peer review, and review of the provisions of the standardized procedure.

   2. In addition to the requirements in paragraph (1), for Schedule II controlled substance protocols, the provision for furnishing Schedule II controlled substances shall address the diagnosis of the illness, injury, or condition for which the Schedule II controlled substance is to be furnished.

d. The furnishing or ordering of drugs or devices by a nurse practitioner occurs under physician and surgeon supervision. Physician and surgeon supervision shall not be construed to require the physical presence of the physician, but does include: (1) collaboration on the development of the standardized procedure, (2) approval of the standardized procedure, and (3) availability by telephonic contact at the time of patient examination by the nurse practitioner.

e. For purposes of this section, no physician and surgeon shall supervise more than four nurse practitioners at one time.

f. 1. Drugs or devices furnished or ordered by a nurse practitioner may include Schedule II through Schedule V controlled substances under the California Uniform Controlled Substances Act . . . and shall be further limited to those drugs agreed upon by the nurse practitioner and physician and surgeon and specified in the standardized procedure.

   2. When Schedule II or III controlled substances . . . are furnished or ordered by a nurse practitioner, the controlled substances shall be

furnished or ordered in accordance with a patient-specific protocol approved by the treating or supervising physician. A copy of the section of the nurse practitioner's standardized procedure relating to controlled substances shall be provided, upon request, to any licensed pharmacist who dispenses drugs or devices, when there is uncertainty about the nurse practitioner furnishing the order.

g. 1. The board has certified that in accordance with Section 2836.3 the nurse practitioner has satisfactorily completed (1) at least 6 month's physician and surgeon-supervised experience in the furnishing or ordering of drugs or devices and (2) a course in pharmacology covering the drugs or devices to be furnished or ordered under this section.

2. Nurse practitioners, who are certified by the board and hold an active furnishing number, who are authorized through standardized procedures or protocols to furnish Schedule II controlled substances, and who are registered with the United States Drug Enforcement Administration, shall complete, as part of their continuing education requirements, a course including Schedule II controlled substances based on the standards developed by the board. The board shall establish the requirements for satisfactory completion of this subsection.

h. Use of the term "furnishing" in this section, in health facilities defined in Section 1250 of the Health and Safety Code, shall include (1) the ordering of a drug or device in accordance with the standardized procedure and (2) transmitting an order of a supervising physician and surgeon.

i. "Drug order" or "order," for purposes of this section, means an order for medication which is dispensed to or for an ultimate user, issued by a nurse practitioner as an individual practitioner, within the meaning of Section 1306.02 of Title 21 of the Code of Federal Regulations. Notwithstanding any other provision of law, (1) a drug order issued pursuant to this section shall be treated in the same manner as a prescription of the supervising physician; (2) all references to "prescription" in this code and the Health and Safety Code shall include drug orders issued by nurse practitioners; and (3) the signature of a nurse practitioner on the drug order issued in accordance with this section shall be deemed to be the signature of a prescriber for purposes of this code and the Health and Safety Code.

Citation: Cal. Bus. & Prof. Code § 2836.1.

Furnishing or ordering of drugs or devices by nurse practitioners is defined to mean the act of making a pharmaceutical agent or agents available to the patient in strict accordance with a standardized procedure. All nurse practitioners who are authorized pursuant to Section 2836.1 to furnish or issue drug orders for controlled substances shall register with the United States Drug Enforcement Administration.

Citation: Cal. Bus. & Prof. Code § 2836.2.

Colorado

An advanced practice nurse who is listed on the advanced practice registry, has a license in good standing without disciplinary sanctions issued pursuant to Section 12-38-111, and has fulfilled requirements established by the board pursuant to this section may be authorized by the board to prescribe controlled substances or prescription drugs as defined in article 22 of this title.

Citation: Colo. Rev. Stat. Ann. § 12-38-111.6(1).

For detailed requirements, see the Colorado Board of Nursing Rules, Ch. XV.

Connecticut

In all settings, the advanced practice registered nurse may, in collaboration with a physician licensed to practice medicine in this state, prescribe, dispense, and administer medical therapeutics and corrective measures and may request, sign for, receive, and dispense drugs in the form of professional samples. . . .

Citation: Conn. Gen. Stat. Ann. § 20-87a(b).

Relative to the exercise of prescriptive authority, the collaboration between an advanced practice registered nurse and a physician shall be in writing and shall address the level of schedule II and III controlled substances that the advanced practice registered nurse may prescribe and provide a method to review patient outcomes, including, but not limited to, the review of medical therapeutics, corrective measures, laboratory tests and other diagnostic procedures that the advanced practice registered nurse may prescribe, dispense and administer.

Citation: Conn. Gen. Stat. Ann. §20-87a(b).

Delaware

Those individuals who wish to engage in independent practice without written guidelines or protocols and/or wish to have independent prescriptive authority shall apply for such privilege or privileges to the Joint Practice Committee and do so only in collaboration with a licensed physician, dentist, podiatrist, or licensed healthcare delivery system. This does not include those individuals who have protocols and/or waiver approved by the Board of Medical Licensure and Discipline.

Citation: Del. Code Ann. tit. 24, § 1902(b)(2).

The "Joint Practice Committee" with the approval of the Board of Medical Licensure and Discipline, shall have the authority to grant, restrict, suspend, or revoke practice or independent practice authorization, and the Joint Practice Committee with the approval of the Board of Medical Licensure and Discipline shall be responsible for promulgating rules and regulations to implement the provisions of this chapter regarding "advanced practice nurses" who have been granted authority for independent practice and/or independent prescriptive authority.

Citation: Del. Code Ann. tit. 24, § 1906(20).

APNs may prescribe, administer, and dispense legend medications including Schedule II-V controlled substances, (as defined in the Controlled Substance Act and labeled in compliance with 24 Del.C. §2536(C), parenteral medications, medical therapeutics, devices and diagnostics.

Citation: DEL. ADMIN. CODE, TIT. 24, §8.18.1.

District of Columbia

An advanced practice registered nurse may initiate, monitor, and alter drug therapies.

Citation: D.C. Stat. § 3-1206.4(1).

The advanced practice registered nurse may perform actions of medical diagnosis, treatment, prescription, and other functions authorized by this subchapter.

Citation: D.C. Stat. § 3-1206.1.

A nurse-practitioner shall have authority to prescribe those drugs on Schedules II through V established pursuant to the District of Columbia Uniform Controlled Substances Act of 1981, D.C. Code §§ 33-501 et seq., that are authorized by the protocol under which the nurse-practitioner is practicing.

Citation: D. C. Municipal Regs. §5910.1.

Florida

The scope of practice for all categories of advanced registered nurse practitioner's (ARNP) shall include those functions which the ARNP has been educated to perform including the monitoring and altering of drug therapies, and initiation of appropriate therapies, according to the established protocol and consistent with the practice setting.

Citation: Fla. Admin. Code Ch. 64B9-4.009.

Georgia

b. 1. A physician may delegate to:
    A. A physician's assistant in accordance with a job description; or
    B. A nurse recognized by the Georgia Board of Nursing as a certified nurse midwife, certified registered nurse anesthetist, certified nurse practitioner, or clinical nurse specialist, psychiatric/mental health in

accordance with a nurse protocol the authority to order controlled substances selected from a formulary of such drugs established by the Composite State Board of Medical Examiners and the authority to order dangerous drugs, medical treatments, and diagnostic studies.

Citation: Ga. Code Ann. 43-34-26.1 (b)(1)(A) and (B).

In addition to and without limiting the authority granted pursuant to Code Section 43-34-23, a physician may delegate to an advanced practice registered nurse in accordance with a nurse protocol agreement the authority to order drugs, medical devices, medical treatments, diagnostic studies, or in life-threatening situations, radiographic imaging tests.

Citation: Ga. Code Ann. § 43-34-25(b).

"Nurse protocol agreement" means a written document mutually agreed upon and signed by an advanced practice registered nurse and a physician, by which document the physician delegates to that advanced practice registered nurse the authority to perform certain medical acts pursuant to this Code section, and which acts may include, without being limited to, the ordering of drugs, medical devices, medical treatments, diagnostic studies, or in life-threatening situations radiographic imaging tests. Such agreements shall conform to the provisions set forth in Subsection (c) of this Code section.

Citation: Ga. Code Ann. § 43-34-26.3(a)(10).

"Order" means to prescribe pursuant to a nurse protocol agreement which drug, medical device, medical treatment, diagnostic study, or in life-threatening situations, radiographic imaging test is appropriate for a patient and to communicate the same in writing, orally, via facsimile, or electronically.

Citation: Ga. Code Ann. § 43-34-26.3(a)(11).

Hawaii

The board shall grant prescriptive authority to qualified advanced practice registered nurses and shall designate the requirements for advanced nursing practice related to prescriptive authority. The board shall determine the exclusionary formulary for qualified advanced practice registered nurses who are granted prescriptive authority.

Citation: Haw. Statutes § 457-8.6(a).

Advanced practice registered nurses shall be considered qualified if they have met the requirements of section 457-8.5(a), and have met the advanced pharmacology requirements for initial prescriptive authority pursuant to rules adopted by the board. Only qualified advanced practice registered nurses authorized to diagnose, prescribe, and institute therapy or referrals of patients to health care agencies, health care providers, and community resources and, only as appropriate, to the practice specialty in which the advanced practice nurse is qualified, may:

1. Prescribe and administer over the counter drugs, legend drugs, and controlled substances pursuant to this chapter and to chapter 329 and request, receive, and dispense manufacturers' prepackaged samples of over the counter and non-controlled legend drugs to patients under their care; provided that an advanced practice registered nurse shall not request, receive, or sign for professional controlled substance samples;
2. Prescribe, order, and dispense medical devices and equipment; and
3. Plan and initiate a therapeutic regimen that includes nutritional, diagnostic, and supportive services including home health care, hospice, and physical and occupational therapy.

Citation: Haw. Statutes § 457-8.6(d).

a. The requirements for prescriptive authority are as follows:
   1. A completed application for prescriptive authority for controlled or non-controlled substances provided by the board and submitted with all appropriate documents (unless currently filed with the board) and required fees;
   2. Proof of a current, unencumbered license as a registered nurse in this State and in all other states in which the nurse has a current and active license;
   3. Proof of a current, unencumbered recognition or license as an advanced practice registered nurse in this State and in all other states in which the nurse has a current and active recognition or license as an advanced practice registered nurse or similar designation;
   4. Proof of a current, unencumbered certification for specialized and advanced nursing practice from a national certifying body recognized by the board;
   5. Proof of successful completion of an accredited graduate-level nursing program with a significant educational and practical concentration on the direct care of patients, recognized by the board, leading to a master's degree as a certified registered nurse anesthetist, a nurse midwife, a clinical nurse specialist, or a nurse practitioner;
   6. Proof of successful completion of at least thirty contact hours, as part of a master's degree program from an accredited, board-recognized college or university, of advanced pharmacology education, including advanced pharmacotherapeutics that is integrated into the curriculum, within the three-year time period immediately preceding the date of application. If completed more than the three-year time period, then one of the following shall be completed within the three-year time period immediately preceding the date of application for initial prescriptive authority:

    A. At least thirty contact hours of advanced pharmacology, including advanced pharmacotherapeutics, from an accredited, board-recognized college or university; or

    B. At least thirty contact hours of continuing education ("CE") approved by board-recognized national certifying bodies in advanced pharmacology, including advanced pharmacotherapeutics related to the applicant's scope of nursing practice specialty; and

7. Payment of a non-refundable application fee.

b. APRNs authorized to prescribe non-controlled substances and who subsequently wish to prescribed controlled substances shall submit the appropriate application for prescriptive authority for controlled substances and meet the requirements of this chapter.

c. Upon satisfying all requirements in chapter 457, HRS, and this chapter, and payment of required fees, the board shall grant prescriptive authority to the APRN.

d. Nothing in this section shall preclude a registered nurse, a licensed practical nurse, or an APRN from carrying out the prescribed medical orders of a license dentist, physician, osteopath, or podiatrist license in accordance with chapters 448, 453, or 463E, HRS, or the orders of a recognized APRN granted prescriptive authority in accordance with this chapter.

Citation: Haw. Admin. R. § 16-89-119.

a. The board of nursing shall consider the recommendations of the joint formulary advisory committee to determine the drugs or categories of drugs listed in the exclusionary formulary for APRNs granted prescriptive authority. The current formulary, attached to this chapter as "Exhibit A", lists the drugs or categories of drugs that shall be prescribed by the APRN.

b. The Exclusionary Formulary, and any revised formularies, shall be made available to licensed pharmacies at the request of the pharmacy at no cost.

c. The APRN shall comply with all applicable state and federal laws and rules relating to prescribing and administering of drugs. The APRN with prescriptive authority shall only prescribe, order, and dispense medical devices and equipment appropriate to the APRN's specialty.

d. Prescriptions by an APRN with prescriptive authority shall be written in accordance with 16-95-82.

Citation: Haw. Admin. R. § 16-89-122.

Prescriptive authority renewal for recognized advanced practice registered nurses.

a. Prescriptive authority for each APRN shall expire on June 30 of every odd-numbered year and shall be renewed biennially. APRNs seeking renewal of prescriptive authority shall also satisfy the renewal requirements for APRN recognition pursuant to section 16-89-87 and submit the following:

1. Evidence of current certification in the nursing practice specialty by a board-recognized national certifying body; and
2. Documentation of successful completion, during the prior biennium, of thirty contact hours of appropriate continuing education as determined by the board in the practice specialty area, eight contact hours of which shall be in pharmacology, including pharmacotherapeutics, related to the APRN's clinical practice specialty area, approved by board-recognized national certifying bodies, the American Nurses Association, the American Medical Association, or accredited colleges or universities. Documentation of successful completion of continuing education required for recertification by a recognized national certifying body, earned within the current renewal biennium, may be accepted in lieu of the thirty hours of continuing education required for renewal.

b. Failure, neglect, or refusal to renew the prescriptive authority by a recognized APRN on or before June 30 of each odd-numbered year shall result in automatic forfeiture of prescriptive authority. Failure of the APRN to renew prescriptive authority shall cause the APRN prescriptive authority to forfeit on the day after the expiration date. The APRN shall not prescribe until prescriptive authority has been restored. Renewal application deadlines shall be as established by the board. Prescriptive authority may be restored within six months from the date of forfeiture, provided the restoration application is in compliance with subsection (a) and is submitted with an additional payment of a restoration fee. Failure to restore within the time frame provided shall constitute an automatic termination of the prescriptive authority. Thereafter, to be eligible for prescriptive authority, the applicant shall meet the requirements of section 16-89-119.

c. Any APRN subject to this chapter who fails to renew his or her prescriptive authority and continues to practice as a recognized APRN with prescriptive authority shall be considered an illegal practitioner and shall be subject to penalties provided for by law.

Citation: Haw. Admin. R. § 16-89-123.

Idaho

Advanced practice registered nurses. . . are authorized to perform advanced nursing practice, which may include the prescribing, administering and dispensing of therapeutic pharmacologic agents, as defined by board rules.

Citation: Idaho Code § 54-1402(1).

Prescriptive and Dispensing Authorization. Means the legal permission to prescribe, deliver, distribute and dispense pharmacologic and non-pharmacologic agents to a client in compliance with Board rules and applicable federal and state laws. Pharmacologic agents include legend and Schedule II through V controlled substances.

Citation: IDAHO ADMIN. CODE §23.01.01.271.15.

An application for the authority to prescribe and dispense pharmacologic and non-pharmacologic agents may be made as part of initial licensure application or by separate application at a later date. Advanced practice registered nurses who complete their APRN graduate or post-graduate educational program after December 31, 2015, will automatically be granted prescriptive and dispensing authority with the issuance of their Idaho licensure.

a. An advanced practice professional nurse who applies for authorization to prescribe pharmacologic and non-pharmacologic agents within the scope of practice for the advanced practice role, shall:
    i.   Be currently licensed as an advanced practice professional nurse in Idaho;
    ii. Provide evidence of completion of thirty (30) contact hours of post-basic education in pharmacotherapeutics. . . .
    iii. Submit a completed, notarized application form provided by the Board; and
    iv. Remit fees prescribed in Section 901 of these rules.

Citation: Idaho Admin. Code § 23.01.01.315.01(a).

Illinois

(Section scheduled to be repealed on January 1, 2018.)

a. A collaborating physician or podiatrist may, but is not required to, delegate prescriptive authority to an advanced practice nurse as part of a written collaborative agreement. This authority may, but is not required to, include prescription of, selection of, orders for, administration of, storage of, acceptance of samples of, and dispensing over the counter medications, legend drugs, medical gases, and controlled substances categorized as any Schedule III through V controlled substances, as defined in Article II of the Illinois Controlled Substances Act, and other preparations, including, but not limited to, botanical and herbal remedies. The collaborating physician or podiatrist must have a valid current Illinois controlled substance license and federal registration to delegate authority to prescribe delegated controlled substances.

b. To prescribe controlled substances under this Section, an advanced practice nurse must obtain a mid-level practitioner controlled substance license. Medication orders shall be reviewed periodically by the collaborating physician or podiatrist.

c. The collaborating physician or podiatrist shall file with the Department notice of delegation of prescriptive authority and termination of such delegation, in accordance with rules of the Department. Upon receipt of this notice delegating authority to prescribe any Schedule III through V controlled substances, the licensed advanced practice nurse shall be eligible to register for a mid-level practitioner controlled substance license under Section 303.05 of the Illinois Controlled Substances Act.

d. In addition to the requirements of Subsections (a), (b), and (c) of this Section, a collaborating physician may, but is not required to, delegate authority to an advanced practice nurse to prescribe any Schedule II controlled substances, if all of the following conditions apply:

   1. Specific Schedule II controlled substances by oral dosage or topical or transdermal application may be delegated, provided that the delegated Schedule II controlled substances are routinely prescribed by the collaborating physician or podiatrist. This delegation must identify the specific Schedule II controlled substances by either brand name or generic name. Schedule II controlled substances to be delivered by injection or other route of administration may not be delegated.

   2. Any delegation must be controlled substances that the collaborating physician or podiatrist prescribes.

   3. Any prescription must be limited to no more than a 30-day supply, with any continuation authorized only after prior approval of the collaborating physician or podiatrist.

   4. The advanced practice nurse must discuss the condition of any patients for whom a controlled substance is prescribed monthly with the delegating physician.

   5. The advanced practice nurse meets the education requirements of Section 303.05 of the Illinois Controlled Substances Act.

e. Nothing in this Act shall be construed to limit the delegation of tasks or duties by a physician to a licensed practical nurse, a registered professional nurse, or other persons. Nothing in this Act shall be construed to limit the method of delegation that may be authorized by any means, including, but not limited to, oral, written, electronic, standing orders, protocols, guidelines, or verbal orders.

Citation: Ill. Comp. Stat. § 65/65-40.

a. A collaborating physician or podiatrist who delegates prescriptive authority to an advanced practice nurse shall include that delegation in the written collaborative agreement. This authority may include prescription of, selection of, orders for, administration of, storage of, acceptance of samples of, and dispensing over the counter medications, legend drugs, medical gases, and controlled substances categorized as Schedule III, III-N, IV, or V controlled substances, as defined in Article II of the Illinois Controlled Substances Act, and other preparations, including, but not limited to, botanical and herbal remedies. The collaborating physician or podiatrist must have a valid current Illinois controlled substance license and federal registration to delegate authority to prescribed delegated controlled substances.

b. Pursuant to Section 65-40(d) of the Act, a collaborating physician may, but is not required to, delegate authority to an advanced practice nurse to prescribe Schedule II or II-N controlled substances under the following conditions:

1. No more than 5 Schedule II or II-N controlled substances by oral dosage may be delegated. For the purposes of this Section generic substitution pursuant to Section 25 of the Pharmacy Practice Act shall be allowed under this Section when not prohibited by a prescriber's indication on the prescription that the pharmacist "may not substitute."

2. The collaborating physician can only delegate controlled substances that the collaborating physician prescribes.

3. Any prescription must be limited to no more than a 30-day oral dosage, with any continuation authorized only after prior approval of the collaborating physician.

4. The advanced practice nurse must discuss the condition of any patients for whom a controlled substance is prescribed monthly with the delegating physician.

c. An APN who has been given controlled substances prescriptive authority shall be required to obtain an Illinois mid-level practitioner controlled substance license in accordance with 77 Ill. Adm. Code 3100. The physician or podiatrist shall file a notice of delegation of prescriptive authority with the Division. The delegation of authority form shall be submitted to the Division prior to the issuance of a controlled substance license.

d. The APN may only prescribe and dispense within the scope of practice of the collaborating physician or podiatrist. Licensed dentists may not delegate prescriptive authority.

e. All prescriptions written and signed by an advanced practice nurse shall indicate the name of the collaborating physician or podiatrist. The collaborating physician's or podiatrist's signature is not required. The APN shall sign his/her own name.

f. An APN may receive and dispense samples per the collaborative agreement.

g. Medication orders shall be reviewed periodically by the collaborating physician or podiatrist.

Citation: Ill. Admin. Code. tit. 68, § 1300.430.

Indiana

An advanced practice nurse may be authorized to prescribe legend drugs, including controlled substances, if the advanced practice nurse does the following:

1. Submits an application with the required fee;

2. Submits proof of an active, unrestricted registered nurse license;

3. Submits proof of having met the requirements of all applicable laws for practice as advanced practice nurse in the state of Indiana;
4. Submits proof of a baccalaureate or higher degree in nursing;
5. If the applicant holds a baccalaureate degree only, submits proof of certification as a nurse practitioner or certified nurse midwife by a national organization recognized by the board and which requires a national certifying examination.
6. Submits proof of having successfully completed a graduate level pharmacology course, consisting of at least two (2) semester hours of academic credit from a college or university accredited by the commission on Recognition of Postsecondary Accreditation:
   A. within five (5) years of the date of application; or
   B. if the pharmacology course was completed more than five (5) years immediately preceding the date of the application, the applicant must submit proof of the following:
      i. completing at least thirty (30) actual contact hours of continuing education during the two (2) years immediately preceding the date of application, including a minimum of at least eight (8) actual contact hours of pharmacology, all of which must be approved by a nationally approved sponsor of continuing education for nurses.
      ii. Prescriptive experience in another jurisdiction within the five (5) years immediately preceding the date of application.
7. Submits proof of collaboration with a licensed practitioner in the form of a written practice agreement that sets forth the manner in which the advanced practice nurse and licensed practitioner will cooperate, coordinate, and consult with each other in the provision of health care to patients. . . .
8. Written practice agreements for advanced practice nurses applying for prescriptive authority shall not be valid until prescriptive authority is granted by the board.

Citation: Ind. Admin. Code tit. 848, r. 5-1-1.

Iowa

"Prescriptive authority" is the authority granted to an ARNP registered in Iowa in a recognized nursing specialty to prescribe, deliver, distribute, or dispense prescription drugs, devices, and medical gases when the nurse is engaged in the practice of that nursing specialty. Registration as a practitioner with the Federal Drug Enforcement Administration and the Iowa board of pharmacy examiners extends this authority to controlled substances. ARNPs shall access the Iowa board of pharmacy examiners Web site for Iowa pharmacy law and administrative rules and the Iowa Board of Pharmacy Examiners Newsletter.

Citation: Iowa Admin. Code r. 655-7.1(152).

Kansas

An advanced practice registered nurse may prescribe drugs pursuant to a written protocol as authorized by a responsible physician. Each written protocol shall contain a precise and detailed medical plan of care for each classification of disease or injury for which the advanced practice registered nurse is authorized to prescribe and shall specify all drugs which may be prescribed by the advanced practice registered nurse. Any written prescription order shall include the name, address, and telephone number of the responsible physician. The advanced practice registered nurse may not dispense drugs, but may request, receive, and sign for professional samples and may distribute professional samples to patients pursuant to a written protocol as authorized by a responsible physician. In order to prescribe controlled substances, the advanced practice registered nurse shall

1. register with the federal drug enforcement administration; and
2. notify the board of the name and address of the responsible physician or physicians. In no case shall the scope of authority of the advanced practice registered nurse exceed the normal and customary practice of the responsible physician. An advanced practice registered nurse certified in the category of registered nurse anesthetist while functioning as a registered nurse anesthetist under K.S.A. 1988 Supp. 65-1151 to 65-1164, including, and amendments thereto, shall be subject to the provisions of K.S.A. 65-1151 and 65-1164, inclusive and amendments thereto, with respect to drugs and anesthetic agents and shall not be subject to the provisions of this subsection. For the purposes of this subsection, "responsible physician" means a person licensed to practice medicine and surgery in Kansas who has accepted responsibility for the protocol and the actions of the advanced registered nurse practitioner when prescribing drugs.

Citation: Kan. Stat Ann. § 65-1130(d).

a. Each written protocol pursuant to which an advanced registered nurse practitioner may transmit prescription orders shall:
   1. Specify for each classification of disease or injury the corresponding class of drugs for which the advanced registered nurse practitioner is permitted to prescribe;
   2. Be maintained in either a looseleaf notebook or a book of published protocols. The notebook or book of published protocols shall include a cover page containing the following data:
      A. The names, telephone numbers, and signatures of the advanced registered nurse practitioner and a responsible physician who has authorized the protocol; and
      B. The date on which the protocol was adopted or last reviewed, and
   3. Be kept at the advanced registered nurse practitioner's principal place of practice.

Each written protocol that an advanced practice registered nurse is to follow when prescribing, administering, or supplying a prescription-only drug shall meet the following requirements:

1. Specify for each classification of disease or injury the corresponding class of drugs that the advanced practice registered nurse is permitted to prescribe;
2. Be maintained in either a loose-leaf notebook or a book of published protocols. The notebook or book of published protocols shall include a cover page containing the following data:
   A. The names, telephone numbers, and signatures of the advanced practice registered nurse and a responsible physician who has authorized the protocol; and
   B. The date on which the protocol was adopted or last reviewed; and
3. Be kept at the advanced practice registered nurse's principal place of practice.

b. Each advanced practice registered nurse shall ensure that each protocol is reviewed by the advanced practice registered nurse and physician at least annually.

c. Each prescription order in written form shall meet the following requirements:
   1. Include the name, address, and telephone number of the practice location of the advanced practice registered nurse;
   2. include the name, address, and telephone number of the responsible physician;
   3. be signed by the advanced practice registered nurse with the letters A.P.R.N.;
   4. be from a class of drugs prescribed pursuant to protocol; and
   5. contain any D.E.A. registration number issued to the advanced practice registered nurse when a controlled substance, as defined in K.S.A. 65-4101(e) and amendments thereto, is prescribed.

d. Nothing in this regulation shall be construed to prohibit any registered nurse or licensed practical nurse or advanced practice registered nurse from conveying a prescription order orally or administering a drug if acting under the lawful direction of a person licensed to practice either medicine and surgery or dentistry, or certified as an advanced registered nurse practitioner.

Citation: Kan. Admin. Regs. § 60-11-104a.

Kentucky

Advanced practice registered nurse shall include prescribing medications and ordering treatments, devices, and diagnostic tests, which are consistent with the scope and standard of practice of the advanced practice registered nurse.

Citation: 201 Ky. Admin. Regs. § 20:057 (Section 4).

KRS 314.011(8)(c) authorizes the Controlled Substances Formulary Development Committee to make recommendations to the Board of Nursing concerning any limitations for the prescription of specific controlled substances by advanced practice registered nurses. This administrative regulation establishes limitations for the prescription of specific controlled substances by advanced practice registered nurses.

Section 1. Specific Controlled Substances. The following controlled substances have been identified as having the greatest potential for abuse or diversion:
1. Diazepam (Valium), a Schedule IV medication;
2. Clonazepam (Klonopin), a Schedule IV medication;
3. Lorazepam (Ativan), a Schedule IV medication;
4. Alprazolam (Xanax), a Schedule IV medication; and
5. Carisoprodol (Soma), a Schedule IV medication.

Section 2. Limitations. Prescriptions for the medications listed in Section 1 of this administrative regulation shall be limited to a thirty (30) day supply without any refill.

Citation: 201 Ky. Admin. Regs. §20:059.

Louisiana

An APRN may be granted prescriptive authority to prescribe assessment studies, including pharmaceutical diagnostic testing (e.g., dobutamine stress testing), legend and certain controlled drugs, therapeutic regimens, medical devices and appliances, receiving and distributing a therapeutic regimen of prepackaged drugs prepared and labeled by a licensed pharmacist, and free samples supplied by a drug manufacturer, and distributing drugs for administration to and use by other individuals within the scope of practice as defined by the board in R.S. 37.913(3)(b).

Requirements for prescriptive privileges:

- Hold a current; unencumbered, unrestricted, and valid RN licensure
- Hold a current, unencumbered, unrestricted, and valid APRN licensure
- Evidence of 500 hours of clinical practice as a licensed APRN within 1 year prior to applying for prescriptive and distributing authority
- 45 hours of education in pharmacotherapeutics
- 45 contact hours of pathophysiology/physiology in formal educational program
- Collaborative practice agreement with one or more licensed collaborating physicians
- Each year . . . six hours of continuing education in pharmacotherapeutics

Citation: La. Admin. Code tit. 46, § XLVII.4513.

Maine

A. Certified nurse practitioners and certified nurse–midwives are authorized to prescribe the following:
1. over the counter drugs
2. appliances and devices
3. drugs related to the specialty area of certification
4. drugs prescribed off label according to common and established standards of practice.
B. Regardless of the schedules indicated on the certificate issued by the Drug Enforcement Administration, the certified nurse practitioner and certified nurse–midwives shall prescribe only those controlled drugs from Schedules II, III, IIIN, IV, and V. A Drug Enforcement Agency (D.E.A.) number is required to prescribe these Drugs.

Citation: Code Me. R. § 02 380 008 (Section 7).

Maryland

A nurse practitioner may perform independently the following functions:

. . . Prescribe drugs. . .

Citation: Md. Regs. Code. 10 § 27.07.02A(12).

"Nurse practitioners certified by the Maryland Board of Nursing as Advanced Practice are automatically given prescriptive authority for non-controlled substances. The Advanced Practice Certification also allows them to apply for permission to prescribe Schedules II through V Controlled Dangerous Substances (CDS)."

Citation: Maryland Board of Nursing, *Instructions for Completing and Submitting the Nurse Practitioner (NP) Attestation Form & Supporting Documents.* Retrieved from http://www.mbon.org /adv_prac/attestation_instructions.pdf

Massachusetts

A nurse practitioner . . . may issue written prescriptions and order tests and therapeutics pursuant to guidelines mutually developed and agreed upon by the nurse and the supervising physician in accordance with regulations promulgated jointly by the board and the board of registration in medicine after consultation with the board of registration in pharmacy. A prescription made by a nurse practitioner or psychiatric nurse mental health clinical specialist shall include the name of the physician with whom such nurse has developed and signed mutually agreed upon guidelines approved by said board and said board of registration in medicine pursuant to Section 80B.

Citation: Mass. Ann. Laws, Ch. 112, § 80E.

A nurse engaged in prescriptive practice means a nurse with: (a) authorization to practice in an expanded role; (b) a minimum of 24 contact hours in pharmacotherapeutics which are beyond those acquired in a generic nursing program . . . , (c) valid registration to issue written or oral prescriptions or medication orders for controlled substances from the Massachusetts Department of Public Health . . . and, where required, by the US Drug Enforcement Administration.

Citation: Mass. Regs. Code tit. 244, § 4.05.

The guidelines for prescriptive practice shall:

- Include a defined mechanism to monitor prescribing practices, including documentation of review with a supervising physician at least every three months;
- Include protocols for initiation of intravenous therapies and Schedule II drugs;
- Specify the frequency of review of initial prescription of controlled substances; the initial prescription of Schedule II drugs must be reviewed within 96 hours;
- Conform to M.G.L. c.94C, the regulations of the Department of Public Health at 105 CMR 700.000 et seq., and M.G.L. c.112 §§ 80E or 80H, as applicable.

Citation: Mass. Regs. Code tit. 244, § 4.22(3).

A supervising physician shall review and provide ongoing direction for the APN's prescriptive practice in accordance with written guidelines mutually developed and agreed upon with the APN pursuant to M.G.L. c. 112, §§ 80B, 80C, 80E, 80G, 80H, and the regulations of the Board of Registration in Nursing (244 CMR) and 243 CMR 2.10. This supervision shall be provided as is necessary, taking into account the education, training and experience of the APN, the nature of the APN's practice, and the physician's availability to provide clinical backup to ensure that the APN is providing patient care in accordance with accepted standards of practice.

(b) A supervising physician shall sign prescriptive practice guidelines only with those APNs for whom he or she is able to provide supervision consistent with 243 CMR 2.10(2) and (3), taking into account factors including, but not limited to geographical proximity, practice setting, volume and complexity of the patient population, and the experience, training and availability of the supervising physician and the APN(s).

(c) A supervising physician shall not enter into guidelines, pursuant to M.G.L. c. 112, §§ 80B, 80C, 80E, 80G, or 80H and 243 CMR 2.10, unless the APN has professional malpractice liability insurance as required by the BORN regulations.

5. a.   A physician who supervises an APN engaged in prescriptive practice shall do so in accordance with written guidelines mutually developed and agreed upon with the APN.

b.   In all cases, the written guidelines shall:

1.   identify the supervising physician and APN;

2.   include a defined mechanism for the delegation of supervision to another physician including, but not limited to, the duration and scope of the delegation;

3.   describe the nature and scope of the APN's prescribing practice;

4.   identify the types of medication(s) to be prescribed, specify any limitations on medications to be prescribed; and describe the circumstances in which physician consultation or referral is required;

5.   describe the use of established procedures for the treatment of common medical conditions which the nurse may encounter;

6.   include provisions for managing emergencies;

7.   include a defined mechanism and time frame to monitor prescribing practices;

8.   include protocols for the initiation of intravenous therapies and Schedule II drugs;

9.   specify that the initial prescription of Schedule II drugs must be reviewed within 96 hours;

10. specify that the guidelines must be kept on file in the workplace and be reviewed and re-executed every two years; and

11. conform to M.G.L. c. 94C, the regulations of the Department of Public Health at 105 CMR 700.000.

Citation: Mass. Regs. Code tit. 243 §2.10 (4) and (5)

Michigan

A licensee who holds a license other than a health profession subfield license may delegate to a licensed or unlicensed individual who is otherwise qualified by education, training, or experience the performance of selected acts, tasks, or functions where the acts, tasks, or functions fall within the scope of practice of the licensee's profession and will be performed under the licensee's supervision. A licensee shall not delegate an act, task, or function under this section if the act, task, or function, under standards of acceptable and prevailing practice, requires the level of education, skill, and judgment required of the licensee under this article.

Citation: Mich. Comp. Laws § 333.16215(1).

A supervising physician may delegate in writing to a registered professional nurse the ordering, receipt, and dispensing of complimentary starter dose drugs other than controlled substances as defined by article 7 or federal law. When the delegated ordering, receipt, or dispensing of complimentary starter dose drugs occurs, both the registered professional nurse's name and the supervising physician's name shall be used, recorded, or otherwise indicated in connection with each order, receipt, or dispensing.

Citation: Mich. Comp. Laws § 333.17212(1).

1. A physician may delegate the prescription of controlled substances listed in schedules 3 to 5 to a registered nurse who holds specialty certification under section 17210 of the code, with the exception of a nurse anesthetist, if the delegating physician establishes a written authorization that contains all of the following information:
   a. The name, license number, and signature of the delegating physician.
   b. The name, license number, and signature of the nurse practitioner or nurse midwife.
   c. The limitations or exceptions to the delegation.
   d. The effective date of the delegation.
2. A delegating physician shall review and update a written authorization on an annual basis from the original date or the date of amendment, if amended. A delegating physician shall note the review date on the written authorization.
3. A delegating physician shall maintain a written authorization in each separate location of the physician's office where the delegation occurs.
4. A delegating physician shall ensure that an amendment to the written authorization is in compliance with subrule (1) (a) to (d) of this rule.
5. A delegating physician may delegate the prescription of schedule 2 controlled substances only if all of the following conditions are met:
   a. The delegating physician and nurse practitioner or nurse midwife are practicing within a health facility as defined in section 20106(d), (g), or (i) of the code; specifically, freestanding surgical outpatient facilities, hospitals, and hospices.
   b. The patient is located within the facility described in subdivision (a) of this subrule.
   c. The delegation is in compliance with this rule.
6. A delegating physician may not delegate the prescription of schedule 2 controlled substances issued for the discharge of a patient for a quantity for more than a 7-day period.
7. A delegating physician shall not delegate the prescription of a drug or device individually, in combination, or in succession for a woman known to be pregnant with the intention of causing either a miscarriage or fetal death.

Citation: Michigan Board of Medicine Rules R338.2305.

Minnesota

A certified nurse practitioner who has a written agreement with a physician based on standards established by the Minnesota Nurses Association and the Minnesota Medical Association that defines the delegated responsibilities related to the prescription of drugs and therapeutic devices, may prescribe and administer drugs and therapeutic devices within the scope of the written agreement and within practice as a nurse practitioner. The written agreement required under this subdivision shall be based on standards established by the Minnesota Nurses Association and the Minnesota Medical Association as of January 1, 1996, unless both associations agree to revisions.

Citation: Minn. Stat. Ann. § 148.235(2).

An advanced practice registered nurse who is authorized under this section to prescribe drugs is authorized to dispense drugs subject to the same requirements established for the prescribing of drugs. This authority to dispense extends only to those drugs dispensed in the written agreement entered into under this section. The authority to dispense includes, but is not limited to, the authority to receive and dispense sample drugs.

Citation: Minn. Stat. Ann. § 148.235(4b).

A licensed doctor of medicine, a doctor of osteopathy, duly licensed to practice medicine, a doctor of dental surgery, a doctor of dental medicine, a licensed doctor of podiatry, or a licensed doctor of optometry limited to Schedules IV and V, and in the course of professional practice only, may prescribe, administer, and dispense a controlled substance included in Schedules II through V of section 152.02, may cause the same to be administered by a nurse, an intern or an assistant under the direction and supervision of the doctor, and may cause a person who is an appropriately certified and licensed health care professional to prescribe and administer the same within the expressed legal scope of the person's practice as defined in Minnesota Statutes.

Citation: MINN. STAT. §152.12.

Mississippi

Certified nurse midwives and certified nurse practitioners may apply for controlled substance prescriptive authority after completing a board approved educational program. Certified nurse midwives and certified nurse practitioners who have completed the program and received prescription authority from the board may prescribe Schedules II-V. The words "administer," "controlled substances," and "ultimate user," shall have the same meaning as set forth in Section 41-29-105, unless the context otherwise requires. The board shall promulgate rules governing prescribing of controlled substances, including distribution, record keeping, drug maintenance, labeling and distribution requirements and prescription guidelines for controlled substances and all medications. Prescribing any controlled substance in violation of the rules promulgated by the board shall constitute a violation of Section 73-15-29(1) (f), (k) and (l) and shall be grounds for disciplinary action. The prescribing, administering or distributing of any legend drug or other medication in violation of the rules promulgated by the board shall constitute a violation of Section 73-15-29(1) (f), (k) and (l) and shall be grounds for disciplinary action.

Citation: Miss. Nursing Practice Law §73-15-20(8).

Missouri

The methods of treatment and the authority to administer, dispense, or prescribe drugs delegated in a collaborative practice arrangement between a collaborating physician and collaborating APRN shall be within the scope of practice of each professional and shall be consistent with each professional's skill, training, education, competence, licensure, and/or certification and shall not be further delegated to any person except that the individuals identified in sections 338.095 and 338.198, RSMo, may communicate prescription drug orders to a pharmacist.

Citation: Mo. Code Regs. Ann. tit. 20, § 2200-4.200(3)(A).

The collaborating physician shall consider the level of skill, education, training, and competence of the collaborating RN or APRN and ensure that the delegated responsibilities contained in the collaborative practice arrangement are consistent with that level of skill, education, training, and competence.

Citation: Mo. Code Regs. Ann. tit. 20, § 2200-4.200(3)(C).

The methods of treatment, including any authority to administer and dispense drugs, delegated in a collaborative practice arrangement between a collaborating physician and a collaborating RN shall be delivered only pursuant to a written agreement, jointly agreed-upon protocols, or standing orders that shall describe a specific sequence of orders, steps, or procedures to be followed in providing patient care in specified clinical situations.

Citation: Mo. Code Regs. Ann. tit. 20, § 2200-4.200(3)(E).

Methods of treatment delegated and authority to administer, dispense, or prescribe drugs shall be subject to the following:

1. The physician retains the responsibility for ensuring the appropriate administering, dispensing, prescribing, and control of drugs utilized pursuant to a

collaborative practice arrangement in accordance with all state and federal statutes, rules, or regulations;

2. All labeling requirements outlined in Section 338.059, RSMo shall be followed;

3. Consumer product safety laws and Class B container standards shall be followed when packaging drugs for distribution;

4. All drugs shall be stored according to the *United States Pharmacopeia* (USP) recommended conditions;

5. Outdated drugs shall be separated from the active inventory;

6. Retrievable dispensing logs shall be maintained for all prescription drugs dispensed and shall include all information required by state and federal statutes, rules, or regulations;

7. All prescriptions shall conform to all applicable state and federal statutes, rules, or regulations and shall include the name, address, and telephone number of the collaborating physician and collaborating APRN.

Citation: Mo. Code Regs. Ann. tit. 20, § 2200-4.200((3)G).

In addition to administering and dispensing controlled substances, an APRN, as defined in section 335.016, RSMo, may be delegated the authority to prescribe controlled substances listed in Schedules III, IV, and V of section 195.017, RSMo, in a written collaborative practice arrangement, except that, the collaborative practice arrangement shall not delegate the authority to administer any controlled substances listed in Schedules III, IV, and V of section 195.017, RSMo, for the purpose of inducing sedation or general anesthesia for therapeutic, diagnostic, or surgical procedures. Schedule III narcotic controlled substance prescriptions shall be limited to a one hundred twenty (120)-hour supply without refill.

Citation: Mo. Code Regs. Ann. tit. 20, § 2200-4.200(3)(G)9.

An APRN may not prescribe controlled substances for his or her own self or family. Family is defined as spouse, parents, grandparents, great-grandparents, children, grandchildren, great-grandchildren, brothers and sisters, aunts and uncles, nephews and nieces, mother-in-law, father-in-law, brothers-in-law, sisters-in-law, daughters-in-law, and sons-in-law. Adopted and step members are also included in family.

Citation: Mo. Code Regs. Ann. tit. 20, § 2200-4.200(3)(G)10.

An APRN or RN in a collaborative practice arrangement may only dispense starter doses of medication to cover a period of time for seventy-two (72) hours or less with the exception of Title X family planning providers or publicly funded clinics in community health settings that dispense medications free of charge.

Citation: Mo. Code Regs. Ann. tit. 20, § 2200-4.200(G)11.

Montana

Initial Application for Prescriptive Authority

1. The APRN shall submit a completed application for prescriptive authority and a nonrefundable fee as specified in ARM 24.159.401. The application for all APRNs except practicing CRNAs must include:

    a. evidence of successful completion of a graduate level course that provides a minimum of the equivalent of three academic semester credit hours (equaling a minimum of 45 contact hours) from an accredited program in pharmacology, pharmacotherapeutics, and the clinical management of drug therapy related to the applicant's area of specialty. The academic credits must be obtained within a three-year period immediately prior to the date the application is received at the board office and must meet the following requirements:

        i.   no more than six of the 45 contact hours may concern the study of herbal or complementary therapies;

        ii. a minimum of 18 of the 45 contact hours must have been obtained within one year immediately prior to the date of application; and

        iii. a minimum of one-third of all contact hours must be face-to-face or interactive instruction.

    b. evidence of the course content and clinical preceptorship;

    c. a copy of the current certification from the APRN's national certifying body;

    d. a description of the proposed practice sites and typical caseload; and

    e. an updated quality assurance plan, if needed, as required by ARM 24.159.1466.

    Citation: Mont. Admin. R § 24.159.1463.

Prescribing Practices

1. Prescriptions must comply with all applicable state and federal laws.
2. All written prescriptions must include the following information:
    a. name, title, address, and phone number of the APRN who is prescribing;
    b. name of client;
    c. date of prescription;
    d. the full name of the drug, dosage, route, amount to be dispensed, and directions for its use;
    e. Drug Enforcement Administration (DEA) number of the prescriber on all scheduled drugs; and
    f. all requirements of state and federal regulations regarding prescriptions.
3. Records of all prescriptions must be documented in client records.

4. An APRN with prescriptive authority shall comply with federal DEA requirements for controlled substances and shall file DEA registrations and numbers with the board.

5. An APRN with prescriptive authority may not prescribe controlled substances for self or members of the APRN's immediate family.

6. In an emergency situation, Schedule II drugs may be phoned in to the pharmacist pursuant to 21 CFR 1306.11(d).

7. An APRN with prescriptive authority may not delegate the prescribing or dispensing of drugs to any other person.

Citation: Mont. Admin. R. § 24-159.1464.

Quality Assurance of APRN Practice

1. Within one month of initiating an APRN practice involving direct patient care the APRN shall submit a quality assurance plan to the board.

2. A quality assurance plan includes the following elements:
    a. location of the APRN's practice site(s);
    b. identification of the APRN's peer-reviewer or peer review organization. Peer review must occur on a quarterly basis and include review of 15 charts or 5 percent of all charts handled by the APRN, whichever is fewer. The peer-reviewer must work in the same practice specialty as the APRN and must hold an unencumbered license. If the APRN has prescriptive authority, the peer-reviewer must also have prescriptive authority;
    c. standards of practice set by the APRN's national professional organization, which the peer-reviewer will use to evaluate the APRN's practice;
    d. criteria for client referrals, patient outcomes, and chart documentation set by the APRN's national professional organization that the peer-reviewer will use to evaluate the APRN's practice; and
    e. description of the method the peer-reviewer will use to address areas in need of attention or improvement, if indicated, and to ensure follow-up evaluation.

3. By December 31 of each license renewal year, the APRN shall submit a quality assurance report to the board on the form provided by the department. The biennial quality assurance report shall:
    a. provide verification that each quarterly peer review has occurred;
    b. provide verification that area(s) identified by the peer reviewer as needing attention and improvement have been appropriately addressed according to the APRN's stated plan; and
    c. inform the board of any change in the location of the APRN's practice site(s), the identity of the peer-reviewer, or the quality assurance criteria

established by the national professional organization in the APRN's specialty area of practice.

Citation: Mont. Admin. R. § 24.159.1466.

Nebraska

2. Nurse practitioner means health promotion, health supervision, illness prevention and diagnosis, treatment, and management of common health problems and acute and chronic conditions, including:
   a. Assessing patients, ordering diagnostic tests and therapeutic treatments, synthesizing and analyzing data, and applying advanced nursing principles;
   b. Dispensing, incident to practice only, sample medications which are provided by the manufacturer and are provided at no charge to the patient; and;
   c. Prescribing therapeutic measures and medications relating to health conditions within the scope of practice. Any limitation on the prescribing authority of the nurse practitioner for controlled substances listed in Schedule II of Section 28-405 shall be recorded in the integrated practice agreement established pursuant to Section 38-2310.

Citation: Neb. Rev. Stat. Ann. § 38-2315.

Nevada

An advanced practice registered nurse may only prescribe controlled substances, poisons, dangerous drugs or devices which are currently within the standard of practice in his or her identified medical specialty.

Citation: Nev. Admin. Code § 632.259.

The State Board of Nursing will issue a certificate to dispense controlled substances, poisons, dangerous drugs and devices to an advanced practice registered nurse if the practitioner:

a. Successfully completes an examination administered by the State Board of Nursing on Nevada law relating to pharmacy; and
b. Submits to the State Board of Nursing his or her affidavit verifying that he or she has made application with the State Board of Pharmacy for a certificate of registration.

Citation: Nev. Admin. Code § 632.2595.

*A protocol must:

1. Reflect the ongoing collaborative relationship between the advanced practice registered nurse and the physician;
2. Reflect the current practice of the advanced practice registered nurse;

3. Reflect established national or customary standards for his or her medical specialty;
4. Be maintained at the place of his or her practice; and
5. Be available for review by the Board.

Citation: Nev. Admin. Code § 632.2555.

This regulation (632.2555) was proposed for repeal as of November 2013 but had not yet been formally adopted as of February 2014.

New Hampshire

An APRN shall have plenary authority to possess, compound, prescribe, administer, dispense and distribute controlled and non-controlled drugs within the scope of the APRN's practice as defined by this chapter. Such authority may be denied, suspended, or revoked by the board after notice and the opportunity for hearing, upon proof that the authority has been abused.

Citation: N.H. Rev. Stat. Ann. § 326-B:11.III.

New Jersey

a. In addition to all other tasks which a registered professional nurse may, by law, perform, an advanced practice nurse may manage preventive care services, and diagnose and manage deviations from wellness and long-term illnesses, consistent with the needs of the patient and within the scope of practice of the advanced practice nurse, by:
   1. initiating laboratory and other diagnostic tests;
   2. prescribing or ordering medications and devices, as authorized by subsections b. and c. of this section; and
   3. prescribing or ordering treatments, including referrals to other licensed healthcare professionals, and performing specific procedures in accordance with the provisions of this subsection.
b. An advanced practice nurse may order medications and devices in the inpatient setting, subject to the following conditions:
   1. the collaborating physician and advanced practice nurse shall address in the joint protocols whether prior consultation with the collaborating physician is required to initiate an order for a controlled dangerous substance;
   2. the order is written in accordance with standing orders or joint protocols developed in agreement between a collaborating physician and the advanced practice nurse, or pursuant to the specific direction of a physician;
   3. the advanced practice nurse authorizes the order by signing his or her own name, printing the name and certification number, and printing the collaborating physician's name;

4. the physician is present or readily available through electronic communications;

5. the charts and records of the patients treated by the advanced practice nurse are reviewed by the collaborating physician and the advanced practice nurse within the period of time specified by rule adopted by the Commissioner of Health and Senior Services pursuant to Section 13 of P.L.1991, c.377 (C.45:11–52);

6. the joint protocols developed by the collaborating physician and the advanced practice nurse are reviewed, updated, and signed at least annually by both parties; and

7. the advanced practice nurse has completed six contact hours of continuing professional education in pharmacology related to controlled substances, including pharmacologic therapy and addiction prevention and management, in accordance with regulations adopted by the New Jersey Board of Nursing. The six contact hours shall be in addition to New Jersey Board of Nursing pharmacology education requirements for advanced practice nurses related to initial certification and recertification of an advanced practice nurse as set forth in N.J.A.C. 13:37-7.2 and 13:37-7.5.

c. An advanced practice nurse may prescribe medications and devices in all other medically appropriate settings, subject to the following conditions:

1. the collaborating physician and advanced practice nurse shall address in the joint protocols whether prior consultation with the collaborating physician is required to initiate a prescription for a controlled dangerous substance;

2. the prescription is written in accordance with standing orders or joint protocols developed in agreement between a collaborating physician and the advanced practice nurse, or pursuant to the specific direction of a physician;

3. the advanced practice nurse writes the prescription on a New Jersey Prescription Blank pursuant to P.L.2003, c.280 (C.45:14-40 et seq.), signs his name to the prescription and prints his name and certification number;

4. the prescription is dated and includes the name of the patient and the name, address, and telephone number of the collaborating physician;

5. the physician is present or readily available through electronic communications;

6. the charts and records of the patients treated by the advanced practice nurse are periodically reviewed by the collaborating physician and the advanced practice nurse;

7. the joint protocols developed by the collaborating physician and the advanced practice nurse are reviewed, updated, and signed at least annually by both parties; and

8. the advanced practice nurse has completed six contact hours of continuing professional education in pharmacology related to controlled substances, including pharmacologic therapy and addiction prevention and

management, in accordance with regulations to New Jersey Board of Nursing. The six contact hours shall be in addition to New Jersey Board of Nursing pharmacology education requirements for advanced practice nurses related to initial certification and recertification of an advanced practice nurse as set forth N.J.A.C. 13:37-7.2 and 13:37-7.5.

d. The joint protocols employed pursuant to Subsections b. and c. of this section shall conform with standards adopted by the Director of the Division of Consumer Affairs pursuant to Section 12 of P.L.1991, c.377 (C.45:11–51) or Section 10 or P.L.1999, c.85 (C.45-49.2), as applicable.

Citation: N.J. Stat. Ann. § 45:11-49.

An advanced practice nurse shall include the following information on each prescription blank issued:

1. The prescribing advanced practice nurse's full name, designation, that is, APN, address, telephone number, and certification number.
2. The full name, date of birth and address of the patient;
3. The date of issuance;
4. The name, strength, route and quality of the medication prescribed;
5. The number of refills permitted or time limit for refills, or both;
6. A handwrittern, original signature;
7. An explicit indication, by initials placed next to "do not substitute," if a specified brand name drug is to be dispensed;
8. The full name, title, address, telephone number, and license number of the collaborating physician
9. Words, in addition to numbers, to indicate the drug quantity authorized if the prescription is for a controlled dangerous substance, for example: "ten (10) Percodan" or "five (5) Ritalin 5mg"; and
10. If the prescription is for a controlled dangerous substance, the advanced practice nurse's DEA number and instructions as to the frequency of use.

Citation: N.J. Admin. Code tit.13, § 37-7.9.

New Mexico

Certified nurse practitioners may . . . practice independently and make decisions regarding health care needs of the individual, family, or community and carry out health regimens, including the prescription and distribution of dangerous drugs and controlled substances included in Schedules II through V of the Controlled Substances Act. . . .

Citation: N.M. Stat. Ann. § 61-3-23.2.B(2).

Certified nurse practitioners who have fulfilled requirements for prescriptive authority may prescribe in accordance with the rules, regulations, guidelines, and formularies for individual certified nurse practitioners promulgated by the board.

Citation: N.M. Stat. Ann. § 61-3-23.2.C.

3. Submit a completed transcript with degree posted from an accredited gradu-ate level advanced practice registered nurse program and which includes evidence of completion of advanced pharmacotherapy, physical assessment, and pathophysiology.
4. Provide evidence of completion of thirty contact hours of education or equivalent in pharmacotherapy related to the applicant's scope of advanced practice that:
    a. Have been obtained within a three-year period of time immediately prior to the date of application for prescriptive authority; or
    b. May otherwise be approved by the board.

Citation: N.D. Admin. Code § 54-05-03.1-9.

The advanced practice registered nurse plans and initiates a therapeutic regimen that includes ordering and prescribing medical devices and equipment, nutri-tion, diagnostic and supportive services including home health care, hospice, and physical and occupational therapy.

1. A permanent advanced practice registered nurse license with the addition of prescriptive authority shall be issued following review and approval of the completed application by the board.
2. Between meetings of the board, board staff may review the prescriptive authority application and grant a temporary permit to prescribe if all the requirements are met.
3. The advanced practice registered nurse with prescriptive authority may pre-scribe drugs as defined by chapter 43-15-01 pursuant to applicable state and federal laws. Notice of the prescriptive authority granted will be forwarded to the board of pharmacy.
4. A prescriptive authority advanced practice registered nurse license does not include drug enforcement administration authority for prescribing controlled substances. Each licensee must apply for and receive a drug enforcement administration number before writing prescriptions for scheduled drugs.
5. The licensee may prescribe, administer, sign for, dispense over-the-counter, legend, and controlled substances, and procure pharmaceuticals, including samples following state and federal regulations.
6. The signature on documents related to prescriptive practices must clearly indicate that the licensee is an advanced practice registered nurse.
7. The advanced practice registered nurse with prescriptive authority may not prescribe, sell, administer, distribute, or give to oneself or to one's spouse or child any drug legally classified as a controlled substance or recognized as an addictive or dangerous drug.
8. Notwithstanding any other provision, a practitioner who diagnoses a sexu-ally transmitted disease, such as chlamydia, gonorrhea, or any other sexually transmitted infection, in an individual patient may prescribe or dispense,

and a pharmacist may dispense, prescription antibiotic drugs to that patient's sexual partner or partners, without there having been an examination of that patient's sexual partner or partners.

Citation: N.D. Admin. Code § 54-05-03.1-10.

Ohio

Under a certificate to prescribe issued under Section 4723.48 of the Revised Code, a . . . certified nurse practitioner is subject to all of the following:

A. The nurse shall not prescribe any drug or therapeutic device that is not included in the types of drugs and devices listed on the formulary established in rules adopted under Section 4723.50 of the Revised Code;

B. The nurse's prescriptive authority shall not exceed the prescriptive authority of the collaborating physician or podiatrist;

C. The nurse may prescribe a Schedule II controlled substance only if all of the following are the case:

a. The Patient has a terminal condition, as defined in section 2133.01 of the Revised Code

b. The collaborating physician of the nurse initially prescribed the substance for the patient

c. The prescription is for an amount that does not exceed the amount necessary for the patient's use in a single, twenty-four period. [Sections omitted.]

E. A ... certified nurse practitioner may personally furnish to a patient a sample of any drug or therapeutic device included in the types of drugs and devices listed in the formulary. . . .[conditions apply].

Citation: Ohio Rev. Code Ann. § 4723.481.

Oklahoma

A Certified Nurse Practitioner shall be eligible, in accordance with the scope of practice of the Certified Nurse Practitioner, to obtain recognition as authorized by the Board to prescribe, as defined by rules promulgated by the Board pursuant to this section and subject to the medical direction of a supervising physician. This authorization shall not include dispensing drugs, but shall not preclude, subject to federal regulations, the receipt of, the signing for, or the dispensing of professional samples to patients.

Citation: Okla. Stat. Ann. tit. 59, § 567.3a.(6)(c).

The advanced practice nurse with prescriptive authority who prescribes Schedule III-V drugs will comply with state and Federal Drug Enforcement Administration (DEA) requirements prior to prescribing controlled substances.

1. The advanced practice nurse with prescriptive authority will submit in writing the assigned DEA number to the Board of Nursing within fourteen (14) days of receipt.
2. No more than a 30-day supply for Schedule III-V drugs shall be prescribed by the advanced practice nurse with prescriptive authority.

Citation: OKLA. ADMIN. CODE §485:10-16-5(c).

Oregon

The Oregon State Board of Nursing may grant to a certified nurse practitioner or certified clinical nurse specialist the privilege of writing prescriptions including prescriptions for controlled substances listed in schedules II, III, IIIN, IV, and V.

Citation: Or. Rev. Stat. § 678.390(1).

The nurse practitioner is independently responsible and accountable for the continuous and comprehensive management of a broad range of health care, which may include:

. . . Prescribing, dispensing, and administration of therapeutic devices and measures, including legend drugs and controlled substances as provided in Division 56 of the Oregon Nurse Practice Act, consistent with the definition of the practitioner's specialty category and scope of practice.

Citation: Or. Admin. R. § 851-050-0005(5)(l).

1. A written prescription shall include the date, printed name, legal signature, specialty category/title, business address, and telephone number of the prescribing nurse practitioner or clinical nurse specialist in addition to the required patient and drug information.
2. An electronically transmitted prescription as defined in OAR 855-006-0015 of the Pharmacy Act shall include the name and immediate contact information of the prescriber and be electronically encrypted or in some manner protected by up-to-date technology from unauthorized access, alteration, or use. Controlled substances have additional restrictions as defined by the DEA, which shall be followed.
3. A tamper resistant prescription shall meet criteria as defined in OAR 855-006-0015 of the Pharmacy Act.
4. Prescriptions may be written for over the counter drugs, durable medical equipment (DME), and devices.
5. Prescriptions shall be signed by the prescriber with the abbreviated specialty title of the nurse practitioner as per OAR 851-050-0005(9) or the title CNS as per 851-054-0015.
6. The nurse practitioner or clinical nurse specialist shall comply with all applicable laws and rules in prescribing, administering, and distributing drugs, including compliance with the labeling requirements of ORS Chapter 689.

7. A nurse practitioner or clinical nurse specialist shall only prescribe controlled substances in conjunction with their own valid and current DEA registration number appropriate to the classification level of the controlled substance.

8. Clinical nurse specialists and nurse practitioners with prescriptive authority are authorized to prescribe legend and controlled substances in Schedule II-V. Additionally, they may prescribe:
    a. Over-the-counter drugs;
    b. Appliances and devices;
    c. Orphan drugs;
    d. Limited access drugs;
    e. Antibiotics to partner(s) of patients diagnosed with a sexually transmitted infection without first examining the partner of the patient, consistent with Department of Human Services guidelines regarding Expedited Partner Therapy;
    f. Off label.

Citation: Or. Admin. R. § 851-056-0010.

1. Evaluation of appropriate prescribing by the Board is constructed based on the following premises:
    a. Nurse practitioners may provide care for specialized client populations within each nurse practitioner category/scope of practice;
    b. Clinical nurse specialists may provide care for individuals and populations within their specialty scope of practice;
    c. Prescribing is limited by the individual's scope of practice and knowledge base within that scope of practice;
    d. Clinical nurse specialists and nurse practitioners may prescribe the drugs appropriate for patients within their scope of practice as defined by OAR 851-050-0005; or 851-054-0020 and 0021;
    e. Clinical nurse specialists and nurse practitioners shall be held independently accountable for their prescribing decisions;
    f. All drugs prescribed shall have Food and Drug Administration (FDA) approval unless mentioned as an exception in OAR 851-056-0010.

Citation: Or. Admin. R. § 851-056-0012.

Pennsylvania

Collaborative Agreement—the written and signed agreement between a CRNP and a collaborating physician in which they agree to the details of their collaboration including the elements in the definition of collaboration.

Citation: 49 Pa Code § 21.251.

b. A CRNP with current prescriptive authority approval from the Board may prescribe, dispense, and administer drugs and therapeutic or corrective measures consistent with the prescriptive authority collaborative agreement and relevant to the CRNP's specialty from the following categories:

1. Antihistamines.
2. Anti-infective agents.
3. Antineoplastic agents, unclassified therapeutic agents, devices, and pharmaceutical aids.
4. Autonomic drugs.
5. Blood formation, coagulation and anticoagulation drugs, and thrombolytic and antithrombolytic agents.
6. Cardiovascular drugs.
7. Central nervous system agents.
8. Contraceptives including foams and devices.
9. Diagnostic agents.
10. Disinfectants for agents used on objects other than skin.
11. Electrolytic, caloric, and water balance.
12. Enzymes.
13. Antitussive, expectorants, and mucolytic agents.
14. Gastrointestinal drugs.
15. Local anesthetics.
16. Eye, ear, nose, and throat preparations.
17. Serums, toxoids, and vaccines.
18. Skin and mucous membrane agents.
19. Smooth muscle relaxants.
20. Vitamins.
21. Hormones and synthetic substitutes.

c. A CRNP may not prescribe or dispense a drug from the following categories:

1. Gold compounds.
2. Heavy metal antagonists.
3. Radioactive agents.
4. Oxytocics.
5. Schedule I controlled substances as defined by Section 4 of the Controlled Substance, Drug, Device, and Cosmetic Act (35 P.S. § 780-104).

d. Restrictions on CRNP prescribing and dispensing practices are as follows:

1. A CRNP may write a prescription for a Schedule II controlled substance for up to a 30-day supply as identified in the collaborative agreement.
2. A CRNP may prescribe a Schedule III or IV controlled substance for up to a 90-day supply as identified in the collaborative agreement.

e. A CRNP may not delegate prescriptive authority.

Citation: 49 Pa Code § 21.284.

Rhode Island

a. Prescriptive privileges for the certified registered nurse practitioner:
   1. Shall be granted under the governance and supervision of the department, board of nurse registration and nurse education; and
   2. Shall include prescription of legend medications and prescription of controlled substances from Schedules II, III, IV, and V that are established in regulation; and
   3. Must not include controlled substances from Schedule I.
b. To qualify for prescriptive privileges an applicant must submit on forms provided by the board of nurse registration and nursing education, verified by oath, that the applicant has evidence of completion of thirty (30) hours of education in pharmacology within the three (3) year period immediately prior to date of application. To maintain prescriptive privileges the certified registered nurse practitioner (R.N.P.) must submit upon request of the board of nurse registration and nursing education evidence of thirty (30) hours continuing education in pharmacology every six (6) years.

Citation: R.I. Gen. Laws § 5-34-39.

South Carolina

A. An advanced practice registered nurse applicant shall furnish evidence satisfactory to the board that the applicant:
   1. has met all qualifications for licensure as a registered nurse; and
   2. holds current specialty certification by a board-approved credentialing organization. New graduates shall provide evidence of certification within one year of program completion; however, psychiatric clinical nurse specialists shall provide evidence of certification within two years of program completion; and
   3. has earned a master's degree from an accredited college or university, except for those applicants who:
      a. provide documentation as requested by the board that the applicant was graduated from an advanced, organized formal education program appropriate to the practice and acceptable to the board before December 31, 1994; or
      b. graduated before December 31, 2003, from an advanced, organized formal education program for nurse anesthetists accredited by the national accrediting organization of that specialty. CRNAs who graduate after December 31, 2003, must graduate with a master's degree from a formal CRNA education program for nurse anesthetists accredited by the national accreditation organization of the CRNA specialty. An advanced practice registered nurse must achieve

and maintain national certification, as recognized by the board, in an advanced practice registered nursing specialty;

4. has paid the board all applicable fees; and

5. has declared specialty area of nursing practice and the specialty title to be used must be the title which is granted by the board-approved credentialing organization or the title of the specialty area of nursing practice in which the nurse has received advanced educational preparation.

B. An APRN is subject, at all times, to the scope and standards of practice established by the board-approved credentialing organization representing the specialty area of practice and shall function within the scope of practice of this chapter and must not be in violation of Chapter 47.

C. 1. A licensed nurse practitioner, certified nurse–midwife, or clinical nurse specialist must provide evidence of approved written protocols, as provided in this section. A licensed NP, CNM, or CNS performing delegated medical acts must do so under the general supervision of a licensed physician or dentist who must be readily available for consultation.

2. When application is made for more than three NP's, CNM's, or CNS's to practice with one physician or when an NP, CNM, or CNS is performing delegated medical acts in a practice site greater than forty-five miles from the supervising physician, the Board of Nursing and Board of Medical Examiners shall each review the application to determine if adequate supervision exists.

D. 1. Delegated medical acts performed by a nurse practitioner, certified nurse–midwife, or clinical nurse specialist must be performed pursuant to an approved written protocol between the nurse and the physician and must include, but is not limited to:

a. this general information:

i. name, address, and South Carolina license number of the nurse;

ii. name, address, and South Carolina license number of the physician;

iii. nature of practice and practice locations of the nurse and physician;

iv. date the protocol was developed and dates the protocol was reviewed and amended;

v. description of how consultation with the physician is provided and provision for backup consultation in the physician's absence;

b. this information for delegated medical acts:

i. the medical conditions for which therapies may be initiated, continued, or modified;

ii. the treatments that may be initiated, continued, or modified;

iii. the drug therapies that may be prescribed;

iv. situations that require direct evaluation by or referral to the physician.

2. The original protocol and any amendments to the protocol must be reviewed at least annually, dated and signed by the nurse and physician, and made available to the board for review within seventy-two hours of request. Failure to produce protocols upon request of the board is considered misconduct and subjects the licensee to disciplinary action. A random audit of approved written protocols must be conducted by the board at least biennially.

3. Licensees who change practice settings or physicians shall notify the board of the change within fifteen business days and provide verification of approved written protocols. NP's, CNM's, and CNS's who discontinue their practice shall notify the board within fifteen business days.

E. 1. An NP, CNM, or CNS who applies for prescriptive authority:

    a. must be licensed by the board as a nurse practitioner, certified nurse–midwife, or clinical nurse specialist;

    b. shall submit a completed application on a form provided by the board;

    c. shall submit the required fee;

    d. shall provide evidence of completion of forty-five contact hours of education in pharmacotherapeutics acceptable to the board, within two years before application or shall provide evidence of prescriptive authority in another state meeting twenty hours in pharmacotherapeutics acceptable to the board, within two years before application;

    e. shall provide at least fifteen hours of education in controlled substances acceptable to the board as part of the twenty hours required for prescriptive authority if the NP, CNM, or CNS has equivalent controlled substance prescribing authority in another state;

    f. shall provide at least fifteen hours of education in controlled substances acceptable to the board as part of the forty-five contact hours required for prescriptive authority if the NP, CNM, or CNS initially is applying to prescribe in Schedules III through V controlled substances.

2. The board shall issue an identification number to the NP, CNM, or CNS authorized to prescribe medications. Authorization for prescriptive authority is valid for two years unless terminated by the Board for cause. Initial authorization expires concurrent with the expiration of the Advanced Practice Registered Nurse license.

3. Authorization for prescriptive authority must be renewed after the applicant meets requirements for renewal and provides documentation of twenty hours acceptable to the board of continuing education contact hours every two years in pharmacotherapeutics. For an NP, CNM, or CNS with controlled substance prescriptive authority, two of the twenty hours must be related to prescribing controlled substances.

F. 1. Authorized prescriptions by a nurse practitioner, certified nurse–midwife, or clinical nurse specialist with prescriptive authority:

a. must comply with all applicable state and federal laws;

b. is limited to drugs and devices utilized to treat common well-defined medical problems within the specialty field of the nurse practitioner or clinical nurse specialist, as authorized by the physician and listed in the approved written protocols. The Board of Nursing, Board of Medical Examiners, and Board of Pharmacy jointly shall establish a listing of classifications of drugs that may be authorized by physicians and listed in approved written protocols;

c. do not include prescriptions for Schedule II controlled substances; however, Schedules III through V controlled substances may be prescribed if listed in the approved written protocol and as authorized by Section 44-53-300;

d. must be signed by the NP, CNM, or CNS with the prescriber's identification number assigned by the board and all prescribing numbers required by law. The prescription form must include the name, address, and phone number of the NP, CNM, or CNS and physician and must comply with the provisions of Section 39-24-40. A prescription must designate a specific number of refills and may not include a nonspecific refill indication;

e. must be documented in the patient record of the practice and must be available for review and audit purposes.

2. An NP, CNM, or CNS who holds prescriptive authority may request, receive, and sign for professional samples, except for controlled substances in Schedule II, and may distribute professional samples to patients as listed in the approved written protocol, subject to federal and state regulations.

G. Prescriptive authorization may be terminated by the board if an NP, CNM, or CNS with prescriptive authority has:

1. not maintained certification in the specialty field;

2. failed to meet the education requirements for pharmacotherapeutics;

3. prescribed outside the scope of the approved written protocols;

4. violated a provision of Section 40-33-110; or

5. violated any state or federal law or regulations applicable to prescriptions.

. . . 4. A person who changes primary practice settings or physician or dentist shall notify the Board of this change within fifteen business days and provide verification of approved written guidelines.

Citation: S.C. Code Ann. § 40-33-44.

South Dakota

A nurse practitioner may perform the following overlapping scope of advanced practice nursing and medical functions pursuant to § 36-9A-15, including:

. . . The prescription of medications and provision of drug samples or a limited supply of labeled medications, including controlled drugs or substances listed on Schedule II in Chapter 34-20B for one period of not more than thirty days, for treatment of causative factors and symptoms. Medications or sample drugs provided to patients shall be accompanied with written administration instructions and appropriate documentation shall be entered in the patient's medical record.

Citation: S.D. Codified Laws § 36-9A-12(2).

Tennessee

The nurse practitioner who holds a certificate of fitness shall be authorized to prescribe and/or issue controlled substances listed in Schedules II, III, IV, and V of title 39, chapter 17, part 4, upon joint adoption of physician supervisory rules concerning controlled substances pursuant to Subsection (d).

Citation: Tenn. Code Ann. § 63-7-123(2).

Any prescription written and signed or drug issued by a nurse practitioner under the supervision and control of a supervising physician shall be deemed to be that of the nurse practitioner. Every prescription issued by a nurse practitioner pursuant to this section shall be entered in the medical records of the patient and shall be written on a preprinted prescription pad bearing the name, address, and telephone number of the supervising physician and of the nurse practitioner, and the nurse practitioner shall sign each prescription so written. Where the preprinted prescription pad contains the names of more than one (1) physician, the nurse practitioner shall indicate on the prescription which of those physicians is the nurse practitioner's primary supervising physician by placing a checkmark beside or a circle around the name of that physician.

Citation: Tenn. Code Ann. § 63-7-123(3)(A).

The Nurse Practice Act T.C.A. § 63-7-101 et seq. requires a certification process for a nurse practitioner to prescribe and/or issue noncontrolled legend drugs.

Citation: Tenn. Comp. R. & Regs. Ch. 1000-4-.01(3).

Texas

A physician may delegate to an advanced practice registered nurse or a physician assistant, acting under adequate physician supervision, the act of prescribing or ordering a drug or device as authorized through a prescriptive authority agreement between the physician and the advanced practice registered nurse or physician assistant, as applicable.

b. A physician and an advanced practice registered nurse or physician assistant are eligible to enter into or be parties to a prescriptive authority agreement only if:
   1. if applicable, the Texas Board of Nursing has approved the advanced practice registered nurse's authority to prescribe or order a drug or device as authorized under this subchapter;
   2. the advanced practice registered nurse or physician assistant:
      A. holds an active license to practice in this state as an advanced practice registered nurse or physician assistant, as applicable, and is in good standing in this state; and
      B. is not currently prohibited by the Texas Board of Nursing or the Texas Physician Assistant Board, as applicable, from executing a prescriptive authority agreement; and
   3. before executing the prescriptive authority agreement, the physician and the advanced practice registered nurse or physician assistant disclose to the other prospective party to the agreement any prior disciplinary action by the board, the Texas Board of Nursing, or the Texas Physician Assistant Board, as applicable.
c. Except as provided by Subsection (d), the combined number of advanced practice registered nurses and physician assistants with whom a physician may enter into a prescriptive authority agreement may not exceed seven advanced practice registered nurses and physician assistants or the full-time equivalent of seven advanced practice registered nurses and physician assistants.
d. Subsection (c) does not apply to a prescriptive authority agreement if the prescriptive authority is being exercised in:
   1. a practice serving a medically underserved population; or
   2. a facility-based practice in a hospital under Section 157.054.
e. A prescriptive authority agreement must, at a minimum:
   1. be in writing and signed and dated by the parties to the agreement;
   2. state the name, address, and all professional license numbers of the parties to the agreement;
   3. state the nature of the practice, practice locations, or practice settings;
   4. identify the types or categories of drugs or devices that may be prescribed or the types or categories of drugs or devices that may not be prescribed;
   5. provide a general plan for addressing consultation and referral;
   6. provide a plan for addressing patient emergencies;
   7. state the general process for communication and the sharing of information between the physician and the advanced practice registered nurse or physician assistant to whom the physician has delegated prescriptive authority related to the care and treatment of patients;
   8. if alternate physician supervision is to be utilized, designate one or more alternate physicians who may:

    A. provide appropriate supervision on a temporary basis in accordance with the requirements established by the prescriptive authority agreement and the requirements of this subchapter; and

    B. participate in the prescriptive authority quality assurance and improvement plan meetings required under this section; and

9. describe a prescriptive authority quality assurance and improvement plan and specify methods for documenting the implementation of the plan that includes the following:

    A. chart review, with the number of charts to be reviewed determined by the physician and advanced practice registered nurse or physician assistant; and

    B. periodic face-to-face meetings between the advanced practice registered nurse or physician assistant and the physician at a location determined by the physician and the advanced practice registered nurse or physician assistant.

f. The periodic face-to-face meetings described by Subsection (e)(9)(B) must:

1. include:

    A. the sharing of information relating to patient treatment and care, needed changes in patient care plans, and issues relating to referrals; and

    B. discussion of patient care improvement; and

2. be documented and occur:

    A. except as provided by Paragraph (B):

       i. at least monthly until the third anniversary of the date the agreement is executed; and

       ii. at least quarterly after the third anniversary of the date the agreement is executed, with monthly meetings held between the quarterly meetings by means of a remote electronic communications system, including videoconferencing technology or the Internet; or

    B. if during the seven years preceding the date the agreement is executed the advanced practice registered nurse or physician assistant for at least five years was in a practice that included the exercise of prescriptive authority with required physician supervision:

       i. at least monthly until the first anniversary of the date the agreement is executed; and

       ii. at least quarterly after the first anniversary of the date the agreement is executed, with monthly meetings held between the quarterly meetings by means of a remote electronic communications system, including videoconferencing technology or the Internet.

g. The prescriptive authority agreement may include other provisions agreed to by the physician and advanced practice registered nurse or physician assistant.

h. If the parties to the prescriptive authority agreement practice in a physician group practice, the physician may appoint one or more alternate supervising physicians designated under Subsection (e)(8), if any, to conduct and document the quality assurance meetings in accordance with the requirements of this subchapter.

i. The prescriptive authority agreement need not describe the exact steps that an advanced practice registered nurse or physician assistant must take with respect to each specific condition, disease, or symptom.

j. A physician, advanced practice registered nurse, or physician assistant who is a party to a prescriptive authority agreement must retain a copy of the agreement until the second anniversary of the date the agreement is terminated.

k. A party to a prescriptive authority agreement may not by contract waive, void, or nullify any provision of this section or Section 157.0513.

l. In the event that a party to a prescriptive authority agreement is notified that the individual has become the subject of an investigation by the board, the Texas Board of Nursing, or the Texas Physician Assistant Board, the individual shall immediately notify the other party to the prescriptive authority agreement.

m. The prescriptive authority agreement and any amendments must be reviewed at least annually, dated, and signed by the parties to the agreement. The prescriptive authority agreement and any amendments must be made available to the board, the Texas Board of Nursing, or the Texas Physician Assistant Board not later than the third business day after the date of receipt of request, if any.

n. The prescriptive authority agreement should promote the exercise of professional judgment by the advanced practice registered nurse or physician assistant commensurate with the advanced practice registered nurse's or physician assistant's education and experience and the relationship between the advanced practice registered nurse or physician assistant and the physician.

o. This section shall be liberally construed to allow the use of prescriptive authority agreements to safely and effectively utilize the skills and services of advanced practice registered nurses and physician assistants.

p. The board may not adopt rules pertaining to the elements of a prescriptive authority agreement that would impose requirements in addition to the requirements under this section. The board may adopt other rules relating to physician delegation under this chapter.

q. The board, the Texas Board of Nursing, and the Texas Physician Assistant Board shall jointly develop responses to frequently asked questions relating to prescriptive authority agreements not later than January 1, 2014. This subsection expires January 1, 2015.

> *Citation:* SB 406 (excerpt), enacted June 2013, with rules under development.

Utah

"Practice of advanced practice registered nursing" means . . . Prescription or administration of prescription drugs or devices, including:

    i.   Local anesthesia;

    ii.   Schedule IV-V controlled substances; and

    iii.   Schedule II-III controlled substances in accordance with a consultation and referral plan.

Citation: Utah Code Ann. § 58-31b-102(13).

Vermont

"Advanced practice registered nurse" or "APRN" means a licensed registered nurse authorized to practice in this state who, because of specialized education and experience, is endorsed to perform acts of medical diagnosis and to prescribe medical, therapeutic, or corrective measures under administrative rules adopted by the board.

Citation: Vt. Stat Ann. tit. 26, § 1572(4).

Virginia

In accordance with the provisions of this section and pursuant to the requirements of Chapter 33 (§ 54.1-3300 et seq.) of this title, a licensed nurse practitioner, other than a certified registered nurse anesthetist, shall have the authority to prescribe controlled substances and devices as set forth in Chapter 34 (§ 54.1-3400 et seq.) of this title as follows: (i) Schedule V and VI controlled substances on and after July 1, 2000; (ii) Schedules IV through VI on and after January 1, 2002; and (iii) Schedules II through VI controlled substances on and after July 1, 2006. Nurse practitioners shall have such prescriptive authority upon the provision to the Board of Medicine and the Board of Nursing of such evidence as they may jointly require that the nurse practitioner has entered into and is, at the time of writing a prescription, a party to a written agreement with a licensed physician, which provides for the direction and supervision by such physician of the prescriptive practices of the nurse practitioner. Such written agreements shall include the controlled substances the nurse practitioner is or is not authorized to prescribe and may restrict such prescriptive authority as deemed appropriate by the physician providing direction and supervision. . . .

Citation: Va. Code Ann. § 54.1-2957.01.A.

The following restriction shall apply to any nurse practitioner authorized to prescribe drugs and devices pursuant to this section:

1. The nurse practitioner shall disclose to his patients the name, address and telephone number of the supervising physician, and that he is a licensed nurse practitioner.

2. Physicians, other than physicians employed by, or under contract with, local health departments, federally funded comprehensive primary care clinics, or nonprofit health care clinics or programs to provide supervisory services, shall not supervise and direct at any one time more than four nurse practitioners. In the case of nurse practitioners, other than nurse midwives, the supervising physician shall regularly practice in any location in which the nurse practitioner exercises prescriptive authority pursuant to this section. A separate office for the nurse practitioner shall not be established. . . .

3. Physicians employed by, or under contract with, local health departments, federally funded comprehensive primary care clinics, or nonprofit health care clinics or programs to provide supervisory services, shall not supervise and direct at any one time more than four nurse practitioners who provide services on behalf of such entities. Such physicians either shall regularly practice in such settings or shall make periodic site visits to such settings as required by regulations promulgated pursuant to this section. . . .

Citation: Va. Code Ann. § 54.1-2957.01.E.

A. A nurse practitioner with prescriptive authority may prescribe only within the scope of the written or electronic practice agreement with a patient care team physician.

B. At any time there are changes in the patient care team physician, authorization to prescribe, or scope of practice, the nurse practitioner shall revise the practice agreement and maintain the revised agreement.

C. The practice agreement shall contain the following:
   1. A description of the prescriptive authority of the nurse practitioner within the scope allowed by law and the practice of the nurse practitioner.
   2. An authorization for categories of drugs and devices within the requirements of § 54.1-2957.01 of the Code of Virginia.
   3. The signature of the patient care team physician who is practicing with the nurse practitioner or a clear statement of the name of the patient care team physician who has entered into the practice agreement.

Citation: 17 Va. Admin. Code § 90-40-90.

Washington

An advanced registered nurse practitioner under his or her license may perform for compensation nursing care, as that term is usually understood, of the ill, injured, or infirm and in the course thereof, she or he may do the following things that shall not be done by a person not so licensed, except as provided in RCS 18.79.260 and 18.79.270:

1. Perform specialized and advanced levels of nursing as recognized jointly by the medical and nursing professions, as defined by the commission;
2. Prescribe legend drugs and Schedule V controlled substances, as defined in the Uniform Controlled Substances Act, Chapter 69.50 RCW, and Schedule II through IV subject to RCW 18.79.240(1)(r) or (s) within the scope of practice defined by the commission;
3. Perform all acts provided in RCS 18.79.260;
4. Hold herself or himself out to the public or designate herself or himself as an advanced registered nurse practitioner or as a nurse practitioner.

Citation: Wash. Rev. Code § 18.79.250.

An ARNP may not . . . prescribe controlled substances in Schedule I.

Citation: Wash. Admin. Code § 246-840-420(3).

1. An advanced registered nurse practitioner licensed under chapter 18.79. RCW when authorized by the nursing commission may prescribe drugs, medical equipment and therapies pursuant to applicable state and federal laws.
2. The ARNP when exercising prescriptive authority is accountable for competency in:
   a. Patient selection;
   b. Problem identification through appropriate assessment;
   c. Medication or device selection;
   d. Patient education for use of therapeutics:
   e. Knowledge of interactions of therapeutics, if any;
   f. Evaluation of outcome; and
   g. Recognition and management of complications and untoward reactions.

Citation: Wash. Admin. Code § 246-840-400.

West Virginia

a. The board may, in its discretion, authorize an advanced practice registered nurse to prescribe prescription drugs in a collaborative relationship with a physician licensed to practice in West Virginia and in accordance with applicable state and federal laws. An authorized advanced practice registered nurse may write or sign prescriptions or transmit prescriptions verbally or by other means of communication.
b. For purposes of this section an agreement to a collaborative relationship for prescriptive practice between a physician and an advanced practice registered nurse shall be set forth in writing. . . .Collaborative agreements shall include, but not be limited to, the following:
   1. Mutually agreed upon written guidelines or protocols for prescriptive authority as it applies to the advanced practice registered nurse's clinical practice;

2. Statements describing the individual and shared responsibilities of the advanced practice registered nurse and the physician pursuant to the collaborative agreement between them;

3. Periodic and joint evaluation of prescriptive practice; and

4. Periodic and joint review and updating of the written guidelines or protocols.

(c) The board shall promulgate legislative rules . . . governing the eligibility and extent to which an advanced practice registered nurse may prescribe drugs. Such rules shall provide, at minimum, a state formulary classifying those categories of drugs, which shall not be prescribed by advanced practice registered nurse, including, but not limited to, Schedules I and II of the Uniform Controlled Substances Act, antineoplastics, radiopharmaceuticals, and general anesthetics. Drugs listed under Schedule III shall be limited to a 72-hour supply without refill. . . .

Citation: W.V. Code Ann. § 30-7-15a.

3.1. The board shall grant prescriptive authority to an advanced practice registered nurse applicant who meets all eligibility requirements specified in W. Va. Code §30-7-15b and the following:

    3.1.a. Prior to application to the board for approval for limited prescriptive authority, the applicant shall:

        3.1.a.1. Successfully complete an accredited course of instruction in pharmacology during undergraduate study;

        3.1.a.2. Successfully complete an advanced pharmacotherapy graduate level course approved by the board of not less than 45 pharmacology contact hours;

        3.1.a.3. Provide documentation of the use of pharmacotherapy in clinical practice in the education program;

        3.1.a.4. Provide evidence of 15 pharmacology contact hours in advanced pharmacotherapy completed within 2 years prior to application for prescriptive authority;

        3.1.a.5. Submit official transcripts or certificates documenting completion of pharmacology and pharmacotherapy course work.

        3.1.a.6. The board may request course outlines and/or descriptions of courses if necessary to evaluate the pharmacology course content and objectives.

    3.1.b. The advanced practice registered nurse shall submit a notarized application for prescriptive authority on forms provided by the Board with the following:

        3.1.b.1. A fee set forth in the board's Fees rule, 19CSR12.

        3.1.b.2. Written verification of an agreement to a collaborative relationship with a licensed physician holding an unencumbered

West Virginia license for prescriptive practice on forms provided by the board. The applicant shall certify on this form that the collaborative agreement includes the following:

3.1.b.2.A.   Mutually agreed upon written guidelines or protocols for prescriptive authority as it applies to the advanced practice registered nurse's clinical practice;

3.1.b.2.B.   Statements describing the individual and shared responsibilities of the advanced practice registered nurse and the physician pursuant to the collaborative agreement between them;

3.1.b.2.C.   A provision for the periodic and joint evaluation of the prescriptive practice; and,

3.1.b.2.D.   A provision for the periodic and joint review and updating of the written guidelines or protocols.

3.1.b.2.E.   Additional documentation at the request of the board.

3.2.   If the board obtains information that an applicant for prescriptive authority was previously addicted to or dependent upon alcohol or the use of controlled substances, the board may grant prescriptive authority with any limitations it considers proper. The limitations may include, but are not limited to, restricting the types of schedule drugs a nurse may prescribe.

3.3.   The board shall forward a copy of the verification specified in Subdivision 3.1.b.2. of this rule to the Board of Medicine or to the Board of Osteopathy, whichever is indicated.

3.4.   Upon satisfactory evidence that the advanced practice registered nurse applicant has met all above requirements for prescriptive authority, the Board shall assign an identification number to that nurse.

3.5.   The board shall notify the Board of Medicine, the Board of Osteopathy, and the Board of Pharmacy of those advanced practice registered nurses who have been granted prescriptive authority, and shall also provide the prescriber's identification number and effective date of prescriptive authority.

3.6.   The advanced practice registered nurse shall file with the board any restrictions on prescriptive authority that are not imposed by W. Va. Code §60A-3-301 et seq., or this rule, but which are within the written collaborative agreement and the name of the collaborating physician for each advanced practice registered nurse on the approved list.

3.7.   The advanced practice registered nurse with prescriptive authority who wishes to prescribe Schedules III through V drugs shall comply with federal Drug Enforcement Agency requirements prior to prescribing controlled substances.

3.8. The advanced practice registered nurse shall immediately file any and all of his or her Drug Enforcement Agency registrations and numbers with the board.

3.9. The board shall maintain a current record of all advanced practice registered nurses with Drug Enforcement Agency registrations and numbers.

3.10. Any information filed with the board under the provisions of this rule shall be available, upon request, to any pharmacist, regulatory agency or board or shall be made available pursuant to other state or federal law.

3.11. The APRN shall maintain with the board a current mailing and, if available, a current e-mail address.

...

5.1. The advanced practice registered nurse shall not prescribe from the following categories of drugs:

   5.1.a. Schedules I and II of the Uniform Controlled Substances Act;

   5.1.b. Antineoplastics;

   5.1.c. Radio-pharmaceuticals; or

   5.1.d. General anesthetics.

   5.1.e. MAO Inhibitors, except when in a collaborative agreement with a psychiatrist.

5.2. Drugs listed under Schedule III and benzodiazepines are limited to a 72 hour supply without refill.

5.3. The advanced practice registered nurse may prescribe drugs from Schedules IV through V in a quantity necessary for up to a 90 day supply, with only 1 refill, and shall provide that the prescription expires in 6 months, with the following exceptions:

   5.3.a. Prescriptions for phenothiazines shall be limited to up to a 30 day supply and shall be non- refillable;

   5.3.b. Prescriptions for non-controlled substances of antipsychotics, and sedatives prescribed by the advanced practice registered nurse shall not exceed the quantity necessary for a 90 day supply, shall provide for no more than 1 prescription refill and shall expire in 6 months.

5.4. Pursuant to a collaborative agreement as set forth in the law governing prescriptive authority the advanced practice registered nurse may prescribe an annual supply of any drug, with the exception of controlled substances, which is prescribed for the treatment of a chronic condition, other than chronic pain management.

5.5. The maximum dosage of any drug, including antidepressants, prescribed by the advanced practice registered nurse shall be consistent with the advanced practice registered nurse's area of practice.

5.6. Each prescription and subsequent refills given by the advanced practice registered nurse shall be entered on the patient's chart.

5.7.   Advanced practice registered nurses shall not prescribe other prescription drugs or refill for a period exceeding 6 months; provided, that this limitation shall not include contraceptives or those treating a chronic condition as defined in WV Code §30-7-15a and section 19-8-5.4 of this rule.

5.8.   An advanced practice registered nurse may administer local anesthetics.

5.9.   The advanced practice registered nurse who has been approved for limited prescriptive authority by the board may sign for, accept, and provide to patients samples of drugs received from a drug company representative.

5.10.   The prescription authorized by an advanced practice registered nurse shall comply with all applicable state and federal laws and regulations; must be signed by the prescriber with the legal designation or the designated certification title of the prescriber and must include the prescriber's identification number assigned by the board or the prescriber's national provider identifier assigned by the National Provider System pursuant to 45 CFR §162.408.

    5.10.a.   All prescriptions shall include the following information:

        5.10.a.1.   The name, title, address and phone number of the prescribing advanced practice registered nurse;

        5.10.a.2.   The name and date of birth of the patient;

        5.10.a.3.   The date of the prescription;

        5.10.a.4.   The full name of the drug, the dosage, the route of administration and directions, for its use;

        5.10.a.5.   The number of refills;

        5.10.a.6.   The Drug Enforcement Agency number of the prescriber, when required by federal laws; and

        5.10.a.7.   The prescriptive authority identification number issued by the board.

    5.10.b.   An advanced practice registered nurse shall at the time of the initial prescription record in the patient record the plan for continued evaluation of the effectiveness of the controlled substances prescribed.

    5.10.c.   An advanced practice registered nurse shall prescribe refills of controlled substances according to current laws and standards.

    5.10.d.   Drugs considered to be proved human teratogens shall not be prescribed during a known pregnancy by the advanced practice registered nurse. This prohibition includes all Category D and X drugs from the Federal Drug Administration Categories of teratogen risks (21 CFR 201.57). Category C drugs should be given only if the patient benefit justifies the potential risks to the fetus and only after consultation with the collaborating physician.

5.11. The board may approve a formulary classifying pharmacologic categories of all drugs which may be prescribed by an advanced practice registered nurse with prescriptive authority.

Citation: W. Va. Code St. R. tit 19 §19-8-3 and 19-8-5.

Wisconsin

The board shall grant a certificate to issue prescription orders to an advanced practice nurse who meets the education, training, and examination requirements established by the board for a certificate to issue prescription orders....

Citation: Wis. Stat. § 441.16(2).

1. Advanced practice nurse prescribers shall communicate with patients through the use of modern communication techniques.
2. Advanced practice nurse prescribers shall facilitate collaboration with other healthcare professionals, at least 1 of whom shall be a physician, through the use of modern communication techniques.
3. Advanced practice nurse prescribers shall facilitate referral of patient health care records to other health care professionals and shall notify patients of their right to have their health care records referred to other health care professionals.
4. Advanced practice nurse prescribers shall provide a summary of a patient's health care records, including diagnosis, surgeries, allergies, and current medications to other health care providers as a means of facilitation case management and improved collaboration.

Citation: Wis. Admin. Code § N8.10(1), (2), (3), and (4).

The advanced practice nurse prescriber:

1. May issue only those prescription orders appropriate to the advanced practice nurse prescriber's areas of competence, as established by his or her education, training or experience.
2. May not issue a prescription order for any schedule I controlled substance.
3. May not prescribe, dispense or administer any amphetamine, sympatho-mimetic amine drug or compound designated as a schedule II controlled substance pursuant to the provisions of s. 961.16(5), Stats., to or for any person except for any of the following:
   a. Use as an adjunct to opioid analgesic compounds for the treatment of cancer-related pain.
   b. Treatment of narcolepsy.
   c. Treatment of hyperkinesis.
   d. Treatment of drug-induced brain dysfunction.
   e. Treatment of epilepsy.
   f. Treatment of depression shown to be refractory to other therapeutic modalities.

4. May not prescribe, order, dispense or administer any anabolic steroid for the purpose of enhancing athletic performance or for other nonmedical purpose.

5. Shall, in prescribing or ordering a drug for administration by a registered nurse or licensed practical nurse under s. 441.16 (3)(cm), Stats., present evidence to the nurse and to the administration of the facility where the prescription or order is to be carried out that the advanced practice nurse prescriber is properly certified to issue prescription orders.

Citation: Wis. Admin Code §N 8.06.

1. Prescription orders issued by an advanced practice nurse prescriber shall:
   a. Specify the date of issue.
   b. Specify the name and address of the patient.
   c. Specify the name, address and business telephone number of the advanced practice nurse prescriber.
   d. Specify the name and quantity of the drug product or device prescribed, including directions for use.
   e. Bear the signature of the advanced practice nurse prescriber.

2. Prescription orders issued by advanced practice nurse prescribers for a controlled substance shall be written in ink or indelible pencil or shall be typewritten, and shall contain the practitioner's controlled substances number.

Citation: Wis. Admin Code §N 8.07.

1. Advanced practice nurse prescribers who prescribe independently shall maintain in effect malpractice insurance evidenced by one of the following:
   a. Personal liability coverage in the amounts specified in s. 655.23(4), Stats.
   b. Coverage under a group liability policy providing individual coverage for the nurse in the amounts set forth in s. 655.23 (4), Stats. An advanced practice nurse prescriber covered under one or more such group policies shall certify on forms provided by the board that the nurse will independently prescribe only within the limits of the policy's coverage, or shall obtain personal liability coverage for independent prescribing outside the scope of the group liability policy or policies.

2. Notwithstanding sub. (1), an advanced practice nurse prescriber who practices as an employee of this state or a governmental subdivision, as defined under s. 180.0103, Stats., is not required to maintain in effect malpractice insurance coverage, but the nurse shall certify on forms provided by the board that the nurse will prescribe within employment policies.

3. An advanced practice nurse prescriber who prescribes under the supervision and delegation of a physician or CRNA shall certify on forms provided by the board that the nurse complies with s. N 6.03 (2) and (3), regarding delegated acts.

4. An advanced practice nurse prescriber who prescribes in more than one setting or capacity shall comply with the provisions of subs. (1), (2) and (3) applicable to each setting or capacity. An advanced practice nurse prescriber

who is not an employee of this state or a governmental subdivision, and who prescribes independently in some situations and prescribes under the supervision and delegation of a physician or CRNA in other situations, shall meet the requirements of sub. (1) with respect to independent prescribing and the requirements of sub. (3) with respect to delegated prescribing.

5. Every advanced practice nurse who is certified to issue prescription orders shall annually submit to the board satisfactory evidence that he or she has in effect malpractice insurance required by sub. (1).

Citation: WIS. ADMIN CODE §N 8.08.

1. Except as provided in sub. (2), advanced practice nurse prescribers shall restrict their dispensing of prescription drugs to complimentary samples dispensed in original containers or packaging supplied by a pharmaceutical manufacturer or distributor.
2. An advanced practice nurse prescriber may dispense drugs to a patient if the treatment facility at which the patient is treated is located at least 30 miles from the nearest pharmacy.

Citation: WIS. ADMIN CODE §N 8.09 (1).

1. Advanced practice nurse prescribers shall communicate with patients through the use of modern communication techniques.
2. Advanced practice nurse prescribers shall facilitate collaboration with other health care professionals, at least 1 of whom shall be a physician, through the use of modern communication techniques.

Citation: WIS. ADMIN CODE §N 8.10(1).

Wyoming

"Advanced practice registered nurse (APRN)" means a nurse who:

A. May prescribe, administer, dispense, or provide nonprescriptive and prescriptive medications including prepackaged medications, except Schedule I drugs as defined in W.S. 35-7-1013 and 35-7-1014.

Citation: Wyo. Stat. Ann. § 33-21-120(a)(i).

a. The board may authorize an advanced practice registered nurse to prescribe medications and devices, within the recognized scope of advanced practice registered nurse and population focus, and in accordance with all applicable state and federal laws including, but not limited to the Wyoming Pharmacy Act [WS 33-24-101 through 33-24-204], the Wyoming Controlled Substances Act of 1971 [WS 35-7-1001 through 35-7-1101], the Federal Controlled Substances Act [21 U.S.C. § 801 et seq.], their applicable Rules and Regulations.

Citation: Wyo. Board of Nursing Rules, Ch. 4, § Section 8(a).

CHAPTER 6

Hospital Privileges

Until about 10 years ago, it was a tradition in the medical field for a patient to be admitted to a hospital by their primary physician, who then visited the patient in the hospital and coordinated the patient's care. Recently, that traditional model has been challenged by the realization that it is highly inefficient. More and more, "hospitalists," that is, physicians and nurse practitioners who specialize in the care of hospitalized patients, are taking over this aspect of practice.

Hospital privileges were so termed because hospitals traditionally "awarded" the status of admitting physician to community physicians who had gone through a hospital's screening process. The screening process, administered by the physicians who already had privileges, was partly focused on credentialing and partly focused on keeping competing specialists out.

With the number of hospital days per hospital stay declining, some hospitals have become interested in broadening their market. While hospitals still want to be sure that the providers ordering hospital care are competent and adequately credentialed, a hospital that wants to maximize its business will also want to maximize the number of providers who can bring in patients. Therefore, hospitals are becoming more open to giving nurse practitioners (NPs) admitting privileges.

Are Hospital Privileges an Issue for NPs?

NPs can perform primary care without hospital privileges as long as they arrange for patients who need hospitalization to be covered by a provider with hospital privileges or a hospitalist. Nevertheless, if a health plan requires that its primary care providers (PCPs) have hospital privileges, NPs will need hospital privileges to be classified as PCPs.

Physicians, when arguing to health plans that only physicians should be PCPs, have used hospital privileges as a way to distinguish themselves from NPs. NPs, they argue, do not have admitting privileges and therefore should not be PCPs. This leaves two important points unsaid. First, many NPs do have admitting privileges. Second, many PCPs no longer pursue hospital practice and hospital privileges because of the inefficiencies of having to be in two places—office and hospital—at once.

Do PCPs Need Hospital Privileges?

A patient in need of hospitalization who is being cared for by an NP or a physician PCP can be accommodated in several ways. One approach is for the PCP who has hospital privileges to admit patients and continue to manage their care during hospitalization. The PCP coordinates specialty consultation, writes admission and discharge orders, takes calls from hospital nurses about the patient's progress, and evaluates the patient onsite once or twice a day, or more as needed.

A second possible approach is for a PCP to turn the care of patients in need of hospitalization over to a physician (or NP) who has admitting privileges and who does hospital-based care, and to have patients admitted under the physician's care. The responsibility for the care of the patient returns to the PCP after discharge. In this case, the PCP might visit the hospitalized patient, but the visit would be a social or courtesy visit rather than a medical visit.

A third approach is for a PCP to admit to a hospital's staff hospitalists. The third approach makes the most sense. The arguments in its favor are as follows:

(1) Patients get round-the-clock access to a physically present provider of medical care.
(2) Hospitalists devote all of their attention, every day, to hospitalized patients.
(3) The community-based PCP need not feel torn between visiting hospitalized patients and conducting office visits.
(4) The expertise of PCPs is not spread thin by the necessity of being an expert on hospital care.
(5) Admission and discharge are more efficient because hospitalists are onsite to do the initial and discharge evaluation and order writing.
(6) Nursing care is more efficient because nurses need not deal with off-site attending PCPs. At a time when hospital days are being monitored by health plans, it is the hospitalists who have the most potential for keeping utilization at a safe minimum.

There is one strong argument against hospitalists, however. A patient may have established a close relationship with his or her PCP and presumably trusts his or her PCP. When hospitalized, the patient may feel more comfortable with the PCP directing their care. The counterarguments are as follows:

1. There is nothing to prevent the PCP from visiting or calling the patient who is hospitalized.
2. The PCP presumably has chosen a competent hospital with a competent hospitalist.
3. Patients are accustomed to being referred to specialists and may likewise feel comfortable with being referred to hospitalists.
4. Many consumers of health care no longer have a close one-on-one relationship with one PCP; because they are signed on with a managed-care plan that may have teams of PCPs.

Do NPs Need Hospital Privileges for Advancement of the Profession?

There are two arguments supporting the assertion that NPs who wish to be PCPs should seek hospital privileges. First, it is a credential that carries weight among professionals. It is something professional groups boast about and battle about, and something that individual professionals strive for. Physicians sometimes use NPs' lack of hospital privileges as an argument that NPs should not be designated PCPs by managed-care organizations. If the majority of NPs had hospital privileges, physicians would not be able to use the hospital privilege argument against NPs.

Second, some health plans and managed-care organizations want their PCPs to have admitting privileges. If that is the case and an NP wants to be a PCP, the NP will need to get hospital privileges.

Do Individual NPs Need Hospital Privileges?

The NP who is not required to have hospital privileges to be a PCP may not want them. For an individual NP weighing the pros and cons of hospital privileges, the issues are as follows:

- Whether the NP is qualified to deliver evaluation/management services to patients who are so ill they require hospitalization
- Whether the NP wants to devote the time it takes to make hospital visits every day
- Whether an NP needs hospital privileges to be an effective PCP
- Whether local health plans require PCPs to have admitting privileges
- Whether patients are better served by hospitalists or by attendance of their PCP
- Whether hospitalists are available in a local hospital
- Whether the NP wants to spend the time necessary to keep up hospital privileges (e.g., to attend medical staff meetings and serve on committees)
- Whether NP applications for hospital privileges are being accepted or denied by a local hospital

An NP debating whether to apply for admitting privileges should consider what privileges will allow them to do, what not having privileges will keep them from doing, how difficult it will be to get admitting privileges, and what alternatives there are to the NP personally admitting patients to hospitals. The following questions may prove helpful in making a decision:

- Does a managed-care organization with whom the provider wants to associate require admitting privileges?

- Is there a physician with admitting privileges who will take on an NP's patients when they need hospitalization?
- Does the local hospital have hospitalists who manage inpatient care?

Some NPs have found that the physicians they work with want them to have admitting privileges and that they support those NPs' applications. In other cases, physicians themselves have decided not to concentrate on admitted patients, but rather to work with other inpatient-oriented physicians to care for admitted patients. Further, while some NPs are educated in acute care–oriented graduate programs, others consider themselves experts on primary care only. Hospital care is, by definition, tertiary, not primary care. An NP may wish to concentrate on primary care and may not wish to spread professional interests too thin.

Finally, an NP should look at the economics of taking on hospital visits. Managing hospitalized patients can take a large portion of an NP's day, and if there are few patients in the hospital, reimbursement may not be rewarding. For example, if a hospital visit can be billed at $75 but it takes 15 minutes to see a patient, 5 minutes to discuss the care with nursing staff and/or write orders and note, and 20 minutes each way to commute between the office and hospital, an NP will net only $75 per hour. In the office, an NP can bring in at least $78 per 20-minute visit, or $234 per hour. A hospitalist can bill the $75 for the 20-minute visit but can also bill at least $75 for visits to other hospitalized patients and can bring in at least $225 per hour.

Who Has Hospital Privileges?

Traditionally, only physicians had hospital privileges. Privileges were granted or denied on the basis of criteria to which only the hospital and physicians involved were privy. Physicians who were denied hospital privileges—often not because of any lack of expertise, but because a hospital already had one endocrinologist, or one radiation oncologist—sought admission by suing the hospital or lobbying for legislation requiring impartial third-party review of hospital privilege denials. For example, the following New York law protects physicians, podiatrists, optometrists, and dentists from discrimination by hospitals in the matter of staff privileges:

> It shall be an improper practice for the governing body of a hospital to refuse to act upon an application for staff membership or professional privileges or to deny or withhold from a physician, podiatrist, optometrist, dentist or licensed midwife staff membership or professional privileges in a hospital, or to exclude or expel a physician, podiatrist, optometrist, dentist or licensed midwife from staff membership in a hospital or curtail, terminate or diminish in any way a physician's, podiatrist's, optometrist's, dentist's or licensed midwife's professional privileges in a hospital, without stating the reasons therefor, or if the reasons stated are unrelated to standards of patient care, patient welfare, the objectives of the institution or the character or competency of the applicant. It shall be an

improper practice for a governing body of a hospital to refuse to act upon an application or to deny or to withhold staff membership or professional privileges to a podiatrist based solely upon a practitioner's category of licensure.

Citation: N.Y. PUB. HEALTH LAW § 2801-b.1.

The law also states that if a hospital does not follow proper procedure, the physician, podiatrist, or other healthcare professional may file a complaint with the public health council, which will make a prompt investigation and may recommend that the hospital review its actions (N.Y. PUB. HEALTH LAW § 2801-b.2 and 3).

Historically, dentists, podiatrists, optometrists, and clinical psychologists did not have admitting privileges. Recently, those professions have made progress in obtaining hospital privileges. Their organizations and individuals applied pressure through the courts and the legislature and eventually, in some states at least, they gained admitting privileges.

Nurse midwives have admitting privileges in some states. For example, in Oregon, nurse midwives (and NPs) have had statutorily permitted hospital privileges since the mid-1970s. The permissive legislation was passed at a time when midwives were needed in rural areas because obstetricians found that malpractice insurance was too expensive and gave up delivering babies. The Oregon legislature was convinced that nurse midwives needed admitting privileges to make sure rural Oregonians could have attended deliveries. When the issue came before the Oregon legislature, the Oregon Nurses Association suggested that the legislature take the opportunity to permit all NPs, not just nurse midwives, to have admitting privileges. The bill passed. The law states the following:

> The rules of any hospital in this state may grant admitting privileges to NPs licensed and certified under ORS 678.375 for purposes of patient care, subject to hospital and medical staff bylaws, rules, and regulations governing admissions and staff privileges.

Rules shall be in writing and may include, but need not be limited to:

- Limitations on the scope of privileges;
- Monitoring and supervision of nurse practitioners in the hospital by physicians who are members of the medical staff;
- A requirement that an NP co-admit patients with a physician who is a member of the medical staff; and
- Qualifications of NPs to be eligible for privileges including but not limited to requirements of prior clinical and hospital experience.

Citation: OR. REV. STAT. § 441.064.

The rules may also regulate the admissions and the conduct of NPs while using the facilities of a hospital and may prescribe procedures whereby an NP's privileges may be suspended or terminated. However, a hospital may refuse privileges to NPs only on the same basis that privileges are refused to other medical providers.

Does Federal Law Support Full Hospital Privileges for NPs?

Federal law states that every hospitalized patient covered by Medicare must be under the care of a physician [42 U.S.C.S. § 1395x(e)(4)]. The federal government has defined physician as a licensed doctor of medicine, osteopathy, dental surgery or dental medicine, podiatric medicine, chiropractic, or optometry (42 C.F.R. § 410.20). In 1994, clinical psychologists pushed through an amendment to the Social Security Act to add language to federal Medicare law that allows hospitalized patients to be under the care of a clinical psychologist [42 U.S.C.S. § 1395x(e)(4)].

Federal regulation allows physicians to "delegate tasks to other qualified healthcare personnel to the extent recognized under State law or a State's regulatory mechanism" (42 C.F.R. § 482.20).

NPs who deliver care to hospitalized patients presumably fall under the delegation rule.

What Does It Mean to Have Hospital Privileges?

When a patient is admitted to a hospital, the admitting provider is the contact person for the hospital regarding the patient's care while hospitalized. Reports are given to the admitting provider, and it is agreed that decisions, such as readiness for discharge, will be made by the admitting provider.

Unless a provider has privileges, some hospitals will not allow that provider to review a patient's chart, much less order treatments. Part of the rationale for this is patient confidentiality. It is the hospital's responsibility to protect the confidentiality of admitted patients. There have to be limits set regarding who can have access to confidential documents. It would be inefficient for an administrator or nurse to have to decide on a visit-by-visit basis whether any particular provider should have access to patient records. Therefore, hospitals have developed systems for granting admitting privileges to providers who have been screened and credentialed. By hospital policy, providers with privileges have full access to information about the patients they admit, as well as decision-making and ordering authority.

Levels of Privilege

Hospitals may have levels of privileges, which they may designate as associate, affiliate, independent, or some other term.

Associate privileges may mean that privileges are less than full. For example, providers who have associate privileges may be able to review the records but not write orders. Or, they may be able to review charts and write orders but not admit. Each hospital has its own policies on this matter. Some NPs who have admitting privileges have full privileges, and some NPs have limited privileges.

The Application Process

The medical staff governing body—traditionally physicians—decides which other providers may have hospital privileges. The medical staff governing body is a separate entity from hospital administration. It may be subject to the requirements of accreditation organizations, state laws, and federal laws.

Competency and experience are the general criteria that a medical staff group will look at in granting or denying privileges. Many hospitals require an applicant to be recommended by a present member of the medical staff, and, after research into credentials is done, a vote is taken on the applicant. This club-type aspect of the privileging process has resulted in some qualified applicants being denied privileges because of noncompetency–related issues, such as competition, personal bias, or prejudice.

Physician-oriented professional associations often have taken on the task of urging that privileging decisions be based on competency rather than friendship or lack thereof. Accrediting organizations also evaluate the emphasis on competency and experience in a hospital's privileging process as part of the accreditation review.

Expense

There may be an application fee or annual fee for hospital privileges.

Denial of Privileges

Some NPs have had admitting privileges for years. Others are applying for and receiving admitting privileges currently. Some NPs have lost their admitting privileges after leaving physician practices. Some NPs have been denied privileges altogether.

While there is a multitude of reported court decisions regarding other classes of healthcare providers who were denied privileges—family physicians, optometrists, and chiropractors, for example—there are no tradition-changing opinions regarding denial of admitting privileges to NPs.

Federal law regarding conditions of participation in Medicare states that a medical staff governing body must ensure that the accordance of staff membership or professional privileges in the hospital is not dependent solely upon certification, fellowship, or membership in a specialty body or society [42 C.F.R. 482.12(a)7]. It is not clear how this law relates to nonphysicians. In 2012, the Centers for Medicare & Medicaid Services (CMS), in a Final Rule, declined to require that hospitals include nonphysician practitioners on medical staff. ["Medicare and Medicaid Programs; Reform of Hospital and Critical Access Hospital Conditions of Participation," *Federal Register*, Vol. 77, No. 95, page 29045, published May 16, 2012.] However, in that Rule, CMS stated "Medical staffs must be representative of all types of health professionals who have privileges, including Advanced Practice Registered Nurses (APRNs) and Certified Nurse Midwives/Certified Midwives (CNMs/CMs), and who provide services to a hospital's patients, and as they are authorized to provide services under State law and to the extent of their full scope of practice."

Change on the Horizon

Hospital admissions are declining around the nation. Hospitals are finding new service lines. Hospitals are consolidating, merging, and closing. It is in the interest of hospitals to draw patients from as many sources as possible. Therefore, hospitals may open their staff privileges to more classes of healthcare providers. If an NP decides he or she needs hospital privileges, the NP should call the intended hospital, ask about the process, and apply.

CHAPTER 7

Negligence and Malpractice

Nurse practitioners (NPs) carrying out their daily routines have one constant on their everyday "to do" list: "Do no harm." Nevertheless, when an NP, or any other healthcare provider, makes hundreds of decisions a day, it is inevitable that mistakes will be made.

For example, researchers studying medical errors at a major teaching hospital followed nurses and doctors for 9 months on three surgical units. They found that some medical error was made with almost half of the patients and that for at least 18% of the patients there was a serious consequence. Only 1% of these patients sued for malpractice, however.[1]

Though malpractice lawsuits against NPs are rare, the financial and emotional sequelae of being sued are so dire that it is worth dealing with this subject in depth. The meaning and incidence of lawsuits against NPs are difficult to state accurately, for a variety of reasons.

First, a filed lawsuit has no meaning other than to state that a person believes himself or herself to have been harmed. The belief may be unfounded. The blame may be placed on the wrong person. The complaint may not even meet the definition of malpractice. Thus, tracking the incidence of filed suits is of very limited value.

Second, some suits that are filed and that name NPs do so not because the plaintiff believes an NP caused harm but because an NP is a member of a team of caregivers who are being sued, and at the early stages of a lawsuit it is not clear who is responsible. On the other hand, some NPs who actually have been negligent may not be sued, for a variety of reasons.

Third, unless an insurance company reports a damage award—a successful lawsuit or a settlement for damages—against an NP to the National Practitioner Data Bank (NPDB), a lawsuit may come to light only through a search of county court or insurance company records. Insurance companies are required to report damage awards to the NPDB. If a suit is filed but the plaintiff is unsuccessful in proving the necessary elements for malpractice, there will be no report filed with the NPDB. Keeping a national tally of unsuccessful lawsuits filed against NPs is almost impossible.

That being said, one study comparing the incidence of successful lawsuits against advanced practice nurses (APNs), physicians, and physician assistants (PAs) found that in 2006, the chances of paying a malpractice award were 1 in 62 for physicians, 1 in 563 for PAs, and 1 in 1016 for APNs, based on the ratio of awards divided by the number of licensed providers.[2]

What Can Happen to an NP Who Is Sued?

An NP who is sued may feel like leaving the profession, may doubt his or her ability to make decisions, or may resort to over-referring and seeking unnecessary consultation. In addition, the NP may find that his or her insurance rates are increased, may miss days of work while testifying, may have to pay some legal expenses, and may have to mount a defense before the state licensing board.

Boards of nursing do not automatically investigate NPs who have lost malpractice lawsuits. However, if someone involved with the case reports the NP to the board of nursing, or the negligence approaches the level of gross negligence, the board of nursing likely will investigate. Gross negligence, for a professional, is the intentional failure to perform a professional duty in reckless disregard of the consequences.

Lifecycle of a Lawsuit

A lawsuit starts with the filing of pleadings with a state court, usually in the county where the incident occurred. Some states direct malpractice actions to an arbitration panel. The case is presented to the panel, and its members make a decision in favor of one party. Depending on state law, either party may appeal, in which case there will be a trial. At trial, a judge or jury decides in favor of one party. Either party may then appeal to a higher state court. Rarely, a party will seek an appeal to a federal court. Federal courts may accept or refuse appeals from the state courts. Although it is possible that a malpractice case could go all the way to the U.S. Supreme Court, it is highly unlikely. Usually, the highest state court of appeals is the highest level of consideration of a malpractice case, and often the parties will let the matter drop after the state trial court case. Because the holdings of state trial courts are not published, the public cannot easily access information on malpractice trials unless there is an appeal. The opinions of appeals courts are published, and that is the information attorneys and professionals can use to gain insight into malpractice cases.

What Is Malpractice?

Malpractice is the failure of a professional to exercise that degree of skill and learning commonly applied by the average prudent, reputable member of the profession. Negligence is the predominant legal theory of malpractice liability. Negligence includes failure to follow up, failure to refer when necessary, failure to disclose necessary information to a patient, and failure to give necessary care.

Elements of Malpractice

A plaintiff in a malpractice suit must prove the following elements:

1. The NP owed the plaintiff a duty.
2. The NP's conduct fell below the standard of care.
3. The NP's conduct caused the plaintiff's injury.
4. The plaintiff was injured.

Duty

A duty is established when there is a provider–patient relationship. A visit to the NP's office by a patient establishes an NP's duty to that patient. However, there need not be an office visit to establish duty. Duty can be established by a telephone conversation or casual discussion with a patient or with someone who is not officially a patient. If an NP gives professional advice or treatment in any setting, a duty may be established. If an injured party has reason to believe that there was a provider–patient relationship, there may in fact be such a relationship, even if the provider did not think of the interaction in that way.

What Is the Standard of Care for NPs?

NPs are duty bound to use such reasonable, ordinary care, skill, and diligence as NPs in good standing in the same general type of practice in similar cases.

An NP is held to the standard of care of a reasonably prudent NP, not necessarily to the standard of care expected of a physician. In many situations, however, the standards of care for physicians and NPs will be identical. For example, an NP providing primary care can be held to the same standard as a physician providing primary care.

If an NP is sued for malpractice, the standard of care will be argued in court. If an NP believes that she or he met the standard of care, the NP's attorney will enlist expert witnesses, usually other NPs, who will give testimony describing the steps that a reasonably prudent NP would take in a similar situation. The plaintiff's attorney also will enlist expert witnesses, who can be expected to testify that the standard of care called for other measures than those performed by the defendant NP. A judge or jury will accept either the plaintiff's or the defendant's explanation of the standard of care and will then decide whether the defendant NP met that standard.

Causation of Injury

For malpractice to have occurred, a breach of the standard of care must have caused an injury to the plaintiff. For example, a patient visits an NP and is diagnosed with otitis media. The NP prescribes penicillin, to which the patient is allergic. This allergy is marked on the patient's chart. The patient leaves the clinic with penicillin, but before she takes it, she is stung by a bee on the front steps of the clinic. She has an allergic reaction to the bee sting and falls and hits her head, causing a permanent scar on her face. The patient sues the clinic and the NP, claiming that the NP had a duty to the patient, the NP breached the standard of care (by prescribing penicillin for a penicillin-allergic patient), and the patient suffered an injury. All of these claims are true, but there is no malpractice because the breach of the standard of care (prescribing penicillin to an allergic patient) did not cause the injury (the wound to the head).

Injury

A provider may be terribly negligent, but if there is no injury, there is no malpractice. For example, if an NP prescribes penicillin to a patient who is allergic, and the patient takes the penicillin but has no reaction that injures them, then there is no malpractice, even though the standard of care has been breached and even though, if an injury occurred, there would have been a causal relationship between breach of the standard of care and injury.

Examples of Lawsuits Against NPs

Missed Diagnosis

Example 1

The patient, a middle-aged man, began experiencing chest pain at work. He called the clinic and got an appointment for 4 PM. He worked until 4 PM and went to the clinic. An NP evaluated the patient, took a history and examined him, and conferred with a physician. The NP diagnosed muscle spasm and initiated treatment with Valium.

The patient went home, went to sleep, and awakened at 1 AM with severe chest pain. He went to the emergency department, where he was examined by a physician. A chest X-ray was taken. The physician diagnosed muscle spasm. He ordered Demerol, intramuscularly, and prescribed oral codeine.

At noon the next day, the patient's chest pain returned and was more severe. He went to the emergency department. An electrocardiogram was done, which showed a myocardial infarction. Finally, a correct diagnosis was made. The patient recovered but did not return to full-time work for 18 months. The patient sued the NP and the medical group for lost wages and won. [*Fein v. Permanente Med. Group*, 38 Cal. 3d 137, 695 P.2d 665, 211 Cal. Rptr. 369 (1985).] This is an old case, but there have been several recent cases in which NPs (and physicians) missed myocardial infarctions because they did not perform electrocardiograms when the patient complained of chest pain.

What NPs Can Learn from This Case

Rule out the worse diagnosis early on, especially if it can be done easily and inexpensively, as with an electrocardiogram.

Example 2

An NP saw a young married female patient for symptoms of cramps, headache, dysmenorrhea, and lesions on the perineum during menses. The NP examined the patient and, on the basis of the physical exam, diagnosed genital herpes. The NP counseled the patient about causes, prevention, and treatment. A physician working with the NP prescribed an antiviral medication appropriate for treating genital herpes.

The symptoms continued, however. The patient saw another physician, who correctly diagnosed the lesions as severe candidiasis.

The patient sued the NP and the employing doctor, claiming pain and suffering and expenses of treatment. The patient's husband claimed loss of society, companionship, and conjugal relationship with his wife.

The court dismissed the case against the NP but found that the doctor associated with the NP had breached the standard of care. The plaintiff won against the doctor.

The physician appealed the case, asking whether the NP's mistake was correctly imputed to the physician. The appeals court said it was. [*Adams v. Kreuger*, 124 Idaho 74, 856 P.2d 864 (1993).]

What NPs Can Learn from This Case:

1. The diagnosis of a sexually transmitted infection carries with it an emotional component. A patient surely will discuss the matter with the partner, and relationships may break up as a result. Always confirm physical exam findings with laboratory testing, especially when diagnosing sexually transmitted infections.

2. Some courts do not consider NPs to be professionally responsible for their judgments. However, most judges and juries find NPs responsible for their own decisions. When an NP is sued, sometimes the physician collaborator also is sued. Usually, if the physician collaborator did not participate in the case, because, for example, the NP did not ask the physician for help, then the physician collaborator is dropped from the complaint. However, there is one recent case where an NP was sued and the physician collaborator was held liable, even though the physician did not participate in the care of the patient. The judge felt that the physician should have exercised more supervision over the NP.

Example 3

A patient saw a family NP for a complaint of discharge and constant scabbing of one of her nipples, of several months' duration. The NP ordered topical and oral antibiotics and a mammogram, which was negative. The patient returned 7 months later with continuing pain and discharge from the same nipple. The NP referred the patient to a dermatologist. The patient did not see the dermatologist.

Four months later, the patient saw her gynecologist, who again treated her breast symptoms with antibiotics and assured her that she did not have cancer.

The patient saw the NP several more times during the year following the first visit. Reasons for the patient's visits were varied. Eighteen months after the first visit, the patient came to the NP with unmistakable masses in her breast. The NP referred the patient to a surgical oncologist, who diagnosed Paget's disease. The cancer had metastasized, and the patient died shortly after the diagnosis. The patient's family sued the NP, the patient's family practitioner, and the gynecologist, and won damages against all three providers. The court said all three providers had breached the standard of care. [*Jenkins v. Payne*, 465 S.E.2d 795 (Va. 1996).]

What NPs Can Learn from This Case

An NP must follow up symptoms from past visits, even when a patient does not continue to complain about the symptoms. In this case, the NP should have continued to ask, on subsequent visits, whether the breast discharge had resolved and whether the patient had followed up with the dermatologist. Unless the patient stated that the breast discharge and scabbing had resolved (in which case the NP should have documented resolution of the symptom), the NP should have followed up with biopsy when the symptoms did not respond to the initial antibiotics.

Failure to Refer
Example 1

A young man went to an emergency room with acute pain caused by testicular trauma after being hit by a softball. He was urinating blood. He was evaluated by a family NP, who prescribed hydrocodone and naproxen. He was discharged 3 hours later with advice to keep ice on the injury and to schedule an elective ultrasound in 2 days. The patient had increasing pain and his right testicle continued to swell. He returned to the emergency department for re-evaluation. An emergency room physician immediately obtained a testicular ultrasound after an examination, which revealed significant bruising, swelling, and tenderness. The ultrasound revealed an adjacent hemorrhage or hydrocele. There also was questionable arterial flow to the right testicle. The physician recommended that the patient see a urologist urgently. The urologist admitted the patient for an immediate scrotal exploration and thereafter concluded that the right testicle was ruptured and not viable. The testicle was removed. The urologist's operative report included a comment that he may have been able to save the testicle if he had seen the patient on the day of the accident. The patient sued the NP, alleging negligence in the failure to order and review a testicular ultrasound before his discharge at the initial presentation. The plaintiff also claimed that the NP should have referred him to a urologist the same day. The defendant argued that the testicle may not have been salvageable even with earlier surgery. The parties settled for $100,000. [Laska, L. editor, *Malpractice Verdicts, Settlements and Experts*, October 2012.]

What NPs Can Learn from This Case

1. Know when to refer. Refer when the possibility of severe patient injury is high (testicular trauma, urinating blood, potential for loss of testicle) and the NP's expertise does not extend to the body area or system affected. (Urologic injuries are not something most primary care providers are expert at evaluating and managing.)
2. If deciding to evaluate an injury yourself, rather than refer, order the test most likely to rule out the worst possibility, and follow up.

Mishandling of Medicine

Example 1

A 49-year-old woman was attacked while at work at a psychiatric clinic. Her attacker was a patient, a schizophrenic woman who had become paranoid, psychotic, and convinced that someone was following her and possibly trying to kill her. The patient entered the clinic, filled out some paperwork, and then pulled a butcher knife out of her handbag and repeatedly stabbed the staff person. The employee suffered wounds to her hands, arms, face, eyes, torso, heart, lungs, liver, bowels, buttocks, and vagina, and she lost her eyesight as a result of the attack. The patient had a well-documented history of chronic schizophrenia and noncompliance with medications. She had a history of violent behavior. Her last psychotic attack had resulted in involuntary commitment. During her hospitalization she did not recognize the need to take medications. She was assessed as a moderately high risk of danger to others. She was released to the care of a community psychiatric clinic and saw an NP there. The NP had not reviewed the patient's history completely and lowered the dosage of antipsychotic medication because the woman said she did not like taking the medications. The injured worker sued the clinic. The parties settled for $5.5 million. A portion of the settlement was paid to an employee who witnessed the attack and suffered post-traumatic stress disorder due to seeing her coworker lying on the floor disemboweled with her eyes gouged out. [(Laska, L., editor, *Medical Malpractice Verdicts, Settlements and Experts*, January 2010.)]

What NPs Can Learn from This Case

Individuals with schizophrenia may not want to adhere to a prescribed regimen for a variety of reasons. While patient requests normally deserve consideration, when the patient is being treated for psychosis, there is justification and even necessity for refusing to comply with the patient's wishes. When a clinician encounters a recently discharged psychiatric patient who has been prescribed a medication regimen, it is a breach of the standard of care to decrease dosages without discussion with and approval by the patient's team, which should include the psychiatrist who supervised the patient's care in the hospital. There are a number of considerations clinicians should address related to decreasing antipsychotic medications, including the following:

- Likelihood of psychotic relapse
- SSRI discontinuation syndrome
- Antipsychotic discontinuation syndrome
- Anticholinergic withdrawal reaction
- Withdrawal dyskinesia
- Rebound dystonia
- Potential for adverse events related to abrupt discontinuation (e.g., dizziness, lightheadedness, nausea, tremors, insomnia, sedation, electric shock-like pains, and anxiety)

Another lesson: Spend the time to get old records on patients.

Failure to Provide Preventive Care

Example 1

A 35-year-old woman visited a primary care physician's office for various ailments in 2001 and 2002. She saw a primary care physician twice and an NP four times. The patient had a history of splenectomy in 1985. She had received Pneumovax following the procedure. She did not receive Haemophilus or Meningococcal vaccination. Subsequent to 2002, the patient developed a pneumococcal infection that required a 3-month hospitalization and a 2-month stay in a rehabilitation facility. During the hospitalization, she became septic, suffered organ failure and necrosis, and had partial amputation of toes. She can now walk only short distances and suffers from chronic infections and pain. The patient/plaintiff contended that the standard of care required the defendants to revaccinate the patient with a Pneumovax booster due to her asplenia. The plaintiff contended that if the defendants had complied with the accepted standard of care, then she would have avoided her subsequent pneumococcal infection. The clinicians argued that the patient's visits had all been for acute sick visits, not annual preventive and wellness physicals, which did not provide them with an opportunity to recommend or administer a pneumococcal vaccination. The defendants also claimed that the pneumococcal vaccination is not the standard of care, is not proven effective, and would not necessarily have prevented the plaintiff's infection. The parties reached a $3 million settlement. [(Laska, L., editor, *Medical Malpractice Verdicts, Settlements, and Experts*, January 2010.)]

What NPs Can Learn from This Case

Generally, patients get one Pneumovax per lifetime. However, patients without spleens need special consideration. The standard of care is to revaccinate asplenic patients. Furthermore, patients who come only for "sick visits" and never get a preventive care evaluation are risks to themselves and to their healthcare providers. The clinician who wants to decrease risk will either make time during sick visits for attention to preventive matters or will insist that all patients schedule a preventive visit every 1–3 years.

Failure to Perform Routine Screening

Example 1

A child visited a primary care center from birth to 9 months. At one visit (the case report does not specify the age of the child at this visit) the child's mother pointed out to an NP that one of the child's pupils was larger than the other. Two months later the parent told the NP that the child's eyes did not move in tandem. The parent claimed the NP said these symptoms were not important. Three months later the NP tested the child for "red reflex." The NP saw no light reflected back and referred the child to an ophthalmologist, who diagnosed retinoblastoma in both eyes. One eye was removed 3 months later and the other 3 years later. The mother claimed that the NP should have tested for red reflex earlier, which would have saved one eye. The mother admitted that one eye would have been lost in any event. The parties settled for $2 million. [Laska, L., editor, *Malpractice Verdicts, Settlements and Experts*, January 2013.]

What NPs Can Learn from This Case

Understand the standard of care for routine screening for your population. The standard of care calls for an NP or physician to perform a red reflex examination at every well child visit until a child can read. One source of the standard of care is the American Academy of Pediatrics (AAP). Here is a summary of the AAP recommendations: "All neonates, infants, and children should have an examination of the red reflex of the eyes performed by a pediatrician or other primary care clinician trained in this examination technique before discharge from the neonatal nursery and during all subsequent routine health supervision visits." [American Academy of Pediatrics, Section on Ophthalmology, American Association for Pediatric Ophthalmology and Strabismus, American Academy of Ophthalmology, and American Association of Certified Orthoptists, "Red Reflex Examination in Neonates, Infants and Children," *Pediatrics* 2008;122;1401 at http://pediatrics.aappublications.org/content/122/6/1401.full.pdf]

The National Practitioner Data Bank

The National Practitioner Data Bank (NPDB) is a repository for damage award data; that is, payments from professional liability insurance companies on behalf of their clients to injured parties for successful malpractice claims. NPDB also records adverse actions against providers by licensing boards, hospitals, and professional quality assurance committees.

The NPDB is the responsibility of the U.S. Department of Health and Human Services. It was established under a law that was intended to encourage hospitals, state licensing boards, and other healthcare entities to discipline those who engage in unprofessional behavior and to restrict the ability of incompetent physicians, dentists, and other healthcare practitioners to move from state to state without disclosure of their previous dangerous performance.

Under the law, any malpractice insurer who pays any amount to a plaintiff on behalf of an NP in a malpractice case must report that payment to the NPDB. If an NP pays an injured patient directly to settle a matter, that payment need not be reported. The insurer must also report damage awards to state licensing boards. A malpractice insurer must report to the NPDB any amount of dollars paid on behalf of a client to a plaintiff. If a healthcare provider pays an injured party directly, that need not be reported. In addition, state licensing boards are required to report adverse licensure actions, hospitals are required to report adverse clinical privilege actions, and professional societies are required to report adverse professional society membership actions.

Hospitals must check the NPDB data every 2 years before granting clinical privileges. Certain agencies may check the NPDB data. The general public does not have access to the NPDB data. Individual NPs may see their NPDB file and add a brief comment to give their version of an incident listed in the database.

Working with Practice Guidelines

An NP may be following practice guidelines as a matter of law, policy, or good practice. Some states require an NP to establish practice protocols or guidelines, with or without a physician's input.

NPs should consult state law to determine whether written guidelines are required. Written guidelines should meet these criteria:

1. Do not write guidelines so detailed that they cannot reasonably be followed in everyday practice.
2. Base guidelines on evidence and widely used resources, and reference those resources in the guidelines.
3. Practices may adopt an already published set of guidelines.
4. Follow the guidelines.
5. If the guidelines are inappropriate for a particular patient, document why an alternative tack is being taken.
6. If guidelines are not followed because a patient will not comply, document efforts to follow guidelines and patient noncompliance.

The federal Agency for Healthcare Research and Quality (AHRQ) establishes guidelines for practice and conducts research into what works and what does not work in healthcare prevention and treatment. AHRQ has established guidelines for the care of certain conditions. An NP who is caring for patients with conditions addressed by AHRQ should follow the AHRQ guidelines or document why the guidelines are inappropriate for a particular patient. AHRQ changes its guidelines fairly frequently to keep up with new evidence. Visit the AHRQ website (http://www.ahrq.gov) to check for new and retired guidelines.

How to Prevent Lawsuits

1. Be careful about establishing patient–provider relationships. If an NP gives medical advice to a person, for example in a social situation, that person is considered a patient and thus the NP should exercise all of the cautions and standards that they would exercise with a patient in an office or hospital setting.
2. Know the standard of care and practice within it.
3. If practice guidelines or protocols have been adopted by the office or agency, follow them.
4. When in doubt, take a conservative approach.
5. Rule out the worst diagnoses early on.
6. Know the limits of training and expertise.
7. Follow up.

What to Do If Sued

1. Call the NP's professional liability insurance company to report the lawsuit.
2. Do not talk about the suit with anyone but the NP's attorney. Specifically, do not talk with the plaintiff/patient or the plaintiff's attorney.
3. Consider retaining the NP's own attorney if the suit is against a group.
4. Never change a record after learning of a lawsuit (or for any other reason).
5. A deposition—a pretrial information-gathering session—can be as important as a trial in terms of the need for preparation. What an NP says in deposition can lock the NP into what he or she may say at trial.
6. Think carefully before agreeing to settle. Settlement awards will appear on an NP's NPDB record.

Communication

Researchers who compared the time physicians spent with patients with malpractice history found that primary care doctors with two or more malpractice claims against them spent 15 minutes on average with each patient, whereas doctors with no malpractice claims against them spent an average of 18.3 minutes with each patient. Quality-of-care ratings for the sued physicians were as good as ratings for physicians who had not been sued.[3]

Experienced NPs know that good provider–patient communication means better outcomes and higher patient satisfaction. Good communication also means fewer lawsuits. Satisfied patients generally do not sue.

Liability of Collaborating Physicians

In the past, some courts have found physicians liable for the negligent acts of NPs. In the majority of these cases, there was some element of physician involvement in the misdiagnosis. Nevertheless, physicians cannot expect to be fully free from the threat of lawsuit for the acts of the NPs they collaborate with or supervise until the legal requirements for collaboration are lifted.

Medical practices and agencies that set policies calling for supervision of NPs and other APNs can expect to be held liable when NPs are not, in fact, supervised.

Consider the following example: A Texas hospital had a contract with a group of anesthesiologists to provide anesthesia services. The anesthesia group employed certified registered nurse anesthetists (CRNAs). The contract between the hospital and the anesthesia group stated that all CRNAs would be supervised by the anesthesia group. The hospital's written policies and procedures required "direct and personal" supervision of CRNAs by physicians. Hospital policy also required that (1) patients be fully informed about the anesthesia providers who would be giving care, (2) an anesthesiologist prepare and evaluate patients about to have surgery, (3) CRNAs document and discuss the evaluation of their patients with a supervising anesthesiologist or surgeon, and (4) the supervising physician countersign all orders for medications.

One night, a CRNA working without an anesthesiologist onsite attempted to intubate a patient having respiratory distress during a Caesarean section. The CRNA called the anesthesiologist on call to come in right away. The anesthesiologist immediately headed for the hospital. The CRNA eventually was able to intubate, but the patient suffered irreversible brain injury.

The patient and her husband settled with the CRNA and physician. The plaintiff's suit against the hospital went to trial. The plaintiffs argued that the hospital was negligent for failing to adopt, implement, and enforce appropriate policies relating to providing an anesthesiologist, having an anesthesiologist evaluate the patient, supervising the CRNA, disclosing that a nurse was providing anesthesia, failing to exercise care in credentialing, and failing to ensure proper quality assurance and peer review in the anesthesia department.

The jury found that the hospital had not followed its own policies. The jury also found that the CRNA and physician were not negligent but found that the hospital was negligent, that the hospital's negligence was the cause of the patient's injuries, and that the hospital was liable for the injury to the patient.

The hospital appealed the case. The appeals court upheld the jury's decision. [*Denton Reg. Med. Ctr. v. LaCroix*, No. 2-95-003-CV (Tex. Ct. App. June 26, 1997).]

A physician is not automatically liable for the negligence of an NP with whom the physician has a written agreement to collaborate when called upon. Generally, some neglect by the physician has to be proven.

On the other hand, if a physician is required, by policy or law, to supervise, then a physician has the responsibilities of supervisors in general. In general, employers and supervisors must determine that their employees or supervisees are adequately trained and competent in the areas in which they practice. If employees or supervisees are not adequately trained or competent, then the employer or supervisor is obligated to provide further training and guidance or to replace the employee or supervisee. If policies are called for, by law or higher policy, supervisors are responsible for ensuring that policies are in place. If supervisors know that policies are not being followed by employees or supervisees, it is their responsibility to monitor supervised personnel until policies are followed, or to replace the personnel.

Guidelines for physicians who are required by law or policy to collaborate with or supervise NPs and who want to avoid malpractice based on the negligence of an employed NP include the following:

1. Ascertain that the NP is licensed, and verify the NP's education, training, and malpractice history.
2. Comanage patients with the NP until the physician can confirm that the NP is professionally competent.
3. Consult state law to determine what is required of a collaborating physician. Conform to state requirements.
4. Consult state law regarding scope of NP practice. Do not encourage the NP to go further than scope of practice allows unless the physician develops written protocols or is physically present.
5. Telephone diagnosis is risky for both the physician and the NP. If an after-hours call is a necessity of practice, establish a second level of call whereby NPs taking calls can get backup.
6. Consult state law to determine whether an NP is independent or dependent upon physician collaboration or supervision. If supervision is required by law, determine whether direct or indirect supervision is required. "Direct supervision" of an NP requires a physician to be immediately and physically available should the need arise. "Indirect supervision" or "general supervision" requires that the physician be on the premises or available by telephone in a timely and consistent manner.
7. If practice guidelines or protocols exist, follow them.
8. Consider supporting NP organizations in their efforts to eradicate legal requirements of supervision or collaboration. Support legal language that places responsibility for an NP's actions squarely on the NP. A physician who employs an NP who is independently responsible for their actions is less likely to be vicariously liable for an NP's malpractice, and a physician can spend less time in supervisory activities.

Malpractice Insurance

An NP cannot control everything. Everyone makes mistakes. Insurance provides a comfort factor that is well worth the money.

Four frequently asked questions about malpractice insurance are: (1) Do I need to have my employer cover me under the hospital/university/practice policy? (2) Will I be more likely to be sued if I have malpractice insurance? (3) Should I get "claims made" or "occurrence" insurance? and (4) Which company's policy is best?

Do I Need Insurance if My Employer Covers Me Under the Hospital, University, or Practice Policy?

NPs who treat patients outside of their work settings or who moonlight definitely need individual insurance policies. For example, many NPs are approached by neighbors, friends, and relatives for prescriptions. The wise NP will not only treat each of these encounters as thoroughly as if the friend was a patient at the office (or decline to become involved at all), but have malpractice insurance to cover the possibility of a mistake.

An NP who neither moonlights nor treats neighbors and friends may still want an individual policy, even if an employer covers an NP under an umbrella policy. Why? Because a lawsuit fractures collegial alliances. The human tendency is to deny one's own liability and blame others. In such an environment, each healthcare provider needs an advocate to protect his or her interests. Insurance will pay for that defense.

Am I More Likely to Be Sued if I Have Malpractice Insurance?

Possibly, but that is not a good reason to forego insurance. Patients do not usually know whether an NP has malpractice insurance. An injured patient who consults an attorney usually files suit before the patient or his or her attorney knows the insured status of the healthcare provider being sued. Information about the insurance usually comes out in the discovery process in preparation for trial.

However, an NP who tells patients about his or her malpractice coverage may provide an incentive for a litigious patient or may relieve a reluctant patient from any feeling of guilt over suing a respected healthcare provider.

Should I Get "Claims Made" or "Occurrence" Insurance?

Get "occurrence" insurance, which covers any incident that occurred while the NP was insured. Under a "claims made" policy, an NP is covered only when the insurance policy is active, no matter when the incident occurred. If an NP retires, leaves the profession, or no longer has need for active insurance, the NP must nevertheless keep a "claims made" insurance policy active (pay the premium) to receive coverage for incidents that happened in years past. A "claims made" policy is extended through purchasing of a "tail" policy.

Which Company's Policy Is Best?

NPs should choose a company that is located in the United States (in case the NP has to sue the insurance company), has been in business at least 10 years, and has a stable financial rating.

An NP will be able to judge the quality of his or her insurer only after a lawsuit is over. There are no surveys of sued NPs that provide guidance about which company provides the best service.

Notes

1. Andrews, L. B. (1997). An alternative strategy for studying adverse events in medical care. *Lancet, 349,* 309–313. A more recent study found that medical errors occurred in half of all hospital admissions for general pediatric surgery. See Proctor, M. L., et al. (2003). Incidence of medical errors and adverse outcomes on a pediatric general surgery service, *Journal of Pediatric Surgery, 38*(9), 1361–1365.
2. Hooker, R. S., Nicholson, J. G., & Le, T. (2009). Does the employment of physician assistants and nurse practitioners increase liability? *Journal of Medical Licensure Discipline, 95*(2),6–16.
3. Levinson, W., Roter, D., Mullooly, J., Dull, V., & Frankel, R. (1997). The relationship with malpractice claims among primary care physicians and surgeons. *JAMA, 227,* 553–559.

Resources

Buppert, C. (2010). Avoiding malpractice. Law Office of Carolyn Buppert, P.C. Available from the author's website at http://www.buppert.com/publications.html

Medical Malpractice Verdicts, Settlements, and Experts, newsletter, Lewis Laska, editor. Contact: 901 Church St., Nashville, TN 37203, 1-800-298-6288.

CHAPTER 8

Risk Management

Risk management is what one does to avoid problems later. Compare risk management to preventive medicine; risk management prevents legal problems.

Nurse practitioners (NPs) are at risk for two categories of professional mishap: clinical mishap and business mishap. There can be great overlap between clinical and business problems; that is, a clinical problem can turn into a business problem and then into a legal problem. For example, when an NP makes a clinical error and a patient discovers the error, the patient is quite likely to tell friends, relatives, and coworkers. Then the problem evolves into a business problem for the NP because the friends, relatives, and coworkers of that patient are unlikely to visit the NP. If the patient is harmed by the NP's error and files a lawsuit based on malpractice, the NP also has a legal problem.

All NPs face certain risks associated with practice:

- Risk of making a clinical error
- Risk of being sued for malpractice when there was no clinical error
- Risk of public perception that the NP is a poor-quality provider
- Risk of breaching patient confidentiality and/or privacy
- Risk of failing to inform patients fully about treatment and to get informed consent to treat
- Risk of failing to disclose information that patients need to get follow-up
- Risk of poor quality ratings
- Risk of disciplinary action
- Risk of being accused of Medicare fraud for upcoding a patient visit
- Risk of business failure as a result of downcoding patient visits

Whether any of these risks becomes an actual problem is largely up to the NP.

Risk of Making a Clinical Error

Medical professionals who have been sued report that the experience soured their attitude toward their profession. NPs are rarely sued. Nevertheless, a lawsuit, even a lawsuit where the NP is not found to be liable, is a devastating personal experience. Therefore, every NP should incorporate into his or her practice an awareness of how to avoid malpractice.

NPs will maintain their positive attitudes toward their profession by practicing litigation avoidance techniques, just as they would advocate preventive medicine and healthcare maintenance to their patients. Avoidance measures include exercising caution about establishing patient–provider relationships and, when a patient–provider relationship has been established, practicing consistently in conjunction with the accepted standard of care for NPs.

What Is Malpractice?

Malpractice is a failure of professional skill that results in injury, loss, or damage. A claim of malpractice requires that a patient/plaintiff prove the following:

1. The existence of a client–professional relationship—a "duty of care."
2. Behavior below the appropriate standard of care for professionals dealing in like circumstances.
3. A causal link between the practitioner's failure to conform to treatment standards and harm to the patient.
4. Actual injury to the patient.

More detailed information on medical malpractice is provided elsewhere in the text.

Existence of a Professional Relationship

A patient–provider relationship is established when a patient arrives at an NP's office for a visit, when an NP undertakes the care of a hospitalized patient, or when an NP makes a home visit to a patient. However, patient–provider relationships also can arise in other less obvious ways, including the following:

- Over the telephone
- At a social gathering
- By supervising another's treatment
- By providing sample medication
- By giving advice or opinions to family or friends

When Is a Person a "Patient"?

Consider the following example: NP Jones receives a message to call Nurse Smith at home. Nurse Smith is a former colleague of NP Jones, and Jones remembers Smith as a very talented and competent nurse. Smith is calling about a personal health matter. Smith's son, James, age 6, has an earache. James has had several earaches in the past, all caused by infections, all cleared by amoxicillin. James is otherwise completely healthy, reports Smith.

Smith is working the evening shift, and James is in first grade all day. Smith does not have time to see James' pediatrician until the end of the month, 2 weeks away. Nor does Smith want to pay the $25 copay to see the pediatrician. NP Jones remembers that he met James once at a picnic, but he has never seen James in the office. Smith recalls that she has always respected NP Jones's judgment. Smith asks NP Jones, a family NP, to prescribe amoxicillin for James. Smith is asking a favor, as she and NP Jones both know that Smith's HMO insurance will not reimburse NP Jones for an office visit.

Is 6-year-old James NP Jones's patient? If NP Jones calls in a prescription for James, the answer is yes.

Managing Risk by Limiting Patient Relationships

If NP Jones gives any advice to Nurse Smith or prescribes any medication to James, NP Jones has taken on a professional relationship with James, and James is now NP Jones's patient. NP Jones will then be liable for any breach in the standard of care that leads to an injury to James. It does not matter that James is the patient of another provider. It does not matter that NP Jones will receive no compensation for treating James. It does not matter that the interaction occurs solely over the telephone.

NP Jones, to protect himself (manage his risk), should either: (1) politely refuse to give advice, other than that Smith should call James's pediatrician, or (2) require Smith to bring James to NP Jones's office to go through the usual new patient evaluation before Jones prescribes an antibiotic or otherwise treats James. NP Jones should then follow up with James as NP Jones would with any of his patients.

For 95 out of 100 times that NP Jones is presented with a situation like this, NP Jones could proceed to treat the child over the telephone with no ill effects to the child or to NP Jones's malpractice history. However, NP Jones will be liable in court for the 5% of cases where: (1) the mother makes an erroneous diagnosis, (2) the mother does not know that the organism in the child's ear is resistant to the antibiotic used in the past, or (3) there is some other problem that NP Jones would have discovered with a careful history and physical examination.

In short, NPs should say "no" to all requests they receive for care that skirt the normal, safe evaluation process. The lesson of this case may seem elementary to experienced NPs. However, it is included because the pressure is great to deliver care to people who "just want a little advice" but are not "patients." It is easy for an NP to forget that they bear professional responsibility for *any* healthcare advice given.

What Is the Standard of Care for NPs?

The standard of care in any clinical situation is discovered by answering the question: What reasonable and ordinary care, skill, and diligence would be given by practitioners in good standing, in the same geographic area, in the same general type of practice in similar cases?

NPs are held to the standard of care of the reasonable and diligent NP. Is this the same standard that pertains to physicians? It may be. If the NP is performing primary care services, for example, the standard of care for an NP and for a physician performing those services will be the same standard.

Consider the example of *Fein v. Kaiser Permanente* (discussed in detail elsewhere in the text). The Fein case is a good illustration of a missed diagnosis. In that case, Mr. Fein, a middle-aged attorney, called a Kaiser clinic at midday complaining of chest pains. He got a 4 PM appointment, at which time he was evaluated by an NP who incorrectly diagnosed musculoskeletal pain. Mr. Fein was having a myocardial infarction. Later in the evening,

Mr. Fein was evaluated by a physician, who also incorrectly diagnosed Mr. Fein's chest pain. It was not until Mr. Fein's third visit that an electrocardiogram was done.

The NP easily could have ruled out myocardial infarction through an electrocardiogram at the first visit. That would be risk management. A prudent NP faced with a middle-aged male patient with chest pain would rule out myocardial infarction before diagnosing musculoskeletal pain. In this case, the NP and physician shared the same standard of care.

How Does an NP Keep Up with the Standard of Care?

Sources of information about standards of care for any specific disease or healthcare maintenance effort include:

- Internet articles
- Newsletters and listserves
- Textbooks and reference books
- Professional journals
- Respected colleagues
- Continuing education presentations
- Government agency–generated guidelines, such as Agency for Healthcare Research and Quality guidelines

An NP who wishes to avoid breaching the standard of care will consult current books and journals on a day-to-day basis, will attend continuing education presentations regularly, will refer patients to specialists when necessary, and will seek consultation from attending or consulting physicians or from other NPs when necessary.

Risk of Being Sued for Malpractice When There Was No Clinical Error

Some patients sue healthcare providers when there was a poor outcome but no actual malpractice on the part of the provider. Whether a provider has, in fact, fulfilled the elements of malpractice is not determined until there is a trial on the matter or the matter is settled out of court.

NPs who have the opportunity to defuse a potential lawsuit through extra time spent with a dissatisfied patient should do so, even if they know that any threatened lawsuit is ultimately without merit. Therefore, risk management efforts aimed at avoiding lawsuits include keeping patients satisfied and appeasing dissatisfied patients. Patients are annoyed by long waits for appointments, long waits in the office waiting room, impersonal treatment, and constant busy signals when trying to call the office. Keeping in mind the estimate that 90% of dissatisfied patients will not complain, it is wise to pay attention to patient complaints and to attempt to resolve problems with patients.

Risk of Public Perception That the Individual NP Is a Poor-Quality Provider

The risk of being perceived as a poor-quality provider is perhaps more of a business risk than a legal risk. How could an NP get a reputation as a poor provider? Like any other professional, an NP can get a poor reputation by failing to follow up with clients; by being inattentive, late, forgetful, or sloppy in appearance, demeanor, language, or intellect; by being unreliable; or by being unable to make a decision.

Risk of Breaching Patient Confidentiality

Patients have a right to confidentiality. Breach of privacy is an intentional tort and can be the basis for a lawsuit by a patient. Breach of privacy also can be malpractice, the basis for a disciplinary action by a state's board of nursing, and a violation of state and federal law. And, under federal regulations, a patient who feels that his or her NP has violated his or her privacy rights can complain to the U.S. Office of Civil Rights. The Office may investigate, and, if an NP has not complied with the government's recommendations aimed at protecting patient privacy, the government may fine the NP.

NPs can breach a patient's confidentiality in the following ways:

- Talking about a patient within earshot of others
- Releasing medical information about a patient without prior written permission
- Leaving a telephone message on a patient's answering machine
- Discussing a patient's condition with family members
- Leaving patient records within view
- Discarding unshredded duplicate records
- Giving a patient's name and address to a vendor
- Accessing a patient's medical record unnecessarily, for curiosity purposes
- Leaving a laptop containing patient information on a subway train
- Faxing patient data to the wrong number, by mistake

It is unusual for patients to sue for breach of confidentiality and it may be difficult for patients to prove. However, patient word of mouth about perceived breaches of confidentiality can harm community perception of a medical practice or provider. Therefore, NPs should seek private places to discuss patients, arrange for discarded records to be shredded, keep records out of view of others, and decline to discuss patient conditions or send written documents on a patient unless the NP has the patient's written permission. An example of an authorization form to use when it is necessary to disclose information about patients to third parties for reasons other than patient treatment, payment, or healthcare operations is given in **Exhibit 8-1**.

Exhibit 8-1   Sample Authorization Form

This form allows a patient to authorize release of protected healthcare information for specified purposes other than treatment, payment, and operations, or to disclose protected healthcare information to a specified third party.

I authorize [Name of provider and/or class of person authorized to make the use or disclosure] to release my:

☐ Name
☐ Address
☐ Telephone number
☐ Email address
☐ Social security number
☐ Insurance policy information
☐ Diagnosis or health status
☐ Laboratory tests or results
☐ X-rays
☐ Immunization record
☐ Physical exam results
or
☐ Other information about my health status, described as follows:

_____

_____

To: [Name of authorized recipients or class of recipients to which information may be released]

via:

☐ Fax to [Name and number]
☐ Mail to [Name and address]
☐ Telephone to [Name and telephone number]
☐ Pick up in person

For the purposes of:

_____

_____

This authorization is effective on the date signed and continues until:

☐ [Provide date]

I understand the following:

 a. If I refuse to authorize release of my health information, [Name of practice and provider] may not refuse to treat me.

 b. I may revoke this authorization at any time by notifying [Name and contact information of privacy officer].

 c. The information disclosed pursuant to this authorization may be redisclosed by the recipient and therefore may be outside the protection of federal rules on privacy.

 d. The healthcare provider named here:

  ☐ will

  ☐ will not

  receive remuneration for disclosing information about me.

_____

Signature

_____

Printed name

_____

Date

Risk of Violating a Patient's Right to Informed Consent

A patient has a right to consent to the care being given and a right to refuse care that is offered. An NP has a legal responsibility to give a patient enough information about the risks and benefits of the care being offered that the patient can make an informed decision about accepting the care.

Informed consent involves disclosure of material risks of care and requires that a patient be competent to understand the risks and make a judgment about accepting care. The doctrine of informed consent requires that there be no coercion in getting a patient to consent to care. The law of informed consent is physician oriented, but the doctrine can be expected to be upheld when an NP is the caregiver.

The doctrine of informed consent arose from a societal desire to discourage persons from unauthorized touching of others. The predisposition against nonconsensual touching expanded when applied to the practice of medicine. In medicine, the requirement is that a physician must inform a patient about what is to be done and obtain the patient's consent before treating. Even though the doctrine of informed consent is grounded in the law of battery, the objective of the courts in applying the doctrine of informed consent has been more involved than the simple avoidance of one person's unauthorized touching of another. The majority of courts have adopted a self-determination rationale for informed consent. That is, a person has a right to determine what shall be done with his or her body.[1]

Many cases where patients have complained that their right to informed consent was violated involved surgery. Of course, surgery is only one of many possible treatments, and physicians are only one of many possible healthcare providers. There are many decisions to be made when a person seeks medical attention, most of which are less dramatic than surgery. For example, prescription drugs have been known to have side effects not discovered until years after the drugs are in common use. Even when a treatment has been used for years with relatively few complications, patients subjected to treatment may want to know that they are taking a risk and that there may be side effects.

An NP who is trying to minimize personal risk and risk to a patient will give as much information as possible to a patient contemplating any therapy. How much information does a patient need? Enough to formulate a reasonable decision.

If an NP failed to get informed consent from a patient before treating the patient, the patient could sue the NP, basing a suit on battery or on negligence. A patient who sued an NP for battery would claim that the patient had not authorized the NP to touch the patient. A patient who sued on the basis of negligence would claim that the NP had not given the patient enough information to consent, in an informed way, to the treatment. In either case, a patient could win monetary damages from an NP.

Does an NP need to get consent for everything? It is well established that before a surgeon performs surgery, he or she must obtain the informed consent of the patient. It is less clear whether an NP must get informed consent before prescribing medication; whether minor but invasive procedures, such as blood transfusion, the starting of intravenous lines, and office incision and drainage, require informed consent; and whether noninvasive treatments carrying some risk, such as office psychotherapy, massage, or even an examination, require informed consent.

At least 25 states have legislation regarding informed consent.[2] An example of an informed-consent statute, one that is oriented toward the physician, is New York's. That law defines lack of informed consent as:

> Failure of the person providing the professional treatment or diagnosis to disclose to the patient such alternatives thereto and the reasonable, foreseeable risks and benefits involved as a reasonable medical, dental, or podiatric practitioner under similar circumstances would have disclosed, in a manner permitting the patient to make a knowledgeable evaluation.

> *Citation:* N.Y. Pub. Health Law § 2805-d.

The law limits the right of action to nonemergent therapies and diagnostic procedures that involve invasion or disruption of the integrity of the body. The statute conforms with New York's case law, which limits the cause of action to procedures that are invasive. The law lists defenses.

Another example of a statute addressing informed consent is Washington's (Wash. Rev. Stat. Ann. Code § 7.70.050). That law states the elements of informed consent as: (1) failure to inform regarding a material fact, (2) patient consented without being aware of the facts, (3) a reasonably prudent patient would not have consented if the information had been adequately conveyed, and (4) injury to the patient.

All states have case law requiring that physicians inform patients of the risks and benefits of surgery and obtain patient consent in writing before doing surgery.

Some courts have defined treatment broadly.[3] Among the nonsurgical treatments around which informed-consent issues have emerged are application of oxygen to a neonate [*Burton v. Brooklyn Doctor's Hosp.* 88 A.D.2d 217, 452 N.Y.S. 2d 875 (App. Div. 1982)],[4] radiation therapy [*Nelson v. Patrick*, 58 N.C. App. 546, 293 S.E.2d 829 (Ct. App. 1982), appeal after remand 73 N.C. App. 1, 326 S.E.2d 45 (1985)], and gastroscopy [*Cooper v. Roberts*, 220 Pa. Super. 260, 286 A.2d 647 (Super. Ct. 1971)]. The courts found that the plaintiffs had causes of action. The Supreme Court of Pennsylvania stated that a physician's duty to disclose a collateral risk involved in treatment is the same "whether or not the treatment can be technically termed operative" (*Cooper v. Roberts*, 220 Pa. Super. 260, 2, 286 A.2d).

Other courts, while not holding that the doctrine of informed consent applies to nonsurgical treatments, have stated in an aside (dictum) that the term "treatment" can be broadly construed [*Pratt v. University of Minn. Affiliated Hosps. and Clinics*, 414 N.W.2d 399 (Minn. Ct. App. 1987)]. The state that defines treatment most broadly is Minnesota. According to the Minnesota Supreme Court, bed rest, when combined with special instructions, would constitute treatment [*Madsen v. Park Nicollet Med. Ctr.*, 431 N.W.2d 855 (Minn. 1988)]. At the opposite extreme is New York, where the need for informed consent is limited to invasive procedures [*Karlsons v. Guerinot*, 57 A.D.2d 73, 394 N.Y.S.2d 933 (App. Div. 1977)].

At least one court has declined to find the need for informed consent in a common, minor, invasive procedure. Informed consent was not applicable to the giving of a flu shot in a Louisiana medical clinic. The court stated that "medical or surgical procedure" did not extend to a flu shot and that to hold otherwise would lead to results in the day-to-day practice of medicine never intended by the legislature [*Novak v. Texada, Miller, Masterson and Davis Med. Clinic*, 514 So. 2d 524, writ denied, 515 So. 2d 807 (La. 1987)]. That one court found bed rest a treatment but another found an injection not a medical or surgical procedure demonstrates the inconsistency of viewpoint among jurisdictions.

The Minnesota Supreme Court, going a step further than most other jurisdictions, stated, "[We] believe there may be some nontreatment situations where the doctrine should be applicable" [*Pratt v. University of Minn. Affiliated Hosps. and Clinics*, 414 N.W.2d 399 (Minn. Ct. App. 1987)]. In *Pratt*, a case about genetic counseling, a plaintiff couple asserted that physicians had been negligent in not disclosing the risk of the couple's encountering a particular genetic abnormality in future children. The physicians, after interviewing the couple and obtaining the tests available, had rejected one possible diagnosis, autosomal recessive disorder, as highly unlikely. Therefore, they did not disclose to the parents the risks of that condition. A subsequent child of the couple was born with autosomal recessive disorder, the diagnosis thought unlikely by the physicians. The plaintiffs asked the Minnesota court to apply to genetic counseling a variation on the doctrine of informed consent [*Pratt v. University of Minn. Affiliated Hosps. and Clinics*, 414 N.W.2d 399 (Minn. Ct. App. 1987)]. Because diagnostic advice and counseling, not treatment, was the medical service involved, the term *negligent nondisclosure* was used. Negligent nondisclosure is discussed more fully in the next section.

The court held that the mere diagnosis of a condition, where all appropriate tests have been performed, does not give rise to a duty to disclose risks inherent in conditions not diagnosed [*Pratt v. University of Minn. Affiliated Hosps. and Clinics*, 414 N.W.2d 399 (Minn. Ct. App. 1987)]. While negligent nondisclosure did not apply in this case, the court stated that the doctrine could be applicable in some other nontreatment situations.

In summary, there is wide disparity among the states regarding how the doctrine of informed consent may be applied. At one end of the continuum, informed consent is needed only for invasive procedures. At the other end, it is needed for counseling.

In *Canterbury v. Spence* [464 F.2d 777 (D.C. Cir. 1972)] [See also *Sard v. Hardy* (281 Md. 432, 379 A.2d 1014)], the U.S. Court of Appeals for the District of Columbia Circuit gave some general advice to physicians that holds true today and can be applied to NPs. The court declined to adopt a standard of full disclosure, saying that it is prohibitive and unrealistic to expect physicians to discuss every risk of a proposed treatment and that such full information generally is unnecessary from a patient's viewpoint. However, the court listed physicians' responsibilities regarding disclosure:

1. Communicate information to the patient when the exigencies of reasonable care call for it.
2. Alert the patient to symptoms of bodily abnormality.
3. Inform the patient when the ailment does not respond to the physician's ministrations.
4. Instruct the patient about any limitations to be observed for his or her own welfare.
5. Inform the patient about precautionary therapy that he or she should seek in the future.
6. Advise the patient of the need for or desirability of any alternative treatments promising greater benefit than that being pursued.
7. Advise the patient regarding risks to his or her well-being that the contemplated therapy may involve.

Citation: Canterbury v. Spence, 464 F.2d 772 (D.C. Cir. 1972).

Many practices cover the risk of a claim of battery by having each patient sign a consent to an examination at the time of registration. Most practices have informed-consent policies that address invasive procedures, such as endometrial biopsy, cervical biopsy, and incision and drainage.

NPs who want to avoid the risk of violating the informed-consent doctrine should do the following:

- Give patients information on risks, benefits, and alternatives to any invasive procedure, and obtain written consent for any procedure.
- Find out what state law requires in the way of informed consent for specific tests, treatments, and procedures.

- Give patients information on the risks, benefits, and alternatives to any treatment, including prescription medications, and ask for their agreement to the treatment.
- Document that information about the risks, benefits, and alternatives to the treatment has been given to the patient and that the patient agrees to the treatment.

Does an NP Need to Get Consent in Writing?

Consent to surgery must be in writing. Consent for invasive procedures that could be considered surgery—endometrial biopsy, for example—should also be in writing. If state law requires consent for specific testing, it must be in writing. In general, however, consent to medical treatment need not be in writing.

Special Cases
Emergency Situations

In an emergency, care may be given to save a patient's life, even if consent cannot be obtained prior to treatment.

Incompetency

A patient who is unconscious or mentally retarded; who has been judged insane; who cannot read, write, or hear; or who is under the influence of sedative drugs or alcohol is not competent to give consent. With the exception of an emergency situation, NPs should avoid treating such patients unless a parent or a court-appointed guardian is available to give consent.

Minors

Minor children cannot consent to treatment. Parental consent is necessary.

Risk of Negligent Nondisclosure

The doctrine of negligent nondisclosure emerged when a physician found an abnormality but failed to sufficiently alert the patient. For example, in *Cornfeldt v. Tongen* [262 N.W.2d 684 (Minn. 1977)], a physician failed to inform a patient of abnormalities in blood testing prior to surgery.

The Minnesota Supreme Court defined the elements of negligent nondisclosure as: (1) nondisclosure of a risk inherent in the treatment, (2) harm materialized from that risk, and (3) proximate causation. The elements of lack of informed consent are the same. The terms *lack of informed consent* and *negligent nondisclosure* refer to the same concept, though they are applicable in different situations. Consent is applicable when a treatment is proposed. Nondisclosure is applicable when an omission of information leads to an injury.

Under the doctrine of negligent nondisclosure, a physician (or an NP), having examined a patient and having found an abnormality, has a duty to inform the patient of the abnormality so that the patient can choose whether to submit to further tests [*Gates v. Jensen*, 92 Wash. 2d 246, 595 P.2d (1979); *Canterbury v. Spence*, 464 F.2d 777 (D.C. Cir. 1972)]. All facts must be disclosed that the doctor (or, by inference, the NP) knows or should know for the patient to make a decision. Some examples include *Truman v. Thomas*, 165 Cal. Rptr. 308, 611 P.2d 902 (Cal. 1980), in which a patient sued a physician for failing to disclose the danger of refusing a Pap smear, and *Lauderdale v. United States*, 666 F. Supp. 1511 (D. Ala. 1987), in which a physician was found liable when he did not inform a patient of a heart problem, the seriousness of the problem, and the necessity for a return visit.

In *Gates*,[5] a physician discovered an increased pressure in a patient's eyes. This suggested glaucoma, a treatable eye disease. The physician failed to inform the patient of the abnormality and of diagnostic procedures that could be undertaken to determine the significance of the abnormality. This resulted in a delay in the diagnosis and treatment of the glaucoma. By the time glaucoma was diagnosed, the patient was functionally blind. The Supreme Court of Washington found that the physician had a duty of disclosure. The court held that the doctrine of informed consent required that the ophthalmologist inform the patient of an abnormality discovered during a routine examination and of diagnostic procedures that could be taken to determine the significance of that abnormality. The court reasoned that a physician has a fiduciary duty to inform a patient of abnormalities in his or her body.[6]

In *Truman*, the issue was whether a physician should have disclosed to his patient the risks of refusing a test. There, a physician had advised his patient to have a Pap smear, a test that detects the presence of cervical cancer, but did not inform her of the risks of refusing the test. She refused to have it. As a result, cancer of the cervix went undiscovered until it had become disseminated. The patient died at the age of 30. The Supreme Court of California held that the trial judge should have given an instruction to the jury that would have allowed the jury to consider whether the physician breached a duty by not disclosing to the patient the danger of failing to undergo a Pap smear.

From a healthcare provider's point of view, there are few guidelines. To give too much detail could be uneconomical. To give too little could be negligent. From a patient's point of view, a requirement that more information be given can be only beneficial.

Right of Patients to Refuse Treatment

Patients may refuse treatment. NPs caring for patients who refuse treatment that the NP believes is necessary should inform such patients of the risks of refusing treatment. After that, it is the patient's right to decide. NPs should document that they have explained the risks, benefits, and alternatives of treatment and the risks of refusing treatment and that the patient nevertheless refuses it.

Risk of Poor Quality Ratings

Increasingly, consumer-oriented groups and Medicare are compiling and reporting data on performance of healthcare providers using various measures. Consumer-oriented groups collect data from health plans, and health plans collect the data from medical practices. The National Committee on Quality Assurance's HEDIS (Health Plan Employer Data and Information Set) is currently the most commonly applied performance criterion among health plans. HEDIS data are gathered from patient surveys, patient charts, and billing forms. For more information or current HEDIS measures, visit the website (http://www.ncqa.org). Medicare collects quality data through its Physician Quality Reporting Initiative (PQRI). For more information on PQRI, visit the Center for Medicare and Medicaid Services (CMS) website (http://www.cms.hhs.gov).

An NP who wants to avoid the risk of poor quality ratings should:

- Understand what performance measures currently are being used
- Develop personal or practicewide systems for complying with performance guidelines and monitoring his or her performance
- Request and obtain feedback on performance

Risk of Disciplinary Action

A state board of nursing approves an NP's right to practice in a state. A board of nursing can suspend or revoke an NP's license.

A court cannot revoke an NP's license. A court can find against an NP in a malpractice lawsuit and direct an NP to pay an injured patient monetary damages, however. If, on the basis of what a judge hears in a case, the judge believes an NP to be grossly negligent, the judge may report the nurse to the board of nursing. *Gross negligence* is indifference to duty or the intentional failure to perform a manifest duty in reckless disregard of the consequences as affecting the life of another.

A board of nursing will respond not only to reports of gross nursing negligence, but also to reports of impairment, fraud, or criminal activity by nurses. Impairment could be reported by a patient, coworker, or supervisor, based on their observation of a nurse. Fraud might include falsifying the nurse's application to the board, falsifying medical records, or documenting that a patient has been seen when the patient has not. A nurse convicted of a felony can expect to be investigated by the board of nursing.

In general, the disciplinary process is as follows:

1. The NP receives a letter stating that he or she is being investigated by the board and requesting that the NP call the board to arrange a meeting.
2. The NP meets with an investigator. The investigator will produce records or other evidence of questionable care given by the NP and ask the NP to respond. The NP may explain why the NP conducted the care or documented the care as they did.
3. The investigator will gather information from other sources. The investigator may talk with auditors, colleagues, patients, or administrators.
4. The investigator will recommend to the board that the investigation be dropped or will recommend a hearing.
5. An administrative hearing, resembling a trial, will be held. The NP should be represented by an attorney. The board of nursing will be represented by a state attorney. Evidence may be presented. Witnesses may testify. Often, the board will give the nurse the option of a prehearing settlement conference. In that case, the nurse, his or her attorney, some board members, and some board staff meet in a less formal setting and discuss the matter. The board representatives may recommend a disposition of the matter without an evidentiary hearing.

6. A hearing officer (or board member present at the prehearing settlement conference) will make a recommendation to the board.
7. The board will decide to drop the matter or discipline the nurse.
8. Discipline may include probation, suspension of a license, or revocation of a license.
9. After the passage of a specified time period, the nurse whose license is revoked may reapply for licensure.

Only a small percentage of registered nurses have been subject to disciplinary action by boards of nursing. The percentage of NPs subject to disciplinary action is probably even smaller. However, NPs are subject to discipline, and it is not unusual for an NP to be called before the board of nursing for an investigatory meeting. For example, an NP might be reported to the board of nursing after an audit of a hospital or nursing home turned up irregularities.

An NP who receives a notice of investigation should be worried. Even if an investigator characterizes the meeting as nonadversarial and states that its purpose is strictly information gathering, an investigation is in fact adversarial and an NP has much to lose. NPs should know that state auditors of nursing homes are not NPs and may not be experienced in evaluating the work of NPs. Furthermore, board of nursing investigators usually are not NPs, though they are probably registered nurses (RNs). An RN investigator may ask such questions as, "This EKG [electrocardiogram] reading says 'abnormal EKG.' Why did you not call in a cardiologist, or send the patient to the emergency room?" The answer may well be: "That abnormality is a left axis deviation that was not clinically significant for that patient at that time. A cardiology consult or an emergency room visit was not clinically indicated." That response may end the inquiry about the abnormal EKG. The RN investigator may not know the nuances of EKG interpretation and may find that answer satisfactory. An NP who can explain all of his or her actions probably will find that the investigation ends with the meeting. However, an NP who is distraught by the nature of the investigation may not give clear explanations. An NP under the pressure and emotional upset of investigatory questioning may not be as assertive in defending his or her actions as is legally prudent.

An NP who receives a letter notifying him or her of an investigation by the board of nursing should retain an attorney immediately. The attorney should represent the NP at the initial meeting with the investigator for the board of nursing. Investigators may tell NPs that an attorney is not necessary. Investigators may also tell NPs that attorneys are not allowed at the meeting. Nevertheless, the NP should engage an attorney, and the attorney can communicate with the investigator about attending the meeting. Attorneys are comfortable with adversarial interactions, are experienced in advocating for clients, and are not likely to dissolve into tears when an investigator questions the NP's professional competency. Furthermore, an attorney will see that an NP's due process rights are protected through the investigation and hearing.

Risk of Medicare Fraud

In the past 15 years, the U.S. Justice Department has increased its investigative efforts into healthcare fraud and abuse. The level of fraudulent billing is such that an estimated 7% to 8% of total healthcare spending goes not for care given, but for care not given.[7]

NPs are responsible for ensuring that the billing for their services matches the level of care given and that their documentation matches the level of care billed. *Upcoding* is billing for a higher level of visit than actually was conducted. Upcoding is healthcare fraud.

Each Current Procedural Terminology (CPT) code has corresponding levels of required history taking, physical examination, and medical decision making, all of which must be supported in an NP's medical record documentation. For example, if an NP meets all of the criteria for a CPT 99214 visit and bills for a 99214 visit but documents only the criteria for a 99213 visit, the NP is at risk of being charged with Medicare fraud. Fraud is intentional deception. Billing a higher code than is supported by documentation may be unintentional. However, NPs are expected to know how to bill correctly. Ignorance is a poor defense. Furthermore, if a provider pleads ignorance but auditors find that more errors were made in overcoding than undercoding visits, a court will find that the upcoding was intentional. On the other hand, providers will not want to undercode. Undercoding will lead to low revenues for a practice.

Consequences of selecting an inappropriate code are Medicare or Medicaid audit failure, loss of Medicare or Medicaid provider status, a fine, and loss or restriction of the NP's license by the board of nursing. Obviously, the consequences also can include loss of one's job.

CMS and the American Medical Association have agreed upon a set of documentation guidelines. These guidelines went into effect in July 1998. Revisions have been proposed since then, but as of the publication of this text, clinicians should abide by the 1995 or 1997 guidelines, whichever the clinician finds to be most useful. The guidelines appear in Appendix 4-A.

Business Risk Management

An NP who starts a business risks business failure. If the NP has partners or fellow directors or stockholders in a corporation, the NP also risks failure of those relationships.

Who Is the Boss?

Consider the following example: Nurse Practitioner Able and Nurse Practitioner Best have agreed to go into practice together. Able is an OB-GYN NP, and Best is a family NP. They are both very experienced. They have known each other for 5 years. They have never worked together, but each knows that the other is well respected in the community. They have carefully planned the business and have decided to be "equal partners."

A friend of Best's told Best that she should have a written agreement with Able. Best called Attorney Clodd, who told Best that he charged $350 an hour and that a partnership agreement usually ran about $900. Clodd also told Best that he would represent only Best and that Able should have her own attorney in the partnership-forming process. Able and Best wanted to forego the expenses of attorneys at this stage. They decided not to draw up a partnership agreement.

The practice opened. Able and Best had no problem choosing the location for the practice, the furniture, or the equipment. They agreed on a receptionist.

After 3 months, Best noticed that half of Able's patients were without insurance and that many did not pay for service at the time of service and owed the practice money. Best's patients had insurance for the most part. Furthermore, the lab was billing the practice for Pap smears and other expensive gynecologic tests, and the lab's bills were mounting. Best had been telling her patients that if there was no insurance to cover the visit and any necessary laboratory work, the patient, not the practice, was responsible for the office visit and lab charges.

Best told Able about the bills and the accounts receivable for Able's patients. Able, who saw her patient roster growing, did not want to offend patients by pressing about the bills. Best wanted to press the patients with outstanding bills for payment. Best's husband was tiring of Best being without a paycheck and was pressuring Best to be a better businessperson.

Who is the boss in this situation? Able and Best did not establish a method of resolving disagreements between them. Therefore, no one is the boss, and they could argue about this issue, or other issues, for years.

How to Avoid a Broken Partnership

When a practitioner starts a business alone, there is no confusion about who makes the administrative and business decisions. Whenever more than one person is involved, however, there will be more than one opinion on how the business should operate. Often, decisions must be made for which there is no "right" or "wrong" answer. Magazines on medical practice management and the civil courts are full of examples of partnerships gone sour. Often, the reasons for the breakup are differences of opinion on how practice collections are made and how practice money is spent. To avoid the risk of deadlocked disagreement, which can lead to hurt feelings, which in turn can lead to "wanting out," it is wise for the members of the group to agree upon a decision-making process from the outset.

Any private practice should have one of the following forms of business: sole proprietorship, partnership, or corporation. If the business is a corporation, the corporation's bylaws (or operating agreement, in the case of a limited liability corporation) describe the chain of command within the company. If the business is a partnership, the partners in the business should have an agreement between them specifying the decision-making process. Partners who fail to specify, early in the process of forming the practice, who is to make what decisions and how a deadlock will be resolved will be facing a short-lived association.

Drawing up an administrative chart should be one of the first tasks in the planning process. At minimum, all principal practitioners should agree to the administrative structure. It is prudent to consult an attorney.

Dealing with High-Risk Patients

Certain patient characteristics should alert an NP to be especially aware of risk management strategies. These characteristics are multisystem failure, low intelligence, polypharmacy, noncompliant behavior, positive review of systems, substance abuse, and litigiousness.

Multisystem Failure

Refer or work closely with a consultant when caring for patients with multisystem failure. The risk is failure to refer when the standard of care would call for referral.

Low Intelligence

Have a guardian present when counseling or teaching a patient with low intelligence. The risk is failure to get informed consent to treatment. A patient who does not have the intellectual capability to process information and make decisions about his or her own care cannot be assumed to have consented to treatment.

Polypharmacy

When patients are on many medications, list the medications, side effects, cautions, and dosing instructions for the patient, or coordinate with a pharmacist who will run computer printouts with the information. Review the dosing schedule with the patient at every visit. Ascertain that the patient can read—that the patient is literate and has adequate eyesight.

Noncompliant Patients

Document attempts and strategies for increasing compliance in the noncompliant patient. Document the patient's verbal responses to the NP's questions about why the patient has not taken the recommended medication, controlled the diet, or changed the dressings.

Positive Review of Systems

When a patient has a generally positive review of systems, consider expanding the patient's problem list even further to include somatization, need for social support, inability to cope with life's pressures, and dependency issues. Consider repeating the review of systems on another visit to see whether the complaints persist. If so, an NP should be prepared to dissect each complaint, taking the more risky complaints first. Whether the problem list is long or short, there is no difference in the standard of care expected of an NP.

Substance Abuse

Do not be lured into becoming a source for a patient who is abusing substances. Patients have sued their healthcare providers for contributing to their substance abuse by prescribing medication.

Litigiousness

Patients who bring up their ongoing lawsuits against another provider can be expected to repeat the performance by suing their current provider.

Notes

1. The right to self-determination was explained by J. Cardozo in 1914: "Every human being of adult years and sound mind has a right to determine what shall be done with his own body; and a [physician who administers treatment] without his patient's consent commits an assault for which he is liable in damages." *Schloendorff v. Society of N.Y. Hospital*, 211 N.Y. 25, 105 N.E. 92 (1914).

2. *Hospital Law Manual, Attorney's Vol. IIB.* (1983). Gaithersburg, MD: Aspen Publishers.

3. For example, in *Head v. Colloton* [331 N.W.2d 870, 875 (Iowa 1983)], the court said, "Treatment is broad enough to embrace all steps in applying medical arts to a person." In *Patrich v. Menorah Med. Ctr.* [636 S.W.2d 134 (1982)], the Missouri Court of Appeals defined treatment as "measures necessary for physical well-being of the patient." Black's Law Dictionary defines treatment as including "examination and diagnosis as well as application of remedies" (6th ed., 1990, p. 1502).

4. In this case, administration of oxygen in high doses caused blindness in the infant.

5. The court used the doctrine of informed consent, even though the issue was not one of consent but of knowledge of an abnormality requiring further evaluation.

6. A duty arises whenever a doctor becomes aware of an abnormality that may indicate risk or danger. The facts that must be disclosed are all those facts that the physician knows or should know that the patient needs to make a decision about treatment. Id. at 923.

7. Sparrow, M. K. (1996). *License to steal.* Boulder, CO: Westview Press.

CHAPTER 9

Reimbursement for Nurse Practitioner Services

Although a small minority of patients pay their own medical bills, most encounters between an NP and a patient include a third-party participant—the payer. Whether an NP is employed by a medical practice or self-employed, the reimbursement policies of third-party payers often will determine whether an NP continues to provide care on a long-term basis.

Payers

There are five major categories of third-party payers:

1. Medicare
2. Medicaid
3. Indemnity insurance companies
4. Managed-care organizations (MCOs)
5. Businesses that contract for certain services

Each type of payer has its own reimbursement policies and fee schedules, and each operates under a separate body of law. Some payers reimburse NPs in the same manner that they reimburse physicians. On the other hand, some payers have NP-specific rules and policies regarding reimbursement. Not every payer will pay every NP for every service.

Medicare

Medicare is a federal program, administered nationally by the Center for Medicare and Medicaid Services (CMS) and administered locally by Medicare carrier agencies. Medicare covers two groups: (1) patients 65 years and older who have enrolled and pay premiums and (2) disabled individuals who qualify for Social Security disability payments and benefits.

Medicare pays for the care of an enrolled patient under one of two arrangements. If a patient covered by Medicare is not enrolled with an MCO, Medicare reimburses the patient's healthcare provider on a fee-for-service basis through a local Medicare carrier agency. If a patient has enrolled in a managed-care health plan, there is an extra payment step between the payer and the provider. Medicare pays the health plan on a capitated basis, an all-inclusive lump sum per month for each patient. Health plans then pay providers on a fee-for-service or capitated basis.

Fee-for-Service Medicare

Fee-for-service reimbursement is payment for specific healthcare services under a fee schedule. A health service might be an office visit, surgery, ear irrigation, suturing of a wound, a Pap smear, or any one of thousands of others. Fees are based on a complex variety of factors, including the number and type of services provided, the Current Procedural Terminology (CPT) and International Classification of Diseases (ICD) codes, the geographic area of service, and certain office and training expenses of the provider. All reimbursable services have a CPT code. CPT is a uniform coding system developed by the American Medical Association and adopted by third-party payers for use in claim submission. All CPT codes have a corresponding Medicare fee. All medical diagnoses have an ICD code.

Fees for CPT codes may vary in different locations and for different providers depending on a complex variety of factors, including the geographic area of service and particular office, malpractice, and the training expenses of the provider. Under Medicare, NPs may be reimbursed at a rate of 85% of the physician fee schedule. Under a fee-for-service system of reimbursement, the more services an NP performs, the more money he or she will generate.

The physician fee schedule is determined using a system called a resource-based relative value scale (RBRVS). The RBRVS, developed by CMS, the federal agency charged with administering Medicare, determines reimbursement for Medicare Part B services. The RBRVS assigns a relative value to each procedural code (CPT code). Under the RBRVS system, services are reimbursed on the basis of resources related to the procedure rather than simply on the basis of historical trends.

There are three components to a relative value: (1) a practice expense component, (2) a work component, and (3) a malpractice component. Each component is adjusted geographically, using three separate Geographic Practice Cost Indexes (GPCIs). The final formula to arrive at an area-specific relative value is:

$$(\text{Practice Expense RV} \times \text{Practice Expense GPCI}) + (\text{Work RV} \times \text{Work GPCI}) + (\text{Malpractice RV} \times \text{Malpractice GPCI}) = \text{Relative Value}$$

The relative value is then multiplied by a single "conversion factor" to arrive at the geographic-specific fee schedule allowable for a given area. The conversion factor is based on whether the service is surgical or medical. RBRVS affects payments made to physicians, NPs, and other providers entitled to Medicare and other forms of third-party reimbursement.

An NP wishing to provide service to a Medicare patient on a fee-for-service basis applies to be a Medicare provider. Once the NP has a provider number, he or she submits bills to the local Medicare carrier agency for each visit or procedure. A standard form, the CMS 1500, is used. NPs who are self-employed receive 85% of the physician charge for the billed procedure. When an NP is employed by physicians and can meet "incident to" requirements, the practice may receive 100% of the physician charge for the billed procedure, subject to the "incident to" rules.

"Incident to" Services

The full term for "incident to" is "incident to a physician's professional service." The term is particular to Medicare. The legal definition of "incident to" services is services furnished as an "integral, although incidental, part of the physician's personal professional services in the course of diagnosis or treatment of an injury or illness."[1] To qualify under this definition, the services of nonphysicians must be rendered in a physician's office under a physician's "direct personal supervision." Nonphysicians must be employees of a physician or physician group or have an independent contractor relationship with the group. Services must be furnished during a course of treatment in which a physician performs an initial service and subsequent services of a frequency that reflects the physician's active participation in and management of the course of treatment. Direct personal supervision in the office setting does not mean that a physician must be in the same room. However, a physician must be present in the office suite and immediately available to provide assistance and direction throughout the time that an NP is performing services. "Incident to" may refer to the services of office nurses and technicians as well as NPs.

Capitated Medicare

Capitation is a fee paid by an MCO to a healthcare provider, per patient, per month, for care of an MCO member. Capitated fees for primary care vary, based on a patient's age and sex. Under a capitated system of reimbursement, NPs and physicians are paid a set fee per patient per month for all services agreed to by contract. If an NP has agreed to provide all primary care services for a patient, then the NP must provide an unlimited number of primary care visits. On the other hand, if a patient never visits, the NP operating under a capitated system of reimbursement still is paid.

An NP wishing to provide care for a Medicare patient enrolled in an MCO applies to the MCO for admission to the organization's provider panel. For information about applying for admission to managed-care provider panels, see **Exhibit 9-1**.

Exhibit 9-1   How to Apply for Provider Status

First, apply for a National Provider Identifier online, through the National Plan & Provider Enumeration System (NPPES).

Medicare
1. Apply on line at http://www.cms.gov.
2. Bill Medicare electronically on a form called the CMS 1500, using the patient's name and identifying information, the diagnosis code (ICD), the procedure code (CPT), the charge, and the NP's provider number.
3. If a Medicare patient is enrolled in managed care, see the "Managed-Care Organizations" section of this exhibit.

Medicaid
1. Apply through the state Medicaid agency. Ask for Provider Relations, and then ask for a provider application as an NP.
2. Bill the state Medicaid agency on a CMS 1500 form, using the patient's name and identifying information, the ICD code, the CPT code, the charge, and the NP's name, provider number, and location.
3. If a Medicaid patient is enrolled in managed care, see the "Managed-Care Organizations" section of this exhibit.

Indemnity Insurer
1. Call the company to inquire whether a provider credentialing number is required. If so, apply. If not, submit a CMS 1500 form to the company for the services rendered.
2. If the company rejects a bill, the company will return the CMS 1500 with a short explanation about why it is being rejected. If the rejection is erroneous, write a letter to the company protesting the rejection and explaining the error, if possible, or supply whatever further information is needed. Sometimes several letters will be necessary before a bill is paid. Sometimes it will be necessary to include a copy of appropriate law with correspondence. Occasionally, intervention by a practice's attorney is necessary. Occasionally, a company will persist in refusing to pay. If so, the patient is liable for the bill.

Managed-Care Organizations
1. Call Provider Relations for each MCO for which admission is needed, and request an application for admission to the panel of providers. Many MCOs want providers credentialed through the Council for Affordable Quality Healthcare. Apply online through that organization's website.
2. If rejected, note the reason for rejection and, if applicable, consult state insurance law. In some states, an HMO or MCO cannot discriminate among providers on the basis of class of license. In other states, HMOs can accept or reject any provider. Ask for an opportunity to present the case for admitting NPs to the provider panel. Pursue a company through letters, presentations, meetings, and telephone calls, going up the supervisory line if necessary.

Individuals covered by Medicare may choose between traditional fee-for-service coverage and managed care.

Medicaid

Medicaid is a federal program, administered by the states, for mothers and children who qualify on the basis of poverty and for adults who are disabled for the short term—1 year or less—and who qualify on the basis of poverty.

Like patients covered by Medicare, some patients covered by Medicaid are enrolled in MCOs and others are not. To serve a Medicaid patient not enrolled in an MCO, an NP must apply and be accepted as a Medicaid provider by the state Medicaid agency. To serve a

Medicaid patient enrolled in an MCO, an NP must apply and be admitted to the provider panel of the MCO in which the patient is enrolled.

Medicaid pays NPs 70% to 100% of the fee-for-service rates set for physicians by state Medicaid agencies. State law controls the rate. Medicaid reimbursement generally is lower than the rates paid by commercial insurers. For information on rates, contact the state Medicaid agency.

Many states have applied to the federal government for "Medicaid waivers." A Medicaid waiver gives permission to a state from CMS to administer Medicaid in ways that differ from the federal laws and regulations; specifically, to enroll patients covered by Medicaid in MCOs. Once a state has received a Medicaid waiver, NPs can expect that most, if not all, patients covered by Medicaid will enroll in MCOs or other managed-care plans. NPs who have served Medicaid patients on a fee-for-service basis must apply for admission to the appropriate managed-care provider panels to maintain reimbursement.

Indemnity Insurers

An indemnity insurer is an insurance company that pays for the medical care of its insured but does not deliver health care. Indemnity insurers pay healthcare providers on a per-visit, per-procedure basis. To obtain reimbursement, an NP submits a billing form to the insurance company (see "Billing" later in this chapter).

Until a few years ago, indemnity insurers had fee schedules based on "usual and customary" charges. "Usual and customary" is an insurance industry term for a charge that is (1) usual and customary when compared with the charges made for similar services and supplies and (2) made to persons having similar medical conditions in the county of the policyholder or such larger area than a county as is needed to secure a representative cross section of fees. "Usual and customary" could be calculated differently from insurer to insurer. Therefore, some insurers pay more than others for the same procedure.

In the past, if a provider charged more than what an insurer considered to be "usual and customary," the insurer paid only the usual and customary charge. In that case, the patient was responsible for the difference between what a provider charged and what an insurer paid. It was up to the provider to collect the difference from the patient. Some providers agreed to accept the "usual and customary" payment and did not pursue patients for the difference. Other providers pursued patients for the provider's full charge, no matter what portion was paid by an insurer.

Today, fee schedules are negotiated between provider and payer. The fee schedule may or may not be based on what is usual and customary. If a payer understands that many providers will accept a fee for a service, then the provider who wants a higher fee will be in a poor negotiating position. On the other hand, where providers are scarce, they are in a better position to negotiate higher fees.

Patients who do not have health insurance and who therefore pay their own medical bills often are in the unfortunate position of paying a much higher price than insurers and health plans, who have negotiated discounts from practice and facility fee schedules.

Managed-Care Organizations

An MCO is an insurer that provides both healthcare services and payment for the services. MCO is an umbrella term that may include HMOs and other forms of health plans. An HMO is a prepaid, comprehensive system of health benefits that combines the financing and delivery of health services to subscribers.

NPs are increasingly gaining admission to MCO provider panels. With panel membership comes the designation primary care provider (PCP), a contract for providing care, credentialing, directory listing, and reimbursement.

A PCP has full responsibility for a patient's primary care, including (1) complying with the MCO's quality, utilization, and patient satisfaction standards; (2) coordinating care with specialists, hospitals, or long-term care facilities; (3) approving or denying referrals for specialty care; (4) keeping costs as low as possible while maintaining quality; and (5) providing a system for 24-hour access to care. "Medical home" is a term associated with many of the same responsibilities as a PCP, with emphasis on attending to the patient's preventive care, coordination of care, and achieving positive outcomes. When a provider is a patient's medical home, the provider may be eligible for enhanced reimbursement. NPs are eligible to provide medical homes under some state programs.

MCOs reimburse PCPs on a fee-for-service basis, a capitated basis, or a combination of fee-for-service and capitation. Each MCO negotiates a payment arrangement with each group, practice, or provider on its panel. (See "Negotiating an MCO Contract" later in this chapter.)

How MCOs Work

MCOs sell a priced package of health services to their clients, who may be employers, individuals, or government agencies, such as the state Medicaid agency or Medicare. A client signs up for a particular plan and offers that plan to patients, or "members," who often share in the cost of the plan. Each MCO has a panel of healthcare providers who may or may not be employed by the MCO.

Group-Model Versus Practice-Model MCOs

There are two types of affiliation between MCO and provider. The first type is an employer–employee arrangement, called the *group-model MCO*. The best known group-model MCO is Kaiser Permanente. A group-model MCO pays a provider a set salary in return for taking care of a panel of patients. In the second type of affiliation, called the *practice-model MCO*, the MCO contracts with independent providers, group practices, or practice associations for a "product line" of services. Contracts between an MCO and a practice govern the relationship. (See "Negotiating an MCO Contract" later in this chapter.)

Some group-model and practice-model MCOs are allowing patients to choose NPs as PCPs. Not all MCOs currently recognize NPs as PCPs, however.

Applying for MCO Provider Panel Membership

NPs should determine which MCOs are prevalent in their geographic area of practice and prevalent among their practice's patients. Once an NP has compiled a short list of MCOs, it is wise to do some research on them.

The NP can ask other providers who have done business with the MCO, or the state agency that oversees MCOs, the following questions:

- Have other providers been paid promptly?
- Who are the specialists in the MCO's referral network? Are you familiar with them?
- Does the MCO have a strong presence in the community?
- Is the MCO financially sound?
- Is the MCO's record with the Insurance Division relatively free of complaints?
- Does the company have decent quality data?

The NP should apply to the MCOs for which all these answers are "yes."

NPs who have been admitted to MCO provider panels are: (1) those whose practice is in a geographic area of interest to an MCO, (2) those who have large numbers of patients who are attractive to the MCO, (3) those who offer a service unavailable elsewhere, or (4) those who have been endorsed and supported by the physicians in a large group practice. In general, these are the same characteristics that distinguish the physicians who have been admitted to MCO provider panels.

In brief, the application process entails (1) calling Provider Relations at an MCO and requesting an application, (2) applying for admission, and (3) following up by telephone or letter.

Provider Credentialing

When an MCO deems a provider "credentialed," it means that they have collected educational, license, malpractice, employment, and certification data on the provider and made a judgment that the provider is adequately prepared to care for the MCO's patients. For the information commonly required of applicants to provider panels, see **Appendix 9-A**.

An MCO interested in an NP as a panel member will verify data submitted on the application and may make a site visit. A site visitor looks for a clean office, safe access, sufficient parking, adequate staffing, and other signs of a well-organized practice. In the case of an NP practice, a site visitor may ask about systems for admitting patients and access to a physician consultant. An offer of admission to a provider panel will come with a contract, to be signed by the NP and the MCO.

Negotiating an MCO Contract

Contractual relationships with MCOs cover not only compensation, but also many other practice areas. Some attorneys specialize in assisting providers to negotiate contracts with MCOs, and NPs are encouraged to seek counsel of an attorney experienced in these matters. A detailed explanation of the contract issues described here is beyond the scope of this text. There are books devoted entirely to negotiating managed-care contracts.

Contract issues to be negotiated include the following:

- What is included? What is excluded?
- What are the carve outs; that is, what patients are treated in special programs because of special needs?
- What is the process for transferring the care of a patient who becomes eligible for a carve out?

- What is the fee schedule or capitation schedule?
- What are the stop-loss provisions?
- Are there withholds?
- Are there referral pools?
- What is the level of distributions from withhold and referral pools to PCPs during the last 5 years?
- What is the bonus system?
- What are the provisions for closing the practice to additional patients from the MCO?
- Is claims processing done in house or contracted out?
- Who does the lab work?
- What will the MCO base renewal upon? What is its renewal rate with providers?
- What is the procedure for the MCO's review of office practices?
- How will the directory listing read?
- Is there any prohibition against joining other MCOs?
- How does the MCO define experimental, emergency, and preexisting conditions?
- Who bears the brunt of the consequences for a mistake regarding eligibility or coverage determination?
- Can preadmission or referral approval be rescinded retroactively?
- What is in the formulary?
- What are the requirements for:
  - Utilization management
  - Quality assurance
  - Credentialing
  - Member grievance
  - Record keeping
  - Claims submission
  - Hours of operation
  - Appointment response times
  - On-call coverage
  - Employing other providers
  - Arranging backup with other groups
  - Minimum/maximum numbers of patients
  - Anti-disparagement
  - Business confidentiality
- What is the system for verifying member eligibility? How often is the provider notified of members who have selected him or her? When in the month is this done?
- What are the provisions for dispute resolution?
- What are the provisions for member grievance?
- What marketing is provided by the MCO?
- Who owns the records/data?

If an NP is an employee of a group practice, then someone within the group will be responsible for negotiating the terms of the MCO contract for the group. An NP who owns a practice will need to negotiate the points just discussed individually or join a practice association in which there is a designated negotiator.

Some providers join provider groups for the express purpose of collectively negotiating contract terms and rates. While some providers enter into a contract with an MCO without experienced legal counsel, it is unwise to do so.

Steps for Dealing with Denial of Provider Status
Gather Information

An NP who is denied a request for an application should ask the following questions of an MCO representative:

- Does the MCO admit NPs to provider panels?
- If not, why not?
- If it is a policy matter, who is the decision maker in the company who could change the policy?
- If state law is given as a reason for denial, ask which law precludes NPs being PCPs.

Strategize

Given that there may be more providers wanting provider status than a MCO wants to credential, the NP needs to analyze his or her strengths and be prepared to convince the MCO that it should credential him or her. The NP should ask for a meeting with an individual at the MCO who is in a position to make a decision and present the reasons why the MCO should take him or her on as a provider. If there are other NPs in the area who are facing the same problem, NPs can enlist the help of their state NP organization. It may also be helpful to hire an attorney to analyze an alleged legal barrier and to determine whether, in fact, it is a true legal barrier. Note, however, that MCOs often have wide latitude to admit the providers of their choice. Persuasion is more likely to be effective than litigation. Sometimes an MCO will be precluded by state law from taking on NPs as PCPs. If there are legal barriers to NPs becoming panel members or PCPs, NPs can hire a lobbyist who will work to change the law.

NPs should research options for using existing state law to encourage MCOs to admit NPs to provider panels. For example, some state laws preclude discrimination by MCOs against classes of healthcare providers who are legally authorized to provide healthcare services. NPs or their attorneys will want to cite such laws when making presentations to MCO executives.

Take Action

If an MCO has a policy against admitting NPs as PCPs, NPs may employ the following actions to effect a policy change:

- Write letters to MCO presidents, stating how NPs can satisfy the business needs of the MCO. Ask for an informational meeting, and present information on NP scope of practice, sources of third-party reimbursement, and arguments supporting NPs as PCPs, backed up by supporting data.

- Ask patients to request, through their employer's benefits office and through their MCO, the services of an NP as PCP.
- Ask colleague physicians to support NP admission to provider panels.
- Testify at hearings and speak at community meetings about the advantages of having NPs as providers.
- Ask for language changes from businesses that use the following message: "Ask your doctor." Ask that the language be changed to "Ask your doctor or NP" or "Ask your healthcare provider."
- In 6 months, request an application, and try again.

Carrying Out an MCO Contract

NPs who are admitted to MCO provider panels will want regular periodic analysis of the income and expense associated with each MCO contract. Such an analysis might reveal that a practice is losing money on one contract while breaking even on another and making a profit on yet another. If there is a discrepancy in reimbursement from various MCO contracts, an NP will want to determine the reason for the unprofitability of certain contracts and either negotiate a different arrangement when the contract expires or cease to deal with an MCO.

NPs also will want to evaluate MCO contracts regarding the effect of the contract on staff and providers. For example, is one MCO's paperwork or procedures for reimbursement overwhelmingly more complicated than another's? If so, then whatever reimbursement is being reaped may be offset by costly staff services. Is the lag time between services and payment greater than 120 days? If so, the practice manager will need to insist upon prompt payment or cease to deal with the offending MCO.

Direct Contracts for Health Services

There are no barriers to the NP who wishes to contract directly with businesses or agencies that need health services. For example, NPs contract directly with some colleges to provide college health services, with businesses to provide occupational health services, and with government agencies to provide school-based health services.

Billing Third-Party Payers

Billing third-party payers includes filing the proper forms, including the appropriate diagnostic and procedure codes, and documenting encounters in the medical record in a manner that justifies a bill.

Standard Form

The standard billing form is the CMS 1500. It can be purchased from the American Medical Association and from other commercial suppliers such as bookstores. The CMS 1500 form asks for ICD codes, CPT codes, date of service, patient identifying information, and provider identifying information. A bill submitted without a CPT or ICD code will be rejected.

Currently the vast majority of billing is done electronically, so most practices are contracting with billing services or purchasing software rather than buying forms.

Coding

The most frequently used CPT codes in primary care are the Evaluation and Management (E&M) Services. Specialty practices use the E&M codes as well. E&M codes represent a healthcare provider's cognitive services, such as office or clinic visits, consultations, preventive medicine examinations, and critical care services. In addition to E&M codes, a primary care practice will use other CPT codes to bill for such procedures as suturing and irrigation of ears.

E&M codes require providers to bill on the basis of the extent and complexity of history taking, physical exam, and medical decision making. For an example of E&M code requirements for a routine visit, see **Exhibit 9-2**.

A typical bill for an office visit could list one or more CPT codes and one or more ICD-9 codes. For example, a bill for a routine annual gynecologic exam would include ICD-9 code V72.3 for a diagnosis of routine annual exam and CPT codes 99213 or 99214 for an office visit for an established patient, 87210 for a wet mount, and 87205 for a Pap smear.

CMS has published *Documentation Guidelines for Evaluation and Management*, which NPs and other Medicare providers will be expected to follow in coding patient visits. (These guidelines are provided elsewhere in the text.) NPs should know that other insurers will expect the same attention to coding and documentation as CMS.

Exhibit 9-2   Selecting an E&M Code

A 99213 visit, the most common E&M code for an established patient, includes the following:

- An expanded problem-focused history
- An expanded problem-focused examination
- Medical decision making of low complexity
- Counseling and coordination of care consistent with the nature of the problem and the patient's needs
- 15 minutes of face-to-face time

The following are examples of office visits:

- A 55-year-old male established patient for management of hypertension and mild fatigue, on hydrochlorothiazide and a beta blocker
- A 50-year-old female established patient with insulin-dependent diabetes mellitus and stable coronary artery disease, for monitoring

Source: CPT five-digit codes, nomenclature, and other data are © 2013 American Medical Association. All Rights Reserved. No fee schedules, basic unit, relative values, or related listing are included in CPT. The AMA assumes no liability for the data contained herein. CPT only © 2013 American Medical Association.

General guidelines for legal coding are as follows:

1. A billable visit involves face-to-face contact between the patient and an advanced practice nurse, physician assistant, or physician. An encounter may occur in the provider's office, a clinic, an inpatient setting, a nursing facility, or the patient's home. Each billable visit must be a diagnostic visit, identified with an ICD code.

2. If care is given in an office, an NP must distinguish between a new patient and an established patient and then select the proper E&M CPT code for the visit. A new patient is one who has not received professional services within the past 3 years from a provider in the same specialty in the same practice. Telephone communication is considered a professional service.

3. History taking, examination, and medical decision making are the key components in determining code selection. Time is the least important factor, unless the visit is a "counseling" visit, there is significant time spent on coordination of care, or the visit qualifies as a "prolonged service." In ambulatory care, only face-to-face time is to be considered in selecting an appropriate CPT code. The nature of the presenting problem also figures into the choice of CPT code, under medical decision making.

4. Medical record documentation must support the level of care billed. Underdocumentation can lead to charges of fraudulent billing or "false claims." For every evaluation and management service billed, the medical record documentation must indicate the medical necessity for the visit.

5. A practice's billing will include a variety of E&M codes because patient encounters vary in the amount of attention required. A provider with a pattern of coding all visits with one of the higher level codes, without documentation to justify the high-level visits, is likely to be identified by the Medicare carrier as an "upcoder"; that is, a provider who bills for a higher level of service than actually provided in order to get a higher fee. Upcoding is false claims. A normal distribution of E&M codes for established patients (99211 through 99215) is a bell-shaped curve, with most visits being 99213.

6. It is important to bill the CPT code that the medical record documentation supports, not a higher level code or a lower level code. Failing to bill for all billable services rendered can mean unnecessarily low revenues for a practice. Consistent overcoding without medical record documentation that supports the level of visit billed can result in an audit by the Medicare carrier, fines, criminal prosecution for Medicare fraud, loss of Medicare provider status, and loss of license.

Table 9-1 shows a comparison for the five levels of visit (99211 through 99215) for an established patient. For a complete discussion of choice of code, see *Current Procedural Terminology* for the current year, published by the American Medical Association. The CMS guidelines will be revised from time to time. A current copy of the guidelines can be found on the CMS website (http://www.cms.gov).

In general, the appropriate documentation for the codes for an established patient mid-level visit (99213) is as follows. Under the documentation guidelines released on the CMS's website in November 1997 and still in effect in 2013, a bill for a 99213 visit will have to be backed up by a medical record entry that includes certain elements of history taking, physical examination, and medical decision making.

TABLE 9-1 A Comparison of Requirements for the Five Levels of Visit for an Established Patient

Level of Visit	History	Exam	Diagnoses	*Two of These Three Components Are Needed		
				Data Reviewed	Risk	
99211	None required	None required	None required	None required	None	
99212	1 descriptor	1	1 minor or established	Order or study 1 lab	1 minor problem, noninvasive labs, home-based management	
99213	1 descriptor 1 ROS	6	2 minor or established, or 1 new	Order or study 2 labs, summarize old records, or personally view tracing	2 minor problems, 1 chronic stable problem, or 1 acute problem; management is minor surgery, over-the-counter drugs, or physical therapy	
99214	4 descriptors 1 PSFH 2 ROS	12	1 new or 1 worse and 1 minor	Order or study 3 labs, order 1 lab and summarize old records, or personally view tracing	1 chronic problem, worse; 1 chronic problem, stable; or 1 acute systemic problem; invasive diagnostic procedures needed; prescription drugs indicated	
99215	4 descriptors 2 PSFH 10 ROS	18	1 new problem needing workup, or 1 new, stable and 1 minor	Order or study 4 labs, order/study 2 labs and summarize old records, or personally view tracing	1 severe chronic problem, 1 life-threatening chronic problem, 1 acute life-threatening problem, or acute mental status change; contrast studies or endoscopy with risk factors as indicated; parenteral therapies, fracture treatment, major surgery or monitoring is indicated	

Abbreviations: PSFH, past, family and social history; ROS, review of systems.

Source: Data from CPT five-digit codes, nomenclature and other data are © 2013 American Medical Association. All Rights Reserved. No fee schedules, basic unit, relative values or related listing are included in CPT. The AMA assumes no liability for the data contained herein. CPT only © 2013 American Medical Association.

For example, CPT 2013 requires a clinician to document, in detail, two of the three key aspects of a visit. Key aspects of an office visit, according to CMS, are history, examination, and medical decision making. The guidelines also address documentation of three other elements of a medical visit—time spent, counseling, and coordination of services. The November 1997 guidelines' requirements to satisfy documentation requirements for history taking, examination, and medical decision making for a 99213 visit are given next, along with the guidelines' discussion of documenting time, counseling, and coordination of services. The November 1997 guidelines are the most current guidelines, as of June 2013.

History Taking

Clinicians must document the following:

- At least one of the symptom descriptors (location, quality, severity, duration, timing, context, modifying factors, and associated symptoms)
- A review of systems for at least one pertinent body area or system; the acceptable body areas and systems are constitutional, eyes-ears-nose-throat/mouth, cardiovascular, respiratory, gastrointestinal, genitourinary, musculoskeletal, skin/breasts, neurologic, psychiatric, endocrine, hematologic, or immunologic

No past, family, or social history is required.

Examination

Clinicians must document at least six elements from a body system or area. Acceptable systems or body areas include constitutional, eyes-ears-nose-throat, neck, respiratory, cardiovascular, breasts, abdomen, genital, lymphatic, musculoskeletal, skin, neurologic, or psychiatric.

Medical Decision Making

According to the guidelines, medical decision making has three components: (1) making a diagnosis, (2) choosing treatment options, and (3) reviewing data. Clinicians are to consider one additional factor when choosing a code and documenting the risk of complications and/ or morbidity or mortality. For a 99213 visit, medical decision making is "low complexity" under the guidelines.

According to the guidelines, the diagnostic component of medical decision making is fulfilled by documenting a "limited" number of diagnoses or management options. Auditors verifying a 99213 visit will be looking for diagnoses for at least two minor problems, or two established stable problems, or one established problem that is documented as worse and one minor problem, or one new problem that is stable or in need of workup.

As for the component of medical decision making that consists of reviewing data, the guidelines give examples of what indicates increased complexity in a visit—a personal review of an electrocardiogram tracing, for example—but the guidelines do not list what documentation is needed to justify a particular level of visit. Auditors' score sheets require, for a 99213 visit, that a clinician document that diagnostic tests have been ordered or reviewed; that an X-ray, tracing, or slide interpreted by another clinician has been reviewed; or that old history has been summarized.

The guidelines appear on the CMS website (http://www.cms.gov; use the search engine to find "Evaluation and Management Guidelines"). The auditors' score sheets are available to clinicians on the websites of Medicare Administrative Contractors.

As for the final component of medical decision making, the risk of complications and/or morbidity or mortality, the guidelines are more specific. For a 99213 visit, the risk is "low." Examples of "low" risk for complications are visits where there are two or more self-limited or minor problems, a stable chronic illness, or an acute uncomplicated illness or injury. Diagnostic procedures that might be ordered during such a visit are physiologic tests not under stress, such as pulmonary function tests, clinical laboratory tests requiring arterial puncture, or skin biopsies. According to the guidelines, management options could include over-the-counter drugs, minor surgery, or physical therapy.

Time

Time is a minor consideration in determining the level of visit to bill, according to the guidelines, if a clinician is billing an office visit for evaluation and management (99211–99215 for an established patient and 99201–99205 for a new patient). If a visit is primarily counseling, however, time matters and should be documented. The visit is billed as a counseling visit, not an evaluation and management visit.

Counseling and Coordination of Services

While clinicians are expected to document patient counseling and coordination of services, there are no specific guidelines for this documentation. The guidelines state that it is expected that documentation will reflect the appropriate level of counseling and coordination based on patient needs.

Rejected Bills

If a bill is rejected by a payer, a member of the medical practice's staff should ask the following questions of the payer, document responses, and follow up by letter:

1. Why was this bill rejected?
2. Is more information needed about the procedure? About the diagnosis? About the documentation? About the NP's practice?

Every practice should have copies of relevant law regarding NP reimbursement. Relevant law includes the state regulation or statute that gives NPs the authority to provide care, the section of the Medicaid and Medicare regulations that apply to NP reimbursement, and any parts of the state insurance law that mandate payment for services provided by NPs. If bills are rejected for reasons related to NPs as a profession, the practice should send copies of relevant laws to insurers, along with any other information the payer requests.

Billing Self-Paying Patients

Though patients who pay their bills themselves are not, by definition, third-party payers, they deserve mention as a source of reimbursement.

Cash at time of service works only when patients are aware of what the bill will be before they arrive for their visit. Many practices are unable to give patients that information, but some can.

Some practitioners take credit cards. Some allow patients to run a balance with the practice and pay a monthly installment. Many practitioners who extend credit to patients have found it necessary to establish a relationship with a collection agency.

Conclusion

Reimbursement is a high-stakes issue for any practice, for without steady income, no practice will survive. Each of the topics discussed in this chapter deserves a book's worth of discussion. In fact, there are publications available on every topic. For sources of more information, see the following section titled "Resources."

Note

1. Medicare Benefit Policy Manual, Chapter 15, Sections 60.1–60.3.

Resources

Billing Nurse Practitioner Services

Buppert, C. (2013). Billing physician services provided by nurse practitioners in specialists' offices, hospitals, nursing facilities, homes and hospice. Law Office of Carolyn Buppert. Retrieved from http://www.buppert.com

Buppert, C. (2011). Safe, smart billing and coding for evaluation and management. Law Office of Carolyn Buppert. Retrieved from http://www.buppert.com

Buppert, C. (2012). Billing and coding critical care: For nurse practitioners. Law Office of Carolyn Buppert. Retrieved from http://www.buppert.com

Buppert, C. (2012). Billing and coding nurse practitioner services in the acute care setting: For nurse practitioners. Law Office of Carolyn Buppert. Retrieved from http://www.buppert.com

Managed-Care Quality Standards

National Committee on Quality Assurance. (n.d.) HEDIS. Retrieved from http://www.ncqa.org/HEDISQualityMeasurement.aspx

Diagnostic Coding

American Medical Association. (2014). *International classification of diseases*. Chicago, IL: Author.
* Always use the most current edition.

Procedural Coding

Buppert, C. *Physicians' current procedural terminology: CPT*. Chicago, IL: American Medical Association.
* Always use the most current edition.

Credentialing Information

A typical credentialing application will ask for the following:

- The NP's name, and other names used in past licensure and certification
- States of licensure
- Type of license
- Specialty
- Subspecialty
- National Provider Identifier (NPI) number
- Social Security number
- Birth date
- Proof of U.S. citizenship
- Place of birth
- Home address and telephone
- Practice status (individual, partnership, or group)
- Practice name, address, telephone, tax identification number, and office manager
- Dates of service at this practice
- Undergraduate and graduate education: institution, address, dates attended, degrees conferred
- Postgraduate training: institution, address, dates attended, type of training, name of program director, specialty
- Fellowship training: institution, address, dates attended, type of training, name of program director, leadership positions held, reason for leaving, type of facility
- Employment history/professional affiliations: institution, address, dates of privileges, position title, leadership positions held, name of department chair, type of facility, reason for leaving
- Current admitting privileges: primary admitting hospital, address, date received privileges, staff category, leadership positions held, name of department chair
- Military service: branch, period of enlistment, discharge status, rank
- Specialty board certification:
  - Board, year certified or recertified, expiration date
  - If you are not certified, whether you have taken the certification examination

- o Number of times you have taken the examination
- o Date that your eligibility to take the examination expires
- o Whether you intend to apply for the certification examination
- o Whether you have been accepted to take the certification examination
- o Date of next certification examination
- Licensure:
  - o States, license number, expiration date, current status
  - o Drug Enforcement Administration (DEA) license number, expiration date, current status
  - o State controlled-substance license number, expiration date, current status
- Professional liability coverage:
  - o Proof of current coverage, name of previous carrier, period of coverage, limits of coverage, type of coverage, reason for discontinuance
  - o Whether you have maintained continuous professional liability coverage since first obtaining coverage
  - o Whether you have been subject to a professional liability suit, including but not limited to malpractice claims, in the past 5 years
  - o Whether there are any restrictions, limitations, or exclusions in your current professional liability coverage
  - o Whether your professional liability insurance coverage has ever been denied, limited, reduced, interrupted, terminated, or not renewed
- Personal information:
  - o Date of last physical examination
  - o Whether you are currently suffering from, or receiving treatment for, any physical or mental disability or illness, including drug or alcohol abuse, that would impair the proper performance of your essential functions and responsibilities as a healthcare provider
  - o Whether you have ever been convicted of, or pleaded guilty to or nolo contendere to, any crime other than traffic violations
- Professional sanctions:
  - o Whether your license to practice any health occupation in any jurisdiction has ever been limited, suspended, denied, subjected to any conditions, terms of probation, or formal reprimand, not renewed, or revoked
  - o Whether you have surrendered your license to practice any health occupation in any jurisdiction
  - o Whether your request for any specific clinical privilege has ever been denied or granted with stated limitations
  - o Whether you have ever been denied membership on a hospital medical staff
  - o Whether your staff privileges, appointment, and/or delineation of privileges at any hospital or other healthcare institution has ever been suspended, revoked, limited, reduced, denied, or subject to any conditions or not renewed

- o Whether your DEA or other controlled-substance authorization has ever been limited, suspended, denied, reduced, subject to any conditions, terms of probation, not renewed, or revoked
- o Whether proceedings toward any of these ends have ever been initiated
- o Whether your controlled-substance authorization has ever been voluntarily or involuntarily relinquished
- o Whether you have ever been subject to disciplinary action in any medical organization or professional society
- o Whether there are any disciplinary actions pending against you
- o Whether you have resigned from any hospital or healthcare institution or professional academic appointment
- o Whether you have ever been placed on probation, suspended, asked to resign, or been terminated while in a training program
- o Whether you have ever been placed on probation, suspended, or asked to resign or been terminated while in a hospital program
- o Whether you have ever withdrawn your application for appointment, reappointment, or clinical privileges or resigned before a decision was made by a hospital's or healthcare facility's governing board
- o Whether you have ever been denied certification or recertification by a specialty board or received a letter of admonition from such a board or committee
- o Whether you have ever been investigated by any private, federal, or state agency concerning your participation in any private, federal, or state health insurance program
- o Whether you have ever been subject to probation proceedings or suspended, sanctioned, or otherwise restricted from participating in any private, federal, or state health insurance program
- o Whether you have received a determination from any professional review organization indicating a "final severity level 3" or a "gross and flagrant" quality concern

- Professional references: List names and addresses of four persons who have worked extensively with you or have been responsible for professionally observing you. Do not list more than two current partners or associates in practice, relatives by blood or marriage, the chief of service to whom you are applying, any person in current or past training programs with you (unless he or she is now a colleague), or persons who cannot attest to your current level of clinical competency, technical skill, and medical knowledge.

CHAPTER 10

The Employed Nurse Practitioner

The majority of nurse practitioners (NPs) are employed by others, rather than self-employed. The advantages of employment by others are:

- A built-in collaborative agreement, in states where these are required
- No struggles for reimbursement from third-party payers, who may balk at paying NPs directly but are comfortable reimbursing physician practices that employ NPs

What Rights Does an Employed NP Have?

At Will Employment

In most states, employment is "at will." This means that employment continues at the will of both parties. Put another way, either party may terminate for any reason at any time. Unless an employee has a contract for a specified term of employment, an employee has no legal right to a job. Likewise, an employee may also end employment at any time, barring a contract for a specified term. The only protections for an employee are those offered by the equal opportunity and disability laws; that is, an employee cannot be terminated solely on the basis of age, national origin, gender, race, religion, or disability.

An NP who is employed but has no contract must negotiate terms of employment on a piecemeal basis, relying on their ability to reach agreement with the employing party as issues arise. If an employer changes the pay scale or work responsibilities for the better, the NP benefits. However, if the employer reduces the pay scale or unreasonably increases responsibilities, the NP has no recourse but to keep working under the new conditions or to leave.

Employment by Contract

Many NPs seeking employment are offered employment contracts. An employment contract is a written agreement under which the employee and employer agree on the terms and conditions of their working relationship.

Employment contracts can be complex and lengthy, and they require careful analysis. The following is a list of some of the issues often addressed in an employment contract:

- Scope of services to be performed
- Compensation

- Duration of employment
- How the agreement can be altered or updated
- Responsibility for maintaining credentials
- Terms of on-call responsibilities
- Benefits
- Time off and expenses for continuing education
- Vacation time
- Number of office hours per week
- Restriction on competition
- Bonuses
- Reasons for termination
- Assistance with continuing education

Some issues that often are not addressed but can be dealt with in an employment contract include the following:

- Extent of support service to be offered to the NP
- Expectations regarding the number of patients seen per day
- Expectations regarding nonclinical (administrative) work to be done by the NP
- Listing of the NP on the door, in directories, and in advertisements
- Use of the NP's name when the office telephone is answered
- On-call responsibilities and backup
- Release to the NP of the NP's quality performance as measured by health plan auditors

An employment agreement can include anything the parties wish to address. Often, agreements are written by attorneys for the practice and therefore are oriented to the needs of the employer. NPs should retain their own attorney to review any proposed contract and respond with counterproposals when the contract language does not mesh with their needs.

Does an NP Need a Contract?

Many NPs practiced for many years without employment contracts. In the past, an employer called to offer a job, and the employer and employee then negotiated a salary, benefits, and the hours of employment. The arrangement was typically sealed with a handshake. Details were worked out as issues arose, but NPs sometimes were unhappy with how they were handled.

Contracts have certain advantages over this informal employment arrangement. First, contract negotiation forces parties to discuss issues. When the parties agree to terms, there is a document that records the agreement and can be referred to as necessary to refresh memories about the details of the agreement. In most cases, an employment agreement is protective to both the employer and the employee.

For an employee, a contract ensures some degree of job security. In most states, unless there is a written contract defining the duration of employment, employment is "at will." As discussed, this means that either party may terminate the employment without cause at any time. For example, a practice that hires an NP and then loses a lucrative patient care contract can terminate an NP who is employed "at will" with no severance pay, even though the NP is not at fault. "At will" employees are often surprised to learn that they have no legal right to their jobs. An NP who has a contract, however, has an agreement for work for the duration of the contract, unless a clause in the contract states otherwise. An employer who wants to end the employment of the NP must wait until the contract terminates or attempt to settle the matter with the NP, possibly by offering severance terms.

For an employer, an employment agreement can afford protection against competition. An employer wants to avoid a situation where a departing NP who has built a patient following takes patients to their next position. An employer can restrict a departing NP from competing with a practice by including a restrictive covenant (discussed shortly) in the employment agreement.

A multitude of issues that affect lifestyle and workstyle can arise among coworker healthcare providers. An employment contract can delineate the expectations of employer and employee before problems arise. A contract also can specify problem-solving procedures.

Three Difficult Clauses

Three clauses commonly found in employment agreements offered by medical practices to NPs are especially difficult for NPs to interpret and can have profound effects on an NP's life. These clauses address restrictive covenants, bonus formulas, and termination clauses. These clauses often bring NPs to attorneys for advice. *Restrictive covenants* require an NP to promise, up front, not to compete with an employer when the present employment ends. *Bonus formulas* specify conditions under which an employer rewards an NP for superior performance. *Termination clauses* specify that an employer may end the agreement, without cause, with 30 days notice.

Restrictive Covenants

A restrictive covenant is a promise not to compete. Specifically, a restrictive covenant is a clause that restricts an employee from practicing within a set number of miles from an employer's business for a set period of time after the employee leaves the employer's business.

Many employers insist on restrictive covenants. An employer wants to avoid a situation where a departing NP who has built a patient following takes patients to their next position, often a neighboring practice.

Restrictive covenants are legal in many states and enforceable as long as they are reasonable. If a former employee challenges the validity of a restrictive covenant by taking the matter to court, a judge will determine whether it is reasonable. A judge will balance the needs of the employer against the harm to the employee. A judge will decide whether the geographic restriction and the time restriction are appropriate to accomplish the employer's needs, but no more. Further, a judge will consider whether there is any potential injury to the public if a restrictive covenant is enforced.

A judge will analyze the past court decisions in the state and compare the facts of those cases with the current case. Such facts include the size of the city or town the practice is in, the severity of the geographic and time restrictions in the clause, what the practice is like, the availability of other healthcare providers, and what the employment climate is like for healthcare providers.

Judges have found restrictive covenants unreasonable when the restraint is greater than necessary to protect the legitimate business interests of the employer. Judges also have found restrictive covenants unreasonable when the restraint is not greater than necessary to protect the business interests but the employer's need for protection is outweighed by the hardship to the employee. Occasionally, judges have found restrictive covenants to be unreasonable when there is neither excessive restraint nor excessive hardship but there is a likely injury to the public. For example, a covenant restricting an oral surgeon from practicing in a particular city for 3 years after termination from a practice was found to be unreasonable. The restraint was greater than necessary. However, a covenant restricting a veterinarian from practicing in a different city for 3 years after termination was found to be reasonable. In that case, the restraint was not greater than necessary. In yet another case, a covenant restricting a physician from practicing in a rural town for 3 years after termination was found to be unreasonable. In that case, there was a potential injury to the public. The injury to the public was a potential shortage of physicians if one of the two town physicians could no longer practice there. The difference in outcome in these three cases can be reconciled only by comparing the factual details of the cases. A decision that one clause was reasonable while a seemingly identical clause was unreasonable was due to differences in profession, practice, city, availability of other providers, and many other factors.

When negotiating the terms of a restrictive covenant, an NP needs to consider the circumstances of the job offer, the severity of the restriction, the potential hardship imposed on them by the covenant, the availability of healthcare providers in the area, and the availability of other practice opportunities.

In agreeing to a restrictive covenant, an NP is giving up something of value—the ability to take any other NP job that is offered to them. However, if an NP refuses to sign a reasonable restrictive covenant their employer may suspect they are looking to start a competing practice nearby. The best practice for restrictive covenants is to negotiate one the NP can live with, one that seems reasonable for all concerned under the particular circumstances of the practice and the NP. **Exhibit 10-1** provides examples of restrictive covenants with comments about their degree of reasonableness.

Bonus Formulas

Some employers offer NPs the opportunity for bonuses. The criteria for bonuses vary greatly. The two most important are that both employer and employee understand the formula and that it be consistent with good patient care.

The most common problem with bonus formulas is vague language. If a formula is vague, it is sure to be interpreted in different ways by different individuals. This can result in disagreements and disappointments at distribution time.

Exhibit 10-1   Restrictive Covenants

Restrictive covenants are enforceable if they balance:

- The employer's need for protection
- Hardship to the employee
- Likelihood of injury to the public

Example 1: "Upon termination of employment for any reason, NP agrees not to practice in any location within 25 miles of any present or future office of this practice for a period of 5 years."

Analysis: Accomplishes employer's need for protection but may be broader than necessary to accomplish employer's need and may put excessive hardship on employee to find alternative work 25 miles away.

Example 2: "Upon termination of employment for any reason, NP agrees not to practice in any location within 1 mile of the Jones Road office of this practice for a period of 1 year."

Analysis: Not a hardship on employee but may not accomplish employer's need for protection, as patients may be willing to travel 1 mile to see the NP.

Productivity-Based Formulas

Many formulas are based on the number of patient visits per year. This makes good business sense under a fee-for-service system of reimbursement. If a practice is at least half fee-for-service, patient visit–based formulas can be a reasonable choice. Tracking patient visits is uncomplicated and is not usually susceptible to vagueness. Generally, an NP who sees large numbers of patients is a productive employee who deserves a bonus.

Bonus formulas based on numbers of patient visits make less sense when reimbursement to the practice is capitated. Under a capitated system of reimbursement, a practice is paid a set fee per patient per month, regardless of the number of patient visits. Under capitated reimbursement, the ultimate goal is not a high number of visits from each patient but good patient care in as few visits as possible. Under capitated reimbursement, bonuses should be given to those providers who demonstrate high-quality care as evidenced by some documented quality measurement tool. Numbers of patient visits should not be relevant when a practice's patients are capitated. Employers have to be careful not to give providers bonuses for withholding care. Aside from the moral and ethical problems involved, there are federal laws that prohibit healthcare providers from profiting by delivering inadequate or inappropriate care.

Many practices have a mix of fee arrangements with patients and payers. Employer and employee should plan for such mixes when devising a bonus formula. A bonus formula should fit the practice's payer mix.

Quality-Based Bonuses

When more than half of patients are covered by some form of managed-care plan, NP performance can be rewarded on the basis of meeting or exceeding quality standards set by the health plan. For example, bonuses could be awarded when the percentage of patients who have met health maintenance criteria—such as childhood immunizations or mammograms for women over 50—exceeds 80%. Or bonuses could be awarded if emergency department visits declined in the past year.

While performance measures are more difficult to track than patient visits, they are more suited to managed care. Some health plans supply performance data to practices, and these data can be used to determine bonuses.

To track this kind of performance data and apportion bonuses based on performance, patients and primary care providers have to be paired. NPs need to have their own panels of patients and be designated as the primary care provider for that panel. Otherwise NP–physician teams have to work together and share bonuses.

Profit-Based Formulas

Some employers share profits with NPs. This can be satisfying to both employer and employee as long as the method for determining profits is clear.

NPs should be aware that there are accounting methods that can maximize or minimize profits and that profit is a word that has modifiers, such as *gross* and *net*, that can mean the difference between a bonus and no bonus. NPs who agree to profit-based formulas should negotiate for the right to audit financial records. NPs should also negotiate for a dispute-resolution process.

Patient Satisfaction–Based Formulas

Bonus formulas are one of the most controversial aspects of provider relationships. Many practices struggle with this issue. One approach taken by employers is to implement a bonus formula with the understanding that it can be altered and improved upon each year.

See **Exhibit 10-2** for some examples of bonus formulas that have been offered to NPs.

Termination Without Cause

Typically, the termination section of an employment agreement will list events that are a basis for termination of the employee "with cause." These events often include conviction of a felony, loss of license, loss of hospital privileges, and gross negligence that compromises patient safety.

Exhibit 10-2   Examples of Bonus Formulas for NPs' Contracts

- Up to 15% of base salary: 5% if practice is profitable, 5% based on meeting a threshold of patient visits, and 5% based on patient satisfaction, staff satisfaction, and citizenship
- The product of "collected billings" multiplied by "total employee billings" divided by "total practice billings," with a cap
- A figure determined by a committee, based on meeting criteria for (1) financial performance; (2) quality of medical services determined by outcomes, medical appropriateness, and extent of health promotion services provided; and (3) level of patient satisfaction

---

Exhibit 10-3   Examples of Termination Clauses

A Termination-with-Cause Clause
The employer may terminate this agreement at the sole discretion of the employer, by written notice to the NP upon the occurrence of any of the following:

 a. The NP dies or becomes disabled. . . .
 b. The NP loses his or her professional license. . . .
 c. The NP is limited or restricted by any governmental authority having jurisdiction over the NP to the extent that the NP cannot render the required professional services. . . .

A Termination-Without-Cause Clause (**Not Recommended for NPs*)
The employer may terminate this agreement at any time, for any reason, after thirty (30) days notice to NP.

In addition to termination-with-cause provisions, some employment agreements include a termination-without-cause clause, which states that an employer can terminate an employee at any time, without cause, with 30 days notice (see examples in **Exhibit 10-3**).

A termination-without-cause clause effectively defeats one of the purposes of a contract for an employee. An employee who can be terminated at any time for any reason or for no reason not only has no job security but also will think twice about pressing for performance of any of the other provisions in the employment agreement. For example, an NP may believe that a bonus was due, while the employer may believe that no bonus was due. If the NP protests too much, an employer can simply terminate the NP. If, on the other hand, an NP can be terminated only "for cause," the NP will feel freer to be assertive about ensuring that the other provisions of the contract are fulfilled.

There are reasons to agree to a "termination-without-cause" clause, however. If an NP cannot commit to a full year's employment, it may be best to agree to the "without-cause" clause. Most employers will not agree to delete a "without-cause" clause unless the employee also gives up the right to leave with just 30 days notice.

How to Negotiate a Reasonable Agreement

Preparing to Negotiate

NPs who have worked for years without contracts are now being offered them. NPs who are currently working without contracts, who foresee an offer in the future, and who want to negotiate a satisfying contract will lay the groundwork a year in advance.

First, an NP should be able to state clearly what he or she has contributed to the practice in the past year and have supporting data. Specifically, the NP should have at hand the total number of patient visits and the dollars billed and received as a result of those visits. If an NP does administrative work, he or she should make a list of administrative projects and determine the dollar worth of the projects to the practice. The NP can contrast the revenues they have brought in with the expenses related to their practice, including salary, benefits, and continuing education. If there are patient satisfaction surveys or quality-of-care data that support the NP, the NP should have those data at hand. While new NPs will not have the option of collecting data in preparation for negotiating first contracts, they should find out everything they can about the practice with which they plan to negotiate. Once employed, new NPs should begin to collect data for future contract negotiations.

First, an NP needs to make the following assessments about his or her speed and comfort level:

- How many patients can I see per hour, day, month, and year?
- How much physician consultation time will I need: a 10-minute consultation on every patient, a 5-minute consultation once a day, or a 5-minute consultation once a year?

Second, an NP should gather basic information on how the practice gets its revenues. The NP should know which insurers pay for NP services and how much they pay. If the payer mix is likely to change in the coming year, the NP must be ready to explain how their value to the practice will continue to increase in the coming year. The NP can propose ways in which the practice can increase its efficiency and revenues in the coming year and offer to help implement plans. An NP embarking on a salary negotiation needs to gather the following data from their employer:

- What is the most frequently billed CPT (procedural) code for the practice? What amount does the practice bill and receive, on average, for that CPT code?
- What percentage of practice income goes to cover practice expenses? If the employer will not reveal that information, the NP can ask how many providers share practice overhead expenses. A solo practitioner pays 43% of their income for office expenses, whereas a practice of 10 to 24 doctors pays 23.5% of their income for office expenses. Determine the appropriate rate to deduct for practice expenses.
- What is the collection rate for the practice? Remember, 90% is good.

Third, the NP should decide which terms of employment are essential and which can be given up. He or she should ask for everything they want but be ready to back down on nonessential terms.

Fourth, the NP must anticipate any drawbacks that an employer might raise in negotiations and prepare to defend or minimize those drawbacks.

Negotiating

Generally, it is best to negotiate individually rather than as a member of a group. For a variety of reasons, some NPs will be more valuable than others to an employer. A more valuable NP should get better offers. On the other hand, some employers have a standard NP offer and will not deviate for an individual NP. In that case, NPs need to negotiate as a group.

Whether negotiating individually or as a group, an NP should read a proposed contract carefully, note areas that are confusing, and get clarification. They should remember that everything is negotiable. While a contract may look intimidating, it was typed on a word processor and can be changed.

NPs should seek legal counsel to review any proposed contract.

Getting Help: What To Look for in a Lawyer

Negotiating is best done by the NP employee, but contract review is best done by an attorney. An attorney who is familiar with NP contracts and business issues is a good first choice. A second choice is an attorney who reviews contracts of other healthcare providers, physicians in particular.

NPs should avoid attorneys who need to research the law regarding NPs. One NP spent $1500 for her attorney to research the law on NPs, only to find that she knew the answers to the questions he was looking up.

Attorneys charge between $150 and $1000 an hour. Many will negotiate a flat fee for reviewing a contract. It is prudent to spend $400 for review of a contract that is worth between $80,000 and $140,000 per year to an NP. If an attorney finds vague wording that needs to be made more specific, the investment in the attorney will be repaid in the long run.

Understanding Business

If an employer has a well-run, profitable practice to which an NP contributes significantly, the NP should expect to be rewarded well under an employment agreement. If a practice is losing money, no NP will be able to negotiate a satisfying agreement, no matter how excellent they are.

NPs are clinicians by nature, not businesspeople. However, all types of clinicians are increasingly finding that they need to understand more about the business of health care. An NP who understands the financial base for a practice is in a better position to negotiate a satisfactory employment agreement than an NP who knows only the clinical side of practice. An employer will respect an NP who approaches negotiations with attention to both business principles and patient care concerns.

Negotiating Salary

New NPs are notorious for asking only two questions of a new employer: (1) What does the position pay? and (2) What are the benefits?

Four methods of payment are currently being used to pay employed NPs:

1. Straight salary
2. Percentage of net receipts
3. Base salary plus percentage
4. Hourly rate

In a straight salary arrangement, an NP is paid a set amount to perform according to a job description. In a percentage salary arrangement, an NP is paid the amount the NP bills minus accounts receivable, minus the NP's portion of practice expenses (which includes the expense of physician consultation). In a base salary plus percentage arrangement, an NP is guaranteed a set salary but can make additional salary if he or she generates practice income over some set amount. NPs working on an hourly basis are paid only for the hours worked.

Straight salary and hourly are more commonly encountered arrangements than percentage or set salary plus percentage. The advantage of percentage-based salaries is the opportunity for productive NPs to have some control over their earnings. The disadvantage is that the method sets up fellow providers in a practice as competitors for patients.

No matter what arrangement an NP chooses, it is wise to focus on hard figures that document an NP's monetary contribution to a practice and the costs of the NP to the practice.

NPs bring in income on a fee-for-service basis or a per-member-per-month basis. Calculating an NP's share of income for a fee-for-service practice is done by multiplying the number of visits by the collected fee per visit. When a practice's patients are capitated, an NP's share of income is calculated by multiplying the number of patients on an NP's panel by the per-member-per-month fee coming into the practice.

The cost of maintaining an NP is calculated by adding together practice expenses and the cost of physician consultation. Practice expenses can be estimated or calculated for a particular practice. For a solo practice, expenses can be 40–50% of the income. For a large practice, expenses are lower, 20–30% of income. Practice expenses include rent, salaries, taxes and benefits of support staff, taxes and benefits of NPs, supplies, laboratory expenses, depreciation, car, continuing education, and insurance (malpractice, workers' compensation, and premises insurance).

An NP who needs a great deal of physician consultation should expect to compensate their employer physicians for their time. An NP who needs little consultation should command a higher salary because he or she needs little of a physician's time. Until NPs no longer need a physician on written agreement, all NPs should expect to pay something for physician consultation. Experienced NPs often pay physician employers/consultants 10–15% of their net income brought to the practice.

Most employers will want a percentage of an NP's earnings as profit. An experienced NP who needs little consultation from an employer physician might consider his or her contribution to profit to be the 10–15% of net income paid for consultation, as noted in the earlier paragraph. A newer NP should expect to contribute 10–15% of net earnings to an employer as profit in addition to 15–25% of net earnings for physician consultation.

To project an appropriate salary for a particular NP, follow these steps:

1. Calculate income to the practice based on NP billings.
2. Subtract 10% for unpaid bills.
3. Subtract:
   a. The calculated figure for practice expenses (20–50% of earnings).
   b. The cost of physician consultation (10–20% of net earnings).
   c. A percentage for employer profit.

Fee-for-Service Practices. For example, an NP who sees 15 patients per day at $70 per patient visit, on average, brings in $1050 per day. Allowing 1 week off for continuing education, 1 week off for illness, and 4 weeks off for vacation, this NP will bring in $241,500 a year, potentially. However, not all bills are paid. With a 90% collection rate—a reasonable collection rate for an efficient practice—this NP actually will bring in $217,350 per year. An NP who sees 24 patients per day will bring in $1680 per day, or $386,400 per year in accounts receivable. With a 90% collection rate, this NP will bring $347,760 to the practice.

Deducting 40% of the NP's gross generated income for overhead expenses (rent, benefits, continuing education, supplies, malpractice, lab expenses, and depreciation of equipment) leaves $130,410 for the 15-patient-per-day NP and $208,656 for the 24-patient-per-day

NP. Further deducting 15% of that figure to pay a physician for consultation services leaves $110,848 in salary for the 15-patient-per-day NP and $177,357 in salary for the 24-patient-per-day NP. Deducting 10% for employer profit leaves $99,763 in salary for the 15-patient-per-day NP and $159,621 for the 24-patient-per-day NP. Note that some practices are compensated more than $70 per visit, on average, and some less. Some practices have a collections rate that is less than 90%. Note also that some practices will be able to justify 50% of generated income for practice expenses and some practices will want more than 10% profit. Ultimately the employer gets to make the final decision about these percentages. The NP's options are to accept, negotiate something better, or to find other employment.

Capitated Practices. In a fully capitated practice, an NP who has a panel of 1000 patients at an average fee per member per month of $10 will bring in $120,000 annually. There should be a 100% collection rate under a capitated system of reimbursement.

Applying 40% to overhead leaves $72,000 for the NP salary, and paying 15% for physician consultation and 10% for employer profit leaves $55,080 for the NP salary. An NP with a larger panel will make more.

The New NP. A newly graduated NP without experience may be able to see only 10 patients a day, with four or five 10-minute physician consultations per day, for the first 6 months. Plugging in the figures from the earlier examples, the NP will bill 2400 visits per year (2 weeks vacation for the new grad) at $70 per visit to total $168,000 in accounts receivable. With a 90% collection rate, the new NP will bring in $151,200.

Deducting 40% for practice expenses brings the net income to $90,720. Because a new NP often requires significant consultation time with a physician (or experienced NP), an additional 25% ($22,680) is deducted for payment for consultation, bringing the NP salary down to $68,040. With a contribution to employer profit, this new NP's appropriate salary is down to $61,236.

After 6 months, when the same NP becomes more comfortable and more efficient, the income numbers should double and consultation requirements should decrease, so that the appropriate salary will more closely approximate the salary of the 15-patient-per-day NP and eventually the 24-patient-per-day NP in the previous examples. Many employers start a new NP at a salary significantly higher than $61,236, expecting that low productivity in the first 6 months will be balanced by high productivity in the second 6 months.

There are experienced NPs who see more than 15 patients per day at CPT code level 99213 (established patient, mid-level visit) or higher who are not making the salary supported by the previous calculations. There are numerous reasons for this. First, the practice may expect more than 10% profit. Many employers expect to make a profit equal to an employee's salary. Second, the NP may have higher expenses than normal. Third, the collections rate may be lower than 90%.

Are These Projections Accurate? One could argue about whether the percentages used in the given examples are correct. In fact, some practices have poor rates of collections, some practices have higher overhead expenses, and some physicians want more payment for consultation. Some employers want more profit than projected here. However, an NP should not be subsidizing a poorly run practice and need not agree to overcompensate a physician or employer. Many practices receive more than $70 per NP visit on average. In these practices, an NP's salary should be proportionately higher.

Reported Median NP Salaries. Comparing these calculated NP salaries with some of the recently reported median salaries for NP salaries is an interesting exercise. Some medical groups use the Medical Group Management Association's (MGMA) median salary data. The median salary for a NP in 2012 was $91,000, according to the MGMA. Advance for Nurse Practitioners reported in its 2012 salary survey that the median NP salary for 2011 was $90,583.

NPs should keep in mind that salary averages are based on surveys. There is no way of knowing whether the respondents are representative of NPs. NPs who believe they are worthy of higher salaries than surveys suggest should present all of the reasons why they deserve the figure they are seeking.

As in all negotiating, there are three things to remember:

1. One who does not ask will not receive.
2. One who does not deserve will not receive.
3. Even when one asks and deserves, one will need to do some selling to get what one wants.

Negotiating Benefits

There are three yardsticks by which to evaluate a benefits package:

1. What benefits does the NP need?
2. What is reasonable?
3. What are other NPs getting?

Only the first two count. It should not matter to either the NP or the employer what others are getting, only what the NP needs, wants, or deserves and what the employer can afford and is willing to cover.

An NP in the late stages of job interviewing should ask a prospective employer the following questions:

- What benefits usually are offered?
- Does the employer pay for continuing education?
- Is time away for continuing education paid time?
- What is the retirement plan?
- What are the basics of the health plan? Is dental included? Is vision coverage included?
- If calls are required, are a cellular telephone, beeper, and car allowance included?
- What vacation time is being offered?
- How is sick time handled?
- Is malpractice insurance paid by the employer? If so, will a separate attorney for the NP be covered? Is the policy occurrence or claims made?
- Are relocation expenses paid?
- Is there a sign-on bonus?
- Are expenses of travel for the interview to be paid?

- Does the employer pay for professional dues? If so, how much?
- Does the employer pay for reference books and subscriptions to professional journals? If so, how much?
- Are there any tuition reimbursement benefits for NPs or for dependents?
- Is there a short- or long-term disability insurance benefit?
- If travel to various sites is necessary, are automobile expenses reimbursed?

Negotiating a Working Environment

Of course, many nonmonetary aspects of an NP's working life affect job satisfaction. An NP contemplating a new job is advised to spend some time thinking about and perhaps listing both the aspects of former jobs that have been most satisfying and most frustrating. Then the NP can briefly summarize the best and the worst of former jobs with the prospective employer and try to maximize the positive in the new position. Here are some appropriate questions:

- Is on-call time required? If so, how are calls shared? What backup will an NP have if consultation is needed for a call?
- What kind of and how many support staff will the practice provide?
- What will support staff do for the NP? What will support staff expect the NP to do for them?
- To whom will the NP report about medical issues? Administrative issues? Payment issues?
- What continuous quality improvement methods does the practice use?
- If the NP finds some aspect of practice organization that he or she would like to change, what is the process be for making suggestions?
- Is the NP expected to build a panel of patients or cover for overbookings of the other providers, or both?

Interviewing

A physician or administrator who is interested in hiring an NP may have significant, little, or no experience working with NPs. Therefore, NPs should be prepared to define NP scope of practice, list state requirements for collaboration or supervision, if any, and identify the sources of reimbursement for NP services.

In an interview for employment as an NP, a candidate should be prepared to answer the following questions:

- Why should I hire an NP?
- Why should I hire you?
- How many patients are you used to seeing in a day?
- Do you have a DEA [Drug Enforcement Administration] number?
- How independently are you used to practicing?
- What can you bring to the practice?
- What is your greatest job strength? Weakness?

- What can an NP legally do in this state?
- What do you want to be doing in 5 years? In 10 years?
- Does working evenings and/or weekends bother you?

Responsibilities of an NP Employee

Whether or not an NP has a contract, an NP has certain ethical responsibilities to their employer. These responsibilities include the following:

- Add to the good will an employer has built in the community by promoting the practice to the public
- Protect the employer's "trade secrets," such as patient mailing lists
- Provide one's best customer service to patients of the employer
- Remain unimpaired by alcohol or drugs
- Maintain one's credentials, knowledge of standard of care, and continuing education
- Maintain patient confidentiality

Employer's Evaluation of the NP's Performance

Some employers evaluate NP performance in highly structured ways—number of patients seen per month or quarter, income generated, detailed evaluation tools—and others use either no measure or very subjective measures.

An NP is advised to ask, in the interview stages, about the employer's expectations for productivity, measures of quality, and other performance measures. If an NP knows how their work will be evaluated, he or she has a better chance of meeting expectations. If there are no set methods of evaluation, an NP may want to offer to develop some standards.

Malpractice Insurance

The best malpractice policy for an NP is an occurrence policy, for at least $1 million per claim and $3 million aggregate, which covers the expense of an attorney for the NP as an individual. If an NP must purchase an individual policy to obtain this coverage, the NP should do so.

Collaborative Practice Agreements

In states where a collaborative agreement is required by law, the NP, the physician, or both are legally responsible for drafting and filing the agreement with the appropriate agency. The most prudent process for drafting a collaborative agreement is as follows:
- Collect information.
  1. *Review the state law regarding NP scope of practice.* Questions to be answered are: Must the practice agreement be approved by the board of nursing and/or board of medicine

prior to beginning practice? Are there qualifications for the collaborating physician? Are there limitations on the collaborating physician (such as a limit on the number of NPs who may collaborate with the physician)? Is the practice agreement required solely for prescriptive authority or for any form of advanced practice?

2. *Determine the functions that the NP will supply to the proposed collaborative practice.* Will there be in-hospital care? Suturing? Surgical assistance? Prescription of controlled substances? Nursing home practice?

3. *Determine whether the physician collaborator's area of specialty matches the NP's.* Interview the physician collaborator, much as you would conduct a job interview, and check references. Ask whether there are any current or past malpractice cases against the physician or practice. Ask whether there has been any loss of hospital privileges or loss of Medicare participation.

- Draft an agreement for the collaborator's review. Often, the board of nursing will have sample written agreements upon which an NP can base the draft.
- Finalize and submit the agreement. Sometimes the board of nursing will return an agreement with a request for more information. If so, simply redraft and resubmit.

An example of a practice agreement is given in **Appendix 10-A**. A sample employment agreement is provided in **Appendix 10-B**.

Sample Nurse Practitioner Collaborative Practice Agreement from the Indiana Board of Nursing

TEMPLATE

Collaborative Practice Agreement for Advanced Practice Nurses Requesting Prescriptive Authority
Rule 848 IAC 5-1-1—Initial Authority to Prescribe Legend Drugs

1. **Complete names, home and business addresses, zip codes, and telephone numbers of the licensed practitioner and the advanced practice nurse.**

Licensed Practitioner:	Advanced Practice Nurse:
Licensed practitioner name and license number	Advanced practice nurse name and license number
Street address of home	Street address of home
City, state, and zipcode of home	City, state, and zipcode of home
Home phone number	Home phone number
Business street address	Business street address
City, state, and zipcode of business	City, state, and zipcode of business
Business phone number	Business phone number

2. **List of all locations where prescriptive authority is authorized by this agreement.**
    Business street address
    City, state, and zipcode of business
    Business phone number

3. **List all specialty or board certifications of the licensed practitioner and the advanced practice nurse.**
    Licensed practitioner is certified as a _____ with a practice specialty in
    _____. The advanced practice nurse is a nurse practitioner, clinical nurse specialist, certified nurse midwife, etc., with a specialized certification as a family nurse practitioner, etc.

4. **Briefly describe the specific manner of collaboration between the licensed practitioner and advance practice nurse. Specifically, how they will work together, how they will share practice trends and responsibilities, how they maintain geographic proximity, and how they will provide coverage during an absence, incapacity, infirmity, or emergency by the licensed practitioner.**

   How they will work together:
   The licensed practitioner and advanced practice nurse shall collaborate on a continual basis, etc.

   How they will share practice trends and responsibilities:
   The advanced practice nurse shall make rounds at the request of the licensed practitioner and consult with the license practitioner as needed, etc.

   How they maintain geographic proximity:
   The licensed practitioner will maintain a physical presence within a reasonable geographic proximity to the advanced practice nurse's practice location.

   How they will provide coverage during absence, incapacity, infirmity, or emergency by the license practitioner:
   In the case of the absence, incapacity, or unavailability of the licensed practitioner, coverage and consultation will be coordinated and maintained by another licensed practitioner as arranged in advance by the licensed practitioner and the advanced practice nurse.

5. **Provide a description of limitations, if any, the licensed practitioner has placed on the advanced practice nurse's prescriptive authority.**
   There are no additional limitations on the advanced practice nurse or there are the following limitations on the advanced practice nurse, etc.

6. **Provide a description of the time and manner of the licensed practitioner's review of the advanced practice nurse's prescribing practices.** *Specifically, the description should include provisions that the advanced practice nurse must submit documentation of prescribing practices to the licensed practitioner within seven (7) days. Documentation of prescribing practices shall include, but not be limited to, at least a five percent (5%) random sampling of the charts and medications prescribed for patients.*
   The advanced practice nurse must submit documentation of the advance practice nurse's prescribing practices within seven (7) days to the licensed practitioner for review. The documentation of prescribing practices shall include at least a 5% random sampling of the charts and medications prescribed for patients.

7. **Provide a list of all other written practice agreements of the licensed practitioner and advanced practice nurse.**
   There are no other practice agreements or list all other practice agreements, etc.

8. **Provide the duration of the written practice agreement between the licensed practitioner and advanced practice nurse.**

Either party may terminate this practice agreement without cause at any time, effective immediately upon notice to the other party, etc.

_____

Signature of licensed practitioner

_____

Signature of advanced practice nurse

_____

Date

_____

Date

Sample Employment Agreement

Note: *The following contract is suited for a particular NP and a particular medical practice. Other NPs and practices may need different or additional provisions. NPs and employers each should seek the counsel of an attorney for drafting a contract suitable to the needs of the particular parties.*

Employment Agreement

THIS PROFESSIONAL SERVICES EMPLOYMENT AGREEMENT (the Agreement) made this _____ day of _____, 2013, by and between Jones Medical Clinic, a professional corporation in the State of Georgia, hereinafter referred to as "the Corporation," and Jane Doe, MS, CRNP, an individual, hereinafter referred to as "the Nurse Practitioner."

Recitals

The Corporation is a professional association formed in Georgia and engaged in the practice of medicine. The services rendered by and on behalf of the Corporation are referred to as the Practice.

The Nurse Practitioner is licensed to practice in Georgia.

The Corporation desires to employ the Nurse Practitioner upon the terms and conditions hereinafter set forth, and the Nurse Practitioner desires to accept such employment.

Article I—Employment

1.1. Professional Services. The Corporation agrees to employ the Nurse Practitioner under this Agreement. The Nurse Practitioner agrees to render professional services for individuals who present themselves as patients of the Practice and to carry out the duties described in Schedule A, which is attached to and made as a part of this Agreement. In performing such services, the Nurse Practitioner shall comply with policies and procedures established by the Corporation, including participation in quality assurance and utilization review activities. The Nurse Practitioner shall render professional services at the Jamestown location.

1.2. Full-Time Employment. The Nurse Practitioner agrees to devote her full time and best efforts to the performance of the duties outlined in Schedule A attached to this Agreement.

1.3. Standards. The Nurse Practitioner shall exercise independent professional judgment with respect to the care and treatment of all patients. The Nurse Practitioner agrees that the patient care services will be provided promptly, efficiently, and in strict accordance with the ethical and professional standards for the provision of healthcare services adopted by the Practice. The Nurse Practitioner agrees that her patient care efficiency and productivity (for example, the number of outpatient visits per week) will be consistent with or better than past experience.

1.4. Authorization for Exchange of Information. The Nurse Practitioner authorizes the Corporation to obtain credentialing information from any necessary source. Credentialing information includes all information related to the Nurse Practitioner's education, training, qualifications, character, and experience, including patient care, quality assurance, utilization review, and risk management records.

1.5. Charges and Accounts Receivable. The Nurse Practitioner assigns to the Corporation the full right to bill for all professional, administrative, and clinical services performed by the Nurse Practitioner. The Nurse Practitioner agrees that all fees, when accrued or paid, are the sole property of the Corporation and that the Nurse Practitioner has no direct interest in any of these fees. All fee schedules shall be established by the Corporation.

1.6. Medical Records. All medical records of the Practice shall be the property of the Corporation, subject to applicable provisions of the medical records law of Georgia.

Article II—Compensation, Benefits, Disability, and Insurance

2.1. Nurse Practitioner Compensation. In consideration of the Nurse Practitioner rendering services under this Agreement, the Corporation will pay the Nurse Practitioner the compensation as set forth on Schedule B.

2.2. Vacation and Employee Benefits. In addition to the monetary compensation, the Corporation shall provide the Nurse Practitioner with the vacation and employment benefits listed on Schedule C.

2.3. Termination of Disability. If the Agreement is terminated because of the Nurse Practitioner's disability pursuant to Subsection 3.2.1, the Nurse Practitioner's compensation shall terminate after the twenty-six (26) week determination period, but the Nurse Practitioner shall have the right to claim benefits under the long-term disability insurance policy provided as an employee benefit.

2.4. Professional Liability Insurance. During the term of this Agreement and thereafter, the Corporation shall continuously maintain in effect professional liability malpractice insurance for the Nurse Practitioner in the amount of $1,000,000 per occurrence/$3,000,000 annual aggregate coverage.

2.5. General Liability. During the term of this Agreement, the Corporation shall include the Nurse Practitioner as a covered employee under the Corporation's general liability insurance policy.

Article III—Term and Termination

3.1. Term. The term of this Agreement shall be 1 year beginning _____, 2013, and, if not sooner terminated as provided below, ending _____ , 2014. Thereafter, this Agreement shall automatically renew on a year-to-year basis, unless sooner terminated as provided below.

3.2. Termination by Corporation—Without Cure Period. The Corporation may terminate this Agreement at the sole discretion of the Corporation by written notice to the Nurse Practitioner (or representative) upon the occurrence of any of the following:

3.2.1. The Nurse Practitioner dies or becomes disabled. As used in this Agreement, disabled means the Nurse Practitioner's inability to perform the material and essential functions of clinical care for patients, despite reasonable accommodations by the Corporation, by reason of any medically determinable physical or mental impairment that has been determined to be terminal or that has lasted or can be expected to last for a period of not less than twenty-six (26) weeks, based on an examination by an independent physician selected by the Corporation.

3.2.2. The revocation, suspension, or cancellation of the Nurse Practitioner's professional license.

3.2.3. The imposition of any restriction or limitation on the Nurse Practitioner by any governmental authority having jurisdiction over the Nurse Practitioner to the extent that the Nurse Practitioner cannot render the required professional services.

3.2.4. A final determination by any board, hospital, or other organization having jurisdiction over the Nurse Practitioner's right to practice that the Nurse Practitioner has engaged in unprofessional or unethical conduct.

3.2.5. The Nurse Practitioner's clinical privileges at a hospital are involuntarily reduced, suspended, or revoked by final action of the hospital board under the bylaws, rules, or regulations of the hospital.

3.2.6. The Nurse Practitioner is convicted in a criminal or civil proceeding of fraud, misappropriation, embezzlement, or Medicare or Medicaid fraud and abuse.

3.2.7. The Nurse Practitioner is excluded from participation in the Medicare or Medicaid program by reason of fraud and/or abuse.

3.2.8. The Nurse Practitioner has misused assets of the Corporation by fraud.

3.3. Termination by Corporation—With Cure Period. The Corporation may terminate this Agreement based upon a failure of the Nurse Practitioner to comply with the terms and provisions of the Agreement after giving the Nurse Practitioner a notice of the alleged deficiency and allowing the Nurse Practitioner thirty (30) days to cure the alleged deficiency. The following are examples of deficiencies subject to the provisions of this Section:

3.3.1. The failure or refusal of the Nurse Practitioner to comply with the reasonable policies, work requirements, standards, and regulations of the Corporation that may be established from time to time.

3.3.2. The Nurse Practitioner breaches any obligation, covenant, or warranty under this Agreement, or the Nurse Practitioner fails to faithfully and diligently perform the services required by the provisions of this Agreement.

3.3.3. Notwithstanding the above, a 30-day notice shall not be required if the same deficiency has occurred more than twice in any 18-month period and written notice to cure was provided with respect to the previous occurrences, or if the deficiency is material and is incapable of being cured.

3.4. Termination by Nurse Practitioner. The Nurse Practitioner may terminate this Agreement:

3.4.1. Based upon a breach by the Corporation for failure to pay the compensation payable under the Agreement or failure to fulfill any other obligations under this Agreement, provided that the Corporation was given written notice of default and thirty (30) days to cure the specified breach.

3.4.2. The physicians of the Corporation are convicted in a criminal or civil proceeding of fraud, misappropriation, embezzlement, or Medicare or Medicaid fraud and abuse.

3.4.3. The physicians of the Corporation are excluded from participation in the Medicare or Medicaid program by reason of fraud and/or abuse.

3.4.4. The Nurse Practitioner moves out of the State of Georgia and gives thirty (30) days notice.

3.5. Effect of Termination. Upon termination of this Agreement as provided in this Article III, neither party shall have any further rights, duties, or obligations under this Agreement, except as otherwise provided herein. The termination or expiration shall not affect any liability or other obligation of either party that accrued prior to the termination or expiration.

Article IV—Management Support Systems and Personnel

4.1. The Corporation shall provide for or secure nonphysician personnel (including administrative, nursing, and other medical support personnel) and services that are reasonably needed by the Practice consistent with sound management standards for similar practices in the community. These services shall include administration, marketing and financial services, computerized management information systems, and computerized billing systems.

4.2. The Corporation shall provide the Nurse Practitioner with monthly statements of billings, collections, and accounts receivables attributable to the Nurse Practitioner. Should the Nurse Practitioner have questions about the data supplied, the Corporation shall provide access to the Corporation's accounting records and a clerk, who keeps these records, will answer the Nurse Practitioner's questions or supply further information as needed.

4.3. If the Nurse Practitioner's own records of patient visits and billings differ from the records of the Corporation, and the discrepancy cannot be resolved by the information seeking covered by Section 4.2, the Corporation agrees to designate one representative to negotiate a settlement acceptable to both parties within thirty (30) days. If no settlement can be reached internally, the Corporation agrees to submit any unresolved dispute to third-party arbitration, with the arbitrator selected from a list provided by the American Arbitration Association. The Corporation agrees to share equally with the Nurse Practitioner the expenses of arbitration.

4.4. The Corporation shall assign one physician to sign the Nurse Practitioner's written agreement, as required by Georgia law. The physician assigned shall be available or shall appoint a designate who will be available for consultation with the Nurse Practitioner when needed.

Article V—Notices

All notices shall be in writing and personally delivered or sent by certified or registered mail, postage prepaid, return receipt requested, addressed to the Corporation and the Nurse Practitioner at the addresses shown below. Any and all notices or other communication given pursuant to this Agreement shall be deemed duly given on the date personally delivered or on the date deposited in the U.S. Postal Service. The parties may change its or his or her address by specifying the change in a written notice to the other:

If to the Nurse Practitioner:
> Jane Doe, CRNP
> 98 Merit Drive
> Jamestown, GA 20000-3000

If to the Corporation:
>Jack Frost, MD
>201 Medical Drive, Suite 100
>Jamestown, GA 20000

Article VI—Miscellaneous

6.1. Entire Agreement. This Agreement embodies the entire agreement between the parties and supersedes all prior agreements, letters of intent, or understandings of any nature whatsoever between the parties with respect to the matters covered herein.

6.2. Amendment: Nonwaiver. Except as otherwise specifically provided, no amendment or modification of this Agreement shall be valid unless it is in writing and signed by the Nurse Practitioner and the designee of the Corporation as named in Article 5. No waiver of any of the provisions of this Agreement shall be valid unless it is in writing and signed by the party against whom it is sought to be enforced. Any waiver of breach of this Agreement shall not be considered to be a continuing waiver or consent to any subsequent breach on the part of either the Corporation or the Nurse Practitioner.

6.3. Counterparts. This Agreement may be executed in counterparts, and each counterpart shall be deemed an original.

6.4. Assignment. This Agreement may not be assigned by the Corporation to any entity without the prior written consent of the Nurse Practitioner. This Agreement is personal to the Nurse Practitioner and is not assignable by the Nurse Practitioner, in whole or in part, without the prior written consent of the Corporation. This Agreement is binding upon and inures to the benefit of the parties respective permitted successors and permitted assigns.

6.5. Governing Law. This Agreement shall be construed in accordance with and governed by the laws of the State of Georgia.

6.6. Governmental Requirements. This Agreement is subject to the requirements of all applicable laws and regulations and any government agency having jurisdiction. The parties agree to negotiate in good faith to amend this Agreement to comply with any governmental requirements affecting the Agreement or either party, including, without limitation, requirements affecting reimbursement for healthcare services. If the parties are unable to negotiate a mutually acceptable amendment to comply with any provision of law, regulation, or ruling, either party may initiate a voluntary termination of this Agreement on thirty (30) days notice.

6.7. Confidentiality. The parties agree not to disclose this Agreement or its contents to any person, firm, or entity, except the agents or representatives of the parties, and except as required by law.

6.8. Further Assurances. The Nurse Practitioner agrees to execute, acknowledge, seal, and deliver further assurances, instruments, and documents and to take such further actions as the Corporation may reasonably request in order to fulfill the intent of this Agreement.

IN WITNESS WHEREOF, the parties have caused this Agreement to be executed as of the day and year first above written, with the intent that this be a sealed instrument.
BY:

>Jack Frost, MD
>Jones Medical Clinic, PC
>Date _____
>
>Jane Doe, MS, CRNP
>Date _____

WITNESS/ATTEST:
>Date _____

Schedule A—Duties

1. The Nurse Practitioner shall provide clinical and professional medical services to patients within the scope of Nurse Practitioner's qualifications and consistent with accepted standards of medical practice and consistent with the reasonable productivity standards adopted by the Corporation and the Nurse Practitioner.
2. The Nurse Practitioner shall provide general patient care at the site specified by performance of accepted procedures and commonly used therapies and provision of appropriate support services. The Nurse Practitioner's duties shall include, but not be limited to, keeping and maintaining (or causing to be kept and maintained) appropriate records relating to all professional services rendered by Nurse Practitioner under this Agreement and preparing and attending to, in connection with such services, all reports, claims, and correspondence necessary and appropriate in the circumstances, all of which records, reports, claims, and correspondence shall belong to the Corporation. The Nurse Practitioner shall do all things reasonably desirable to maintain and improve her professional skills, including attendance at professional, postgraduate seminars and participation in professional societies. In addition, the Nurse Practitioner shall perform the following administrative, teaching, or professional services for the Corporation:
   a. Order medical supplies for the office.
   b. Review lab and radiology reports of office patients, and take appropriate follow-up action.
   c. Precept students from Georgia State University.
3. The Nurse Practitioner shall be responsible for the quality of medical care rendered by Nurse Practitioner to the patients of the Practice and for ensuring that such care meets or exceeds currently accepted standards of medical competence.
4. The Nurse Practitioner shall participate in the quality assurance and risk management program.

5. The Nurse Practitioner shall assist in the recruitment and hiring of professional personnel and support staff to work in the practice.
6. The Nurse Practitioner will relate to colleagues, staff, patients, and the public in a collegial manner and will abide by standards of conduct appropriate to the workplace.
7. The Nurse Practitioner shall assist in the marketing of the Practice and participate in the professional activities that promote the Practice.

Schedule B—Compensation

1. During the year of this Agreement (_____, 2013 to_____ , 2014), the Nurse Practitioner shall be paid a salary of $91,000, payable in biweekly installments. Salary is understood to include the Nurse Practitioner's share of collected billings, as determined in Paragraph 2 below, and the Nurse Practitioner's performance of administrative, teaching, and other professional duties as specified in Schedule A, Paragraph 2, previously listed.
2. Billings shall be apportioned as the Nurse Practitioner's share as follows:
   a. The Corporation and the Nurse Practitioner agree that efficiency at collections is outside of the control of the Nurse Practitioner, but within the control of the Corporation. Therefore, the Corporation and the Nurse Practitioner agree to apply a 95% collection rate (percentage of billings collected, as of 120 days after billing) for the purposes of determining the Nurse Practitioner's collected billings. The Corporation agrees to take responsibility for maintaining a 95% rate of billings collected. In the event that the Corporation does not collect 95% of its billings during the term of this Agreement, Corporation agrees to pay the Nurse Practitioner salary as if the Corporation had maintained a 95% collections rate.
   b. The Corporation and the Nurse Practitioner agree to a fee schedule for the Nurse Practitioner's services, which is attached.
3. The Nurse Practitioner agrees to bill a minimum of $270,000 per year.
   a. Billings shall include self-paying patients, third-party payers, and internal billings, which shall include surgical follow-up visits handled by the Nurse Practitioner for the Corporation.
   b. Surgical follow-up visits are assigned a value of $70.00.
4. The Corporation shall retain all but $91,000 of collected revenues from the first $270,000 of billings generated by the Nurse Practitioner.
5. The Nurse Practitioner shall receive bonus payments to be determined as follows:
   a. If the Nurse Practitioner's billings exceed $68,000 in any quarter, collected revenues exceeding $68,000 per quarter shall be shared jointly and equally by the Nurse Practitioner and the Corporation, and the Corporation shall pay the Nurse Practitioner's 50% share to the Nurse Practitioner as a bonus within 30 days of the last day of the quarter.
   b. If the Nurse Practitioner bills less than $68,000 in any quarter, the Nurse Practitioner shall receive no bonus for that quarter, and the difference between the

amount billed by the Nurse Practitioner in the deficient quarter, and $68,000 shall be deducted from any bonus the Nurse Practitioner shall receive in a future quarter. There shall be no deduction from the Nurse Practitioner's salary.

c. In the event that this Agreement is terminated prior to receipt of any bonus payment due the Nurse Practitioner, the Corporation agrees to pay the Nurse Practitioner the bonus earned within 15 days of termination. In the event that termination occurs mid-quarter, both parties agree that neither bonus nor deficiency will apply for the final quarter.

Schedule C—Benefits

1. The Nurse Practitioner shall be entitled to the following benefits:
   a. Health insurance: The Corporation shall pay directly to the health insurance company up to $5000 per year for premiums for health insurance.
   b. Malpractice insurance: The Corporation shall pay the malpractice insurance premiums for the Nurse Practitioner.
   c. Pension benefits: The Corporation will fund the Nurse Practitioner's pension benefits.
   d. Vacation: Four (4) weeks per year.
   e. Continuing medical education time: One (1) week.
   f. Continuing medical education expenses: Up to $1500.00 per year, paid for by the Corporation.
   g. Life insurance: In an amount equal to annual base salary.
   h. Salary continuation plan: Short-Term Disability—full pay continuation until Long-Term Disability coverage begins at ninety (90) days.
   i. Sick leave: Ten (10) days per year.
   j. Professional fees and medical staff dues: Professional journals in the amount of $350 per year, medical staff dues at hospitals where the Nurse Practitioner attends patients of the Practice, state license fee, state Controlled Dangerous Substances and DEA license fees, and Basic Cardiac Life Support/Advanced Cardiac Life Support recertification fees.

CHAPTER 11

Practice Ownership: Legal and Business Considerations for the Nurse Practitioner Owner

Some state laws are more conducive to nurse practitioner (NP) practice ownership than others because of collaboration requirements, or lack thereof, and reimbursement practices. Nevertheless, a number of NPs are starting their own practices, and many others have owned practices for over 25 years, hiring physicians where necessary to conform to the law.

The NPs who have been in practice for more than 20 years often bought an existing practice from a physician. In such cases, the NP was initially an employee or partner of the physician, and the physician opted to leave the area and sold the practice to the NP. In that situation, the NP had to make many adjustments, but he or she did not have to start from scratch.

In the past 15 years, NPs serving Medicaid enrollees have started practices from the ground up. Some of these have started faculty practices associated with nursing schools. Others have been strictly private entrepreneurs.

As this edition is being written, there are proposals and plans for changes to the nation's healthcare delivery system. It is impossible to predict how these changes will affect the landscape for NPs who want to start their own practices. Those considering practice start-up should be monitoring the state and national news to gain perspective on how their business ideas fit into their state's and the nation's plans.

Advantages of Practice Ownership

Even without a general redesign of primary care, NPs who wish to run their own practices have been able to do so in many states. The advantages to an NP of practice ownership are as follows:

- The NP decides upon the length of patient visits.
- The NP decides how the practice is run.
- The NP chooses employees.
- The NP controls quality.
- The NP controls referrals.

- The NP may titrate workload to income.
- The NP keeps profits.

There are also advantages for the public when NPs own practices:

- The patient gets the benefit of combined nursing and medicine.
- The patient gets more face time with the provider.
- The patient may pay less or get more for the same amount of money.
- The patient may have better access to health care.

In an NP practice, physicians are called in when necessary, but not all patients have to pay for a physician visit or wait for physician to be available when a nurse could fulfill the patient's needs.

Examples of NP Practices

NPs own the following types of practices:

- Travel medicine clinics
- Pediatric primary care
- Wound care consultations
- Home visits
- Family health centers
- Urgent care
- Cosmetic procedures

Barriers

It is true that NPs have more obstacles to overcome than physicians when starting a practice. These include the following:

- Getting on commercial insurance provider panels
- Getting and keeping a collaborating physician, if required by state law or if billing Medicare
- Getting referrals from hospital emergency rooms
- Getting privileges at hospitals
- Lack of legal authority to admit patients to nursing homes, to order home care, or to direct hospice services

This chapter is for the NP who has started a practice or who has considered or may in the future consider opening an NP practice and requires an understanding of the legalities and knowledge of the details involved. **Appendix 11-A** offers a checklist of considerations relevant to opening a practice.

Decisions Before Starting a Practice

There are eight major business considerations when starting a practice:

1. With whom will I practice?
2. Where will reimbursement come from?

3. Will reimbursement cover expenses?
4. How will I get patients to come to the practice?
5. Where will the practice be located?
6. If the state requires a collaborative agreement, how will that be handled?
7. What sort of quality and productivity measures will the practice institute?
8. How will patient flow be handled?

Also important, though somewhat less important than the eight major considerations, are the following considerations:

1. What form will the business take?
2. What systems need to be set up for getting supplies, equipment and repairs, depositing cash, and disposing of hazardous waste?
3. Who will the practice hire to help?

With Whom Will I Practice?

There are advantages to both solo practice and group practice. Advantages of solo practice include:

- Autonomy
- Efficiency of one-person decision making
- Less income necessary to support one person than multiple people
- No chance that another person's lack of productivity will affect one's business

Advantages of group practice include:

- Possible greater access to capital
- Possible shared call and office coverage
- Another source of expertise
- Social support
- Possible economies of scale

There are many potential partners for NPs and many ways of aligning practices. In addition to the traditional solo practitioner or group practice of professionals, where patients come to the office and providers collect from insurance companies, there are hospital-affiliated practices, nursing home–based practices, employer-affiliated practices, and agency-affiliated practices.

Where Will Reimbursement Come From?

Reimbursement might come from any or all of four sources:

1. Government payers: Medicaid and Medicare
2. Private insurers: Health maintenance organizations (HMOs), managed-care organizations (MCOs), and indemnity insurers
3. Patients who pay their own bills
4. Contracts

(Reimbursement for NP services is discussed in more detail elsewhere in the text.)

A practice owner should look into any and all sources of reimbursement. For example, some government and private agencies will contract with healthcare providers for health services. A pediatric NP might contract with the county school system to give immunizations or conduct school physicals. Certain procedures and diagnostic testing can be billed separately from visits, and a potential practice owner will want to see what opportunities there are for getting that income.

Will Reimbursement Cover Expenses?
Practice Expenses: Crunching the Numbers

Many an employed NP has thought, "If I was in charge, I would never run the practice like this." Before going too far with this line of thought, an NP considering opening a practice, and even an NP who expects to remain employed, needs to know how the numbers crunch in the business of primary care. Simply put, it takes a large number of patient visits to support a practice.

It costs about $200,000 a year to run a primary care physician practice, not including physician compensation. Expenses include the following:

- Rent
- Payroll and employee benefits
- Quarterly state and federal taxes
- Office equipment
- Telephone and Internet connection
- Utilities
- Answering service
- Supplies
- Hazardous waste disposal
- Payment on start-up loan
- Professional dues and subscriptions
- Fee to register lab with federal and state governments
- Accounting fees
- Attorney fees
- Business travel (local—to nursing homes, patients' homes, educational seminars—and also for continuing education)
- Gifts to staff
- Cleaning
- Insurance (professional liability, umbrella policy, workers' compensation, unemployment)
- Application fee for hospital privileges
- Beeper and cellular telephone
- Advertising

Office Expenses. In addition to equipment, office expenses can include lab expenses, the lease of a car used only for business, depreciation of equipment, equipment rental, equipment maintenance, and continuing education tuition.

Compensation and Charges. Primary care physicians earn, on average, $160,000 per year, according to several recent surveys. Keep in mind that physicians in private practice take as compensation the difference between income and expenses. How they apportion this compensation—retirement, health insurance, vacation pay—is up to them.

For the sake of illustration, assume the average cost of running a solo primary care physician practice is $360,000 per year: $200,000 in expenses and $160,000 in physician compensation. To cover salary and expenses, a physician has to conduct 4562 patient visits a year at a charge of $80 per visit. This assumes that payment is received for each visit. In reality, not all bills are paid.

NP Practice Compared

Now let's run the numbers for a practice where the owner/provider is an NP. Assume that the NP pays a physician to be the collaborator on a written agreement required by state law.

An NP practice will have all of the same office expenses, plus the expense of paying the physician who signs the NP's written agreement. Malpractice insurance costs considerably less for an NP than for a physician, but the cost to cover a practice is about $2500 a year. Thus, for the sake of this example, assume the expenses are equal for an NP and a physician.

Reasonable NP compensation, considering the responsibility of a private practice, would be at least $100,000 per year. The total expense of running an NP practice, based on these projections, would be $300,000.

Assume 4285 patient visits a year, which translates to a daily load of 18 to 19 patients, 5 days a week, 47 weeks a year. An NP could charge $70, on average, per visit, and make the salary and expenses listed earlier. If an NP charged less than $70 per visit, he or she would have to: (1) take less compensation; (2) pay less for office, supplies, and so on; (3) have fewer office personnel than the average physician; (4) see more than 19 patients per day, 5 days a week; or (5) work more than 5 days a week, 47 weeks a year.

Twenty patients a day is a fairly reasonable load, but that volume may or may not be attainable, and $70 per visit may or may not be attainable. More than 20 patients a day, every day, is a taxing patient load. That is not counting the time it takes to return telephone calls, deal with personnel problems, do payroll, and so on.

Still, the economics are favorable for NPs who want to be their own bosses, and they may not be working any harder than employee NPs. Those NPs who work for someone else are usually expected to see about 20 patients a day, but it will be someone else's decision that they do so, and the majority of employed NPs will not make $100,000 per year.

For examples of practice expenses and revenues of a physician practice and an NP practice compared, see **Exhibit 11-1** and **Exhibit 11-2**. Exhibit 11-1 demonstrates that an NP practice could be run on approximately $100,000 less per year than a physician practice, due largely to the differential in salary between NPs and physicians.

How Will I Get Patients to Come to the Practice?

An NP who starts a new practice, as opposed to buying an established practice, will need to bring in patients with whom the NP has already established a relationship or attract new patients. Either way, there are costs involved.

If an NP has signed an employment contract with a previous employer in which the NP has agreed not to compete with the previous practice under specified conditions, the NP must honor the agreement or face the possibility of a lawsuit. If the NP has not signed such

---

Exhibit 11-1 Primary Care Practice Expenses (in $): NP Versus MD

NP Practice Expenses		MD Practice Expenses	
Rent	20,700	Rent	20,700
Utilities	7400	Utilities	7400
Supplies	25,300	Supplies	25,300
Depreciation	3400	Depreciation	3400
Equipment rental	3500	Equipment rental	3500
Equipment maintenance	2300	Equipment maintenance	2300
Continuing education	1600	Continuing education	1600
Advertising/promotion	1700	Advertising/promotion	1700
Cleaning	10,000	Cleaning	10,000
Insurance	2500	Insurance	12,400
Answering service	4500	Answering service	4500
Licenses	1200	Licenses	1200
Car	2000	Car	2000
Legal	1000	Legal	1000
Lab	7900	Lab	7900
Dues	600	Dues	2000
Taxes	14,000	Taxes	15,700
Other expenses	3000	Other expenses	5000
	112,600		127,600

NP Practice Salaries		MD Practice Salaries	
NP, 1.2 FTE	102,600	MD, 1.0 FTE	150,000
RN, 1.0 FTE	45,000	NPs, 1.2 FTE	80,000
Business manager, 1.0 FTE	45,000	RN, 1.0 FTE	40,000
Receptionist, 1.2 FTE	25,000	Receptionist, 1.2 FTE	25,000
MD consultant	5000	Clerks	10,000
	222,600		305,000

Benefits at 25%	55,600	Benefits at 25%	76,250
Total personnel	278,250	Total personnel	381,250

Total yearly expenses	390,850	Total yearly expenses	508,850

Abbreviation: FTE, full-time employee.

---

a "noncompete" clause, then the NP is legally free to take established patients to the NP's own practice. However, the previous employer, who has lost patients, is quite likely to be upset, and this nonmonetary "cost" is certainly worth considering.

Whether the NP is seeking new or old patients, some marketing efforts will be necessary. Marketing can take the form of word of mouth, letters, flyers, advertisements, health fair appearances, speaking engagements, television appearances, radio announcements or talk shows, social media, web pages, or newspaper articles.

Exhibit 11-2 Primary Care Practice Revenues, NP or MD

Assumptions:
Practice size: 3000
Office hours: 48 hours per week
Number of visits/year: 7488

Included Services:
Healthcare maintenance and preventive care, all episodic visits including primary care gynecology, primary care, mental health care, suturing, nebulization of asthmatics, skin biopsies, incisions and drainages, outpatient detoxification, hospital medical visits, home visits, 24-hour on-call, venipuncture, lab services as allowed under CLIA exemption

Excluded Services:
Diagnostic labs other than CLIA-exempt, pharmacy, emergency department visits, physical therapy, obstetrics, emergency transport, patient transportation, hospitalization, medical specialist care, surgery, chemotherapy, sigmoidoscopy, fracture repair

Excluded Patients:
Pregnant, AIDS, ALS, MS, paraplegics, quadriplegics, spina bifida, chronic nursing home, hospitalized mentally ill

Capitation and Patient Mix:

Age	%	N	Rate	Income/Month
0–2	5	150	29.09	4364
2–4	5	150	10.75	1613
5–11	10	300	8.46	2538
12–20	10	300	7.08	2124
21–64	60	1800	11.67	21,006
65+	10	300	29.00	8700
				$40,345

Yearly income: $484,140

Through marketing the practice, potential patients learn what services it provides and the advantages of visiting. Advantages of a particular practice to a patient may be convenient location, ease of getting an appointment, acceptance of the patient's insurance, an especially personable provider, extraordinary personal attention, or a reduced fee for cash-paying patients.

Some general principles of practice marketing include the following:

- The marketing message must be repeated many times—some say 12, some say 27 times—before a person learns it.
- Create a sense of affiliation with the practice.
- Create an image for the practice and a marketing message.

- Strive to exceed the patient's expectations, and the patient not only will stay with the practice but also will tell others about it.
- A new patient is worth the price of a visit; a patient kept is worth thousands of dollars.

Where Will the Practice Be Located?

The location of the practice will determine how easy or difficult it is for patients to come. If the patient base that the NP is looking for is using public transportation or traveling on foot, then the practice must be on a bus line or in a neighborhood. If it is an inner-city practice but the patients are coming by car, then convenient and inexpensive parking is a consideration. If a practice is looking for walk-in traffic, then a storefront location would be better than a second-story office in a large building.

Location also can have implications for practice income. In rural areas, there could be more opportunity due to less competition. On the other hand, there could be too few patients to support a practice. In certain urban areas, there is actually a dearth of healthcare providers, while in other urban and suburban areas, there is an oversupply. A study of locations of other providers is a prerequisite for choice of practice location.

If the State Requires a Collaborative Agreement, How Will That Be Handled?

If a collaborative agreement is required by state law, a practice will need to find a collaborator before opening.

The first step is to find out what the state law requires in the way of physician collaboration. Is it a signature on a written agreement and an agreement to consult when necessary, or is it more involved, such as quarterly review of charts, cosignatures on charts and prescriptions, and monthly meetings?

The second step is to make a list of possible collaborators. NPs will want to look for a collaborator who is competent, has a similar philosophy of patient care, will be accessible when necessary, and will do what is needed for a reasonable price.

The third step is to discuss the NP's needs, the state's requirements, and fees with the potential collaborator(s). Many potential collaborators are worried about increasing their liability for malpractice suits if they collaborate with an NP. Therefore, an NP may want to suggest that potential collaborators discuss any such increased liability with their malpractice insurer. If a physician's premiums will go up, then that cost will have to be borne by the NP. It is unlikely that an insurer will raise a physician's premium for collaborating with an NP, however.

The fourth step is to weigh the potential contributions and expense of various possible collaborators.

The fifth step is to draft, or have an attorney draft, a professional services contract between the physician collaborator and the NP. If there are few willing and available collaborating physicians in the area, then a practice's longevity is threatened if a collaborator bows out after the practice has opened. Therefore, it is wise to hire a collaborator and seal the arrangement with a written contract with a term of at least 1 year and 60 days notice before the collaborator terminates the relationship. See **Appendix 11-B** for an example of an NP–collaborator agreement.

Finally, draft the written agreement as required by state law. If written practice protocols or guidelines are required by law, obviously those must be drafted also.

What Sort of Quality and Productivity Measures Will the Practice Institute?

If quality measures and systems to collect data on performance are set up at the time a practice opens, then data collection will proceed from day one, and attention to quality will be built into the structure of the practice.

At what sort of quality and productivity measures should a practice look? Practices will be interested in quantity—productivity—because the practice must do enough business to cover costs. Practices will be equally interested in high-quality clinical care, so that they can build their reputation for quality, satisfy patients, and avoid medical errors.

Productivity

Productivity directly affects income. In a fee-for-service system of reimbursement, the more visits made and billed for, the more a practice makes. In a capitated system of reimbursement, the more patients enrolled with a practice, the more monthly fees the practice receives, and the more patients potentially will need attention. Providers and staff who generate lots of work should be rewarded accordingly, and providers and staff who generate little work should be encouraged to be more productive.

Therefore, a prudent practice owner will build systems for tracking productivity into a practice from day one. Most software systems for practices track provider productivity. As for office staff productivity, measures should be agreed to by staff members and practice administrators at the time of hiring, with periodic review and revision, if necessary, of the standards that are set.

Clinical Performance

A good start when attempting to measure clinical performance is the Healthplan Employer Data and Information Set (HEDIS) put out by the National Committee on Quality Assurance (NCQA). Because NCQA audits health plans, and health plans audit practices to collect data to submit to HEDIS, the HEDIS measures are becoming the industry-wide standards for comparing quality among providers.

Another source to review when thinking about measuring clinical performance is Medicare's Physician Quality Reporting System (PQRS). Information on this program is available through Medicare's website (http://www.cms.hhs.gov). If a practice will be seeing Medicare patients, it makes sense to incorporate participation in the PQRS from the day it opens.

In addition, new practice owners will want to take part in electronic prescribing, not only as a quality improvement and quality maintenance measure, but also to take advantage of payment incentives. Medicare's Electronic Prescribing (eRx) Incentive Program is a reporting program that uses a combination of incentive payments and payment adjustments to encourage electronic prescribing by eligible professionals. The program provides an incentive payment to practices with eligible professionals (identified on claims by their individual National Provider Identifier and Tax Identification Number) who successfully e-prescribe for covered Physician Fee Schedule services furnished to Medicare Part B Fee-for-Service

Beneficiaries. As of 2012, the program applied a payment adjustment to those eligible professionals who are not successful electronic prescribers on their Medicare Part B services. For more information on this program, visit Medicare's website (http://www.cms.hhs.gov).

How Will Patient Flow Be Handled?

From day one, there must be an agreed upon way of setting up appointments, greeting patients, getting insurance or other payment information, obtaining clinical intake information (e.g., history, old records, chief complaint, vital signs), visiting the provider(s), and arranging follow-up as needed.

Appointments

Appointment-making software is available. Appointment books from office supply stores remain a good option as well.

Payment Intake Information

For each patient, the intake staff person will need to obtain the following information:

- Name
- Address
- Telephone number
- Social Security number
- Date of birth
- Method of payment: insurance, cash, credit card
- Insurance company name, address, and telephone number
- Copy of insurance card
- Emergency contact name, address, and telephone number

Clinical Intake Information

A practice should have a clinical intake form—a history and physical form—suited to the patient. An example of such a form for the college-age patient is included as **Exhibit 11-3**.

Provider Visits

A system for dealing with patient flow should address the following questions:

- Does the provider see one patient at a time or work multiple rooms?
- Does the provider get the patient from the waiting room or does an assistant get the patient into the examination room?
- Does the provider talk to the patient while the patient is dressed or does an assistant get the patient into a gown prior to the arrival of the provider?
- Does the provider chart and make telephone calls in a separate office or is the provider's office space within the exam rooms?
- When the provider is finished, who takes care of ordering referrals and laboratory tests?
- Does the provider do all of the history taking and teaching or will registered nurses do these things?

Exhibit 11-3 New Patient History

Family history

	Age	Health	Occupation	Alive?	Age and/or Cause of Death
Father	____	____	_____	_____	_____
Mother	____	____	_____	_____	_____
Brothers	____	____	_____	_____	_____
Sisters	____	____	_____	_____	_____

State any blood relative, including parents, grandparents, and siblings, who have/had any of the following:

Alcoholism _____   Diabetes _____
Asthma _____   Tuberculosis _____
Cancer or leukemia _____   Stroke _____
Infectious disease _____   Epilepsy/seizure _____
   State disease: _____   Bleeding disorder _____
High blood pressure _____   Psychiatric illness _____
Kidney disease _____   Other familial disease: _____
Heart disease _____

Personal health history:
Give the approximate age at which you had any of the following:

Chicken pox	Pneumonia	Attention deficit disorder
German measles	Pleurisy	High cholesterol
Measles	HIV infection	Diarrhea, chronic
Hepatitis	Tonsillitis	Hernia
Mononucleosis	Diabetes	Overweight
Malaria	Kidney disease	Joint injury/disease
Mumps	Thyroid disease	Gonorrhea
Rheumatic fever	Concussion	Syphilis
Meningitis	Seizures	Herpes
Tuberculosis	Bleeding disorder	Other infectious disease
Asthma	Fainting	Heart murmur
Allergies	Migraine	Heart disease
Hay fever	Mental illness	Circulatory problems

Hospitalizations for injury, illness, surgery, or diagnostic testing:

_____ Age _____
_____ Age _____
_____ Age _____

Females:
Menstrual history:
Age of onset _____ Interval _____ Duration _____
Current menstrual problems _____
Contraceptive method, if any _____
Date of most recent Pap smear _____ Normal? _____ Yes _____ No
Date of most recent mammogram _____ Normal? _____ Yes _____ No

Please rank the following by circling severity in the last 3 years:
0 for absent, 1, 2, 3 for increasing severity or frequency.

Acne	0 1 2 3	Fatigue	0 1 2 3
Allergy injection	0 1 2 3	Frequent urination	0 1 2 3
Anxiety	0 1 2 3	Headaches	0 1 2 3
Back trouble	0 1 2 3	Health worries	0 1 2 3
Blood in urine	0 1 2 3	Heart racing	0 1 2 3
Blurred vision	0 1 2 3	Indigestion	0 1 2 3
Boils	0 1 2 3	Lack of energy	0 1 2 3
Chest pain	0 1 2 3	Loss of hearing	0 1 2 3
Chronic cough	0 1 2 3	Nausea	0 1 2 3
Constipation	0 1 2 3	Nightmares	0 1 2 3
Depression	0 1 2 3	Sexual abuse	0 1 2 3
Diarrhea	0 1 2 3	Sexual problems	0 1 2 3
Difficulty concentrating	0 1 2 3	Short of breath	0 1 2 3
Difficulty or pain swallowing	0 1 2 3	Sinus trouble	0 1 2 3
		Skin problems	0 1 2 3
Difficulty making friends	0 1 2 3	Sleeplessness	0 1 2 3
Discord with parents, spouse	0 1 2 3	Sleepwalking	0 1 2 3
		Sore throat	0 1 2 3
Dizziness	0 1 2 3	Stuttering	0 1 2 3
Domestic violence	0 1 2 3	Suicidal thoughts	0 1 2 3
Earaches	0 1 2 3	Tension	0 1 2 3
Fainting spells	0 1 2 3	Trouble falling asleep	0 1 2 3
		Use of laxatives	0 1 2 3

When did you last see your dentist for an oral exam? _____
Do you smoke?_____ If so, what and how much? _____

How much alcohol do you drink? _____
Have people annoyed you by criticizing your drinking? _____
Have you ever felt bad or guilty about your drinking? _____
Have you ever had a drink first thing in the morning to steady your nerves or to get rid of a hangover? _____
Are you using street drugs? _____ If yes, drug? _____

Have you used street drugs in the past 2 years? _____

If yes, drug? _____

A positive answer to any of the previous seven questions is highly indicative of having an alcohol or drug problem. You are invited to discuss your answers with the nurse practitioner or physician.

Do you have an eating disorder? ___Type? _____

Are you allergic to cats, dust, trees, grass, or other substances in the environment? If so, what? _____

If you are ALLERGIC TO ANY MEDICINE, please list here _____

Has your physical activity been restricted during the past five years? ___
Give reason and explanation _____ _____

Do you have any physical or emotional disability that interferes with your daily activities? If so, detail _____

Have you been physically violent with yourself or others? _____ Yes _____ No
If so, detail _____

Have you consulted a primary care provider recently for any illness or health problem? _____ If so, detail _____

Have you consulted a psychiatrist or psychologist in the last 2 years? If yes, for how long? _____ Please provide the name, address, and telephone number of your therapist _____

Previous primary care provider's name, address, and telephone number
_____

Do you take any medication regularly? _____ If so, what?

IMMUNIZATION RECORD
Tetanus booster within 10 years. Date_/_/_
Measles vaccine, two doses required after 12 months of age.
Dose 1, date _/_/_ Dose 2, date_/_/_
Mumps, one dose required. Date_/_/_
Rubella, one dose required. Date_/_/_
Polio Date_/_/_
How would you usually rate your health?
Excellent ____ Average ____ Poor ____

Would you estimate that health problems keep you from your day's work or activities _____ Never _____ Occasionally _____ Sometimes _____ Often

If health problems keep you from your daily activities, what health problem bothers you the most? _____
_____

Would you say that your health in the past six weeks has ____ improved ____ stayed the same ____ declined.

Date ____ Signed _____

Follow-Up

Review and follow-up of laboratory testing, telephone calls to patients who need follow-up contact, and telephone calls to other providers about patient issues all are tasks that providers or some staff member who is integrally involved in patient care must be responsible for. If a provider is to do these things, there must be time built into the schedule. If another staff member is to do these things, there must be systems for communication between the provider, helper, and patient, as well as documentation in medical records.

What Form Will the Business Take?

There are four options for the business structure of a practice: sole proprietorship, partnership, limited liability company (LLC), and corporation.

Sole Proprietor

In a sole proprietorship, the business and the individual are one and the same. Any debts or legal liability are the responsibility of the individual owner. The owner files tax information on a Schedule C, along with their tax return. Year-end losses can be deducted from the individual's taxable income. Year-end profits are added to other income the individual may have and are taxed accordingly.

Advantages of a sole proprietorship include the following:

- The owner makes all decisions.
- Losses can be deducted from personal/family income.
- There is no potential liability for purchases, mistakes, or bad judgment of a partner.
- There is no double taxation as is possible with a corporation.

There are disadvantages of a sole proprietorship as well:

- There is no one to help with expenses of start-up and maintenance.
- Ups and downs are dealt with alone.

Partnership

A partnership is a business relationship involving two or more individuals or business entities. Most partnerships spell out the relationships between or among the parties in a partnership agreement. If there is no partnership agreement, state law governs the relationships.

Partners are liable for the debts and legal liabilities of one another. Partners share profits, decision making, administration, and workload in some way that is agreeable to all.

Profits and losses in a partnership are divided and deducted or added to an individual's tax forms. The partnership has a tax form, and the partnership's distributions of profits or losses to the individuals involved appear on the individuals' tax forms.

A lawsuit against a partnership implies liability for all partners. A debt incurred by one partner is a debt shared by all partners.

The major decisions to be made by partners are as follows:

- What happens if one partner wants out?
- Who inherits if one partner dies?

- How will profits and losses be divided?
- What contribution to start-up expenses will each partner make?
- How will duties be carried out?
- How will decisions be made?
- How will disputes be settled?

Advantages of a partnership include the following:

- Risk is shared.
- Success and failure are shared.
- Losses can be deducted from individual partners' taxable income.
- There is backup for individual partners in the practice.

There are also disadvantages of a partnership:

- The debts incurred by one partner are the debts of the partnership.
- A partner may be liable for another partner's mistakes.
- There are many opportunities for disputes between partners.
- A less productive partner will affect all other partners.

Limited Liability Company

An LLC combines some of the best attributes of partnership with the best attributes of a corporation. State laws vary regarding the specifics of LLCs. The general provisions, however, are as follows:

- Income passes through to the individual members of an LLC, as in a partnership.
- Losses pass through to the individuals, as in a partnership.
- Individual members are liable for the debts of the company only up to a limit.
- Members agree on operational matters through a written document. If there is no written agreement, differences are settled according to state law regarding LLCs.
- Professionals may form LLCs.

The main advantage of an LLC is that this business form combines the best of partnerships and corporations. There are also disadvantages, however, including the following:

- A state may not include the LLC in its legal forms of business entity.
- The law is not as extensive in addressing this form as the other forms.
- States may have specific conditions that must be met before forming an LLC.

A professional forming an LLC is still liable for professional malpractice. However, in other forms of lawsuits against an LLC, the business entity affords protection against individual liability as in corporations.

Corporation

A corporation is a business entity with its own identity. Although one individual may be the sole stockholder, director, and officer—the owner—the corporation is nevertheless a separate legal entity.

Under state law, professionals often must form a specific type of corporation with specific laws. Called a professional corporation or professional association, this form of company resembles a general corporation in many ways. The corporation has its own identifying number with the Internal Revenue Service (IRS) and files a tax return. Decisions are made by officers, a board of directors, and stockholders. In some states, stockholders must be like-licensed professionals.

Advantages of a corporation are as follows:

- When several individuals have ownership interest in the business, there are mechanisms for decision making and dispute resolution.
- There are set mechanisms for dividing profits and losses, based on capital contribution and professional work done.
- Many corporations like to deal with other corporations.
- The expenses of doing business are taken from a central pool before distribution of profits to stockholders.
- There are legal limits on the personal liability of individuals.

There are disadvantages as well:

- A great deal of paperwork is required by state and federal governments.
- Corporate profits are taxed, and, thus, an owner could pay tax on corporate profits and pay again on a distribution of profits.

Liability Ramifications. A corporation is often liable for corporate debts, rather than each individual stockholder being liable. Professionals are not shielded from malpractice liability, however.

Professional Corporations. Some states' laws prohibit the forming of a professional corporation by professionals with differing forms of licenses—for example, nurses and physicians. Before an NP attempts to form a corporation with a physician, he or she should consult state law.

Choice of Corporate Structure. State laws governing partnerships, corporations, and LLCs differ. Consult a local attorney about choosing a business form and drafting the necessary legal documents.

Corporate Practice of Medicine Doctrine. This doctrine is based on a tradition that medicine and business do not mix. Some states have ignored or dispensed with this doctrine. In other states, it is still on the legal books. Nevertheless, professional corporations are an option in every state.

What Systems Need to Be Set Up?

In addition to systems for tracking quality and quantity of care provided, systems will be necessary for these items:

- Tracking inventory of supplies
- Purchasing supplies
- Purchasing equipment
- Getting equipment repaired

- Depositing cash at day's end
- Disposing of hazardous waste
- Protecting patient confidentiality and privacy

There will be local vendors with whom accounts can be opened and arrangements made for each of these tasks.

Who Will the Practice Hire to Help?

An early decision to be made is the necessary number of support staff. What kind of talents and skills will be needed? Where can these employees be found?

New practice owners are likely to use past experience to judge how much employed help will be needed. Minimum services include these:

- Reception/appointment making
- Billing
- Cleaning
- Accounting
- Payroll
- Legal
- Medical assistance

Many of these services can be obtained on an as-needed basis as opposed to hiring employees. In many communities, medical billing is done by billing services, as is payroll. Reception and appointment making, however, are almost always done by employees of the practice.

Business Planning

The success of a practice is closely related to several factors that can be researched prior to opening the business. Those factors include the following:

- The need for the services in the community
- Community interest in the services to be provided
- The size of the potential patient pool in the community
- The willingness of the community to use the services of an NP
- The willingness of third-party payers to reimburse NPs for services

The best way to plan for a practice is to produce a business plan. A business plan is a written document that answers these questions:

- What do you plan to offer?
- How will you market the services?
- Who will purchase the services?
- Where will the business be located?
- How big will the practice be?
- How will the practice's activities, policies, and procedures be organized?
- How will expenses be covered?
- What are the potential problems with the business?

- How will those problems be dealt with?
- What start-up money is needed, if any?
- What form will start-up funds take: equity, debt?
- How will start-up costs be repaid?

Often used to convince investors to invest or lenders to lend money to get the business started, a business plan is also an exercise that forces someone who is considering starting a business to research its feasibility and organize a plan for carrying out the business goals.

Writing a Business Plan for an NP Practice

A business plan can run 25 to 40 pages and can cost thousands of dollars in consulting fees. A short version may be satisfactory if a business owner is looking for a rather small start-up loan and few investors are needed. Some NPs who have started practices have enlisted students in graduate business programs to create business plans for them as part of a class project. In these cases, the NPs have gotten a business plan for a much lower rate than is often commanded. For the do-it-yourself enthusiast, there are business plan software programs that an NP can adapt to suit their purposes.

At a minimum, a business plan for an NP practice should include these items:

- A list of services provided to patients
- Evidence of the need for those services
- Projections for the practice's income compared with expenses
- A description of the principal movers who are starting the business, including their relevant experience and skills
- An organizational plan
- A plan for managing the day-to-day operations
- Investment needs
- Potential problems and critical risks

A sample business plan is given in **Appendix 11-C**.

Services Provided

In a business plan, an NP contemplating a practice venture lists the services to be offered. For example, in a primary care practice, the likely services might include the following:

- Health assessment (histories and physicals)
- Management and treatment of acute episodic illnesses and chronic stable illnesses
- Preventive education and counseling
- Screening for health maintenance
- Urgent care, such as stitching of lacerations and incision and drainage of certain lesions

Evidence of the Need for Those Services

If a proposed location for the practice is in a community that has been documented as underserved for the services just listed, the business plan should cite the documents evidencing lack of primary care services. On the other hand, if the location is adequately served but the practice is offering some more attractive way of providing the service, the business plan should describe how the new practice will participate in the current market.

Projections for the Practice's Income Compared with Expenses

This part of a business plan requires the writer to estimate. Some knowledge of the economics of private practice will be necessary to complete this section. In the case of an NP practice, one would need to know the number of people in the community who are potential patients, the income that could be expected per enrolled patient or per patient visit, the going rate of collected billings in similar practices, and the projected expenses of the practice. Expenses such as rent would be documented by citing classified ads for business space or by an oral quotation from a commercial realtor based on number of square feet needed and location.

Description of the Principal Movers Who Are Starting the Business

This section is résumé material. It answers the question: "Do these potential business owners have the relevant experience and skills to make a go of the business?"

Organizational Plan

If there is to be more than one owner/director, the principal movers should draw up an organizational chart that shows how authority will be distributed.

Plan for Managing the Day-to-Day Operations

Practice owners who also are providers may want to have a nonprovider—an office manager—handle the day-to-day operations.

Investment Needs

If outside funds are needed for start-up, the business plan should include an estimate of what is needed. If partners or corporate codirectors are contributing start-up funds, the business plan should state who is contributing and how much and should state a plan for return on or repayment of investment.

Potential Problems and Critical Risks

If there are known risks to the business, the owners should state these risks in the business plan and state a plan for addressing these risks. For example, if an NP knows that managed-care organizations (MCOs) are reluctant to admit NPs to provider panels, thereby a potential inability to collect reimbursement, the NP should include this risk in the business plan and offer a strategy for addressing or minimizing it. An example would be meeting, prior to the opening of the practice, with MCO executives and obtaining a letter that one or more MCOs are willing to admit NPs as providers.

A Business Plan's Top 20 Questions

Usually a business plan answers 20 questions, the questions that most people will ask about the business. The 20 questions that are most asked of owners of new businesses and that an NP thinking of opening a practice should be prepared to answer are these:

1. What type of business do you have?
2. What is the purpose of this business?
3. What is the key message or one-sentence phrase that can describe your business?
4. What is your reason for starting your own business?
5. What is your product or service?
6. What are three unique benefits of your product?
7. Do you have data sheets, brochures, diagrams, sketches, photographs, related press releases, or other documentation about your product/service?
8. What is the product?
9. What led you to develop your product?
10. Is this product or service used in connection with other products?
11. What are the top three objections to buying your product/service immediately?
12. When will your product be available?
13. Who is your target audience?
14. Who is your competition?
15. How is your product differentiated from that of your competition?
16. What is the pricing of your product versus that of your competition?
17. Are you making any special offers?
18. What plans do you have for advertising and promotions?
19. How will you finance company growth?
20. Do you have the management team needed to achieve your goals?

Sections of a Business Plan

The following are the customary sections of a business plan:

- Executive summary
- Vision/mission statement
- Background information on the business
- Objectives
- Capital requirements
- Management team (in-house and outsourced)
- Product strategy
- Current product/service
- Research and development
- Key factors in delivery of service
- Analysis of the market
- Definition of the market
- Profile of clients

- Competition
- Business risks
- Plan for marketing the practice
- Advertising and promotion
- Publicity strategies
- Financial plan
- Repayment plan for loans/dividends to investors

A typical way to begin is to answer the top 20 questions. From the answers, it is possible to develop the executive summary, and then to work on the details of the sections one at a time.

An NP entrepreneur (or any entrepreneur) is not expected to be an expert on writing a business plan. An entrepreneur should be prepared to answer these 20 questions, however, so that a business consultant will have some substance to use as the framework for developing the plan.

It is common for someone with an idea for a business to give it up after considering all of the questions brought up by a business plan. If this happens, the exercise of producing a business plan will have saved substantial time and money.

Getting a Business Loan

A prospective practice owner may want a bank loan or a venture capitalist's investment to cover the expenses of start-up. A business plan will set out the start-up costs and a plan for repayment.

Multiple Uses of a Business Plan

In addition to helping a potential future practice owner decide whether a practice will be profitable and helping lenders decide whether to participate, a business plan can be used to orient employees, suppliers, and other people with whom the business will deal. A strong business plan points out to the practice owner potential adversities and weak areas, giving an opportunity to respond before there is a business failure.

Resources for Getting Help with a Business Plan

Among the resources for more information on business plans are the Small Business Administration and the Service Corps of Retired Executives, both of which are listed in the telephone book and can also be found through an online search. Other possible resources are business consultants, business-oriented community groups, professional organizations and professional journals, business consultants, web articles, and public libraries. Every local library should have at least one book on writing a business plan.

Looking at the Big Picture

An NP planning to start a practice will need to take a look at the healthcare industry in general, and particularly the climate in the NP's geographic area. Whether there is a need for the NP in practice to fill, whether there will be enough business to support the practice, and whether there are any barriers to overcome are three issues that an assessment of "the big picture" can address. The big picture includes the business climate, the competition, the law regarding NPs, and patient and public perceptions of NPs. All of these considerations will affect how the practice does and whether it will survive. An investor or lender reviewing a business plan will be impressed by a plan that takes the big picture into account.

Looking at the Smaller Picture

An NP considering starting a practice also will need to consider how entrepreneurship and business ownership will affect their life. Possible effects of small business ownership on an individual include the following:

- Lack of a separation between work life and personal life
- Necessity of an investment of time and money in start-up
- Inconsistent income while the practice is growing
- Uncertainty about success of the business
- Anxiety about the ability of partners or coworkers to hold up their end

Doing Business

Several responsibilities come with being a practice owner:

- Protecting the confidentiality of and storage of patient records
- Carrying out the responsibilities of an employer (discussed shortly in more detail)
- Registering the practice name with local government
- Disposing of hazardous waste produced in the course of business
- Complying with fire marshal inspections and building codes
- Maintaining the laboratory facilities in accordance with federal and state law
- Credentialing providers
- Ensuring that hiring and firing are done in accordance with the nondiscrimination provisions of law
- Providing malpractice coverage for the providers or company
- Providing general liability for the practice (against slip-and-fall or other injuries to patients)
- Providing after-hours contact information and coverage

Responsibilities of an Employer

Employers have legal and practical responsibilities. Legal responsibilities include the following:

- Withholding and paying employment taxes
- Ascertaining that a hiree is an American citizen or legal immigrant
- Paying workers' compensation and unemployment insurance premiums for employees
- Ensuring that employees actually have the credentials and licenses that they say they have
- Conducting background checks before hiring to decrease the risk that an employee might cause harm to a patient, have been barred from Medicare or Medicaid, or will otherwise adversely affect the quality of or finances of the practice

- Training employees to provide safe care or ensuring that hired employees are already adequately trained
- Ensuring that employees have a safe working environment
- Complying with the provisions of the Americans with Disabilities Act, which prohibits discrimination against a prospective hiree with a disability who needs only "reasonable accommodation" to do the proposed job

Practically, employers want to hire employees who have social skills, are motivated to perform, and will either make decisions or take direction, depending on the need.

Employment Agreements

In most states, employment is "at will." In an "at will" state, an employer may end an employee's job at any time. Likewise, an employee may leave a job at any time. Good public relations dictates reasonable notice, but there is no legal requirement for notice. Except for a few protections provided by federal law—protection against firing on the basis of race, age, gender, or exercise of free speech—employees are employees at the will of the employer. Therefore, an employer who wants to ensure that an employee will stay with the practice for a specified length of time will want to have employment agreements with employees. Employees will find employment agreements useful as well. For more information about employment agreements, see "Negotiating Terms of Employment," a book available at http://www.buppert.com.

Employee Rights

The rights of an employee include coverage by workers' compensation and unemployment insurance, a safe working environment to the extent specified by the Occupational Safety and Health Act, and freedom from discrimination on the basis of race, gender, national origin, religion, age, or disability. An employee has a right to health insurance according to some state laws, under certain conditions. A new employer should check the laws of the state regarding employer responsibilities.

Employer Rights

An employer has no legal rights.

Independent Contractors

A practice owner may want hire some staff as independent contractors. An independent contractor is not an employee. An employer's responsibilities to independent contractors are only those specified by a contract between the practice owner and independent contractor. An independent contractor is responsible for his or her own taxes, insurance, health benefits, tools, and possibly supplies and workspace.

An employer must withhold payroll taxes—income, Medicare, Social Security, and unemployment—for employees. An employer is responsible for paying workers' compensation of an employee injured on the job. In some states, small businesses must offer health benefits to employees. An employer may be held responsible for the malpractice of an employee and therefore should have professional liability insurance covering employees. All of these employer responsibilities are expensive to maintain.

An employer cannot avoid the legal responsibilities connected with being an employer by calling an employee an independent contractor, however. The IRS and other governmental agencies may investigate an employer who appears to be avoiding insurance and taxes by claiming that workers are independent contractors. To minimize unpleasant contact with the IRS, an employer should know the important, but subtle, legal distinctions between employees and independent contractors.

Employee Versus Independent Contractor

In determining whether an individual is an employee or independent contractor, the following matters are considered:

- The extent of control that, by agreement, the employer may exercise over the details of the work
- Whether the one employed is engaged in a distinct occupation or business
- The kind of occupation, with reference to whether, in the locality, the work is usually done under the direction of the employer or by a specialist without supervision
- The skill required in a particular occupation
- Whether the employer or the worker supplies the instruments, tools, and place of work for the person doing the work
- The length of time for which the person is employed
- The method of payment, whether by the time spent or by the job
- Whether the work is a part of the regular business of the employer
- Whether the parties believe they are creating the relationship of employer and employee
- Whether the principal is or is not in business

What Is an Employee?

NP Jones, after working for Physician Smith for 5 years, noticed that a nearby town, growing in size, was lacking a healthcare provider. NP Jones, familiar with the current sources of reimbursement for NPs, drew up a business plan and determined that he could, in fact, support himself if he left the employ of the physician and set up a private practice.

NP Jones asked Dr. Smith to supply, for a fee, medical backup for his practice and to collaborate via a written agreement. Dr. Smith agreed to provide those things and offered to cover one session a week at the new practice for a percentage of the reimbursed charges.

Is Dr. Smith now an employee of NP Jones? Can NP Jones avoid the responsibilities of being an employer? Under the circumstances described here, Dr. Smith is considered an employee of NP Jones.

These are the factors that make Dr. Smith an employee:

- NP Jones will control when the job is done and the place where it is done.
- NP Jones will hire the medical assistant with whom Dr. Smith will work.
- NP Jones will supply the equipment necessary to do the job.
- NP Jones, not Dr. Smith, will suffer financial losses if the work does not produce income for the practice.

Clearly, an independent contractor would be less expensive. A physician who provided consultation as needed, at an hourly rate, over the telephone, would be an independent contractor. To ensure that the IRS will view the physician as such, the NP should have the physician do the following:

- Bill the NP periodically on the physician's stationery for work done
- Bill the NP varying amounts, corresponding with the work performed (a standard weekly or monthly fee sounds like a salary)
- Not work at the NP's place of business

In addition, the NP and physician should draft and sign an independent contractor agreement, spelling out, at minimum, the duties and responsibilities of both parties, the duration of the agreement, and the rate and method of payment. See **Appendix 11-D** for a sample contract between an NP and a physician for consultation services.

Note that a contract alone will not transform an employment situation into an independent contractor arrangement. Some business owners have attempted to make employees independent contractors by writing a contract stating that the arrangement is one of independent contractors, not employer–employee. The IRS is unimpressed with this maneuver. The IRS, if it determines that the NP was an employer and did not provide proper coverage for employees, could fine the NP and create other business headaches. Furthermore, returning to the previous example given, if Dr. Smith suffers a needle stick at NP Jones' place of business, Dr. Smith will want workers' compensation. The Workers' Compensation Commission is likely to find that Dr. Smith was an employee, and NP Jones will be liable for compensating Dr. Smith for his or her injuries and lost wages.

Employment Contracts and Independent Contractor Contracts

Prospective practice owners should consult attorneys when drafting employment or independent contractor agreements. They are different contracts. A contract for an independent contractor should not only state that the relationship is one of independent contractor but also show how the relationship fits the definition of independent contractor. An employer who attempts to avoid employer responsibilities by calling an arrangement an independent contractor arrangement when it actually fits the definition of employment will find need an attorney for representation before the IRS.

Evaluating Performance

An employer will want to evaluate the performance of all employees on a regular basis. Employees who are adding value to a practice should be rewarded, and employees who are not worth the money paid to them should be encouraged to improve performance or leave. To approach performance evaluation rationally, a set of expectations should be drafted and agreed upon by both employer and employee. In some organizations, a new employee has an evaluation at 90 and 180 days and then yearly. In other organizations, a yearly performance review is the standard.

Terminating Personnel Legally

An employer who wants to terminate a staff member should consider legal necessities and public relations realities. Legally, an employer may not terminate an employee solely on the basis of race, age, gender, religion, national origin, or disability. That is not to say that an employer may never terminate a minority or older employee. The law simply requires that termination not be solely on that basis. Independent contractors, on the other hand, can be terminated for any reason, pursuant to the conditions of a contract between contractor and contractee.

Getting Paid for Services

Practices have three general sources of income: patients who self-pay for services, insurance, and contracts.

Self-Paying Patients

Patients who pay their own bills are in the minority. However, patients who either are uninsured (estimated at 17% of the population of the United States) or prefer to go to a provider who is out of their plan but attractive for reasons of convenience or service appreciate a provider who can offer medical services at a reasonable rate. An NP may want to market to such patients.

For convenience to both the patient and the practice owner, a practice may want to set up a charge account with a major credit card company. A practice owner also must decide whether to extend credit to patients and if so, how to deal with delinquent payments.

Insurers

Insurers fall into two categories: MCOs and indemnity insurers. MCOs contract with an employer to provide, for a set sum, all health services, with some exceptions, needed by employees for a year. MCOs contract with practices or groups to provide health services on a capitated or fee-for-service basis. A practice must be admitted to panels of MCO providers and have a contract that contains the details of the arrangement between the provider and the MCO. Indemnity insurers likewise contract with employers to provide health services, with exceptions, for employees. Indemnity insurers pay providers' bills, according to a fee schedule, on a fee-for-service basis. Indemnity insurers have no relationship with providers other than to pay bills presented by the provider to the insurer for the care of a covered patient.

Obtaining payments from third-party payers is not necessarily any easier than obtaining payment from patients directly. It can be 3 months between the time the provider bills the insurer and when the provider receives the insurer's payment. When payment is capitated, practices sometimes have trouble establishing that a patient is, in fact, enrolled with the individual provider and with the MCO at the time the care was given.

Contracts

Practices may contract with businesses to provide certain health services, under any sort of arrangement that is agreed upon by both parties.

Applying for Provider Status

It is important for NPs opening a practice to gain admission to some managed-care provider panels for the following reasons:

- If NPs do appear in MCO directories of providers, and if an NP's name is not on the patients' cards as the primary care provider (PCP), patients are going to think that the NP is some sort of assistant provider. They will not take the NP's advice as seriously as they would take advice from a "real provider."
- It is necessary to get paid.

There are other sources of direct reimbursement: Medicare, Medicaid, indemnity insurers, and direct payments from patients or companies. However, many patients covered by Medicare and Medicaid and more and more patients previously covered by indemnity insurers are now enrolling in MCOs.

If NPs do not become providers for those MCOs, they will not have access to a large portion of the patient population. Of course, NPs with their own practices can see the patients under the auspices of a physician practice. But with the competition high for patients, physicians who will agree to such an arrangement are few and far between. The goal of NPs realistically should be to see patients as full-fledged providers, not under the auspices of physicians. The relationship should be one of consultation, not supervision.

Attaining the designation of PCP from MCOs, with all of its attendant authority and responsibilities, is now one of the most important professional goals for NPs. Some NPs have attained the goal. Others are still trying, and in the meantime they are working on NP–MD teams where an MD is the designated PCP. Some NPs do not want the responsibilities attached to being a PCP and are content to assist a physician or other NP.

The argument that NPs should be admitted to MCO panels as PCPs can be tailored to the target of the persuasion. Next are some of the arguments supporting NP admission to provider panels as PCPs. There are specific arguments to make to physicians, MCOs, practice managers, and other NPs.

Arguments to Physicians

The following points may be helpful to raise with physicians:

- If an NP works under a written agreement with a physician, but only the physician may be a PCP, then the physician will have to sign all of the referral forms for the NP's patients. It is unwise for a physician to sign a referral unless he or she has reviewed the patient's chart. Chart review for every referral written by an NP will require a significant time investment. On the other hand, if the NP is a PCP, then the NP can make referrals without investment of physician time.
- If an NP with whom a physician is associated is a heavy referrer, and if all of the NP's referrals are attributed to the physician (because the physician is the PCP), that will reflect poorly on the physician's utilization rates with an MCO. An NP should be responsible for the NP's referrals and a physician for the physician's referrals.
- If an NP does not make a necessary referral for a patient or misdiagnoses a problem, a physician who is the PCP for the patient involved bears ultimate responsibility and is

much more likely to be liable in any future malpractice case than if the NP were the PCP. If the NP is the PCP, then it is far less likely that a physician will be found liable for any errors made by the NP.

Arguments to MCOs

Perhaps the toughest audience is the MCOs, whose executives may have little experience with NPs and are used to dealing with physicians. When attempting to convince MCOs of the need to admit NPs to provider panels, consider using the following arguments:

- NPs fill MCOs' needs of getting the job of patient care done in a high-quality and cost-effective manner. NPs are the appropriate providers of first-level care—that is, primary care. They are educated specifically for this role, enjoy this role, and are well accepted by patients. The top ten reasons for "visits to the doctor" are hypertension, diabetes, acute upper respiratory infection, bronchitis, chronic sinusitis, acute pharyngitis, routine medical exam, inner ear infection, depressive disorder, and urinary tract infection. All of these illnesses are appropriate for NP management. It makes no sense to use a physician when an NP is perfectly suited for this role.
- In virtually every study done on the matter, NPs have been found to be high-quality providers, at least as safe and effective as physicians.
- In virtually every study done on the matter, NPs have been found to be cost-effective—more cost-effective than physicians.
- Patients are highly satisfied with NPs.
- NPs focus on the kind of care that the agencies that accredit MCOs are looking for. For example, NCQA has a set of standards for measuring clinical performance in primary care: HEDIS. HEDIS measures include:
  - Keeping childhood and adolescent immunizations current
  - Advising smokers to quit
  - Giving annual flu shots to older patients
  - Screening appropriately for cervical cancer
  - Screening appropriately for breast cancer
  - Checking on postpartum women within 6 weeks of delivery
  - Maintaining patients who have had myocardial infarctions with beta blockers.[1]
- Use physicians where necessary. Have NPs take care of patients where it makes sense to use NPs.

Certain arguments can backfire, for example, the argument that NPs can provide care for a lower fee than physicians. NPs in private practice do not want to undercut physician charges because they have to pay physicians to be their collaborators, as is required by the law of most states and by Medicare. If the NP is earning less than a PCP earns to care for a patient, where is the NP going to find the money to pay the physician collaborator?

Another thorny argument is that NPs have less malpractice litigation than physicians. It is true that claims against NPs are minuscule compared to claims against physicians. However, to be fair, there are many reasons for that. Yes, NPs have good relationships with their patients and are very conscientious, but NPs are not perceived by the public to be wealthy.

Further, the reporting requirements are somewhat different for NPs, so the data may be misleading.

Arguments to Practice Managers

The following points may be persuasive with practice managers:

- It is unreasonable for an NP to stop in the middle of clinical sessions and interrupt a physician to present a case, when it is otherwise unnecessary, in order to get a signature for a referral. Some system must be set up to deal with referrals. If only physicians can be PCPs, it will ultimately fall on the practice manager to make sure that when there are physician–NP teams, the physicians are notified of what the NP is doing about referrals.
- Physicians cannot have panels of unlimited size. At some point, to keep patients within a practice, there will have to be NP PCPs.

Arguments to Other NPs

Being deemed a PCP by an MCO may seem like a semantic issue rather than a substantive issue. Granted, the issue is more professional than clinical. An NP can provide primary care whether or not they are formally designated a PCP. For example, patient Smith may see NP Jones several times a year and may consider NP Jones to be her healthcare provider, whether or not an MCO has designated NP Jones as patient Smith's PCP. However, if NP Jones does not hold PCP status with patient Smith's MCO, the NP is invisible to the MCO. To the MCO, patient Smith's PCP is NP Jones' employer, Dr. Doe. In some clinics, the patients have physicians whom they have never met named on their file as PCP. The clinic simply assigns some physician, any physician, to a patient who actually is cared for by an NP. Even though NP Jones evaluates patient Smith, orders diagnostic tests, makes referrals, and follows up, to the MCO, this all is done by Dr. Doe.

This arrangement works well for patient Smith. As long as NP Jones does a good job, the MCO, patient, physician PCP, and clinic all will be happy with the arrangement. But to the "invisible provider," NP Jones, the arrangement means three things:

1. NP Jones is a ghost provider. His or her work is seen only through Dr. Doe's statistics and is indistinguishable from Dr. Doe's. The NP is a "helper."
2. Without data on NP Jones' work, the situation never will change. An MCO will never know how many patients NP Jones sees; never know the effectiveness of his or her diagnosis, treatment, preventive efforts, and teaching; and never know that NP Jones draws patients to the practice.
3. NP Jones always will be working for Dr. Doe or another physician. NP Jones cannot ever have his or her own practice, because he or she can never prove that he or she is an effective healthcare provider. NP Jones is forever tied to Dr. Doe.

The dynamics of human nature will begin to work as soon as Dr. Doe understands that NP Jones is forever tied to a physician, unable to care for MCO patients as a PCP. Dr. Doe will not give NP Jones as high a level of professional respect as if NP Jones were an equal PCP, able to take his or her patients and start his or her own practice down the block. A deficit in professional respect may reveal itself on a daily basis or only at contract negotiation time. At some point, however, it is sure to manifest.

The selfless NP who only wants to take good care of patients and has no interest in challenging the physician's role as captain of the healthcare ship should realize that the implications here reach far beyond issues of pecking order. Patients will see their MCO's directory of providers and notice that NP Jones' name is not listed. Patients will notice that a physician's name, not NP Jones' name, appears on their referral forms and their medical card. Patients eventually will become aware that NP Jones is a "helper" rather than the PCP. The subtle message to patients is that NPs are not worthy of being relied on for advice about serious matters and not deserving of full attention when healthcare teaching is underway. The message may be completely erroneous, especially when an NP really is the patient's primary decision maker, diagnostician, teacher, gatekeeper, confidant, and advisor—in effect, the PCP.

How to Apply for Panel Admission

First, answer the following questions:

- Is the law in place?
- Does state law permit an NP to be a managed-care provider?
- Is the practice ready for scrutiny?
- Will the practice physically present well during a site visit? Are health maintenance efforts well documented? Are records orderly?
- Are policies written, recently reviewed, and organized?
- Are the required relationships in place with a physician?
- If a written collaborative agreement is required by law, is it signed and approved by the appropriate board?
- Are the arguments ready? (See the arguments previously detailed.)

Give MCOs general information on NPs, such as educational requirements, malpractice actuarials, information on insurers that reimburse for NP services (e.g., Medicare, Medicaid, and Blue Cross), and scope of practice. Include articles on studies that demonstrate the cost-effectiveness and quality of NP practice. Also, give MCOs information on the specific practice, including credentials of each provider, description of the practice, location, and size.

What To Do If Rejected

If rejected, rework the arguments or address the counterarguments, wait 6 months, and try again. The climate may have changed, or the presentation may be better the second time.

Effective Negotiation of Managed-Care Contracts

Once an MCO agrees to admit an NP, it will offer a contract. This section provides basics on negotiating such contracts. The following basics about managed-care contracting should be understood:

- Under capitated-care contracts, everything the provider does is paid for in one lump sum, with exceptions.
- "Everything" means everything that is included in the contract and everything that is not excluded or excepted by the contract.

- Some MCOs pay providers on a fee-for-service basis.
- Some MCOs pay providers through a combination of fee-for-service and capitated fees.
- Currently, most MCOs and most physicians are using the fee-for-service model of care provision, superimposed on the capitated payment system.

Preparing to Negotiate

A practice owner should ask other providers, and possibly the state insurance commissioner's office, the following questions about an MCO with whom a practice is considering a contract:

- Have other providers been paid promptly?
- Are there specialists in the MCO's referral network with whom the provider is familiar?
- Does the MCO have a strong presence in the community?
- Is the MCO financially sound?
- Is there a history of complaints about the company with the Insurance Division?
- Does the company have decent quality data?

Use of Actuarial Data

Actuaries make predictions about risks, usually insurance risks. An actuary can predict such practice variables as how many visits patients will make per year and what the average payment per visit will be. If possible, an NP seeking a contract with an MCO should obtain actuarial data on the group of patients whom the contract would cover. Sometimes MCOs can provide actuarial data on their patients. If not, an NP could hire an actuary. If an actuary is unaffordable and the MCO cannot supply actuarial data, an NP who has data from their own practice and/or access to charts can make some actuarial predictions on how many patient visits to expect per year and what the average payment per patient visit has been.

- *Research the costs of the practice.*
  1. Add up all salaries, rent, material costs, insurance costs, legal costs, cleaning costs, that is, all the costs of doing business. See Exhibit 11-1.
  2. Divide by the number of patients for which a practice can reasonably expect to get a year's capitation. The result will be the average yearly cap rate, per patient, needed to support the practice.

- *Research the demographics of the practice.*
  1. Age and gender will make a difference in the cap rate.
  2. Age and gender will make a difference in the time spent per patient.

- *Decide upon the product line to be offered.* Will the practice offer primary care service to all age groups? Will the practice offer full well-woman care? EKGs on site? Suturing? Sigmoidoscopies? Incision and drainage? Outpatient detoxification? Asthmatic nebulization? A practice that offers a wider range of services can expect to refer fewer patients to other providers and can argue for a large capitation rate when a capitation form of payment is being negotiated.
- *Research the capitation and fee-for-service rates for that payer.* Ask insurers for their capitation rates and fee-for-service schedules early on. If data on capitation rates offered to other practices nearby are obtainable, obtain that information.

Negotiating

Here are some tips on negotiating a managed-care contract. They were suggested by physicians who signed whatever came their way in the first round and later learned from their mistakes.

- Think of the unsigned contract as the presenter's opening offer. It is a biased offer. Understand that it is only a starting point in negotiations.
- Do not assume that any provision is non-negotiable. It was written on a word processor and can be easily changed. Make counteroffers to strike unfavorable provisions and insert others that are favorable. Much will depend upon how much the MCO wants the practice.
- Read the whole contract carefully—even the fine print. Make a photocopy and write notes and questions on it. Have an attorney answer any questions in plain English. If the contract refers to manuals or "rules and regulations," review these before signing.
- Make certain the contract covers all important business. If something is not covered in the contract, the provision does not exist. Make sure oral promises are included in the written document.
  1. Ask: Is there a way out for the provider if the dealings with the MCO turn out to be unbearable?
  2. Watch the billing and payment provisions, details of quality and utilization reviews, restrictions on coverage arrangements, and limitations on referral and admission. Get it in writing that the MCO will pay "clean claims" within 30 days. Include a provision for regular utilization reports. Determine how the beginning and end of coverage for a client affects a provider's duty to give care. Determine the limitations on and procedures for referral and admission. Determine what the MCO expects as far as quality data.

- Pay attention to the definitions at the beginning of the document, as definitions sometimes include substantive information, such as what is meant by "medically necessary services."
- Hold-harmless clauses usually work against an NP provider. They can be applied to a variety of situations. For example, a contract might state that "provider holds enrollee harmless for charges," even if the MCO becomes insolvent and does not pay the provider. Or it might state that "the provider holds MCO harmless in regard to any lawsuit filed by a patient against provider." Do not agree to such a clause unless the practice's liability insurance carrier signs off on it.
- Indemnification clauses: Indemnification means make whole or compensate for some loss or damage. Do not agree to indemnify the MCO for any loss by the MCO.
- No-cause termination: Try to avoid a situation where an MCO could terminate the relationship at any time, without good cause. Instead, insert a due-process clause, which allows a hearing in front of peers to determine whether termination has good cause.
- Do not negotiate jointly with anyone other than practice partners or other members of an integrated network. Practices differ greatly and need practice-specific contracts.
- Once the parties sign, the contract is binding.

In addition, here are four self-assessment questions to ask:

1. Can I live with this MCO's rates?
2. Can I live with the other requirements?
3. Can I negotiate with the MCO on any of the issues important to me?
4. Can I alter the system of care from the traditional model to a more efficient and effective model?

Enlist the help of an experienced attorney in negotiating the terms of the contract. The practice's accountant should review the payment mechanisms. The practice's business manager should evaluate the mechanics of payment, the timing of reimbursement, and the requirements for approvals of referrals.

Notes

1. National Committee on Quality Assurance. http://www.ncqa.org

A Checklist for Setting Up a Practice

NPs who are contemplating going into private practice have few role model colleagues to consult with, and those NPs who do run their own practices have little free time to consult with fledgling entrepreneurs.

This checklist fills in gaps in knowledge, giving NPs a description of things to do, think about, and decide on before setting up a practice. Some of the things to do will vary from state to state, and some are common to NPs in all states.

Administration

A practice may have one owner or many. The three basic business forms are sole practitioner, partnership, and corporation. Each of these forms suggests an administrative structure. If an NP is starting a business alone, there will be no confusion about who makes administrative decisions. Whenever more than one person is involved, however, there is the question of who should make the many decisions necessary to run a practice and how the decision making will be done. Draw up an administrative chart as one of the first tasks in the planning process.

Billing

Many practices have a billing clerk. Others hire outside companies to do the billing. An outside billing company may take a percentage of the income or charge a fee per bill.

Blue Cross/Blue Shield and Other Private Insurers

Each insurance company has a procedure for enlisting providers. Develop a list of insurers' names, addresses, and telephone numbers. Call each company's provider relations office and ask the following questions:

- What is the policy of the company regarding reimbursement for NP services?
- What is the process for reimbursement?
- How does an NP apply for a provider number?

Ask for an application to become a provider, fill out and return the application, and deal with the responses one by one.

If a rejection comes in the mail, follow up with telephone calls or letters to find out why. Some states have laws that require third-party payers to reimburse NPs for services performed. If there is such a law in your state, include a copy of it with your correspondence.

Business Associates

Under the Health Insurance Portability and Accountability Act (HIPAA), the business associates of healthcare providers are required by contract to protect the privacy of patient information, if a business associate has access to this information. Therefore, a practice must have an agreement with business associates to this effect.

Business Form

A sole proprietor is solely responsible for the business. Legal liability and liability for taxes lie with the sole proprietor. In a partnership, each partner shares the profits and liabilities. Each partner pays taxes on their own earnings. Each partner has personal liability for debts and judgments against the business.

There are several forms of corporations. A corporation is an entity apart from the individuals involved in the business. A corporation pays taxes on profits, the employees pay taxes on their income, and the shareholders pay taxes on their dividends. The corporation is liable for debts and judgments against the company. However, if corporate assets are insufficient to cover debts or other liabilities, corporate officers or directors may be personally liable. A corporation that provides medical services usually is required by state law to be a particular form of corporation: a professional corporation (PC) or professional association (PA).

A limited liability company (LLC) combines some aspects of the corporation and some aspects of partnership. In some states, an LLC may have the corporate purpose of delivering medical care. An LLC should be considered when there is more than one provider and the providers are considering partnership.

Consult an attorney when choosing a business form.

Call

Set up a system for ensuring that patients have 24-hour access to providers.

Chaperones

The need for a chaperone during a patient visit is based on the nature of the visit and the gender of the provider and the patient. The provider often will not know the nature of the visit until the patient is in the room.

Consider the following patient–provider combinations:

- Male provider, female patient
- Same-sex provider and patient
- Female provider, male patient
- Unaccompanied minor patient of either sex with provider of either sex

The need for chaperones should be kept in mind when considering staffing.

Calling in chaperones for all patient visits may inhibit the back-and-forth between the NP and patient. On the other hand, practitioners who forget to call in a chaperone may later find themselves accused of improper behavior by a patient and have no witnesses to refute these accusations. The most reasonable policy regarding chaperones is to offer the patient the option of having one.

Computer System

Answer the following questions:

- What software will be used for billing? For medical records? For tracking quality data?
- Is the software compatible with Medicare and Medicaid systems?
- Does it meet the federal standards for e-prescribing?
- How many terminals are needed?
- Will providers enter medical record data, and if so, will entry be done in the exam room with the patient present or later?
- What sort of networking is needed?
- Will Internet service be needed? Email?
- What are the provisions for patient confidentiality of data kept on a computer?

Point-of-care medical data entry is new. It requires that practitioners be well versed in the data entry system or that a transcriptionist be hired. In the future, a computerized medical records system likely will be a requirement of practice.

Confidentiality

Each practice should have a HIPAA compliance plan. To learn specifics, consider completing the Medscape continuing education module, "Patient Privacy: A Guide for Providers" (http://www.medscape.org).

Answer these questions:

- How will patient confidentiality be maintained?
- Will patients have privacy when announcing the reason for their visit at the receptionist's desk?
- Will discarded notes and lab results be shredded?
- Is there an area where the provider and assistants can talk about plans for patients without other patients hearing the discussion?
- Are exam and conference rooms reasonably soundproof?
- Are rooms laid out such that a patient in a gown cannot be seen by waiting patients?

Concerning release of medical record information: Any provider, clinic, or hospital needs written permission from a patient to give out medical information about that patient, for any reason other than treatment, payment, or healthcare operations. When a patient's medical problem is substance abuse, federal law requires that certain language be used in the consent for release of information.

All employees should be aware of the need to protect patient confidentiality when responding to telephone inquiries from or about patients and the need for keeping progress notes, incoming lab tests, and mail about patients private.

Copy Machines, Fax

Some practice management consultants recommend that providers each have fax and copying machines within arm's reach. Every practice needs at least one of each. (Smart phones and computers may eventually replace fax and copying machines but the new technologies require attention to compliance with federal and state privacy regulations.)

Credentialing

For each NP, the clinic manager should have the following items:

- A copy of the NP's current state license as an advanced practice nurse
- A copy of the NP's current certification by a certifying organization
- A copy of two professional references, including name, address, telephone number, title, nature of professional association with employee, and recommendation regarding the employee's clinical competence and ability to work with a team
- A statement signed by the NP declaring that the NP has never been convicted of a felony, is not under investigation for suspected commission of a felony, is not under investigation by the board of nursing for a licensing offense, and has not been suspended from Medicaid or Medicare provider status
- A statement of the NP's malpractice history. The National Practitioner Data Bank (NPDB) keeps records of all damage awards for medical malpractice paid by a practitioner (MD, DDS, or NP). A practitioner can get his or her own report by requesting a form from the NPDB. Hospitals can subscribe to the service. Actions by state boards of nursing are not required to be reported by NPs, but reporting is required for MDs and DDSs.
- The practice agreement under which the NP is practicing. In many states, each NP must have a written practice agreement with a physician specifying what the NP may do, what kind of oversight the physician will give, and the site of practice. The agreement must be signed by each party and approved by the board of nursing.
- Prescribing authority. Providers need to obtain Drug Enforcement Administration (DEA) numbers and may need state controlled dangerous substance (CDS) numbers. Contact the state health department and the DEA for an application.
- A copy of the NP's current cardiopulmonary resuscitation card
- The NP's National Provider Identifier

Disability

Patients with Disabilities

Each place of business should be wheelchair accessible in order to avoid unlawful discrimination against the patients with disabilities.

Screening Patients for Medicaid Eligibility

Clients may receive Medicaid because they are low income with children or because they, as adults, have disabilities. NPs may be asked to do disability evaluations. In the disability determination process, the client obtains a form from his or her local Department of Social Services (DSS) office, fills out the required information, and brings it to the clinic. The NP does a history and physical exam to determine whether the client has a disability and is unable to work and how long the client will be disabled. The client's eligibility for services depends upon the projected length of disability. A clinic may obtain the financial criteria that qualify a family for welfare from the local DSS and make referrals to the DSS accordingly.

Screening Patients for Medicare Disability

As of the publication date of this text, NPs do not have the legal authority to determine disability under the Medicare program.

Employee Disability

Employees of the practice who injure themselves on the job will seek workers' compensation. Practices should carry insurance to cover such claims.

Doctors, Medical

If a state requires physician collaboration, an NP may hire or contract with a physician to provide consultation services and develop and sign a written agreement as required by law. A physician's fee might be an annual or monthly retainer payment, a percentage of collections, a rate per hour of consultation time, or another arrangement that is agreeable to the parties.

An NP may want to establish a partnership with a physician, contract with a physician for specific consulting services, or hire a physician as an employee. For an example of a contract between an NP and a physician for physician consultation services, see **Appendix 11-D**.

When an NP hires or contracts with a physician, the parties agree that the profits, as well as the liabilities, are the NP's. In a partnership, profits and liabilities are shared among the partners.

The owners of a new practice may find it most economical to engage a physician as an independent contractor rather than hire the physician as an employee. When taking on a physician consultant, specify in the contract that the physician is an independent contractor, specify an hourly rate of payment and terms of payment, and specify the duties and responsibilities of the physician and of the NP. In addition to a practice agreement that fulfills the requirements of state law, the NP and physician should have an employment or professional services agreement. The former is the professional collaboration agreement; the latter is the business arrangement between the two individuals.

Emergency Plan

Establish a written emergency plan that answers these questions:

- How much emergency care will the NP give?
- What are the criteria for referral to the nearest emergency department?
  - For calling 911?
  - For ambulance transport?

Each practice also needs a plan for emergencies, such as:

- Patient loss of consciousness or other life-threatening emergency
- Fire on the premises
- Threats to safety from intruders or unruly patients
- Uncontained hazardous wastes

Employees

Anyone who hires another person legally must determine that the employee is an American citizen or a legal alien and that the employee is certified or licensed as necessary. An employer may be held liable for any injuries that an employee causes to a patient.

Employers should consider checking state registries of sexual offenders before hiring an individual.

Employers are responsible for keeping records of employees' Social Security wages, Medicare wages, and income tax wages. Most employers pay at least a portion of employees' Social Security. All employers are required to withhold income tax from employee wages. In some states, employers must register their employees in a state registry, for the purpose of tracking individuals who owe child support.

Employers should carry workers' compensation insurance, payroll insurance, and health insurance for employees in accordance with state laws.

Forms

Forms should be developed for these items:

- Intake (name, address, telephone, insurance company and numbers, birth date, etc.)
- History and physical
- Tracking of healthcare maintenance and screening
- Care plan/problem list
- Progress note
- Referral
- Return to work
- Appointment slips
- Appointments (calendar)
- Encounter/billing

- Release of medical information
- General consent to treatment
- Consent to procedure
- Patient instructions
- Lab report flowsheet
- Vital sign flowsheet
- Patient contact
- Notice of patient privacy rights

Guardians

Any patient who has a legal guardian may not sign consent forms (or give consent) for care.

Health Maintenance Organizations

Many health maintenance organizations (HMOs) are contracting with NP practices, but some are not. When the practice's address and telephone number are set, contact local HMOs about becoming a panel member.

Hours of Practice Operation

Some managed-care organizations (MCOs) require by contract that a practice maintain certain hours. Barring that requirement, a practice is free to set its own hours.

Housekeeping

Housekeeping includes the following areas:

- Cleaning: Contract for a service, specifying how often cleaning is done and what is done. Three times a week is the minimum.
- Extermination: Twice a month is reasonable.
- Snow removal: Businesses are usually responsible for removing snow or ice from the entranceway and parking lot.
- Hazardous waste removal: Separate red bag trash cans need to be in each examination room. When those are filled, the bags are stored in a larger marked box or can. Hazardous waste disposal companies pick up at a monthly minimum rate.

Information Sheets for Patients

Collect effective patient handouts, videos, website references, and tapes on an ongoing basis. Display them in waiting rooms, bathrooms, or offices.

Insurance

Practices will need premises, professional liability, payroll, workers' compensation, and employee health insurance.

Justifying NP Existence

Compile, on an ongoing basis, as many facts about the practice and clients as possible for use with insurers and other providers and for marketing purposes.

Laboratory

Compliance

The laboratory, even for a small practice that does only urine dipsticks and pregnancy tests, must be approved by the state and federal governments. Obtain and fill out the paperwork needed to comply with state (State Laboratory Administration) and federal (CLIA) requirements. This means applications, fees, and, most likely, a designated "laboratory director." In some states, the forms state that the laboratory director must be an MD, but on questioning, one may discover that a PhD in microbiology or biochemistry will be accepted as laboratory director.

Equipment

Buy a refrigerator with ice-making capabilities. Medications should be kept in a separate refrigerator from staff lunches and separate from specimens. Calibrate all equipment at least annually.

Laundry

Linens can be rented and laundered by an outside company, or paper gowns and drapes can be used. Laundries often require a monthly minimum charge, which may not be cost-effective for a new clinic.

Library

Some books are indispensable:

- Primary care handbook
- Dermatology book with pictures
- Lab test reference book
- *Drug Facts and Comparisons* or *Physicians' Desk Reference*
- *Sexually Transmitted Disease Guidelines* from the Centers for Disease Control and Prevention for current year

- *Guide to Antimicrobial Therapy* from the Centers for Disease Control and Prevention for current year
- A current algorithm for healthcare maintenance and screening

Malpractice Insurance

Several companies sell malpractice insurance to NPs. Promotions for these companies are found in any of the journals for NPs.

Marketing

Consider generating newspaper articles about the opening of the practice, and ask for television coverage if an NP practice is a novel idea in your area. See that the practice is listed in provider directories. Consider purchasing advertisements in local newspapers. Consider having a website, and consider using social media. Send direct mail or email flyers or have someone distribute flyers in local neighborhoods. Announce your practice to colleague NPs, in NP publications, and at NP meetings, and ask for referrals. Notify local physicians of your practice and ask for referrals. When you refer patients to MDs, dentists, podiatrists, or optometrists, send a letter with the patient so that the provider knows that the referral comes from you.

Nurses

Family NPs are the most useful type of NP for a small clinic because they can see all age groups. In terms of noneducational assets, experience in primary care, productivity, compatibility, resourcefulness, and flexibility are essential.

Depending upon patient needs, a practice may want to offer the services of addiction counselors and nurse psychotherapists.

Researchers

If there is a local nursing school, a connection for research expertise can be valuable.

RNs, LPNs

If payment for visits is not tied to NP or MD providers, a practice may find that visits to RNs or LPNs can be useful to patients.

On-Call Service

Twenty-four hour on-call service is required by some insurers. Some practices use an answering machine that gives the telephone or beeper number of the person on call. Others use an answering service.

OSHA Compliance

The major requirements under the Occupational Safety and Health Act (OSHA) are: wearing protective wear—gloves, gowns, masks, and goggles—when at risk for blood and other body fluid handling; collection of hazardous waste in separate, clearly marked trash cans; and proper disposal of hazardous waste.

In some states, the state administers the occupational health and safety program; other states have federal oversight. Inspectors generally concentrate on one of two areas: building safety or safe clinical practices.

Patients

Think about sources for new patients and ways to keep established patients. Word of mouth about good experience of care is the best form of advertising. Also, see "Marketing."

Pharmaceuticals

Stock

State law may control the NP's authority to dispense medications and the conditions of dispensing. The practice may want to have a limited stock of commonly used pharmaceuticals. Or, if a pharmacy is nearby, the practice may not need to stock pharmaceuticals. As for stocking controlled substances, a practice that does so increases the risk of robbery and drug-seeking behavior on the premises.

Samples

Drug representatives supply many practices with samples of the newest and most expensive pharmaceuticals. However, if patients do not have pharmacy insurance, it is unlikely that they will be able to afford to keep taking the medications dispensed as a starter dose.

Cost of Prescriptions

Some reference books give comparison cost information on medications. Pharmacists are good sources of such information as well. Some insurers cover pharmaceuticals, and other insurers do not. Some patients are uninsured. Unless a patient has insurance that covers pharmaceuticals, patients will want to know the cost of prescriptions being written and the cost of alternative remedies. It is useful to establish a relationship with a pharmacy that can supply price lists for the prescribing NP.

Storage

Vaccines must be refrigerated, with a thermometer/thermostat keeping them at whatever temperature they require. Other noncontrolled medications should be kept out of public display. Controlled substances should be behind double locks. Records of on-hand supply and the dispensing of each dose should be kept.

Physical Plant

Consider the need for the following types of space:

- Conference room
- Play area for children
- Exam rooms
- Waiting area
- Laboratory
- Utility room
- Offices
- Storage

Prescribing

In some states, NPs need to obtain prescriptive authority separate from licensure. NPs who will be prescribing controlled substances need a DEA number and a state CDS number. There is a fee for DEA registration. There also may be a fee for the state registration.

State law may require that NPs follow specific procedures when prescribing or dispensing medications. The state board of nursing is a good starting point for information about prescribing requirements.

Purchasing

Set up standing accounts with the following companies: medical supply company, pharmacy, medical waste disposal, answering service, telephone, utilities, medical equipment, equipment repair, printing, office supplies, and cleaning.

Quality Assurance Plan

Write a mission statement for the practice, and post it. Set up a method of evaluation for staff, and conduct periodic self-evaluations. Adopt a set of clinical practice guidelines and a set of healthcare maintenance and screening guidelines. Do periodic chart reviews to see that the practitioners are following the clinic's guidelines.

Referrals

Keep a referral directory, updated on a continuing basis, including names and phone numbers of referral sources for the following:

- Cardiac evaluation
- Chest X-rays
- Counseling regarding unwanted pregnancy
- Dentistry
- Dermatology evaluation

- Drug and alcohol counseling
- Genetic counseling
- Gastrointestinal/genitourinary evaluation
- Head, eyes, ears, nose, and throat evaluation
- HIV testing
- Mammograms
- Marriage/family counseling
- Neurologic evaluation
- Orthopedic evaluation
- Psychiatric care
- Sexually transmitted infection screening
- Social work
- Surgical evaluation
- Counseling
- Protective services

Regulatory Matters

Every medical office lab needs either periodic inspection by CLIA or a letter of exception that states that an inspection is not required. For information, call the state department of health's laboratory division.

States do not necessarily require clinics to be licensed. However, the fire marshal will probably need to inspect and sign off on every public space.

Reimbursement

Develop a patient intake procedure by which the practice can ensure that insurance information is current. For example, check the patient's insurance card, copy the card, and verify current coverage through a telephone number on the card. If the patient has no insurance, obtain his or her credit card, or work out the payment process. Collect copays.

Develop a fee schedule for visits and procedures, using appropriate CPT codes. Base the fee schedule on the income needs of the practice and the current reimbursements being paid by insurers.

Security

Most clinics do not need a security guard, but it is something to contemplate. Consider drafting a policy about after-hours use of the clinic by staff members. Develop a policy for handling cash collected during the day. Do not keep narcotics or large sums of cash in the clinic.

Standard of Care

Consult books, journals, and other providers, and attend at least one conference a year.

Start-Up Funding

Write a business plan, or hire a consultant to write a business plan. Take the business plan to a bank and ask for a business loan. If turned down, contact the local Small Business Administration and request a loan.

Supplies

Disposable Medical Supplies

No matter what a clinic starts with, additional supplies always will be needed. Any clinic needs a running account with a medical supply company and a pharmacist, with a turn-around delivery time of no more than 48 hours.

Durable Equipment

Every state has durable medical equipment companies. Used medical equipment also is available through brokers or through the web.

Stationery

The practice will need letterhead and envelopes, business cards, appointment cards, prescription pads, promotional brochures, and patient education brochures.

Diagnostic Lab Supplies

Laboratories supply specimen collection materials. State health departments often provide supplies for infectious disease testing and sometimes offer free diagnostic testing, with specimens sent by mail. Commercial labs provide all of the materials and vessels necessary to transmit lab specimens.

Support Staff

A receptionist is the most important employee, followed closely by the billing manager. Other staff to consider include a lab technician, a marketing specialist, a handyman, and a housekeeper.

Volunteers

States differ on whether volunteers are liable for their own acts or whether a clinic is responsible for the acts of volunteers. Managers should follow the same credentialing process in taking on volunteers as they do with employees.

Waste, Hazardous

Red plastic containers specially made for sharp instruments and needles and clearly marked as hazardous waste containers are required by law. Sharp instruments and needles are deposited in the red containers, which then go in boxes supplied by a waste disposal company and are picked up monthly, at a minimum. Diapers and bloody materials are deposited in red bags. The red bags are tied and put into larger boxes. Personnel who pick up the hazardous waste must be certified in that area; that is, a staff person cannot cart it away. Therefore, clinics must hire waste disposal services.

Written Agreement

In many states, each NP must have a written collaborative agreement with a physician specifying the scope of practice of the NP, what kind of oversight the physician will give, and the site of the practice. The agreement must be signed by each party and approved by the board of nursing.

Yellow Pages Advertising

Advertising is expensive, yet for some practices it will be the major source of clients. It is a budgetary item to be considered and balanced among other necessary expenditures.

Sample Independent Contractor Agreement

Note: This is a sample contract for a situation in which an NP is contracting for NP services with a business entity. It should not be used as a template because every arrangement is different and thus needs its own contract. Consult an attorney to draft a contract to suit a particular arrangement.

THIS AGREEMENT made _____, 2013, by and between Jane Doe, an individual, hereinafter referred to as "the Nurse Practitioner," and Heathrow School, a nonprofit educational institution in Maryland, hereinafter referred to as "the School."

Recitals

1. The School is an educational institution.
2. Jane Doe is an individual Nurse Practitioner certified to practice in Maryland.
3. The School has a health center, hereinafter referred to as "the Center," that serves the needs of enrolled students when school is in session. The purposes of the health center is to (a) improve the health of children and adolescents by providing comprehensive physical and mental health services and (b) work with school faculty, parents, and students to create health-promoting environments.
4. The school year is September 5 to June 15, not including December 12 to January 4 and March 15 to 27.

NOW, THEREFORE, the parties agree as follows:

1. The School, through the Nurse Practitioner, will offer the following services: general primary health care; mental health, psychosocial, and family counseling; drug and alcohol abuse programs; treatment of minor injuries; sexuality education and counseling; gynecological exams and treatment of sexually transmitted infections; AIDS education and counseling; nutrition education and weight reduction; health education; routine physical exams (including sports physicals); diagnosis and treatment of acute and chronic illnesses; referrals for illnesses and injuries not suitable for treatment in the school clinic; pregnancy tests, early periodic screening, and development testing; case management and support services for mainstreaming and preventing complications for children who have chronic health problems and special healthcare needs; and sick care for students with minor injuries and illnesses.

2. The School will have the following responsibilities for operations of the Center:

   2.1. The School shall maintain physical plant, to consist of two rooms, including two telephone lines, copy machine, fax machine, desk, lamps, exam table, sink, and file cabinets, all in safe working order.

   2.2. The School shall arrange and pay for disposal of hazardous waste, compliance with state and federal requirements for health centers and laboratories, security, utilities, cleaning, and durable medical equipment and supplies.

   2.3. The School will arrange and pay for physician consultation services, if needed.

   2.4. The School will maintain storage and confidentiality of medical records to the extent required by state law.

   2.5. The School will bill for services provided by the Nurse Practitioner.

3. The Nurse Practitioner will have the following responsibilities:

   3.1. Maintain her own certification, licensure, malpractice insurance, and continuing education.

   3.2. Provide her own tools and examination instruments.

   3.3. Pay her own taxes, Social Security, Medicare, workers' compensation, and unemployment contributions.

   3.4. Set her own hours within the following parameters: she must be on premises 5 hours on school days, with a schedule prearranged and posted.

   3.5. Provide on-call services for school hours when she is not on site.

   3.6. Attend two school meetings per year.

   3.7. Report to school authorities any student who is a danger to self or others, in accordance with the state laws regarding patient privacy.

   3.8. Maintain patient confidentiality.

   3.9. Maintain the accepted standard of care of school-aged patients.

   3.10. Follow up outstanding diagnostic and treatment problems even if school has gone out of session.

4. Jointly, the parties will:

   4.1. Establish procedures to adopt protocols and standards to evaluate quality and appropriateness of care provided at the health center.

   4.2. Work cooperatively to generate reports and analyses required as a condition of grant or contract funding of the health center and submit to each other data and other information required by regulatory or funding agencies.

   4.3. Work in concert to ensure compliance with all regulatory requirements relating to clinical services.

5. Term and termination.

   5.1. This Agreement shall become effective September 1, 2013, and continue through June 15, 2014, and will be renewed annually, for a term beginning September 1. By agreement of the parties, this Agreement shall be amended to be effective for any subsequent school years in which the parties agree to continue the Agreement with compensation to be adjusted in such years in accordance with the procedure specified in clause 7.1.

5.2.   Either party may terminate this Agreement upon the material default of the other party, provided that the party in default is given at least five (5) business days notice of intention to terminate and fails to cure the default, or, if the default is such that it cannot be cured within five (5) business days, fails to undertake substantial efforts to begin cure and to continue such efforts until the default is cured. For this purpose, "business day" is defined as a day the School is open for regular business.

5.3.   Either party may terminate this Agreement for any cause by giving the other party at least six (6) months written notice.

5.4.   If the parties agree that there are irreconcilable differences regarding the standard of care to be upheld at the health center, either party may give the other party thirty (30) days notice of termination.

5.5.   Either party may terminate this Agreement immediately if its performance becomes impossible, and is expected to remain impossible for an indefinite period of time, as a result of a cause described in clause 6.12.

6.   Administrative and legal matters.

6.1.   The School shall hold title to any equipment purchased by it. The Nurse Practitioner shall hold title to any equipment purchased by the Nurse Practitioner.

6.2.   The parties shall comply with all federal, state, and local laws, ordinances, rules, and regulations that are applicable to the operation of the school health center.

6.3.   Amendments to this Agreement must be stated in writing and executed by the authorized officials of the School and the Nurse Practitioner.

6.4.   The relationship of the School and the Nurse Practitioner is that of independent contractor. Nothing in this Agreement shall be deemed to create or constitute a partnership, joint venture, employment, or agency relationship between the parties.

6.5.   The parties agree that each is responsible for the actions and failures to act on the part of each party's own employees and agents in the performance of this Agreement and that each party shall have no responsibility for costs, judgments, or obligations resulting from or in any way connected with the actions and failures to act on the part of the other party's employees.

6.6.   All notices, official correspondence, and requests for permission required by this Agreement to be sent from one party to the other shall be sent in writing by first-class mail, return receipt requested, or by any overnight courier or same-day delivery service that provides a receipt of delivery, to the address set forth in this paragraph or to such other address as a party may establish in the future by proper notice:

For the School:
Barbara Johnson
Headmistress
Heathrow School
Fulton, MD
For the Nurse Practitioner:

Jane Doe
11 Janeway Ct.
Fulton, MD

6.7. Each party represents that it has authority to execute and deliver this Agreement and to perform its obligations hereunder and that all necessary approvals for execution of this Agreement have been obtained.

6.8. This Agreement is not assignable, in whole or in part, by either party without the prior written consent of the other party.

6.9. This Agreement, the rights and obligations of the parties, and any claim or dispute arising from this Agreement shall be governed by and construed in accordance with the laws of Maryland.

6.10. If any part of any provision of this Agreement becomes invalid or unenforceable under applicable law, that provision shall be ineffective to the extent of the invalidity or unenforceability only, without in any way affecting the remaining provisions of this Agreement.

6.11. Any payment due the School that is rendered more than fourteen (14) calendar days after the date due shall accrue interest at the rate of ten percent (10%) per annum from the date due until the date paid.

6.12. Neither party shall have liability for breach of contract or delay in performance of its contractual responsibilities if the party is unable to perform required services under this Agreement as the result of performance becoming impossible due to governmental regulation, request or order, or due to circumstances beyond the reasonable control of the party, including, without limitation, acts of God, fire, flood, accident, labor strike, war or civil disobedience, inability to obtain supplies, or interruption of utility services, where such circumstances make it impossible to perform or to perform in a timely manner.

6.13. A party's waiver of any right under this Agreement, including without limitation the right to terminate for default, shall not be construed as an agreement to continue such waiver indefinitely or to grant a waiver in the event of a repetition of the action or omission in question.

7. Payment.

7.1 The School agrees to pay Nurse Practitioner $81,000 per year, payable in ten payments of $8100, due on the first of the month starting September 1 and continuing through June 1.

7.2. The School agrees to mail payments to Nurse Practitioner at the address listed in clause 6.6.

IN WITNESS WHEREOF, the parties, by their undersigned representatives, have caused this Agreement to be executed.

Barbara Johnson
For Heathrow School
Date _____
Jane Doe, NP
Date_____

Sample NP Business Plan

The following is an example of a basic business plan for a very simple NP practice. Any individual who is considering starting a business should research the income and expenses of the business to determine whether it has potential for success. A business plan can be much more detailed than this example and should include a balance sheet. An NP should engage a business consultant to write or review their business plan, using research and projections supplied by the NP. An NP also should engage an accountant to compute a balance sheet and other computations based on the NP's research of income and expenses. The information given here is what an NP should expect to supply to the business consultant and accountant.

Assumptions

Assume that the business is a well women clinic in a small town.

The business will be staffed by one NP, who will be assisted by a receptionist and a medical assistant.

The hours are noon to 4 PM, Monday to Friday, and 9 AM to 1 PM on Saturdays.

The NP starting the practice has 15 years of experience as an OB-GYN NP but will not do obstetrics. She will refer pregnant patients to her collaborator.

Assume that the business is in a state where a written physician collaboration agreement is needed. The physician collaborator will be paid for reviewing and signing the written agreement and being available for consultation at the discretion of the NP.

The NP has elected not to bill insurance. The services will be provided on a fee-for-service, payment-at-time-of-service basis. The practice will accept credit cards. The fee for an exam is $75. Cultures (i.e., gonorrhea, chlamydia, and herpes) and HIV tests will be sent to the state public health lab, which will do the tests at no charge. The clinic will do urine pregnancy tests and wet mounts onsite at charges of $20 and $25, respectively. Pap smears will be read by a local laboratory, which has agreed to charge $30 each. If blood work is needed, the blood will be drawn by the NP and sent to a local laboratory. Bills for any blood work are sent from the laboratory directly to the patient.

Main Street Well Women Care

111 Pinetree Lane
Bristol, CT 06010
(300) 333-1212

Jane Jones, CRNP

July 30, 2013

1

Executive Summary

Main Street Well Women Care (WomenCare) is a new business, to open January 2, 2014. The business will offer women who are essentially healthy routine annual gynecologic examinations, Pap smears, diagnosis and treatment of gynecologic infections, birth control, and pregnancy tests.

With the closing of Bristol Planned Parenthood in June 2013 due to financial and management restructuring of that organization, there has been a lack of well women services in Bristol. Not only is the Hartford office of Planned Parenthood inconvenient to the women of Bristol, but also that office is not prepared to handle the volume of patients from Bristol.

WomenCare will replace the services of the Bristol Planned Parenthood office and will market itself differently so that women who would not go to Planned Parenthood will visit WomenCare. WomenCare will be located in a storefront location next to the town's main grocery store. WomenCare will offer basic gynecologic services, such as annual exams, breast exams, infection checks, prescription of birth control, and pregnancy tests. There will be no surgical services, no prenatal services, and no abortion services. Visits will be by appointment and on a walk-in basis.

Jane Jones, CRNP, is the owner and practitioner of WomenCare. Ms. Jones is an OB-GYN nurse practitioner, certified nationally and licensed in Connecticut. Ms. Jones has 15 years of experience providing primary care to women at Planned Parenthood of Hartford. John Evans, MD, an obstetrician-gynecologist in Hartford, will provide consultation and sign the written agreement, as is required by Connecticut law for nurse practitioner practice. Patients who need surgery, or further consultation, or who are pregnant, will be referred to Dr. Evans or another obstetrician-gynecologist of the patient's choice.

The business strategy of WomenCare is to offer low-cost, high-quality primary care women's health services in a convenient storefront setting. WomenCare will operate on a cash or credit card payment basis, with fees paid at time of service. WomenCare will not bill insurance companies. The strategy underlying this payment system is that avoiding the clerical work necessary to establish provider status and bill multiple insurers will allow WomenCare to offer services at a rate below that of other local providers. Furthermore, WomenCare's services will be performed by a nurse practitioner, whose services can be offered at less cost than a gynecologist's services.

The charge for a routine annual examination from a private physician in Bristol is $140. WomenCare will offer the exam for $75 and therefore will be attractive to uninsured women. Forty percent of the women in Bristol do not have health insurance ("Uninsured Lack Care in Area," *Hartford Courant*, January 2, 2013, p. 2). Women who are insured may visit WomenCare, pay the bill, and attempt to obtain reimbursement from their insurer.

Start-up funding is needed in the amount of $50,000.

Mission Statement

To provide convenient, high-quality, affordable primary women's healthcare services to generally healthy women aged 13 and over.

Background Information on the Business

During her 15 years of practice in Bristol, Jane Jones has established a following of patients. She is now working at the Hartford Planned Parenthood but will leave that position on December 30 to open WomenCare. The location for WomenCare has been secured. An agreement has been reached with the consulting physician. Opening publicity has been planned.

Hours will be noon to 4 PM, Monday to Friday, and 9 AM to 1 PM on Saturdays, 50 weeks of the year. Patients will be scheduled for half-hour appointments. Therefore, the volume will be 48 visits per week, or 2400 visits per year. The charge will be $75 per visit, $20 for a pregnancy test, and $25 for a wet mount.

Objectives

1. Secure start-up funding by October 15, 2013.
2. Sign lease on December 1, 2013.
3. Purchase equipment for delivery on December 15, 2013.
4. Outfit office from December 15 to 30, 2013.
5. Hire two employees to start December 26, 2013.
6. Open WomenCare on January 2, 2014.
7. Repay start-up loan by December 31, 2015.

Capital Requirements

Start-up funding of $50,000 is needed to cover initial rent, furnishings, equipment, legal fees, initial salaries, cleaning, and other business expenses. It is not anticipated that further business loans will be needed unless expansion occurs.

Management Team

Jane Jones is the provider/manager. Because there is no billing of insurers, there is little need for a professional office manager. Ms. Jones will be assisted during office hours by a part-time medical assistant. A receptionist will cover the front desk during office hours.

4

Attorney Carolyn Buppert will provide legal services, including contracts between Ms. Jones and Dr. Evans, review of the lease, and laboratory contracts; filing of the CLIA application; and employment contracts for the staff.

Accountant James Edwards will provide accounting services. Payroll will be handled by PayCheck, a local payroll service.

Product Strategy

Every woman needs a yearly gynecologic exam. The strategy of WomenCare is to provide that service in a convenient neighborhood location at a reasonable cost through a provider already well known to many neighborhood residents. Women will be reminded of WomenCare's services every time they visit the grocery store, which is located in the same strip shopping center as WomenCare.

Current Product/Service

There is no current service by WomenCare. The services to be offered by WomenCare when it opens are currently offered at a higher cost by three local obstetrician-gynecologists, who are located in a less convenient location in the Bristol Medical Park. Similar services to WomenCare are also offered currently through Planned Parenthood of Hartford, which is 30 miles away from the proposed WomenCare location.

Research and Development

Ms. Jones surveyed the patients who visited Planned Parenthood of Bristol in the final 3 months of that clinic's operation. Two hundred patients responded. Patients responded that they did not have an alternative provider in mind at the time of the survey, that they were interested in continued service from Ms. Jones, and that they were primarily in need of the following services:

- Annual gynecologic exam (100% of patients)
- Infection checks, approximately once a year (25% of patients)
- Exam for menstrual pain or dysfunctional menses, approximately once every 3 years (10% of patients)
- Renewal of birth control pills every 6 months (20% of patients)
- Pregnancy test approximately once every 6 months (10% of patients)

Planned Parenthood of Bristol had 800 patients at the time the center closed.

A survey conducted at the local YWCA in April 2011 of 200 women attending a seminar for unemployed women revealed that 50% of the women would visit a women's health office every year if the cost were $75 or less. Seventy-five percent of surveyed women stated that they would prefer a woman provider. Ninety-eight percent of women surveyed were amenable to having their primary care services provided by a nurse practitioner. Two percent preferred a physician.

Of the five internists in Bristol, only three do gynecologic examinations. Two internists refer their patients to gynecologists for annual examinations. Ms. Jones met with the two internists who do not do gynecologic exams and asked whether they would consider referring to WomenCare. Both internists agreed to refer "some" of their patients to WomenCare.

Key Factors in Delivery of Service

Key factors distinguishing WomenCare that will contribute to its success are:

- Convenience
- Service by one well-known nurse practitioner
- Reasonable cost

Definition of the Market

The market for WomenCare is all females aged 13 and over living in Bristol, CT, or within a 15-mile radius of WomenCare.

Analysis of the Market

Fourteen thousand people live in Bristol. Approximately 35% of Bristol's residents are females aged 13 and over. The potential market in Bristol, therefore, is 4900 people. If WomenCare acquired one-half of the potential market, WomenCare would have 2450 patients, each visiting at least once per year.

Southington and Plainville are neighboring communities with 10,000 and 15,000 residents, respectively. If 35% of Southington and Plainville residents are women over 13 years of age, and 10% of the eligible population visit WomenCare, then Women-Care will have an additional 875 patients who will visit at least once a year.

Profile of Clients

There are three subsets of "average patients" who will patronize WomenCare.

One subset of clients will be sexually active females of childbearing age who are employed without health benefits or who are unemployed. Such clients will be seeking birth control services for some portion of their childbearing years and will be seeking diagnosis of symptoms that they suspect are due to a sexually transmitted infection.

6

A second set of average patients will be menopausal women who will need attention to menopause-related symptoms and hormone replacement therapy or alternative therapies.

A third subset of patients will be teenagers who are seeking care for complaints that they would prefer not to discuss with their parents. These patients are considered emancipated under Connecticut law for issues of birth control and sexually transmitted infection screening, and parental consent is not required.

Competition

There are three obstetrician-gynecologists in Bristol. Two are male, and each has been in practice for approximately 20 years. The third is female and has been in practice approximately 5 years. Approximately 50% of the practice of each physician is obstetric care. The two male physicians have approximately 3000 patients each. The female physician has 2000 patients. The physicians draw patients from Southington, Plainville, and Worthington.

WomenCare could be expected to draw approximately 500 patients from the physicians. These patients would be those who are uninsured and do not want to pay $140 per visit.

Planned Parenthood of Hartford offers the same services proposed by WomenCare and therefore is a competitor as well. However, because Ms. Jones practiced in Bristol with Planned Parenthood until June 2012 and now practices at the Planned Parenthood in Hartford, it is reasonable to expect that Ms. Jones has former patients in Bristol and that a portion of the Hartford patients will visit WomenCare.

Business Risks

The biggest risk is insufficient patient visits, primarily because of inability of patients to afford the $75 fee plus lab fees when necessary. Another risk is the withdrawal of Dr. Evans as collaborator. This risk is minimized for the first year, because Dr. Evans has agreed to sign a yearlong contract.

Plan for Marketing the Practice

A direct-mail announcement will be sent to all of Ms. Jones' former patients at Bristol Planned Parenthood. Ms. Jones will email individuals in her own address book, to announce the opening. Ms. Jones will enlist several of her trusted colleagues to email their contacts about WomenCare. Flyer-type advertisements will be posted at the grocery stores and on the high school and community college bulletin boards. WomenCare will have a website, to include a video of Ms. Jones talking about her approach to care and welcoming new patients.

Because of WomenCare's storefront location next to the grocery store, WomenCare will be seen by almost everyone in the neighborhood. An "Opening Soon—WomenCare" sign will appear on December 1, 2013, at the location.

Dr. Evans has agreed to refer patients to WomenCare when they are uninsured and cannot afford the $140 he charges.

Marketing Strategy

The strategy for marketing WomenCare is to get a core number—approximately 250 patients—through direct mail to former patients of Ms. Jones at the now-defunct Planned Parenthood of Bristol, through the flyers at the store and schools, and through the "Opening Soon" sign at the business location. It is anticipated that each of the core 250 patients will tell one other potential patient of WomenCare in the first 3 months of operation and that one-half of the word-of-mouth contacts will visit. Therefore, by month 4, WomenCare will have seen approximately 375 women. Each quarter, it is estimated that a patient will tell at least one friend, neighbor, or family member about WomenCare and that a significant portion of those contacts will visit within the year.

Advertising and Promotion

No advertising will be purchased. However, the WomenCare sign at the location in the strip shopping center will advertise the business.

Ms. Jones and her staff will attempt to make every patient a permanent patient through close attention to personal service and attention to individual needs.

One Saturday a month will be "Teen Day," when female teenagers will be encouraged, through an announcement posted on the door of the business location, to come and ask any question of Ms. Jones, free of charge. Through this promotion, teenage girls will begin to establish a relationship with Ms. Jones so that when they are in need of services, they will think of WomenCare.

Publicity Strategies

Each visitor to WomenCare will receive a business card that includes the services provided and their prices, along with the usual business card information.

Ms. Jones will do one presentation per year at the high school on a topic of interest to female high school students and one presentation per year at the local college on a topic of interest to female college students.

Financial Plan

Table 11-1	Projected Operating Expenses, Year 1
Expense	**Cost**
Rent	$24,000
Utilities	$6000
Supplies	$2500
Continuing education	$1000
Cleaning	$6000
Insurance	$2500
Hazardous waste disposal	$1200
MD consultant	$10,000
Total nonsalary expenses	$53,200
Salaries, annual	
NP, 0.6 FTE	$54,000
Medical assistant, 0.6 FTE	$16,800
Receptionist, 0.6 FTE	$16,800
Social Security/Medicare, contributions for 1.8 FTEs	$6701
Total salary expenses	$94301
Total operating expenses	$147,501
Expenses of start-up (equipment, attorney, licenses, etc.)	$20,500
Abbreviation: FTE, full-time employee.	

Source: © Jones & Bartlett Learning

Table 11-2　Projected Expenses, Month by Month, Year 1 ($)

	Jan	Feb	Mar	Apr	May	Jun	Jul	Aug	Sep	Oct	Nov	Dec
Operating Expenses												
Rent	2000	2000	2000	2000	2000	2000	2000	2000	2000	2000	2000	2000
Utilities	500	500	500	500	500	500	500	500	500	500	500	500
Salaries	7858	7858	7858	7858	7858	7858	7858	7858	7858	7858	7858	7858
Supplies	1500					500			500			
Cont. ed.					1000							
Insurance	2500											
Cleaning	500	500	500	500	500	500	500	500	500	500	500	500
MD consult	1000	1000	1000	1000	1000	1000	1000	1000	1000	1000	1000	1000
Haz. Waste	1000	1000	1000	1000	1000	1000	1000	1000	1000	1000	1000	1000
Expenses/mo	16,858	12,858	12,858	12,858	13,858	13,358	12,858	12,858	13,358	12,858	12,858	12,858
YTD expenses	16,858	29,716	42,574	55,432	69,290	82,648	95,506	108,364	121,722	134,580	147,438	160,296
Loan Payments	800	800	800	800	800	800	800	800	800	800	800	800

Source: © Jones & Bartlett Learning

Table 11-3		Projected Income, Month by Month, Year 1 ($)										
	Jan	Feb	Mar	Apr	May	Jun	Jul	Aug	Sep	Oct	Nov	Dec
Visits	200	200	180	205	195	205	190	180	205	200	190	190
Test, preg.	80	80	70	50	40	50	50	50	50	45	40	40
Tests, wet mount	50	50	60	50	45	45	45	35	50	45	45	45
Income	17,850	17,850	16,400	17,625	16,550	17,500	16,375	15,375	17,625	17,025	16,175	16,175

Projected total income, year 2   202,525

Projected operating expenses, year 2*   168,310

Loan payments, year 2   12,000

Total expenses, year 2   180,310

Profit, year 2   22,215

*It is projected that operating expenses will increase at 5 % per year.

Source: © Jones & Bartlett Learning

11

Table 11-4   Projected Income, Month by Month, Year 2 ($)

	Jan	Feb	Mar	Apr	May	Jun	Jul	Aug	Sep	Oct	Nov	Dec
Visits	60	80	100	110	120	120	120	100	140	160	180	192
Test, preg.	8	10	10	15	20	20	20	25	30	40	60	72
Tests, wet mount	15	20	25	26	30	30	30	25	35	40	44	48
Income	5035	6700	8325	9200	10,150	10,150	10,150	8625	11,975	13,800	15,800	17,040

Projected total income, year 1	126,950
Projected operating expenses, year 1	160,296
Year 1 operating loss	(33,346)
Loan payments, year 1	(9600)
Year 1 loss	(42,946)

Table 11-5	Projected Income, Month by Month, Year 3 ($)											
	Jan	Feb	Mar	Apr	May	Jun	Jul	Aug	Sep	Oct	Nov	Dec
Visits	200	200	180	205	195	205	190	180	205	200	190	190
Test, preg.	80	80	70	50	40	50	50	50	50	45	40	40
Tests, wet mount	50	50	60	50	45	45	45	35	50	45	45	45
Income	17,850	17,850	16,400	17,625	16,550	17,500	16,375	15,375	17,625	17,025	16,175	16,175

Projected total income, year 3   202,525

Projected operating expenses, year 3   176,725

Loan payments, year 3   12,000

Total expenses, year 3   188,725

Profit, year 3   13,800

13

Payback Plan

Loan of $50,000 on October 1, 2013.

  Repay nothing until January 1, 2014, at which time payments will be made as follows:

January 1 to December 31, 2014:	$800/month
January 1 to December 31, 2015:	$1000/month
January 1 to December 31, 2016:	$1000/month
January 1 to December 31, 2017:	$1500/month

Total repaid: $51,600

Sample Professional Services Agreement

Note: *This is a sample contract between an NP and a physician collaborator. It is not meant to be a template. Each agreement between two parties is different, and participants should consult an attorney to determine the best contract to suit their particular agreement.*

THIS AGREEMENT ("Agreement"), effective _____, 20__, is between C.B. Bosco, CRNP, PC, an Indiana professional corporation (the "Nurse Practitioner") and George Oaks, MD, PC, an Indiana professional corporation (the "Physician").

RECITALS

WHEREAS, the Physician is engaged in the practice of medicine in Indiana;

WHEREAS, the Nurse Practitioner is engaged in practice of a nurse practitioner in Indiana;

WHEREAS, the Nurse Practitioner is required by law to have a collaborative association with a physician;

WHEREAS, the Physician wishes to collaborate with the Nurse Practitioner;

NOW, THEREFORE, for good and valuable consideration, the receipt and sufficiency of which is acknowledged, the parties agree as follows:

1. Definitions
    1.1. "Contract Year" shall mean the twelve (12)-month period following the effective date of this Agreement. Thereafter, each additional twelve (12)-month period during the term or any successive term shall constitute a Contract Year.
    1.2. "Nurse Practitioner" shall mean C.B. Bosco, located at 102 Goldleaf Ave., Suite 2, Jasonville, IN.
    1.3. "Physician" shall mean George Oaks, located at 102 Goldleaf Ave., Suite 3, Jasonville, IN.
    1.4. "Term" shall mean the period from_____, 20__ through _____, 20__, unless sooner terminated or extended as provided herein.

2. Representations and warranties
   2.1. The Nurse Practitioner represents:
      2.1.1. That she holds a current license from the state of Indiana as an Adult Nurse Practitioner;
      2.1.2. That her license or certificate to practice as a registered nurse or nurse practitioner in Indiana has never been revoked, suspended, restricted, or subject to possible disciplinary action;
      2.1.3. That her privileges to practice as a nurse practitioner at a hospital or other healthcare facility have never been revoked, suspended, restricted, or subject to possible disciplinary action;
      2.1.4. That there has never been entered against the Nurse Practitioner a final judgment in a malpractice action, and that there has never been an allegation of malpractice by the Nurse Practitioner that has been settled by payment to the plaintiff;
      2.1.5. That the Nurse Practitioner has never had malpractice liability insurance canceled, restricted, or not renewed;
      2.1.6. That the Nurse Practitioner has never been found guilty of a crime of any nature;
      2.1.7. That the Nurse Practitioner has never been reported to any state or federal healthcare program for alleged violations of state or federal health laws or regulations or been found by such program to be in violation of such laws or regulations.
   2.2. The Physician represents:
      2.2.1. That the Physician holds a current license from the State of Indiana as a physician;
      2.2.2. That the Physician's license to practice as a physician in Indiana has never been revoked, suspended, restricted, or subject to possible disciplinary action;
      2.2.3. That the Physician's privileges to practice as a physician at a hospital or other healthcare facility have never been revoked, suspended, restricted, or subject to possible disciplinary action;
      2.2.4. That the Physician has never been found guilty of a crime of any nature;
      2.2.5. That the Physician has never been reported to any state or federal healthcare program for alleged violations of state or federal health laws or regulations or been found by such program to be in violation of such laws or regulations.

3. Duties of the Nurse Practitioner. The Nurse Practitioner shall:
   3.1. Practice the profession of a nurse practitioner in accordance with the laws and regulations governing the practice of a nurse practitioner in Indiana.
   3.2. Provide all medical services within reasonable and accepted medical standards and in conformance with all requirements that may be imposed from time to time by the applicable health licensing boards.

3.3. Maintain neat, timely, and legible medical records for all patients evaluated and treated by the Nurse Practitioner.

3.4. Maintain Nurse Practitioner's own malpractice insurance; maintain a license to practice as a nurse practitioner in Indiana in good standing during the term of this Agreement or any renewal thereof; maintain nurse practitioner board certification; and maintain nurse practitioner continuing education credits according to the prevailing standard, which is a minimum of seventy-five (75) credits every five (5) years.

3.5. Maintain her own schedule of patients.

3.6. Pay the Physician a sum of $5000 per contract year, with one payment made on the date this Agreement is signed and one payment made six (6) months after the signing of this Agreement, plus $200 per hour for consultation time initiated by the Nurse Practitioner.

  3.6.1. Consultation time includes telephone consultations, in-person, face-to-face consultations, and review of charts.

  3.6.2. The minimum segment billed for a consultation is ten (10) minutes.

  3.6.3. Nurse Practitioner will pay consultation fees monthly, within thirty (30) days of receiving a bill from the Physician.

  3.6.4. When patients are admitted to a hospital, Nurse Practitioner shall pay Physician for consultation time until such time as the patient is admitted. After hospital admission, Physician may bill patient or patient's insurance company for services provided the patient in the hospital until such time as the patient is discharged.

4. Duties of the Physician. The Physician shall:

  4.1. Respond to a telephone call from Nurse Practitioner within two (2) hours, unless Nurse Practitioner characterizes the call as an emergency, in which case the Physician will respond to a call within fifteen (15) minutes.

  4.2. Keep a record of consultations and bill the Nurse Practitioner once a month.

  4.3. Sign the Nurse Practitioner's written agreement as required by Indiana law.

  4.4. Meet with the Nurse Practitioner once a month, for one half hour, for discussion of clinical guidelines and management of difficult patients.

    4.4.1. Agree that the meeting shall take place at a mutually agreed upon location, which may vary from time to time.

    4.4.2. Agree that payment for monthly meeting time is included in the $5000 per contract year that Nurse Practitioner pays Physician.

  4.5. Agree to conform, in Physician's consultations, to the standard of care of a reasonably prudent Physician practicing as an internist in suburban Indiana.

  4.6. Assist Nurse Practitioner, to the best of Physician's ability, in any other requirements for physician collaboration that may arise and that are necessary to conform to the laws and regulations governing the practice of a nurse practitioner in Indiana

4.7.   Agree not to bill a patient's insurance company directly for any consultative services Physician provides a nonhospitalized patient of the Nurse Practitioner unless the Nurse Practitioner and Physician agree that the Physician, and not the Nurse Practitioner, will bill the services.

4.8.   Bill a patient of the Nurse Practitioner or the patient's insurance company for visits to such patient while the patient is hospitalized.

4.9.   Return the care of hospitalized patients of the Nurse Practitioner to the Nurse Practitioner after discharge from the hospital.

4.10. Cosign charts where the Nurse Practitioner and Physician are comanaging patients.

4.11. Maintain Physician's own malpractice insurance; maintain a license to practice as a physician in Indiana in good standing during the term of this Agreement or any renewal thereof; maintain physician board certification; and maintain physician continuing education credits according to the prevailing standard.

4.12. Maintain hospital admitting privileges at at least one hospital within a 20-mile radius of the Nurse Practitioner's office.

4.13. Physician agrees that this is not an employment relationship.

  4.13.1. Physician agrees that Physician is responsible for federal and state income taxes on any amount paid to Physician by Nurse Practitioner; for Physician's own health insurance, workers' compensation, and unemployment insurance; and for Physician's own expenses of practice.

5. Term

5.1.   The Term of this Agreement shall be from_____ , 20___ and shall automatically renew for successive one (1)-year terms unless terminated earlier as provided herein.

5.2.   In the event that either party intends not to renew, such party shall give the other party ninety (90) days notice of its intent not to renew, and the term or renewal term shall end upon the completion of the applicable contract year.

6. Termination

6.1.   The Agreement shall be terminated immediately upon the happening of any of the following events:

  6.1.1. The death of Nurse Practitioner or Physician;

  6.1.2. Nurse Practitioner is legally disqualified or restricted in Nurse Practitioner's ability to render professional medical services in the State of Indiana as a nurse practitioner, or disciplinary action is taken against Nurse Practitioner's license in any other jurisdiction. For purposes of this section, the lapse of license for nonpayment of applicable licensing fees in a jurisdiction other than Indiana shall, by itself, not be considered disciplinary action;

  6.1.3. Physician is legally disqualified or restricted in his ability to render professional medical services in the State of Indiana as a physician, or disciplinary action is taken against Physician's license in any other jurisdiction. For purposes of this section, the lapse of license for non-payment of applicable licensing fees in a jurisdiction other than Indiana shall, by itself, not be considered disciplinary action;

6.1.4. Physician's loss or restriction of staff membership or professional privileges at any hospital or healthcare facility at which Physician has privileges, unless such loss or restriction was due to the occasional violation of the facility's record-keeping requirements or Physician shall have previously notified Nurse Practitioner that such loss or restriction will not terminate this Agreement;

6.1.5. Physician's disability as defined by federal or state law, or to the extent that the Physician cannot reasonably or competently perform the Physician's duties;

6.1.6. Nurse Practitioner's disability as defined by federal or state law, or to the extent that Nurse Practitioner cannot reasonably or competently continue to practice;

6.1.7. Ninety (90) days after Nurse Practitioner or Physician gives written notice to the other of termination without cause;

6.1.8. At any time by mutual agreement of the parties;

6.1.9. Nurse Practitioner's material breach of this Agreement, provided, however, that if Nurse Practitioner's breach of this Agreement is of a type and nature that may be cured, Nurse Practitioner shall have the opportunity immediately to cure breaches to the reasonable satisfaction of the Physician;

6.1.10. Physician's material breach of this Agreement, provided, however, that if Physician's breach of this Agreement is of a type and nature that may be cured, Physician shall have the opportunity immediately to cure breaches to the reasonable satisfaction of the Nurse Practitioner;

6.1.11. Upon Physician's conviction of a crime;

6.1.12. Upon Nurse Practitioner's conviction of a crime;

6.1.13. Upon adjudication that Nurse Practitioner is insane or determined to be legally incompetent;

6.1.14. Upon adjudication that Physician is insane or determined to be legally incompetent;

6.1.15. In the event that professional malpractice insurance for Nurse Practitioner is denied or lost or is limited by restriction or endorsement;

6.1.16. In the event that professional malpractice insurance for Physician is denied or lost or is limited by restriction or endorsement;

6.2. Upon termination of this agreement, the original records of patients followed by Nurse Practitioner or in Nurse Practitioner's office are understood by the parties to be the property of Nurse Practitioner.

7.   Notices

    7.1   All notices provided in this Agreement shall be directed to the parties in writing, by registered or certified mail, return receipt requested or by hand delivery at the following addresses.

If to Nurse Practitioner:

C.B. Bosco, NP

102 Goldleaf Ave. Suite 2

Jasonville, IN

If to Physician:

George Oaks, MD

102 Goldleaf Ave. Suite 3

Jasonville, IN

8.   General terms

    8.1.   Applicable law. This Agreement shall be construed and enforced under Indiana law.

    8.2.   Nonassignment.

        8.2.1.   The Physician shall not be entitled to assign any of the benefits or burdens imposed on the Physician hereunder.

        8.2.2.   The Nurse Practitioner shall not be entitled to assign any of the benefits or burdens imposed on the Nurse Practitioner hereunder.

    8.3.   Binding effect. This Agreement shall be for the benefit of and be binding upon the parties hereto, their respective representatives, heirs, assigns, and successors-in-interest.

    8.4.   Execution. This Agreement shall be executed in duplicate, and each executed copy shall constitute an original, but the two copies shall be deemed one and the same instrument, and this Agreement shall not be modified or changed, except in writing, signed, and acknowledged by the parties hereto.

    8.5.   Entire agreement. This Agreement contains the entire understanding between the parties hereto and supersedes any prior written or oral agreement between the parties. There are no representations, agreements, or understandings, oral or written, between or among the parties hereto relating to the subject matter of this Agreement that are not fully expressed herein.

WITNESS the following signature and seals;

Nurse Practitioner: _____

Date: _____

Physician: _____

Date: _____

CHAPTER 12

Lawmaking and Health Policy

Health care is regulated for the public good, to ensure quality to a public that is powerless to assert quality control as individuals. That is the theory, at least. In the real world, health care is regulated for quality reasons, and because professional groups lobby for regulations that support their profession and businesses lobby for regulations that help their businesses. Regulation is imposed through statutes, regulations, and policies, and when a statute or regulation is challenged in court, through the judicial system.

The Legal Process

Statutes

A statute is a law enacted by a state legislature or Congress. Laws are found in state and federal codes. For example, Maryland statutes are found in the Maryland Code Annotated, and federal statutes are found in the U.S. Code Annotated (U.S.C.A.).

Citizens can influence the statutes that are enacted by electing representatives who they think will vote as they would and by lobbying those representatives for passage of bills about specific issues.

For example, in many states, nurse practitioners' (NPs') prescriptive authority is found in a statute. In those states, the legislatures have considered the issue of NP prescribing and have approved it.

Regulations

A regulation is law written by a state or federal agency in accordance with a statute. Agencies are a part of the executive branch of government. A regulation cannot directly contradict a statute but may expand upon a statute, supplying details not included in it. The divided responsibility—between the legislature to enact statutes and the executive branch agencies to write regulations—is part of the balance of power created by the U.S. Constitution.

Citizens have input into regulations in that regulations, prior to being adopted, usually are published for public review, with an opportunity for public comment. Agencies may or may not accept the comments. Further, citizens who are unhappy with a current regulation can enlist their legislators to enact laws that require agencies to change the regulations. For example, if state regulations addressing nursing homes do not address NP practice in nursing homes, a state NP organization can ask the director of the appropriate state agency for a change of regulation to include NPs as providers in nursing homes, ask legislators to request a regulation change, and, if necessary, ask legislators for a statute that requires the agency head to change regulations to allow NPs to practice in nursing homes.

Policies

Policies are rules made by companies or government agencies that do not have the force of law but that dictate day-to-day decisions. Citizens have input regarding policies only insofar as they can convince whomever has authority over a policy to change it. Citizens may also lobby legislators for a law that requires companies or government agencies to change a policy. For example, a health plan may have a policy of credentialing physicians only. Local NPs who want to be on a plan's provider panel will want to persuade the appropriate health plan decision maker, through facts, figures, and a presentation of projected benefits to the health plan, of the need to change policy and include NPs on the panel.

The Judicial System

A state court may hold that a state law is unconstitutional, and a federal court may hold that a federal law is unconstitutional. Courts may interpret laws and determine whether laws have been applied as the legislature, or Congress, meant them to be. A citizen who believes that a law has been misapplied and who has suffered damage as a result may bring suit in court in an effort to force correct application of a law. For example, in 1983, the medical board in Missouri brought legal action against two NPs practicing in a women's services clinic, arguing that the NPs were practicing medicine without medical licenses. The lower court agreed that the NPs were practicing medicine without a license, but the NPs took the case to the highest court in Missouri, and after reviewing historical documents, this court held that the intent of the legislature in expanding the nurse practice act had been to expand the scope of practice to include the activities performed by the NPs.

Health Policy

Policy is defined by the *Merriam-Webster Collegiate Dictionary* as "a definite course or method of action selected . . . to guide and determine present and future decisions."[1] Presidents and governors have policies on health care. Executive branch policies may influence the activities of federal and state agencies. However, unless policy becomes law, policy is like nursing theory: it may or may not have any effect on the way people do things.

An example of the influence of policy on the healthcare industry is President Clinton's 1994 effort at healthcare reform. The president had a definite course of action, a move toward a one-payer system; that is, government-run health care. The president's plan was not enacted, however. In fact, it was criticized so soundly that it was never even introduced as a bill in Congress. But the threat implied by the Clinton healthcare reform policies—that if the healthcare industry did not change itself, the government would impose changes—encouraged the private sector to reform. Health care today is quite different from health care in 1993. "Managed care" is now a household phrase. President Obama followed up on

President Clinton's efforts to reform health care, advocating for the Affordable Care Act (ACA), which passed Congress in 2010 and included some aspects of the Clinton plan. To date, however, it is unclear how the provisions of the ACA will ultimately change health-care policy and/or the industry and practice of health care.

Laws and Rules That Affect NPs

NPs are affected by laws, regulations, policies, and court decisions that address the following:

- The scope of NP practice
- Reimbursement for health services
- Qualifications for NP licensure and renewal
- Delegation of authority by physicians
- Quality of care
- Requirements for collaboration
- Confidentiality and patient privacy
- Electronic medical records and e-prescribing
- Medical homes

NPs have found laws, regulations, and policies to be barriers to the practice for which they were educated. How can NPs change these legal barriers?

Changing Laws

NPs who seek to change laws generally do so because they find that a statute, regulation, or policy keeps them from doing something necessary for practice. For example, NPs who were enrolled as Medicaid providers found that once Medicaid patients began enrolling in managed-care health plans, the NPs could no longer be the primary providers for their patients because the policies of the managed-care organizations (MCOs) precluded NPs from being admitted to primary care provider (PCP) panels.

In some states, the quest to change MCO policy has turned into an effort to enact new statutes. That is because MCOs, when asked to admit NPs to provider panels, said that the state law was unclear. Therefore, NPs have sought to clarify state laws such that they are specifically designated by statute as PCPs.

Understanding the Big Picture

Managed care is one aspect of the big picture that has and will affect NP practice.

What Is Going on in Managed Care?

Simply put, managed care is a system where the insurer is not only the payer, but also the provider of health care. Prior to managed care, insurance companies paid bills submitted by providers. The insurer had no control over the quality or quantity of care being given and had no responsibility to patients other than to pay bills. Under managed care, the insurer is responsible for the care given. The insurer keeps close tabs on the services provided. The insurer monitors how the healthcare services are utilized, as well as the costs of care, and sometimes denies, in advance or retrospectively, payment for services. Under fully developed managed care, insurers agree with purchasers to give care—whatever care is needed—for a fixed fee (monthly, yearly, or per procedure) and clinicians agree with insurers to give whatever care is needed for that fee. The clinician shares the financial risk that a patient will need more care than a payment covers with the insurer.

The bottom line is that insurers are not only concerned with cost; they now also monitor the quality of care given by providers and practices.

The healthcare industry has recently come under scrutiny regarding quality of care from the people who purchase the most services—employers who buy health care for employees—and from consumer-oriented groups. Employers are beginning to base decisions about which health plan services to offer employees based upon quality data gathered by such organizations as the National Committee for Quality Assurance (NCQA). Employers monitor the NCQA data, NCQA monitors health plans, health plans monitor practices, and, often, practices monitor individual providers.

State and national legislators, wanting to ensure that citizens' best interests are not overshadowed by the goals of employers and insurers to make money, are introducing bills to improve quality and to make sure that citizens get the care they want or need. For example, some state legislatures have passed bills requiring that health plans allow postpartum mothers to stay overnight in the hospital for 24 hours after delivery in response to the practice of health plans requiring mothers to go home shortly after delivery. Citizen groups felt that good care required that postpartum mothers have at least a 1-night hospital stay. Thus, legislatures have been delving into healthcare decisions formerly made only by clinicians, and lately made by insurers and clinicians.

Stages of Managed Care

An NP's place in the healthcare landscape depends on many factors. One factor is the stage of managed care in the region. In the early stages of managed care, most patients are covered by traditional insurers, and MCOs try to encourage employers who purchase health plans to enroll employees by offering premiums that cost less than those of traditional insurers. In the middle stages of development of managed care, more patients are enrolled, and MCOs try to control costs by decreasing the number of hospital visits, the length of stay in hospitals, and the number of emergency department visits, and by bargaining with medical practices for reduced rates on visits. In the advanced states of managed care, most patients are enrolled in managed care, and medical practices have agreed to share the risks. In other words, medical practices agree to take care of patients for a fixed amount of money per year. If care costs more than the set fee, providers lose money. If care costs less than the set fees, providers make a profit. In the later stages of development, much attention is paid to providing care that will prevent hospitalization and other high costs in the future, and to providing the nuts and bolts of care most cost effectively. It is at these later stages that NPs are most likely to fulfill the needs of MCOs.

Where Do NPs Appear in the Managed Care Landscape?

The position of NPs is well described by a favorite quote of the late Congressman Sonny Bono, "We have good soap to sell, but we have to go out and sell it." NPs are likely candidates for the position of PCPs, responsible for their own panels of patients. Consider the endorsement of NP practices given by Dr. Stephanie Seremetis, Director of the Women's Health Program at Mount Sinai Medical Center, "Probably in the future the best use will be nurse practitioners in independent practice, using a physician as a backup for complex conditions and for system analysis."[2] Or consider the endorsement by Joseph A. Califano, Jr., former U.S. Secretary of Health, Education, and Welfare:

> We should develop a three-tiered medical system: nonphysician practitioners, primary care physicians, and physician specialists. The first tier—the front line of delivery—should be the nonphysician practitioners: physician assistants, nurse practitioners, and certified nurse midwives. These professionals are capable, reliable and cost efficient.... They should be licensed to diagnose ailments, treat common diseases, prescribe drugs, admit patients to hospitals, and release them.... The second tier should be composed of primary care physicians: the family doctors, pediatricians, and general internists, including geriatric practitioners. These physicians should handle the more complex cases that do not require specialist care and be available to consult, guide, and, where appropriate, supervise the nonphysician practitioners.... The third tier should be specialists.[3]

Now that the United States, under the ACA, is in a situation where many previously uninsured people will soon become insured, many who follow health policy have begun to see NPs as a solution to an impending shortage of healthcare providers. Here is one comment to this effect, from a health policy brief in *Health Affairs*:

> With a predicted shortage of primary care as the population grows and as millions of people become newly insured starting in 2014, one proposed solution is to expand the role of nurse practitioners in many more areas of the country, and to allow them to provide a wider range of preventive and acute health care services.[4]

The views expressed by Dr. Seremetis, Mr. Califano, and *Health Affairs* concern the general welfare. What about the welfare of the NP? Consider the view of Joseph Tommasino, a physician assistant writing about both physician assistants and NPs:

> Our professional growth ... is essentially stunted by the simple fact that we have nowhere to go. We all grapple with, but seldom talk about, our lack of vertical mobility.... Want to change jobs? Submit your curriculum vitae and join the throng of PAs or NPs that apply for the job. True, your experience should ultimately speak for itself, but even if it does, will you get the salary you deserve? I doubt it, especially given the propensity of administrators to fill slots with the least expensive PAs or NPs.... One thing is certain, NPs and PAs must be proactive in designing their own career tracks.[5]

Salary aside, NPs who are practice owners have the opportunity to design a flow of care that makes sense from their point of view. It is not cast in stone that care must be given through an office visit. The office visit mode of healthcare delivery came about because of a physician-driven effort to tie reimbursement to physician services. Under capitated managed care and under the part of the ACA describing Accountable Care Organizations, a good model of care delivery is any model that keeps patients satisfied, meets quality standards, and is cost-effective. That could mean increased use of community health nurses, home visits, and school-based health care. Groups of creative NPs with open minds are capable of designing effective models that get out of the box established by fee-for-service medicine. Currently, however, in the majority of states, NPs are giving primary care under the auspices of a physician. The present situation is a function of past history, the present law, and public perceptions of physicians as givers of medical care.

Past History

Physicians "professionalized" their practice before nurses or other healthcare practitioners did and before the NP role even existed. Physicians convinced lawmakers to draw the legal lines such that only physicians could diagnose and treat and only physicians could order and perform tests and procedures, and prescribe medication. For many years, nurses went along with physician dominance.

NPs are now trying to climb a hill where physicians work at the top. The entrances are barricaded and are being shored up on all sides by physicians, who want to maintain their status as "king of the hill." Many state laws governing the practice of medicine and health care still contain protectionism for physicians, while other healthcare providers have had to fight for the right to provide the services they have been educated to provide. In some states, NPs are winning those fights.

Present Law

Third-party reimbursement goes to PCPs and specialists. Therefore, if NPs want to have their own practices, they need to be legally designated as PCPs or have cash-based practices.

In many states, physician collaboration is a matter of law, although it should be a matter of clinical and professional judgment. Nevertheless, the majority of states require physician collaboration for NP practice, especially if prescription writing is involved. Most states allow NPs to prescribe if they have a collaborative agreement with a physician.

Public Perceptions

While research indicates that patients are highly satisfied with the care given by NPs, and while some patients specifically request NPs as their providers, it is unclear whether there is a general awareness that NPs could be PCPs in their own right without physician oversight or collaboration.

Television shows have impressed the image of the kindly family physician on the minds of the public. The American Medical Association and the American Academy of Family Physicians have active public relations campaigns that seek to maintain the public perception of the physician as PCP.

MCO policies initially called for physician PCPs, even though NPs were delivering much of the care of patients enrolled in MCOs. Some MCOs, however, are changing their policies.

What Must Happen for NPs to Be PCPs?

For NPs to achieve PCP status, three things must happen. Laws have to permit NPs to be PCPs, the public must accept and be comfortable with the concept of the NP as PCP, and MCOs must agree to designate NPs as PCPs. States that do not define a PCP as an NP will need to be convinced to add this legal permission. Public relations efforts should be aimed at convincing the public that they are safe with NPs. Simultaneously, MCOs need to be convinced of the advantages of having NPs as PCPs.

Laws can prohibit NPs from practicing, say nothing about NPs, or permit NPs to practice and protect that NP practice. An example of a prohibitive law is: "A separate office for the nurse practitioner shall not be established." This language was enacted in 1995 by the Virginia legislature, but the legislature eliminated it in 2012. An example of a permissive law is: "APRNs may serve as primary care providers of record." (VT. Nursing R. §15.2[f]).

An example of a protective law (protective of physicians) is:

> It shall be an improper practice for the governing body of a hospital to refuse to act upon an application for staff membership or professional privileges or to deny or withhold from a physician, podiatrist, optometrist, dentist or licensed midwife staff membership or professional privileges in a hospital, or to exclude or expel a physician, podiatrist, optometrist, dentist or licensed midwife from staff membership in a hospital or curtail, terminate or diminish in any way a physician's, podiatrist's, optometrist's, dentist's or licensed midwife's professional privileges in a hospital, without stating the reasons therefor, or if the reasons stated are unrelated to standards of patient care, patient welfare, the objectives of the institution or the character or competency of the applicant. It shall be an improper practice for a governing body of a hospital to refuse to act upon an application or to deny or to withhold staff membership or professional privileges to a podiatrist based solely upon a practitioner's category of licensure.
>
> *Citation:* N.Y. Pub. Health Law §§ 2801-b.1.

NPs need to work to erase the laws that are prohibitive. NPs need more laws that are permissive and protective. An example of a law protective of NPs would be:

> A managed-care organization may not refuse to act upon an application for staff membership or professional privileges, or deny privileges for a nurse practitioner, without stating the reasons therefor, or if the reasons stated are unrelated to standards of patient care, patient welfare, the objectives of the institution or the character or competency of the applicant.

This is a slight alteration of New York's law quoted here, which protects physicians, dentists, podiatrists, optometrists, and nurse midwives from being denied hospital privileges without fair reason.

The first step for state and national NP organizations is to have an attorney analyze the law to identify barriers. Sometimes, when arguing about a professional issue, competitors will cite laws of which NPs were not even aware as the basis for barring NP participation.

The top priority areas where laws need to be changed to reflect NP training and practice are as follows:

- Authorization of PCP status
- Reimbursement
- Hospital privileges
- Loosening of legal requirements for physician collaboration
- Authorization to admit patients to skilled nursing facilities
- Authorization to order home health services
- Authorization to serve as medical director for hospice
- Authorization for NP practices to be "medical homes"

Once prohibitions are erased from the law, and once permission is certain, NPs will want to work toward legal protection. Other professions, notably physicians, have remarkable professional legal protection. The legal protection of physicians has been so great that the public associated "healthcare provider" with "physician" until recently, when other providers began to be assertive about their roles.

The stage is set for more permission and protection of professions other than physicians. For example, Medicaid law requires an insurer to offer a variety of choices to enrollees. Some state laws require insurers to pay NPs for services.

The Process of Changing the Law

Law change involves certain steps, including these:

- Developing a set of goals and legislative strategies for achieving the goals
- Developing relationships with lawmakers
- Analyzing present state law for barriers to NP practice
- Monitoring law changes proposed by other groups
- Responding to proposed law that affects NPs adversely
- Following up to see how bills that have been introduced have progressed
- Arranging testimony when bills come up for a hearing
- Arranging for communication with legislative representatives
- Drafting and arranging support for legislation that supports the NP agenda
- Following through until the bill is written into regulations
- Debriefing to see how the process can be done better next time

Developing Goals and Strategies

Clinicians know what gets in their way. NPs who have considered starting practices or who have actually done so know what stopped them from getting paid, know how difficult it can be to get a good physician collaborator, and whether they need hospital privileges. NP organizations should poll their members to develop a list of goals for the organizations. Then, keeping in mind that law must be in place, public perception must be favorable, and payer policies must be permissive, organizations can develop strategies for overcoming barriers. Strategies might include hiring a lobbyist, drafting a bill, hiring a public relations firm, brainstorming about ideas for news articles on NPs, meeting with researchers about data collection on NP practices, meeting with groups to ask for support, or meeting with MCO executives to explain the benefits to their business of having NPs as providers.

Developing Relationships with Lawmakers

NPs who attend fundraisers, assist candidates at election time, and otherwise get to know the lawmakers in their districts find that cooperation is there when it comes time to sponsor and vote for a bill important to NPs.

Analyzing Law for Barriers to NP Practice

An attorney familiar with the NP role should analyze the law of each state for each state organization. First, the attorney will analyze the law that names NPs to determine whether any prohibitions exist or whether permission or protection is needed. The attorney will also look for laws that do not name NPs but that regulate health care in a way that affects NPs. For example, the attorney will analyze state insurance law even if it does not name NPs as reimbursable providers. The attorney can locate the clause that should name NPs as reimbursable providers. The attorney should also analyze state law that addresses healthcare quality. If a law says a physician must oversee all care of patients in MCOs, the attorney can locate the clause that neglects NPs and suggest language changes that will remedy the barrier for NPs.

Monitoring Changes to the Law Proposed by Other Groups

NPs are not the only group looking to change the law. NP organizations need to have someone monitoring proposed statutes and regulations to see how incoming law might affect NPs. Physicians have historically sought protective language and will continue to do so, as will physical therapists, physician assistants, chiropractors, and other professionals. It is frustrating enough that NPs must change laws that were enacted before NPs existed. It is doubly frustrating when NPs are caught off guard and a new law is made that excludes NPs.

Collaborating with Other Stakeholders

Sometimes a law is proposed that adversely affects NPs but is not a result of professional competition. Instead, the proposed law is aimed at solving some unrelated problem. For example, the agency that administers Medicare, the Center for Medicare and Medicaid Services (CMS), sets the rates of payment for visits by Medicare patients. Physicians, NPs, physical therapists, chiropractors, and many other groups all may be working toward the same end: increasing those rates. In such situations, NPs may find allies in other professional groups. Again, to participate, NPs must be aware of the proposed law changes.

Following Up on Bills in Progress

A bill may be changed many times between introduction and passage. The job of the lobbyist includes checking on bill status nearly every day to determine when the hearings are, what amendments have been proposed, when the votes will be held, who is in favor and who is opposed, and what bills have been introduced that may counteract any given bill. Sometimes an NP organization, to get the legislative support to pass its bill, will need to agree to support another group's bill. In that case, a lobbyist must know who backs which bills, who will give what support in return for support, and what the NP organization's parameters are in terms of what can be supported and what cannot.

Arranging Testimony

Legislative committees hear testimony on a bill before a vote is taken to pass the bill out of committee and to the full legislative body, house, or senate. At hearings, citizens are permitted to address the committee or legislative body about the effect a bill will have on a citizen or a group. Committee members may question those who testify. Often there are many people who want to testify on a particular bill. There may be several hearings in a day. Keeping in mind that legislators can only digest so much information, parties are advised to keep testimony short and to the point. Three minutes is often all an individual has to make their point.

Legislators will be more affected by testimony that a bill will affect many people or will affect some people greatly. For example, a legislator is likely to be more swayed by testimony that a particular bill will open health care to 17,000 uninsured citizens than by testimony that a bill will give reimbursement to five self-employed NPs. On the other hand, if an NP can show legislators how the number of self-employed NPs could, with release of barriers, soon grow to 2500 self-employed NPs who can participate in a state program for the uninsured by offering reduced rate services, legislators' interest is likely to be stimulated. Legislators, like the population in general, are moved by issues that affect mothers and children, the elderly, public safety, and public expenditures. Testimony that shows how a bill touches on these issues can be very effective.

Lobbyists often help NP organizations develop testimony and testifiers. If a bill affecting NPs also affects patients, it is often helpful to have patients testify on behalf of the bill.

Arranging for Communication with Legislative Representatives

Citizens can communicate their opinions to legislators through telephone calls, emails, and visits, as well as in hearings. Legislators make themselves available to citizens at such gatherings as "nurses' night at the legislature" and other receptions. All legislators have aides who can hear citizen concerns and pass those concerns along to the legislator. NPs who want to communicate with legislators about professional issues can arrange for a personal visit with their individual legislators in their districts, telephone the legislator or aide, ask patients to contact their legislators about an NP issue of interest to the patient, and/or hire a lobbyist to communicate with the legislators.

It is a fact of life that legislators need money to conduct reelection campaigns. Legislators do, in fact, take the time to listen to contributors. Legislators remember the individuals and groups who contribute to their campaigns. Many NP organizations have political action committee funds that they use to support legislative campaigns. This is an important use of association funds.

Drafting and Arranging Support for Legislation That Furthers the NP Agenda

The drafting of legislative language is an art. Lobbyists, legislators, and attorneys do it. Citizens and associations do not do it, or rather, they usually do not do it well. A bill has to take into account the existing law, the form that state law takes, possible unintended consequences of particular language, the state-defined meaning of particular words, the possible reaction to opponents and competitors to specific language, and the need for conciseness and clarity of expression.

NP associations usually begin a bill-drafting process by discussing the problem NPs are trying to solve with a lobbyist. The lobbyist then locates the section of law that needs to be changed and proceeds to draft language changes that will solve the problem. Lobbyists, when drafting bills for NPs, often will get opinions from selected legislators and other professional groups about possible language in an attempt to pretest reactions to specific language. Often, between the time a bill is conceptualized and the time it is introduced, the bill's language has been changed and rearranged many times. And after the bill is introduced, the language may be changed several times through amendments.

After there is a draft of language for a proposed bill, or during the drafting process, a lobbyist seeks sponsors. A bill's sponsor introduces it and shepherds it through the legislature. There can be companion bills in both houses of the legislature, in which case there should be a sponsoring senator and a sponsoring representative. The selection of a sponsor is crucial because their personality, committee position, affiliations, and popularity will affect how the bill progresses. For example, a well-positioned sponsor may decline because the legislator is trying to curry favor from an opposing group. It is not uncommon to "shop" for sponsors.

After a lobbyist gets a bill sponsor, the search is on for cosponsors. A bill with many cosponsors is likely to get passed. No legislator likes his or her name on a bill that fails. So, cosponsors can be expected not only to support the bills they cosponsor, but also to work for passage of those bills.

After obtaining sponsors and cosponsors, a lobbyist's next task is to line up testimony for committee hearings. Then, after a hearing, a lobbyist turns attention to locking in votes. Lobbyists ask legislators directly whether they intend to vote for or against a bill. If the vote is "no," a lobbyist can ask why. If something about the bill can be tweaked to change a "no" vote to a "yes," a lobbyist can draft an amendment and seek the approval of sponsors, cosponsors, and other favorable voters on the amended language.

Finally, a bill comes to a vote. A bill must pass each house of the legislature. A bill that passes both houses then goes to the governor for approval. The final hurdle is escaping a gubernatorial veto. Lobbying is done even at this final stage to convince the governor and his or her staff of the worth of the bill.

After a bill becomes a law, the bill is codified—that is, written into the state's code of laws. Many bills are further expanded upon in regulations written by the state agencies that carry out the laws. Regulations may include detail not specified in the law, but regulations cannot directly contradict a statute.

NPs who are working toward legal change will want to work closely with their lobbyist all the way through regulation writing. After it is over, they can debrief to see how things could be done better next time.

Hiring Lobbyists and Attorneys

Lobbyists and attorneys often serve many clients and may or may not know the issues that are most important to NPs. An NP association that is fortunate enough to have a lobbyist and an attorney who are well versed in NP issues and already familiar with the law regarding NPs has a head start.

When interviewing an attorney, or lobbyist, ask these questions:

- What is your experience with NP issues?
- Have you personally experienced the care of an NP?
- Who are your other clients? Might their issues conflict with NP issues?
- Do you have any opinions about NPs?
- What does an NP do?

One would think a lobbyist or attorney who has scheduled an interview with an NP organization would have done enough research to answer this last question. But surprisingly, that is not always the case. A prospective lobbyist or attorney who cannot answer this question should not be hired.

Do-It-Yourself Lobbying

Some NPs are very good at testifying. Usually the best testifiers are those who have had the most practice. When called to testify, ask who the committee members are and whether any are healthcare providers. Ask about a time limit. Ask who else will be testifying, and coordinate the testimony if possible. The best testimony has an introduction, a middle, and a conclusion, just like a speech. Polish is not a necessity, but preparation is essential.

Should NPs Join with the State Nurses' Association for Lobbying?

In some states, the NP association is a separate organization from the state nurses' association. In other states, NPs are an interest group within the state nurses' association. Ideally, from the point of view of an outsider, the state nurses' association would take care of legislative issues for all nurses. However, NPs sometimes find that their issues are a lower priority for the state nurses' association than they would like. NPs have sometimes formed their own organizations and hired their own lobbyists for this reason.

It is worth noting that in Oregon, where state law is quite favorable to NPs, lobbying has always been done by a strong state nurses' association, of which NPs are an interest group. Officers of NP associations should attempt to work with the state nurses' association on legislative issues. If, after attempting to work with the state nurses' association, NPs find they cannot get what they need, then NPs can hire their own lobbyist.

Dealing with Government Agencies

Many people who work for government agencies lack an understanding of health care and specifically the role of NPs. Though an NP might expect that a state or federal agency would research an issue when knowledge is lacking, many state agencies rely on citizens and their representatives to bring problems to light and to do the legal research to support the proponent's position. When NPs or their hired representatives become familiar with the personnel of state and federal agencies and seek person-to-person communication about an NP issue, questions and problems can often be taken care of efficiently at the agency level without resorting to legislative action. Further, NPs will be included in government policy making when they sit on the advisory panels and commissions making the policies. It is part of a lobbyist's job to know the influential policy-making commissions in a state and attempt to get NPs appointed to these commissions and boards.

The Competition

Change would be easy if there were no competition. There is competition, however, and it is useful to know where it comes from and what competitors' interests are.

Physician Competition

Physicians fought hard for their position in health care and now fight to maintain it. The fight is by no means limited to NPs. Physicians have fought against other providers, such as homeopathic physicians and optometrists, and now they fight against MCOs, which physicians perceive as threatening physician autonomy.

Through capturing the mechanisms of reimbursement, physicians were able to secure and maintain a dominant position among healthcare providers. They are not going to give up their position now.

Although NPs made significant strides in the 1970s because of a physician shortage in certain areas, and although NPs made some progress in the 1990s because of a funds shortage, there are still many legal and policy barriers to NPs, many of which were established by and are now maintained through physician influence.

Whereas the climate in the early 1970s was conducive to the proliferation of "physician extenders" due to the physician shortage, in recent years the NP has been increasingly viewed by some physicians as a competitor rather than simply an extender of physician services.

Competition is something NPs always will need to budget for in terms of time, energy, and money.

Competition from Physician Assistants

Physician assistants (PAs) have many of the same goals as NPs: professional recognition and respect, the ability to make a good living, and the ability to control one's work product. PAs will have to fight their own battles, as their profession was set up differently from its inception. By nature of their name and mission, PAs are not meant to be independent providers. While individual NPs may compete with individual PAs for specific jobs, it is not fruitful for NP professional organizations to engage PA organizations in competition in the public arena.

Competition from Other Nurses

Some NP associations find that when they go for inclusion in the law as PCPs, other nurses, particularly clinical nurse specialists (CNSs), want to be included as well. At that point, there is a possibility that the legislature will be hearing competitive arguments from NP and CNS groups about the relative merits of each group. As with PAs, NPs and CNSs have many of the same goals. It will not serve either group well to fight, and public fighting will definitely cause harm. Peaceful coexistence is the key. If NPs only put forth efforts to further their profession and do not engage in efforts to hold back other professions, not only will time and expenses be saved, but public relations will be better.

How Can Individual NPs Make a Difference?

Individuals can influence lawmakers and lawmaking in the following ways:

- Ask candidates in local elections about their position on NPs, and vote accordingly. Support good candidates with campaign contributions, noting on the check that you are an NP.
- When a bill concerns NPs or health issues of concern to NPs, call or write legislators, noting that you are an NP.
- When regulations are proposed that affect NPs, write and send comments on how the proposed regulations will affect NPs.
- Join an NP association.
- Write letters to the editor of the local newspaper about news events affecting NPs or affecting your patients.

Conclusion

The process for making law conform to NP goals for the profession is this:

1. Analyze the current law for prohibitions, lack of permission, and lack of protection where it matters. Have an attorney work with the NP organization to do the analysis.
2. Draft a bill that erases prohibition, gives permission, or affords protection for NP practice. Have an attorney, lobbyist, or legislator work with the organization to do this.
3. Gather support for the bill among lawmakers and the public. Enlist the participation of association members in each legislative district.
4. Introduce the bill, and follow its progress, testifying when necessary, educating lawmakers when necessary, and arranging give-and-take with other groups when necessary. At this stage, professional lobbyists should be running the show.
5. Follow the bill through to the regulation-writing stage, monitoring the language of proposed regulations and commenting on the proposed regulations through letters. Have an attorney do this.
6. Refine the approach, based on what was learned with previous law changes. Association officers, attorneys, and lobbyists should do this.

Notes

1. Merriam-Webster. (2005). Policy definition. In *Merriam-Webster collegiate dictionary* (11th ed., p. 960). Springfield, MA: Author.
2. Freudenheim, M. (1997, November 2). The future wears white: Nurses treading on doctors' turf. *The New York Times Week in Review*. Retrieved from http://www.nytimes.com/1997/11/02/weekinreview/the-future-wears-white-nurses-treading-on-doctors-turf.html
3. Califano J. A., Jr. (1994). *Radical surgery: What's next for America's health care?* (p. 218). New York, NY: New York Times Books.
4. Health policy brief, Health Affairs. (2013, May 15.). Nurse practitioners and primary care. Retrieved from http://www.healthaffairs.org/healthpolicybriefs/brief.php?brief_id=92
5. Tommasino, J. (1998). The dilemma of the one-rung ladder. *Clinician Reviews, 8,* 31.

CHAPTER 13

Promoting the Profession to the Public

According to studies of patient satisfaction, most patients who have seen nurse practitioners (NPs) like them. But not everyone has seen an NP. People who are healthy and rarely visit any healthcare provider may not have experienced care given by an NP. Those who have had a long relationship with a physician also may not have experienced NP care.

NPs have had little, if any, exposure in popular culture. For example, there are no equivalents of the "Grey's Anatomy" primetime television doctors for the NP profession. These TV characters, doing their work on the air week after week, have given the average viewer the sense that they know what physicians do.

There are no well-known figures in literature who are NPs. Children do not grow up reading books about NPs. There are no NP dolls. There are no NP senators or congressional representatives.

Furthermore, no advertising campaigns keep NPs in the public eye (in the way that, for example, advertising keeps Coca-Cola at center stage). In contrast, however, the American Medical Association budgets millions for major public relations (PR) efforts.

NP organizations and NP business owners are just beginning to realize the necessity of organized PR plans to promote the profession and its agenda. NPs who want to see the passage of legislation favorable to their practice and NPs who have their own practices and want to see them thrive will want the public to have an opinion about NPs, and they will want that opinion to be favorable. NPs have made great progress on a one-on-one basis. In fact, the main way the public currently comes to understand what an NP does is by experiencing their care. Those who have not experienced the care of an NP can be encouraged, through PR efforts, to seek the care of an NP.

Public Relations Steps

There are systematic ways of raising public awareness about NPs. Marketing, PR, and sales all have the same process:

1. Develop a message.
2. Determine who the message should reach.
3. Determine the best way to disseminate the message.
4. Disseminate the message.
5. Evaluate the success of the effort and fine tune the process.

The specific steps in a PR strategy for NPs are as follows:

1. Set a goal.
2. Develop a plan.
3. Develop a budget.
4. Work the plan.

Setting the Goal

A likely PR goal for the NP profession is to establish NPs as experts on primary care, and the ultimate goal might be getting primary care provider (PCP) status for NPs. An alternative goal for an individual NP with a private practice may be getting patients to come in the door.

There is also a place for specialist NPs. At least one NP has taken on pediatric enuresis as a specialty, for example. Others have taken on nonsurgical treatment of incontinence in women. These NPs have the goal of establishing themselves as experts for patients with specific problems.

Developing the Plan

Whatever goal is selected, the plan will revolve around establishing NPs in general, or individual NPs, as high-quality professionals. The most effective forms of publicity show the expertise of NPs in a way the public can understand. NPs can convey expertise in a number of ways:

- By providing high-quality care to each patient, on a one-on-one basis
- Through word of mouth, such as when a friend or family member has a good experience of care and shares it
- By including testimonials from patients in brochures, promotional videos, or paid advertising
- By arranging for articles written by NPs on health topics to appear in local newspapers or on popular blogs or websites
- By arranging for radio or television talk show appearances by NPs
- By speaking on healthcare topics at community forums
- By serving on healthcare advisory boards in the area and nationally
- By endorsing, as an association, particular sets of preventive care guidelines and standards

A simple PR plan that focuses on a series of news releases is described in **Appendix 13-A**.

Developing the Budget

PR can be done with a million-dollar budget or with a hundred-dollar budget. Either way, there must be a budget, or nothing will happen. The majority of a PR budget will go toward services. The researching and writing of news releases, communication with reporters, and follow-up via telephone calls will consume the most monetary resources. One year, a state NP organization spent its PR money on a billboard on one of the major highways in Georgia.

Even a small NP organization should count on spending about $15,000 a year on PR. Besides membership dues, this money can be generated from other business ventures. One job of a PR professional, for example, can be to promote an NP educational conference with a registration fee. Such an event would presumably turn a profit. Another job of a PR professional is to develop written materials—brochures and fact sheets on NPs—that can be sold to individual NPs and practices and distributed to patients.

Working the Plan
Proactive PR

In a proactive PR plan, an NP organization seeks to generate articles or television pieces about NPs or to showcase the expertise of NPs, not in response to attacks, but rather as a regular, systematic promotion strategy. For example, an NP organization might arrange for an article to appear in the local newspaper giving an NP's advice for staying well during the flu season. The article serves three purposes: (1) It keeps NPs in the news in a positive light, (2) it demonstrates the information an NP can offer, and (3) it gives people useful information. In addition to satisfying the needs of NPs and patients, such an article satisfies the needs of newspaper editors to run informative articles.

A message about NP expertise in primary care can be disseminated on television, in newspapers and magazines, at health fairs, by word of mouth, through advertising, and through websites and blogs. It is generally agreed that television stories, newspaper articles, and websites are effective ways of getting a message to a large segment of the population with little expenditure.

When developing a PR plan, NPs need to keep in mind that newspapers, television station owners, and websites need readers (or viewers) and advertisers. An NP organization may not be able to offer advertisers to a newspaper, but it can offer readers, particularly if a contributing NP is providing information on a topic of interest to many people. Health, and particularly primary care, is interesting to many people.

To generate an article in a newspaper or on a website, the following things have to happen:

1. Generate an idea for an article.
2. Generate the information to be conveyed.
3. Write the news release.
4. Identify the appropriate vehicle for the article.
5. Identify the decision maker (editor) who can ensure that the article will get into the paper or on the website.
6. Give the editor the name of a contact if the editor wants more information.
7. After the release is sent to the editor, follow up by telephone call.
8. Arrange for more information to be given to the editor, or arrange for accompanying photographs or art.

A statewide media campaign might, for example, involve sending a news release to every newspaper in the state once a month. When the process just described is undertaken 12 times a year and multiplied by 50 or 100 newspapers, it is close to a full-time job.

Each NP organization and each private practice needs a person designated to handle PR. PR services may be purchased or performed by a volunteer NP. An NP volunteer is less expensive, is likely know more about NPs than a PR professional, and will be highly motivated. However, an NP volunteer probably have a full-time job, and as a result the volunteer PR efforts may not get the regular attention that is needed. Further, when NPs organize into associations and there is a treasury, it makes sense for all NPs to share in contributing to PR efforts, and that is best done by purchasing PR services, rather than imposing on one NP to do the work.

Reactive PR

PR is reactive when it is in response to a particular event or criticism. For example, if a physicians' group came out with a statement that only physicians should be PCPs, the rebuttal of an NP organization would be reactive.

The keys to effective reactive PR are speed and a consistent and logical message. Therefore, NP organizations should have a set of "talking points" ready for use in the event that such a timely reaction is needed. Talking points are a PR method for ensuring that a spokesperson for a group has something to say and that their message is consistent with the group's goals. For examples of talking points for NP organizations, see **Appendix 13-B**.

The Substance of the Message

When NPs are asked how they differ from physicians and why they should be incorporated into payment systems, they must be ready to support their answer with hard facts and data.

Compare the following two statements: "NPs are good listeners and are safe and effective providers of health care" and "A health services research team studying 799 episodes of otitis media and sore throat in a Columbia, Maryland HMO found that NPs were more effective at resolving the problem. And NPs' care was 20% less expensive than MDs." Which statement will more effectively persuade business people and lawmakers that NPs are value-added providers? The second statement is what an NP should tell an insurance executive, an employer, or a congressperson. NPs know that the first statement is true, but to convince others, they must have hard facts and numbers.

Supporting Data

Here is an excerpt from a health policy brief – "Nurse Practitioners and Primary Care" — published in *Health Affairs* on May 15, 2013:

> Studies comparing the quality of care provided by physicians and nurse practitioners have found that clinical outcomes are similar. For example, a systematic review of 26 studies published since 2000 found that health status, treatment practices, and prescribing behavior were consistent between nurse practitioners and physicians. What's more, patients seeing nurse practitioners were also found to have higher levels of satisfaction with their care. Studies found that nurse practitioners do better than physicians on measures related to patient follow up; time spent in consultations; and provision of screening, assessment, and counseling services. The patient-centered nature of nurse practitioner training, which often includes care coordination and sensitivity to the impact on health of social and cultural factors, such as environment and family situation, makes nurse practitioners particularly well prepared for and interested in providing primary care.

Recent studies (and not so recent studies) have found NPs to be as good as or better than MDs as PCPs. These studies should be on the tip of the tongue of anyone trying to "sell" the concept of the NP as the preferred healthcare provider.[1]

Study 1: NPs Match MDs on Primary Care Tasks

Hall et al. set up audit criteria, with input from the practitioners being studied, and then audited charts of 426 MDs and NPs in 16 ambulatory care practices.[2] The researchers looked at eight tasks:

1. Follow-up on a low hematocrit to detect patients with anemia caused by colorectal cancer or other serious gastrointestinal disease
2. Screening for cancer using breast examination and Pap smears in women
3. Follow-up on a high serum glucose to detect and treat diabetes
4. Monitoring of patients on digoxin to detect drug toxicity or symptomatic relapse
5. Follow-up on a positive urine culture to treat persistent bacteriuria
6. Compliance with the American Academy of Pediatrics standards for screening and immunization of infants
7. Assessment of the risk of dehydration in children at the start of an episode of gastroenteritis
8. Monitoring and follow-up of children with otitis media to detect and treat failure to resolve the middle-ear effusion

The findings: NPs' performance was comparable or superior on seven of the eight tasks. Female MDs were better at cancer screening for women, but male MDs were worse at this than NPs. The sample of male "nonphysicians" was too small to make any generalizations and was therefore excluded from the results.

Study 2: NPs Are Cost-Effective

Salkever et al. compared NPs and MDs on cost and effectiveness.[3] To study costs, Salkever paid observers to time NP and MD visits with patients. The research team then analyzed costs of office space, costs of follow-up visits, and costs of ancillary services and drugs ordered by the providers. To study effectiveness, the researchers randomly surveyed patients regarding problem severity and changes in problem status after treatment. The researchers then computed the cost per episode of care for two conditions, sore throat and otitis media.

The findings: NPs were 20% less costly in their care.[4] NPs were at least as effective as MDs at resolving the problem.[3, p.152]

Study 3: NPs Get to the Root of the Problem

Avorn et al. asked 799 MDs and NPs to consider the following case vignette and answer two questions:[5]

> A man you have never seen before comes to your office seeking help for inter-mittent sharp epigastric pains that are relieved by meals but are worse on an empty stomach. The patient has just moved from out of state and brings along a report of an endoscopy performed a month ago showing diffuse gastritis of moderate severity but no ulcer. Is there a particular therapy you would choose at this point, or would you need additional information? What more do you want to know? What would you do?

The findings: Nurses were far more likely to collect more historical information about the patient before deciding upon therapy. The NPs asked an average of 2.6 questions about the patient as opposed to 1.6 for physicians. A third of physicians (and 19% of NPs) chose to initiate therapy without any additional information. Nurses were far more likely to ask about the patient's diet and psychosocial information (but less likely to ask about alcohol intake). NPs were more likely to suggest nonprescription approaches to therapy, such as a change in diet or counseling to help the patient deal with stress. NPs were far less likely than physicians (20% versus 63%) to recommend a prescription drug.[6] NPs were much less likely to state that a prescription drug would be the single most effective therapeutic intervention for this patient (12% versus 46%).[7]

No analysis of the cost of therapy was done. However, when the cost of the MDs' treatment plan (prescription medication but no counseling about unhealthy lifestyle) was compared to the NPs' treatment plan (no prescription but counseling regarding aggravating factors), the NPs' treatment plan certainly showed itself to be the more economical approach to care.

Study 4: Patients Are Satisfied with NPs

Medical Economics, a magazine written for physicians, conducted a survey of patient satisfaction with NPs and MDs.[8] The magazine found that patients were as satisfied with NPs as with physicians.

Study 5: Patients Are Satisfied with NPs

Harrocks et al. systematically reviewed randomized controlled trials and prospective observational studies and found that patients were more satisfied with care by an NP, that there were no differences in the health status of patients treated by NPs versus medical doctors, and that the quality of care was in some ways better for NP consultations.[9]

Study 6: NPs Are More Successful at Getting Patients' Blood Pressure Down

Mundinger et al. conducted a randomized trial comparing outcome measures for care provided by NPs and medical doctors. Among other things, Mundinger found a statistically significant difference in the diastolic value of patients treated for hypertension by NPs. NPs' patients had a lower diastolic blood pressure after treatment than physicians' patients.[10]

Further Data on the Value of NP Practice

A survey study ($N = 3257$) comparing OB-GYN practices that used nonphysician providers to physician-only practices found that patients preferred the "collaborative" practices.[11] Of the nonphysician providers, 45% were NPs, 19% were midwives, 16% were physician assistants, and 9% were clinical nurse specialists. Reasons for preferring practices with nonphysician providers were as follows:

- The patient got an appointment faster.
- More time was spent with the provider.
- More health information was given.
- More diet information was given.

Patients felt that nonphysicians were less rushed in their care. However, patients believed that physicians provided more complete information.

For a quick reference to substantive arguments supporting NP practice and citations for the arguments, see **Exhibit 13-1**.

Exhibit 13-1   Effective Arguments for NPs

Argument 1: Effective care requires a proper match between provider and patient problem. NPs are the appropriate first-line provider.

Data: Hall, Salkever, and Avorn studies (see notes 2, 3, and 5 of this chapter)

Argument 2: Patients are highly satisfied with NPs.

Data: Perry and Harrocks studies (see notes 8 and 9)

Argument 3: NPs have been proven cost-effective in their evaluations/treatments.

Data: Avorn and Salkever studies (see notes 3 and 5)

Argument 4: NPs give high-quality primary care.

Data: Hall, Salkever, Avorn, and Mundinger studies (see notes 2, 3, 5, and 10)

Argument 5: NPs emphasize disease prevention and healthcare maintenance.

Data: Hall and Avorn studies (see notes 2 and 5)

Other Studies Documenting Quality of Care Provided by NPs

NP vs. Physician Outcomes in Patients Treated by Either Provider

Aigner, M. J., Drew, S., & Phipps, J. (2004). A comparative study of nursing home resident outcomes between care provided by NP/physicians versus physicians only. *Journal of the American Medical Directors Association, 5*(1), 16–23.

Ettner, S. L. (2006). An alternative approach to reducing the costs of patient care? A controlled trial of the multidisciplinary doctor-NP (MDNP) model. *Medical Decision Making, 26*, 9–17.

Lambing, A. Y., Adams, D. L., Fox, D. H., & Divine, G. (2004). NPs and physicians' care activities and clinical outcomes with an inpatient geriatric population. *Journal of the American Academy of Nurse Practitioners, 16*(8), 343–352.

Lenz, E. R., Mundinger, M., Kane, R. L., Hopkins, S. C., & Lin, S. X. (2004). Primary care outcomes in patients treated by nurse practitioners or physicians: Two year follow up. *Medical Care Research and Review, 61*(3), 332–351.

Lenz, E. R., Mundinger, M. O., Hopkins, S. C., Lin, S. X., & Smolowitz, J. L. (2002a). Diabetes care processes and outcomes in patients treated by nurse practitioners or physicians. *Diabetes Education, 28*(4), 590–598.

Lenz, E. R., Mundinger, M. O., Hopkins, S. C., Lin, S. X., & Smolowitz, J. L. (2002b). Put into practice. Diabetes care processes and outcomes in patients treated by NPs or physicians. *Diabetes Education, 28*(4), 566–569.

Litaker, D., Mion, L., Planavsky, L., Kippes, C., Mehta, N., & Frolkis, J. (2003). Physician-nurse practitioner teams in chronic disease management: The impact on costs, clinical effectiveness, and patients' perception of care. *Journal of Interprofessional Care, 17*(3), 223–237.

Mundinger, M. O., Kane, R. L., Lenz, E. R., Totten, A. M., Wei-Yann, T., Cleary, P. D....Shelanski, M. L. (2000). Primary care outcomes in patients treated by nurse practitioners or physicians. *Journal of the American Medical Association, 283*(1), 59–68.

Rudy, E. B., Davidson, L. J., Daly, B., Clochesy, J. M., Sereika, S., & Baldisseri, M. (1998). Care activities and outcomes of patients cared for by acute care nurse practitioners, physician assistants, and resident physicians: A comparison. *American Journal of Critical Care, 7*(4), 267–281.

Sox, H. C. (1979). Quality of patient care by nurse practitioners and physician assistants': A ten year perspective. *Annals of Internal Medicine, 91,* 459–468.

Spitzer, W. O., Sackett, D. L., & Sibley, J. C. (1974). The Burlington randomized trial of the nurse practitioners. *New England Journal of Medicine, 290,* 251–256.

Wardrope, J., & Rothwell, S. (2000). Primary care outcomes in patients treated by nurse practitioners or physicians: A randomized trial. *Journal of Accident and Emergency Medicine, 17*(4), 290–291.

Wilson, I. B., Landon, B. E., Hirschhorn, L. R., McInnes, K., Marsden, P. V., & Cleary, P. D. (2005). Quality of HIV care provided by nurse practitioners, physician assistants and physicians. *Annals of Internal Medicine, 143*(10), 729–736.

Acute Care

Christmas, F. B., Reynolds, J., Hodges, S., Franklin, G. A., Miller, F. B., Richardson, J. D., & Rodriquez, J. L. (2005). Physician extenders impact trauma systems. *Journal of Trauma and Acute Care Surgery, 58*(5), 917–920.

Hoffman, L. A., Tasota, F. J., Scharfenberg, C., & Donahoe, M. P. (2005). Outcomes of care managed by an acute care nurse practitioner/attending physician team in a subacute medical intensive care unit. *American Journal of Critical Care, 14*(2), 121–132.

Jensen, L., & Scherr, K. (2004). Impact of the practitioner role in cardiothoracic surgery. *Canadian Association of Critical Care Nurses, 15*(3), 14–19.

Meyer, S. C., & Miers, L. J. (2005). Cardiovascular surgeon and acute care nurse practitioner. *AACN Advanced Clinical Care, 16*(2), 149–158.

Geriatric

Baherjian, D. (2008). Care of nursing home residents by advanced practice nurses: A review of the literature. *Research in Gerontological Nursing, 1*(3), 177–185.

Barrow, C. R., & Graber, R. B. (2000). Nurse practitioner care versus physician care: An analysis of recent outcomes research. *Advance for Nurse Practitioners,* 17–18.

Lambing, A. Y., Adams, D. L. C., Fox, D. H., & Divine, G. (2004). Nurse practitioners' and physician' care activities and clinical outcomes with an inpatient geriatric population. *Journal of the American Academy of Nurse Practitioners, 16*(8), 343–352.

Pediatrics

Woods, L. (2006). Evaluating the clinical effectiveness of neonatal nurse practitioners: An exploratory study. *Journal of Clinical Nursing, 15,* 35–44.

Primary Care

Brooten, D., Youngblut, J. M., Kutcher, J., & Bobo, C. (2004). Quality and the nursing workforce: APNs, patient outcomes and health care costs. *Nursing Outlook, 52*(1), 45–52.

Cooper, R. A. (2001). Health care workforce for the twenty-first century: The impact of nonphysician clinicians. *Annual Review of Medicine, 52,* 51–61.

Horrocks, S., Anderson, E. & Salisbury, C. (2002). Systematic review of whether nurse practitioners working in primary care can provide equivalent care to doctors. *BMJ, 324,* 819–823.

Iliffe, S. (2000). Nursing and the future of primary care: Handmaidens or agents for managed care. *BMJ, 320,* 1020–1021.

Kleinpell, R. & Gawlinski, A. (2005). Assessing outcomes in advanced practice nursing practice. *AACN Advanced Critical Care, 16*(1), 43–57.

Laurant, M., Reeves, D., Hermens, R., Braspenning, J., Grol, R., & Sibbald, B. (2006). Substitution of doctors by nurses in primary care. *Cochrane Database of Systematic Review,* 2.

Ohman-Strickland, P. A. (2008). Quality of diabetes care in family medicine practices: Influence of nurse practitioners and physician assistants. *Annals of Family Medicine, 6*(1), 14–22.

Seale, C., Anderson, E., & Kinnersley, P. (2005). Comparison of GP and nurse practitioner consultations: An observational study. *British Journal of General Practice, 55,* 938–943.

Seale, C., Anderson, E., & Kinnersley, P. (2006). Treatment advice in primary care: A comparative study of nurse practitioners and general practitioners. *Journal of Advanced Nursing, 54*(5), 534–541.

Venning, P., Durie, A., Roland M., Roberts, C., & Leese B. (2000). Randomised controlled trial comparing cost effectiveness of general practitioners and nurse practitioners in primary care. *BMJ, 320,* 1048–1053.

Collecting Impressive Facts

Not all hard facts and data come from research studies. Under Medicare's Physician Quality Reporting System, clinicians report (on the claim forms used to obtain reimbursement) their performance for each patient on specific measures. The practice receives cumulative data periodically on these performance measures. When a practice gets a contract as a provider with a health maintenance organization (HMO), the practice receives quarterly performance reports from the HMO. The reports compare the practice to the aggregate (average practice) on such qualities as the number of emergency department visits by covered patients, the number of admissions, the length of stay of admitted patients, and the monthly cost of care per patient.

NPs who have their own practices can use Medicare's data for marketing. Because NP-only practices are rare, it is difficult to find aggregate data on such practices. NPs who do not have their own practices but who work as employees of MDs or HMOs may find that practice managers are collecting data to compare NPs' performance with that of local MDs. NPs who collect such data and pool it with other NPs will have substantive answers to such questions from businesspeople and legislators as "Why should we want NPs?"

Not-So-Impressive Facts About NPs

While some of the problems NPs experience with regard to acceptance are brought on by physicians who are guarding their professional territory or by the response of the public to physicians' successful and persistent PR, some NP problems are based on fact. The argument put forth by physician organizations that the education required for entry into NP practice is less than the education required for physician entry into practice is true. Likewise, the argument that the continuing education requirements of NPs are less than physician requirements is true. *The Washington Post* gave this advice to NPs in an editorial:

> If nurses' role is to go on changing as quickly as it has, it will be up to nursing schools to look closely at that training—as some clearly have done—and make sure it corresponds to reality. It remains true that nurses receive far less medical training than doctors (typically two years or less) and a far lower proportion have been to college.[12]

Dealing with the Downside

NPs need to be able to respond positively to comparisons between NP and MD educational paths. There are two ways of dealing with this problem. The first is upgrading the entry into practice requirement to a master's degree. Thirty-two states already have done this. The second is to upgrade continuing education requirements. The present continuing education requirements of NPs differ depending on the certifying organization. A wise move on the part of NPs would be to match continuing education requirements to those of family physicians.

At least one pharmacology course needs to be on every nursing graduate school's list of required courses. Nursing graduate schools would also do well to add physicians to their faculty, specifically for the illness management portion of the program. (Medical schools also would benefit from adding NPs to their faculty teaching primary care.) Finally, nursing schools could offer a clinical doctorate in primary care. The curriculum logically might include pharmacology, physiology, clinical psychology, and advanced medical management.

Even when a master's degree is required for entry into practice, NP education will be of shorter duration than physician education. However, no data exists to support the necessity of 4 years of medical school and 3 years of residency to perform primary care. Physicians set those educational requirements without research to support that level of education. The data showing that NPs are excellent PCPs support an argument that master's-level preparation is appropriate education for PCPs.

A coalition of nursing organizations has recommended that the entry-level degree for new NPs be a clinical doctorate as of 2015. This recommendation, until adopted by all state legislatures, is simply a recommendation.

A second not so impressive fact about NPs is that some feel there is a lack of assertiveness among NPs. Timidity does not serve nurses well in day-to-day work situations, such as when nurses defer to physician dominance.[14] Nor does taking a backseat serve researchers well when they fail to approach journalists with their findings.[15] It is time for NPs to state, publicly and consistently, that "NPs are experts in primary care," not that "NPs do primary care in a collaborative relationship with a physician."

NP organizations should consider spending some of their budget on PR services to deal with these issues. Among the projects for a PR professional hired by an NP organization is generating publicity, particularly through news releases that establish NPs as experts in primary care. Another project is to generate a fact sheet or brochure on NPs, for publication online and on paper, to give out to anyone who expresses interest in and has questions about NPs. See **Appendix 13-C** for an example of the information that could be included in a fact sheet on NPs.

Finally, each NP organization should designate an NP in the organization who will be the spokesperson when a reactive comment is needed. This NP should be familiar with the organization's talking points and should be unafraid of talking with the news media.

Notes

1. The Salkever study was done by two public health PhDs, an MSW, and an MD. The Hall study was done by four PhDs, an MB, and an MA, from departments of psychology, health policy, biostatistics, and information technology. The Avorn study was done by MDs.

2. Hall J., Palmer R. H., Orav E. J., Hargraves, J. L., Wright, E. A., & Louis, T. A. (1990). Performance quality, gender and professional role: A study of physicians and nonphysicians in 16 ambulatory care practices. *Medical Care, 28,* 489–501.

3. Salkever, D. S., Skinner, E. A., Steinwachs D. M., & Katz, H. (1982). Episode-based efficiency comparisons for physicians and nurse practitioners. *Medical Care, 20,* 143–153.

4. For otitis media, the NP cost per episode was $14.98; the MD cost was $18.22. For sore throat, the NP cost per episode was $11.80; the MD cost was $15.64.

5. Avorn J., Everitt D. E., & Baker M.W. (1991). The neglected medical history and therapeutic choices for abdominal pain: A nationwide study of 799 physicians and nurses. *Archives of Internal Medicine, 151,* 694–698.

6. A month's supply of both ranitidine and Tagamet cost close to $100.

7. There was no relationship between nurses having prescription authority in their state and their reliance upon prescription versus nonprescription therapy.

8. Perry, K. (1995). Patient survey: Physician extenders. Why patients love physician extenders. *Medical Economics*, 72, 58, 63, 67.

9. Harrocks S., Anderson E., & Salisbury C. (2002). Systematic review of whether nurse practitioners working in primary care can provide equivalent care to doctors. *BMJ*, 324, 819–823.

10. Mundinger, M. O., Kane, R. L., Lenz, E. R., Totten, A. M., Wei-Yann, T., Cleary, P. D…,.Shelanski, M. L. (2000). Primary care outcomes in patients treated by nurse practitioners or physicians: A randomized trial. *Journal of the American Medical Association*, 283, 59–68.

11. Hankins G. D., Shaw S. B., Cruess D. F., Lawrence, H. C., & Harris, C. D. (1996). Patient satisfaction with collaborative practice. *Obstetrics & Gynecology*, 88, 1011–1015.

12. Doctors vs. nurses? Editorial. (1993, December 13). *The Washington Post*, pp. A20. Retrieved from http://pqasb.pqarchiver.com/washingtonpost/search.html

13. Medical education was a mishmash of courses and apprenticeships until standardized at its present form in the early 1900s by the American Medical Association. See Starr, P. (1982). *The social transformation of American medicine* (pp. 116–123). New York, NY: Basic Books, Inc.

14. Buresh, B., & Gordon S. (1996). Subtle self-sabotage. *American Journal of Nursing*, 96, 22–23.

15. Buresh, B., & Gordon, S. (1996). Publicizing nursing research. *American Journal of Nursing*, 96, 62, 64.

16. Chesanow, N. (1998). How one group builds market leadership. *Medical Economics*, 75, 84–86, 92–94, 98–100.

A Simple PR Plan for a State NP Organization

This plan can work for a state organization or for an individual NP. It is a simple plan, using newspapers only. Much more elaborate plans can be made with the aid of a good PR expert. More elaborate plans might explore websites, television news coverage and features, prime-time shows featuring NPs, public television pieces on NPs, national magazine pieces, radio talk show appearances, speaking engagements, and/or advertising.

For each of the topics that follow, four things need to happen:

1. Develop the substance of the news release. Two or more NPs should be able to do this in less than 30 minutes.
2. Write the news release in the form that news editors are used to seeing. Have a PR professional do this.
3. Place the release. Decide which newspapers and to whom at the newspapers to send it, and send it. A PR professional should do this.
4. Arrange for follow-up. Have a contact name on the release. The contact should place a follow-up telephone call if there is no response in 2 weeks. The contact should deal with any responses that come in by helping to arrange interviews and photos and answering questions.

January

It is a new year. Place an article with NP advice on annual health maintenance. Suggestions include the time to schedule a mammogram, Pap smear, and yearly cholesterol check.

February

It is flu season. Place an article with NP advice entitled, "The Five Best Ways to Avoid Passing the Flu."

March

It is spring break time. Place an article with NP advice on avoiding ruining spring break, covering points such as wearing seat belts, consuming alcohol only in moderation, and not skiing alone.

April

It is pollen season. Place an article with NP advice for allergy sufferers.

May

It is prom season. Place an article with NP advice on avoiding the consequences of unprotected sex. Recycle the information from March because it applies to prom season and can never be said too many times.

June

It is sunbathing season. Place an article with NP advice on maintaining healthy skin.

July

It is poison ivy season. Place an article with NP advice on treating and avoiding poison ivy.

August

It is hot. Place an article with NP advice on avoiding dehydration and overheating, especially for individuals with other medical problems.

September

It is back-to-school time. Place an article with NP advice on up-to-date immunizations.

October

It is Halloween. Place an article with NP advice for parents on how to oversee safe trick-or-treating.

November

It is Thanksgiving. Place an article with NP advice on the benefits of moderate diet and exercise.

December

It is holiday season. Place an article with NP advice on how to recognize depression and discuss current treatments.

Some Talking Points for NPs

1. Every study of NP cost-effectiveness has shown that NPs are cost-effective primary care providers.
2. Every study of NP quality of care has shown that NPs provide effective and safe care.
3. Every study of patient satisfaction with NPs has shown that patients are very satisfied with them.
4. Research has been corroborated, no matter whether the researchers were nurses or physicians.
5. New York [change to your state, if applicable] law does not preclude NPs being on HMO provider panels. In the case of Medicaid and the Child Health Insurance Plan, NY law specifically names NPs as PCPs.
6. Federal law does not preclude NPs as PCPs. In fact, the Centers for Medicare & Medicaid Services policy for Medicaid patients mandates that managed-care organizations (MCOs) offer NP services.
7. MDs are fighting NP admission to provider panels because of the pressures of economic competition.
8. The American Medical Association surveyed physicians who employ NPs and found that the physicians think NPs operate with a high level of autonomy. In practice, physicians who hire NPs do not supervise NPs, but rather provide consultation when the NP requests it. It is only when it is suggested that the flow of money go straight to the NP that physicians begin to protest.
9. Experts agree that NPs are the way to go.
10. Unless NPs are admitted to provider panels, there will be no real world data on NP costs, effectiveness, attention to preventive measures, outcomes, or utilization. That research cannot be done unless NPs have a panel of patients and their practice patterns are tracked, as is done with physicians.
11. Patients deserve to have a choice of NP as provider. Let the customers decide what kind of healthcare provider they want.
12. Take the reins for controlling NPs out of the hands of physicians. Physicians have an economic conflict of interest.

13. Put the reins for controlling the quality of the NP profession in the same hands that control quality over other healthcare providers:
 (a) Licensing boards
 (b) Consumer-oriented groups (such as the National Committee for Quality Assurance and The Joint Commission)
 (c) The MCO credentialing process
 (d) MCO audits
 (e) Health Employer Data and Information Set (HEDIS) report cards
 (f) Medicare's Physician Quality Reporting System (PQRS)
14. NPs provide a perfect fit of provider and patient need.
15. There is still a shortage of PCPs in the Northeast [fill in your region].
16. The position of NPs is that NPs do primary care. If physicians want to do it too, fine. But do not try to impede NPs from practicing their profession.

Counterarguments to Medical Society Talking Points

Here are some arguments that physician organizations will make in attempting to erect barriers:

Admitting Privileges

Argument: NPs don't have admitting privileges. How will they care for hospitalized patients?
Answer: Many NPs have admitting privileges. In addition, some physicians don't have admitting privileges but still get on provider panels by arranging with hospitalists to take care of admitted patients. Some family practice physicians assert that they do a better job by concentrating on office visits and turning over admitted patients to hospitalists. NPs without admitting privileges arrange with a provider who does cover hospitalized patients.

Credentialing

Argument: We don't know how to credential NPs.
Answer: The following is the credentialing information most often asked of NPs:

- Geographic area of practice
- Work history
- Types of patients cared for (i.e., adults, pediatric, OB-GYN)
- Procedures done
- Partners practicing with
- MD collaborator
- States where licensed as NP, license number
- DEA number
- Degrees, year of graduation, and schools attended
- Certification (year, type, and granting agency)

- Specialty training (year and agency giving training)
- Three references
- Are there any suits against you that have resulted in damages? Are you listed with the National Practitioner Data Bank? Are you currently being sued for malpractice?
- Malpractice insurance policy number, carrier, limits, claims made, or occurrence

Malpractice Insurance

Argument: If we allow NPs to be PCPs, then their employer physicians will be more likely to be sued.

Answer: Ask your insurer about that. Our experience is that insurers have the policy that an NP is responsible for the NP's actions and a physician is responsible for the physician's actions. If an NP is the PCP, it makes sense that the NP, not the employer physician, is likely to be found liable. The physician employing an NP PCP is actually safer than if the NP is caring for the physician's patients, when if the NP makes a mistake, the physician is the official PCP.

Example Fact Sheet on NPs

About NPs

NPs are registered nurses with advanced preparation who provide primary healthcare services in offices and clinics, specialty care in physician offices, and acute care in hospitals and other facilities. NPs provide medical and educational services such as these:

- Complete physical examinations
- Health assessments and screenings (e.g., monitoring blood pressure, monitoring blood sugar levels for diabetic patients, giving routine gynecologic exams, and screening for high cholesterol levels)
- Treatment of common acute illnesses (e.g., bronchitis, skin infections, urinary tract infections, and gynecologic infections)
- Treatment of chronic stable medical conditions (e.g., diabetes, high blood pressure, asthma, ulcers, and high cholesterol levels)
- Health counseling services (e.g., smoking cessation, weight reduction, diet and exercise, medications and their side effects, effects of heavy drinking, and effects of high blood pressure on long-term health)

Education Requirements

NPs must complete a 2-year master's degree program in addition to obtaining an undergraduate college degree. Many NPs have or are getting doctoral degrees. All NPs have advanced training beyond their license as a registered nurse, but some may not have received a master's degree because this is a relatively new requirement.

Laws Regulating Activities for NPs

Licensure

NPs have licenses as registered nurses for which they must pass a national board examination. They must then pass an additional national board examination to become certified as an NP.

Diagnosis and Treatment

NPs may diagnose and treat patients under their own license. The NP determines when consultation with a physician or other health professional is necessary.

Scope of Practice

All primary care evaluations, procedures, and treatments are within the scope of practice for NPs. In addition, NPs may assist with surgery, do sigmoidoscopies, oversee exercise stress testing, excise skin lesions, suture and perform many of the procedures needed in acute care. NPs in most states may write for both controlled and noncontrolled medications without the cosignature of a physician.

Malpractice Actuarials

Lawsuits against NPs are rare. The rate of lawsuits against NPs is low, compared with a rate for physicians. For state-by-state comparisons, see The Pearson Report. (Online access is available for purchasers of this book.)

NPs may be sued for malpractice, and the physician affiliated through the written agreement (if one exists) may be named as codefendant. However, the physician is not automatically considered to be liable for a colleague NP's negligence.

Reimbursement

Medicare and Medicaid reimburse NPs directly, as do Blue Cross and many other insurers. Although out-of-state third-party payers are not required by law to reimburse NPs, many do so.

Employer Familiarity with NP Services

A recent informal survey of employers revealed that:

- Company presidents are familiar with NPs because they are seeing NPs when they themselves "visit the doctor."
- Company presidents have reported satisfaction with the care that they received from NPs.
- Employers are hungry for quality healthcare plans that offer savings on premiums.

CHAPTER 14

Standards of Care for Nurse Practitioner Practice

The traditional definition of standard of care has been, "such reasonable, ordinary care, skill, and diligence as used by practitioners in good standing in the same general type of practice, in similar cases."[1] Today, nurse practitioners (NPs) and other clinicians are judged not only by what other clinicians would do, but by what is best for the patient. Today, the standard of care addresses these questions:

- Did the clinician do the right thing at the right time?
- Was effective care provided to the patient?
- Was care provided safely and in an appropriate time frame?
- Was the outcome as good as expected, given the patient's condition and personal characteristics and the current state of medical science?

Who Is Monitoring the Standard of Care?

In the past, compliance with the standard of care was voluntary, performance was not measured or reported to the public, and often, the standard of care for a particular set of circumstances became clear only after a mistake was made, a lawsuit was filed, expert witnesses were hired, dual versions of the "standard of care" were argued by both sides of a malpractice case, and a jury accepted one side's version. Today, while the standard of care for NPs still may be scrutinized in a court of law, it is recognized that a minimum acceptable level of care can be determined outside the judicial system by consensus, with participation by consumers, providers, and agencies. The standards that are being developed will be continually reassessed and reset on the basis of research outcomes, analysis of costs and benefits, and the results of patient satisfaction measures.

The 1990s brought increased attention to quality standards for health care from people outside the medical profession, namely consumers and government agencies. That initiative has continued in the 21st century. Corporate and government purchasers of health services have joined medical and nursing professional organizations, licensing boards, and the judicial system in setting standards for healthcare providers. Standards of care are being monitored, publicized, and changed by the government and by several national

http://www.aanp.org/images/documents/publications/standardsofpractice.pdf; Courtesy of American Association of Nurse Practitioners.

consumer-oriented groups. Traditionally, standards of medical and nursing care were developed by clinicians and monitored by these groups:

- Professional societies
- State legislatures and state agencies
- Licensing boards
- Accreditation commissions
- The judicial system
- Employers

Standards of care are now being set, modified, monitored, and publicized by certain self-appointed consumer-oriented agencies, as well as government agencies. Those groups include:

- The National Committee for Quality Assurance (NCQA)
- The Joint Commission
- The Agency for Healthcare Research and Quality (AHRQ)
- Medicare

Professional Societies

The American Academy of Nurse Practitioners (AANP) has written the following standards for the process of care:[2]

Assessment of Health Status

The nurse practitioner assesses health status by:

- Obtaining a relevant health and medical history.
- Performing a physical examination based on age and history.
- Performing or ordering preventive and diagnostic procedures based on the patient's age and history.
- Identifying health and medical risk factors.

Diagnosis

The nurse practitioner makes a diagnosis by:

- Utilizing critical thinking in the diagnostic process.
- Synthesizing and analyzing the collected data.
- Formulating a differential diagnosis based on history, physical examination, and diagnostic test results.
- Establishing priorities to meet the health and medical needs of the individual, family, or community.

Development of a Treatment Plan

The nurse practitioner, together with the patient and family, establishes a mutually acceptable cost awareness plan of care that maximizes health potential. Formulation of the treatment plan includes:

- Ordering additional diagnostic tests.
- Prescribing/ordering appropriate pharmacologic and nonpharmacologic interventions.
- Developing a patient education plan.
- Appropriate consultation/referral.

Implementation of the Plan

Interventions are based upon established priorities. Actions by the nurse practitioner are:

- Individualized.
- Consistent with the appropriate plan of care.
- Based on scientific principles, theoretical knowledge, and clinical expertise.
- Consistent with teaching and learning opportunities.

Actions include:

- Accurately conducting and interpreting diagnostic tests.
- Prescribing pharmacologic agents and nonpharmacologic therapies.
- Providing relevant patient education.
- Making appropriate referrals to other health professionals and community agencies.

Follow Up and Evaluation of the Clients' Status

The nurse practitioner maintains a process for systematic follow up by:

- Determining the effectiveness of the treatment plan with documentation of patient care outcomes.
- Reassessing and modifying the plan as necessary to achieve medical and health goals.

Care Priorities

The nurse practitioner's practice model emphasizes:

A. Patient and Family Education
   The nurse practitioner provides health education and utilizes community resource opportunities for the individual and/or family.
B. Facilitation of Patient Participation in Self Care
   The nurse practitioner facilitates patient participation in medical and health care by providing information needed to make decisions and choices about the:

- Promotion, maintenance, and restoration of health
- Consultation with other appropriate healthcare personnel
- Appropriate utilization of healthcare resources

C. Promotion of optimal health
D. Provider of continually competent care
E. Facilitation of entry into the healthcare system
F. The promotion of a safe environment

Interdisciplinary/Collaborative Responsibilities

As a licensed, independent practitioner, the nurse practitioner participates as a team leader and member in the provision of health and medical care, and interacting with professional colleagues to provide comprehensive care.

Accurate Documentation of Patient Status and Care

The nurse practitioner maintains accurate, legible, and confidential records.

Responsibility as Patient Advocate

Ethical and legal standards provide the basis of patient advocacy. As an advocate, the nurse practitioner participates in health policy activities at the local, state, national, and international levels.

Quality Assurance and Continued Competence

Nurse practitioners recognize the importance of continued learning through:

- Participation in quality assurance review, including systematic review of records and treatment plans on a periodic basis
- Maintenance of current knowledge by attending educational programs
- Maintenance of certification in compliance with current state law
- Applying standardized care guidelines in clinical practice

Adjunct Roles of Nurse Practitioner

Nurse practitioners combine the roles of provider, mentor, educator, researcher, manager, and consultant. The nurse practitioner interprets the role of the nurse practitioner to individuals, families, and other professionals.

Research as Basis for Practice

Nurse practitioners support research by developing clinical research questions, conducting or participating in studies, and disseminating and incorporating findings into practice.

State Legislatures and State Agencies

Some states address NP standards of care in their laws.

In Montana, for example, the board of nursing must approve the method of an advanced practice nurse's quality assurance prior to issuance of prescriptive authority. Montana law mandates that the quality assurance method include the following:

(1) Within one month of initiating an APRN practice involving direct patient care the APRN shall submit a quality assurance plan to the board.
(2) A quality assurance plan includes the following elements:
    (a) location of the APRN's practice site(s);
    (b) identification of the APRN's peer reviewer or peer review organization. Peer review must occur on a quarterly basis and include review of 15 charts or 5% of all charts handled by the APRN, whichever is fewer. The peer reviewer must work in the same practice specialty as the APRN and must hold an unencumbered license.

If the APRN has prescriptive authority, the peer reviewer must also have prescriptive authority;

(c) standards of practice set by the APRN's national professional organization, which the peer reviewer will use to evaluate the APRN's practice;

(d) criteria for client referrals, patient outcomes, and chart documentation set by the APRN's national professional organization that the peer reviewer will use to evaluate the APRN's practice; and

(e) description of the method the peer reviewer will use to address areas in need of attention or improvement, if indicated, and to ensure follow-up evaluation.

(3) By December 31 of each license renewal year, the APRN shall submit a quality assurance report to the board on the form provided by the department. The biennial quality assurance report shall:

(a) provide verification that each quarterly peer review has occurred;

(b) provide verification that area(s) identified by the peer reviewer as needing attention and improvement have been appropriately addressed according to the APRN's stated plan; and

(c) inform the board of any change in the location of the APRN's practice site(s), the identity of the peer reviewer, or the quality assurance criteria established by the national professional organization in the APRN's specialty area of practice.

Citation: MT Admin. R. § 24.159.1466.

Indiana law sets the following standards for each NP:

1. Assess clients by using advanced knowledge and skills to:
   a. Identify abnormal conditions.
   b. Diagnose health problems.
   c. Develop and implement nursing treatment plans.
   d. Evaluate patient outcomes.
   e. Collaborate with or refer to a practitioner as defined in IC 25-23-1-19.4 in managing the plan of care.

2. Use advanced knowledge and skill in teaching and guiding clients and other health team members.

3. Use appropriate critical thinking skills to make independent decisions, commensurate with the autonomy and responsibilities of an NP.

4. Function within the legal boundaries of their advanced practice area and have and utilize knowledge or the statutes and rules governing their advanced practice area, including the following:
   a. State and federal drug laws and regulations
   b. State and federal confidentiality laws and regulations
   c. State and federal medical record access laws

5. Consult and collaborate with other team members.

6. Recognize the limits of individual knowledge and refer as appropriate.

7. Retain professional accountability for any delegated intervention, and delegate only as authorized by IC 25-23-1 of this title.
8. Maintain current knowledge and skills in the NP area.
9. Conduct assessment of clients and families which may include health history, family history, physical examination, and evaluation of risk factors.
10. Assess normal and abnormal findings obtained from the history, physical examination, and laboratory results.
11. Evaluate clients and families regarding development, coping ability, and emotions and social well being.
12. Plan, implement, and evaluate care.
13. Develop individualized teaching plans with each client based on health needs.
14. Counsel individuals, families, and groups about health and illness and promote attention to wellness.
15. Participate in periodic joint evaluation of services rendered, including but not limited to chart review, client evaluations, [and] outcomes statistics.
16. Conduct and apply research findings appropriate to each area of practice.
17. Participate when appropriate, in the joint review of the plan of care.

Citation: Ind. Admin. Code tit. 848, r. 4-2-1.

Licensing Boards

Licensing boards carry out the statutes of the state and write and administer rules and regulations for nursing practice, based on statute.

Licensing boards enforce standards in the following ways:

- Ensuring that qualifications are up to date by authorizing licensing
- Responding to complaints from consumers, employers, colleagues, or patients
- Following up on malpractice awards monitored through the National Practitioner Data Bank to determine whether a nurse was grossly negligent in providing care

Boards of nursing do not test NPs or do audits of NP practices. An NP who is sued for malpractice will not necessarily be investigated by the state board of nursing. If, however, a judge, attorney, or plaintiff reports a nurse for suspected gross negligence, the board of nursing will investigate.

Accreditation Commissions

The Joint Commission has accredited and monitored hospital practice and now evaluates health plans, clinics, and medical groups through an accreditation program. The accreditation program is voluntary; however, hospital accreditation has become synonymous with staying in business. Health plan accreditation is also becoming a business necessity. Clinics and medical practices are not routinely accredited, but it is reasonable to expect that accreditation may become a standard in the future.

Through accreditation, committees set standards and conduct site visits to ensure that the standards are met. Providers of health care want to publicize the fact that they are accredited, so they make sure they meet the current standards.

The Judicial System

The judicial system becomes involved in NP practice only when a patient is injured and files a lawsuit. A healthcare provider's negligence (or lack thereof) is decided by a judge or jury on the basis of the law and the facts of the case. In a court case, each side may present, through expert witnesses, their interpretation of the "standard of care." The plaintiff will argue that the standard of care has been violated. The defendant is likely to argue that there has been no violation of the standard of care.

When a judge or a jury accepts one side's version of the standard of care, that version is affirmed for future cases, and for healthcare providers, because previous case decisions (precedent) affect future decisions.

Although one organization may publish one standard of care and an expert may testify to an alternate version of the standard of care, the judicial system is a final arbiter of standards.

Employers

Some employers develop performance standards for NPs. The following is an example of an employer-generated performance standard for NPs, addressing patient education:

> Criterion for evaluation: Provides health education to patients about ways to improve, promote, and maintain their health status, including but not limited to providing educational information on disease/disease processes, self-care practices, and positive lifestyle choices.
>
> Performance standards:
>
> 1. Assesses learning capabilities and readiness of population or individuals, and tailors education to meet age, developmental, and educational needs.
> 2. Prioritizes learning needs and documents them accordingly.
> 3. Ensures that time frame and subject matter are appropriate for target audience/individual.
> 4. Utilizes appropriate teaching materials.
> 5. Initiates, designs, and completes educational programs for patients, families, and targeted audiences.
>
> (Exceeds) Demonstrates a high degree of effectiveness in fulfilling standard as observed by supervising physician.[3]

The National Committee for Quality Assurance (NCQA)

The NCQA is a consumer-oriented group directed by representatives from major employers, insurers, and the government. The NCQA accredits managed-care organizations (MCOs) and health plans. It has developed a set of clinical performance measures and patient satisfaction surveys that the group believes represents the consumer's interests. Those performance measures are being applied to health plans around the country, and the results of the measures are being reported in the news media. Health plans voluntarily collect the performance data, hoping to rate high, receive accreditation, receive media attention, and attract more enrollees.

Health plans and MCOs turn to medical groups and physician practices for much of the performance data. One prominent set of performance measures is the Health Plan Employer Data and Information Set (HEDIS). The NCQA changes HEDIS measures from time to time, so NPs must order their materials or check their website to ascertain the current measures. Some examples of HEDIS measures follow:[4]

1. Breast cancer screening
   Measure: Female patients aged 40 to 69 had at least one mammogram in the past 2 years.

2. Cervical cancer screening
   Measure: Women aged 21 to 64 had at least one Pap smear during the past 3 years.

3. Prenatal care in the first trimester
   Measure: Pregnant women had prenatal care in the first trimester.

4. Checkups after delivery
   Measure: Women who had a postpartum visit 21 to 56 days after delivery.

Agency for Healthcare Research and Quality (AHRQ)

The AHRQ is a government agency with the mission of improving quality, safety, and efficiency in health care. The AHRQ has convened panels of experts that developed standards on certain illnesses, including the following:

- Myocardial infarction (April 2005)
- Acute pain management (February 1992)
- Urinary incontinence in adults (March 1992)
- Prevention of pressure ulcers (May 1992)
- Cataract in adults (February 1993)
- Depression in primary care (April 1993)
- Sickle cell disease in infants (April 1993)
- Early HIV infection (January 1994)
- Benign prostatic hyperplasia (February 1994)
- Management of cancer pain (March 1994)
- Unstable angina (March 1994)
- Heart failure (June 1994)
- Otitis media with effusion in children (July 1994)
- Quality determinants of mammography (October 1994)
- Acute low back problems in adults (December 1994)
- Treatment of pressure ulcers (December 1994)
- Poststroke rehabilitation (May 1995)
- Cardiac rehabilitation (October 1995)
- Smoking cessation (October 1996)
- Recognition and initial assessment of Alzheimer's and related diseases (October 1996)

Some of these standards have been changed or retired as new evidence has become available. For access to current guidelines, visit the website (http://www.ahrq.gov). One AHRQ project is the National Guideline Clearinghouse, which is a web-based resource for information on evidence-based clinical practice guidelines. The clearinghouse describes guidelines developed by professional societies and associations, as well as the U.S. Preventive Services Task Force. An example of one such guideline is "Management of Newly Diagnosed Type 2 Diabetes Mellitus (T2DM) in Children and Adolescents," developed in 2013 by the American Academy of Pediatrics.[5] The clearinghouse website (http://www.guideline.gov), while encouraging clinicians to use the guidelines, states that the recommendations may not be appropriate for use in all circumstances and that decisions to adopt any particular recommendation must be made in light of available resources and circumstances presented by individual patients.

Medicare

As part of an initiative to increase the quality of care to beneficiaries, Medicare, in 2006, asked physicians to voluntarily report their performance on specified quality measures. Information on these measures is available online (http://www.cms.gov). Search for "Physician Quality Reporting System."

How Should NPs Keep Current on Standard of Care?

NPs should use traditional methods of keeping current, including the following:

- Books
- Newsletters and list-serves
- Websites, such as Medscape.com, Epocrates.com, guideline.gov, and those of relevant professional societies
- Continuing education seminars
- Journals
- Other practitioners

In addition, and in light of newly emerging standards, NPs should also consult these sources:

- Audit tools used by MCOs
- Accreditation guidelines supplied by accrediting organizations
- NCQA standards
- AHRQ standards or guidelines
- State law, if standards are mandated by law

Credentialing

Another standard being developed under managed care is credentialing. Credentialing for most health plans is now being conducted largely by one nonprofit organization, the Council for Affordable Quality Health Care (CAQH). For more information about the organization and about how to get credentialed through CAQH, visit the website (http://www.caqh.org). Given the quantity and detail of questions being asked about applications for admission to provider panels, it is reasonable to expect that a set of standards based on credentials will emerge.

Utilization

Under managed care, not all standards for clinicians are related to the quality of patient care. Some standards look at quantity of care delivered. For example, NPs can expect that health plans will be looking at NP utilization of emergency room visits, hospitalization, specialist visits, and diagnostic testing.

Patient Satisfaction

There are emerging standards regarding patient satisfaction. For example, some health plans want practices to answer a telephone call within five rings, want patients to be able to get appointments within 72 hours, and do not want patients to have to wait more than 20 minutes after arrival for their appointment. These standards have evolved from research showing that patients are annoyed by unanswered telephones, long waits for appointments, and sitting in waiting rooms. Because health plans compete for patients, and because medical practices compete for admission to provider panels, it is reasonable to expect that certain customer service standards that are currently informal will be more forthrightly stated in the future.

Notes

1. Robert E. Shepherd, Jr., *The Law Of Medical Malpractice In Virginia*, 21 Wash. & Lee L. Rev. 212, 214 (1964), http://scholarlycommons.law.wlu.edu/wlulr/vol21/iss2/5
2. American Association of Nurse Practitioners. (2013). Standards of practice for nurse practitioners. Retrieved from http://www.aanp.org/images/documents/publications/standardsofpractice.pdf
3. Smith, M. A. (1996). Job description for primary care nurse practitioners. *The Nurse Practitioner, 21*, 160, 162–163.
4. National Committee for Quality Assurance. (n.d.). The Health Plan Employer Data and Information Set (HEDIS). Retrieved from http://www.ncqa.org/HEDISQualityMeasurement.aspx
5. Agency for Healthcare Research and Quality, National Guideline Clearinghouse (2013) Retrieved from http://www.guideline.gov

CHAPTER 15

Measuring Nurse Practitioner Performance

Standards of care and measures of performance are interrelated. Measures of performance are used to determine the extent to which standards of care are met. Measuring performance without standards is like playing a game without rules. Setting standards without measuring performance is like making laws when there are no police to enforce the laws.

Measuring Quality

In general, the quality of clinical care is assessed by asking and answering the following questions:

- Did the clinician do the right thing?
- Was the care effective?
- Was care given in an appropriate time frame?
- Was the outcome as good as could be expected, given each patient's condition and personal characteristics and the current state of medical science?

The standard of care for a particular episode of illness is assessed by asking and answering these questions:

- What was the correct treatment?
- What was the correct timing of treatment?
- What was the correct teaching or counseling?

Measures of the standard of care ask and answer these questions:

- Did the clinician follow the standard?
- Did the patient's problem resolve?
- Did the problem resolve within the expected time frame?
- If the problem did not resolve and the clinician did not expect that it would resolve, did the patient's quality of life improve or did bothersome symptoms decrease in severity?
- Were the resources used to solve the problem in line with what would be expected for that problem?
- Was the patient satisfied with the experience of care?
- Was the patient satisfied with the outcome?

Multiple Measures, Multiple Measurers

Nurse practitioner (NP) performance is evaluated on several levels: productivity, utilization, and patient satisfaction, as well as the quality of clinical decision making. An NP's performance is judged by employers, patients, health plan auditors, peers, and possibly even researchers.

If an NP's performance is employer defined, then the NP will need to ascertain the values of the employer. To one employer, good performance might be synonymous with high billings, which could, because of time constraints, preclude giving adequate attention to each patient. For another employer, good performance might mean high scores on surveys of patient satisfaction. An NP who satisfies patients might not be a high biller. To yet another employer, good performance might mean close communication with the physician consultant, while in another practice it might mean independent functioning without the need for communication with a physician.

If performance is defined by the health plan, then a good performer is one who uses expensive resources—hospitals and emergency rooms—relatively infrequently.

If an NP's performance is defined by present performance measures developed by consumer-oriented groups, such as the National Committee for Quality Asurance (NCQA), an NP who sees that all children are properly immunized, who gets patients to quit smoking, and who raises the functional status of elderly patients will be seen as a good performer.

If an NP's performance is defined by peers, a good performer is likely to be an expert diagnostician who shares knowledge willingly with other NPs and who is compatible with other clinicians and staff.

If performance is defined by researchers, a good performer is one who meets the particular testing criteria studied by the researcher.

Finally, if performance is defined by patients, a good performer is one who does not make the patient wait more than 20 minutes in the waiting room before being seen, who is patient and polite, and who does not miss a serious diagnosis.

There is no single, widely accepted set of measures of an NP's worth or performance. In this chapter, several measures of performance are summarized.

Productivity

Definitions

A definition of productivity may depend upon the setting and the method of payment to the practice.

In a practice that gets reimbursed according to a fee-for-service structure, a productive NP is one who sees many patients, at a 99213 level or above, and who bills often for additional services that generate revenue, such as suturing, incision and drainage, and endometrial biopsy.

In a practice that receives mostly capitated payments, an NP who efficiently handles a large panel of patients with little use of the practice's resources—staff, materials, time—is a good performer.

If an NP is employed by a nursing home, productivity may mean keeping elderly patients out of the hospital, while imparting to their families the feeling that their loved one is being closely monitored and well cared for.

Measurement

In a fee-for-service practice, a simple way of measuring performance is to set the number of visits conforming to the evaluation and management Current Procedural Terminology (CPT) codes. For example, good performance could be set at 20 visits at levels 99211 to 99215 per day. One would not want to set a specific code as a performance measure because it is the patient's need for evaluation and management services that determines the CPT code billed, and a provider cannot predict what level of visit will be needed.

In a capitated practice, good performance could be set at maintenance of an 1800-member panel of patients, with patient satisfaction, as measured by a particular tool, at 80% or above.

In a nursing home practice, good performance could be measured by decreasing, over a previous year, the number of hospital visits among the nursing home's residents.

For a detailed discussion of NP productivity, see "Productivity Incentive Plans for Nurse Practitioners: How and Why" by Carolyn Buppert (http://www.buppert.com).

Housekeeping Performance Measures

NPs may have more experience with "housekeeping" forms of performance measurement than with substantive forms such as the Physician Quality Report System or the Health Plan Employer Data and Information Set (HEDIS). For example, many NPs' charts are audited for such things as clear labeling of allergies, initialing and dating of laboratory results, patient name on every page, and a completed problem list. While these are important matters, in the future, NPs should expect that audits will become increasingly more oriented toward outcomes.

NCQA Measures of Clinical Performance

Nonclinicians have begun to get involved in measuring clinical performance. After putting out a call for performance measures, NCQA received 800 suggestions and developed HEDIS and a set of clinical performance measures aimed largely at primary care providers. Presumably HEDIS is some indication of what employers, consumers, and health plan executives think is important for healthcare providers to accomplish. The HEDIS measures are still being refined.

Among the evaluation measures set by HEDIS for primary care providers are these:

- At least 80 percent of female patients age 40 to 69 had at least one mammogram in the past 2 years.
- Eighty-two percent of women age 21 to 64 had at least one Pap smear during the past 3 years.
- Ninety-seven percent of pregnant women began prenatal care during the first trimester of pregnancy.

Some of these data are collected from the Center for Medicare & Medicaid Services 1500 (billing) forms. Other data are collected by auditors who review charts or from surveys. HEDIS also looks at these indicators:

- Whether women had a postpartum visit 21 and 56 days after delivery
- Whether patients who were hospitalized for mental illness and were seen on an outpatient basis by a mental health provider within 30 days after discharge

HEDIS measures change from time to time. For the current measures and benchmarks, visit the website (http://www.ncqa.org/HEDISQualityMeasurement.aspx).[1]

Other Measures

HEDIS is not the only set of performance measures, and NCQA is not the only organization looking after consumer interests and rating health plans and providers. Among the other organizations publishing performance measures are the Centers for Medicare & Medicaid Services, The Joint Commission, certain managed-care plans, certain state health departments, and the Agency for Healthcare Research and Quality. The performance measures advocated by these organizations overlap to some extent.

Formal Research

Researchers who have studied NP performance and compared it with physicians' performance have looked at the following measures:

- Whether NPs took a thorough history and gave appropriate treatment to a patient with a particular set of symptoms and history.[2]
- Whether NPs performed or followed up on a set of primary care tasks, such as follow-up on a low hematocrit and obtaining appropriate cancer screening tests.[3]
- Whether patients reported, on a survey, that their experience of care was satisfactory.[4]
- Whether NPs' care was cost-effective when all of the costs of care were tallied.[5]
- Whether the level of care in nursing homes was improved by NP participation.[6]
- Whether NPs controlled the blood pressure of patients diagnosed with hypertension to below 140/90.[7]

The performance of NPs was found to be at least as good as physicians' on these measures.

Patient Ratings

Many difficulties and intervening factors become apparent when one attempts to get patients to rate NP performance. Patients have their own set of beliefs about health and illness, which may affect their interpretation of the quality of care given to them. Patients may focus on nonclinical aspects of care that affect their experience. Patients may feel compelled to give a provider a good rating, fearing a turn in the relationship if they are critical. And surveys may reach a patient at a date much later than the care was given, when a patient has forgotten the bad or the good aspects of the care.

Nevertheless, patient-rated measures of performance are to be taken seriously. Whether or not an NP believes a patient's rating to be valid, much information can be gleaned from patient survey results. For example, if a patient's experience of care was influenced negatively by a grouchy receptionist, then attitude adjustment on the part of the receptionist is a relatively easy alteration for a practice to make.

Health plans, practices, and facilities often conduct patient surveys, and NPs would be wise to get copies of these various surveys and their results and to conduct visits and make corrections in problem areas accordingly.

Consumers are able to review other patients' experience with clinicians through commercial websites and through health plan sites. NPs thus are also advised to search such sites for comments about themselves and to make adjustments if needed.

Peer Review

Some accrediting organizations require that medical offices conduct regular peer review. There are many peer review tools in the NP literature.

Utilization

Because hospitals, emergency rooms, and specialists are high cost centers for health plans, health plans want providers to keep admissions and referrals to the emergency room and specialists at a minimum. Whether an NP works for a physician or is in independent practice, the NP can expect that in the world of managed care, someone will be looking at the numbers of admissions and referrals.

How to Get an "A" on Performance Report Cards

An NP who wants to shine on performance evaluations will determine who in a work setting is interested in what measures and will adapt his or her practice accordingly. If there are no adopted performance measures, the NP may want to adopt the self-evaluation routine given in **Appendix 15-A**.

The number of hoops through which NPs must jump continues to rise. Many more tasks are coming under scrutiny than ever before.

NPs who are only given 15 minutes to take care of a patient's episodic problem know the frustration of quickly leafing through a patient record to check on details. Whether a patient has been a smoker, whether a patient has been advised to quit, or whether a patient is up to date on healthcare maintenance—mammograms, immunizations, and Pap smears—often takes longer than 15 minutes to ascertain, even when the patient is sitting in the adjacent chair. Electronic medical records may decrease the amount of time NPs spend on healthcare maintenance in that some systems alert the clinician about tests needed and questions to ask. On the other hand, NPs may spend more time in the future on healthcare maintenance because they are reminded what is needed and attend to these needs.

Documentation of health maintenance checks was a problem long before HEDIS, NCQA, and even the term primary care provider came into common usage. Every primary care provider is familiar with the feeling of uneasiness that comes from scanning a chart for an established patient that contains no record—all in one place—of routine screening efforts and results. Occasionally, some thoughtful physician assistant, NP, or physician will have summarized a patient's chart in a progress note. The trick then becomes finding that progress note.

Some practices keep flowcharts to document healthcare maintenance. Some electronic medical records track and/or remind clinicians to attend to healthcare maintenance tasks. Practices that track health maintenance are far ahead of those that do not keep such information in a central place. But even practices that keep flowcharts need to know how health plans and Medicare have decided to "grade."

Ensuring Compliance

A simple tool, kept in the front of a chart or in a special section called "Performance Measures" or some similar title, can prompt busy providers to ask the pertinent questions; arrange the pertinent screens, tests, medications, classes, or counseling; and note the date when the work was done. Some electronic medical records are programmed to prompt clinicians to address health maintenance. One format for a tool is given in **Appendix 15-B**.

NPs who are employees can be motivated to keep checklists and flowcharts up to date by tying compliance to bonuses, conducting internal quality assurance audits and giving feedback to providers on their performance, and including this activity in job descriptions and evaluation tools.

Self-employed NPs will find their own rewards in keeping up with outside measures of performance. Finding a healthcare provider is no longer a matter of word of mouth. Patients usually go to providers who will be reimbursed by the patient's health plan. Retention on provider panels is likely to be contingent on satisfaction of performance measures. Those providers who meet the standards now being set by consumer-driven groups will end up with a thriving practice, which, after all, is the most traditional measure of performance.

The organizations doing the measuring, grading, and reporting have the mission of helping consumers. How logistically difficult it is for health plans and providers to comply with these measures is not the main concern of these organizations.

The hoops are not limited to clinical performance measures. HEDIS has included measures of access and availability of care, patients' satisfaction with their care experience, health plan stability, utilization of selected services, cost of care, and such services as new member orientation and translation services.

HEDIS details are not particularly accessible to consumers, health plans, or providers. Anyone can purchase HEDIS reports and explanations from the NCQA, but they are expensive.

Strategies for complying with the performance criteria set by the NCQA and Medicare include increasing clinicians' and administrators' knowledge of specific performance measures, delegating responsibility for continuous quality improvement, implementing systems for tracking compliance, attending to patient satisfaction, addressing the functional level of elderly patients, and rewarding clinicians and practice managers for compliance and high scores.

Notes

1. National Committee for Quality Assurance. (n.d.). The Health Plan Employer Data and Information Set (HEDIS). Retrieved from http://www.ncqa.org/HEDISQualityMeasurement.aspx
2. Avorn, J., Everitt, D. E., & Baker, M. W. (1991). The neglected medical history and therapeutic choices for abdominal pain: a nationwide study of 799 physicians and nurses. *Archives of Internal Medicine, 151,* 694–698.
3. Hall J. A., Palmer R. H., & Orav, E. J. (1990). Performance quality, gender and professional role. A study of physicians and nonphysicians in 16 ambulatory care practices. *Medical Care, 28,* 489–501.
4. Perry, K. (1995). Patient survey: Physician extenders. Why patients love physician extenders. *Medical Economics, 72,* 58, 63, 67.
5. Salkever D. S., Skinner E. A., Steinwachs D. M., & Katz, H. (1982). Episode-based efficiency comparisons for physicians and nurse practitioners. *Medical Care, 20,* 143–153.
6. Mahoney, D. F. (1994). The appropriateness of geriatric prescribing decisions made by nurse practitioners and physicians. *Image, 26,* 41–46.
7. Mundinger, M. O., Kane, R. L., Lenz, E. R., Totten, A. M., Wei-Yann, T., Cleary, P. D....Shelanski, M. L. (2000). Primary care outcomes in patients treated by nurse practitioners or physicians: A randomized trial. *Journal of the American Medical Association, 283,* 59–68.

NP Self-Evaluation

To fare well on clinical performance evaluations, an NP should set up a routine for self-evaluation. Tailor the questions to your own patients and practice. For example:

1. For each visit, have I asked the patient:
   - Are you smoking? (If so, advise patient to quit.)
   - Did you get an appointment promptly?
   - How long did you spend in the waiting room? Was the wait too long or was it acceptable?
   - Has this visit satisfied your expectations?

2. On each visit, have I consulted the chart for:
   - Up-to-date immunizations?
   - Up-to-date cancer screening: Pap, mammogram, colonoscopy?
   - Eye exam in the past year for diabetic patients?
   - Follow-up visit within 6 weeks of giving birth for postpartum patients?

3. If a patient has been hospitalized:
   - If for mental illness, was the patient seen by a mental health clinician within 30 days after discharge?

   To do utilization self-monitoring, for each quarter, keep a notebook with this information:

   - Patient admissions to hospitals
   - Referrals to the emergency department
   - Referrals to specialists
   - Number of patients seen per day

Health Maintenance Flowchart

Name: _____

Patient number: _____

Date of Birth: _____

Female Cancer Screening	Date	Result	Date	Result	Date	Result
Pap (21–64)						
Mammo (50–69)						

Adult Immunizations	Date	Result	Date	Result	Date	Result
Tetanus (all patients, q 10 yrs)						
Flu (q yr. > 50 y.o.)						
Pneumococcal (only for individuals > 65 y.o.)						

Childhood Immunizations	Date	Date	Date	Date
Diphtheria-tetanus-pertussis				
Polio				
MMR				
HIB				
Hep B				
Chicken Pox				
Pneumococcal conjugate				

CHAPTER 16

Resolving Ethical Dilemmas

There are a multitude of ethical issues that come up in nurse practitioner (NP) daily practice, including these:

- Whether or not to disclose to a patient that the NP or someone else at the practice made a mistake regarding the patient's care
- Whether the availability or lack of reimbursement should determine if a service is provided
- Whether participation in a research study is the best thing for a patient
- Whether a promise to a patient or family member not to disclose information to a family member or patient best serves that individual
- Whether and when curative treatments should be stopped
- When and how to terminate a relationship with a patient
- Whether or not to accept a gift or meal from a vendor or pharmaceutical representative
- Whether to discuss the deficiencies of a patient's insurance coverage with a patient
- Whether and how to tell a patient you are moving to another practice
- Whether and how to inform a patient that you believe the surgeon he or she has chosen is not competent

Examples

Consider these four situations.

Situation 1

While standing in line at the grocery store, you hear someone yell, "Help! This lady is having a seizure!" Behind you, a woman is on the floor, jerking around in a way you know is characteristic of a grand mal seizure. Several people are standing over her, calling out for help. You feel compelled to help but worry that you will get sued if something goes wrong and/or be accused of practicing medicine without a physician collaborator.

Situation 2

You get a letter from a pharmaceutical company inviting you to participate in a round table discussion hosted by the company. There will be 15 attendees, all NPs who provide women's health care. The topic will be treatment of hypercholesterolemia in the older woman.

The company has a prescription product for reducing cholesterol. The letter offers you $500 plus a gourmet dinner. The writer wants to send you a consulting contract.

Situation 3

You are arranging the annual conference for NPs in your state. You have heard from past conference chairs that some pharmaceutical manufacturers will engage in any and all of the following sponsorship activities:

- Purchase booth space in the exhibit hall
- Provide unrestricted grants for general conference overhead in return for a listing as sponsor on the program
- Fund specific speakers, including their speaking fee, travel expenses, slides, and handouts
- Purchase books as gifts for attendees
- Fund the travel expenses of some high-volume prescribers

You have the names and telephone numbers of several drug reps in your area. You are not sure what to ask for or what is appropriate under the new federal compliance program guidance for pharmaceutical manufacturers.

Situation 4

A patient of yours wants to quit smoking. His health plan will pay for Wellbutrin (buproprion), which is prescribed for depression, but not Zyban (buproprion), the same drug marketed for smoking cessation. You wonder whether it is "insurance fraud" to save the patient money by treating smoking cessation with a prescription for Wellbutrin, given that the medication and dosing is the same as Zyban.

Analyzing the Ethical Choices Inherent in These Situations

Situation 1: Providing Care on the Street

When faced with a scenario similar to Situation 1, an NP who ignores the person having a seizure is doing nothing illegal. There is no legal requirement that a healthcare provider pay attention to patients, even when a patient is sitting in front of the provider in a clinic. However, most healthcare providers feel an ethical, as well as business, responsibility to provide care for patients who come to the office. As for the individual who falls down in the street, has a seizure in public, or has had an automobile accident, the individual clinician may make his or her own decision about whether to become involved. The decision will be based on the clinician's analysis of whether he or she is ethically obligated to respond and whether other considerations outweigh any ethical dictates. Two NPs in the same situation may come to opposite conclusions.

Four forces encourage clinicians to provide care:

1. Fear of a lawsuit for malpractice, if he or she neglects to treat an illness
2. Fear of a charge of patient abandonment, if one does not give care

3. The need for compensation
4. The clinician's own values, which include the clinician's sense of ethical responsibility

Malpractice

For a successful malpractice lawsuit, four elements have to be satisfied. First, there must be a duty of care owed to the patient by the clinician. Second, the clinician has to have breached the standard of care. Third, there must be an injury to the patient. Fourth, the patient's injury must be causally related to the clinician's breach of the standard of care.

A clinician who provides care or advice for a person on the street establishes a duty of care. A clinician who walks by without offering advice or a service does not establish a duty of care. Thus, the clinician who chooses not to become engaged is shielded from a lawsuit for malpractice, because there is no duty of care.

Patient Abandonment

In the case of the woman seizing in the grocery store, a clinician cannot be charged with patient abandonment if the clinician never becomes engaged in the woman's care. Patient abandonment is defined slightly differently from state to state. It is often addressed on the websites for the board of nursing. For example, the Colorado Board of Nursing states that for patient abandonment to occur, the registered nurse has to have accepted the assignment and severed the relationship without giving reasonable notice to the appropriate person (such as a supervisor or patient) so that arrangements can be made for care by others. It is not patient abandonment, therefore, to refuse to accept an assignment or a patient–nurse relationship. Therefore, a nurse who walks by a person in distress on the street cannot be accused of patient abandonment.

Reimbursement

In a roadside assistance situation, reimbursement is not an issue, as there is no system under which a clinician can submit a bill for such care. The reimbursable settings of care are office, hospital, nursing home, patient's home, and domiciliary facility, and there are no procedure codes for the settings "sidewalk" and "grocery store."

Ethics

The clinician faced with a decision to ignore or become involved with an individual in distress will weigh his or her assessment of right and wrong and attempt to come to a decision in which his or her behavior conforms to a standard of right behavior. Some considerations might be as follows:

- Are there other people already helping the individual?
- Are my skills any more helpful than what is already being done for the individual? The NP can help shield the patient's head from hard or sharp surfaces, but so can the nonclinician bystander. If the NP has no education or experience in emergency medicine, the NP may not be any more qualified to help than another bystander.
- What, exactly, can I do for the patient? For example, the treatment for seizures is intravenous valium. The NP on the street has no valium to offer a patient. On the other hand, if

the situation is that an individual has fallen to the ground, apparently unconscious, and an NP knows cardiopulmonary resuscitation, then there is something the NP can offer.

- Do I have the legal authority to diagnose and treat in this situation? In most states, an NP needs a collaborative agreement with a physician to diagnose and treat, and those agreements do not usually extend to on-the-street encounters.
- Will I feel that I did not meet my own expectations of myself if I pass by without offering help?
- If I were the patient, and an NP walked by and saw me, would I want the NP to offer to help?

NPs make situation-by-situation decisions about whether to become involved with clinical care during "off" hours. There is no legal mandate to offer services. A clinician may choose to become involved or not, depending upon the situation and the clinician's analysis of what is the humane and reasonable thing to do.

Situation 2: Accepting Gifts or Payment from a Pharmaceutical Company

When a pharmaceutical company offers a clinician substantial remuneration for minimal work, it raises suspicions that the company is looking to create a situation where a clinician feels obligated to prescribe the company's medication.

Both the pharmaceutical industry and the federal government recently have adopted guidelines addressing the relationships between clinicians and pharmaceutical companies. The guidelines attempt to provide pharmaceutical companies with a yardstick by which to judge whether a gift or payment from a pharmaceutical company is a kickback to a clinician or a payment at fair market value for personal services rendered.

The questions that separate a kickback from a business arrangement for services are as follows:

- Is the clinician in a position to generate healthcare business for the manufacturer directly or indirectly?
- Is any one purpose of the remuneration to induce or reward the referral or recommendation of business payable in whole or in part by a federal healthcare program?[1]
- Does the arrangement have the potential to interfere with or skew clinical decision making?
- Does the arrangement or practice have the potential to increase costs to the federal healthcare programs, beneficiaries, or enrollees?
- Does the arrangement or practice have the potential to increase the risk of overutilization or inappropriate utilization?
- Does the arrangement or practice raise patient safety or quality of care concerns?[1]

The pharmaceutical industry's own "Code on Interactions with Healthcare Professionals" provides the following guidance:

> It is appropriate for consultants who provide services to be offered reasonable compensation for those services and to be offered reimbursement for reasonable travel, lodging, and meal expense incurred as part of providing those services.

Compensation and reimbursement that would be inappropriate in other contexts can be acceptable for bona fide consultants in connection with their consulting arrangements. Token consulting or advisory arrangements should not be used to justify compensating healthcare professionals for their time or their travel, lodging, and other out-of-pocket expense. The following factors support the existence of a bona fide consulting arrangement:

- A written contract specifies the nature of the services to be provided and the basis for payment of those services;
- A legitimate need for the services has been clearly identified in advance of requesting the services and entering into arrangements with the prospective consultants;
- The criteria for selecting consultants are directly related to the identified purpose and the persons responsible for selecting the consultants have the expertise necessary to evaluate whether the particular healthcare professionals meet those criteria;
- The number of healthcare professionals retained is not greater than the number reasonably necessary to achieve the identified purpose;
- The retaining company maintains records concerning and makes appropriate use of the services provided by consultants;
- The venue and circumstances of any meeting with consultants are conducive to the consulting services.[2]

The Office of the Inspector General (OIG) "Federal Register Notice on the Compliance Program Guidance for Pharmaceutical Manufacturers" issued in 2003 states the following: "In general, fair market value payments to small numbers of physician for bona fide consulting or advisory services are unlikely to raise any significant concern. Compensating physicians as 'consultants' when they are expected to attend meetings or conferences primarily in a passive capacity is suspect."[1] The OIG Guidance applies to healthcare professionals other than physicians.[1]

Both the Pharmaceutical Research and Manufacturers of America (PhRMA) Code and the OIG Guidance are targeted to the pharmaceutical industry. It is up to clinicians to get a sense of what is considered right and wrong on their part.

Hence, a clinician faced with Situation 2 should apply the tests now accepted as standard in the industry before accepting the invitation. Specifically, will the NP, having accepted the $500 and a fine dinner, be more likely to prescribe the company's medication, even though it will cost the patient or the patient's insurer much more than a generic product, than if the NP did not accept the money and dinner? And, if the answer is "no," is the NP being ethical accepting the money and dinner? Will the NP provide $500 worth of consultative services to the pharmaceutical company at the dinner?

Note that the latest edition of the PhRMA Code prohibits the provision of meals to clinicians, except when accompanied by an educational session in the clinician's office, hospital, or at a speaker event such as a conference, and it also prohibits the distribution of non-educational items such as pens. The organization decided that even a very small token can influence a clinician.[2]

Situation 3: Accepting Financial Support from a Pharmaceutical Company

The PhRMA Code has these caveats about pharmaceutical company involvement in third-party educational or professional meetings:

- Financial support should be given to the conference's sponsor rather than to an individual participant.
- Responsibility for and control over the selection of content, faculty, educational methods, materials, and venue should remain with the conference organizers.
- Pharmaceutical companies should not provide direct support for conference meals, though a conference director may decide to use general support money to pay for meals.
- Pharmaceutical companies may not support the expenses of participants.

For arrangements between physicians and other persons in a position to make or influence referrals, orders, or prescriptions that do not fit a safe harbor from the anti-kickback rule, the analysis that the OIG recommends is as follows:

- What degree of influence does the physician have, directly or indirectly, on the generation of business for the manufacturer?
- Does the remuneration take into account, directly or indirectly, the volume or value of business generated?
- Is the remuneration more than trivial in value?
- Do fees for services exceed the fair market value of any legitimate, reasonable, and necessary services rendered by the physician to the manufacturer?
- Does the remuneration have the potential to affect costs to any of the federal health-care programs or their beneficiaries or to lead to overutilization or inappropriate utilization?
- Would acceptance of the remuneration diminish, or appear to diminish, the objectivity of professional judgment?
- Are there patient safety or quality of care concerns?
- If the remuneration relates to the dissemination of information, is the information complete, accurate, and not misleading?

A safe harbor from violation of the anti-kickback is described as follows:

> Personal services and management contracts. As used in Section 1128B of the Act, "remuneration" does not include any payment made by a principal to an agent as compensation for the services of the agent, as long as all of the following seven standards are met:
>
> (1)   The agency agreement is set out in writing and signed by the parties.
> (2)   The agency agreement covers all of the services the agent provides to the principal for the term of the agreement and specifies the services to be provided by the agent.
> (3)   If the agency agreement is intended to provide for the services of the agent on a periodic, sporadic, or part-time basis, rather than on a full-time basis for the term of the agreement, the agreement specifies exactly the schedule

of such intervals, their precise length, and the exact charge for such intervals.

(4) The term of the agreement is for not less than 1 year.

(5) The aggregate compensation paid to the agent over the term of the agreement is set in advance, is consistent with fair market value in arms-length transactions and is not determined in a manner that takes into account the volume or value of any referrals or business otherwise generated between the parties for which payment may be made in whole or in part under Medicare, Medicaid, or other federal healthcare programs.

(6) The services performed under the agreement do not involve the counseling or promotion of a business arrangement or other activity that violates any state or federal law.

(7) The aggregate services contracted for do not exceed those which are reasonably necessary to accomplish the commercially reasonable business purpose of the services.

For purposes of Paragraph (d) of this section, an agent of a principal is any person, other than a bona fide employee of the principal, who has an agreement to perform services for, or on behalf of, the principal.

Citation: 42 C.F.R. § 1001.952(d).

As described in Situation 3, an NP arranging the annual state conference may arrange for pharmaceutical manufacturers to do the following:

- Purchase booth space in the exhibit hall at which they will distribute information
- Provide unrestricted grants for general conference overhead, in return for a listing as sponsor on the program
- Fund specific speakers, including speaking fee, travel expenses, slides, and handouts, as long as the information the speakers provide is educational and consistent with patient safety

Situation 4: Prescribing Medications

It may be ethical to try to save the patient money, but it is illegal—fraud—to diagnose depression in a patient whose mood is normal so that the patient can get a prescription covered by insurance.

Here is what the U.S. Code says about fraud:

Whoever knowingly and willfully executes, or attempts to execute, a scheme or artifice (1) to defraud any healthcare benefit program; or (2) to obtain, by means of false or fraudulent pretenses, representations, or promises, any of the money or property owned by, or under the custody or control of, any healthcare benefit program, in connection with the delivery of or payment for healthcare benefits, items, or services, shall be fined under this title or imprisoned not more than 10 years, or both. If the violation results in serious bodily injury (as defined in Section 1365 of this title), such person shall be fined under this title or imprisoned not more than 20 years, or both; and if the violation results in death, such person shall be fined under this title, or imprisoned for any term of years or for life, or both.

Citation: 18 U.S.C. § 1347.

Is it fraud if you diagnose "smoking," and prescribe Wellbutrin? Probably not, because you are not deceiving anyone. However, the insurer is likely to deny payment for the Wellbutrin.

Is it fraud if you diagnose "depression" and omit any reference to smoking? Yes. Is it fraud if you diagnose "depression" and "smoking" and prescribe Wellbutrin? Probably not. However, ask yourself if you can make the argument, with a straight face, that the patient is both depressed and a smoker, or that he is using nicotine to self-medicate for depression, or that he may be depressed about his smoking. In addition, before taking that route, consider that unless a patient is truly depressed, you may not want to enter that diagnosis unless the patient agrees that he is depressed. In the future, the patient may want to authorize release of his medical record to a prospective employer. If that happens, you do not want the patient to be surprised and upset to find that he has a documented history of depression. Furthermore, are you ready to follow up your diagnosis of depression by addressing that problem in subsequent visits by performing and documenting one of the depression scales? Are you prepared to follow the standard of care for treatment of depression, that is, to treat for 12 months?

A clinician may have the best intentions—to relieve the patient's problem and save the patient money—but the risk probably outweighs the benefits in these situations.

Ethical Analyses

In general, NPs might approach a situation with ethical considerations in the following manner:

- Gather information.
  - Is this a legal, rather than ethical question?
  - Is there a law governing this situation?
  - Consider laws governing:
    - Scope of practice
    - Kickbacks
    - Patient privacy and confidentiality
    - Billing Medicare, Medicaid, and commercial insurers
    - Good Samaritan laws
    - End-of-life issues such as the decision not to resuscitate
  - Who is benefitting from this situation? How?
  - Who is being hurt or could be hurt by this situation? How?
  - Do I have a gut feeling about what is the right or wrong course of action in this situation?
  - Am I being swayed by what is beneficial to me or my group?

- What would other ethical practitioners do?
- Does my state board of nursing have any guidance regarding this situation on their website?
- Does my malpractice insurance cover me in this situation?

- Structure a plan.
  - Identify the course of action you would like to take.
  - Identify alternate approaches.
  - Identify the pros and cons of the preferred course of action, as well as the alternative approaches.

- If it is a patient care matter, present the issue to the patient, if appropriate.
- Tell the patient that you would like him or her to direct you in this situation.
- If it is a business matter, consult with your partners, committee members, employer, and/ or employees.
- If there is a code of conduct from a governmental agency, a professional society, or your own institution that applies, then follow the dictates of that code.

- Make a decision.
  - Prepare, for yourself, an argument that supports your decision. Carry out your plan.
- If you decide later that you made the wrong decision, learn from your mistake.

Of course, every situation is different and is accompanied by nuances that are beyond the scope of this text. To explore medical ethics and problem solving, an excellent reference is a recent book by Dr. Bernard Lo.[3]

Notes

1. Department of Health and Human Services, Office of the Inspector General. (2003, April 18). Compliance Program Guidance for Pharmaceutical Manufacturers. Retrieved from http://oig.hhs.gov/authorities/docs/03/050503FRCPGPharmac.pdf
2. Pharmaceutical Research and Manufacturers of America. (2009). PhRMA Code on Interactions with Healthcare Professionals. Retrieved from http://www.phrma.org/code-on-interactions-with-healthcare-professionals
3. Lo, B. (2013). *Resolving ethical dilemmas: A guide for clinicians*. Philadelphia, PA: Lippincott, Williams & Wilkins.

CHAPTER 17

Strategies for Nurse Practitioners

The difference between making do and advancing is like the difference between eating all of what is put on one's plate and deciding what to have for dinner. Unfortunately, many of today's nurse practitioners (NPs) are simply making do.

NPs faced with restrictive or outdated laws often report at professional meetings that they are proud of how they are able to function despite the law. For example, NPs who want to own their own businesses can construct a private practice that conforms to the law by hiring a physician consultant. NPs practicing in states where the law requires physician oversight to prescribe can do so as long as a physician takes the necessary steps to conform to the state's requirements. NPs who cannot be designated as primary care providers (PCPs) and handle panels of managed-care patients may actually perform the patient care if a physician is designated as the PCP. In these cases, NPs say their reward is that patients know that they are providing their care and appreciate NPs' efforts.

Although many NPs are making the best of existing law, in many states, the law is still unsatisfactory. The states where NPs are free to practice their profession without mandatory participation by physicians are still in the minority.

Opportunities in a Changing Field

In states where barriers to NP practice have been lifted and where reimbursement is attainable from third-party payers, there are opportunities for healthcare delivery systems that increase attention to preventive medicine, increase access to citizens, and provide alternatives to expensive physician-oriented systems.

Under a see-a-nurse-first system, patients initially are seen by a registered nurse or NP. The nurses take care of as many of a patient's healthcare problems as is prudent, and then seek consultation and referral for those problems that exceed the scope of their practice. **Figure 17-1** depicts a see-a-nurse-first system.

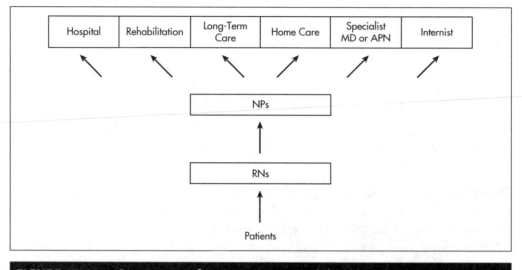

FIGURE 17-1   See-a-nurse first primary care delivery system.

Source: © Carolyn Buppert. Reprinted by permission.

Opponents of the See-a-Nurse-First System

Physicians often oppose the see-a-nurse-first system of healthcare delivery. The American Academy of Family Physicians (AAFP) issued the following policy regarding NP practice: "The nurse practitioner should not function as an independent health practitioner. The AAFP position is that the nurse practitioner should only function in a collaborative practice arrangement under the direction and responsible supervision of a practicing, licensed physician."[1]

Some patients may be suspicious of a see-a-nurse-first system as well. For that reason, patients should be offered a choice of nurse and/or physician providers. Once the law offers a level playing field, both physicians and NPs will have incentives to improve their services to patients and will advance their respective professions.

Challenges for NPs Attempting to Advance the Profession

First, there is the matter of the energy required. NPs are accustomed to relying on volunteer organizations. Now is the time to hire professionals, however. Public relations experts, not volunteers, develop public relations campaigns for physician organizations. Physicians do not expect to see 30 patients at the office, stop by the hospital on the way home, and then get together at 8 PM to develop public relations campaigns. Physician organizations hire public relations firms or retain in-house staff whose sole job is to attend to the public image of physicians. NPs can hire professionals, too, and they should. Much publicity can be gained with a small budget and creative public relations professionals.

Second, there is the challenge of publicizing the good in NPs and comparing NP services to physician services without denigrating physicians. The solution to that challenge is to continue to publicize the studies that have shown that NPs are as competent providers of primary care as physicians.

Third, there is the phenomenon that every action generates a reaction. When physicians see NPs step up efforts to advance the profession, they may feel it necessary to react with more aggressive efforts. NPs who are intimidated by this should focus on their goal of advancing the profession to stay on course.

The major focus of physician arguments—that only physicians should have the authority to direct primary care—is the educational differential between NPs and physicians. However, physicians set their own educational level, and there has been no major study of physician education and training since 1910, when Abraham Flexner published a report commissioned by the Carnegie Foundation that called for medical training to be university-affiliated programs rather than 8-month programs where students came without a high school diploma.[2] There are no studies showing that the appropriate education for providing primary care is 4 years of medical school and 3 years of residency, which is the education for all physicians, whether they are brain surgeons, researchers into neurotransmitters, or providers of primary care. On the contrary, there are many studies showing that NPs are quite appropriate providers of primary care.

Strategies to Implement Collectively

NPs are familiar with the advantages of working collectively toward change. First, individuals can pool money and thus gain more purchasing power than an individual NP. Second, groups are taken more seriously by lawmakers and political parties than are individuals.

Marshalling support of even homogeneous groups is no small accomplishment. In the case of NPs, a stumbling block to collective action is the heterogeneity of NPs, as not every NP has the same professional interests, the same viewpoint, or the same goals. For example, NPs who are professors have professional goals that include getting government funding for their educational programs. NPs who are clinicians do not have educational funding as a top-priority goal. Instead, they have the goal of being able to practice with few barriers.

Nevertheless, organizations are necessary for the advancement of the NP profession. NPs inspire, encourage, and rejuvenate other NPs, which is necessary when the goals are long term.

Ten Organizational Strategies

The following ten strategies are suggested for NPs who want to advance the profession and/or their own opportunities.

Set a Goal

For example, one NP set herself a goal of becoming a PCP credentialed by health plans. She built up a base of loyal patients, became an excellent clinician, and worked with the state's organization of NPs to change the law so that an NP could be designated by a health maintenance organization (HMO) as a PCP. She succeeded.

Of course, NPs work not only in primary care, but also in specialty practices and tertiary care. In every setting, NPs need to choose an achievable and reasonable goal, one that affects not only themselves, but also other NPs.

Analyze the Law for Barriers

There is much ignorance and confusion about the law as it affects NPs. Some NPs say, "The law says we need to be supervised, but we really practice independently." By participating in a practice situation where the limits of the law are stretched, NPs are taking a risk. In some states, the law puts responsibility squarely on the NP for ensuring that supervisory requirements are met. Clinics, hospitals, and medical groups have little to lose if they provide little or no supervision and let NPs go as far as their desire for intellectual adventure and their professional judgment allows. NPs are bringing in at least $150 per hour and getting paid about $40 per hour. If an NP makes few mistakes and no one enforces the law, everything runs smoothly. However, the better an NP does with independent decision making, the more momentum builds for more independence, and pretty soon the NP is out on a limb, with no physician available to answer telephone calls to help, much less supervise. As soon as an NP makes a mistake, the burden is back on the NP for not seeking supervision. If the NP is a practice owner making $150 per hour and willing to take a risk, that is one thing, but if the NP is an employee earning $40 per hour, the risk outweighs the benefits.

Some NPs have argued that current law and custom permit them to practice in a satisfying manner and ask, "Why open a can of worms by attempting to change the law?" This argument not only offends a sense of legal "neatness," where law and current practice jibe, but also condones a timidity that is incongruent with the level of assertion needed to perform as an NP. Why would NPs participate in life-and-death decisions for patients and yet retreat from challenging statutory omissions that relegate NPs to the invisible category of "others" or "nonphysicians"?

Every NP needs a copy of every law that affects their practice. That includes law that does not mention NPs but that affects NPs because of the omissions. For example, every NP needs a copy of the NP scope of practice in the state where they are licensed and practicing.

National NP organizations need fact sheets that cover federal law regarding:

- Delegation of duties in nursing home care
- Direction of the care of hospitalized patients
- Anti-kickback laws
- Definition of medical care and medical care provider
- Application for Drug Enforcement Administration numbers
- Reimbursement by Medicare and Medicaid
- Coding and billing of Medicare and Medicaid visits
- Documentation guidelines
- Definition of collaboration

Because the officers and board members of NP organizations change from year to year, NP organizations should maintain a current file of the relevant law for each new officer to review at the start of the term. Much anxiety will be avoided if NPs have copies of the exact language of the law.

Lobby for Eradication of the Barriers

Once the barriers are known, organizations can enlist lobbyists to help eradicate them. NPs may make progress in one area, such as convincing managed-care organizations (MCOs) to admit NPs to panels, only to find that there is some phrase in state law that a state administrator interprets as barring NPs from becoming PCPs.

NPs should not expect to win passage of new legislation the first time it is introduced. Each time an issue is lobbied, more information comes out about NPs, and the idea of NPs becomes more familiar and palatable to lawmakers.

NPs may argue that if certain issues are brought up, they may lose ground in the law rather than gain it. NPs ask, "What if we introduce a law, but it is amended and passed at the last minute, and our authority to prescribe is lost?" While that is a possibility, it is not probable. Compare a situation an NP faces every day in clinical practice: A patient arrives complaining of low back pain. In 99% of cases, the back pain is due to musculoskeletal strain and will respond to rest and nonsteroidal anti-inflammatory drugs. In one case out of 100, the back pain will be something else, and in a very minuscule percentage of cases, the low back pain will be cancer. Does the NP rush all patients who complain of low back pain to magnetic resonance imaging at the first visit? No. Likewise, the chance that NPs, by introducing legislation to advance the profession, will actually fall backward is minuscule, for the following reasons. First, NPs are valuable to medical groups, hospitals, HMOs, and health departments. Second, a good lobbyist, as well as a sponsor of a bill, will follow it very closely. It is unlikely that a bill that was introduced on behalf of NPs will be amended without the knowledge of the NPs' lobbyist. Because the lobbyist is hired by an NP organization, it is unlikely that a lobbyist will be caught unaware or will fail to rally the NP organization client when necessary. Third, there is virtually no opposition to NPs as healthcare providers other than from organized physician groups, and then only when NPs are striving to release the legal apron strings that tie NPs to physicians. NPs should not be deterred by the prospect of introducing a bill five times before it is passed. If it takes 5 years to get a bill passed, so be it.

Sell MCOs and Purchasers of Health Services on NPs as PCPs

NPs can offer MCOs and employers, who purchase healthcare services for their employees, quality services at a reasonable cost. However, NPs cannot depend on health plan purchasers to know what NPs can do unless they educate them.

MCOs and business executives are used to listening to business presentations from those who want to sell services. NPs are not used to giving business presentations, but they can learn. Alternatively, NP organizations can retain the services of professionals who make business presentations to do the work on their behalf.

The basic message of a business presentation on why MCOs and businesses should contract with NPs as PCPs is that NPs give high-quality care at a reasonable price. The message should be supported by data demonstrating the quality of NP care and numbers demonstrating the rationale of the pricing schedule. Finally, MCOs and businesses need to know how they can contract with NPs, that is, where the NPs are located and whom to contact.

Promote NPs to the Public

For the most part, individuals who have experienced the care of an NP have been satisfied. However, there is still too great a number of people who have never experienced the care of NPs. Promotional efforts need to be aimed at the "unconvinced" segment of the population.

Further, some individuals who have experienced the care of NPs and been satisfied may not know that NPs are responsible for the care they provide. People may believe that NPs simply relay what a physician has decided and that NPs are simply physician helpers. NPs need to establish themselves as experts. That can be done, for example, through newspaper articles where NPs give advice on healthcare topics, through talk radio, through television public service announcements, through paid advertising, through presentations at community events, through journal articles, and through one-on-one interactions between NPs and patients.

Work the Data

All studies done on the care given by NPs are supportive of NPs. This includes many studies done by physicians and operations researchers, as well as studies done by nurses. NPs need to cite and recite the data in language that a layperson can understand. NPs also need to compile their own data on the effectiveness of their care. For example, electronic medical records systems now allow clinicians who treat diabetes to produce data that compare the effectiveness of individual clinicians at controlling patients' HgAlc. While physicians are hashing and rehashing the educational differences between NPs and physicians, NPs need to be repeating the data that support the assertion that NPs give good care. Therefore, the educational differential, while significant, must not be relevant. As mentioned earlier, to date, physicians have no data to prove that their additional years of education make them better PCPs than NPs.

Hire Professionals to Do the Association's Work

It is time to hire professionals and time for NP associations to act like businesses. It is time for board members to be relieved of the hands-on "doing" of association business so they can do what board members are supposed to do: decide how the association money is spent and evaluate the performance of the hired help.

Why? Because NPs are operating in an industry where changes are coming fast. NPs stand to gain ground, but progress will not come easily. Other professional groups are spending large sums to have experts monitor changes and ensure that their members' interests are represented when policy is made, law is enacted, and contracts are signed.

NPs have great potential because they combine nursing and medical knowledge. In volatile times, there are great opportunities. However, no laws will be enacted that designate NPs as PCPs unless bills are drafted expertly, hard lobbying is done successfully, and public relations efforts are increased and well targeted. No state regulations will be changed in NPs' favor without carefully drafted, persistent requests to state agencies. No health plans will open themselves to additional providers unless they can be shown how doing so will benefit them.

How are NP organizations going to fund all this expert help? By developing revenue streams other than membership dues. Each NP organization that does not have an annual continuing education conference for which the registration fee is at least $150 per day should work on creating one. Putting on a conference may require hiring a part-time conference coordinator. The budget for a conference should support a conference coordinator, the speakers' time, and the expenses of room rental and coffee, and the conference should make a profit. Each organization should charge for the use of its name and the use of its directory. When files of laws are sent out on request, the organization should charge for that service.

NP organizations need public relations specialists, lobbyists, and attorneys, either on retainer or on a per-project basis. Each organization also needs a paid executive director who answers to the board of directors.

Volunteer officers, board members, and committee chairs of NP organizations are running themselves ragged and burning out. These volunteers are making the day-to-day decisions about their organizations; often they also are talking with newspaper reporters, trying to recruit new members, trying to make sense of laws, folding flyers, licking stamps, and answering nonstop questions from individual NPs.

At a time when NPs are defending themselves, in the press and to the legislatures, and fighting for their spot in the managed-care landscape, they need to hire expert assistance, not rely on do-it-yourself operations. It is time to hire professionals and to get appropriate service.

Do Not Be Timid

Nurses, as a group, have lacked confidence and assertiveness in the past. NPs are trying to overcome barriers that were erected long before their title and position existed, barriers that resulted from this history of timidity in nursing. For example, in 1955, the American Nurses Association's (ANA's) model definition of nursing stated that nursing "shall not be deemed to include any acts of diagnosis or prescription of therapeutic or corrective measures."[3] In 1955, however, nurses were already performing acts that clearly were within the definition of diagnosis and prescription of corrective measures. Nevertheless, by 1967, 22 states had incorporated the ANA model language into state law.[4] To cover hospitals and agencies where nurses were engaging in "acts of diagnosis or prescription of therapeutic measures," joint statements of hospital, medical, and nursing associations were written that allowed nurses to perform certain acts, such as venipuncture or initiating intravenous fluids.[5] The joint statements were at odds with the law, yet no one challenged the law or the policy statements.

Today, NPs find that they can practice independently, meaning that they make decisions about patient care without consulting physicians. However, if state and federal regulations call for collaboration and define collaboration as supervision, NPs who push the envelope without also pushing for changes in legal language that supports their independent practice will be going nowhere.

It is time for NPs to affirm that NPs are experts in primary care. They should make statements such as "I am an expert in managing diabetes," rather than "NPs do primary care in collaboration with physicians."

Erase Collaboration from the Legal Vocabulary

NPs, like other healthcare providers, cannot function without collaboration with other experts. Nevertheless, nurses are virtually the only profession that has "collaboration" as a legal mandate.

NPs have considered the word collaboration an improvement on the word supervision. However, a close reading of federal law reveals that the law defines collaboration as supervision.

When arguing for erasure of barriers to NP practice, NPs have had difficulty convincing legislators of the difference between collaboration and supervision, and with good reason. Although there is a difference in the definitions of the two words—the dictionary defines collaboration as "work jointly with others" (and alternatively as "cooperate with or willingly assist an enemy force occupying one's country")[6] and supervision as "superintend, oversee"[7]—a legal mandate to collaborate suggests that the group given the mandate is not the final authority on a matter. Although NPs are not so arrogant as to consider themselves final authorities on all matters of health care, certainly NPs can and should consider themselves final authorities on primary care and other areas of medicine where they have specialized and have extensive education and experience. Consultation is appropriate, but a legal requirement for collaboration is not.

Insist Upon Legal Clarity of NP Authority to Practice

Compare Laws A and B on NP scope of practice:

Law A:

The board recognizes advanced and specialized acts of nursing practice as those described in the scope of practice statements for nurse practitioners certified by national certifying bodies recognized by the board.

Citation: Alaska Admin. Code tit. 12, § 44.430.

Law B:

The nurse practitioner provides holistic health care to individuals, families, and groups across the life span in a variety of settings, including hospitals, long-term care facilities, and community-based settings. Within his or her specialty, the nurse practitioner is responsible for managing health problems encountered by the client and is accountable for health outcomes. This process includes:

    a. Assessment
    b. Diagnosis
    c. Development of a plan
    d. Intervention
    e. Evaluation

The nurse practitioner is independently responsible and accountable for the continuous and comprehensive management of a broad range of health care, which may include:

a. Promotion and maintenance of health
b. Prevention of illness and disability
c. Assessment of clients, synthesis and analysis of data, and application of nursing principles and therapeutic modalities
d. Management of health care during acute and chronic phases of illness
e. Admission of his/her clients to hospitals and long-term care facilities and management of client care in these facilities
f. Counseling
g. Consultation and/or collaboration with other care providers and community resources
h. Referral to other healthcare providers and community resources
i. Management and coordination of care
j. Use of research skills
k. Diagnosis of health/illness status
l. Prescription and/or administration of therapeutic devices and measures including legend drugs and controlled substances ... consistent with the definition of the practitioner's specialty category and scope of practice...

The nurse practitioner is responsible for recognizing limits of knowledge and experience, and for resolving situations beyond his/her nurse practitioner expertise by consulting with or referring clients to other healthcare providers. The nurse practitioner will only provide healthcare services within the nurse practitioner's scope of practice for which he/she is educationally prepared and for which competency has been established and maintained. Educational preparation includes academic course work, workshops or seminars, provided both theory and clinical experience are included.

Citation: Or. Admin. R. § 851-050-0005.

There is no question what an NP in Law B can do. Many questions are left unanswered by Law A, however. For example: What is "advanced and specialized acts of nursing practice?" Do such acts include medical services, or is an advanced practice nurse the same as a registered nurse? While Law B is specific and permissive of NP practice, Law A is unclear.

NPs need to insist upon clarity. Without clarity, other groups may decide what the law addressing NPs means.

Notes

1. American Academy of Family Physicians. (2009). Policy statement on nurse practitioners. Retrieved from http://www.aafp.org/about/policies/all/nurse-practitioners.html
2. Starr, P. (1992). *The social transformation of American medicine* (Chapter 3). New York, NY: Basic Books.
3. American Nurses' Association. (1955). ANA board approves a definition of nursing practice. *American Journal of Nursing, 55,* 1474.

4. Phillips, R. S. (1985). Nurse practitioners: Their scope of practice and theories of liability. *Journal of Legal Medicine, 6*, 391–414.

5. Bullough, B. (1975). The first two phases in nursing licensure. In: *The law and the expanding nursing role*, Vol. 7. New York, NY: Appleton-Century-Crofts.

6. Merriam-Webster. (2005). Collaboration definition. In: *Merriam-Webster collegiate dictionary* (11th ed.). Springfield, MA: Author.

7. Merriam-Webster. (2005). Supervision definition. In: *Merriam-Webster collegiate dictionary* (11th ed.). Springfield, MA: Author.